FDR and Reagan

FDR and Reagan

Transformative Presidents
with Clashing Visions

John W. Sloan

 UNIVERSITY PRESS OF KANSAS

Published by the University Press of Kansas (Lawrence, Kansas 66045), which was
organized by the Kansas Board of Regents and is operated and funded by Emporia
State University, Fort Hays State University, Kansas State University, Pittsburg State
University, the University of Kansas, and Wichita State University

Library of Congress Cataloging-in-Publication Data

Sloan, John W., 1940–
    FDR and Reagan : transformative presidents with clashing visions / John W. Sloan.
       p.   cm.
    Includes bibliographical references and index.
    ISBN 978-0-7006-1615-2 (cloth : alk. paper)
    1. Roosevelt, Franklin D. (Franklin Delano), 1882–1945—Political and social views.
2. Reagan, Ronald—Political and social views. 3. Roosevelt, Franklin D. (Franklin Delano),
1882–1945—Influence. 4. Reagan, Ronald—Influence. 5. Social change—United
States—Case studies. 6. United States—Politics and government—1933–1945.
7. United States—Politics and government—1981–1989. 8. Presidents—United States—
Biography. I. Title.
    E807.S55 2008
    973.917092—dc22   2008014478

British Library Cataloguing-in-Publication Data is available.

Printed in the United States of America

10 9 8 7 6 5 4 3 2 1

The paper used in this publication is recycled and contains 30 percent postconsumer
waste. It is acid free and meets the minimum requirements of the American National
Standard for Permanence of Paper for Printed Library Materials Z39.48-1992.

To my wife, Patty, for a lifetime of love
To my grandson, Will, for the brightest of futures

CONTENTS

Preface *ix*

1 Reconstructive Presidents as Principal Agents of Regime Change *1*

2 The Collapse of the Republican Regime *18*

3 Erosion of the Liberal Regime *44*

4 The Life, Personality, and Political Philosophy of Franklin Roosevelt and Ronald Reagan *66*

5 Advising FDR *101*

6 Advising Reagan *150*

7 Core Policies of the New Deal *178*

8 Reagan's Core Policies *223*

9 Legitimating the New Deal *246*

10 Legitimating Reagan's Conservative Regime *287*

11 FDR's Reconstructive Party Leadership *321*

12 Reagan's Reconstructive Party Leadership *340*

Conclusion *356*

Notes *369*

Index *403*

PREFACE

Clashing Visions has two sources. The first was my experience as a young boy in Brooklyn in the late 1940s, listening to my aunts and uncles tell vivid tales of how the exuberance of the 1920s was obliterated by the Depression. Their description of the brutal despair of the 1930s seemed so different from the life I was observing, in which most adults I knew were working, owned their own home, and were planning to buy a new car. The second source was the election of Ronald Reagan in 1980, which I believed was going to play a major role in the political future of the nation. During the 1980s, I changed my major field of study from comparative politics to the presidency and began an analysis of the reasons for Reagan's successes (and a few disasters), which resulted in the publication of *The Reagan Effect* in 1999. In studying Reagan's efforts to create a conservative regime, I found that there was a natural tendency to compare his administration to Franklin Roosevelt's in the 1930s. Stephen Skowronek's book, *The Politics Presidents Make*, explained why this is so: FDR and Reagan played similar roles in American political development: each of them came into office replacing failed presidents, and each was able to dominate politics and institute significant policy reforms. Their visions, philosophies, and electoral coalitions affected the presidential regimes that came after them and still influence the politics and policies of today. That is precisely why examining the FDR and Reagan administrations in terms of the regimes each of them forged in the heat of political battle is so valuable for students of presidential policy making.

My goal in writing *Clashing Visions* is to educate readers about the key role of presidents in promoting the progress of the United States. The presidency is certainly not the sole initiator of change in American politics, but it is probably the most important one. The campaign for the presidency every four years provides a national evaluation of where we are as a nation and whether we should continue on the same track, that is, whether we should prolong the existing regime or create a new one. More than any other individual or group of individuals, the chief executive is pressured both during the campaign and while in office to imagine how the promise of America can be fulfilled. And because the public perceives the White House to be the center of power and authority in the American political system, we expect the president to be successful as he works to fulfill that promise.

Yet many presidents fail. In trying to account for presidential success or failure, most studies on leadership stress the qualities of an individual president's leadership skills; Skowronek, however, shifts the focus to the context in which an aspiring politician assumes the White House. In Skowronek's model, presidents like Herbert Hoover and Jimmy Carter, who came to power affiliated with a declining regime, are destined to fail because they lack the authority to either repudiate the vulnerable regime or create a new one. Their tragic fate is to set the stage for their far more fortunate successors. Presidents like Franklin Roosevelt and Ronald Reagan, who come to office opposed to a weakening regime, are more likely to achieve success because they have the widest warrants of authority to denounce the failing regime and to build a new one. Reconstructive presidents, such as Jefferson, Jackson, Lincoln, FDR, and Reagan, perform a vital function in periodically overcoming the inertia of exhausted regimes and producing a reenergized political system.

As I have worked to produce this book, I have received grants to conduct research at the FDR and Reagan libraries, taught special topics courses comparing both presidents, and presented papers at numerous professional conferences. I want to thank the three chairmen of the Department of Political Science at the University of Houston, Professors James Anderson, Kent Tedin, and Harrell Rodgers, for supporting my research. I also want to express my gratitude to Professors Robert Carp, Robert Lineberry, and Richard Murray, for reading different chapters and providing helpful criticisms. To Michael Briggs, the editor-in-chief of the University Press of Kansas, I owe a special thanks for encouraging my research projects and not laughing when I promised him that I would produce the manuscript several years before I actually completed it. Working with the exceptionally friendly and competent crew at the University Press of Kansas has been a pleasure. I am most indebted to my wife Patty, who encouraged and improved every phase of this project with great love and skill.

1

Reconstructive Presidents as Principal Agents of Regime Change

Scholars have become increasingly intrigued with how American presidents such as Franklin Roosevelt and Ronald Reagan attempt to promote change in a governmental system that was constitutionally designed to limit political leadership. A chief executive's endorsement of change is further complicated by the tacit understanding that such action should appear to renew many of the traditional values of our heritage. Hence, visionary politics in the United States requires massive social engineering while preserving cherished foundations.

Stephen Skowronek, in his book *The Politics Presidents Make*, presents a historically based model for comparing the leadership efforts of chief executives from John Adams to Bill Clinton. He asserts that the leadership endeavors of presidents are the major force transforming American politics because the office creates compelling incentives that induce its incumbents to engage in large leadership projects that inevitably threaten existing governing arrangements. Both the political and economic systems are often disrupted and sometimes transformed by the battering ram of order-shattering, order-affirming, and order-creating presidential decisions.

In Skowronek's model, the politics presidents make are largely determined by the context in which the presidents operate. He classifies past presidents according to whether they were opposed to or affiliated with the prevailing regime. Regimes (the dominant orthodoxy—for example, the New Deal) are defined in terms of whether the previously established institutional arrangements are vulnerable or resilient. The resulting two-by-two table (Table 1.1) constitutes a cycle of political time, which allows scholars to compare presidents in different time periods facing similar leadership challenges.

Franklin Roosevelt and Ronald Reagan are in the first cell of this typology because both came into office opposed to a vulnerable regime and engaged in the politics of reconstruction. Presidents who come to office in this context (that is, opposed to a vulnerable regime) have the advantage of receiving the widest warrants of authority to practice the politics of reconstruction, a clarion call to repudiate the failing political order and construct a new one. Simply put, they are licensed to destroy and rebuild. Reconstructive presidents, such as Jefferson, Jackson, Lincoln, FDR, and Reagan, played a vital role in the evolution of the U.S. political system by resetting the clock of political time. This is the process through which the political system rejuvenates itself by replacing the exhausted regime, now viewed as blocking progress, and creating a new one that promises to usher in a better life for millions of Americans.

It is significant and rewarding to compare the presidencies of Roosevelt and Reagan. First, these were the most recent reconstructive presidents, and their policies and politics still have major effects on the way we live today. Second, comparing these two leaders reveals the wide variation in practicing the politics of reconstruction. As an obvious example, FDR was a liberal reformer supporting the idea of an activist federal government in solving the problems of the Depression, whereas Reagan was a conservative reformer believing that a powerful federal government was the source of the nation's problems, not its solution. A less obvious variation is that FDR, not being sure about how to deal with the Depression, was willing to recruit a variety of advisers and to experiment with a diverse set of programs. He created an advisory system that was designed to supply him with numerous options, and he was confident in his wisdom to select the most politically feasible one and nurture it into public policy. Reagan, on the other hand, believed he knew the causes and remedies of the malaise of the late 1970s, but he did not know how to get his vision enacted into law. Hence, FDR needed advisers to provide him with a variety of proposals, whereas Reagan was dependent on his advisers to supply him with the guidance to bring his vision into reality.

Table 1.1. Recurrent Structures of Presidential Authority

	President's Political Identity	
Previously Established Commitments	Opposed	Affiliated
Vulnerable	Politics of reconstruction	Politics of disjunction
Resilient	Politics of preemption	Politics of articulation

Source: Stephen Skowronek, *The Politics Presidents Make* (Cambridge, Mass.: Harvard University Press, 1993), 36.

Finally, the New Deal and the Reagan Revolution emphasized fundamentally different policy prescriptions for the economic problems that still reverberate early in the twenty-first century. For the Roosevelt administration, the Depression had demonstrated the precariousness of economic life, which meant that the federal government would have to provide more security for its citizens. Thus, there were New Deal programs to help the farmers, the workers, the unemployed, the aged, the homeowner, the investor, and the poor on relief. Market solutions were less relied on; business, banks, and the stock market were less trusted and thus had to be regulated. For the Reagan administration, however, the stagflation of the late 1970s proved the futility of the liberal regime's Keynesian economics. Federal programs designed to provide security smothered individual initiative, increased the size of the bureaucracy, and had to be financed by high taxes. Reagan's vision was to emphasize economic freedom for the individual by providing lower tax rates and deregulation. He believed that individuals should be free to decide what is best for themselves rather than be shepherded by federal bureaucracies.

Skowronek's Theory

Stephen Skowronek's theory is based on the idea that the presidency is "a singularly persistent force driving the transformation of American politics." He identifies chief executives "with a persistent pattern of political disruption, a recurrent pattern of political breakthrough, breakup, and breakdown, and an emergent pattern of expanding executive resources and responsibilities in governance. . . . Eventually I came to see at the heart of the politics presidents make an institutional imperative to resolve the inherently disruptive effects of the exercise of presidential power in the reproduction of political order."[1] The paradox of presidential power is that while the chief executive takes an oath to preserve order, his actions often have order-shattering effects. The president's challenge is to legitimate both the mayhem he has caused and the new political order he has created.

For Skowronek, presidential behavior is guided by one of four recurring contexts. In essence, context determines the politics presidents will practice. Presidents can be classified according to whether they are opposed to or affiliated with either a resilient or vulnerable regime. Table 1.1 provides us with a heuristic device to study the patterns of presidential politics. Each of the four contexts provides a rational script to follow for the president operating within its parameters. For a president who is opposed to a declining regime, the context-derived guideline will "instruct" him (someday her) to engage in the politics of reconstruction—namely, to destroy the old regime and create a new one. The success of a reconstructive president resets the cycle of political time in which presidents who are affiliated with a resilient regime practice the politics of articulation; presidents who are opposed to a resilient regime practice the politics of preemption; and presidents who are affiliated with a vulnerable regime practice the politics of disjunction.

The presidency is an order-shattering institution because it prods each incumbent to exercise the independent powers of the office in his own right, which has an unsettling effect on our tightly integrated check and balance system. It is an order-affirming institution because the disruptive consequences of the exercise of presidential power must be legitimated in constitutional legality. It is an order-creating institution because it motivates each occupant of the White House to employ his powers to assemble new political arrangements that can meet the tests of legitimacy. Skowronek stresses that chief executives have enormous difficulty in making these three exercises in power work harmoniously together. Reconstructive presidents are in the best position to utilize their power in such a manner that their order-shattering, order-affirming, and order-creating impulses operate in tandem. In a reconstructive context, what the president (and many others) believe must be done to remedy the salient problems of the day cannot be done under the existing rules and procedures of the present regime. Old formulas no longer work. The classic reconstructive posture is encapsulated by Abraham Lincoln's words: "As our case is new, so we must think anew and act anew. We must disenthrall ourselves, and then we shall save the country."[2]

A reconstructive period will be preceded—and accompanied—by intense ideological debate. Supporters of the old regime will stress their allegiance to the traditional and eternal truths and will proclaim that to violate these verities will destroy our liberty and bring about the tyranny Americans always fear. If Jackson is allowed to kill the national bank, if Lincoln is able to eradicate slavery, if FDR's New Deal is permitted to regulate agriculture and business, if Reagan is authorized to deregulate the economy, then proponents of the preexisting regime will predict the end of the American experiment. Supporters of the new regime will emphasize the antiquated nature of the old one; it is holding back the progress that Americans believe is their birthright. Additionally, it is not supported by the people; instead, it has been upheld by powerful but selfish special interests. In their moral outrage, these proponents of reform may also allege corruption of the political process by notorious individuals who symbolize the old regime. Champions of the new order will extol a visionary construct that will solve the nation's problems and bring about a much better life for the majority of its citizens. Opponents will condemn this construct as utopian, impractical, and likely to lead to tyranny.

For the reconstructive leader, the crisis that brought him into office is the principal source of his legitimacy. The critical situation that delegitimized his predecessor authorizes the reconstructive president to search for new policy solutions. But reconstructive presidents do not necessarily have to solve all the problems that face them as they take office in order to be successful. Lincoln did not prevent the Southern states from withdrawing from the Union; Roosevelt's New Deal policies did not lead the economy out of the Depression; and Reagan never came close to balancing the federal budget. Little blame will be placed on a reconstructive president if he is skillful in providing the public with a plausible narrative that justifies his decisions. The chief irony for a reconstructive leader is that his continuing failure to resolve some of the problems that helped get him elected may not cause his demise, but may operate to fuel further reforms. For example, Lincoln's initial goal was to stop the spread of slavery to the new states, but by 1863, his more radical aim was to abolish slavery. Similarly, the early failures of several New Deal programs, especially the National Industrial Recovery Act of 1933, encouraged Roosevelt to engage in a wider variety of experimental programs.

To explain one reconstructive president is not to explain them all. Patterns of reconstructive politics and reform can vary. In Skowronek's words, "We have yet to escape the circuit of political time, but in each successive cycle the roller coaster has taken a slightly different loop. The basic patterns are altered and the political range of presidential leadership in all its various modes reshaped."[3] Skowronek claims that in the evolution of American history, reconstructive presidents have been faced with an increasing number of entrenched institutions and interests, which means their possibilities of success in both destroying the old regime and creating a new one have decreased. Jefferson's reconstructive politics resulted in the demise of the Federalist party; Reagan's reconstructive politics could not bring about the Republican control of the House of Representatives during his eight years in the White House. The thickening milieu of institutions reflected in Skowronek's concept of the waning of political time suggests that reconstructive leaders are no longer able to direct their repudiative thrusts at such strategic objects as the Federalist party, the national bank, or slavery. Although it is true that elements of a reconstructive coalition may focus on one part of an existing regime as the principal target—for example, business monopolies for leftist New Dealers and the progressive income tax for supply-siders—reconstructive administrations now have to deal with multiple options in selecting which of their desired goals is achievable.

The waning of political time influences reconstructive politics through the constraints of political feasibility. Pragmatic politicians and advisers search for issues that they can win; they avoid conflicts where they are likely to lose. Hence, even if some conspicuous residue of the old regime is still present, presidents may decide not to launch a frontal attack against it if they believe such an onslaught will be too costly. There are always plenty of other targets. The result is unfulfilled agendas by reconstructive presidents that frustrate the true believers of the new regime.

The waning of political time also implies that the victories of reconstructive presidents will be less decisive because there will be more compromises with interests associated with the previous regime. Big business survived the New Deal; the welfare state survived the Reagan Revolution. Because of the constraints of the waning of political time, the success of reconstructive executives is measured in terms of more or less instead of totally obliterating one institution and another. Indeed, by the end of Skowronek's book, he is suggesting that the waning of political time is eroding the capability of reconstructive presidents to perform their historical function of bringing about fundamental change. When reconstructive presidents can no longer destroy the old regime and create a new one, chief executives will be forced into the role of practicing preemptive politics.

Revising the Concept of Regime

It is accurate to view the creation of the United States as an experiment in republican government. The "Founding Brothers" had many, often diverse, visions concerning how the nation should develop.[4] They designed a Constitution that was flexible enough to accommodate different interpretations and a variety of governing arrangements known as regimes. The ambiguity and brevity of the Constitution allows a variety of regimes to develop, disintegrate, and be reconstructed. In essence, the Constitution provides a legal, procedural framework for governing; the concept of regime bestows a substantive framework for politics and policy making. The Constitution regulates how law should be made; a regime ordains what kind of law should be passed. By allowing regime change within the Constitution, the U.S. political system provides avenues for significant reform without the need for violent revolutions.

The U.S. political system is constantly changing, but we can view the prevailing political order for a limited number of years as a regime. Regimes refer to enduring institutional arrangements bolstered by ideology. Skowronek explains: "The government's basic commitments of ideology and interest have tended to congeal institutionally around relatively durable partisan regimes, and those orderings frame the recurrent pattern of founding, fragmenting, and disintegrating governing coalitions and party systems."[5] Regimes are temporary governing devices; there is no final regime. Because of our dynamic economy and society, an existing regime will inevitably be seen as blocking progress instead of promoting it. This triggers the process of calling forth the construction of a new regime, which must simultaneously repudiate the old one. The destruction of the old order and the building of a new one constitute turning points in political evolution and are the basis for the cyclical periodization of American history.

As the proponents of a new regime achieve success in destroying the old one, they attempt to institutionalize their enterprise. In trying to make the fruits of their victory permanent, they will attempt to bring about changes in constitutional and statutory law, the federal bureaucracy, and national government–state government relations. For a regime to become institutionalized, it needs to:

1. Elect a president that delegitimizes the existing regime and that personifies and mobilizes support for the new one.
2. Create a majority electoral coalition that will elect presidents and Congress members who will continue to support the regime's policy agenda for at least a decade or more.
3. Construct a political philosophy that legitimates and guides its policy choices.

4. Enact a core of public policies that define what the regime is most committed to.
5. Gain the legal backing of the Supreme Court to demonstrate that the new regime is compatible with the Constitution.

A regime is associated with a mode of thought. The proponents of a new regime undermine and ridicule the intellectual foundations of the old order and begin the process of creating the new conventional wisdom that will uphold the evolving one. Eldon Eisenach stresses, "a regime perspective should examine the institutions, practices, and policies that constitute the present regime, and then look to the sets of ideas that institute, direct, and legitimate them."[6] A regime needs a political philosophy to both guide and justify its actions. That philosophy must handle the tricky task of explaining that the new regime is actually based on the traditional values that have steered the nation since 1776. By restoring the traditional values that have been violated by leaders in the discredited regime, the political system can be rejuvenated.

A regime helps to determine which policy proposals will be seriously considered and which will be rejected as out of bounds. Each regime has typical policy responses to problems. For example, during the New Deal, a recommendation for the creation of a new federal agency to deal with an economic problem would be considered plausible by many liberal policy makers. Similarly, during the Reagan presidency, a proposal to deal with a problem with a tax cut would be viewed as reasonable by many conservative legislators. The rise of a new regime means new parameters concerning what can and cannot be done. A successful regime change will refute much of what had been considered the truth by many experts.

Regimes deteriorate because they cannot accommodate economic, social, and political changes. These changes occur more rapidly than the existing order can adjust to them. Regimes are programmed to become static; the economy and society are more dynamic. Hence, regimes inevitably clash with alterations taking place in the economy and society. What is originally an energetic flexibility in the rise of a new regime eventually hardens into dogma. Each regime develops its own partisan ties, supportive interest groups, political philosophy, and constitutional law; together, these represent a reasonable settlement for a particular period, which will eventually be overtaken by events. Rebel reformers, if they live long enough, will find themselves accused of being reactionaries.

When an existing regime appears to be blocking progress, the pressures for political change will increase. In the twentieth century, the pressures emanating from economic change were particularly important. The U.S. political system is expected to aid the economy in providing the growth and the social mobility we associate with the fulfillment of the American Dream. The public holds high expectations because America has vast resources, and it has the burden of living up to its mythical reputation of being the land of opportunity. A regime that fails to meet its responsibilities will be replaced.

Because our political system allows regime change, we do not need violent revolutions or new constitutions to adapt to changing conditions. We enjoy the benefits of continuity and change. However, the conflict over regime change represents a higher level of conflict than the politics of interest. Regime politics is a contest over philosophy and beliefs, that is, about how the world works or should work. The contesting philosophies and beliefs may be abstract, but the argument itself is more than academic and is capable of rousing intense passions. The difficulty of replacing a regime may be appreciated when one comprehends that we are talking about changing things (institutions, procedures, policies, values) that were considered fundamental and moral. These institutions will have supporters who will strongly resist any attempt to eliminate or modify what they consider vital to their way of life. For example, slave owners in the South could not imagine how their economy and social life would function without slavery. Similarly, many businessmen in the 1930s worried that capitalism could not survive if workers were allowed and encouraged by the federal government to organize. The destructive component of reconstructive politics will outrage the beneficiaries of the old order, who will view the slaughter of their sacred cows—a national bank, slavery, the gold standard, states' rights—as a lethal threat to civilized life.

A vulnerable regime suffers from declining ideals. It can no longer depend on the idealism that inspired its early adherents; therefore, it must increasingly depend on naked self-interest, which makes the regime look corrupt to its opponents. A viable regime must depend on both self-interest and idealism for its continuity.

When a regime is being dismantled, and before a new one can set the parameters of policy orthodoxy, the range of policy options is likely to expand. A regime change is punctuated by major departures in policy. Ironically, the changes in policy are sometimes foreshadowed by policies in the declining regime. Thus students who associate Herbert Hoover with laissez-faire are surprised that he created the Reconstruction Finance Corporation in 1932, and students who look at Jimmy Carter as a liberal are perplexed that he championed the policy of deregulation in the late 1970s.

The end of a regime and the transition to a new one create an intellectually liberating period. Freed from the timeworn shackles of conventional thought, new ways of looking at the political system and of deciding what policy remedies should be tried multiply. Charlatans and demagogues, such as Huey Long and the Townsend movement in the 1930s, are likely to thrive in this milieu. The normal monitors that keep seriously considered options within a reasonable range are not operating. What would previously be considered heretical views may now appear sensible and may become popular.

Proponents of regime change will always be accused of being impractical, visionary, radical, and utopian by supporters of the old one. The present order has met one of the tests of practicality: it exists. We know the weaknesses of the present regime; the proposed new one may make matters worse. Moreover, the supporters of a new regime will be challenged to prove that their proposal is feasible and compatible with the nation's traditions and values.

A new regime promises the necessary innovations to resolve a national crisis. It promises to reinvigorate the political system by claiming it possesses greater capabilities and sensitivities toward the many Americans who were neglected and exploited by the previous governing arrangements. The New Deal promised to remember and help "the forgotten man"; the Reagan Revolution vowed to lower oppressive tax burdens for all citizens and lift the deadweight of regulation from business.

The potential radicalism of a new regime is diluted as it accommodates itself to the exigencies of governing. Hence, the institutionalization or consolidation of a regime may appear to be reactionary to some of its original, radical supporters. Orren and Skowronek stress, "political regimes will never be as coherent as the ideas that inspire them. The clearest and most arresting of reform ideas are likely to be those that are universal and holistic, while the accomplishments of even the most radical reform episodes are likely to be specific and partial."[7] Regimes strive for philosophical consistency but never achieve it. The waning of political time means more stumbling and less success in bringing about congruity. Segments of previous regimes may possess staying power; they become embedded with budget lines, protected by powerful Congress members, and continue to receive pressure group support. A regime represents a temporary tide; it rarely is an irresistible force. Because it is subject to contingency, countercurrents, and fortuitous factors, there will always be elements within a regime that do not seem to fit. The new order never becomes totally consistent; it never totally destroys the old one; it never totally creates a new one.

Although an inconsistent or hybrid regime may present problems for scholars who prefer clear-cut categories, such systems are functional for governing such a vast and diversified federal republic. Just as individuals are not totally consistent in their political beliefs, neither are regimes. When a regime is deconstructed and examined closely, its "motley composition" is exposed. Orren and Skowronek conclude, "Regimes . . . are among other things mechanisms for holding together in the same orbit interests and ambitions that in other circumstances could be expected to be regularly at loggerheads."[8] Thus the motley crew of the FDR coalition included supporters of Woodrow Wilson's New Freedom and Teddy Roosevelt's New Nationalism, free traders and protectionists, prolabor groups and antilabor groups, and advocates for African American civil rights in the North and opponents of minority rights in the South. Similarly, the strange bedfellows in the Reagan Revolution included budget balancers and supply-siders, libertarians and the religious right, and members of the corporate elite and white male workers. This lends support to John Karaagic's point that "American politics is about loose coalitions rather than ideological cohesion."[9] A regime, therefore, is like a holding company that manages a polity composed of multiple orders.

Because of its dynamic and static qualities, a regime is not easily understood or described accurately. Descriptions of regimes are heavily influenced and sometimes distorted by personal, partisan, class, and ideological perspectives. It is easier to describe regimes of the past than the one—or more accurately, the mixture of several—that we may be living under today.

Presidents and Public Policy

The presidency is not the sole initiator of change in American history; an accurate explanation of any particular change would have to analyze the contributions of many other factors. Obviously wars, economic developments, demographic trends, and social movements can be as important, if not more so, in accounting for policy change than the activities of the chief executive. Yet, as Skowronek points out, the presidency "has been a singularly persistent source of change, a transformative element ingrained in the

Constitution itself. In the presidency, change is generated routinely by incumbents, trying to legitimate themselves."[10] The most important changes are generated by reconstructive presidents because they possess the widest warrants for disruption.

The lack of substantive requirements in the Constitution makes regime change possible, but its complex, interdependent procedures mean that regime replacement can only occur under an infrequent, unique constellation of forces. One of those forces—the most important one—is a president committed to regime change. Power and authority must be concentrated and used effectively to destroy the old regime and construct the new one. There is more concentrated power and authority in the White House than anywhere else in the American political system, which is precisely why its role in policy making is so vital. Contrary to Skowronek's argument that the cycle of political time is wearing down, I believe that reconstructive presidents will continue to play a major role in bringing about changes in regime and policy.

Much of the cyclical history of the nation can be analyzed in terms of presidents. The White House is still the most coveted and competitive prize for the most ambitious politicians in the Democratic and Republican parties. The campaigns for the presidency every four years provide a convenient and compelling evaluation of where we are as a nation and whether we should continue on the same track (prolong the existing regime) or change direction (create a new one). The issues that presidential candidates highlight in their campaigns and the concerns that presidents emphasize in their state of the union addresses and in their special messages still play significant—and perhaps the dominant—role in explaining public policy in the United States. More so than any other individual or group, the president is pressured, both during the campaign and while in office, to imagine how a better world could be created. Indeed, that is the required public justification for a presidential campaign. Although candidates will have private motivations in running, they must publicly legitimize their ambitions by asserting their alleged superior ability to solve the problems that are impeding the country from enjoying the progress it deserves. In essence, the presidency has the incentives and resources to think and act anew.

The strategic position of the president in promoting change is recognized by scholars and politicians. One leading expert in public policy, John Kingdon, suggests that the chief executive occupies the preeminent position in agenda setting. The agenda refers to the short list of problems policy makers are focusing on in hopes of creating solutions:

No other single actor in the political system has quite the capability of the president to set an agenda in a given policy area for all who deal with those policies. . . . When a president and his top appointees decide to place a high priority on a given item, agendas are set all over town. Members of Congress, bureaucrats, and lobbyists all pay attention to that priority item. Conversely, by virtue of such an administrative decision, other subjects that could be prominent agenda items in different administrations are put on the shelf for the time being. This blocking of issues is at least as important on agenda-setting as positively promoting an item.[11]

Presidential support imbues a reform proposal with publicity, resources, and energy; it empowers a reform project with the claim of a national interest rather than a special interest.

To bring about regime change, one must combine and mobilize several streams of discontent into an electoral coalition. The president, especially during his electoral campaign, is the critical agent in deciphering the meaning of elections and converting electoral opportunities into new patterns of politics. Reconstructive presidents have all been skillful party leaders and spent considerable time in party-building activities. FDR's presidency made the Democratic party more liberal, and Reagan's led the Republican party to a more conservative stance. Hence, a reconstructive president, who may initially believe that his visions possess almost universal appeal, will soon find himself under attack and will need to identify his key allies and reward them.

A reconstructive president attempts to be the architect of his times. He will try to educate the public to change some of its convictions and accept new ones. This requires that the president move beyond the usual strategy of followership—that is, of carefully assessing public opinion and group attitudes and then expediently assuming the optimum position on a set of issues that amass the most votes on election day. In contrast, what is periodically needed, according to James MacGregor Burns, is a transforming leader who "actively shapes his political context; he seeks to change the constellation of political forces about him in a direction closer to his own conception of the political good. The genius of great party leaders [like Jefferson and Jackson] lies in their power to forge a majority combination of voters around burning issues of government, and through their personal qualities of leadership to put this combination behind some philosophy of government and program of action."[12] Reconstructive presidents overcome the usual contradiction between being the nonpartisan leader of the nation, expected to promote the public interest, and the head of his political party, sponsoring its partisan interests. Reconstructive leaders have the rare opportunity to convince the public (and probably themselves) that their partisan goals are really reflections of the public good. This combination of moral and partisan passion energizes the reconstructive presidency.

The election of a reconstructive president reflects the public's belief that prevailing conditions require major (rather than incremental) policy changes; thus he enters office with the power to mobilize a shift in the national mood. Beyond the mandate given him to create change, however, a reconstructive president must have the skill to unite and lead such an idea-based majority. Liberalism prevailed in the 1930s, but only Roosevelt was able to lead it. Conservative ideas predominated in the 1980s, but only Reagan was able to unite the movement.

Skowronek talks about the vision of the reconstructive president, but in looking back on the twentieth century and forward into the twenty-first, one should also consider the visions of key members of a presidential administration. In the complex milieu of modern times, the singular perspective of the chief executive is clearly inadequate. To see the nature and problems of the existing regime and to envision the creation of a new one require great intellectual capabilities. Most presidents, however, are not intellectuals; they are politicians. As politicians, their focus is on short-term opportunities rather than on fulfilling the logic of regime change. That part of a reconstructive president that is a politician will yearn to win elections, build up popularity, make as few enemies as possible, and take advantage of short-term windows of opportunity. These immediate pressures are a threat to the reconstructive enterprise because they have the ability to "drive out grand designs and long-term plans."[13] In neglecting regular politics and focusing on long-term plans, the president may develop such a reputation as a loser that he will not accrue the political capital to achieve his major goals. By emphasizing regular politics, the president runs the risk of winning many little battles but losing the war. Thus, reconstructive presidents must balance their needs to be successful politicians with their aspirations to launch a new regime. No one was better at achieving this balance than Abraham Lincoln.

The logistics of fighting along multiple fronts will require advisers and administrators with varied talents. Not all presidential advisers need to be driven by reconstructive visions. Indeed, most will be motivated by the routine tasks of getting the president elected, guiding his legislative proposals through Congress, writing speeches, and vetting presidential appointees to the bureaucracy and the federal courts. But a few advisers will be motivated by—and will attempt to inspire the president with—their reconstructive visions. These advisers usually have a core idea that they are fully committed to. In the FDR administration, there were advisers devoted to planning, balanced budgets, Keynesian economics, antitrust, public power, conservation, and public relief. In the Reagan administration, there were zealous supporters of supply-side tax cuts, monetary policy, returning to the gold standard, market rationality, decentralization, and religious fundamentalism. These advisers will fiercely compete with one another for the president's attention and commitment because the window of opportunity that allows for major changes is open for a short time and the stakes are so high. They will frequently lament that the president is not as dedicated to their cherished positions as they initially believed. There will be much debate about the meaning of the New Deal or the Reagan Revolution; charges of policy inconsistency and even betrayal will be heard. Reconstructive presidents will inevitably confront the internal conflicts of clashing visions because there are conflicting perspectives and priorities within the liberal and conservative viewpoints.

Because reconstructive presidents will attract and recruit a large number of visionary-inspired advisers, these chief executives will have the task of managing them. Being true believers, most of these aides will not be satisfied merely because their candidate has been elected or because they have been appointed to a patronage position. Because they are fully committed to their policy proposals, such advisers have difficulty working in an organizational context and accepting the need for compromise that a checks-and-balances system usually requires. In addition, as the number of presidential advisers has multiplied, the propensity for policy-oriented factions to form within the administration has increased. This group dynamic is also influenced by personality factors and political ambition. Supporters of the president claim that they are good soldiers and anxious to serve him in any way they can. But they customarily want to serve as generals rather than privates. And usually the positions and policy outcomes they espouse will benefit their own ambitions and interests. Many of them are likely to believe that they have made decisive contributions to the president's success, that he would have failed without their advice, campaign contribution, speech, or key vote in Congress. Hence, it will be a real challenge for the chief executive to make sure these advisers are serving *his* political purposes, rather than their own. A reconstructive president will not only face the obvious challenge of defeating the supporters of the old regime, but he will also confront the unexpected test of keeping his competing sets of advisers in line. The breadth of presidential constituencies guarantees that different components of these constituencies will have divergent views over visions, policy, issues, and personnel.

Conclusion

The purpose of this chapter is to outline the approach I will use to compare the presidencies of Franklin Roosevelt and Ronald Reagan. Both of these leaders came into office opposed to a vulnerable regime and therefore engaged in the politics of reconstruction. The context-derived script for reconstructive politics calls for the president to repudiate the existing regime and to construct a new one. Although the Constitution furnishes a legal, procedural framework for governing, a regime renders a substantive framework for politics and policy making. A regime is a temporary institutional arrangement, supported by a political philosophy and an electoral coalition, that dominates the policy agenda for a period of time. Regimes inevitably deteriorate because they cannot adapt quickly enough to economic, political, and social changes. Regimes begin their careers as the "solution" to the nation's major problems; they end them by being considered the problem. Because of the nature of our checks-and-balances system, a regime will never be as coherent—or as radical—as the ideas that inspired them. The resulting regime is similar to a holding company that administers a polity composed of multiple orders. Because no reconstructive president will be able to completely destroy the old regime or create a totally new one, a functioning regime can best be described as a hybrid.

The destruction and construction of regimes by reconstructive presidents play a significant role in explaining how the United States periodically produces major policy changes and rejuvenates its political system. This pattern of tearing down and rebuilding constitutes a well-trod pattern of reform in American politics. Although Skowronek suggests that the waning of political time is eroding the capability of reconstructive presidents to bring about fundamental changes, I argue that they are still the most powerful force driving American politics. Authority and power must be consolidated and effectively used to dismantle the existing regime and erect a new one, and there is no better place to orchestrate "shrewd political strategy and responsive policy" than in the White House.[14] Reconstructive presidents will continue to be required to overcome the inertia of tired regimes and to imagine the better life that can be launched by a new, dynamic regime.

Skowronek's approach helps us to understand why presidents personalize for much of the public the declining regime (Herbert Hoover and Jimmy Carter practicing the politics of disjunction) and the new regime (Roosevelt and Reagan practicing the politics of reconstruction). A reconstructive president symbolizes the new regime; he helps to legitimize it; he becomes its mythical father and creator. He has the unique ability to appear as both a reformer opening the doors to a new political order and a supporter of the traditional ways and values. His words and actions will take on mythical significance as they are cited by his political heirs to support further fulfillment of the regime's expectations.

In order to understand the effectiveness (as well as the limitations of) reconstructive presidents in practicing reforms, it is beneficial to compare the two most recent practitioners: the creators of the New Deal and the Reagan Revolution. A study of the FDR and Reagan presidencies reveals how they exerted their authority and power to create bursts of reform energy that produced major changes in policy and politics. Because they constructed regimes that extended their influence beyond their own administrations, Roosevelt and Reagan affected the political development of the United States more significantly than any other presidents in the twentieth century.

2

The Collapse of the Republican
Regime

Chief executives who come into office supporting a declining regime are likely to pursue the politics of disjunction. Presidents in this category—John Adams, John Quincy Adams, Franklin Pierce, James Buchanan, Herbert Hoover, and Jimmy Carter—are typically portrayed as being politically incompetent. Skowronek provides a deeper, structural explanation for their failures. These presidents are confronted with an "impossible leadership situation," doomed to have their activities fail because of a dismal choice: "To affirm established commitments is to stigmatize oneself as a symptom of the nation's problems and the premier symbol of systemic political failure; to repudiate them is to become isolated from one's most natural political allies and to be rendered impotent."[1] The politics of disjunction are destined to fail because the president can neither fully support the integrity of the existing regime nor strongly repudiate it. In this no-man's-land, the president is subjected to a withering crossfire from opponents of the declining regime and increasingly rabid supporters of a new one. His authority to control the political definition of these activities is denied, which means that he is unable to establish credibility as a leader. The foreordained failure of these presidents creates the conditions for the next stage in the cycle of political time: the politics of reconstruction.

It is ironic that the presidents who assume office in this ungovernable situation usually have weak ties to the establishments they represent. As semi-outsiders, these leaders often propose major departures from the standard formulas and priorities. But, as Skowronek points out, "The political impact of these departures is disjunctive: they sever the political moorings of the old regime and cast it adrift without anchor or orientation."[2] These presidents also attempt to legitimize their authority by claiming special expertise in resolving the pressing problems of the day. Skowronek suggests that "the reification of technique as the central justification for political action — the elevation of proper administrative methods into a political cause and the claim of special insight into the mechanics of government — is a hallmark of the politics of disjunction."[3] However, as the history of the Hoover and Carter administrations demonstrates, the reification of technique cannot compensate for the failure of public policies; instead, this approach toward governing is the final and futile refuge of leadership ambitions that cannot be sustained by a governing coalition.

Because regimes are durable governing mechanisms, it takes powerful forces to dislodge them. The Republican regime was shattered by the earthquake of the Depression; the foundations of the liberal regime were eroded away by the multiple discontents of the 1970s. To understand the behavior of FDR and Reagan, one must study the failures of Hoover and Carter.

The 1920s

During the 1920s, the Republicans were politically and economically successful. They gained control of Congress in the 1918 elections and won the presidency by a landslide in 1920. The probusiness message of the Republicans may have alienated the Lost Generation of writers and intellectuals, but it obviously appealed to voters, who elected Warren Harding, Calvin Coolidge, and Herbert Hoover to the White House. When Coolidge declared that "The business of America is business," he elicited the ridicule of H. L. Mencken, but as long as the Republicans were providing prosperity, they would continue to trounce the Democrats in congressional and presidential elections. Not even the Teapot Dome scandal in 1923, which involved Cabinet officials of the Harding administration, could prevent Coolidge from being reelected by a wide margin in 1924.

The Republican economic policy was largely designed by Secretary of the Treasury Andrew Mellon, who served in all three GOP administrations.

Mellon advocated lowering income tax rates, raising high protective tariffs, and using government surpluses to pay off the national debt, which had expanded because of the Great War from over $1 billion in 1915 to over $25 billion in 1919. By 1930, the national debt had been slashed to $15.9 billion. After enduring a postwar recession in 1921, Mellon's policies (tax cuts in 1924, 1926, and 1928) provided impressive economic growth with low inflation. From 1922 to 1929, the economy grew at an annual rate of 4.7 percent and unemployment averaged 3.7 percent. The gross national product (GNP) soared from over $59 billion in 1921 to over $87 billion in 1929, while per-capita income increased from $522.00 to $716.00.[4] No wonder conservatives in the Reagan era resurrected Mellon as an early practitioner of supply-side economics.

Under Coolidge, an arrangement was jerry-built to handle the thorny issues of German war reparations and allied war debts owed to the United States. Under Article 231 of the Versailles Treaty, Germany was required to pay the allies $33 billion in war reparations. Its inability to meet this obligation led Germany to pursue policies that caused hyperinflation in 1923. By the mid-1920s, the allies, mainly Great Britain, France, and Italy, owed the United States over $22 billion in principal and interest. The postwar international financial system was further handicapped by the Republican administrations' high tariff policies that blocked both the allies and the Germans from earning dollars in American markets, which would have helped them fulfill their debt obligations. Michael Parrish explains, "With only modest encouragement from the State Department, American bankers and businessmen, led by Charles Dawes and Owen Young, took the initiative to shore up the faltering international financial structure. Dawes and Young negotiated settlements in 1924 and 1929 that trimmed German reparations to $26 billion, put them on a regular payment schedule over fifty-nine years, and provided new loans to underwrite the loans and stabilize the German currency. Germany paid reparations to the allies, the allies in turn paid the Americans—all with money borrowed from the United States."[5] This system would break down after 1929, when American banks would no longer make the loans, and both the allies and Germany could not meet their debt obligations.

The Dawes Plan required the cooperation of the Federal Reserve Board to provide the loose monetary policy that would help European rehabilitation. "By keeping the interests rates low and credit cheap," according to Arthur Schlesinger, "the Board both discouraged the import of gold from Europe and made more American money available for foreign loans."[6]

However, cheaper credit in the United States had an unanticipated consequence that may have contributed to bringing about the Depression. When the Fed cut the discount rate (the interest rate charged by Federal Reserve banks for loans to commercial banks) from 4 to 3.5 percent in the summer of 1927, it encouraged a speculative bubble in the stock market.

But few Republican leaders were worried about the dangers of the genuine prosperity of the 1920s overheating into an unsustainable speculative bubble. They believed their probusiness policies were launching a new era of perpetual prosperity because most of the economic trends of the 1920s interacted in a positive way. One major trend that profoundly transformed everyday life was the expansion of electricity use. "In 1902, the United States used 6 billion kilowatt-hours of electricity, about 79 kilowatt-hours per person. In 1929, it was 118 billion, and 960 kilowatt hours per person, well over ten times as much per person."[7] The availability of electricity slashed production costs and generated new markets for appliances, such as irons, toasters, stoves, refrigerators, washers, vacuum cleaners, and especially radios. By the end of the decade, over 16 million homes, mainly in urban areas, sheltering almost two-thirds of the population, had been wired for electricity. Over 90 percent of the nation's electric power production was controlled by sixteen holding companies, which operated largely free from state regulatory authority.[8]

A second trend was the growth of the automobile industry, which, like the railroads in the last thirty years of the nineteenth century, fueled the economy during the 1920s. In 1914, there were 1.26 million cars on the road; by 1929, there were 26 million. Between 1920 and 1929, car registrations tripled. The industry produced 5.6 million vehicles in 1929. America's love affair with the automobile spurred satellite industries: filling stations, repair shops, highway construction, steel, glass, rubber, and roadside motels.[9] A large portion of the workforce was now dependent on consumers' having the money to buy new cars each year.

The consumption problem appeared to be resolved by the accelerated use of advertising and installment buying during the 1920s. The business and techniques of advertising rapidly expanded, thus increasing its ability to convince consumers that they needed to buy a variety of products. Stuart Chase, a popular economist of the period, was offended that more money was spent during the 1920s on advertising than on public education. Bruce Barton, one of the founding fathers of modern advertising, wrote a series of best-selling books promoting the dubious thesis that Jesus was "a master of business organization and public relations." Unlike the Puritan God, Jesus wanted us to live the good material life. Barton is generally given credit — or blamed — for having "reconciled Christianity and consumption."[10]

Although advertising would increase the desire to consume, installment buying would augment the means. Until the 1920s, the availability of credit to buy now and pay later had been a perquisite of the well-to-do. By extending this privilege, merchants were expanding the purchasing power of millions of Americans. In 1919, General Motors initiated installment purchase plans to buy its cars. By 1929, 60 percent of all cars sold in the United States were financed with installment credit. Lendel Calder reports, "from 1920 to 1929, the volume of consumer debt soared upward 131 percent, from $3.3 billion to $7.6 billion outstanding."[11] The expansion and interaction of radio, movies, advertising, and installment buying appeared to work together to support a consumption-driven prosperity. It was also producing a social transformation that disturbed many religious people and intellectuals. Parrish argues, "We began to experience in these years the virtues and vices of a consumer society, in which the production, marketing, and individual accumulation of a seemingly endless stream of goods and services threatened to become the chief preoccupation of daily life, a virtual secular religion."[12]

Groups that were not sharing in the prosperity of the 1920s were also disturbed. Farmers, who had their group consciousness raised by the previous Populist and Progressive eras of reform, believed they were being exploited by urban-industrial groups. During World War I, the agricultural sector had expanded to meet international demands, but after the war, this market had collapsed. Moreover, the growing use of trucks and tractors on farms meant that the estimated 25 million acres devoted to growing feed for horses and mules now was available for other agricultural use. The result was an agricultural sector overwhelmed by excess production, falling prices, and stifling debt. The foreclosure rate on farms accelerated from 3.2 per thousand farms between 1913 and 1920, to 17.0 per thousand from 1926 to 1930.[13] "For the first time in American history," according to David Hamilton, "the total number of farmers declined during the decade, falling from 6.5 million in 1920 to 6.3 million in 1930."[14] In brief, the agricultural sector, representing about one-fourth of the workforce, was in deep trouble before the Depression.

For farmers, their demand for equality became associated with the concept of parity. George Peek and Hugh Johnson, two executives from the Moline Plow Company who would later occupy top positions in the FDR administration, created a plan designed to assure that a bushel of, say, corn, sold in the 1920s would be able to buy the same nonfarm products that a similar bushel had bought before the war. Their plan was presented to Congress by Senator Charles McNary of Oregon and Representative Gilbert Haugen of Iowa in 1924. It authorized a federally created Agricultural Export Corporation to buy eight basic farm commodities at prices that would restore the farmer's purchasing power to pre–World War I levels. Surpluses would be sold (dumped) on foreign markets at the prevailing lower price.[15] The McNary-Haugen bill passed Congress twice, but Coolidge vetoed it both times, claiming it was unconstitutional.

Workers were also dissatisfied. With union strength declining, the bargaining power of labor for obtaining higher wages and benefits was weak. Although businessmen and economic theorists still talked about the American economy's being based on small, freely competing units, the reality was an economy dominated by large, publicly financed corporations. According to McElvaine, "In 1929, 200 corporations controlled nearly half of all American industry. The $81 billion in assets held by these corporations represented 49 percent of all corporate wealth in the nation. . . . Moreover, the trend was rapidly in the direction of even more concentration."[16] These corporations produced impressive rises in productivity but allowed much slower increases in wages. The result is summarized by McElvaine: "With production costs falling rapidly, prices remaining nearly stable, and wages rising slowly, the bulk of the benefits went into profits."[17] The increasingly skewed distribution of income meant that the bulk of the population could not participate in the prosperity of the 1920s. Although the Bureau of Labor Statistics estimated that a family of four needed an income of $2,500 a year in 1929 to maintain a decent standard of living, more than half the population was earning less.[18] Obviously, a structural conflict was developing. By the end of the decade, production was still increasing, but consumption was stagnating. During the 1920s, the United States developed a mass production economy, but because of the unequal distribution of income, it could not sustain a mass consumption economy. The Republican regime had no answer to this dilemma.

The Stock Market Crash

Probably no decade in American history has avoided speculative booms and busts, but the 1920s seemed particularly susceptible to them. In their desire to become rich in this land of many opportunities, Americans often allow their greed to overcome their common sense. Charles Ponzi set the tone for the Roaring Twenties by creating an investment business in Boston in 1919 that promised a 50 percent return in 45 days. By 1920, 30,000 people had invested in Ponzi's scheme, and he ended up in jail.[19] Five years later, a new speculative land boom occurred in Florida. In this venture, real estate interests were able to enlist the rhetorical talents of William Jennings Bryan. Leuchtenburg writes, "The land-speculation mania in Florida reached its high point one day in the summer of 1925 when the Miami *Daily News*, crowded with real estate advertisements, printed an issue of 504 pages, the largest in newspaper history. In 1926, after a hurricane had driven the waters of Biscayne Bay over the cottages of Miami, the land boom collapsed."[20] But neither of these episodes can compare, in scope and consequence, with the stock market boom and ruin of the 1920s.

Before World War I, only railroads and a small number of corporations tried to attract capital by selling stock to the public. Most corporations financed their capital needs with loans from commercial banks. During the war, "the United States government created a new market of middle-class investors by selling $27 billion in Liberty Bonds and Victory Bonds to finance the war against Germany. Few decisions did more to create the stock market boom of the next decade. Over 22 million Americans from all walks of life, responding to the patriotic calls of the United States Treasury, bought war bonds and received their first initiation into the mysteries of the securities market."[21]

The securities market was characterized by many mysteries and few regulations. Investors entered this "casino" at their own risk because it was almost impossible to obtain accurate financial information about the corporations whose stock one wanted to buy or sell. Even the New York Stock Exchange (NYSE), the largest one of the twenty-nine in the United States, "imposed minimal disclosure requirements on its listed companies. . . . Investment bankers, lawyers, and accountants who prepared financial statements as well as brochures for prospective customers wanted a quick sale of stock, not a careful inventory of a company's assets and liabilities."[22] The lack of governmental regulation and reliable information meant that the stock market could be manipulated by insider trading, false rumors, and secretive pools of investors.

Nevertheless, the economic growth of the 1920s, the increase in corporate profits, and the lure of making a killing attracted many new investors to the stock market. As the nation quickly recovered from the 1921 recession, a reasonable economic optimism escalated into a financial euphoria. Businessmen, financiers, and Republican leaders talked about — and took credit for — a new era, where there were fewer chances for economic downturns and more opportunities to get rich. Indeed, John Raskob wrote an article in the *Ladies' Home Journal* in August 1929 entitled, "Everybody Ought to Be Rich." The risks of stock market investing were underestimated; the rewards were overestimated; and thus the prerequisites for a bubble were created.

During the mid- to late 1920s, it may have seemed that everyone was speculating in the stock market, in part because it was a widely covered story in the newspapers. However, the truth was, the actual number was small. McElvaine estimates, "Roughly 4 million Americans owned stock in 1929, out of a population of approximately 120 million. Only 1.5 million of these stockholders had a sufficiently large interest to have an account with a broker. The bulk of the 'stockholders' owned only a few shares. . . . Almost 74 percent of all 1929 dividends went to the fewer than 600,000 individual stockholders with taxable incomes in excess of $5,000."[23] This small number of investors sustained a bull market from 1921 until 1929. During that period, the market experienced an extraordinary increase in both volume and volatility. In 1921, the volume of trades on the NYSE was 162,433,000 shares; by 1925, it was 466,615,000; and it peaked in 1929 at 1,124,610,000. Before 1928, the daily volume of trades had surpassed 3 million shares 8 times; in 1928 it did so 159 times.[24] As the value of the 1,200 stocks listed on the NYSE reached $90 billion in September 1929, the game spiraled out of control.

The rise in stock market prices seemed to generate a momentum of its own. Normally, one would expect to see a relationship between the real economy and stock prices, but "while the GNP increased by 59 percent in the 1920s, the Dow Jones went up by 400 percent."[25] The speculative frenzy was increasingly financed by call loans. Operating under the illusion that the price of the stocks they were buying would only go up, many investors bought stocks on margin. As Maury Klein explains, to gain control of more stock with less of their own money,

> they paid only a portion of the price in cash—anywhere from 10 to 70 percent—and borrowed the rest from a broker, who in turn usually got the funds from a bank loan. The purchased stock served as collateral for the loan, and the buyer received all gains or losses in price. If the stock's price dipped below the amount needed to cover the loan, the margin became impaired, meaning the buyer had to put up more margin to make up the difference. If he could not "cover" this additional margin, the broker could "sell him out"—in effect foreclosing the loan and selling the stock used as collateral for whatever it would buy.[26]

As long as stock prices went up, this system generated income for all participants. Commercial banks could borrow at the discount window of the Federal Reserve at 5 percent and lend it at 12 percent to brokers, who would then lend it to investors at 20 percent. A nightmare would occur, however, if stock market prices fell; brokers would call in their loans, and if investors could not cover their margins, brokers would sell their stock. The market would be flooded with stocks whose prices would be rapidly sinking; thousands of investors would be wiped out. Because so much of the stock had been bought with borrowed money, this unregulated market created a precarious situation that threatened more than Wall Street.

By 1928, the Federal Reserve, and especially Benjamin Strong, the head of the Fed's New York District Bank, became worried that the volume of brokers' loans from commercial banks was fueling a speculative bubble. But the Fed, according to Kettl, was faced with a dilemma that hindered decisive action: "how could it limit the flow of credit for stock speculation without drying it up for other purposes? . . . To tighten money enough to slow the speculative boom would stir up attacks from farmers and small businessmen who would have great trouble in securing credit. Not to tighten credit would give license to speculators."[27] Following Strong's recommendation, the Fed tightened the money supply beginning in January 1928 by selling treasury bonds to commercial banks and raising the discount rate from 3½ to 5 percent. This contractionary policy failed to restrict the call loan market because brokers were successful in tapping into resources outside of the Federal Reserve, such as corporations.[28] A split emerged between the Federal Reserve Board in Washington, D.C., and the Federal Reserve Bank of New York over how to respond. Although the board advocated denying access to the discount window to member banks making loans to brokers, the Federal Reserve Bank of New York argued that it was impossible to control credit selectively. It recommended that speculation could only be decreased by raising the discount rate.[29] Some scholars suggest that Strong would have found a way to stop this runaway train of speculation, but he died in October 1928. The New York Federal Reserve Bank voted to raise the discount rate eleven times in the first half of 1929, but the Federal Reserve Board would not allow it. The board finally relented in August 1929 and permitted its New York bank to raise its discount rate to 6 percent.[30] It was too late.

The Dow closed at 381.7 on September 3, 1929, "a peak that would not be reached again until November 1954."[31] During the next six weeks, a jittery market trended downward and oscillated between greed—the feeling that there were still more opportunities to make easy money—and fear—the attitude that the exceptional length of the bull market meant a "correction," perhaps a collapse of stock prices, was likely. It was ominous that a number of knowledgeable Americans, such as Herbert Hoover, Joseph P. Kennedy, Bernard Baruch, Owen Young, and Paul Warburg, had withdrawn their money from the stock market for safer havens. Some investors became even more wary when indexes of industrial production began to decline in the summer of 1929. Early in September, an economist named Roger Babson predicted a stock market crash and a devastating depression, a forecast that was widely circulated and resulted in a dip in stock prices. Babson had made similar predictions before, however, and the market soon recovered most of its losses. The final refuge of the optimists was their faith that the big moneyed interests would simply not allow the stock market to crash. Just as the legendary J. P. Morgan had mobilized private bankers to resolve the Panic of 1907, it was hoped that a similar effort could prevent a disaster this time.[32]

No one was able to head off the disaster of October 1929. On the morning of October 24, Black Thursday, an avalanche of sell orders caused the stock prices to plummet. Within the first few hours, $9 billion was lost. In response to this panic, a group of bankers met in the offices of J. P. Morgan and agreed to pool their resources to prop up prices. Early in the afternoon, Richard Whitney, vice president of the NYSE and brother of the Morgan partner, walked out on the trading floor and bought 25,000 shares of U.S. Steel at 205 (it had been selling at under 200) and several other stocks. "The mood on the floor," according to Klein, "transformed at once. Organized support had arrived! . . . Prices rallied almost at once and cut deeply into the day's losses. When trading ceased at 3:00 P.M., the Dow was down only 6.38."[33]

For several days, the prices of stocks seemed to stabilize, but then on Monday, October 28, the Dow plunged over 38 points on a volume of 9.2 million shares. The next day, Black Tuesday, an unprecedented 16.4 million shares were traded, a record that would stand for almost forty years. The Dow declined by over 30 points to 230.07. This time there was no rescue party: "The bankers met again at noon and agreed that even their buying could not deflect the enormous wave of selling. Any attempt to support the market was, as an analyst said, 'like trying to stem the falls of Niagara.'"[34] At the end of October, the crash had eliminated $26 billion of paper wealth from its September value of $90 billion. Despite assurances from businessmen that the economy was fundamentally sound, stocks continued to decline; by July 1932, "total stock values were only 17 percent of their peak in September 1929."[35] On July 8, 1932, the Dow measured at 41.22.

Because few Americans had money invested in the stock market, most historians do not view the October 1929 crash as the sole or even the major cause of the Depression. As was correctly stressed after the collapse, not a single factory or farm was destroyed on Black Tuesday. Indeed, one could make the plausible argument that the crash was a necessary correction that would rechannel funds from speculative to productive purposes and aid the real economy. However, when economic conditions deteriorated in the early 1930s and Senate investigations revealed the selfish behavior of bankers and businessmen, it became clear that the crash had destroyed more than the bull market. It had shattered the foundations of the Republican regime. In Clyde Weed's words, "During the 1920s, business leadership reached a zenith in public esteem that led to its portrayal as a kind of ultimate American profession; business leaders were thought to be producing a technological revolution that utilized new patterns of both industrialization and science."[36] The Republican strategy of promising continuous prosperity by giving business and Wall Street a free hand had resulted in producing billions in stock profits that suddenly vanished and was replaced by lasting misery. The titans of business and finance had proven to be false gods; they proved unable to control the business civilization they had created. Confidence had been replaced by fear and uncertainty.

The Depression

Explaining the Depression to a contemporary audience is difficult and can be compared with describing a foreign country. With the freedom provided by dramatic license, McElvaine suggests, "It began in New York City on a series of days in October 1929, and decisively ended on December 7, 1941, near Honolulu."[37] Visually, the Depression can be portrayed in black-and-white photos and newsreels that display bread lines, hobos living under bridges, labor riots, dust storms, Okies trekking to California, and young men traveling in boxcars, futilely seeking jobs. Economically, the Depression can be outlined in a set of grim statistics. For farmers, who never recovered from the collapse of prices for their produce after the Great War, the Depression was a second calamity. Between 1929 and 1932, the prices of crops and livestock nosedived by nearly 75 percent, causing farm income to plunge from $13.8 billion to $6.5 billion. Between 1929 and early 1933, the GNP was sliced in half, and unemployment rose from 3.2 percent to nearly 25 percent. At the end of Hoover's presidency, about 13 million workers were unemployed. Although the unemployment rate for labor in manufacturing was 40 percent, it measured 73 percent among construction workers. During these years, investment dropped 98 percent, 5,000 banks crashed, wiping out $7 billion in depositors' cash, and more than 500,000 homeowners were not able to meet their mortgage obligations and lost their homes.[38] Allan Meltzer reports, "From the peak of the cycle in the summer of 1929 to the bottom of the depression in March 1933, the stock of money—currency and demand deposits—fell by 28 percent, and industrial production fell by 50 percent."[39] The combination of the stock market crash and bank failures triggered a "spiral of deflation" in which consumer prices declined 18 percent between 1929 and 1933.[40] In brief, this is not the America most of us have known since the end of World War II.

It is easy to accumulate statistics and anecdotes about how terrible the Great Depression was, but the reader knows that the United States recovered and prospered. The challenge is to convey the spirit of despair that gripped the nation and made many fear the country might never recuperate. The irrational euphoria of 1929 had metamorphosed into the profound pessimism of 1932. In the words of one observer, "We are in the doldrums, waiting not even hopefully for the wind which never comes."[41] Another witness asked a question that reflected the basic dilemma of the Depression: "We are not able to purchase the abundance that modern methods of agriculture, mining, and manufacture make available in such bountiful quantities. Why is mankind being asked to go hungry and cold and poverty stricken in the midst of plenty."[42] The fact that there was no generally accepted answer to this question contributed to the despondent mood and occasional rage of citizens during the Depression.

The United States had experienced a number of recessions before (in 1819, 1837, 1857, 1873, 1893, and 1921), but the nation was totally unprepared for what began in late 1929. An urban-industrialized society turned out to be more vulnerable to an economic slump than the more rural economy of the nineteenth century. In an agrarian economy, a greater portion of the population could ride out the downturn by living on the farm and getting help from family, friends, and local charities. In the more mobile urban environment, there was less family to fall back on, and when workers lost their jobs and could not pay their grocery bills, their rent, or their mortgage, the negative effects were more severe. Experiencing unemployment and stomach-churning insecurity had certainly weakened the faith of many citizens in the value of self-reliance and made them more receptive to relying on government programs to help them with their problems.

Although many extreme leftists hoped that the economic breakdown would precipitate a revolt against capitalism, this did not happen. Indeed, the victims of the Depression probably experienced more self-loathing than a rise in revolutionary consciousness.[43]

The Depression created a self-sustaining system that would be difficult to dislodge. Just as prosperity is propelled by optimism, the Depression was fueled by pessimism. Despite assurances from politicians and businessmen that everything was fundamentally sound, the reality was that workers were losing their jobs, businesses were closing, mortgages were being foreclosed, and banks were collapsing. Insecurity bred behaviors that prevented recovery. Capitalists, anxious about conserving their wealth, were no longer looking for investment opportunities; fearing runs on their banks, bankers were reluctant to lend their money; workers, worried about losing their jobs, restricted their consumption. "More and more Americans," according to McJimsey, "diverted their energies from producing to surviving. Clothes were stitched and mended again and again, mothers extended meals with watery soups, farmers who could not sell their corn burned it for fuel."[44] The struggle for survival is always the plight of the poor; during the Depression, it became the predicament of a much larger proportion of the population. The attempts of individuals to respond rationally to the problems of the Depression were proving irrational.

The Depression was a seminal event in American history. In altering our politics and policies, it was as significant as the Civil War. If abolishing slavery and preserving the union were the most challenging political problems ever faced by the United States, recovery from the Depression was the most severe economic one. The Depression took on the appearance of an irrepressible force that no human efforts could impede; it swamped the endeavors of leaders of both private enterprise and government to control it. Leuchtenburg pointed out several ways people tried to make sense of what was happening: "Sometimes people thought of the Great Depression as a breakdown of a system, sometimes as the product of the machinations of evil or stupid men, sometimes as the visitation of a plague like the Black Death. But from the very first, many conceived the depression to be a calamity like war or, more specifically, like the menace of a foreign enemy who had to be defeated in combat."[45] Whatever metaphor they used to describe their situation, the victims of the Depression yearned for someone to devise a strategy that would lead them out of this valley of despair.

The economic collapse meant there would have to be big changes, but many of the new proposals sounded un-American. What values and traditions would we have to sacrifice in order to rid ourselves of this alien force that had taken over our nation? Would the new remedies be compatible with democracy, federalism, capitalism, and our cherished individuality? As the Depression persisted and spread its misery among a number of nations, the lack of adequate responses became a national security concern. In 1931, the British historian Arnold Toynbee wrote that "men and women all over the world were seriously contemplating and frankly discussing the possibility that the Western system of Society might break down and cease to work."[46] How long would the public support democratic procedures when they seemed to prolong the crisis? Were fascism and communism the waves of the future? "'Even the iron hand of a national dictator,' said [Republican Governor] Alfred Landon of Kansas, 'is in preference to a paralytic stroke.'"[47]

The Depression created an environment in which it was difficult, if not impossible, to formulate strategic priorities in public policies. It seemed that everything had broken down, which meant that everything had to be fixed. Part of the dilemma was that there was no consensus as to what caused the collapse, and even less agreement on how to navigate the economy out of this morass. In July 1932, Walter Lippmann, one of the most astute observers of the period, wrote, "Our danger is neither from radicalism nor conservatism but from incoherence and paralysis. What we have to fear is the inability of government to determine policies and to execute them."[48] The task of seeing through this fog of confusion and orchestrating an effective response to the crisis was in the hands of Herbert Hoover.

Herbert Hoover

When Herbert Hoover was elected president by a landslide in 1928, few would have predicted that he would be trounced by Franklin Roosevelt four years later. Given his background and administrative skills, Hoover appeared to be the best-qualified protector of the Republican regime. But the Depression shattered the foundations of the regime and overpowered his impressive administrative skills. Hoover was tied to a declining regime and pursued the politics of disjunction to its bitter end. That end found Hoover unintentionally delegitimizing the Republican regime and paving the road to a new liberal one based on ideas and policies that he vehemently opposed.

In terms of experience, Hoover would appear to be better equipped to deal with the Depression than Roosevelt was. He was born August 10, 1874, in West Branch, Iowa, to a Quaker family. His father, Jesse, a blacksmith, died in 1880; three years later, Hoover's mother, Huldah, passed away, leaving Herbert an orphan. Hoover was then moved to Newberg, Oregon, and raised by an uncle. Being bright in math, Hoover went to the newly created Stanford University and majored in mining engineering, graduating in 1895. He was soon hired by a British mining company, which sent him to work in Australia, China, Burma, Peru, Russia, and Mexico. By 1908, he was a millionaire, and he decided to leave the British firm and set up his own consulting firm in London.

When the Great War began in August 1914, Hoover was asked to head a relief effort to help nearly 120,000 Americans living in Great Britain return to the United States. After successfully completing this mission, Hoover was then given a number of difficult tasks that established his reputation as a great humanitarian. He directed the Commission for Relief in Belgium, which fed and clothed hundreds of thousands in that war-torn country; after the United States joined the war in April 1917, President Wilson put him in charge of the distribution, export, and storage of food; after the war, he directed postwar relief.[49] This shy man with progressive credentials was now ready to play a major political role in the United States during the 1920s.

Some Democrats, including FDR, hoped that Hoover would declare himself a Democrat and replace the ailing Wilson as president. But early in 1920, Hoover announced he was a Republican and sought that party's nomination. Senator Warren Harding won the Republican nomination and was easily elected president by a wide margin, reflecting the new conservative mood of the nation. In 1921, Harding appointed Hoover as secretary of commerce, but with a broad grant of authority that allowed him to become involved in a variety of subjects. He was involved in a number of conferences that sought to help farmers and businessmen prevent waste and promote efficiency. He called for a major government role in regulating radio and aviation. He supported the proliferation of national voluntary associations, which grew from approximately seven hundred in 1919 to about two thousand by 1929.[50] When there was extensive flooding along the Mississippi River in 1927, President Coolidge put Hoover in charge of the relief efforts. Hoover's activities bred the joke that he was the secretary of commerce "and the Under-Secretary of everything else."

Throughout the 1920s, Hoover and his supporters were successful in filling media space with favorable stories and images of the Great Engineer. Hence, when Coolidge announced he would not run for reelection in 1928, Hoover, despite some reservations from conservatives who worried about his progressive background and inclinations, was nominated for president on the first ballot. Although Hoover had never run for elected office before, given the combination of peace and prosperity, and a natural Republican majority in the electorate, there was never any doubt that he would defeat Governor Al Smith from New York.

However, just as the owners of the *Titanic* had tempted fate when they claimed that their ship was unsinkable, Hoover's campaign rhetoric proved to be prophetically perverse. In accepting the Republican nomination, Hoover declared, "We in America today are nearer to the final triumph over poverty than ever before in the history of any land. The poorhouse is vanishing from among us. We have not yet reached the goal, but given a chance to go forward with the policies of the last eight years, we shall soon with the help of God be in sight of the day when poverty will be banished from the nation."[51] Hoover's failure to either prevent the Depression or cushion its effects during his four years in office allowed his opponents to throw these words back at him with lethal sarcasm.

Hoover did not fail in office because he believed in laissez-faire, the doctrine that stressed that government should not meddle in economic affairs. Whereas Coolidge was inclined to "Do Nothing," Hoover was disposed to "Do Something." He believed that the market results "of the 'invisible hand' in classical economics could be improved upon by developing institutions with managerial and regulatory capacities."[52] Hoover's biographer, David Burner, suggests, "His writings put expertise and cooperation in the central place that classical economists had assigned to competition and price."[53] To verify Hoover's attitude toward laissez-faire, Herbert Stein cites a letter that the ex-president wrote to his friend and economic adviser, Arch W. Shaw, on July 26, 1933:

> I notice that the Brain Trust and their superiors are now announcing to the world that the social thesis of laissez faire died on March 4. I wish they would add a professor of history to the Brain Trust. The 18th century thesis of laissez faire passed in the United States a century ago. The visible proof of it was the enactment of the Sherman Act for the regulation of all business, the transportation and utility regulation, the Federal Reserve System, the Eighteenth Amendment, the establishment of the Farm Loan Banks, the Home Loan Banks, and the Reconstruction Finance Corporation. All are but part of the items marking the total abandonment of that social thesis.[54]

Hoover's alternative to laissez-faire was voluntary cooperation among the components of private enterprise and the different levels of government.

He pictured himself as helping the nineteenth-century industrial system become more rational by utilizing the expanding pool of scientific information now available. The new knowledge should be disseminated and used to prevent recessions and to promote efficiency, raise living standards, and humanize industrial relations.[55] The proper use of technical proficiency and nonstatist machinery (promotional conferences, expert inquiries, cooperating committees) could foster "a kinder, gentler" form of capitalism. A more compassionate form of capitalism was dependent on the encouragement of forces outside of government, which were imbued with a sense of public responsibility and which would not succumb to the temptation of becoming dependent on federal bureaucracies. According to Burner, Hoover's "aversion to national bureaucracy was not one symptom of a pro-business orientation but a concern shared by many progressives. What he desired was some system of balances: a government just large enough to regulate, harmonize, and effect arbitrations in American business, and small enough to preserve its efficiency and independence. To a great extent it was the old progressive ideal of Woodrow Wilson."[56]

In examining Hoover's philosophy, one becomes aware of how central morality was to his thought and behavior. As a Quaker, he had been taught to be guided by an inner light. The moral values of self-reliance and individual initiative had helped him overcome the tragedies of his youth and become a millionaire. He was fearful that the expansion of government would destroy the self-reliance of the American people. This moral concern of violating traditional values competed with—and was sometimes more powerful than—his compassion for helping the victims of the Depression. Hoover was not blessed with the moral flexibility of FDR.

Hoover's opposition to laissez-faire is demonstrated by his behavior as president. As soon as he was inaugurated, Hoover summoned Congress into special session in April 1929 to deal with the farm problem. He informed congressional leaders that he would not support mandatory production controls and export subsidies. By June 15, 1929, Congress passed, and the president signed, the Agricultural Marketing Act, which committed the federal government to placing "agriculture on a basis of economic equality with industry." The law created the Federal Farm Board to administer the lending of $500 million out of a fund set up to encourage farmers' cooperatives and, if necessary, to establish stabilization corporations to buy and sell surpluses. Because the law assumed that farm prices would follow a normal pattern of sometimes going up and sometimes going down, it was totally unprepared when they collapsed. The stabilization corporations tried to maintain farm prices by buying and storing surpluses while waiting in vain for prices to recover. Their efforts "succeeded" in filling warehouses with grain and cotton, a costly undertaking that exerted downward pressure on prices. By mid-1931, the Federal Farm Board conceded its inability to uphold farm prices and stopped making loans. The failure of the Agricultural Marketing Act helped make the case for the need of compulsory mechanisms to curtail production in order to raise farm income. FDR's Agricultural Adjustment Act would do that.

Hoover's commitment to activist economic policies was also demonstrated by his initial responses to the October 1929 stock market crash. While Treasury Secretary Mellon advocated the orthodox view of allowing economic forces to run their downward course after the speculative orgy, namely, "Liquidate labor, liquidate stocks, liquidate the farmers, liquidate real estate," Hoover was determined to prevent the contagion of Wall Street from infecting other parts of the economy that he believed were healthy.[57] To bolster business confidence, he immediately stressed that the real economy of production and distribution, as opposed to the paper economy of trading stocks, was still sound and prosperous. Hoover also recognized the need for action. By the end of November 1929, he had met with the leaders of business and finance in a series of highly publicized conferences and obtained pledges that they "would not reduce wages, lay off employees, engage in price-cutting, or lower production."[58] The president secured similar pledges not to cut back from the country's mayors and governors, who managed the lion's share of public expenditures at the end of the 1920s. Finally, Hoover promised that his administration would accelerate spending for construction, praised the Federal Reserve for lowering interest rates, and proposed cuts in taxes. The significance of these first steps was that Hoover was accepting a more significant role for the president as manager of the economy than any other previous chief executive.

Hoover continued the core commitment of the Republican regime to protectionism by signing the Smoot-Hawley tariff on June 17, 1930. He had originally advocated a narrower bill that protected farmers, but once on the floor of the House and Senate, the legislation snowballed into a monstrosity that raised tariffs on a wide variety of goods to the highest levels in American history. Over a thousand economists submitted a petition to Hoover asking him to veto this bill, but he felt morally bound to sign it. Internationally, Smoot-Hawley triggered retaliatory measures that stifled global trade. In the United States, "Exports declined from $5,200,000,000 in 1929 to $1,647,000,000 in 1933. Imports fell off from $4,399,500,000 in

1929 to $1,450,000,000 in 1933."[59] The results of Smoot-Hawley were so disastrous that they delegitimized protectionism and provided arguments for the reciprocal trade agreements in the New Deal.

As millions of Americans lost their jobs during the 1930s, the debate over how to provide relief for the destitute became a major issue. Hoover was no social Darwinist; he wanted to help the unemployed. He believed that the first line of defense should be the nation's private charities: the Red Cross, the Salvation Army, the Community Chest, the YMCA, Traveler's Aid, and many others. The second line should be the agencies of state and local governments. This was the traditional American way of providing relief. Hoover was extremely reluctant to use a direct federal role in relief for a variety of reasons: "it would delay the natural forces at work to restore prosperity, it impaired the credit and solvency of the government, it stifled voluntary giving, it was inflexible and thus could not respond to local needs, it established politicized bureaucracies, it undermined free enterprise, it was illegal—a violation of local responsibility and states rights—and it ultimately endangered democratic government."[60] Hoover's philosophy about public relief was demonstrated in December 1930, when he supported a congressional appropriation to feed the drought-stricken livestock of Arkansas farmers but opposed additional money to aid the starving farmers.

When the unprecedented massive misery produced by the Depression overwhelmed the capabilities of both private charities and local governments, Hoover was forced to retreat from the "American way." In October 1930, he created the Emergency Committee for Employment, headed by Colonel Arthur Woods. A year later, the committee was reorganized as the President's Committee on Unemployment. These two committees relied on public relations strategies to encourage private contributions to charity. Katz points out, "With no funds for relief, the committee accomplished little, and Hoover rejected its recommendations for 'federal road building, rural electrification projects, . . . urban housing . . . , a national bureau for gathering unemployment statistics, a nationwide system of public employment offices, and a national plan for unemployment insurance.'"[61] Pressures for New Deal programs were being generated by Hoover appointees.

On July 21, 1932, Hoover signed the Emergency Relief and Construction Act, which had been sponsored by Democratic Senator Robert Wagner of New York. The legislation allowed the Reconstruction Finance Corporation to lend money to the states to finance local public works for the purpose of relieving unemployment. But because most of the states were already in debt and were reluctant and sometimes legally forbidden to take on more debt, few states applied for the loans, and little federal money helped the poor. In brief, Hoover's failure to prove that local efforts could handle the relief problem only served to amplify the pressures for a substantial federal relief effort.

Hoover's philosophy was also wounded when he attempted to deal with the banking problems. In October 1931, the president, at a meeting in Secretary Mellon's Washington home, pressured the heads of several large banks to create the National Credit Corporation (NCC), with a capital fund of $500 million. In Parrish's words, "the NCC was a perfect expression of Hoover's philosophy. Bankers, not government, would help other bankers weather the storm. The NCC would use its reserves to break the liquidity crisis by purchasing the dubious assets of banks on the verge of insolvency and some of those already closed."[62] Again, Hoover's reliance on voluntarism did not work because the NCC, reflecting the prevailing mood of insecurity, only lent out a tiny proportion of its funds.

Hoover then felt compelled to accept the recommendation of Eugene Meyer, the chairman of the Federal Reserve Board, to create the Reconstruction Finance Corporation (RFC). The RFC was modeled on the War Finance Corporation's experiences in financing industry during the Great War and reflected (to Hoover's surprise) what the bankers wanted: federal help. The bill passed Congress quickly and was signed by Hoover in January 1932. It authorized the RFC to lend up to $2 billion to help banks, savings banks, railroads, and insurance companies. This new capital saved some banks from closing, but it did not reverse the deflationary spiral that was preventing recovery. According to Schlesinger, the "RFC, grudgingly accepted and grudgingly employed, was a reluctant breach in the voluntarist philosophy. Hoover used the new powers with the utmost conservatism, and his RFC had little impact on the depression."[63]

The persistence of the Depression had negative effects on the budget, which increasingly worried Hoover. Between 1929 and 1931, federal receipts diminished by almost 50 percent, and expenditures rose by almost 60 percent, resulting in a budget deficit in July 1931 of $461 million. In 1930, the president had persuaded Congress to pass a $160 million tax cut; now he was worried about the effects of a growing budget deficit on business confidence and the fear that the United States, like Great Britain, might be forced to abandon the gold standard.[64] With the Depression getting worse despite his monumental efforts, and with his chances for reelection in November 1932 rapidly declining, Hoover became obsessed with balancing the budget. Perhaps that was the key that would open the door to recovery.

Hence, Hoover rejected the arguments that raising taxes in the grim conditions of 1932 would decrease consumption and increase unemployment. Instead, in December 1931, he proposed a tax increase that was projected to bring about a balanced budget in 1933. Congress, reflecting traditional attitudes, was also committed to the goal of balancing the budget. Initially, both Hoover and the new Democratic Speaker of the House, John Nance Garner, recommended a national sales tax, but this was rejected. After a great deal of compromising, the president signed the Revenue Act of 1932 on June 6, 1932. This legislation raised the top rate for taxing those with the largest incomes to 55 percent; it also increased estate, corporate, and excise taxes. Burner concludes, "The Revenue Act of 1932 was the most progressive tax law of the decade; Hoover called it a natural extension of the graduated income tax 'one of the most just and efficient methods of taxation.' The new rates were left essentially unchanged throughout the New Deal and for a generation after."[65] Hoover had retreated from Mellon's tax policy.

Reexamining the Hoover presidency is like watching a good man futilely struggling against his inevitable doom. The story is tragic because Hoover was moral, intelligent, and hardworking; he deserved a better fate. Hoover reacted to the crash as a conscientious executive who accepted the responsibilities of making sure that the paper losses on Wall Street did not spread havoc throughout the rest of the economy. His unprecedented efforts were rewarded with unprecedented failure. In responding to the unique problems of the Depression, so much of his morality, knowledge, and hard work was either useless or counterproductive. The intellectual and physical resources of the existing regime were totally inadequate to handle the multiple problems of the Depression. When Hoover said he felt like he was fighting on one hundred fronts, he was giving us an accurate description of the politics of disjunction. When a regime is unraveling, the president is overwhelmed by the hopeless task of trying to maintain the legitimacy of the existing governing arrangements.

Hoover viewed the crash and the ensuing economic decline as an aberration, a temporary setback that could be rectified. Both his personality and his philosophy determined that he would reject a laissez-faire strategy and opt for an activist response. Hoover's policies were designed to save the existing regime, not transform it. The prevailing system had given him (and many others) the opportunity to become wealthy. It was the American way; any new regime would be alien and threaten individual liberty. Moreover, the present economy was fundamentally sound and would soon recover if the country followed his recommendations and avoided radical proposals.

By December 1930, in Hoover's second annual address to Congress, he developed the self-serving argument that the causes of the Depression were international, the lingering financial problems bred by the Great War and its aftermath. Hence, the regime was not responsible for the Depression, and there was no need for it to be replaced by a New Deal. But to blame the Depression on foreign sources was difficult to explain to the public. More importantly, Hoover and the Republicans could not escape the logic—and the Democratic accusation—that because they claimed credit for the prosperity of the 1920s, they could not avoid blame for the Depression in the early 1930s.

When teaching about this period, I am often asked why Hoover didn't utilize more of the powers of the federal government to fight the Depression. The answer is that the federal role in America was limited in 1929; for most citizens, the major federal agency that they interacted with was the post office. The limited economic role of the Republican regime is revealed in the following statistics: "In 1929 total federal expenditures were about 2.5 percent of the GNP, federal purchases of goods and services about 1.3 percent, and federal construction less than .2 percent. . . . Receipts were about 3.7 percent of the GNP in 1929, but by 1931 they had fallen 50 percent in dollar amounts to 2.7 percent of the diminished GNP. A very large percentage change in the revenue or expenditure side of such small budgets would have been required to make a significant dent in the national economy."[66] David Kennedy adds, "State and local government expenditures were about five times larger than the federal budget in 1929; by century's end, these figures would be nearly equal."[67] Maury Klein points out, "The federal government spent only about $200 million on construction projects in 1929, while the states spent $2 billion, or ten times as much, and private industry $9 billion."[68] Under these conditions, it was rational in the short term for Hoover to try to mobilize state and private resources to counter the effects of the Depression. But these resources quickly dried up because of the prolonged economic collapse, and Hoover was not willing to expand the federal role through deficit financing. Congress members could propose spending billions on public works in order to provide jobs, but Hoover knew that neither the federal government nor local governments had a set of well-prepared projects sitting on their shelves waiting to be financed. In the old regime, there was no way massive amounts of federal money could be spent wisely and honestly.

In confronting the challenges of the Depression, Hoover was not helped by his strict moral code. In 1930, the president felt morally bound to sign the Smoot-Hawley tariff bill; by 1932, his moral indignation toward bankers and Wall Street led him to demand a Senate investigation. It was part of both his philosophy and his morality that the leaders of business and finance in a time of economic crisis should increase their efforts to promote the public interest. Although many captains of industry did this, too many did not. Hoover was initially frustrated that the stock exchange did not undertake any significant reforms after the crash. What incensed him later were the bear raids that allowed investors to make profits from falling stock prices. In the spring of 1932, the Senate Banking and Currency Committee began its investigation of bankers and investors. The committee hearings, which were widely publicized in the press, produced revelations that disgusted the public. These hearings "revealed that the most respected men on Wall Street had rigged pools, had profited by pegging bond prices artificially high, and had lined their pockets with fantastic bonuses. The leading financial houses, the committee learned, invited insiders to purchase securities at a price much below that paid by the public. When officers of Charles Mitchell's National City Bank faced ruin because they could not cover their investments, the bank gave them interest-free loans while ruthlessly selling out their own customers."[69] Although not all businessmen who testified were Republican, most of them were affiliated with the GOP. Their greed was now blamed for the collapse; their recommendations for recovery were now treated with suspicion. Writing in 1934, Walter Lippmann declared, "In the past five years the industrial and financial leaders of America have fallen from one of the highest positions of influence and power that they have ever occupied in our history to one of the lowest."[70] One of the principal props supporting the Republican regime had been seriously weakened, but Hoover had no strategy for replacing it. The stage was set for federal regulation of the stock market, which FDR provided with the creation of the Securities and Exchange Commission in 1934.

Hoover was also hampered by his lack of political skills. He was a great engineer and administrator, but no one ever described him as an outstanding politician or communicator. His dilemma was that he was facing crises caused by the Depression that required the political capabilities of a Lincoln. The Depression demanded imaginative political responses that were beyond Hoover's capabilities. His speeches, which he insisted on writing himself, were fact-filled, ponderous, and dull. Barry Karl suggests, "He was essentially a managerial technician and proud of it. He sought facts—facts to organize and analyze. . . . From his point of view, experimentation was a public danger. No responsible engineer would use real people to test the stresses on a bridge or the safety of a machine in a mine."[71] Therefore, while FDR viewed the Depression as a crisis that required imaginative experimentation, Hoover did not.

Hoover's political ineptness was reflected in a number of ways. Given his background and humane achievements, it would have shocked Hoover during the 1920s that any political opponent could successfully label him a do-nothing reactionary. But that is precisely what FDR was able to do in the 1932 presidential elections. Despite his working sixteen-hour days, organizing thirty conferences to deal with economic problems, and doing more than any previous president in response to an economic slump, Hoover was perceived by the public as not having been aggressive enough in fighting the Depression. His concern about promoting business confidence led him onto the ruinous road of predicting too many upturns that did not happen. As the Depression worsened, Hoover's words seemed increasingly detached from reality. By proclaiming the economy was sound while standing next to millionaire businessmen, he was distancing himself from the millions of citizens whose blighted prospects demonstrated that something was profoundly wrong. Hoover was not confronting the wolf at the door—unemployment. It was futile for him to claim that he was saving us from inflation and socialism.

The failure of Hoover's initial efforts to stem the onslaught of the Depression generated pressures for expansive federal programs, pressures that he felt morally obligated to oppose. He was seen more often blocking reforms than promoting them at a time when significant changes were clearly needed. While Hoover was stressing that relief should still be the major concern of private charity, Governor Roosevelt, in August 1931, was declaring that unemployment relief "must be extended by government—not as a matter of charity but as a matter of social duty."[72] In trying to hold the line against progressive reforms, Hoover found himself defending several contradictory positions: supporting federal relief for bankers with RFC funds while opposing federal help for the unemployed; providing foreign governments with a one-year moratorium on their debts to the United States but denying mortgage relief to farmers and homeowners; supporting the Boulder Dam project in Arizona but vetoing Senator George Norris's proposal for the Tennessee Valley Authority. By the end of his administration, Hoover seemed more frightened by proposed solutions than by the problems of the Depression.

The longer the Depression lasted, the more the legitimacy of the Republican regime came into question. Under these conditions, Hoover found himself increasingly defending the existing regime because he (correctly) feared that a new one would be even less to his liking. Shielding the regime made Hoover appear less progressive and more conservative at a time when the political spectrum was moving to the left.[73] The more Hoover defended the old regime, the more the president and the struggling regime became entangled in an embrace that benefited neither one. The grim symbols of the Depression became associated with him: a shantytown was called a Hooverville; a newspaper that covered a sleeping man in the park was called a Hoover blanket. Schlesinger suggests that in defending the regime, Hoover had undermined it: "For all his faith in individualism, he brought great areas of the economy—the banks, the railroads, the insurance companies, the farmers, even, toward the end, the unemployed—into the orbit of national action. No doubt, he entered on these programs grudgingly, and did as little as he could to develop their possibilities. Yet he breached the walls of local responsibility as had no President in American history."[74] Hoover's presidency, in conformity with the politics of disjunction, was truly a tragic one.

Conclusion

To understand FDR and the New Deal, one must analyze the Depression and the inept efforts of Herbert Hoover to handle it. The industrial machine produced by the alliance of business and the Republicans had produced prosperity in the 1920s and promised abundance in the near future. However, the stock market crash of 1929, and increasing poverty in the midst of plenty, wiped out the political benefits of the Republican regime's achievements in industrializing America. The inability of the Republicans to prevent or cure the Depression meant that the gospel of the new era was now false. The search for a new public philosophy was begun. A large capitalist economy could not be left to capitalists to control; it needed more governmental regulations to ensure that the public interest was maintained. As a result of the stock market crash and the Depression, the prestige of businessmen and financiers nosedived, preparing the way for Americans to shift their faith to the talented New Dealers recruited by FDR.

As Hoover struggled to deal with the problems generated by the Depression, he was entrapped by the dilemmas of the politics of disjunction: his proposals were considered too little and too late, and they were more "successful" in delegitimizing the existing regime than in solving problems. He became the personal symbol of a failed regime. Under these conditions, Hoover's impressive administrative skills were useless. He could organize conferences attended by the captains of industry and finance, and he could issue statements confirming that the economy was sound and that prosperity would soon return. But what was needed was a president not shackled by the perspectives of the old regime. New visions and much greater national resources were needed to combat the Depression. This required an imagination and a set of political skills that Hoover did not possess.

Hoover's decision making was cross-pressured between progressive inclinations to help the victims of the Depression and conservative fears that such efforts would create a bureaucratic leviathan that would destroy the American way. Although the search for political solutions was a natural goal for FDR, it was an immoral temptation for Hoover. No president alienated more citizens and Congress members by adhering to his moral principles than did Hoover. Most people are astonished that he could believe that it was acceptable for the government to feed starving livestock but immoral to help desperate farmers. By being more dismayed by proposed solutions than he was about the deepening problems of the Depression, he ruined his reputation as a humanitarian and opened the door for a politician who was comfortable with experimenting with a number of new programs.

3

Erosion of the Liberal Regime

Reagan's presidency was as much a reaction to the failures of Jimmy Carter's four years in the White House as Franklin Roosevelt's was to Herbert Hoover's. If Carter had been planted as a mole in his own administration by conservative Republicans to deliberately wreck his presidency and prepare the way for Reagan's political successes, he could hardly have been more effective in accomplishing that feat. As Peggy Noonan writes, "There was no Reagan without Carter. Only four years of steady decline and lack of clarity could have lurched the country over to this . . . actor."[1] Michael Foley suggests, "Reagan's election, his political agenda, his style of leadership and the level of success achieved in his term of office was to a large extent attributable to President Carter. Without Carter, the presidency of Ronald Reagan would be unimaginable, not just because the latter simply followed the former in time, but because . . . Carter prepared much of the ground for Reagan and provided many of the prior conditions that Reagan was later to capitalize on."[2] Thus, a number of scholars have mentioned one or two ways in which Carter forged a path for Reagan, but that subject was not the focus of their studies. It *is* the focus of this chapter.

My purpose here is not to present a comprehensive review of the Carter administration but to analyze how his presidency set the stage for his successor. Consequently, some of Carter's successes, such as the Camp David

Accords and the Panama Canal Treaty, will not be dealt with. Instead, the following sections examine the context of the late 1970s during which Carter served as president, the leadership style of Jimmy Carter, and Carter's political ineffectiveness.

The 1970s

By the end of the 1970s, the American people's confidence in their ability to deal with the major problems of the day was shattered. Political assassinations, political corruption, the defeat in South Vietnam, Organization of Petroleum Export Countries (OPEC)-dictated oil price increases that raised the cost of a barrel of oil from $4 in 1973 to $37 in 1980, the collapse of the exchange-rate system, the kidnapping of American embassy staff in Iran, the Russian invasion of Afghanistan, and the frightening economic news about budget deficits, inflation, and unemployment led many citizens to fear that the United States was declining. After the Kennedy assassination in 1963, a series of failed presidencies only added to the cycle of hope and gloom. Presidential candidates could exploit the problems of incumbents during the campaign, but once in office, they could not govern effectively. Whereas in the 1960s, problems seemed solvable (the 1964 Civil Rights Act) and great tasks manageable (traveling to the moon in 1969), in the 1970s, the country lost faith in its ability to deal with crime, education, inflation, poverty, competition with the Japanese, third world nationalism, and the containment of communism.

Underlying much of this despair was a decline in productivity. From 1947 to 1973, the average annual increase of output per worker hour had been 3 percent, but from 1973 to 1979, it dropped to 0.8 percent. The lessening of productivity occurred in many nations, but whereas in other industrialized countries the decline went from fast to modest growth, in the United States, it collapsed from modest to almost zero growth. The result was stagnation in standards of living for more than half the population in a country that expects economic progress. Government figures indicated that "growth in real GNP per capita was cut to one-half of the 1948–73 rate, to a 1.1 percent annual rate despite the growth in the proportion of two-earner families. A real differential began to show up in the 1970s, however, with the lowest groups in the distribution of income faring the worst. The poverty rate increased from 11.1 percent in 1973 to 14.0 percent in 1981."[3]

A number of explanations were offered to account for the downturn: an increase in the female proportion of the labor force, decreasing growth of capital per worker, stifling government regulations, mammoth increases in oil prices, and the growing proportion of the economy devoted to services. Conservative market-oriented economists argued that the slowdown reflected the inadequacy of Keynesian economics and that what the country needed were public policies that would increase the incentive to save and invest. Michael Boskin, a Stanford economist, wrote, "Among all explanations advanced, the decline in incentives to produce wealth and income is perhaps the most important. The reasons for this decline include high and rising inflation, which increased uncertainty in returns to investment and saving; rising marginal tax rates, especially on the returns to savings and investment, aggravated by the interaction of inflation and the unindexed tax system; and the growth of government regulation, which increased costs and uncertainty in long-term investment planning."[4]

The economic problem felt most severely by the public was inflation. During the 1970s, the price level as measured by the Consumer Price Index (CPI) doubled; this was four times as large an increase as occurred during the 1960s. In 1979 and 1980, unemployment rates went up along with the CPI. The double-digit inflation rates in 1979 and 1980 were devastating for the Carter administration and one of the major reasons why Reagan was able to win the presidential election. James Alt reports, "by 1979, the cost of living was seen as the most important problem facing the country by 60 percent of the public; it was the seventh straight year it had led the list, beating Watergate, energy and unemployment in turn."[5] The fact that inflation was condemned by the public and politicians yet continued to spread like some insidious plague heightened fears that the government had lost its ability to protect the purchasing power of currency.

Accelerating inflation also had the effect of shoving taxpayers into higher marginal tax brackets, thus forcing them to pay more taxes even though they were not enjoying real income gains. The proportion of the population subject to high marginal tax rates quadrupled between 1965 and 1980. When the effects of bracket creep combined with increases in social security taxes, many families found themselves struggling with less disposable income. Hence, there was a growing alienation from the tax system, highlighted by the passage of a property tax–cutting constitutional amendment in California known as Proposition 13 on June 6, 1978. After Proposition 13 won in California by a 2-to-1 margin, it "quickly inspired successful crusades against property taxes in thirty seven states and against income taxes in twenty eight states."[6] By 1980, according to Boskin, "the United States tax system had reached a crisis, creating pressure for fundamental tax reform. . . . Our tax system was widely perceived to be pro-consumption and anti-saving, in a society that had an extremely low saving rate."[7]

The economic conditions at the end of the 1970s set the stage for Reaganomics, with its emphasis on supply-side tax cuts to promote economic growth and monetarism to control inflation. In 1980, interest rates were high (the prime rate reached 21.5 percent), and the budget deficit doubled from the previous year to $59 billion. High interest rates were partially blamed on the crowding-out effect of the federal government's borrowing to finance its budget deficit, which borrowing amounted to almost 36 percent of the $348 billion in U.S. credit markets.[8] The Carter administration was overwhelmed by economic trends that saw unemployment grow, industrial production decline, and the dollar fall in value.

The liberal-Keynesian formula of economic growth and moderate inflation financing the incremental growth of social programs no longer worked. During the Kennedy-Johnson years (1961–1969), Keynesian economics had produced an outstanding record of economic growth, high employment, and low inflation. The declining productivity and rising inflation of the 1970s terminated this self-perpetuating system. In the long run, Keynesianism collapsed into stagflation—a condition of high inflation and high unemployment that Keynesianism could neither explain nor provide a policy remedy for.[9] In brief, both the public and the politicians were ready to pursue different economic strategies.

The 1970s were also hard on the unity, philosophy, and effectiveness of the Democratic party. Franklin Roosevelt's New Deal had created a coalition of workers, Southerners, farmers, ethnics, minorities, and intellectuals that made the Democrats into the majority party, the organization most likely to control Congress and the presidency. Its philosophy was based on the idea that the federal government had the expertise and the compassion to tax, spend, and regulate society in order to bring about maximum employment and social progress. By the mid-1960s, liberal Democrats could claim an impressive list of achievements. Their foreign policy had rebuilt the war-torn economies of Europe and Japan and contained communism; their Keynesian-inspired economic policy had prevented a depression and was promoting cycles of economic growth, low inflation, and high employment, marred only occasionally by mild and short recessions; their domestic policies had promoted civil rights, health care for the elderly and the poor, federal aid to education, and a large variety of welfare programs.

But by the end of the 1960s and into the 1970s, the prospects for the Democrats darkened considerably. The war in Vietnam was lost and had severely split the party; the war against poverty, initiated with such high hopes, degenerated into trench warfare, with some progress but no major victories; school integration produced white flight and a decline in public education; the crime rate soared; welfare dependency increased; and the economy that liberals in the 1960s believed they could fine-tune with the help of the Phillips curve became a constant source of worry in the 1970s. The slowdown in the economy meant that Democrats could no longer finance the expanding budgets of their New Deal and Great Society programs. "Declining growth rates," according to Steven Gillon, "created a zero-sum game where further expansion of the welfare state required shifting resources among groups."[10]

The Democrats found it difficult to adapt to the altered environment of the 1970s. Older liberals tried to maintain the FDR coalition, whereas newer liberals felt that an alliance of campus, ghetto, and suburbs could constitute a new majority. The new liberal strategy was tested by George McGovern's 1972 campaign and was buried by the Nixon landslide. There were racial, cultural, and regional cleavages within the broad-based Democratic party that could be exploited by the opposition. The sons and daughters in many working-class families went to college and became more culturally liberal and more economically conservative than their parents. Perceptive politicians such as Richard Nixon and George Wallace discovered a number of wedge issues, such as law and order, busing, abortion, and prayer in schools, that appealed to the more culturally conservative Democrats, thus splitting the party. As the economy soured in the 1970s, "A working class threatened by inflation had little sympathy for 'the powerless' who demanded their tax money. . . . Just as ominous, a struggling middle class watched as inflation consumed much of its purchasing power. By the early 1970s, postwar prosperity along with many successful Democratic programs had created a growing middle class, which now fought to protect its hard-earned status."[11] In this new milieu, many members of the working and middle classes viewed Republican promises of lower taxes, law and order, and deregulation as being more compatible with their interests than were liberal Democratic programs.

The Democratic party was hurt as much by its successes as by its failures. Decades of economic prosperity helped many laborers move up into the middle class, thus weakening a major constituency of the Democratic party and increasing the market for those attracted to Republican calls for cuts in taxes. Civil rights programs aided many blacks but also alienated many white voters and allowed the Republicans to become increasingly competitive in the formerly solid Democratic South. Gillon points out, "despite the massive mobilization of black voters since passage of the Voting Rights act in 1965, the increase of white registration between 1960 and 1980 surpassed black by almost five to one. The mobilization of southern blacks and the defection of white southerners from the Democratic Party dramatically transformed the demographic composition of the Democratic coalition in the south."[12] Even the Democratic victory of forcing Nixon to resign because of the Watergate scandal had unforeseen costs, in that it fueled the public's paranoia about how corrupt politicians and government are.

By the end of the 1970s, liberal policies were seen as a major cause of high taxes, budget deficits, inflation, and stifling bureaucracies. Democrats were shocked that populist conservative allegations that a liberal elite was benefiting from policies that hindered social mobility were being accepted by a growing proportion of the electorate. Skowronek writes, "By 1976, the liberalism of Roosevelt had become a grab bag of special interest services all too vulnerable to political charges of burdening a troubled economy with bureaucratic overhead. . . . The energies that once came from advancing great national purposes had dissipated. A rule of myopic sects defied the very notion of governmental authority."[13] The historian Alonzo Hamby suggests that liberalism "increasingly became open to attack as a conglomerate of diverse special interests—labor unions, blacks, feminists, homosexuals, environmentalists, disarmers, counterculturalists—that had little support in the larger body politic and no compelling vision of a general public interest."[14]

Blinded by sectarian squabbles, liberal Democrats allowed conservatives, long associated with privileged interests, to make the stronger claim for representing the public interest. By pandering to narrow constituencies, the Democrats lost the ability to mobilize majorities. During the 1930s, Roosevelt had articulated a vision and a program when the bulk of the citizenry was needy, but no Democratic leader was able to construct a similar project for the 1970s and 1980s, when the majority was middle class and the issues were more morally ambiguous. The Democratic party's problems and ineptness are painfully revealed in a series of statements by E. J. Dionne:

When the poor are seen as a "special interest" while the wealthy are not, something very peculiar has happened to the national political dialogue. When such values as family and work are perceived as the exclusive province of one party to the political debate, the other party has clearly made some fundamental blunders. When the party of racial harmony creates conditions that encourage racial division, something is awry in its program. When constituencies who had gotten jobs, gone to college, bought houses, started businesses, secured health care, and retired in dignity because of government decided . . . that "the government was the problem"—when this happened, it was clear a political revolution was in process.[15]

Thus, when James Earl Carter was inaugurated on January 20, 1977, as the thirty-ninth president of the United States, he was likely to be challenged and constrained by a troubling economy and by an intellectually exhausted and fragmented political party.

The Carter Presidency

For Skowronek, Carter had assumed a doomed mission: he was attempting to rejuvenate rather than repudiate a declining liberal regime. Others believed that Carter lacked the political skills to govern successfully during the difficult and uncertain times of the 1970s. Whatever the case, the challenge for any study of the Carter presidency is to explain why such a good, intelligent, and hardworking man failed so miserably in office.

Jimmy Carter looked far more promising in 1976, when he transformed himself from "Jimmy Who?" to president. The son of a peanut farmer in Plains, Georgia, a graduate of the Naval Academy, a naval officer who worked under Captain (later Admiral) Hyman Rickover as a nuclear submariner, governor of Georgia from 1970 to 1974, Carter defeated a number of more liberal Democratic candidates in 1976 to win the Democratic nomination for president. The fifty-two-year-old Carter was an ideal candidate in a country still affected by Watergate and the defeat in South Vietnam. Carter was an outsider; he had nothing to do with the mess in Washington. He was a religious Southern Baptist who solemnly promised to never tell a lie and to fulfill all his campaign promises.

Carter was considered a liberal in the South because he was committed to the civil rights of blacks, but he was also conservative in that he promised to balance the budget within four years and to do away with unnecessary bureaucracy and government regulations. He thought that government could be revitalized if the executive branch installed zero-based budgeting, as he had done as governor of Georgia, and if it streamlined the bureaucracy by reducing the number of federal agencies from 1,900 to 200. He pledged major reforms of the tax and welfare systems, and he vowed to replace the realpolitik of Henry Kissinger's foreign policy with an approach that stressed moral purpose and human rights, less fear of communism, and more concern with aligning the United States with progressive forces in the third world.

Carter's experiences in 1976 foreshadowed problems that would plague his presidency. The self-inflicted wounds of the *Playboy* interview, in which Carter gratuitously criticized Lyndon Johnson and admitted that he frequently had "lust in his heart" for women, demonstrated a lack of political wisdom. Party professionals were dismayed that Carter blew most of his 33-point lead over President Gerald Ford in the summer of 1976 and was able to win in November by a margin of only 2 points. Carter would have heavy Democratic majorities in the House and Senate, but his influence over Democratic Congress members would be limited by his lack of electoral coattails. In the congressional elections of 1976, the Democrats gained only one additional seat in the House and one in the Senate. The resulting 95th Congress had 292 Democrats and 143 Republicans in the House; the Senate was composed of 62 Democrats and 38 Republicans. The president-elect ran ahead of only twenty-two successful House Democrats and only one successful Senate Democrat.[16] Hence, there were early anxieties among Democrats about whether Carter was ready for prime time.

There was also a fuzziness about his leadership and political identity. Was Carter a liberal or a conservative, a populist or a technocrat, a politician or a preacher? Theodore Lowi captured the paradox of Carter's position when he wrote, "In 1976 Jimmy Carter ran against the party he wanted to lead and against the government over which he would preside."[17] Skowronek makes a similar point: "It is Jimmy Carter's peculiar genius to treat his remoteness from his party and its institutional power centers as a distinctive asset rather than his chief liability in his quest for a credible leadership posture. . . . This curiosity afforded neither the regime's outsider's freedom to oppose established interests nor the regime's insider's freedom to support them."[18] Carter was an "antiparty outsider" who was more committed to "enlightened administration" than to the Democratic party.[19]

The new president's views on leadership were largely influenced by his deeply held religious beliefs and by his training as an engineer. He often quoted a line from Reinhold Niebuhr that encapsulated the former governor's grim view of political leadership: "The sad duty of politics is to establish justice in a sinful world." According to Gillon, "For Carter, 'the people' were his flock and he was the shepherd elected to protect them from the narrow interest groups scheming to corrupt their democratic institutions."[20] Considering himself to be a virtuous leader, Carter thought that he could communicate directly with the public and decipher what was best for it in the long run; he didn't need the Democratic party or interest groups to serve as intermediaries.

As a trained engineer, Carter expected to lead through mastering the mechanism of government rather than through rhetorical eloquence. Rickover had insisted that submariners be fully knowledgeable about a variety of tasks on their ships, and Carter attempted to apply this philosophy in the White House. Professor Erwin Hargrove writes, "For Carter the cognitive aspect of political style was most strongly manifested in his drive for competence. He wished to understand thoroughly the issues for which he assumed primary responsibility, and he characterized his cognitive processes as those of an engineer."[21] The problem here was that Carter assumed responsibility for a multitude of issues, which meant that the cognitive demands on him were overwhelming.

Carter thought that it was his duty to search for hard problems, study them diligently, then seek comprehensive solutions to them. He was ambitious and tenacious, and he expected to be politically rewarded for his unconventional behavior in tackling the most difficult issues. He sought to achieve major reforms in the policy areas of energy, welfare, tax, urban development, hospital cost containment, and the environment. His successes in negotiating an accord between Israel and Egypt at Camp David and in passing the Panama Canal Treaty through a skeptical Senate were truly personal triumphs. James Sterling Young asserts that Carter believed that "the point of presidential leadership . . . was to achieve good policy. In a political system that was tilted in favor of policies that were expedient, constituency-oriented, costly, and good for the short run, it was the president's job to push for policies that were problem-solving, goal-oriented, cost-effective, and best in the long run."[22] The tragedy for Carter was that such noble intentions and prodigious efforts led to more failures than successes.

Carter had the analytical skills to recognize that the liberal regime was no longer economically viable. A slowdown in economic growth and existing budget commitments were placing old liberal aspirations on a collision course with present economic realities. True to his leadership perspective, Carter did not shirk his responsibility in analyzing this problem and trying to formulate a solution. Constrained by his moral code and analytical capabilities, Carter was not afforded the luxury of avoiding painful trade-offs by selecting "voodoo" remedies. As a late-regime president, Carter was concerned about limits; no miracles could be expected.

In an overreaction to the Nixon administration and complaints about an imperial presidency, Carter decided that he would not have a chief of staff in the White House and would reconstitute the Cabinet to its proper role as the president's top tier of advisers. By not selecting a chief of staff, Carter was in reality taking on the onerous and time-consuming duties of being chief of staff himself. The new president would be the hub of a circle of advisers who would report directly to him. Carter's administrative system, according to Hargrove, "called for diversity of advice within a collegial setting emphasizing homework and knowledge."[23] The Democratic party could certainly provide diversity.

As an outsider who had never served in Washington, Carter was overly dependent on his advisers from Georgia. Major advisers from his home state included Hamilton Jordan, his principal political adviser; Jody Powell, his press secretary; Bert Lance, director of the Office of Management and Budget (OMB); James McIntyre, who replaced Lance because of a scandal in September 1977; Frank Moore, congressional liaison; and Griffin Bell, a conservative, who became attorney general. For his national security adviser, Carter appointed Professor Zbigniew Brzezinski, an expert on the Soviet Union whom Carter had met during meetings of the Trilateral Commission. Most of Carter's non–White House appointments came from the liberal wing of the Democratic party. Former senator Walter Mondale was chosen as vice president to be an expert on and liaison with Congress, the Democratic party, and labor. Carter's decision to staff his administration with both insiders and outsiders was probably designed to increase its representation and flexibility; instead, it augmented its unmanageability. Rather than being praised for appointing a wide variety of Democrats, Carter was criticized, according to Sidney Milkis and Michael Nelson, as "an irresolute leader who was eager to accommodate all sides."[24] For the most part, Carter's appointments were individually talented but collectively ineffective.

Carter's White House advisers developed many of the problems associated with collegial systems. Burke notes, "They put a heavy burden on the president's time and attention and called for unusual interpersonal skills, which Carter was unable to provide, in mediating differences and maintaining teamwork. . . . Meetings of the Cabinet proved unproductive, forcing Carter to work individually with Cabinet members or in task forces and placing increasing authority for coordinating the policy process on the White House staff, which was ill-equipped to handle it."[25] The lack of a chief of staff until mid-1979—combined with the fact that neither

Stuart Eizenstat, as head of the domestic policy staff, nor Brzezinski had the authority to control the centrifugal forces of the presidency—meant that the Carter administration frequently appeared to be at war with itself. The numerous publicized disputes within the administration—between Cyrus Vance and Brzezinski, Mondale and Griffin Bell, Eizenstat and Patrick Caddell (Carter's pollster), McIntyre and all the liberal appointees— projected the deflating image that Carter could not lead his own team.

The usual White House procedures did not compensate for Carter's handicaps as a leader and decision maker; they magnified them. Thus Carter's system did not help him establish priorities or impose order. The president was inundated with time-consuming details that should have been settled at lower levels. Midway through his presidency, forty advisers were reporting directly to Carter, and he was reading 300 to 400 pages a day. This problem was recognized but could not be solved. Brzezinski reports that "whenever I tried to relieve him of excessive detail, Carter would show real uneasiness, and I even felt some suspicion that I was usurping authority."[26] In Carter's commitment to "conquer the office," he felt compelled to master the details of a wide variety of subjects.[27] By submerging himself in trivia, he lost sight of the big picture.

This lack of strategic vision was noted by Carter's contemporaries. He was ridiculed for monitoring the White House tennis courts. In 1978, Emmet John Hughes, a journalist who had been an aide in the Eisenhower White House, wrote, "there has been no President since Hoover so absorbed and fascinated as Carter by the 'machinery' of his government and the monitoring of all its details. There has been no President since Hoover so devoted to 'running a desk' with an industry decreed by a presidential work-ethic of exhaustive briefings and exhausting hours."[28] Perhaps no chief executive learned more about how the government works and understood less about how a president succeeds.

Carter's intelligence and hard work seemed capable only of publicizing how complex and difficult his problems were; his lack of political skills meant that he could not provide solutions. Hargrove provides the most perceptive critique of Carter's leadership style:

> Carter did not manage the seamless web of purpose, politics and
> process smoothly. His strategic leadership had a disjointed character
> in which discrete decisions jarred and jostled each other. He fastened
> too much on particular decisions without relating them to decisions
> that had come before and those that would follow. . . . He reversed his

course often in response to immediate situations. . . . Constant reversals in economic policy confused everyone. Carter did not know how to extract a strong strategic sense of direction from a welter of discrete decisions. The decisions rather than the direction were his focus.[29]

This focus on individual decisions and neglect of direction meant that the Carter administration often appeared to be adrift, buffeted by shifting political winds, with no clear set of priorities. Unlike that of most modern presidents, Carter's presidency could not be defined by a catchy term such as "New Deal" or "Great Society." When Carter failed to provide a unifying theme, the Republicans stuck him with one: Carter was the personification of failed liberalism. This labeling was effective but unfair, because Carter's decision-making style did not adhere to any ideology. Indeed, as Stephen Hess suggests, "many of Carter's policies seemed inordinately at cross purposes. Complicated tax proposals belied attempts at tax simplification, new social programs compromised the vision of a balanced budget, the creation of new federal departments [Energy and Education] scuttled the promise to reduce the size of the bureaucracy. The Domestic Policy staff proposed a liberal task, and the OMB pursued a conservative one."[30] In other words, because the president lacked a guiding political philosophy, his policy recommendations fluctuated between the liberal and the conservative.

Carter believed that if he diligently searched for the best solution to a problem, he had the intelligence to find it. He resented the fact that his decisions had to be sold to politicians who were less knowledgeable and less moral than himself. Their petty interests frustrated him. The fact that other politicians did not consider their interests petty and were not moved by Carter's appeals to morality and the public interest caused him constant grief. Only a politically naive person could believe that good policy would automatically sell itself.[31] What Carter considered a higher form of leadership seemed to many other politicians merely sanctimony.

Unlike most politicians, Carter liked substantive discussions about important issues but disliked debates about political feasibility. However, in stressing how nonpolitical he was, Carter unintentionally created incentives for the media to focus on the role of politics in his decisions. When the media found evidence of political concerns in Carter's behavior, it made him look like a hypocrite. Because of Carter's holier-than-thou attitude, no president ever received less credit for negotiating a compromise. A Carter-engineered compromise tended to be viewed as "politics as usual"—the very thing he was pledged to change. A member of his own administration was quoted as saying that he did "good things badly."[32] Carter's moral posturing had the effect of reducing the effectiveness of his political activities. When he engaged in personal attacks against Senator Edward Kennedy during the 1980 Democratic primaries and Ronald Reagan in that year's presidential election, the result was to raise the issue of his own "meanness." The press quickly changed its image of him from Christian Carter to Jungle Jimmy.[33] Charles Jones points up the president's leadership dilemma when he writes that "Carter's style and techniques suggest that his first instincts were to try to make Washington less political. Failing that, he was forced to engage in the very behavior that upset him. It is understandable that problems developed for him, both in pursuing his natural instincts and in trying to be somebody else."[34] In brief, Carter was not effective when he was himself or when he tried to act like a conventional politician. That did not give him much opportunity to be productive.

In publicizing the standards of efficiency and honesty by which it wished to be evaluated, then selecting the most difficult issues to address, the Carter presidency was setting the stage for its own downfall. The more Carter stressed his competence, the more incompetent he looked. The more he pointed out that there were no easy answers, the more it looked like he had no answers at all. The more he pronounced that he was a moralist and not a politician, the more he appeared to be neither. "The final irony," according to Hargrove, "was that he became the scapegoat for all unresolved national and international problems. Everybody—politicians, the public, interest groups, and media—piled on him."[35] Whereas ridiculing Reagan often did not work, caricaturing Carter paid dividends for the Republicans. No one accused Carter of being a Teflon president.

Carter's problems were aggravated by his administrative system. The absence of a chief of staff for the first two and a half years of his administration reinforced Carter's inability to establish priorities. And when Carter finally did establish a chief of staff in July 1979, he appointed Hamilton Jordan to the position, even though this young Georgian lacked the organizational aptitude for the job. Moreover, the organizational structure of the Carter White House did not shield the president from issues and problems that should have been handled at lower levels.[36]

Carter lacked both the Washington experience and the political wisdom to make political judgments about policy decisions. The president desperately needed help here, but his determination to keep top decisions in his own hands prevented him from delegating authority and seeking more assistance. This meant that Carter was frightfully exposed and alone in the making of too many decisions. Whereas most modern presidents have used certain advisers as lightning rods (think of how Reagan used David Stockman, Caspar Weinberger, and James Watt), Carter's style all too often highlighted himself as the scapegoat when things went wrong. And because Carter's decisions often appeared to be directionless, he did not even get credit for having the courage to take on so much responsibility.[37]

Both Carter and his staff were deficient in the political skills needed to deal effectively with Congress, especially during their first year in office. Thomas "Tip" O'Neill, the Speaker of the House, believed that Carter was the smartest public official he had ever encountered in terms of the range and depth of his knowledge about policy. However, O'Neill complained that Carter did not know how Congress worked and wasn't interested in learning. The new president naively expected Congress to adjust to his style of leadership. Nothing reveals Carter's ineptness more sharply than his attempt in February 1977 to cancel nineteen water and dam projects, including several in Louisiana, the state represented by Senator Russell Long, the chairman of the Finance Committee. Additionally, O'Neill and many Democratic congressmen found that Frank Moore, Carter's congressional liaison, "didn't know beans about Congress." But O'Neill was particularly enraged by what he considered the arrogance and ignorance of Hamilton Jordan, whom he nicknamed "Hannibal Jerken." The Speaker claims, "When it came to helping out my district, I actually received more cooperation from Reagan's staff than from Carter's."[38]

By not taking advantage of its honeymoon period with a Democratically controlled Congress in 1977, the Carter administration became trapped by a reputation of failure from which it never escaped. Even Hamilton Jordan later conceded, "by the end of the first year there were a number of perceptions about the Carter administration. Fair or unfair, the perception was that he didn't know how to deal with the Congress, that he was not successful getting things through the Congress, that he was surrounded by too many people from Georgia who were in over their heads, and that he was overwhelmed by all the details of issues in his presidency. . . . Those perceptions never changed."[39] That negative image weakened the leverage of the Carter administration in every bargaining situation after 1977.

Carter's administration was equally ineffective in dealing with the Democratic party. The Democratic party and its constituent groups were not willing to coalesce behind Carter and follow him in a new style of politics. They liked the traditional way of the New Deal and the Great Society. They wanted more; Carter was offering them less. For them, liberal progress had been temporarily derailed by the Kennedy assassination and the Vietnam War. After eight years of Republican leadership, it was time to complete the liberal agenda. Each liberal constituency felt that it had supplied the margin of victory for Carter in 1976, and each threatened to withdraw its assistance unless his administration rewarded it in terms of recruitment and policies. Blacks, Hispanics, women, environmentalists, and labor unions wanted their people appointed to administrative positions, and they demanded big increases in social spending.

After Carter's defeat, Eizenstat viewed Carter as a transitional president valiantly attempting to induce the Democratic party to adapt to the milieu of the 1970s. Carter was the nominal leader of a party that was philosophically based on aid to various factions and that had a particular concern with helping low-income and disadvantaged groups. But how could the Democrats maintain their majority rule when labor and the poor were a declining proportion of the electorate? In Eizenstat's words, "What you had is an institution . . . whose constituent members refused to recognize the economic realities, [and who] continued to make maximal demands on the administration, and therefore governance became very difficult for a Democratic President at a time of high inflation and inadequate resources."[40] Eizenstat praises Carter for recognizing that the Democratic party had to move beyond Great Society liberalism because economic conditions could no longer finance it, but he concedes that his boss was never able to construct a compelling vision to transform enough traditional Democrats. The Democratic party was not going to be revived by civil service reform and zero-based budgeting.

What did excite many traditional Democrats, at least for awhile, was Senator Edward Kennedy. Kennedy's challenge to Carter's leadership exacerbated the philosophical, religious, and regional cleavages in the Democratic party. In December 1978, at the midterm Democratic party convention in Memphis, Kennedy told a cheering crowd that the party ought to "sail against the wind" of public opinion and reject "drastic slashes" in domestic expenditures. The senator declared, "The party that tore itself apart over Vietnam in the 1960s cannot afford to tear itself apart over budget cuts in basic social programs."[41] In May 1979, Kennedy proposed a $100 billion national health plan several weeks before Carter presented his less comprehensive health program. That same month, when enraged motorists were enduring long lines at the gas pumps to buy gasoline selling at over a dollar a gallon for the first time ever, polls showed Kennedy leading Carter among Democrats by 2 or 3 to 1. Kennedy was even leading the president in the South.[42] The bubble of Kennedy's popularity burst quickly after he formally announced his candidacy for the Democratic nomination in November 1979. A few days after Kennedy became a candidate, the Iranians took over the U.S. embassy in Tehran, and the nation rallied around the president, doubling his public approval rating to 61 percent. When the press reminded the public about the Chappaquiddick scandal, and when Kennedy was not able to duplicate the inspiring campaigns of his fallen brothers, John and Robert, Carter was able to defeat his liberal antagonist. But the fact that a morally blemished politician like Ted Kennedy could command more support than Carter in 1979 spoke volumes about the lack of rationality in the Democratic party and the dearth of political skill in Carter's leadership.

Throughout most of his term in office, Carter was also criticized for the contradictions of his policies. As a candidate, he had promised to cut the military budget, but he soon found himself compelled to promote major increases in defense expenditures. His assertions that he could achieve more cooperation with the Soviet Union were denied by its invasion of Afghanistan in late 1979. His administration's response to the energy crisis, which he declared constituted "the moral equivalent of war," was eventually so delayed and watered down that it was satirized by the acronym MEOW. His belief in human rights and in the idea that the United States could develop a better relationship with progressive forces in the third world was undermined by the Ayatollah Khomeini in Iran and the Sandinistas in Nicaragua.

According to Hargrove, Carter "wished for new balance between equity and efficiency in domestic programs, for a fiscally responsible economic expansion and for subordination among nations through cooperation. He deliberately incorporated these contradictions into his political appeals and in so doing embodied in his presidency the contradictions of public policy of the 1970s. This incorporation was accomplished by the confidence that hard issues could be resolved by goodwill and homework."[43] It did not work. Carter saw the contradictions and tried to reconcile them, but they ended up overwhelming his presidency. Because of the way Carter was positioned, even when he responded to the policy preferences of the times—such as increasing the defense budget or signing a tax bill in 1978 that cut the rate on capital gains—he did not receive any credit. Indeed, Carter's policy changes were usually belittled as too little, too late and flip-flopping.

Carter's economic policy was especially prone to criticism. In the election year of 1976, the unemployment rate was a little over 7 percent, inflation was under 6 percent, and the federal government had a budget deficit of about $66 billion. During the campaign, Carter promised to lower the unemployment rate, reduce inflation, and balance the budget within four years. As a Democrat, Carter thought that his first duty was to propose a $30 billion economic stimulus program, which was less than half of what union leaders advocated. With so many unemployed, Carter's economic advisers were not worried that the stimulus package would generate more inflation. However, when the economy grew faster than expected early in 1977, Carter withdrew the consumption-inspired $50 rebate portion of his program. This initial flip-flop created immediate doubts about the economic and political wisdom of the Carter administration.

Because FDR had taught the Democrats to see unemployment as a more significant economic problem than inflation, it took several years before Carter reluctantly decided that inflation would have to be addressed. The CPI rose 6.5 percent in 1977, 7.7 percent in 1978, 11.3 percent in 1979, and 13.5 percent in 1980. By not attacking inflation in 1977, the administration allowed rising prices to gather momentum that would prove electorally lethal in 1980. If the administration had cut the budget and enforced a tighter monetary policy in 1977, the economy might have encountered a mild recession in 1978, but with economic recovery and low inflation, it would have been in better shape in 1980. This strategy was not pursued, however, because most of Carter's economic advisers underestimated the inflationary forces operating in the economy and were fearful that any strong attempt to control inflation would result in rising unemployment, which would cause suffering among Democratic constituencies. Carter responded to his dilemma by being tentative, by splitting the difference in terms of the advice he received from conservatives such as Secretary of the Treasury Michael Blumenthal and OMB Director James McIntyre and from more liberal advisers such as Charles Schultze, Walter Mondale, and Stuart Eizenstat. Hargrove explains the president's predicament in these words: "Carter's economists could not give him a policy strategy for the inflation problem that he could pursue as a Democratic president. The centrist political strategy did not work, either with Democratic interest groups or with diffuse publics."[44]

Carter began targeting inflation in 1978. He set up a Council on Wages and Price Stability (COWPS), directed by Barry Bosworth, to monitor wages and prices. The goal was to use public pressure (jawboning) on business and labor to voluntarily keep their prices and wages below the average of the previous two years. The program was bitterly opposed both by business, which suspected that this was a forerunner to mandated controls, and by labor, which feared that restricting wages would turn out to be the principal means of curbing inflation. Republican economists ridiculed wage and price controls by claiming that invoking such a policy was like commanding the tides to stop moving. Jawboning was a total flop; COWPS merely ended up publicizing the inflationary figures thus making the administration look even more impotent. Similarly, the moderate budget cuts the administration undertook were, according to Eizenstat, "enough to make all the constituencies mad without accomplishing the desired result."[45] In brief, just as Hoover underestimated the threat of unemployment, Carter miscalculated the problem of inflation. In 1977, inflation was the wolf at the door that required the immediate and focused attention of the administration.

Ironically, the most effective decision Carter made in confronting inflation was to appoint Paul Volcker as chairman of the Federal Reserve Board in July 1979. Volcker believed that inflation was the major threat to the health of the economy and was therefore willing to take strong and unprecedented steps to subjugate it. On October 6, 1979, the chairman announced a new monetary policy that would emphasize controlling the supply of money and credit instead of interest rates. Volcker's strategy of tightening the money supply caused interest rates to soar during the election year of 1980; only after the recession of 1981–1982 did the inflation rate finally drop back to acceptable levels. Fighting inflation with monetary weapons meant rising unemployment during an election year; it opened up an opportunity for Reagan to appropriate what has traditionally been the Democratic party's best issue — full employment — and attract a significant portion of the labor vote. Carter's electoral support from union households decreased from 59 percent in 1976 to 49 percent in 1980. According to Dionne, "Working class voters weighed Carter's policies of retrenchment against Reagan's buoyant optimism and decided that Reagan really did sound more like Franklin Roosevelt than the Democratic nominee."[46] Thus, in the 1980 election, Carter absorbed much of the political heat for the rise in interest rates, inflation, and unemployment levels, and in the 1984 election, Reagan received much of the political reward for taming inflation and overseeing a robust economic recovery.

By 1980, the political identity and direction of the Carter presidency had become blurry, but its failures were clear. Richard Neustadt, the preeminent presidential scholar, wrote, "Watching Jimmy Carter in early 1979 sparked the question, is the Presidency possible?"[47] Throughout Carter's four-year term, his presidency exhibited a propensity for self-inflicted wounds, from the vetoing of nineteen water projects in 1977 to the grain embargo and the Olympic boycott in 1980.

The biggest self-inflicted wound endured by Carter was the Crisis of Confidence speech he delivered on July 15, 1979. This speech was triggered by a June announcement from OPEC that it was raising its oil prices for the fourth time in the last five months. With Americans already livid about the gasoline shortages causing long lines at the pumps, this OPEC price hike posed a major challenge to the declining fortunes of the Carter presidency. Carter cancelled his planned vacation and initiated staff work on an energy speech that was scheduled for national delivery on July 5. But on July 4, without giving any explanation, the president cancelled the speech and retreated to Camp David. Over the next eleven days, Carter met with almost 150 representatives of business, labor, government, universities, and religion as he reevaluated his presidency. He also secretly flew to the homes of two middle-class families in Pennsylvania and West Virginia.[48]

In meetings at Camp David with his top advisers, Carter revealed that he was impressed by the arguments his young pollster, Patrick Caddell, had set forth in a 107-page memo. Caddell had persuaded the president that underlying the energy crisis was a deeper, psychological problem—a crisis of confidence characterized by a declining faith in the future. "Caddell's solution," according to Stephen Gillon, "required a new type of leadership. Adopting James MacGregor Burns' distinction between transitional and transforming leadership, Caddell argued that the time was ripe for Carter to 'become the relevant, thriving center of national revival, a popular leader [of] enormous personal consequence for every American.'"[49] Mondale vehemently opposed Caddell's analysis because it would lead to the president's scolding the American people while doing nothing to cure the problems that were causing the despair. The vice president felt so strongly that Caddell's advice would wreck Carter's presidency and Mondale's political future that he threatened to resign. For the next few days, Mondale and Eizenstat worked feverishly to formulate an energy program that Carter could incorporate in his speech.

After all this drama, the president was guaranteed a large audience and a rare opportunity to reverse his declining public approval ratings when he spoke to the American public on Sunday evening, July 15. The speech he gave set forth Caddell's perspective but also included specific policy recommendations to deal with the energy problem. However, it came to be called the Crisis of Confidence speech, and it was remembered for a word that was not used in the text—*malaise*. In the speech, Carter stressed that the despair that had gripped the country during the 1970s was more significant than inflation, recession, or the energy shortage. A crisis of confidence was undermining faith in our institutions, leaders, and future. It perpetuated divisiveness and failure. He ended the speech by calling for "a rebirth of the American spirit" that would provide the unity necessary for progress.[50]

The initial responses to Carter's speech were positive. But within a few days, Carter used a Nixon technique of asking for the resignations of his entire Cabinet and accepting the resignation of five department secretaries, including Joe Califano, who was popular among liberal Democrats. Carter also reversed a previous pledge that he would never have a chief of staff in the White House by promoting Hamilton Jordan to that position. The headlines gave the appearance that Carter's administration was falling apart.

More importantly, the effectiveness of Carter's speech boomeranged when its arguments were reviewed and publicized. Carter was blaming the American people for lacking confidence in him and failing to follow his leadership. During the 1976 campaign, Carter had promised to provide a government as good as the American people; in 1979, he was scolding the public for not living up to their civic responsibilities. The arguments in his "malaise" speech were as self-serving as Hoover's were in blaming the Depression on international causes. Carter was claiming that the public was not supporting his recommendations in the energy crisis because they were too selfish and consumer oriented. The criticisms of Carter's speech were lethal, causing his public approval scores to plummet into the mid-20s. Carter was now as unpopular as Nixon was during the Watergate scandal.

Carter had hoped to legitimize his leadership on the basis of his competence. But the economic, political, and international situation in 1980 indicated that for all of Carter's hard work, the public thought that conditions had deteriorated since he had entered office. His personal identification with so many problems that did not get solved—the energy issue, welfare reform, the tax system, inflation, and especially the kidnapping of U.S. embassy personnel in Tehran—made it easy for the Republicans to campaign against Carter in 1980. By that year, the public had less faith in government programs than in 1976, and the target of much of their alienation was Carter.[51] Reagan exploited this sentiment by asking voters, "Are you better off now than you were in 1976?" Carter's leadership projects were rejected by the voters because, according to Foley, "they evoked an image of passivity; of a leader attempting to mobilize a people downward to lower expectations, when their traditions and culture were rooted in progress and optimism."[52] Reagan would not make that mistake.

By the end of the 1970s, Carter was vulnerable to the accusation that he was passively presiding over the decline of the United States. His "leadership" style was to explain to the public the complexity of problems, the limits of U.S. power, and the need for sacrifices. In 1980, the country seemed unable to preserve the purchasing value of its currency, to supply gasoline for its motorists at a reasonable price, to check Soviet aggression, or to maintain the safety of its embassy officials. James Baker later wrote, "The Iranian hostage crisis . . . contributed greatly to the election of Ronald Reagan in 1980. Jimmy Carter's inability to secure the release of American diplomats held hostage by Iran for 444 days had become a metaphor for a paralyzed presidency and the decline of American power throughout the world."[53]

Carter was not able to sell his argument, and in 1980, he became the fifth straight president to serve only one term. Reagan defeated Carter in forty-four states.

Conclusion

Carter's disappointing performance set the stage for Reagan's politics of reconstruction by bolstering the latter's authority to repudiate the liberal regime. Carter came into office trying to rejuvenate a tired liberal regime through a combination of hard work and administrative reforms. The president failed because "locating the salvation of the nation in the machinery of the government, Carter was unable to anchor his leadership project in any bedrock of constituency support."[54] He was impeded as much by his ostensible allies as by his opponents.

In struggling with the problems of the late 1970s, Carter was moving away from Keynesian economics, and toward monetarism to prevent inflation and deregulation to encourage entrepreneurial activities.[55] His fatally delayed anti-inflation policy managed to be ineffective against rising prices while it antagonized most Democratic constituencies and delivered its economic and political benefits to Reagan.

Carter tried to communicate that the United States now lived in an age of uncertainty and limits but succeeded only in conveying his limitations for the job of president. In highlighting his own incompetence to deal with the complex problems of the day, he became the personification of a paralyzed presidency and of spent liberalism. His style was personal, moral, issue oriented, difficult to grasp, and not likely to inspire. His pessimism clashed with our sanguine political culture, and his complex message did not resonate with public opinion. He left himself open to attacks (by Kennedy on the left and Reagan on the right) that he was blaming the American people for the nation's problems. He became vulnerable to the lethal charge that he lacked the qualities of leadership that constitute the essence of what we expect in a president. In brief, Carter's failures fulfilled the conditions that allowed Reagan, as the leader of the conservative movement, to enter from stage right.

4

The Life, Personality, and Political Philosophy of Franklin Roosevelt and Ronald Reagan

Skowronek argues that scholars have been prone to explain presidential behavior in terms of their subject's background and personality. He suggests that a president's performance can be better understood by studying the context in which he entered the White House rather than his biography. However, no one who becomes president is a blank slate; each brings with him certain qualities, formed by his personal history, his personality, and his political philosophy, that will help or hinder him while he engages in presidential politics. The purpose of this chapter is to summarize the backgrounds of FDR and Reagan so that we can see what kind of man each was when he assumed the role of a reconstruction president.

Franklin Delano Roosevelt

A review of FDR's life reveals that he would not be deterred by the paradox of the reconstructive leader's task of promoting fundamental change while extolling the virtues of ancient truths. Nor would he lack the self-confidence to lead the nation into the uncharted waters that others would find frightening. FDR probably considered himself "luckier" than his cousin, Theodore Roosevelt, because the Depression and World War II confronted him with greater challenges than the problems of 1901 to 1909, thus providing FDR with more opportunities to be a greater president.

FDR was born in 1882 as the only child of loving and wealthy parents on the Roosevelt estate in Hyde Park, New York. His father, James Roosevelt, was a wealthy Democrat who owned major interests in railroads and real estate. His first wife died in 1876; four years later he married Sara Delano, who was twenty-six years his junior. The Delano family's Hudson River estate was located twenty miles south of Hyde Park. Their wealth had been generated from trade with China, especially opium, and from Appalachian coal mines. Sara, in giving birth to Franklin, was in labor for twenty-four hours; she could never have another child. Franklin became the focus of her overwhelming maternal love; he responded to this affection by developing a supreme self-confidence.

Leuchtenburg stresses, "He [Franklin] was a member of the landed gentry and the old mercantile class who could claim ancient lineage. . . . Both the Roosevelts and the Delanos were prosperous merchant families who had derived much of their fortune from seafaring. As a landowner with a Hudson River estate, a man from a family that moved easily in the Edith Wharton universe of Knickerbockean society, Roosevelt approached economic problems with different preconceptions from those of the industrialist or the financier on the make."[1] His privileged but challenging life at Hyde Park and his education at Groton School in Massachusetts and at Harvard combined to develop in him a world view of noblesse oblige.

Franklin was taught by nannies at home. He was close to his father, whom he called "Popsy," and they spent time together supervising the estate, traveling in James's private railroad car, and touring Europe. James instilled in his son a love of the land, a commitment to planting trees, and a fondness for sailing. As a prominent New York Democrat, James was able to take his son to meet President Grover Cleveland in the White House in 1887. When James suffered a heart attack in 1890 at the age of sixty-two, his feigned good cheer for the remaining ten years of his life probably served as a model for Franklin when he later was struck by polio.

In 1886, at the age of fourteen, Franklin left the cloister of Hyde Park and began his formal education at Groton. This Episcopal boarding school was begun by Endicott Peabody; it stressed "a classical curriculum with Spartan living and strenuous sports. [Peabody's] emphasis was upon physical and moral vigor in the pursuit of religious and civic responsibilities."[2] Because most of the other boys had begun their Groton education at the age of twelve and had already formed their cliques by the time Franklin arrived, he had some trouble fitting in. He never wrote about any of these difficulties in the two letters he sent his parents each week. Instead, his communications were filled with details about his vigorous participation in a variety of school activities. Franklin, who was most comfortable with adults and his cousins, may have tried too hard to be popular with his schoolmates. He did admire Peabody, however, and sent all four of his sons to Groton.

In September 1900, FDR enrolled at Harvard. Three months later, his father died of a heart attack; he left his estate to Sara and provided Franklin with a trust fund of $120,000. Roosevelt was an average student at Harvard, earning C's in most of his classes. No professor inspired him as Peabody had at Groton. His biggest disappointment at Harvard was being rejected by its most prestigious club, the Porcellian. His major achievement was to become editor of the school newspaper, the *Harvard Crimson*. As editor, he championed school spirit; there was nothing in his editorials to suggest that he would eventually become a great reform president.

Franklin watched and admired Teddy's career even as a student at Groton. At Harvard, FDR had joined the Young Republican Club and cast his first presidential vote for Teddy. He saw TR's political success as a roadmap for his own ambitions. In 1902, Franklin became romantically interested in his cousin, Eleanor Roosevelt, the president's favorite niece. While TR favored the marriage of Franklin and Eleanor, Sara thought that they were too young and tried to delay it. But FDR soon had his way. With Endicott Peabody performing the ceremony and the president giving away the bride, Franklin and Eleanor were married on March 17, 1905, in New York City. As a wedding present, Sara gave the couple a townhouse adjoining her own, on East Sixty-fifth Street in Manhattan. Between 1907 and 1916, the couple had one daughter and five sons (their second son died when he was eighteen months old).

After graduating from Harvard in 1904, FDR became a law student at Columbia University. Again, his academic record was mediocre—he flunked two classes—but he was able to pass the bar exam in 1907. That same year, Roosevelt was hired as a law clerk by Carter, Ledyard, and Milburn, a prominent Wall Street law firm, but he was bored with legal work. In a conversation with his fellow law clerks in 1908, he declared his goal was to replicate his cousin Teddy's political career and become president.[3]

In November 1910, FDR was elected as a Democratic state senator from Hyde Park and the surrounding rural counties. Normally, attention would not be focused on a twenty-eight-year-old freshman state senator, but this politician had the nationally recognized name of "Roosevelt." Hence, both the newspapers and politicians watched FDR closely. He immediately identified himself as a reform Democrat by opposing Tammany's candidate for U.S. Senate, William "Blue-eyed Billy" Sheehan. Tammany responded by accusing Roosevelt and his Democratic reformers of being anti-Catholic. After a delay of several months, Charles Murphy, Tammany's boss, substituted a new candidate with ties to the Democratic machine, James A. O'Gormand, who was elected senator by the state legislature. To avoid the anti-Catholic label, Roosevelt felt compelled to vote for O'Gorman. FDR had received national publicity for opposing Tammany, but he had been outfoxed by Murphy.[4]

In his first year as a legislator, FDR had to adapt to the changing political environment brought about by the Triangle Shirtwaist Company fire in Manhattan on March 25, 1911, which killed 146 people, mostly young female immigrants. In response, the state legislature created the New York Factory Commission, headed by two Tammany politicians, state senator Robert Wagner as chairman, and state assemblyman Alfred Smith as vice chairman. The commission's chief investigator was Frances Perkins, who became FDR's secretary of labor in 1933. During the next few years, this commission issued a series of reform bills to regulate wages and hours, improve building codes, and ban child labor. In the spring of 1912, Perkins tried to enlist FDR's vote for a bill limiting the hours of work for women and children; initially he refused, but then he reluctantly cast his vote for it. The bill eventually passed because it received enthusiastic help from Tammany politicians, not FDR. "This inconvenient fact," according to Geoffrey Ward, "evidently bothered Franklin" because "in later years . . . as he so often did, he simply altered the past to suit the present."[5] That is, as his political career blossomed, FDR, in order to enhance his credentials as a prolabor reformer, claimed to have championed this piece of legislation.

Roosevelt's reelection as a state senator in 1912 — as well as his election to the presidency in 1932 — was largely the work of Louis Howe. In 1912, Howe was a forty-one-year-old small-town newspaperman who regularly covered the state legislature. He had reported on FDR's efforts to block Sheehan, first with skepticism and then with respect. The newspaperman saw almost immediately that with the proper guidance, FDR could become president, and Howe could achieve the success that had so far eluded him. The two men spent hours together discussing politics and developed a trusting relationship. When Roosevelt fell ill with typhoid fever in the autumn of 1912, he asked Howe to run his campaign, which he did with great success. A political partnership was forged that would last until Howe's death in 1936.[6]

The contrast between Roosevelt and Howe could have hardly been greater. While FDR was tall (six feet, one inch) and elegant, Howe was short and sickly. Howe was constantly smoking and coughing; his face was scarred because of an accident. Roosevelt's family initially found Howe repulsive, but FDR saw a man who would totally dedicate himself to serving Roosevelt's political needs. According to Schlesinger, "FDR found in Howe an astuteness in political operation which supplemented his own inexperience, and an astringent attitude toward life, which stimulated his own high spirits. Howe was indifferent to political ideology, beyond a commitment to the Democratic party . . . ; but he was a master of political technique, and here Roosevelt needed assistance."[7] Ward adds: "Paperwork was Howe's specialty. He read fast, wrote fast, dictated fast, scattering cigarette ashes over everything as he went, and his newspaperman's training had taught him how to deal with the press, how to distill from vast amounts of material those essential facts which his boss needed to function at his best."[8] Choosing Howe as his helpmate reflected FDR's skill in recruiting advisers who could serve his political purposes.

In 1911, FDR began to shift his attention to a new national figure: Governor Woodrow Wilson of New Jersey. Roosevelt was impressed by how the Princeton professor had been able to gain the backing of Democratic machines in New Jersey while attracting the support of the growing progressive movement. Because progressives were united in their hatred of corrupt machines, this was the kind of political magic that FDR appreciated and aspired to duplicate. Roosevelt admired Wilson's practical skill in winning elections and his ability to pose as a moral leader for the progressive cause. Accordingly, FDR supported Wilson's quest for the presidential nomination in 1912 and voted for him in the election, even though his cousin Teddy was running as a third-party (progressive) candidate. When Wilson was elected, FDR campaigned to be appointed assistant secretary of the navy—the same position Teddy had received in the McKinley administration. President Wilson gave him the job, and history was ready to repeat itself.

FDR nominally served under Josephus Daniels, the secretary of the navy. Daniels was a North Carolina newspaper publisher; he was an isolationist and pacifist with no maritime experience. Roosevelt was raised in a house where he played with model ships, studied maritime maps, perused the naval logs of his grandfather Delano, read the naval histories of Admiral Alfred Mahan, and sailed his own boat. More importantly, his ambition to be noticed by making daring decisions was not likely to be compatible with being loyal to his superior. Roosevelt's job as assistant secretary was concerned with the business affairs of the navy, such as procurement, supply, and civilian labor. This gave him the opportunity to interact with businessmen like Joseph Kennedy and labor representatives in many different ports. Roosevelt was particularly proud that no major strikes occurred during his eight years in office.[9] However, FDR did generate strife within the administration by calling for a larger navy than either Daniels or Wilson wanted. And when the Great War erupted in August 1914, Roosevelt urged that the United States join Great Britain and France to fight German militarism, a position closer to Teddy Roosevelt's than to Wilson's initial policy of neutrality. FDR was lucky that neither Wilson nor Daniels fired him for insubordination.[10]

While serving in the Navy Department, Roosevelt, aided by his assistant, Louis Howe, never neglected his political interests and ambitions in New York. He attempted to influence patronage decisions in his home state, but President Wilson channeled most jobs through Senator O'Gormand. In the summer of 1914, FDR challenged Tammany by running against its candidate, James W. Gerard, in the New York primary senatorial race. Roosevelt was trounced in the primary by a 3-to-1 margin, but Gerard was defeated in the November election. This outcome taught both FDR and Boss Murphy a painful lesson: in order to win a statewide election, Roosevelt needed Tammany support, and Tammany required the help of upstate Democrats. Recognizing their mutual interests, Murphy, in 1917, invited FDR to deliver a speech to a Tammany Fourth of July celebration, and Roosevelt gladly accepted. The next year, he supported Al Smith's successful run for governor. A wary alliance had been forged.[11]

In 1920, with President Wilson incapacitated by a stroke, the Democrats nominated Governor James Cox of Ohio to be their presidential candidate, and he selected FDR as his running mate. Cox hoped that Roosevelt, with Teddy now dead and the Republicans having nominated Warren Harding and Calvin Coolidge, would attract progressive Republican votes for the Democratic ticket. FDR demonstrated his exuberance for campaigning, traveling 8,000 miles, and giving, on average, seven speeches a day, but to no avail. The electorate responded to Harding's conservative call for a "return to normalcy," and the Republicans won by a landslide.[12]

In 1921, Roosevelt was hired to head the New York office of the Fidelity and Deposit Company of Maryland, a surety bonding firm, for $25,000 a year, five times his salary as assistant secretary of the navy. His secretary was Marguerite "Missy" LeHand, who would continue to work faithfully for FDR until she was incapacitated by a stroke in 1941. In August 1921, while vacationing at his family's summer home on Campobello Island in New Brunswick, Canada, Roosevelt suddenly fell ill with fatigue, fever, pain, and spreading paralysis. The first doctor who examined Roosevelt misdiagnosed his disease, never thinking that his malady was the one known as "infantile paralysis." The doctor recommended that Eleanor and Louis Howe massage Roosevelt's legs, but that only caused the patient excruciating pain and made his condition worse. Finally, FDR was diagnosed accurately; his thirty-nine-year-old body had been invaded by the polio virus, which was weakening and destroying nerve cells. Barely able to move, many of his body functions no longer working, Roosevelt briefly lost his faith in God. Louis Howe arranged for his transportation to Manhattan and hospital care in a manner that minimized his crippling condition for the press and maximized the chances for his full recovery. Once the disease was correctly diagnosed and he was presented with exercises to promote recovery, FDR's faith and optimism were restored, and he believed that he would be able to walk again. He resisted his mother's efforts to get him to return to Hyde Park and live as an invalid[13] and accepted the encouraging opinion of Eleanor and Louis Howe that he could still achieve political success.

Regaining his physical capabilities was necessary because Roosevelt felt that a show of good health was indispensable for renewing his political career. The language of electoral politics used metaphors of mobility. Candidates "ran" for office; the campaign was a "race"; if you were likely to win, you were a "front runner."[14] One could not be elected to higher office on the basis of pity. This led to a simple goal in Roosevelt's life throughout the 1920s: he would learn to walk again so he could run for office.

There has been controversy over the effect of FDR's illness on his political career. His wife suggested that it made him more sensitive toward those who were wounded by the different hazards of life. Burns argued that polio did not change FDR's political philosophy: he was still a Wilsonian progressive who believed in the kind of dramatic executive leadership exemplified by his cousin Teddy.[15] In this debate over the consequences of polio on FDR's life, however, nothing can measure up to the analysis provided by Geoffrey Ward. Perhaps because the author had had polio, his chapters on how Roosevelt struggled to cope with the indignities of being handicapped while fulfilling his personal and political ambitions are the best available. Ward documents FDR's mistaken optimism that he would fully recover and walk again. When that plan failed, Roosevelt substituted the illusion of being able to walk. After many hours of practice, with the aid of steel braces on his legs, a cane, and the trained support of someone like his son, James, walking beside him, FDR appeared to be walking. To complete the illusion, despite the prodigious effort it required to carry this off, FDR camouflaged this feat by smiling, laughing, and carrying on animated conversations. Ward points out that in both public and private meetings, FDR had "consummate skill at pretending that his disability did not bother him and that it therefore need not bother anyone else."[16]

Nothing demonstrates FDR's resilience better than his success in changing the disaster of his paralyzing disease from a career stopper to a career enhancer. Before suffering the ravages of polio, FDR appeared to many contemporaries as a spoiled and self-absorbed young man who was capitalizing on his mother's money and his cousin's reputation. But after recovering from polio, Roosevelt's aristocratic cheerfulness was often regarded as inspiring. Polio helped change FDR's image from a privileged dilettante to a heroic humanist. Conkin explains, "In many ways his legs became a major political asset, appealing to all who suffered, who had calamities, and who aspired to overcome them. Polio made an aristocratic Roosevelt into an underdog. For him it replaced the log cabin."[17] This resilience was also reflected in his development of Warm Springs, Georgia, to which he traveled in 1924 to recover strength in his legs in the naturally warm waters, and which he then developed into a treatment facility for crippled children and adults. This second home helped FDR to pose as a son of the South and helped to overcome the North-South split in the Democratic party.

In brief, FDR never conquered polio; he transcended it. He performed a magical illusion in his recovery. Although he was never able to walk again, he was able to run again and win the top political prize.

FDR launched his political comeback in 1924 by nominating Al Smith for president before the national Democratic party convention in New York City. The party was split between Smith's urban-wet supporters and William McAdoo's southern and western dries. It took 103 ballots over fourteen days before the party could nominate a compromise candidate, John W. Davis, a conservative Democrat, who was destined to be defeated by Calvin Coolidge. Four years later, Roosevelt again nominated Smith at the Democratic convention in Houston, and this time, the governor gathered more than the required two-thirds vote of the delegates and was nominated on the first ballot. After his nomination, Smith orchestrated a campaign to pressure FDR to run for governor of New York in hopes that Roosevelt would help him win the electoral college vote of New York by expanding his support with upstate Protestant voters. Roosevelt initially declined the offer because he claimed he needed more time for his physical recovery. However, when Smith's campaign manager, John J. Raskob, offered to make a major donation to Warm Springs, FDR disregarded Howe's advice and accepted Smith's offer to run for governor.[18] Smith, the first Catholic to be nominated for president, was beaten badly by Herbert Hoover, not even carrying his own state, but Roosevelt was elected governor by a small margin of 25,000 votes out of over 4 million cast.

Smith had inadvertently created an awkward position for himself: he was now out of a job, and Roosevelt, having been elected governor in a key state, was now the most prominent Democrat in both New York and the nation. Underestimating Roosevelt, Smith mistakenly believed he could run the state through his old political advisers, Belle Moskovitz and Robert Moses, but FDR, determined to be governor in his own right, quickly put his own loyalists in office. Smith had also assumed that for health reasons Roosevelt would spend most of his time at Warm Springs and would neither aspire to be nor be capable of being a dynamic executive. Smith was wrong again. Roosevelt responded skillfully to the new challenges of the Depression, and in the 1930 governor's race, he campaigned vigorously and defeated his Republican opponent by 725,000 votes, almost doubling Smith's 1924 majority of 387,000.[19] FDR was now ready to run for president, a story that I will cover in Chapter 11.

FDR's Personality

Eleanor Roosevelt described her husband's personality in these words: "'You made up your mind to do a thing and you did it to the best of your ability. If it went sour, why, then you started in all over again and did something else. . . . ' And she added significantly: 'I have never heard him say there was a problem that he thought it was impossible for human beings to solve.'"[20] For Roosevelt, where there was a problem, there was a solution that a good politician like himself could eventually find.

All of Roosevelt's biographers cite Oliver Wendell Holmes's quip that FDR had "a second class intellect, but a first class temperament." Kenneth Davis writes, "Possessed of an intellect that was broad but shallow, he collected facts and ideas as he did stamps and naval prints, letting them lie flat, distinct, separate in his mind, never attempting to combine them into any holistic truth. Indeed, he shied away from generalized thinking and abstract ideas."[21] Driven by undisciplined curiosity and immune to the allure of ideology, FDR was open to a wide variety of ideas and people.[22] By being free of the constraints of dogma, he was an exceptionally flexible politician who could adapt to changing conditions.

The most famous attack on FDR's intelligence and his qualifications for the White House was issued by the prestigious pundit Walter Lippmann. The journalist was personally familiar with FDR and was aware of his reputation as an intellectual lightweight and his nickname, "Featherduster." If the Depression was overwhelming the efforts of someone as bright and hardworking as Herbert Hoover, what would it do to a dilettante like FDR? Lippmann believed that a successful president required the intellectual credentials of a Teddy Roosevelt or Woodrow Wilson, and FDR obviously did not have those qualities. What particularly disturbed Lippmann was that FDR appeared to be tolerating the corruption of Jimmy Walker, the Tammany-supported mayor of New York City. Lippmann publicized his concerns about FDR, the odds-on favorite to win the Democratic nomination, in his column on January 8, 1932. "Roosevelt, Lippmann warned, 'is a highly impressionable person without a firm grasp of public affairs, and without very strong convictions . . . an amiable man with many philanthropic impulses, but he is not the dangerous enemy of anything. He is too eager to please.' In total, charged Lippmann: 'Franklin D. Roosevelt is no crusader. He is no tribune of the people. He is no enemy of entrenched privilege. He is a pleasant man who, without any important qualifications for the office, would very much like to be President.'"[23] FDR never publicly reacted to this criticism, but he did create the Brains Trust to tutor him on the major policy issues that he would have to deal with in both the 1932 campaign and as president.

One source of his personal security was his religious beliefs. Paralleling his political eclecticism, Roosevelt was raised as an Episcopalian but preferred Baptist, Methodist, or Presbyterian sermons. According to Schlesinger, "His faith was non-theological, a matter of tradition and propriety, something which he felt but did not care to formulate. 'I think it is just as well not to think about things like that too much!' he admonished his wife. . . . The divisiveness of dogmatic theologies bothered him."[24] Davis argues, "the root and core of his conception of self and world was the inward certainty that he was a chosen one of the Almighty, his career a role assigned him by the Author of the Universe."[25] Roosevelt felt that even his more Machiavellian moves were moral because his ultimate goals were good. In his mind, God was part of the FDR coalition.

There is little doubt that FDR carefully crafted his public persona to achieve his ambition of becoming president. With his easy laugh, boyish enthusiasm, and teasing style of conversation, FDR believed in the effectiveness of his charm. He wanted to be liked and worked hard at trying to gain the affection of others. Although he had many acquaintances, and thanks to Louis Howe and Missy LeHand he maintained an extensive correspondence with a wide variety of people, he had few intimate friends who thought that they knew him well. Sixty years before there were friends of Bill Clinton's, there were friends of Roosevelt who sometimes wondered whether they were recruited to serve his political purposes. Among both his friends and opponents, the idea took hold "that a political implication underlay his every move, and that the man could manipulate the different aspects of his own personality for political advantage. Everything about the President—his wife, his children, his dog Fala, his stamp collection, his fishing trips—seemed to have a public quality."[26] His desire to become a successful president meant that his public self largely replaced his private self. Political calculations dominated Roosevelt's personality.

Because personality affects presidential behavior, both supporters and opponents of FDR were constantly trying to decipher his character. One of the most insightful contributions to this debate was provided by Robert Sherwood, the prize-winning playwright, who also served as one of FDR's major speechwriters. According to Sherwood, Roosevelt's

character was not only multiplex, it was contradictory to a bewildering degree. He was hard, and he was soft. At times he displayed a capacity for vindictiveness which could be described as petty, and at other times he demonstrated the Christian spirit of forgiveness and charity in its purest form. He could be a ruthless politician, but he was the champion of friends and associates who for him were political liabilities. . . . He could appear to be utterly cynical, worldly, illusionless, and yet his religious faith was the strongest and most mysterious force that was in him. Although he was progressive enough . . . to be condemned as a "Traitor to his class," . . . he was in truth a profoundly old-fashioned person with an incurable nostalgia for the very "horse and buggy era" on which he publicly heaped so much scorn. He loved peace and harmony in his surroundings and . . . greatly preferred to be agreed with, and yet most of his major appointments to the Cabinet and to the various New Deal and War Agencies were peculiarly . . . quarrelsome . . . men. He liked to fancy himself as a practical, down-to-earth, horse-sense realist . . . and yet his idealism was actually no less empyrean than Woodrow Wilson's.[27]

FDR's Political Philosophy

Some scholars will deny that FDR's presidency was guided by any political philosophy. For them, Roosevelt was too much of a political opportunist to be shackled by a doctrine. Leuchtenburg writes, "Herbert Hoover called him a 'chameleon on plaid,' while H. L. Mencken declared, 'if he became convinced tomorrow that coming out for cannibalism would get him the votes he sorely needs, he would begin fattening a missionary in the White House backyard come Wednesday.'"[28] One of FDR's early biographers portrays him as a practical politician, lacking a transformative vision, who wanted to build a number of projects. According to Burns, FDR "had ideas such as the tree shelter belt in the drought areas; transcontinental through-highways with networks of feeder roads; huge dams and irrigation systems; resettlement projects for tenant farmers; civilian conservation work in the woods; a chain of small hospitals across the country; rural electrification; regional development; bridges and houses and parks. . . . What excited Roosevelt was not grand economic or political theory but concrete achievements that people could touch and see and use"[29]—and that would influence their voting decisions.

One could also make the case that FDR believed in some basic conservative ideas. He accepted the Burkean idea of the organic continuity of the past, present, and future. Roosevelt also gave credence to the notion that reforms were necessary to conserve enduring ends. His conservatism was reflected in his lifelong concern with his ancestors, the history of Dutchess County, land conservation, tree farming, and the national heritage.[30] FDR loved the land much more than the city, and he nurtured a romantic, almost reactionary, infatuation that many urban residents could be lured back to the countryside by inducements like rural electrification. If Roosevelt had a utopian vision of what kind of America his New Deal policies should produce, it might have been the tranquility of his estate in Hyde Park. It is ironic that the man who brought about so many changes in the United States and the world preferred for things to remain the same in Hyde Park, in his office, and on his immediate staff.

Although FDR did not have a clear-cut philosophy in 1932, he did have a sense of direction in how he wanted to govern. As an ambitious politician, he had constructed his philosophy more from experience observing such dynamic leaders as Teddy Roosevelt, Woodrow Wilson, and Al Smith than from studying books. Both his personality and philosophy called for vigorous executive action to deal with the major problems of the day. As a young man, he was attracted to the progressive idea that morally inspired government, led by executives who fought against special interests to promote the public interest, was essential to improve society. With his famous name, self-confidence, and political experience, he felt qualified to be president. With the advent of the Depression, he saw that the progressive philosophy (soon called modern liberalism) could be rejuvenated and become the guiding light of both his administration and the Democratic party.

FDR publicly stressed that the presidency is primarily an office of "moral leadership." In 1932, he declared, "All our great Presidents were leaders of thought at times when certain historic ideas in the life of the nation had to be clarified. So Washington had personified the idea of federal union, Jefferson and Jackson the idea of democracy, Lincoln union and freedom. . . . Isn't that what the office is—a superb opportunity for reapplying, applying in new conditions, the simple rules of human conduct we always go back to?"[31] The idea that FDR personified and tried to legitimate for the American people was that positive government was both good and necessary; it could provide for the general welfare without endangering individual liberty.

For many historians, Roosevelt's New Deal was deeply influenced by two strands of progressivism, the New Nationalism of Teddy Roosevelt and the New Freedom of Woodrow Wilson. Each of these doctrines had helped their proponents to achieve some success; they had proven their value on the political battlefield. Yet there were conflicts between the New Nationalism, with its acceptance of bigness and its emphasis on a planned and disciplined business system, and the New Freedom, with its stress on the restoration of competition through antitrust policies. But in Roosevelt's imaginative mind, these competing visions of progressive thought could be woven together to serve as a policy guide. Schlesinger points out, "He never could see why the United States had to be all one way or all the other. 'This country is big enough to experiment with several diverse systems and follow several different lines,' he once remarked to Adolf Berle. 'Why must we put our economic policy in a single systematic strait jacket?'"[32]

Certainly FDR's wandering and experimenting mind could never be constrained by any philosophical straitjacket. Witness how FDR could claim to be both liberal (promoting change) and conservative (protecting institutions): "The most serious threat to our institutions," he once said, "comes from those who refuse to face the need for change. Liberalism becomes the protection for the far-sighted conservative. . . . 'Reform if you would preserve.' I am that kind of conservative because I am that kind of liberal."[33] There is some truth in FDR's statement, along with some sophistry.

FDR's philosophy and general intentions were reflected in how he governed New York from 1929 to 1932. David Kennedy suggests that his record indicated that he

> shared his cousin Theodore's belief in the supremacy of the public interest over private interests and in the government's role as the active agent of the public interest; that he meant to preside over a government even more vigorously interventionist and directive than Hoover's; that he intended to use government power to redress what he judged to be harmful and unfair imbalances in the American economy, especially the huge income gap between the agricultural and industrial sectors; that he had long been seeking for ordinary Americans some measure of the economic security and predictability of life's material circumstances that his own patrician class took for granted; that he had a lover's passion for the cause of conservation; and that he was a champion of public waterpower.[34]

Much of FDR's New Deal was also forecast in his 1932 campaign for the presidency.[35] His speeches during that period demonstrated that he believed the old system had produced the Depression and would therefore have to be replaced with a new one that would provide a more stable and equitable economy. To bring this change about, the status of business would have to be lowered while the authority of the federal government to work for the public interest would have to be raised. In his "Forgotten Man" speech of April 7, 1932, Roosevelt accused Hoover of being concerned with only "the top of the social economic structure" while the present crisis called for "bottom up" plans that would aid the farmer, worker, and homeowner.[36] When the "Forgotten Man" speech generated controversy over whether FDR was demagogically encouraging class conflict, the candidate responded with a Jefferson Day address on April 18 that called for governmental action in the form of national planning to deal with the present crisis and to prevent future ones. "I am not speaking of an economic life completely planned and regimented," declared Roosevelt. "I am speaking of the necessity, however, that, in those imperative interferences with the economic life of the Nation, there be a real community of interest, not only among the sections of this great country, but among its economic units and the various groups in these units. . . . In much of our present plans there is too much disposition to mistake the part for the whole, the head for the body, the captain for the company, the general for the army. I plead not for a class control but for a true concert of interests."[37] In brief, FDR portrayed the contrasting philosophies of the Republican regime and his new one by claiming that Hoover promoted policies to help the privileged, while his administration would be more socially fair because it would aid a broader array of interests.

A month later, Roosevelt delivered an unusually candid speech to the graduating students of Oglethorpe University in Georgia. He pointed out how different conditions were when they entered college in 1928 than when they were graduating in 1932. In FDR's view, the Depression—a man-made calamity, not a natural one—had eroded the security that citizens were entitled to and that the nation was rich enough to provide. He suggested that the economic machine we had created had broken down and that we were presented with a multitude of proposals to promote economic recovery. FDR rejected the option of laissez-faire, which he ridiculed as doing nothing. He advocated the need for innovative thinking and daring experimentation. Roosevelt called for new thinking that would be more concerned with consumption than with production. For the economic order to survive, he argued, we will have to "bring about . . . an equitable distribution of the national income." That would require farmers and workers to receive a larger share of the national income and capitalists to attain less. The key lines in the address were the following: "The country needs and, unless I mistake the temper, the country demands bold, persistent experimentation. . . . The millions who are in want will not stand by silently forever while the things to satisfy their needs are within easy reach. . . . We need to correct, by drastic means if necessary, the faults in our economic system from which we now suffer." He ended his speech with a peroration that was both a reflection of reconstructive thinking and a challenge to his audience, his supporters, and himself: "We need the courage of the young. Yours is not the task of making your way in the world, but the task of remaking the world which you will find before you. May every one of us be granted the courage, the faith, and the vision to give the best that is in us to that remaking!"[38]

The Depression wrecked so many lives and created such a sense of precariousness for millions of Americans that it elevated the value of security. Hence, in his July 1932 speech accepting the Democratic nomination for president, FDR proclaimed that work and security "are the spiritual values, the true goal toward which our efforts of reconstruction should lead. These are the values that this program is intended to gain; these are the values we have failed to achieve by the leadership we now have."[39] David Kennedy concurs: "Security was the touchstone, the single word that summed up more of what Roosevelt aimed at than any other. 'Among our objectives,' he declared, 'I place the security of the men, women, and children of the Nation first.' People wanted, indeed they had a 'right'—a significant escalation of the rhetoric of political claims—to three types of security: 'decent homes to live in,' 'productive work,' and 'security against the hazards and vicissitudes of life.'"[40]

Roosevelt believed that because the Depression demonstrated that capitalism could not provide economic security for the bulk of the nation's population, protection would have to be supplied by the expanded role of the federal government. Although conservatives argued that the quest for security would lead to regimentation, FDR and his liberal supporters believed that security was a prerequisite for being free. In Roosevelt's view, the freedom of the few rich had to be restricted—or, more accurately, taxed and regulated—for the benefit of the many. "The choice," according to Clinton Rossiter, "was not between liberty and security any more than it had been between liberty and Union [in Lincoln's presidency]. The two are inseparable, said Roosevelt, and it was his particular task to remind us of the hollowness of liberty for a man who lacks security."[41]

FDR's most ambitious attempt to lay out his political philosophy was his speech to the Commonwealth Club in San Francisco on September 23, 1932. The Commonwealth speech was largely written by Adolf Berle (in three drafts) and was edited by Moley and Roosevelt. In this address to an elite audience, FDR was attempting to live up to his self-proclaimed standard that "the greatest duty of a statesman is to educate." What he wanted to teach his audience—and the nation—was that democracy is a never-ending quest for a better life. In McJimsey's words, "Roosevelt proposed an economic social contract based on the principles of the Declaration of Independence—life, liberty, and the pursuit of happiness—updated for the modern economic order."[42] With the closing of the frontier and the rise of the giant corporation at the turn of the century, it became evident to progressives like Teddy Roosevelt and Woodrow Wilson that we had to renovate the social contract that Jefferson and the Founding Fathers had instituted. The equality of opportunity to start a farm or business that so characterized America no longer existed. With our industrial plant already built, there was no longer a need for financial titans; the new challenge was to deal with the problem of underconsumption by adjusting production to consumption (perhaps through economic planning) and "distributing wealth and products more equitably." The socially just society could no longer be provided by competitive markets and overly limited government;

it now required "enlightened administration." FDR's speech, according to Milkis, "revealed clearly the progressive concern to give new meaning to the Hamiltonian tradition [of energetic administration] by infusing it with a democratic purpose. . . . With the decline of conditions favoring an expansion of the economic sector, . . . the impetus for the national welfare would now have to shift from the shoulders of the productive private citizen to the government; the guarantee of equal opportunity now required that individual initiative be restrained and directed by the national government."[43]

Given the nature of the new economic order, private economic power was now a public trust and would have to be publicly regulated. Irresponsible manipulation of markets and greedy speculation would have to be legally prohibited. In Roosevelt's mind, the Depression proved that public power would have to restrain the rights of the few "princes of property," who were creating an oligarchy, to benefit the security interests of the many, which was necessary for the continuation of democracy. "As I see it," proclaimed FDR, "the task of Government in its relation to business is to assist the development of an economic declaration of rights, an economic constitutional order. This is the common task of statesman and businessman. It is the minimum requirement of a more permanently safe order of things."[44] In short, FDR's Commonwealth discourse displayed his pessimism about whether capitalists could provide economic growth and distributive justice and his optimism concerning the ability of the public sector to supply security for citizens while maintaining democracy.

Ronald Wilson Reagan

While FDR enjoyed the benefits of being born to a rich and prominent family, Ronald Reagan began his life on February 6, 1911, above a bakery in Tampico, Illinois. His father, Jack, was a Catholic Democrat whose parents had died of tuberculosis when he was only six years old. Jack was raised by an aunt and uncle in Iowa and dropped out of school when he was twelve. He grew up to be a witty raconteur and shoe salesman who futilely dreamed about owning his own store and house, but his ambitions were handicapped by his alcoholism.

In November 1904, Jack married Nelle Wilson, a Protestant and teetotaler. Although they were married in a Catholic church, Nelle soon joined the Disciples of Christ Church. Reagan was raised in his mother's religion. Nelle taught her son that God has a positive plan for each of us; Reagan's experiences seemed to confirm that. Because of her own love of dancing and acting before audiences, she taught her son how to perform—reciting poetry and acting in plays—at an early age, thus nurturing one of Reagan's skills: his ability to perform before an audience.

The Reagan family moved from town to town, finally settling in Dixon, Illinois, in 1920. With neighboring farmers suffering a decline in income after the Great War and Jack occasionally engaging in binge drinking, the family could only afford to live in an apartment. But despite his family's financial struggles and conflicts over alcohol, Reagan remembered growing up in Dixon as a happy period. When Ronald was sixteen, he went to work as a lifeguard at Lowell Park on the Rock River, and during the six years he held that job, he demonstrated his physical courage by saving seventy-seven people from drowning. He also did well in high school, playing on the varsity football and basketball teams, acting in a number of school plays, dating the attractive and intelligent daughter of a minister, earning a low B average, and being elected president of his senior class. His sunny disposition was reflected by a poem he wrote entitled, "Life," in which the key line is: "We make our life a struggle, when life should be a song."[45] Reagan graduated from high school in 1928, then attended Eureka College, a Disciple of Christ Church school of 187 students located 200 miles south of Dixon. Jack could not afford to help his son financially, but Reagan was able to obtain a half-tuition football scholarship and a job washing dishes at one of the two female dormitories. He majored in sociology and minored in economics; both subjects were taught by the same professor. With his photographic memory, Reagan did not have to study hard to pass—and he didn't. He maintained a C average, played guard on the football team, helped his brother get a football scholarship, and appeared in a number of plays. As a freshman, he gave a speech supporting a student strike against the college president's proposal for budget cuts; as a senior, he was elected class president. When Reagan graduated in June 1932, in the midst of the Depression, he could not afford to buy a class ring.[46]

After graduation, Reagan decided he wanted to become a sports announcer. In October 1932, at a time when millions were unemployed, Reagan got a sportscasting job for radio station WOC in Iowa, first in Davenport, later in Des Moines. He got the position by impressing the WOC program director with an enthusiastically imagined play-by-play announcement of the final quarter of a Eureka College football game. "During the next four years," according to Tygiel, "Ronald Reagan became one of the most celebrated sportscasters in the Midwest. Best known for his work on major league baseball games [excitedly recreating Chicago Cubs and Chicago White Sox games based on pitch-by-pitch reports via telegraph], he also gave twice-daily sports reports and commentaries and wrote a regular sports column in the *Des Moines Dispatch*."[47]

In 1932, Reagan cast his first of four votes for FDR. Reagan's father, as a well-known Democrat in Dixon, was helped by New Deal relief agencies. Jack was awarded patronage positions in the Civil Works Administration in 1933 and the Works Progress Administration in 1935. Given how much help his family received from these programs, it is troubling that Reagan became so adamantly opposed to welfare in the 1950s.

In 1937, Reagan traveled to Southern California, where the Chicago Cubs were conducting their spring training. A female friend helped Reagan get a screen test with Warner Brothers, and he was promptly signed to a seven-year contract. By June 1937, he was starring in a B movie. His career was aided by Hearst columnist Louella Parsons, who was also from Dixon. Reagan was soon making enough money to bring his parents out to Hollywood, where Nelle joined the Hollywood-Beverly Christian Church and Jack worked for Warner Brothers, handling his son's fan mail. In 1939, Reagan and a young actress named Jane Wyman costarred in several B films and fell in love. Their romance and marriage in January 1940 was highly publicized by Louella Parsons and the movie magazines. The young couple had a daughter named Maureen in January 1941 and adopted a son, Michael, in April 1945.

Although Reagan never became a top star in Hollywood, he did have a successful career. He appeared in fifty-four movies, typically playing the star's best friend in A movies and the lead in B films. His two most famous roles were as the mythic George Gipp in the 1940 movie, *Knute Rockne — All American*, in which he delivers the famous deathbed line, "Win one for the Gipper," and as Drake McHugh in the 1941 film, *Kings Row*, in which he wakes up to find his legs have been amputated and calls out, "Where is the rest of me!" As an actor, he had a limited range, but within that sphere he was likable and authentic. Tygiel describes the strengths and limitations of Reagan's talent in these words: "He was a dependable worker who showed up on time, knew his lines, rarely required a stunt man, and did whatever the studio asked of him, either on the set or in publicity settings. He performed best when playing himself—a likable All American type, 'boyish of face and gleaming of teeth.' . . . Unlike other actors, . . . Reagan never sought out acting lessons or joined a theater group that might help him to hone his craft."[48]

After the Japanese attack on Pearl Harbor, Reagan was ordered to report to the army in April 1942. Although the movie magazines, and even

Reagan's autobiography, *Where's the Rest of Me?*, suggested that he was ful-filling his patriotic duty far from Jane Wyman, he was actually serving in the First Motion Picture Unit in Culver City near Hollywood. His service during the conflict was as a "celluloid commando," making war movies and training films. Reagan did see the early films of the liberation of the Nazi concentration camp at Buchenwald and later proudly but falsely claimed that he had participated in the liberation of Buchenwald.[49] He did earn out-standing performance evaluations, and by the end of the war, he had been promoted to captain.

Reagan was discharged from the army in July 1945. Although Lew Was-serman, Reagan's agent, had negotiated a lucrative new contract for him with Warner Brothers, it was Jane Wyman's career that took off after the war, while Reagan's, as a result of a series of bad movies, declined. In De-cember 1947, the Reagans separated; six months later, Wyman filed for divorce.[50]

Meanwhile, Reagan had become interested in the activities of the Screen Actors Guild (SAG). This union emerged from the employment codes in FDR's National Industrial Recovery Act of 1933 and was institutionalized in 1937 with the assistance of the National Labor Relations Board.[51] Rea-gan replaced Robert Montgomery as president of SAG in March 1947; he served as its head from 1947 to 1952. During these early years of the cold war and the red scare, SAG was deeply involved with the issues of loyalty oaths, blacklisting, and violent jurisdictional disputes between the International Alliance of Theatrical Stage Employees and Motion Picture Operators (an allegedly corrupt union with ties to gangsters) and the Con-ference of Studio Unions (a union with alleged ties to communists) over who would represent carpenters laboring on movie sets. As a result of these experiences, including what he considered threats on his life by commu-nists, Reagan, who had been a left-wing Democrat during the war, now shifted to the right and became a more conservative Democrat, willing to work as an informer for the FBI. Although he still publicly supported Tru-man in 1948, by 1952 he was leading a "Democrats for Eisenhower" group. This conservative transformation was also abetted by his outrage that he was being taxed at the top income tax rate—91 percent.

In 1949, Reagan met a young actress named Nancy Davis, whom he married on March 4, 1952; seven and a half months later, they had a daugh-ter, Patti. In May 1958, a son, Ronald Jr., was born. The combination of Ronnie and Nancy's love for each other and his political ambitions meant that Reagan had little time for any of his children, nor was Nancy a very caring mother. Nevertheless, the Reagans had a highly successful and happy marriage, and Mrs. Reagan helped her husband fulfill his political goals in many ways. Although it is said that Reagan never worried about anything, Mrs. Reagan worried about everything and continually brought vital information to his attention. While Reagan would rarely take the initiative and call an adviser to see if things were proceeding according to plan, Mrs. Reagan terrorized the staff by frequently using the phone to make sure that Reagan's aides were serving his purposes. One long-term aide, Lynn Nofziger, who was sometimes the target of Mrs. Reagan's wrath, nevertheless wrote that "when she latched onto Ronald Reagan, her career became Ronald Reagan, and if any one person besides Reagan is responsible for the success of his political career, it is Nancy."[52]

As the door closed on Reagan's movie career, another one opened, allowing him to launch a career in television. In the early 1950s, MCA, a talent agency representing many movie actors, including Reagan, created Revue Productions to develop programs for television. These plans were impeded, however, by a SAG rule that prohibited talent agents from also acting as producers. In 1952, Lew Wasserman, head of MCA, petitioned SAG "for a blanket waiver allowing MCA to continue to represent actors, while allowing its Revue subsidiary to produce shows." Wasserman offered two incentives to obtain SAG's agreement: Revue Productions would be located in Southern California and provide work to many actors; and MCA would become the first studio to pay residuals to performers when a show was repeated. In July 1952, Reagan signed the blanket waiver that granted Revue Productions permission to produce television programs. As a result of this agreement, "MCA could now offer its clients steady work in Revue Productions. Since SAG granted a blanket waiver to no other agencies, actors began abandoning their representatives and flocking to MCA. MCA came to dominate television production . . . and Lew Wasserman became the most powerful man in Hollywood."[53]

Although hosting *General Electric Theater* rescued Reagan from financial ruin, it was a subsidiary component of his contract that put him on the road to the White House. As part of his contract, he was obligated to spend sixteen weeks a year on the road—literally on the road because Reagan was afraid of flying—visiting the 185 GE plants throughout the nation. His public relations role was to meet with GE executives, talk with the workers, and give inspiring speeches celebrating the virtues of America, free enterprise, and the company. This kind of activity might be considered a chore for many celebrities, but for Reagan it was pure delight. He loved performing on the "mashed potato circuit," writing his own speeches, generating laughter with his wit, and educating his audience about the evils of big government and the virtues of his evolving conservatism. Reagan, the former ardent New Dealer, was transforming himself in this speech-by-speech process to a committed conservative who was dedicated to bringing about a similar conversion of the audiences he was addressing. "By the late 1950s," according to Tygiel, "Reagan had developed both the speaking style and much of the content that would characterize the remainder of his political career. He collected and presented a dazzling string of facts, quotations, statistics, and anecdotes that endorsed his antigovernment message. Reagan never questioned that the 'facts' he had come across might be false, the quotations misattributed, or the stories unrepresentative. He presented them as, and believed them to be, the unvarnished truth."[54] Through trial and error, before hundreds of audiences, Reagan was creating "The Speech," which crystallized his conservative beliefs, and by repeatedly giving that speech (with slight variations) for the rest of his public career, he established his credentials as a conviction politician.

GE ended its relationship with Reagan in 1962. In the late 1950s, Reagan had added criticism of the Tennessee Valley Authority (TVA) to his speech, not realizing that it was a major customer of GE. Reagan offered to cut references to the TVA from his discourse, but there were a growing number of GE executives who feared that their spokesman's growing conservatism might hurt the company. In early 1962, Robert Kennedy's Justice Department was investigating the MCA-SAG relationship to see if any antitrust laws were being violated. Reagan was questioned by a federal grand jury about this in February 1962. This investigation resulted in a civil indictment of MCA for violations of the Sherman Antitrust Act in July 1962. When NBC slotted a popular western, *Bonanza*, against Reagan's program, causing the latter's ratings to decline, GE withdrew its sponsorship. *General Electric Theater*'s last show appeared on September 1962.

Over the next few years, Reagan's television career limped along with a few guest appearances and his hosting of *Death Valley Days*. His big break came in 1964 during Senator Barry Goldwater's futile campaign against President Lyndon Johnson. Reagan had finally registered as a Republican in 1962 and was now campaigning for Goldwater in California. Prominent California Republicans bought a half hour of prime time on NBC so that Reagan could deliver "The Speech," now labeled "A Time for Choosing," to a national audience on October 27. Reagan's talk endorsed conservatism more than it did Goldwater and was favorably received. With Goldwater buried by the LBJ landslide, the leadership of the conservative movement within the Republican party was now opening up for Reagan. Suddenly an over-the-hill actor was being talked about by many conservatives as a candidate for governor of California in 1966, and eventually for the presidency.

Many Democrats were delighted when Reagan announced he was running for governor in 1966 because they believed that like Goldwater, he could be labeled a right-wing extremist and easily defeated by the usual liberal voting coalition. But conditions in 1966 were different than in 1964; liberal visions had lost their majority appeal because of the Vietnam War, the African American riots in the Watts sector of Los Angeles, and the student demonstrations at the University of California at Berkeley. Moreover, Reagan had the capability to deliver the conservative message to a broader range of voters than Goldwater did. Reagan turned his lack of political experience into an asset by proclaiming himself to be a "citizen politician," a moral outsider who was not corrupted by inside politics. He defeated the liberal San Francisco mayor, George Christopher, in the Republican primary and then trounced two-term incumbent Democrat Governor Pat Brown in the general election by almost 1 million votes. With the help of a well-financed campaign and the political consulting firm of Stu Spencer and Bill Roberts, Reagan "had managed to create a fusion between economic and traditional conservatives and to reach out to moderates, unifying the Republican party. Campaigning as an outsider and a representative of hard-pressed, white middle- and working-class Americans, he had helped to transform the message of conservatism from an ideology of the privileged elites to one with a populist base."[55] Reagan had discovered the formula for his political success.

By being elected governor at the age of fifty-five, Reagan had demonstrated his skills as a campaigner; he now faced the challenge of governing. His problem was that he did not know anything about how California's state government worked, a handicap that might be expected to frighten anyone assuming the responsibilities of the job. But Reagan did not feel insecure. From his perspective, his responsibility was setting the right direction of state policies in his speeches; he was confident that his administration would hire personnel who knew the necessary nuts and bolts of state government well enough to carry out his conservative agenda.

With Democrats predicting disaster and conservative Republicans looking forward to miracles, Reagan turned out to be a good governor. His administration did not produce miracles, but it did leave California in better shape than when he took office. During his eight years as governor, the state budget doubled and the number of state employees increased from 163,000 to 204,000. Because the California constitution required a balanced budget, Reagan, in his first year in office, was compelled to sign the largest tax increase in California history, but in his second term, he was able to provide significant tax relief. In 1971, Reagan personally engaged in negotiations with the new Democratic speaker of the state assembly, Bob Moretti, to get the legislature to pass the California Welfare Reform Act (CWRA). Lou Cannon suggests that the CWRA reflected many of the best features of Republican and Democratic welfare recommendations:

> While increasing aid to most recipients [80 percent], the new law also tightened eligibility. . . . Antifraud measures included a state cross-check between county welfare records and employer earnings records. Counties were given financial incentives to recover support payments from absentee fathers. A demonstration project called the Community Work Experience Program was introduced in some cities. It required fathers and AFDC mothers without young children to work at public service jobs. . . . Within three years, the AFDC caseload [in California] dropped from a high of 1,608,000 to 1,330,000.[56]

With the exception of Reagan's signing an abortion bill in 1968, conservatives were pleased with his record as governor and hoped he could obtain the Republican nomination for president in 1976.[57]

Reagan's original plan was predicated on Nixon serving two full terms, but the Watergate scandal forced Nixon to resign in August 1974. This meant that when Reagan participated in the primaries in 1976, he was in the awkward position of running against an incumbent Republican president, Gerald Ford. But because Reagan was already sixty-five in 1976, it was believed that it was now or never for him to fulfill his political ambitions. When Ford defeated Reagan in the first four party contests, the pressure on him to withdraw was enormous. Instead of bowing out, however, Reagan demonstrated both his stubborn perseverance and competitive drive by staying in the race and defeating the president in a number of primaries, especially in the Southern states. Ford was forced to employ the full authority and prestige of the White House to win the nomination by the barest majority on the first ballot at the Republican convention. Reagan's valiant effort and his crowd-pleasing concession speech at the convention made it clear that he still harbored strong desires for the presidency.

After Carter defeated Ford in the 1976 elections, Reagan renewed his quest for the nation's top office. This time, almost everything that weakened

Carter and strengthened Reagan fell into place. Under Carter, the economy was wounded by stagflation, and the nation's pride was humiliated by the Iranian students' storming of the American embassy in Tehran and the Russians' invasion of Afghanistan. Carter's failures and pessimism contrasted unfavorably with Reagan's optimistic faith in his proposals. Reagan's fortunes were bolstered by his support of tax cuts, a faster military buildup, and the rise of the religious right. After George H. W. Bush defeated Reagan in the 1980 Iowa caucus, the governor went on to win twenty-nine out of thirty-three primaries and earned the nomination on the first ballot. In a three-way race, Reagan defeated President Carter and John Anderson by attracting 51 percent of the popular vote and winning the electoral votes of forty-five states. Reagan had somehow overcome the circumstances of his birth and work experiences and succeeded in climbing to the top of the greasiest and most competitive pole in America. He was in a position to perform the same kind of reconstructive politics that his hero, FDR, had engaged in during the 1930s.

Reagan's Personality

For politicians who must interact with him, as well as for journalists and scholars who try to explain his behavior, the personality of a president is a subject of intense interest. Because Reagan was already a Hollywood celebrity, the curiosity about what kind of person he was and whether he would succeed in performing the role of president was immense. Some were concerned (a few were terrified) that Reagan's political successes were due to a combination of rich benefactors in California, a pleasing personality, an attractive voice, and a great deal of luck, and that the unforgiving realities of making decisions in the White House would reveal that he was totally unqualified for the job. But to the surprise of many students of the presidency, including myself, Reagan proved capable of meeting the many challenges of the office.

In discussions about Reagan's personality, one point was beyond dispute: he was likable. Having an attractive personality is obviously a vital asset for anyone aspiring to the presidency; Reagan was naturally friendly; he had a sunny, easygoing disposition; he rarely lost his temper; and he had a repertoire of jokes and quips for every occasion. Reagan was self-assured without appearing conceited or self-centered. Even his adversaries conceded that he believed in what he was saying, which distinguished him from most other politicians. He seemed to be comfortable and unpretentious, whether he was delivering a speech to a joint session of Congress, riding a horse on his ranch, or hosting the queen of England. He succeeded in all these roles without appearing to be working hard; although he was an ambitious politician striving to accomplish big goals, he came over as more relaxed than driven. In short, Reagan had the mass appeal that political consultants look for in candidates for higher office.[58]

As is true when any personality is put under a microscope, there were contradictions in Reagan's character. As a performer, Reagan loved to be in the limelight, but he also enjoyed being alone writing a letter or fixing a fence on his ranch. He was friendly and courteous to all who came in contact with him, but with the exception of his wife, Nancy, he had no close friends. One of his biographers suggests, "The totality of his embrace of and by Nancy seems to have relieved him of the need for other intimacies (even with his children)."[59] Some of his critics charged that while he championed family values, he headed a dysfunctional family.[60] One of his long-term aides, Martin Anderson, argued that although Reagan's easygoing nature often conveyed the impression that he was passive and could be easily persuaded, the reality was that he was stubbornly determined to do what he believed to be morally correct. In Anderson's words, "Reagan may be unique in that he is a warmly ruthless man."[61] It might be more accurate to describe Reagan as blithely detached rather than warmly ruthless. Like FDR, he avoided internal family problems and let his wife handle them.[62] Cannon notes, "Reagan craved harmony and inevitably withdrew from conflicts among his advisers. In this respect he was a classic adult child of an alcoholic who had learned early in his life to retreat from discord and unpleasantness."[63] Reagan's distance from many of the people who worked harder for his success than he did may account for why a number of them—Michael Deaver, David Stockman, Donald Regan—wrote kiss-and-tell memoirs that praised their boss but also included material that was critical of him. For example, Donald Regan's book revealed that Reagan and his wife believed in astrology, an accusation that generated a lot of ridicule for the president.[64]

Discussions about Reagan inevitably lead to controversies over his intelligence. For conservatives, Reagan was a perceptive leader because in the early 1950s he saw that the logical results of the prevailing liberalism would cause disastrous domestic and international problems for the United States. Moreover, Reagan was later able to enter the liberals' den of iniquity in Washington, D.C., as president and continue to articulate and fight for conservative causes. His official biographer, Edmund Morris, thought that Reagan as a young man was anxious to learn about national and world affairs. Morris believed that Reagan possessed "considerable intelligence," but that his "most regrettable characteristic in later years was his incuriosity, compounded . . . by a refusal to be budged from any shibboleth that suited him."[65] Another biographer writes, "Reagan remained an avid reader [during the 1970s] and continued to take delight in writing most of his own speeches, allowing him to advance his ideals and beliefs. But his reading seemed designed not to accumulate information or stimulate his intellect, but rather to identify quotations and examples that he might use to support his existing viewpoints. These views had grown ossified, virtually impermeable to change."[66] Historian James Patterson summarizes the contrasting views toward Reagan: "Knowing where he wanted to go, he steered a straight and usually predictable course. . . . Reagan's stubborn certitude continued to appall his opponents, but it fortified an ideological constancy, as his supporters perceived it, which was to be a major source of his considerable political popularity."[67] Reagan may have assumed office with a closed mind, but his achievements as governor of California and president of the United States support the case that liberals underestimated his intellectual capabilities.

Another controversy concerns Reagan's truthfulness. The Great Communicator was prone to give speeches in which many of the facts and stories he used, often derived from friends and conservative publications, were not correct. He falsely claimed, for example, that the Russians had no word for freedom, that Vietnam veterans could not receive benefits under the GI Bill, that governments that taxed its citizens beyond one-third of their gross domestic product inevitably went socialist, and that the Occupation Safety and Health Administration had 144 regulations on ladders (it had only two).[68] Garry Wills points out:

> There is one story he has told so often over the years that it seems
> to have a special meaning for him—the tale of a B-17 pilot in World
> War II, who told his crew to bail out after his ship was hit. The belly
> gunner was too badly wounded to move; the pilot, finding him in tears,
> said, "Never mind, son, we'll ride it down together." After hearing
> Reagan deliver this story, with quivering voice, in Racine, Wisconsin,
> during the 1980 campaign, reporters noticed that, if the two men died
> together, no one could have repeated their last words or actions.[69]

Such logic meant nothing to Reagan; in his mind, this anecdote was true because he had used it with great dramatic effect many times. At a 1981 Gridiron Club dinner, the press satirized Reagan's disregard for verifying his facts by paraphrasing the song "Something Wonderful" from the Broadway show, *The King and I:*

> He knows a thousand things that aren't quite true;
> And you know that he believes them
> And that's enough for you.[70]

Conservatives grudgingly admitted that Reagan sometimes told "whoppers," but they laughed it off by claiming that Reagan was not really lying because he believed he was telling the truth. Indeed, conservatives argued that Reagan's anecdotes, which might not be technically correct, were serving a moral cause by reflecting eternal truths. Liberals, on the other hand, were outraged that Reagan was not bound by the truth; they complained he had the dramatic license to supplement his talent as the most gifted storyteller in American politics with exaggerated tales and falsehoods.

Reagan's Political Philosophy

Politicians—especially presidents—rarely have the time or inclination to be philosophical. For most politicians and chief executives, a political philosophy is more often used to justify what has already been decided rather than determining what will be done. This was not true of Reagan. Reagan's commitment to conservative philosophy since the early 1950s elevated him to the status of a conviction politician; unlike most other office seekers, he believed in what he was preaching. For Reagan, ideas were more important than government programs, rhetoric was more significant than deeds. Richard Reeves, a liberal journalist, writes that Reagan "was an ideologue with a few ideas that he held with stubborn certainty. His rhetorical gift was to render these ideas into values and emotions."[71] Andrew Busch, a conservative scholar, suggests that Reagan "was a practical politician—but his politics were driven by a clear set of interlocking ideas, supported by an even more fundamental set of moral and religious convictions."[72]

Like FDR, Reagan aspired to change how Americans thought about the legitimate role of government. While Roosevelt constructed a liberal public philosophy to justify an expanded federal government designed to provide economic security, Reagan articulated a conservative public philosophy oriented toward promoting individual freedom. In Reagan's mind, the United States in the 1970s faced its worst crisis since the Depression because domestic and foreign policies had been guided since 1933 by liberalism. Reagan's heroic mission was to popularize a new (old?) political philosophy based on traditional American values that could get the nation back on its righteous path.

Reagan claimed that the United States had been lured off the correct path of limited government by FDR's New Deal and Lyndon Johnson's Great Society. Reagan believed in limited government because he had a negative view of the capabilities of bureaucrats in Washington, D.C., and a positive, romantic attitude toward the talents of the American people. In Reagan's world, the more we relied on big government, the more our problems multiplied. He rejected the claims of expert competence that warrant the existence of the various agencies in the modern administrative state. Reagan frequently proclaimed, "If no one among us is capable of governing himself, then who among us has the capacity to govern someone else?"[73] He ridiculed the rationality of the liberal administrative state by characterizing its policies in the following way: "If it moves, tax it. If it keeps moving, regulate it. And if it stops moving, subsidize it."[74] He fantasized in 1976 that if federal bureaucrats left their offices, most of the people in the nation wouldn't miss them for quite some time.[75] In his 1981 inaugural address, Reagan declared, "It is no coincidence that our present troubles parallel and are proportionate to the intervention and intrusion in our lives that result from unnecessary and excessive growth of government."[76] Hence, for Reagan, government was not the solution to our problems; it *was* the problem.

Although liberals saw the expansion of the federal government as a major mechanism to bring about social justice, Reagan viewed it as a troubling transformation that threatened democracy and impeded economic growth. For him, the more government does for us, the more it can do to us. Reflecting a rigid, dichotomous perspective, Reagan argued that either the people run the government or the government runs the people. The incremental growth of government meant creeping socialism that would reach a tipping point, leading to the end of the free enterprise system. At a conservative rally in 1961, Reagan declared, "one of the foremost authorities on communism in the world today has said we have ten years. Not ten years to win or lose — by 1970 the world will be all slave or all free."[77] In 1962, Reagan wrote a friend that "we can no more have partial socialism than a person can be a little bit pregnant."[78] Most liberals were blind to where their philosophy was leading the country, but Reagan, as only a true believer can, saw that the nation was headed for disaster and was determined to change its course.

Reagan's new direction called for the United States to shift authority from the federal government to the people and the states. He believed in limited government because he also had faith in the unlimited capabilities of the American people and private enterprise. Citizens unleashed from bureaucratic regulations and high taxes would be free to pursue their individual dreams and would perform miracles. For Reagan, the magic of the marketplace always works.[79] His unrealistic optimism was displayed in his televised address to the nation endorsing tax reform in May 1985:

> To young Americans wondering tonight, where will I go, what will I do with my future, I have a suggestion: Why not set out with your friends on the path of adventure and try to start up your own business? Follow in the footsteps of those two college students who launched one of America's great computer firms from the garage behind the house. You, too, can help us unlock the doors to a golden future. You, too, can become leaders in this great new era of progress—the age of the entrepreneur.[80]

Reagan's commitment to limited government naturally led to his emphasis on reducing taxes. Because taxes fueled the growth of the administrative state, the way to halt its expansion and reduce its size was to slash tax rates. Reagan believed that the progressive income tax, which he mistakenly thought was invented by Karl Marx, inhibited both economic growth and social mobility. It was morally and materially wrong to punish the success of hard work by taxing it at a higher rate. According to Reagan, for the past forty years under the liberal regime, the United States had tried to tax and spend our way to prosperity, which had led to the economic crises of the late 1970s. It was now time to try a simple idea that had worked well in the past: cutting tax rates for both individuals and businesses. Before he became president, Reagan supported the supply-side-inspired Kemp-Roth tax bill, citing the success of the Andrew Mellon tax cuts in the 1920s and the Kennedy tax cut in the 1960s in increasing revenues without inflation. Hence, both as a candidate and as president, Reagan advocated cutting tax rates because that would bring about prosperity and increased tax revenues.[81] Why Mellon's tax policy did not prevent the Depression was the type of question Reagan never considered.

Although Reagan was identified with supply-side economics, he tried to separate himself from that school of thought. To correct the record about his relationship with the supply-siders, Reagan wrote in his memoirs, "At Eureka College, my major was economics, but I think my own experience with our tax laws in Hollywood probably taught me more about practical economic theory than I ever learned in a classroom or from an economist, and my views on tax reform did not spring from what people called supply-side economics."[82] Reagan defined his basic view about limited government and taxes in a letter to R. Emmett Tyrell, the conservative editor of the *American Spectator.* "It's always seemed to me that when government goes beyond a certain percentage of what it takes as a share of the people's earnings, we have trouble. I guess a simple explanation of what I've been trying to do is to peel government down to bare essentials—necessities if you will, and then set the tax revenues accordingly."[83] For Reagan, it was just a simple matter of common sense, not economic theory, that cutting everyone's taxes would benefit everyone.

While the forgotten man for FDR was the poor worker threatened with unemployment, for Reagan, he was the more affluent but overburdened taxpayer—a category that included most Americans in the late 1970s. While FDR made millions feel they might be the beneficiary of a New Deal policy, Reagan made millions feel they were the victims of unfair taxes that were too often financing welfare programs for the undeserving poor (welfare queens). In responding to a letter accusing him of a lack of compassion for the poor, Reagan replied, "I'm sure everyone feels very sorry for the individual who has fallen by the wayside or who can't keep up in our competitive society, but my own compassion goes beyond that to those millions of unsung men and women who get up every morning, send the kids to school, go to work, try to keep up with the payments on their house, pay exorbitant taxes to make possible compassion for the less fortunate, and as a result have to sacrifice many of their own desires and dreams."[84] This conservative message resonated positively with the American voter throughout the 1980s.

Reagan communicated another message reflecting his religious and patriotic views that proved effective. Hugh Heclo argues that Reagan was a rare political leader who was competing with secular liberals to define the American public philosophy. Reagan had a "sacramental vision" of the United States; he believed that "God had chosen America as the agent of His special purposes in history."[85] Although most secular scholars would consider this idea as mythical, Reagan believed it was literally true. He talked about the United States as a "City on a Hill," a divinely purposed nation that, in Thomas Paine's words, has in its "power to begin the world over again." The United States was a consecrated nation assigned by God to circumvent history's pattern of growth and decay. Our unique nation was forever young, persistently renewing its moral purposes, continually reviving itself as the land of opportunity. Reagan's ideas about American exceptionalism were derived from many of the Founding Fathers, "but in the aftermath of the 1960s, in a world characterized by modernism, skepticism, and secularism, they seemed fresh in Reagan's optimistic rendering."[86] Reagan's belief in this sacramental vision helped to reach and inspire the religious and patriotic groups in America. As the proponents of a tired political philosophy, Democrats could not match the glory and romance of Reagan's story. Nor could they publicly attack Reagan for his religious and patriotic beliefs without alienating a multitude of voters. Extolling the sacramental vision helped Reagan assume the moral high ground in political conflict.

Much of Reagan's political success can be attributed to his ability in communicating his philosophy to the public through speeches.[87] In analyzing four decades of his speeches, one is struck by how little they changed over time. A typical Reagan oration was composed of humor, heroes, nostalgia, anecdotes, statistics, symbols, and mythic visions. He used simple sentences and stark choices (slavery versus freedom) to convey his message. Wills suggests that Reagan saw "issues in moral terms, where the choice is clear."[88] Reagan was particularly effective at boiling abstractions down to concepts that the public could understand; the United States was threatened externally by communism and internally by the seductive appeal of big government, but the nation could thrive if we returned to honoring the traditional values that made us great. He presented these concepts not as a philosopher, but as a citizen who felt it was his patriotic duty to warn his neighbors that they were headed for disaster. Although Reagan's speeches presented a grim message prophesying the demise of American democracy if we continued on the liberal path, his confident demeanor, appealing humor, and sanguine determination also communicated his expectation of a happy outcome. God's chosen people would not fail.

Reagan's attacks on the role of the state were more radical than the criticisms of other Republican chief executives. According to D'Souza, "All the Republican presidents of the postwar era—Eisenhower, Nixon, and Ford—criticized the excesses of the federal government and spoke of making it more efficient, but they did not question in principle the ability of the government to remedy the ills of society."[89] For Reagan, the administrative state was not only too big and inefficient, it was also the primary source of the nation's domestic problems.

To get a feel for Reagan's thinking, it is worthwhile to examine the version of a speech, "A Time for Choosing," that he delivered on national television endorsing Barry Goldwater for president on October 27, 1964. Reagan began his talk by ridiculing President Lyndon Johnson's assertions that liberal policies were providing prosperity and peace. The truth, according to Reagan, was that our prosperity was unsustainable because of budget deficits, a growing national debt, and a tax burden that would inevitably destroy our economy. After mentioning the conflict in South Vietnam, he proclaimed, "We are at war with the most dangerous enemy that has ever faced mankind in his long climb from the swamp to the stars."

After telling an anecdote about a Cuban refugee coming to the United States to escape Castro's oppression, Reagan declared that America was the last bastion of freedom in the world. That freedom, however, was being threatened. As he saw it, the issue of the 1964 election was: "Whether we believe in our capacity for self-government or whether we abandon the American Revolution and confess that a little intellectual elite in a far-distant capital can plan our lives for us better than we can plan them ourselves." The choice of voters was whether they wanted "individual freedom consistent with law and order" or security provided by the welfare state that would eventually lead to "the ant heap of totalitarianism."

The liberal assertion that providing for the material needs of the American people requires "the full power of centralized government" was precisely the arrangement the Founding Fathers sought to prevent. "They knew that . . . a government can't control the economy without controlling people. And they knew when a government sets out to do that, it must use force and coercion to achieve its purpose. They also knew . . . that outside of its legitimate functions, government does nothing as well or economically as the private sector of the economy."

To substantiate his criticism of big government, Reagan provided statistics and told stories about the farm program, urban renewal, unemployment, and welfare. He criticized liberals for claiming that they can "solve all the problems of human misery through government and government planning. Well, now if government planning and welfare had the answer, and they've had almost thirty years of it . . . , shouldn't they be telling us about the decline each year in the number of people needing help?" But, Reagan stipulated, the reverse is true and is used as a justification for bigger and more expensive programs. Reagan concluded, "Our national, inalienable rights are now considered to be a dispensation from government, and freedom has never been so fragile, so close to slipping from our grasp as it is at this moment." His hyperbolic peroration used a famous phrase from FDR: "You and I have a rendezvous with destiny. We will preserve for our children this, the last best hope of man on earth, or we will sentence them to take the last step into a thousand years of darkness."[90]

The Speech was an influential polemic that raised campaign money for Goldwater and elevated Reagan's stature among conservative Republicans, but such a speech did not permit nuance and contradiction. To maintain its ideological consistency that liberal policies always fail, The Speech ignored the success of social security in reducing poverty for senior citizens, the 1944 GI Bill of Rights in helping millions of servicemen to buy a house and earn a college degree, and the fact that Keynesian-inspired post–World War II policies kept the country from suffering another depression and promoted prosperity until the 1970s. Reagan also condemned liberal government for not "solving" the problems of poverty, unemployment, and education, when a more realistic standard would be whether policies, liberal or conservative, had improved these situations. And most importantly, although Reagan argued that the growth of the federal government threatened individual rights (especially property rights), he conveniently avoided dealing with the notion that the expansion of the central government and a liberal Supreme Court had brought about long-overdue advances for minorities.

Conclusion

The backgrounds of FDR and Reagan prepared them to perform the role of a reconstructive president in different ways. For Roosevelt, being raised in an aristocratic family and having a cousin who was a popular president meant that he developed the highest political ambitions at an early age. He wanted to be president before he knew what he wanted to accomplish in the White House. When he was struck by polio at the age of thirty-nine, it appeared that paralysis would thwart his ambitions, but in overcoming the disease, FDR demonstrated his courage and resilience. What might have ended his political career enhanced it. He became a more compassionate politician, creating the Warm Springs Foundation for victims of polio and the New Deal for victims of the Depression.

If FDR had a clear-cut vision of the New Deal in 1932, no one has ever been able to clearly explain it in a manner that most scholars would agree with. However, as a student of Teddy Roosevelt and Woodrow Wilson, FDR knew he was a liberal progressive with a belief in strong executive leadership, and that he wanted to steer the nation in a more socially just direction. For Roosevelt, the Depression proved that the Republican regime's dependence on private enterprise, which increasingly meant large corporations, did not work. What was now needed was a broader concert of interests that would bring about a better balance between the cities and the countryside, between business and labor. Enlightened administration could provide citizens with greater security from the hazards of life. Roosevelt had faith that American ingenuity could concoct a more positive state and still preserve democracy.

Despite having an alcoholic father, Ronald Reagan had an optimistic view of life, which helped him to succeed as a sports announcer, actor, president of the Screen Actors Guild, public speaker, and politician. The communication skills he developed before going into politics served him well when he began to run for office. The irony of Reagan's role as a reconstructive president is that he was originally a liberal Democrat who cast four votes for FDR, but who evolved into a conservative during the 1950s and became a moral crusader against the liberal regime his hero had built.

Reagan's vision of a conservative regime was a response to the prevailing liberal one. While FDR had created the modern presidency to launch a more activist federal government that could combat the Depression and provide security for the nation's citizens, Reagan wanted to use the modern presidency to rejuvenate the private sector by reducing tax rates and deregulating the economy. The magnitude of what Reagan was trying to accomplish is summarized by William Muir: the Reagan presidency "was organized to achieve a moral revolution—moral in the sense of affecting the animating ideas of the American people, a revolution in the sense of returning the nation to its intellectual starting point. . . . He set out to define a philosophy of freedom to distinguish it from a philosophy of equality, and to plant it in the soul of the nation."[91]

In terms of their ability to fulfill the reconstructive role, both FDR and Reagan had the communication skills and the desire to educate citizens about why the nation needed an updated public philosophy to deal with its present crises. FDR felt secure because he assumed he could find the right answers; Reagan was secure because he believed he already had the answers. The key difference between them was that FDR lacked faith in the private sector and believed that experts in the administrative state could formulate solutions to many of the nation's problems, whereas Reagan had great faith in the magic of the marketplace and, with the exception of the military, no confidence in the "dead hand" of bureaucracy. The clash of their visions still dominates American politics.

5

Advising FDR

Popular historical memory erodes away nuances and inconsistencies. In popular memory, there is a tendency to think of Franklin Roosevelt and his New Deal advisers as liberals sharing common views toward both the problems of the Depression and the policy remedies that would bring about recovery and reform. We forget the conflicts of vision and personalities that made observing and trying to make sense of what the New Deal was doing and where it was headed such a controversial issue for the people of the 1930s and for historians and social scientists ever since.

The men and women who counseled Roosevelt were not confined to a single school of thought. And the competition among them—which was mischievously encouraged by the president—was fierce. "Indeed," according to Arthur Schlesinger Jr., "they represented divergent and often clashing philosophies."[1] Roosevelt's advisers can be classified in a variety of ways. Schlesinger talks of laissez-faire liberals (Cordell Hull and Lewis Douglas), agrarian Democrats calling for monetary inflation, trust busters reflecting Louis Brandeis's "big is bad" perspective, planners calling for government business collaboration, and Keynesian spenders advocating that the federal government pump money into the depressed economy. Thomas Langston suggests that the three major groups advising Roosevelt were "the anti-monopolistic spenders; the industrial, agricultural, and social planners;

and the corporatists."[2] Because of the depth and scope of the Depression, Roosevelt recognized that he needed to surround himself with "adventurous minds," people who would provide him with the options he needed in order to be in control and to stay on the political offensive.[3] The paradoxical consequence of all this ideological activity, combined with Roosevelt's propensity to try to keep his advisers satisfied by following some of their recommendations, was that the New Deal was an ideological stew, rarely dominated by a coherent and consistent set of beliefs for any significant length of time.

My purpose here is to portray the conflicting advice FDR received and how he interacted with a small sample of his top advisers—Raymond Moley, Rexford Tugwell, Adolf Berle, Henry Morgenthau, Henry Wallace, and Harry Hopkins—in making decisions. I will analyze each adviser's view toward the causes of the Depression, his major policy proposals, and his value to Roosevelt. I will also provide a summary of Roosevelt's decision-making style.

The Brains Trust

Governor Roosevelt created the Brains Trust in the spring of 1932 as he prepared to campaign for the Democratic nomination for president and to compete against the Republican president, Herbert Hoover. FDR was obviously concerned by the criticism of Walter Lippmann, who claimed that the New York governor did not have the intellectual status to lead the entire nation. Given the omnipresence of the Depression in 1932, it was imperative for Roosevelt to demonstrate in his speeches that he had the knowledge to lead the country to economic recovery. The job of the Brains Trust was to provide the candidate with a tutorial focusing on policy solutions to the many problems caused by the worst Depression in history. Meetings of the Brains Trust afforded Roosevelt the opportunity to think out loud and to test ideas and possible speech phrases in the midst of skeptical but loyal advisers.

On the one hand, the Brains Trust consisted of three professors from Columbia University tutoring a student in order to prepare him for the tests of a campaign and presidential office. On the other hand, their student was a Roosevelt, accustomed to selecting his help. Moreover, this student was in the market for advisers who could serve his political and policy purposes. To compete successfully for Roosevelt's attention, an adviser had to prove his usefulness to the politician's needs. Moley, Tugwell, and Berle, each in his own way, for a limited period of time, did exactly that.

RAYMOND MOLEY

Raymond Moley was born in 1886 into an Irish Catholic family in the Western Reserve area of Ohio. His father was a partisan Democrat, and Moley became enamored with the progressive reform politics of Mayor Tom Johnson in Cleveland and President Woodrow Wilson. In his education and work experiences, Moley was determined to become a practical political expert. After studying under the distinguished progressive professor, Charles A. Beard, Moley received his Ph.D. from Columbia in 1918, and in 1923, he became professor of government at Columbia, with a specialty in the study of the police and the courts. In his memoirs, Moley wrote, "As the thoughtlessness and aimlessness of the twenties became more apparent, I'd grown convinced that someone must be found who could do on a national scale what Tom Johnson had done in Cleveland."[4]

In 1928, he met Louis Howe, Franklin Roosevelt's closest adviser, who recruited him to work in FDR's gubernatorial campaign. Early in 1932, Roosevelt asked Moley to set up an advising mechanism that would eventually be called the "Brains Trust." Its function would be to conduct policy research and write speeches. Moley explains, "When Roosevelt asked me to assist him in his quest for the nomination in January 1932, I was confident that my study, observation and professional interest in national affairs could play a role in the formulation of campaign issues. Also, my experience in directing . . . various research projects had equipped me to organize the ideas and knowledge of others."[5]

A Roosevelt biographer suggests that the candidate found Moley "eminently useful" because he was "hard-working, self-disciplined, and well-organized in all his operations." Moley possessed "practical intelligence," and "his pragmatic, flexible, anti-ideological attitudes" were compatible with Roosevelt's. His knowledge extended far beyond his academic specialty of criminal law administration. Moreover, Moley could provide the hungry candidate with "occasional literary eloquence and the mastery of the telling word."[6] In brief, Moley had the invaluable talent to clarify complex issues and transform Roosevelt's vague visions into vivid language, as illustrated in the governor's "Forgotten Man" speech of April 1932. Through skill and ambition, Moley was able to move from the outer rim of Roosevelt's advisers to the inner circle.

Moley's role with the Brains Trust implies something interesting about Roosevelt. He understood that assuming the Oval Office in March 1933 would require a wide-ranging policy expertise considerably beyond the capability of either the president or one or two major advisers. Responding to the Depression would demand fighting a multifront war to deal with the problems of agriculture, industry, unemployment, banking, Wall Street, and relief. Roosevelt's political advisers, Louis Howe, Ed Flynn, and James Farley, could help him attain the Democratic nomination and win the election, but Moley's job was to ensure that the new president would be prepared to govern as the activist, progressive leader FDR longed to be.

As a progressive, Moley had no doubts about the need for positive government. While in graduate school, he had read Charles Van Hise's *Concentration and Control* and accepted its thesis regarding the irresistible growth of large corporations and the necessity for them to be regulated by the federal government.[7] Moley rejected the Louis Brandeis–Felix Frankfurter recommendation to break up the monopolies through antitrust policies. However, Moley believed that the United States could no longer tolerate the unpredictable results of unregulated competition, which, as the Depression demonstrated, led to economic instability and social insecurity. It was his view, given that "economic bigness was here to stay, that the problem of government was to enable the whole people to enjoy the benefits of mass production and distribution (economy and security); and that it was the duty of government to devise, with business, the means of social and individual adjustment to the facts of the industrial age—these were the heart and soul of the New Deal."[8]

According to Elliot Rosen, the basic outlines of both the first and second New Deals were forecast in a memo Moley submitted to Governor Roosevelt on May 19, 1932. Moley wrote:

> And what do people want more than anything else? To my mind, two things, first work with all the moral and spiritual values that go with it. . . . Second, they want a reasonable measure of security for themselves and for those who depend upon them. Work and security are the spiritual values toward which our efforts for reconstruction should lead. . . . It is all very well for those who speak for the present administration to speak of economic laws. But men starve while economic laws work out. And it is a fair question as to whether economic laws exist which cannot be controlled by the laws of man. Our economic system is a human thing built by human beings. I believe that it can likewise be controlled by human beings for the general good.[9]

Moley's memo specifically recommended $2.5 billion for relief, public works, and housing subsidies; liberalization of the Democratic party; taxation of undistributed corporate income; the separation of the national budget into a regular budget and an emergency budget (a euphemism for an unbalanced budget); regulation of utility holding companies; and reforms of the banking and security businesses.[10] Reviewing this list, one can see that although Moley did not consider himself (or FDR) an expert in economics, he was not hesitant to challenge the conventional economic wisdom of the Republican regime. Indeed, Moley considered his and Roosevelt's lack of economic knowledge an advantage because it freed them to see that the old system was not working and to seek new remedies. The list also indicates that the ambitious Moley was willing to expand his advising responsibilities from policy to politics by advocating that Roosevelt regenerate the Democratic party so that it would be motivated by a liberal agenda, justifying humane purposes and serving a more lower-class constituency.[11]

Given the role Moley performed before the election and the period before the inauguration on March 4, 1933, he probably should have been named administrative assistant to the president. But Louis Howe, ever jealous about access to Roosevelt, had abolished that office. Instead, Roosevelt appointed Moley as one of the four assistant secretaries of state, an office that had no assigned responsibilities and that would therefore free Moley to provide the president with a variety of services. This was not the best of solutions: while Moley was an economic nationalist, Secretary of State Cordell Hull was a fervent believer in free trade.

Moley was obviously proud of his intimacy with Roosevelt. He cites a *New York Times* reporter, Arthur Krock, who, in April 1933, wrote, "there is no adviser in whom the President reposes more confidence."[12] He outlined his responsibilities in March 1933 in these words:

> In addition to two major assignments in the field of foreign relations, I had a roving commission to watch over the formulation of legislation, to unravel the snarls that delayed that formulative process, to cull out of the thousand and one schemes that came pouring into Washington the few that deserved presidential examination, to work up the basic material for FDR's speeches and messages with the appropriate officials, to assume the literary role after these preparatory chores were done, to be on hand when there were such special headaches as the Thomas amendment to be handled, and, with Louis Howe, to 'sit on the lid' when Roosevelt's less happy impulses threatened to break loose. . . . I tried to see as many people as I could, since I was Roosevelt's unofficial sieve on policy.[13]

Contemplating this list, no one would be surprised that Moley often felt overwhelmed and irritated. According to Schlesinger, "The new confusion [during the first hundred days] disturbed him, as did the sense of unresolved purposes; so too perhaps did the feeling that each new official appointed, each new adviser welcomed at the White House, threatened his position and diminished his authority."[14] It was probably dangerous for Moley's future that a joke circulating through Washington, D.C., early in 1933 claimed that you had to go through Roosevelt to get an appointment with Moley.

Moley admired Roosevelt's courage, optimism, self-confidence, empathy for those who were suffering, magical voice, and incomparable ability to judge public opinion. But there were aspects of FDR's administrative style that exasperated Moley. Moley tells the story of being asked by Roosevelt in December 1932 to prepare stock exchange and securities legislation. In March 1933, Moley was surprised to find out that Roosevelt had asked another group to work on the same project. Roosevelt's "often-used technique" in this situation was to order everyone to sit around a conference table and "compromise all differences."[15]

Moley also became increasingly peeved by Roosevelt's belief that he could reconcile the irreconcilable. During the campaign, the governor had flabbergasted Moley by instructing him to weave together a speech that called for protectionism and a speech that advocated free trade. What appeared to be dichotomous choices to many people—and especially to Moley—were, to Roosevelt's playful mind, challenges to create politically acceptable hybrids. Similarly, Moley felt that the president could not resolve his support for the conflicting ideas of Theodore Roosevelt's "partnership" of business and government and Woodrow Wilson's advocacy of antitrust.[16]

After the partnership policy was tried in the National Industrial Recovery Act and had failed, the president shifted to trust busting, which facilitated the rise of one of Felix Frankfurter's so-called hotdogs, Thomas Corcoran, as a major adviser to FDR. Moley viewed Corcoran as a young lawyer on the make, whose antibusiness attitudes inhibited the encouragement of business confidence that was so necessary for economic recovery. In 1934, when they were discussing appointments to the newly created Securities and Exchange Commission, Moley was angered that Corcoran classified four of the appointees as being "for us" and one, Joe Kennedy, "for business." He complained that the Brandeisians "see government operating successfully not through the process of consultation, compromise, and harmonious adjustment but rather through the litigation process. This implies that the art of government is a battle between the lawyers of the Lord and the lawyers of business."[17] The radicalization of the New Deal in 1935 increasingly alienated Moley.

The intimate relationship forged by Moley and Roosevelt in 1932 and 1933 was not likely to last. Initially, Moley was pleased that Roosevelt was "so receptive to the new and unorthodox," but in the reconstructive context of the 1930s, Roosevelt's openness meant he was subject to a bewildering array of reform proposals by many different advisers. Roosevelt found this situation stimulating; Moley considered it chaotic. Moley grumbled, "Since I was so near the center of the new Administration during the months after the inauguration and since the climate of Washington at that time was so pregnant with the spirit of reform, I saw as strange an influx of visitors as has been witnessed since the days of Jackson."[18] Roosevelt was not equipped to handle this situation, according to Moley, because his open-mindedness was not monitored by a critical and disciplined intelligence. Moley longed to provide that disciplined intelligence, but Roosevelt would never let anyone play that role.

Moley claimed he was free of any political ambitions and the usual jealousies that affect advisers competing to influence the president. But Tugwell suspected that Moley was wounded when Roosevelt, celebrating his election victory at the Biltmore Hotel, publicly thanked Howe and Farley for their contributions, and neglected to mention Moley. There is also no doubt that Moley wanted to continue to control his own shop of advising Roosevelt about policy. Tugwell noted that Moley "was constantly worried about Roosevelt's insouciance, irritated by loose ends and half-materialized ideas. . . . In his own way, and for a different purpose, Ray was as jealous as Louis Howe or Henry Morgenthau. He was annoyed, sometimes to the point of fury, when he discovered that an important study we had been assigned to make had been let out to someone else as well."[19] While Tugwell and Berle had more interest in specific policies, Moley was more concerned that policies assumed an orderly and consistent structure.

Moley also indicted Roosevelt for succumbing to the vice of overly personalizing reform politics. Anticipating George Reedy's thesis about the potentially negative effect of the White House on the man who occupies it, Moley argued that Roosevelt increasingly assumed the posture that he personified the reform movement and the public interest. He suggested that Roosevelt's success during the first hundred days nurtured a growing and dangerous appetite for personal authority. In a meeting with the president in late May 1936, Moley was shocked when Roosevelt told him, "There's one issue in the campaign. It's myself, and people must be either for me or against me."[20]

While Roosevelt continued to use the war analogy of fighting against "economic royalists," Moley stressed that successful cooperation depended on reform, not bitter conflict. After Roosevelt's militant acceptance speech at the 1936 Democratic party convention, Moley delivered a different message:

> People are tired of battle. . . . People will call businessmen names until the public realizes, as some of us realize, that modern business, through efficient production, is bringing closer to the average man not only the things that he needs in his daily life, but the things that made his life more pleasant. . . . As I see it, the only way to save the house we live in from . . . fundamental conflict is to convince the American people by word and deed that our economic system is inherently decent; . . . that our business and industry are serving the public, and that the interests of business and the interests of the public, far from being antagonistic, are inseparable.[21]

The end of Moley's intimate relationship with Roosevelt was triggered by events at the London Economic Conference in June 1933. At this international meeting, Moley attempted to serve as the president's agent, trying to fathom what he wanted to achieve in terms of international cooperation. Moley negotiated a tentative agreement that was then torpedoed by a blunt telegram of rejection from Roosevelt. This telegram was written while Roosevelt was on vacation, sailing off the New England coast in the company of two of Moley's enemies, Howe and Morgenthau, who may have taken advantage of this opportunity to slash Moley's influence. Moley was publicly humiliated by this experience, and in September 1933, he resigned from his position in the State Department. He became involved in the creation of two newsmagazines—first *Today*, then *Newsweek*. Moley continued to write speeches for Roosevelt and supported him in 1936, but they became increasingly estranged. He opposed FDR's Supreme Court–packing scheme in 1937 and then supported Wendell Wilkie in 1940. The extent of Moley's political migration can be measured by the fact that in 1964, he was advising Barry Goldwater.

REXFORD TUGWELL

Rexford Tugwell was born in 1891 in Sinclairsville, New York, a small town twelve miles from Lake Erie. His father was an orchard farmer and cannery owner. His mother had been a teacher and encouraged her only son, who suffered from asthma and allergies, to read and develop his intellectual skills. Tugwell became an outstanding student and eventually earned a bachelor's, a master's, and a doctoral degree from the University of Pennsylvania. After receiving his Ph.D. in economics in 1920, he was hired to teach at Columbia University, where he quickly became a full professor. During his twelve years at Columbia, he wrote four books, conducted a study in the Soviet Union, and penned forty-five articles for professional journals and for magazines like the *New Republic*. Obviously he never suffered writer's block, but his voluminous publications provided his enemies with plenty of ammunition to use against him and the New Deal.

Tugwell was the first professor Moley brought up to Albany to meet with Governor Roosevelt. The candidate and Tugwell found each other's company stimulating. According to Moley, "While Roosevelt rejected many of Tugwell's ideas, the professor's range of interest provided for him a sort of intellectual cocktail. Tugwell's reaction to Roosevelt from the first meeting . . . was the beginning of an admiration that almost approached a romantic dedication."[22] What thrilled Tugwell was the possibility, provided by access to Roosevelt, that his academic advice might be transformed into public policy.

Although Tugwell's academic credentials and commitments hold some appeal for a number of scholars studying the New Deal, his style of operation created more enemies than allies. His fastidious dress and manners alienated him from the agricultural interests he was supposedly serving in the Department of Agriculture. He also antagonized Henry Morgenthau and Eleanor Roosevelt and felt contempt for what he called the "moneyed interest" represented by Bernard Baruch and Joseph Kennedy. Ideologically, he felt closest to the LaFollettes in Wisconsin (progressive Republicans) and was highly critical of the Brandeis school of thought within the Democratic party. Like Moley, he claimed not to have any political ambitions. Tugwell considered political activities to be morally inferior to his efforts to promote policy change. He stressed, "all I wanted was to see my conclusions embodied in policy."[23] The professor was frequently disdainful and tactless when dealing with people who disagreed with him.[24] Armed with the truth, feeling self-assured and morally superior, Tugwell was probably destined to fail in the treacherous politics of the 1930s.

Tugwell became one of the most controversial of the New Dealers. He opposed the use of force and believed that reason could promote evolutionary progress. The professor claimed that his knowledge of the past qualified him to predict the future. His understanding of economic trends and political thought enabled him to make recommendations that would, if followed, bring about a more rational and socially just future. According to his biographer, "Tugwell was concerned with efficiency as an economic objective (Taylor), planning as a means of achieving that objective (Patten and Veblen), experimentation as the technique of planning (Dewey). This technique neither rejected capitalism nor accepted socialism. It was not dictatorial but evolutionary."[25] Taylorized industry was capable of expanding product while virtually eliminating onerous labor. Tugwell believed he understood the imperatives of technological advance and that he could recommend the necessary policy changes to bring about a more efficient and humane society. Namorato points out, "There was a tension in him between practical, hardheaded economics and more sentimental, romantic idealism."[26]

Tugwell believed that the prosperity of the Roaring Twenties had been a seductive mirage, blinding the public to what needed to be done to assure sustainable economic growth. Farmers during the 1920s had not shared in the good times, and the political system did not respond to their growing needs. The selfishness of business meant that industrial efficiency and profits increased, but prices remained high (hurting consumers) and wages stayed low (hurting workers). Corporate profits financed unplanned expansion and speculative activities. By 1929, the unregulated and unplanned economic system had inevitably created an enterprise of overproduction and underconsumption that crashed by virtue of its own inexorable logic. From Tugwell's perspective, the one redeeming virtue of the Depression was, "There was no escaping any longer the responsibility of government—for recovery from it, for relief while it went on, and for taking measures to prevent recurrences. This last we [the Brains Trust] felt to be the most important."[27] In brief, the reconstructive project for Tugwell was not to get the economy back on its old track, but to get it on a new and planned one.

In Tugwell's mind, the Depression proved that laissez-faire did not work, that the competitive, profit-seeking mechanism would have to be fundamentally changed. The United States' economy was no longer characterized by the competition of small business; it was now dominated by some two hundred large corporations. Because the competition among firms could no longer promote the public interest, the federal government would have to intervene and provide the visible, guiding hand. Hence, Tugwell argued, "The American system was ready for social management; actually it *was* managed, but for private benefits rather than for a public one."[28] The long-run solution was national planning that would guarantee an equilibrium among business, labor, consumers, and farmers.

The logic of Tugwell's argument that underconsumption was the major cause of the Depression involved a significant redistribution of income and political power. In Tugwell's planning mechanism, the federal government, as the senior partner, would force outcomes in which the compensations for workers and farmers would be greater and the rewards for capital (profits and interest) would be less.[29] In Tugwell's vision of a planned economy, price fixing would serve the public interest rather than private profit. For the government to perform this role, the antitrust laws would have to be abolished because they prevented social management and encouraged destructive competition. Tugwell was urging that the state move from its traditional negative role in regulation to what he viewed as a more positive one. According to Namorato, "Instead of being the traditional policeman of the Wilson-Brandeis school, [the government] had to exert more authority over capital uses, profits, and prices so as to assure an equitable adjustment of production to consumption, cost to prices, and profits to wages."[30] Tugwell was advocating that the present stage of industrial development had created an imperative for it to be publicly managed as an integrated whole.[31]

Although Tugwell considered this new coordinated system to be the next logical step in the evolution of capitalism and democracy, his enemies claimed that his reforms would destroy both. Different opponents labeled his proposals as state capitalism, corporatism, fascism, socialism, and communism. This is not surprising because, as Conkin suggests, "In Tugwell there were faint echoes of technocracy, a hint of a corporate state, and a near arrogant contempt for such traditional values as competition, [and] small economic units."[32] What was sacred to businessmen was treated with contempt by Tugwell, who wrote about the "carnivorous competitive system," "the fetish" of government noninterference, and "the gargantuan vulgarities of the newly rich."[33] From his point of view, the immoral, irresponsible, and selfish behavior of businessmen had brought on the Depression, and they were incapable of providing the guidelines to lead the nation out of it. Despite Tugwell's protestations that his concept of "bottom-up" planning was compatible with democracy, his right wing adversaries stigmatized him as "Rex the Red" and "Rex the Regimenter."

Tugwell shared Moley's feeling that working for Roosevelt was both exhilarating and frustrating. While Moley found Roosevelt too unorthodox, Tugwell had the opposite complaint. Tugwell lamented, "In spite of his inquiring mind and experimental temper, the inquiring and experimentation were still confined . . . within old boundaries, some of them obsolete and obstructive. I had a foreboding that this would limit his range."[34] Tugwell believed that much of Roosevelt's resistance to his proposals could be blamed on the governor's continued adherence to the traditional progressive program.

Despite all of Roosevelt's apparent candor and openness, there was something mysterious about him. The members of the Brains Trust heard Roosevelt thinking out loud on one point or another, but they were not allowed to see or hear his constructing the grand strategy (assuming he had one) to guide his decisions. Tugwell wrote, "I suspected that he was making policy pictures in his mind, arranging and rearranging. We sometimes had glimpses of the pictures when he talked, but they were mostly beyond our sight. What we were suggesting had radical implications, and I thought he was fitting our notions to political possibilities. That, it became clear in time, was exactly what was taking place."[35] Tugwell desperately wanted to convince Roosevelt to champion economic planning, but FDR simply refused to commit himself fully to any school of thought. While Roosevelt was determined to attain certain objectives, such as more security from the hazards of life for a wider portion of the population, he was searching for a variety of methods to achieve them.

While Tugwell was trying to educate Roosevelt about policy imperatives, the candidate may have been trying to enlighten the professor about political priorities. Tugwell wanted Roosevelt to be a statesman, while Roosevelt was emphasizing that he had to practice politics first before he could assume that role. FDR tried, in vain, to convince Tugwell that the less encumbered the candidate was with specific commitments, the freer he would be to experiment in the presidency. As the 1932 Democratic convention drew nearer, the candidate became less interested in long-run policies and more concerned with political expediency. Although Moley accepted that "ideology must yield to political necessity," Tugwell did not.[36] He was anxious for Roosevelt to exploit the platform of a presidential candidate to educate the public about what ought to be done to overcome the Depression.

However, FDR was determined not to engage in any behavior that would threaten his chances to gain the Democratic nomination and then win the general election. In a political campaign, what should be done "could not compete with what voters would like to think ought to be done." Roosevelt told Tugwell, "A President . . . could educate in the interest of his program, but a candidate had to accept people's prejudices and turn them to good use."[37] The most notorious example of this was Roosevelt's October 1932 speech in Pittsburgh, written by Hugh Johnson, in which the candidate accused Hoover of being a profligate spender and promised, if elected, that the New Deal would cut the federal budget by 25 percent.

Tugwell believed that national planning was such a new and necessary addition to the political economy that Roosevelt ought to play an educative role and make it the centerpiece of his 1932 campaign. For Roosevelt, planning was one, but not necessarily the only, instrument he would use to combat the Depression. There was no guarantee that Tugwell had found the key to solving the riddle of the Depression, and therefore, Roosevelt listened carefully to the Columbia professor but always hedged his commitments. The reality was that Tugwell was a policy expert and Roosevelt was the political expert, and when the two competed, politics inevitably trumped policy. FDR tried to console (or to co-opt) Tugwell by telling him in February 1933, "You know we ought to have eight years in Washington. At the end of that time we may or may not have a Democratic Party, but we will have a Progressive one; and some day we will have the planning you want."[38] But Elliot Rosen concludes, "The projection of a stringently regulated, organic economy made by Rexford Guy Tugwell was rejected by Berle and Roosevelt in August 1932. It was never realized, even for a moment, in the New Deal period."[39]

In his frustration, Tugwell realized that he was not as fully committed to Roosevelt as several other advisers were. While Louis Howe, Samuel Rosenman, and Basil "Doc" O'Connor had come to the conclusion that what was best for Roosevelt was best for the nation because their interests were identical, Tugwell, motivated by his progressive causes and academic independence, was not as sure. The discipline of loyal service to Roosevelt's candidacy and then presidency threatened his intellectual integrity. He was the most likely adviser to tell Roosevelt that he was making a mistake, as Tugwell did in March 1933 when he complained that the administration had missed an opportunity to take advantage of the banking crisis by setting up a national banking system.[40]

In 1935, with both the National Industrial Recovery Act and the Agricultural Adjustment Act being declared unconstitutional, Tugwell's star descended, and he was replaced by his ideological opponents, Thomas Corcoran and Ben Cohen. By 1936, Tugwell had become such a political liability that Roosevelt accepted James Farley's advice to keep "Rex the Regimenter" quiet and hidden during the election campaign. After the election, Tugwell resigned. He later wrote, "I made the mistake of attempting too much at once — of undertaking battles on more fronts than were necessary or could be successfully fought; and once engaged, I could not or would not withdraw. So I would become not so much a symbol of progressivism as a kind of crackpot radical. . . . By the end of my first year I was confirmed as a notorious character."[41]

ADOLF A. BERLE JR.

Adolf Berle, perhaps the most brilliant member of the Brains Trust, was born in the Boston suburb of Brighton in 1895. Ted Morgan points out, "His grandfather was a German immigrant, his father was a Congregational minister, and his mother was the daughter of another Congregational minister who had done missionary work with the Sioux in South Dakota. From his father and his maternal grandfather, he had examples of religious vocations combined with social activism."[42] Berle was home schooled, entered Harvard at the age of fourteen, and graduated with honors three years later. By the age of twenty-one, he had his Harvard law degree and had begun practicing law in Louis Brandeis's law firm. In 1917, Berle enlisted in the Army Signal Corps and later attended the Paris Peace Conference. In the 1920s, he spent three years at the Henry Street Settlement House in New York City, three years teaching at the Harvard Business School, and then in 1927 was hired as a professor of law at Columbia University. Burns writes that Berle was "a child prodigy who, his enemies said, had continued to be a child long after he had ceased being a prodigy. [In 1932] Berle was still a brash young man of 37, who could overwhelm banker and bureaucrat alike with his biting tongue and his vast information on financial practices."[43] His ambition was to make an intellectual contribution reflecting the policy space and possibilities between Adam Smith's laissez-faire and Karl Marx's total public control.

Berle was difficult, but he was extremely valuable to Roosevelt and the Brains Trust because of his knowledge of the American economy. In 1932, Berle and Gardner Means, an economist, published *The Modern Corporation and Private Property*, in which they stressed first that big business was an inevitable part of modern society because of its efficiency, and second that power had shifted from stockholders to managers and bankers. Although Berle had voted for Hoover in 1928, he was pleased to be recruited by Moley because advising Roosevelt gave him the opportunity to see his scholarship transformed into public policy. Berle yearned to have a positive social impact and was certain that he was intellectually and morally qualified to perform the role of policy adviser.

Berle delivered his first memo (coauthored by Louis Faulkner) to Roosevelt in late May 1932. He based his argument in the memo on the growing concentration of industry in the United States. Six hundred corporations then controlled 65 percent of American industry, which meant that six thousand men, as directors of these organizations, dominated the business world. But despite this oligarchic power, this "handful of dominant individuals do not agree on a policy; assume little responsibility to the country, to their customers or to their labor; have no cohesion; and fight among themselves for supremacy within their industry." The increasing concentration of industry was making the periodic depressions in the business cycle deeper and longer, and therefore more menacing to American democracy. To illustrate this point, Berle compared the effects of an economic downturn on an agrarian society and an industrial one:

> When most people are on farms, and business is small, a depression merely means a bad time. When most people are concentrated in cities, and most industry is concentrated in a few hundred very large units, depression means dislocation of the entire mechanism; millions of people literally without food and shelter; savings temporarily or permanently wiped out; wholesale misery and disturbance. . . . Unless there is some reversal of trend, or some residual control, some depression will ultimately cause a wholesale dislocation amounting to a revolution in fact, if not in name. . . . For the first time the United States has come within hailing distance of revolution along continental European lines.[44]

Berle was warning Roosevelt that depressions were more than an economic problem—they were a lethal threat to national security.

From Berle's perspective, the Depression made individuals feel insecure, which caused them to act in a way that made a bad situation worse. Insecure workers restricted their consumption; insecure businessmen laid off their employees; insecure bankers would not lend money to businessmen; and insecure investors would not invest in the stock market. This insecurity was turning the great wealth of the nation into a sterile, inert mass; wealth was no longer fueling consumption, economic growth, jobs, and investment. Hoarded dollars in banks or under mattresses were sterile dollars. If insecurity was the cause of the Depression, the cure was for the federal government to provide security through public policies. A more secure population would reverse the present downward cycle to an upward cycle, leading to economic recovery. To provide more "individual safety" would require the federal government to expand its functions into new policy areas, such as old-age pensions, unemployment insurance, and stricter regulation of banks and Wall Street. Berle argued that effective reforms could be formulated that reflected sound economics and humanitarian concerns.[45] He did not warn Roosevelt that in providing more security for the individual, the federal government might make business feel more insecure.

As a member of the Brains Trust, Berle advised Roosevelt on railroads, employment, banking, and securities legislation, but perhaps his most important activity was composing the candidate's Commonwealth Club of San Francisco speech, which was given on September 23, 1932. Beginning in August, Berle urged Roosevelt, for the sake of his political career and influence, to deliver a speech that would outline his political philosophy in the same way Woodrow Wilson's New Freedom discourse did in 1912. Over the next month, Berle produced three drafts of this "New Deal Manifesto," with the final version being edited by Moley and Roosevelt.

The Commonwealth Club speech placed FDR in the direct line of presidential reformers: Thomas Jefferson, Theodore Roosevelt, and Woodrow Wilson. Wilson is praised for recognizing that the closing of the American frontier (no more free land) and the growing concentration of industry meant the end of equality of opportunity. The world war in 1914 prevented Wilson from being able to deal with this threat to one of the nation's most cherished values. Citing Berle's statistics concerning industrial concentration, Roosevelt warned, "we are steering a steady course toward economic oligarchy, if we are not there already." He described conditions in 1932 in these words: "A glance at the situation today only too clearly indicates that equality of opportunity as we have known it no longer exists. Our industrial plant is built; the problem just now is whether under existing conditions it is not overbuilt. . . . More than half of our people do not live on the farms or on lands and cannot derive a living by cultivating their own property. . . . We are now providing a drab living for our own people."

The present crisis required a reappraisal of the roles of government and the capitalist economy. The United States no longer needed "the great promotor or the financial titan" to create progress. "Our task now is . . . [the] less dramatic business of administering resources and plants already in hand, of seeking to reestablish foreign markets for our surplus production, of meeting the problem of under consumption, of adjusting production to consumption, of distributing wealth and products more equitably, of adapting existing economic organizations to the service of the people. The day of enlightened administration has come."

Although large corporations had undoubtedly abused their power under the old system, the Commonwealth Club discourse did not call for their demise. Using one of Berle's historical analogies, Roosevelt said, "We did not think because national government had become a threat in the 18th century that therefore we should abandon the principle of national government. Nor today should we abandon the principle of strong economic units called corporations, merely because their power is susceptible of easy abuse." Instead, Roosevelt claimed the new conditions called for a new relationship between government and business that would be focused on their joint responsibility to provide security. "As I see it," proclaimed Roosevelt, "the task of government in its relation to business is to assist the development of an economic declaration of rights, an economic constitutional order. This is the common task of statesman and businessman. It is the minimum requirement of a more permanently safe order of things."[46]

The Commonwealth Club speech had a difficult message to sell because it asked the public to accept the "new terms of the social contract," which implied living with (under) more intrusive bureaucracies. While in the past the prevailing belief was that the individual was best protected by limited government, Roosevelt was now arguing that the citizen would be best served by a more extended government. The economic freedom that existed under the old regime was now defined as freedom for corporations and subjugation for the individual. Under the proposed New Deal regime, the state would provide more services to protect the individual and to prevent large corporations and financial institutions from engaging in the kind of activities—exploiting labor and speculating in the stock market—that had brought about the Depression.

These new terms would create a larger and more powerful bureaucracy, dominated by experts, that would challenge traditional constitutional principles, the independence of Congress, and the local orientation of political parties. The significance of the Commonwealth Club speech is nicely summarized by Sidney Milkis: "The traditional emphasis in American politics on industrial self-reliance should . . . give way to a new understanding of the social contract, in which the government guaranteed individual men and women protection from the uncertainties of the marketplace. Security was to be the new self-evident truth of political life in the United States."[47] However, for many conservatives and libertarians, the need for security provided by public bureaucracies never became a self-evident truth; instead, it became the most contentious issue between liberals and conservatives because it implied the redistribution of income and political power.

The Commonwealth Club speech and Berle's early relationship with Roosevelt also had a significant influence on the subsequent New Deal economic policies. In reading this speech, one is struck by its pessimistic tone concerning the potentially dynamic capabilities of capitalism. We now know that the economy of 1929 was not a ceiling on the nation's potential; there were still possibilities of growth based on new inventions, ambitious entrepreneurs, and innovative ways to increase investment and consumption. But Berle—the recognized expert on the economy—did not educate Roosevelt about these prospects. Hence, despite all the emphasis on the experimental nature of New Deal policies, the bulk of them gave priority to restricting production rather than increasing it. It took the exogenous shock of rearming for World War II to unleash the economy from its Depression mentality and restraints.

Although Berle agreed to continue advising the president on a freelance basis, he did not accept a position in the first Roosevelt administration. Instead, he went to work for Fiorello LaGuardia when he was elected mayor of New York City in 1933 and served as a liaison between Roosevelt and the progressive Republican mayor. In 1938, Berle was appointed by Roosevelt as assistant secretary of state and later became ambassador to Brazil. Berle was active in politics and policy until his death in 1971.

HENRY MORGENTHAU JR.

Henry Morgenthau Jr. was born in New York City on May 11, 1891. His parents, Henry and Josephine Sykes Morgenthau, were German Jews who had become wealthy through investing and real estate. His father had a progressive social conscience, supporting the Henry Street Settlement House in New York City and contributing to Woodrow Wilson's campaign in 1912. Young Henry was not successful in school; he dropped out of Phillips Exeter after two years and withdrew from Cornell after three semesters. After contracting typhoid fever, Morgenthau went to Texas, where he developed an interest in farming. He reenrolled in Cornell but again withdrew. He did work at the Henry Street Settlement House and served as his father's secretary when President Wilson appointed him ambassador to Turkey. In 1913, young Henry purchased several hundred acres in East Fishkill, New York, and became a neighbor and friend of Franklin Roosevelt. In 1922, Morgenthau purchased the *American Agriculturist*, a trade journal for farmers, in which he, as editor, advocated the need for cheaper credit for the rural sector, rural electrification, and conservation. When Roosevelt was elected governor of New York in 1928, he appointed Morgenthau as head of the Agricultural Advisory Commission. After Roosevelt became president in March 1933, Morgenthau aspired to be secretary of agriculture, but the president appointed Morgenthau chairman of the Federal Farm Board and later chairman of the Farm Credit Administration, which granted low-interest loans to farmers. Later in 1933, when Secretary of the Treasury William H. Woodin was gravely ill and was replaced by Dean Acheson, who was extremely skeptical about the wisdom and legality of Roosevelt's monetary experiments, FDR shocked everyone by firing Acheson and appointing Morgenthau as acting secretary, and then in January 1934 making Morgenthau the secretary of the treasury. Given the difficulties Roosevelt experienced when Acheson was acting secretary of the treasury, it is likely that the president decided he did not want anyone in that crucial post who might defy him. Morgenthau held this powerful position until after FDR's death in April 1945.

Morgenthau was forty-two years old in 1933. Schlesinger describes him as a "tall, heavy-set, nearsighted, partly bald man, slow in speech, often hesitant in reaction, but possessed of great stubbornness and drive. In his private relations, he was a person of delicacy and warmth; in public he tended toward worry and suspicion, displaying in official relations a pervading mixture of insecurity and aggressiveness, which never quite fully interfered with his effectiveness."[48] As governor, Roosevelt had groomed Morgenthau for Washington assignments and thought that he had demonstrated administrative talent and loyalty. As president, Roosevelt also valued Morgenthau's views that blended "orthodoxy in economics with humanitarianism in social policy."[49] In short, Roosevelt trusted Morgenthau to provide him with loyal service.

Grace Tully, the president's personal secretary, wrote, "There was a close bond between the Roosevelt and Morgenthau families. . . . When the younger Morgenthau came to Washington, the close family associations continued, and Henry and his wife, Elinor, were frequent guests at informal parties and dinners at the White House. Henry probably had more personal appointments with the Boss than any other Cabinet member; he saw him frequently before he had left his bedroom in the morning and it became a custom for Henry to have a Monday desk-side lunch with the President."[50] Thus, as a friend, neighbor, and adviser to both Governor and President Roosevelt, Morgenthau is a particularly good source in helping us to understand the ever-elusive FDR. He not only experienced the rewards and frustrations of advising Roosevelt over a long period, but he also recorded them meticulously in his diary.

Morgenthau was certainly one of FDR's more moderate—many New Dealers would say conservative—advisers. He believed that the Depression was caused by a combination of factors that included the shortchanging of farmers, the overconcentration of business, and the speculative fever that fueled the stock market crash of 1929. From his perspective, recovery was dependent on stimulating the nation's free enterprise economy in a more sound and equitable manner. John Blum, Morgenthau's authorized biographer, summarized his philosophy in these words: "Morgenthau was determined to use federal authority to ensure honest business behavior, to prevent the growth of clusters of private economic power so large that they overwhelmed potential competition, and to protect the funds of small stockholders and depositors. . . . Morgenthau belonged to the antimonopoly tradition which had flowered in Washington since 1935. He was solicitous of small business, suspicious of big business, and especially wary of the motives of the giant institutions of American finance."[51]

Roosevelt, who always believed that fiscal conservatism should be a component in his policy-making procedures, also appointed a committed budget balancer, Lewis Douglas, a rich Democratic Congress member from Arizona, to be the director of the Bureau of the Budget, an agency that was then located in the Treasury Department. Roosevelt explained Douglas's role at a press conference on December 13, 1933: "Douglas' job is to prevent the Government from spending just as hard as he possibly can. . . . Somewhere between his efforts to spend nothing . . . and the point of view of the people who want to spend ten billion additional on public works, we will get somewhere."[52] FDR understood that the viability of the New Deal was dependent on significant budget restraints.

As fiscal conservatives, both Douglas and Morgenthau feared the effects of budget deficits on consumer prices, national savings, and the foreign exchange value of the dollar. They worried whether New Deal budget deficits could be financed—that is, would the Treasury Department be able to sell its bonds? Their bureaucratic positions made them much more sensitive about budgetary costs and tax burdens in policy decisions than those advisers who were more concerned about social needs. For Douglas and Morgenthau, fiscal restraints were vital for recovery because they limited the potentially insatiable needs of the state and of interest groups and renewed the faith of citizens in a disciplined government. According to Julien Zelizer, "Both saw fiscal conservatism as the moral obligation of current politicians to future generations as well as beneficial to investment and business leaders. Fiscally conservative policies would enable Roosevelt to build a sizable federal government *and* maintain relatively low tax rates in a nation hostile to taxation."[53]

Yet there were significant differences in the style and ideas of Douglas and Morgenthau that compelled one to resign and allowed the other to play a significant role in the evolution of the New Deal. Given Douglas's ideological rigidity, he believed that New Deal liberalism and fiscal conservatism were incompatible. In his view, Roosevelt's policies were preventing recovery and would eventually produce some form of authoritarian government, as had happened in Germany. Despite falling prices brought about by the Depression, Douglas was most worried about inflation caused by budget deficits, which would ruin the middle class and undermine our democratic form of government.

Douglas was an early favorite of the president. He attended cabinet meetings and helped Roosevelt formulate the Economy Act during the first hundred days. But the budget director was eventually shocked when he realized that every dollar he cut in the regular budget was being swamped by increases in expenditures in the emergency budget for relief and public works. His value to Roosevelt declined because of his ideological rigidity, moral certitude, and threats to resign. His biographers write, "For Douglas, a balanced budget, sound money, an international gold standard, and low tariffs were articles of faith. . . . A contemporary observer wrote that Douglas saw disaster at every turn, 'and confused the principle of laissez faire with the Word of God.'"[54] When Roosevelt took the United States off the gold standard in April 1933, Douglas warned that it "was the end of Western civilization."[55] When Roosevelt asked for Dean Acheson's resignation in the fall of 1933, Douglas wrote to his father: "The Administration lost real ability in Acheson, nothing in Woodin, and has acquired Hebraic arrogance and conceit in Morgenthau."[56] Obviously, Douglas was not likely to form a conservative alliance with his nominal boss, the secretary of the treasury.

The flavor of Douglas's advice is revealed in a 10-page memo he submitted to the president on December 30, 1933. In this memo, he lectured Roosevelt that "history demonstrates . . . that huge expenditures eventually plunge governments . . . into paper inflation." Such inflation, he argues, destroys the middle class and leads to the creation of either a communist or fascist political system. For Douglas, once a leader violated the principle of laissez-faire, he launched a malevolent set of changes that inexorably led to catastrophe. Douglas was warning FDR that he was unwittingly leading the country not in the direction of recovery and reform, but toward economic and political disaster.[57] Eventually, Roosevelt resented Douglas's bullheadedness, his simplistic and self-serving view of history's lessons, his lack of imagination in believing that the only two paths open to the United States were to preserve the old capitalist system or create one characterized by state socialism, and his demands that the president proclaim long-term commitments to Douglas's policy views. With the exception of his commitment to free trade, Douglas was actually closer to Hoover and the old Republican regime than to Roosevelt and the New Deal. With greater loyalty to the old regime than the one Roosevelt was struggling to create, Douglas became alienated and felt compelled to resign on August 30, 1934.

Morgenthau lasted until 1945 because he believed that fiscal conservatism and the New Deal, although not an easy fit, were compatible. His connections to agricultural interests and Cornell made him more open to monetary experiments and less committed to gold. Morgenthau accepted that the Depression was a special condition that justified more government programs and less fiscal restraint. His loyalty and faith in Roosevelt's leadership allowed him to accept—sometimes with anguish—the zigzags of the New Deal. Zelizer argues that Morgenthau's concern for fiscal conservatism helped legitimate the New Deal.[58]

Nonetheless, it was frustrating for Morgenthau, an adviser with a consistent policy point of view, to work for the ever-shifting FDR. Morgenthau argued that it was essential for the administration to demonstrate that it was making progress toward the goal of balancing the budget. Unbalanced budgets were a function of the emergency conditions of the Depression; it was morally imperative for the federal government to finance relief for the millions of unemployed. But recovery meant less reliance on government spending and more on business spending. Approaching a balanced budget would reduce fears about inflation and the expansion of government and encourage investors to take risks with their capital. For Morgenthau, many New Deal programs could be cut, or even eliminated, because they were not effective in promoting recovery. The secretary understood that the president, as an elected official, had to respond to political pressures, which usually meant new and expensive programs that postponed the achievement of a balanced budget. Morgenthau's challenge was to convince Roosevelt that balancing the budget would reap economic and political rewards.

Morgenthau cultivated his staff (Herman Oliphant, Herbert Gaston, Roswell Magill, and Harry Dexter White) more than most of the other cabinet secretaries. He was handicapped in dealing with Roosevelt because he had few allies (Cordell Hull was one of the few) who could reinforce his arguments. Moreover, in an administration filled with intelligent and articulate men with outstanding academic records, Morgenthau was a college dropout. His appointment as secretary of the treasury, a position that he did not appear qualified for, drew criticisms from many New Dealers.[59] Years later, Morgenthau responded to these criticisms by explaining, "Mr. Roosevelt often asked me to do things for the government which had nothing to do with regular Treasury work. He would usually ask these things of me after some other Cabinet member had failed, with the result that I made many enemies. Many times Mr. Roosevelt needed a whipping boy and he favored me [?] with that role. But then, he had to run for office and be re-elected and I didn't."[60] Providing loyal service to Roosevelt was not for the fainthearted.

The incident that best reveals the relationship between Morgenthau and Roosevelt and the president's decision-making style involves how the administration chose to respond to Congressman Wright Patman's bill in 1935 to give World War I veterans their bonus, which would be financed by greenbacks. Morgenthau led the fight for a presidential veto, but when he went to the White House on May 20, he found the president wavering. Roosevelt said, "Patman asked me point-blank whether I had an open mind and I told him that I had an open mind because how could I know what they might pass." Morgenthau wrote of his response:

> I had a sort of sinking feeling and found myself sort of gradually crumpling up and I said, "If you want me to go on please do not talk that way to me because I am building a bonfire of support for you in your veto message." He said rather quickly with a smile, "Let's agree that I will not talk to you about any compromise if you will not talk to me about any bonfire." He said, "In other words, never let your left hand know what your right hand is doing." I said, "Which hand am I, Mr. President?" And he said, "My right hand. . . . But I keep my left hand under the table." This is the most frank expression of the real FDR that I ever listened to and that is the real way that he works—but thank God I understand him.[61]

In brief, Morgenthau accepted, with considerable anguish, that Roosevelt could occasionally be devious, that he could simultaneously and comfortably pursue opposing policies on different tracks, and that shifting political calculations could mean the withdrawal of the president's support.[62]

It became even tougher for Morgenthau in 1938, and he almost resigned. During most of 1937, the economy had continued to revive, and

Morgenthau was able to convince Roosevelt to consider reductions in expenditures in hopes of achieving a balanced budget in 1939. Morgenthau believed it was time "to strip off the bandages and throw away the crutches" because private enterprise could now stand on its own feet. If the New Deal could provide relief, reform, recovery, and a balanced budget, FDR would deprive the Republicans of a legitimate issue. But in the autumn of 1937, the economy and the stock market turned sour, which prompted the Republicans to pounce on a new issue—the Roosevelt recession. Morgenthau attributed the economic decline to the lack of business confidence, doubts about the administration's commitment to reducing the budget deficit, anxieties about war in Europe, and the tight monetary policy of the Federal Reserve Board. Nevertheless, Morgenthau continued to advocate a policy of budgetary austerity. He was opposed by a group of New Dealers, known as the spenders, who blamed the recession on fiscal restraint.

The spenders (or consumptionists) were led by Marriner Eccles, Lauchlin Currie, Harry Hopkins, Leon Henderson, Tom Corcoran, and Ben Cohen. These "big spenders" supplied the president with competing advice and a different vision than that offered by Morgenthau. "Consumptionists argued," according to Zelizer, "that spending, not investment, was the key to a healthy economy. Rejecting the traditional belief that production created its own demand, they insisted that under-consumption had caused the depression. To solve this problem, the government should compensate for inadequate private spending through increased public spending."[63] Eccles, the banker from Utah, was the leader of this group stressing the need for a compensatory fiscal policy (pumping money into the economy to increase aggregate demand) to correct for underconsumption. The Fed chairman and his adviser, Lauchlin Currie, who had a Ph.D. in economics from Harvard, were bringing a Keynesian perspective to New Deal policy making. Eccles's vision emphasized that because the economy had evolved into a stage of maturity, it could no longer grow fast enough to provide full employment, and thus the government would have to transform federal spending from a temporary, emergency measure to a permanent, regularly used instrument. This vision meant that the mature economy of the United States would continue to need crutches and pumps.

At the end of March 1938, while Roosevelt was vacationing in Warm Springs and Morgenthau was vacationing on Sea Island, the stock market took another ominous plunge. Hopkins, fortified by memoranda from Leon Henderson and Aubrey Williams, took advantage of this period and provided FDR what he yearned for—an action program of increased spending. The president, whose vacillation about how to respond to the recession had frustrated both himself and many New Dealers, now was re-invigorated by his decision to spend his way to recovery.

When Morgenthau returned to Washington on April 10, he was stunned and personally hurt that Roosevelt and his spending advisers had formulated a whole new fiscal program without consulting him or the Treasury Department. When Morgenthau met with the president, Hopkins, and Jimmy Roosevelt on the evening of April 10, FDR used his propensity to avoid unpleasant subjects and blithely informed his treasury secretary that big decisions had been made over the previous week and that Morgenthau would have to work quickly to inform himself about the program. Morgenthau expressed his dismay about the costs of the program, its negative effects on business confidence, and the question of whether it would be possible to finance such large budget deficits. He presented a memo to the president that outlined his less expensive suggestions. The next morning, Morgenthau bitterly complained to his staff that they had not been consulted and that the spenders had "stampeded [Roosevelt] like cattle." On April 13, Morgenthau met with Roosevelt and threatened to resign. Roosevelt responded with a lecture on the solidarity of the British cabinet, meaning that each member was bound by the decision of the majority. The president praised Morgenthau for doing a "magnificent job" and argued that if the secretary resigned, it would destroy the Democratic party, lead to the creation of a third party, and end the possibility of passing the New Deal reforms through Congress. During this conversation, Morgenthau recalled that Roosevelt had used similar words and arguments with Lewis Douglas in 1934 in a futile effort to prevent the budget director from resigning. The president was obviously uncomfortable and tried to end the conversation by pointing out that Bernard Baruch was waiting outside for his appointment. Morgenthau reluctantly withdrew from the Oval Office and spent the next few hours agonizing over whether he should resign.[64]

During these hours, Morgenthau rationalized why he should remain in the administration. He and Roosevelt had differed over a controversial issue that had plausible arguments on both sides. This was only one of many issues the administration faced, and they were in agreement on most of the fundamental questions. As Blum explained,

> They shared the same deep conviction that the first concern of
> government should be for the masses of the people. They shared the
> same deep conviction that the democracies of the world had to prepare

for an impending war with the forces of aggression. Morgenthau asked himself whether he should jeopardize those common objectives . . . because of his opposition to one phase of the President's program. He still had . . . a splendid opportunity to make relief efficient, to improve the banking system and tax structure, to mold a foreign economic policy helpful to the democracies. More important, was he to desert the man he admired and loved second only to his father, because of a single disagreement? At the bottom of his heart, he knew his greatest usefulness was in the service of Franklin Roosevelt, and he could not abandon him. So he stayed on.[65]

Henry Morgenthau provided FDR with a vision of moderate fiscal conservatism. The politically astute Roosevelt recognized that the liberal regime he was constructing needed a fiscally sound system. Because many New Deal advisers were big spenders, motivated by concerns for social justice, Roosevelt insisted that policy proposals be subject to at least a few advisers who were cost conscious. Morgenthau was not brilliant, but he always did Roosevelt's bidding by finding ways to finance New Deal programs and deficits. Zelizer concludes, "Although he suffered some major losses, Morgenthau also shaped the design of several key policies such as Social Security, veterans' pensions, and income taxation. By being flexible about when fiscal conservatism was politically obtainable or economically desirable, and by packaging fiscal conservatism as an ongoing objective rather than a fixed requirement, Morgenthau gained legitimacy for himself and his beliefs."[66]

HENRY AGARD WALLACE

Henry A. Wallace was born on October 7, 1888, in Iowa. His family was active in agriculture, religion, publishing, and politics. Wallace's grandfather, Henry Wallace (1836–1916), was a Presbyterian minister, a major landholder, a supporter of Theodore Roosevelt, and the editor of Iowa's most influential farm journal, *Wallace's Farmer*. On the front page of each issue was the credo: "Good farming, clear-thinking, right living." Wallace's father, Henry Cantwell Wallace (1866–1924), was a professor at Iowa State College, an editor of *Wallace's Farmer*, and one of the founders of the American Farm Bureau Federation in 1919, and had been appointed secretary of agriculture by President Warren Harding in 1921. As a child, the insatiably curious Henry A. Wallace, who was more comfortable with plants than with people, began experiments to increase corn yields. Young

Henry went to Iowa State in 1906 and graduated at the top of his class in 1910. In his senior thesis, Wallace advocated that the federal government should support soil conservation. He taught himself calculus in order to analyze the relationship between corn and hog prices. In 1914, he married Ilo Browne; they eventually had three children. Wallace helped his father edit *Wallace's Farmer,* and he also contributed many articles championing scientific farming. In the Harding and Coolidge cabinets, Henry Cantwell Wallace supported the McNary-Haugen bill to help farmers, but Coolidge accepted the advice of Herbert Hoover, then secretary of commerce, to veto the bill. Henry Cantwell Wallace died in October 1924, and his son developed a strong dislike for Hoover and a number of Republican policies, such as high tariffs and protectionism.

In 1926, Wallace and several of his friends created a company to develop, produce, and sell hybrid corn, which was later known as the Pioneer Hi-Bred Company. After a rough start, this company provided Wallace a steady income and would eventually make him and his grown children rich.

Wallace supported Al Smith in his race against Herbert Hoover in 1928. Four years later, Henry Morgenthau came to Iowa to solicit Wallace's support for Roosevelt. After the Democratic party convention nominated Roosevelt, he invited Wallace to visit him in Hyde Park. Their scheduled thirty-minute meeting ballooned to almost two hours as FDR both charmed Wallace and surprised him with his knowledge about the farm problem. In September, Wallace and H. L. Wilson, a professor of agriculture at Montana State Agricultural College, drafted a campaign speech for Roosevelt touting the virtues of the domestic allotment plan. FDR did not use their draft in his Topeka, Kansas, speech, but he did discuss raising farm prices. After the election, Roosevelt offered the position of secretary of agriculture to Wallace on February 6, 1933, and after six days of deliberation, he accepted. Wallace was secretary of agriculture until September 1940, when he resigned to run for vice president under Roosevelt, who was running for president for the third time. In 1944, Democratic party leaders convinced Roosevelt to drop Wallace from the ticket in favor of Senator Harry Truman. In 1945, Roosevelt appointed Wallace as secretary of commerce. After FDR died and Truman became president, Wallace objected to the administration's cold war policies toward the Soviet Union. Truman asked for Wallace's resignation in September 1946. Two years later, Wallace ran for president as the head of the Progressive party and received only 2.4 percent of the vote. This quixotic adventure ended Wallace's public career. He died of Lou Gehrig's disease in 1965.

Although Wallace's enemies labeled him a dreamer, he accepted the term because he believed progress was dependent on the visions of dreamers who could imagine a better world. David Kennedy points out that Wallace was "a magnet for controversy." "To his partisans he was an agrarian intellectual, a scientist and a visionary. . . . To his detractors he was a dreamy rustic, an awkward and swankless bumpkin, a pixilated hayseed who dabbled in fad diets, consulted Navaho shamans, and proved a sucker for the enchantments of spiritual snake-oil merchants like his confidant and guru, the émigré Russian mystic Nicholas Roerich."[67] Wallace's biographers, Culver and Hyde, stress that "he struck many people as a walking paradox: a registered Republican in a Democratic administration, a vegetarian from a hog producing state, a reserved and private soul in the most garrulous and public of professions. There was about him something unknowable, an odd coolness, a baffling diffidence that associates found hard to fathom."[68] It is particularly hard to understand how Wallace, a man who was more interested in plants than people, who would prefer to exercise with boomerangs than consult with party leaders, developed ambitions to succeed Roosevelt as president.

Although the Republican opposition in the 1930s accused the Roosevelt administration of being driven by political, socialist, communist, and even fascist aspirations, Wallace was more likely to cite prophets from the Bible than Gallup, Marx, or Mussolini. Wallace thought that troubled times called for prophets, and he yearned to play that role by living an ascetic life and articulating religion-inspired visions. While other cabinet secretaries were driven to their offices by chauffeurs, Wallace walked two and a half miles to work, engaged in regular exercise, denied himself the pleasures of alcohol and tobacco, and experimented with strange diets. Throughout his life, he looked on religion as the authentic promise of the future rather than the dead hand of the past. Schlesinger writes, "This sense of closeness to what he called 'that blissful unmanifested reality which we call God' gave him his mission in life. . . . The vision of Micah was forever in his mind, when swords were beaten into plowshares . . . , when nations no longer warred against nation. . . . Micah and Jeremiah, Elijah and Amos were almost as real to him as Senator Norris; he cited their views as he might those of elder liberal statesmen with whom he lunched the day before."[69] Culver and Hyde suggest that in 1933, "The prophet of reform had become the agent of change; the thinker had become the doer. Few men knew more about agriculture than Wallace; and no man anywhere burned with greater zeal to rescue farmers from their cruel misfortune."[70] But no problem during the Depression was more difficult to resolve than trying to improve the conditions of the farmers.

The big problem, according to Wallace, was that the supply-and-demand system punished farmers because demand for agricultural products was inelastic and farmers had no workable means of controlling supply.[71] While industry, dominated by large corporations, responded to declines in demand by reducing production, individual farmers were likely to increase production in a futile attempt to compensate for lost income, therefore worsening their condition. Wallace thought that capitalism had created an imbalance between city and country because of the economic and political weaknesses of farmers. The Depression demonstrated that capitalism distributed too much income to business owners and too little to labor and farmers. To save capitalism, profits would have to be limited, and more of the national income would have to be channeled to workers and farmers. Wallace advocated four steps to promote recovery: "the reduction of crop acreage through the domestic allotment plan; the scaling down and refinancing of farm indebtedness; the expansion of the means of payment through . . . 'controlled inflation' . . . ; and the search for new foreign markets by regional trade agreements."[72]

In essence, Wallace was trying to bring security for the farmer — a sector that was chronically subject to volatility because of the unpredictable effects of weather, insects, and crop disease. He believed that security for farmers was largely dependent on developing their political unity and strength. The political clout of the agricultural sector was diluted because with six million farms scattered over forty-eight states, it was unable to bargain successfully with groups that were more organized. Farmers needed to develop a group consciousness that would be reflected in public policies specifically designed to promote their interests. As Stanley High wrote in 1937, "[Wallace] believes that, in the long run, economic improvement will greatly depend upon political strength. His first consultation with farm leaders in March, 1933, and all the succeeding meetings, . . . have been intended . . . both to get agreement on farm legislation and, by the process of agreeing and in the united front that such agreement results in, develop the habit of unity among the farm forces and make it plain what political victories can be won when they have united."[73] Wallace also argued that American ingenuity could design policies to provide security and prosperity for farmers without regimenting them under authoritarian bureaucracies or violating the nation's democratic traditions.

It is worth noting that Wallace avoided some of the pitfalls of his philosophy. For example, in contrast to most Midwestern progressives, who were isolationists, Wallace was an internationalist. His biographers point out, "Unlike William Borah of Idaho or George Norris of Nebraska or the La-Follettes of Wisconsin, all firmly isolationist, Wallace tended toward internationalism. Fostering international trade was not only a means of helping American farmers, Wallace thought, but the surest path to world peace. In the cabinet, he had been Secretary of State Cordell Hull's strongest ally in the effort to reduce trade barriers through negotiation of reciprocal agreements."[74] Similarly, although Wallace was an expert on genetics, he avoided the racism of those who dreamed of breeding a higher form of the human race.

Being the youngest member (age forty-five) of Roosevelt's original cabinet did not inhibit Wallace's activities and keep him from expressing his views on a wide range of topics. His energy level was astounding; he typically worked fourteen- to sixteen-hour days. In his first year as secretary of agriculture, he authored numerous speeches and pamphlets outlining his visions of a "new frontier" of cooperation between the government and the farmer. Culver and Hyde stress, "Most striking of all, however, was his zeal and sense of purpose. He brought to his task the solemn dedication of a crusading reformer. It was this quality that let Wallace rise above his personal reticence."[75] Roosevelt's private secretary writes, "In Cabinet meetings, Wallace took an active part in most discussions on the whole range of problems that faced the Administration. The Boss liked this quality and preferred it to the reticence or indifference of some Cabinet members when discussions turned on matters outside their own departments."[76]

Roosevelt valued Wallace. Not only did Wallace provide the eastern Roosevelt a means of communicating with farmers in the Midwest, he was an appreciated adviser. As Schlesinger suggests, "talking agriculture, Wallace could be exceedingly crisp, hard-hitting, and impressive. For all his turmoil within and his vagaries without, the fact remained that few Americans in 1933 were so steeped in the agricultural crisis, or had brooded over it so thoughtfully, or brought to it such acute and informed judgement."[77] Culver and Hyde concur that Roosevelt prized "Wallace's agile mind," his advice on diverse subjects, and his expertise on farm problems. They add that FDR "took an almost childlike delight in trying to catch Wallace in an error of fact" (whether the price of cotton yesterday was 11.5 cents a pound or 10.74 cents). They argue that Wallace appealed to Roosevelt's better nature: "There was something very genuine about a man who gave the president seed corn as an Easter gift, along with clear instructions about when and how it should be planted at Hyde Park."[78] There was also something real about Wallace's contributions to the New Deal; in its support, he traveled over 40,000 miles, made public appearances in all 48 states, delivered 88 speeches, authored 20 articles for magazines, published 2 books, and held numerous press conferences.[79]

One of Wallace's administrative challenges was that his department was split between pragmatic and social reformers. The pragmatic agrarians emphasized that their priority was to restore the economic health of commercial agriculture. That goal meant cooperating with the agricultural establishment—the Southern committee chairman in Congress, the big food distributors, the packing houses, the American Farm Bureau, the land-grant colleges, and the extension agents. The social reformers viewed their role as bringing fundamental change to a system they considered corrupt and obsolete. The reformers were anxious to expand the rights of Southern tenant farmers, many of whom were African Americans, an obviously explosive issue. According to Culver and Hyde,

> Both sides . . . claimed Wallace as their own. His leadership in the
> crusade for farm relief, his solid credentials as farm editor and plant
> scientist, his family's long association with land grant colleges, and the
> farm establishment's top echelon stood him in good stead in the eyes of
> the Agriculture Adjustment Administration's agrarians. The reformers,
> on the other hand, saw in Wallace a reflection of themselves: young,
> idealistic, open-minded, comfortable with intellectual give-and-take,
> and repulsed by the excesses of capitalism. Wallace himself knew he was
> part of both camps.[80]

For two years, Wallace attempted to operate above both contesting groups, but when Chester Davis, the agrarian who replaced George Peek as the head of the AAA, fired a number of reformers (Jerome Frank, Lee Pressman, and Gardiner Jackson) in February 1935, Wallace was forced to take sides. He supported Davis's decision and incurred the wrath of the reformers. The publicity from these firings generated debate about the nature of the New Deal: how committed was it to fundamental reform? Wallace privately blamed FDR's leadership style, with its emphasis on experimentation and lack of clear-cut objectives, for the problem because it encouraged intrigue among warring factions within the administration. Wallace was later to conclude that Roosevelt was a water man: "He looks in one direction and rows the other with the utmost skill."[81]

Wallace came to believe that to do good, to fulfill the prophet's visions and his own, he would have to be in a position of higher authority. He campaigned for Roosevelt in 1932 and was rewarded by being appointed secretary of agriculture. Within a few years, it was widely rumored that he harbored ambitions to succeed Roosevelt as president in 1940. But many of Wallace's enemies thought that he "was a man whose judgment could never be trusted when he strayed more than six feet from a manure pile."[82]

Wallace believed that social justice could be achieved through some combination of ethical and scientific formulas. Religion and science could be reconciled to produce social justice and fulfill the American promise. American ingenuity should be utilized to bring about balanced prosperity for the city and country. Because of Wallace, the Department of Agriculture was deeply imbued with New Deal ideas and enthusiasms. *Time* magazine reported in 1938 that just "as Harry Hopkins' Works Progress Administration is filled with social workers and reminds visitors of a settlement house, so Henry Wallace's Agriculture looks like the agricultural extension bureau of a mid-western university."[83] The New Deal agricultural policy bore the stamp of Wallace more than the fiscal program reflected the views of Morgenthau. However, Wallace was dealing with a dilemma that he understood but could not resolve: "Even as he was teaching Iowa farmers how to produce more corn, Wallace was in Washington wrestling with the problem of overproduction. And as he was bringing scientific advancement to the farm, he was setting in motion forces that would drive more farmers off the land."[84] Neither Wallace's practical nor visionary side could solve this puzzle.

HARRY HOPKINS

Harry Hopkins was born in 1890 in Sioux City, Iowa. His father was a harness maker and his mother was a teacher and a religious Methodist (president of the Iowa Methodist Home Missionary Society). Hopkins graduated from Grinnell College with a double major in history and political science. After graduation in 1912, he attended both the Democratic and Republican party conventions as a spectator. He then got a job at the Christadora House, a settlement house in New York City, where he began his long career as a social worker. In 1913, Hopkins married Ethel Gross, a Jewish immigrant who also worked at the Christadora House. They had three sons. Hopkins was a social worker from 1912 to 1918, a Red Cross administrator from 1918 to 1921, and director of health agencies from 1921 to 1931. He divorced his first wife in 1930 and immediately married

Barbara Duncan. They had one daughter. In 1931, Governor Roosevelt created the Temporary Emergency Relief Agency (TERA), which was initially headed by Jesse Isador Strauss, the president of Macy's department stores. Strauss appointed Hopkins as his deputy; when Strauss resigned the next year, Roosevelt named Hopkins to direct TERA. As president, Roosevelt appointed Hopkins to head the Federal Emergency Relief Administration (FERA) in May 1933, the Civil Works Administration (CWA) in late 1933, the Works Progress Administration (WPA) in 1935, and in 1938, he named him secretary of commerce. In 1937, Hopkins's wife died, and he had a cancerous part of his stomach removed; the disease had killed his father in 1930. For a short period, Hopkins believed he had FDR's private endorsement to be the Democratic party's nominee for president in 1940, but Hopkins's divorce and chronic health problems (as FDR must have known) made this outcome extremely unlikely. In 1940, a physically frail Hopkins and his daughter moved into the White House, where they lived for three and a half years. Hopkins was Roosevelt's personal representative at the 1940 Democratic party convention, where the president was nominated for the third time. In 1942, Hopkins married Louise Macy, the former Paris editor of *Harper's Bazaar*. During World War II, Hopkins was one of Roosevelt's major advisers and was used as an envoy to negotiate arrangements with Winston Churchill and Joseph Stalin. Shortly after the war, Hopkins's frail body broke down, and he died on January 29, 1946. The man who distributed billions to the American poor and to wartime allies died a poor man.

Students of the New Deal have been fascinated by the personality of Harry Hopkins. His great-granddaughter, June Hopkins, wrote, "From his Iowa roots, Hopkins absorbed some of his mother's Methodist teachings, his father's cynicism, his sister's commitment to social service, and his college's Social Gospel message that rallied Christians to the cause of reform and combined them with his own idealism and ambition."[85] In David Kennedy's words, "Like the track touts with whom he frequently kept company, he affected a hell's-bells air that caused others to appraise him as both shrewd and faintly ominous. Yet compassion suffused his nature, tempered by a piercing intelligence that would one day lead Winston Churchill to dub him 'Lord Root of the Matter.'"[86] No higher compliment can be paid to an adviser. The most vivid description of Hopkins was provided by Schlesinger.

Hopkins was a lean, loose-limbed, disheveled man, with sharp features and dark, sardonic eyes. He talked quickly and cockily, out of the side of his mouth; his manner was brusque and almost studiously irreverent;

his language, concise, pungent, and often profane. . . . He was at his best under pressure. . . . He would screw up his face and fire a volley of short, sharp questions until he had slashed through to the heart of a problem. Understanding what had to be done, he wasted no time in formalities, but assumed responsibility, gave orders, and acted. He expended nervous energy carelessly and restored it by chain-smoking and by drinking cup after cup of black coffee. Beneath his air of insouciance and cynicism, he had a buoyant . . . conviction that all walls would fall before the man of resource and decision.[87]

In brief, Hopkins was the kind of personality New Dealers could love and Republicans could hate as a left-wing Rasputin.

Hopkins's philosophy was equally controversial. He believed that social workers were in the best position to understand social problems and work for social justice. Hopkins thought that his work among the poor in New York qualified him to propose and administer national solutions for relief as a New Deal policy maker. However, he also feared that his becoming a top presidential adviser was precarious because his role as the distributor of relief made him the target of conservatives determined to find waste and corruption in his program. He had angrily rejected President Hoover's belief that relief was a local problem and responsibility. Social workers were aware that the breadth and depth of the Depression overwhelmed the financial capabilities of both local governments and charities. Nor could Hopkins "agree with the [Hoover] administration's assumption that so long as the top of the financial structure was taken care of with credit and subsidy," sufficient benefits would trickle down to the bulk of the population. In June Hopkins's words, "Concerned for the economic security and the morale of those on the lowest rung on the economic ladder, he insisted that, with over ten million American workers unemployed, people needed jobs more than industry needed credit."[88]

When FDR was elected president in 1932, Hopkins was anxious to serve in Washington as a national relief administrator. Hopkins believed the country desperately needed a federal relief program, and he was confident that he was the best man for the job. As a social worker, Hopkins believed that the federal government could help the unemployed without destroying them or the nation. For Hopkins, the practical idealist, the problem had a simple solution: if business could not provide enough jobs, then the federal government would have to supply them. His relief philosophy remained consistent throughout the New Deal decade: "Give a man a dole and you save his body and destroy his spirit; give him a job and pay him an assured wage, and you save both the body and the spirit."[89] Work relief was more expensive than providing cash allowances (the dole), but Hopkins thought that jobs provided self-respect for its recipients. Because the bulk of the unemployed had lost their jobs through no fault of their own, they ought not be socially ostracized. They were not useless; they were worthy of receiving a living wage. And by earning money, the people on work relief would now be able to contribute to recovery by increasing consumer demand. "To Hopkins," according to his great granddaughter, "jobs and wages for the unemployed seemed the most effective way to preserve the traditional American values of independence and self-sufficiency and the most direct road to full economic health for the nation."[90] For Hopkins, there was no conflict between relief and recovery.

Many conservatives were not so sure. During a speech Hopkins delivered explaining how government-sponsored jobs on public projects would provide income for the unemployed and demand for business, a frustrated member of the audience shouted out, "Who's going to pay for all that?" In response, "Hopkins, with his charismatic flair for the dramatic, slowly took off his coat and tie, rolled up his sleeves, and looked at the now fascinated audience. . . . 'You are,' Hopkins shouted, 'and who better? Who can better afford to pay for it? This is America, the richest country in the world. We can afford to pay for anything we want. And we want a decent life for all the people in this country. And we are going to pay for it.'"[91] It is hard to imagine a more polarizing statement.

Hopkins also tried to convince the public to accept a more activist government. For him, government was not an alien force; in a democracy, it represented the instrument of our collective aspirations. In the past, the government had bestowed its benefits in order to develop commerce, agriculture, and industry. The proponents of laissez-faire conveniently neglected to mention the public policies designed to promote development: high tariffs; free land for war veterans, settlers, and railroad companies; and the construction of dams, roads, and internal improvements. Helping the unemployed in the Depression was not a violation of our political tradition, it was a humane extension of it. However, he also stated that the old order of rugged individualism and laissez-faire were "definitely past and finished."[92] Hence, Hopkins tried to legitimate his relief policies by arguing that they were compatible with our political heritage and that they constituted core policies in a new liberal regime that emphasized economic security instead of rugged individualism.

It is easy to understand why Hopkins thought that the New Deal should look on poverty as a permanent problem and not just a temporary emergency brought about by the Depression. Although many policy makers had become concerned with the poor and the unemployed only since 1929, Hopkins had been dealing with the poor since 1912. For him, poverty preceded the Depression and would continue to be a major issue after the Depression. In 1937, he predicted that even after recovery, there might still be 5 million unemployed. Hopkins never gave up his vision of "a permanent program of counter-cyclical government projects to absorb unemployed industrial workers. . . . Government jobs would prime the economic pump."[93] This vision, however, was more radical than FDR was willing to accept in his 1935 social security bill.

The idea of analyzing his visions and philosophy would probably have made Hopkins smile. Among FDR's advisers, he assumed the role of the doer, not the thinker. His language was blunt and frequently quoted by the press; it often delighted his liberal supporters and frightened his conservative adversaries. For Hopkins, "When a house is on fire, you don't call a conference, you put it out."[94] The poor, in his words, were people who had been dealt "deuces and threes" in the game of life. When an assistant came to Hopkins with a proposal that would help the unemployed "in the long run," Hopkins snapped, "People don't eat in the long run. They eat every day."[95] When Hopkins was questioned about extending benefits to writers, artists, and musicians in 1934, he responded, "Hell, they've got to eat just like other people."[96] Schlesinger writes that "when Harry Hopkins lightly said in 1934, 'The country does not know what real heavy taxation is,' he sent a chill of horror through the business community"[97] — and probably through the more politically astute Roosevelt.

But the most famous line attributed to Hopkins is something he might not have said. In August 1938, while at the Empire racetrack in Yonkers, New York, Hopkins allegedly remarked, "We shall tax and tax, and spend and spend, and elect and elect." Arthur Krock, the conservative reporter for the *New York Times*, wrote that this phrase was a "concentrated gem of Mr. Hopkins' philosophy." During Hopkins's senatorial confirmation hearings for secretary of commerce, he categorically denied ever saying this.[98] Whether or not Hopkins ever made this statement, the important point is that the Republicans had an effective caricature of the liberal regime created by the New Deal. The accusation that FDR created a self-sustaining system fueled by taxes, spending, and elections, but that did not solve problems, appealed to Republicans, and still does. For them, Hopkins's statement exposed the ugly truth that the driving force of the New Deal was neither compassionate nor moral, but political.

While Hopkins became a negative symbol for conservatives, he was destined to become FDR's closest adviser. Hopkins did not become a member of Roosevelt's administration until May 22, 1933, the seventy-ninth day of the first hundred days, when he resigned his $13,500 TERA job in New York and accepted the $8,500 position as head of the new Federal Emergency Relief Administration in Washington, D.C. Within two hours of assuming his new office, he dispersed $5 million in relief funds and established his reputation as "the speediest spender" in the New Deal.[99] "Within two days," according to Kenneth Davis,

> drawing upon his wide acquaintance among social workers and aided by soft-spoken, hard-working 42-year-old Aubrey Williams, who became his chief assistant, he threw together a remarkably efficient staff, whose members were not only fanatically devoted to him personally but also imbued with his determination to bring relief to suffering humanity *fast*, at a minimum overhead cost. Within two weeks he had made his impress upon official Washington and, through the Washington press corps, upon the nation as a distinctly different kind of federal bureaucrat if, indeed he was not one of a kind. Within two months, initially sponsored by Eleanor Roosevelt, Hopkins was to be introduced into the inner circle of presidential advisers.[100]

Hopkins's success can be attributed to his skill in distributing relief money quickly and widely, which served Roosevelt's purposes—namely, by demonstrating that in contrast to the tradition-bound Hoover administration, the New Deal was both activist and compassionate.

As an innovative administrator with a keen sense of the president's political needs, Hopkins was highly motivated and comfortable working within Roosevelt's unconventional administrative procedures. Raymond Moley, perhaps reflecting some jealousy that Hopkins had replaced him as a top confidante, later wrote, "Hopkins combined vigorous dispatch in distributing the funds entrusted to him with unorthodox, not to say radical, political and social ideas, most of which were derived from the emotional impact he had experienced in dealing with the poor and unfortunate in his social work. There was never any evidence that he had studied these questions in any depth."[101] But what was compelling to Roosevelt was that Hopkins was willing to act decisively in support of the president's leadership and the shifting goals of the New Deal. For example, when the president ordered

Hopkins to shut down the CWA early in 1934, it was done without critical leaks to the press or threats to resign. By carrying out this unpleasant order, Hopkins had demonstrated his loyalty to Roosevelt.

A number of people have tried to explain why Hopkins emerged victorious from the fierce competition to be Roosevelt's top adviser. Access to Roosevelt was valued because it meant influence over New Deal policies. Labor Secretary Frances Perkins, who had worked for Governor Roosevelt, wrote, "Hopkins became not only his relief administrator but his general assistant as no one had been able to be. In many ways he filled the gap left by Louis Howe's death, but he had a much larger grasp of national and international affairs than did Howe."[102] The "temperamental sympathy" between the two men was spelled out in a *New Yorker* profile in 1943: "Roosevelt and Hopkins think alike on an astonishing number of points; they share a concern for the average man and a preference for the society of the rich, the gay, the talented, and the wellborn . . . ; they share intuitiveness, a mixture of idealism and political shrewdness and a relish for fairly ribald anecdotes and the exercise of irony."[103] By being an excellent social companion to the socially needy Roosevelt, Hopkins multiplied his opportunities to be a major political adviser. Schlesinger stresses that Hopkins "was highly intelligent but non-ideological, far more interested in results than in doctrines. He stayed aloof from the debate between Brandeis/Frankfurter and Berle/Tugwell except as that debate affected his ability to do his job—an exception that allied him with the Keynesian compensatory spenders. He remained friendly with all New Deal sects from Tugwell to Frankfurter and regularly played cards with Jesse Jones."[104] But Schlesinger adds that Hopkins was jealous of his competitors' efforts to move into Roosevelt's inner circle and willing to "throw sand into every competitor's machine." Both Harold Ickes and Thomas Corcoran believed their relationship with Roosevelt was sabotaged by Hopkins's machinations.

Robert Sherwood, a dramatist who worked for Hopkins and wrote speeches for Roosevelt, received his fourth Pulitzer Prize for his 1,000-page book on the relationship between FDR and Hopkins. In comparing the two, Sherwood wrote, "When Roosevelt contemplated a subject, his mind roamed all around it; he considered it in its relation to past, present and future. Hopkins, contemplating the same subject, was interested only in thrusting straight through to its heart and then acting on it without further palaver. In that respect, Hopkins was remarkably useful to Roosevelt."[105] Sherwood suggested that the best explanation for Hopkins's worth was provided by Roosevelt in a conversation with Wendell Willkie on January

19, 1941. The Republican presidential candidate in 1940 asked Roosevelt, "Why do you keep Hopkins so close to you? You surely must realize that people distrust him and they resent his influence." The president responded, "I can understand that you wonder why I need that half-man around me. [The half-man was an allusion to Hopkins's physical frailty.] But someday you may well be sitting here where I am now as President of the United States. And when you are, you'll be looking at that door over there and knowing that practically everybody who walks through it wants something out of you. You'll learn what a lonely job that is, and you'll discover the need for somebody like Harry Hopkins who asks for nothing except to serve you."[106] Roosevelt recognized Hopkins as a rare gem.

For personal and political reasons, Hopkins grappled his way up to become FDR's most versatile and intimate adviser. His final triumph was to live in the White House, just as Louis Howe had done, from 1940 to 1943. He provided the politically and socially needy Roosevelt with administrative energy, skill, and honesty, compassion for the unemployed, loyal service, and witty and amusing friendship. During the Depression, the 1940 Democratic Convention, and World War II, Roosevelt gave Hopkins the vitally important missions of supplying billions for the unemployed, passing along political instructions to party leaders, and providing billions to our military allies. But as close as Hopkins was to Roosevelt, the former was not able to convince the president to include his vision of a permanent government job assurance program in the 1935 social security proposal. In the New Deal, Roosevelt's concern about what was politically feasible always prevailed.

FDR's Decision-Making Style

It is difficult for a contemporary audience to appreciate the effect of Roosevelt's optimism and his aura of self-confidence in his leadership during a period of extreme economic and political insecurity. While President Hoover was diminished by the Depression, Roosevelt was enlarged. The Depression provided the ambitious Roosevelt the "grandest" opportunity to win the presidency and put his personal stamp on a wide variety of public policies. Instead of being frightened by facing the country's most severe economic crisis, he saw it as presenting a perfect stage for heroic performance. With his flair for the dramatic and his optimism that all problems had solutions, Roosevelt had no doubt that he could perform brilliantly under these conditions. Reflecting an Ivy League casualness, he worked hard at projecting an image that he was not working hard—that making decisions was easy and natural for him. George McJimsey describes Roosevelt's mood and style in these words: "Through it all he was a cheerful optimist, capable of lifting others' spirits by showing them small kindnesses and sympathies, taking in their ideas and manners as part of life's continuing adventures and newness, as something to be treasured and enjoyed. . . . Roosevelt's style conveyed an urbanity and polish that revealed his eastern patrician background, but also a genuine warmth and delight."[107] In brief, Roosevelt's optimistic personality suggested to the public that he would not be overwhelmed by the burden of making decisions to deal with the complex issues of recovering from the Depression.

In recruiting his advisers, what Roosevelt wanted most were counselors who were innovative thinkers and who could provide him with practical solutions to the mammoth problems of the Depression. He did not limit himself to the usual white male Anglo-Saxon Protestants, but expanded his "family" to include Catholics, Jews, and women. He also sought advice from professors from a wide variety of universities. As times and needs changed, he moved from one favorite adviser to another—from Louis Howe, to Raymond Moley, to Rexford Tugwell, to Thomas Corcoran, to Harry Hopkins. Each of his advisers had to prove his value in a chaotically competitive system described by Schlesinger: Roosevelt's "favorite technique was to keep grants of authority incomplete, jurisdictions uncertain, charters overlapping. The result of this competitive theory of administration was often confusion and exasperation on the operating level; but no other method could so reliably insure that in a large bureaucracy filled with ambitious men, eager for power, the decisions, and the power to make them, would remain with the President."[108] This competitive system kept FDR well informed, but whether it promoted better policy is debatable.

Roosevelt's self-confidence was also bolstered by his religious faith. "So sure was he of the rightness of his aims," asserts James MacGregor Burns, "that he was willing to use Machiavellian means; and his moral certainties made him all the more effective in struggle. To the idealists who cautioned him, he responded again and again that gaining power—winning elections—was the first indispensable task. He would use the tricks of the fox to serve the purposes of the lion."[109] Thus, because in his own view he was working to achieve moral ends, Roosevelt felt free to employ morally ambiguous means, such as negotiating compromises with William Randolph Hearst and Huey Long in order to gain the Democratic nomination for president in 1932.

Roosevelt's religious posturing also aided him in performing the paradoxical roles of a reconstructive leader. By publicizing his religious orientations, Roosevelt could reassure Americans that he was not a home-grown Hitler or Stalin, but that he was tapping into the great reform potential of the social gospel—a traditional source of rehabilitation in the United States. However, Roosevelt's use of religious rhetoric also possessed radical ramifications in that it morally delegitimized the beneficiaries of the old order. In analyzing Roosevelt's inaugural address in March 1933, Stephen Skowronek stresses, "Christian sentiments framed ruthless images of the degenerate regime Roosevelt sought to displace. He stood against the 'money changers.' He would 'apply social values more noble than mere monetary profits,' and cleanse the temple of the stewards who had disgraced it.'"[110] Hence, Roosevelt's religious stance helped him occupy the moral high ground, which is the position a reconstructive leader must utilize if he is to be successful. Roosevelt generally enjoyed the advantages of operating from this exalted position until he decided to pack the Supreme Court in 1937.

Scholars have debated whether any particular ideology guided Roosevelt's decision making.[111] This debate indicates that if Roosevelt was guided by an ideology, it was probably eclectic and nebulous—a little left of center, but too conservative for his more liberal supporters. And even then he was not fully committed to it. His decision-making rule was not to place all his eggs into one ideological basket; he was inclined to place more eggs in the political basket than in any other. The New Deal was vulnerable to the charge that it was guided more by political opportunism than by political philosophy.

Despite this debate, most scholars agree that FDR was a pragmatist rather than a radical ideologue. However, what is frequently overlooked is that being a pragmatist political leader in the context of the 1930s possessed radical implications.[112] The depth and length of the Depression created conditions in which many aspects of the society, the economy, and the political system were subject and vulnerable to critical attacks. A president operating in such a context was free to launch multiple probes and experiments to bring about relief, recovery, reform, and realignment. FDR's open mind and his ambitious staff had the capacity and opportunity to be imaginative in creating such hybrid solutions as the Tennessee Valley Authority and social security. The usually imposing constraints of political feasibility were less operative; a much greater variety of proposals became possible, which made the New Deal a beacon of hope for many but also a symbol of fear for a sizable and powerful minority. While FDR was not driven by radical beliefs, the fact that his pragmatic decisions might lead to revolutionary proposals explains why such a wide coalition could support the New Deal and a powerful minority could fear it.

As a reconstructive president, Roosevelt had the proper attitude toward the experts: he was skeptical. In order for a president to discard the existing order, he must defy a great deal of the conventional wisdom. Schlesinger writes, "His attitude toward economists was typical. Though he acknowledged their necessity, he stood in little awe of them. 'I brought down several books by . . . leading American economists,' he once told a press conference. . . . 'I suppose I must have read different articles by 15 different experts. Two things stand out: The first is that no two of them agree, and the other thing is that they are so foggy in what they say that it is almost impossible to figure out what they mean.'"[113] His attitude seemed to be, why should he follow any one theory when economists could not agree among themselves?

Roosevelt's attitude toward experts was determined by his needs as a practical politician; he wanted specific solutions, not abstract theories. Burns points out that Roosevelt was "exasperated with the tendency of his business friends to take refuge in abstractions. Again and again he chided them for their failure to address themselves to specific issues. When the dean of Harvard Business School criticized the president in the New York *Sun*, Roosevelt wrote a friend sadly that he had talked with the dean for an hour once. "I put several problems up to him and he had not one single concrete answer to any of them."[114] When in 1934 the banker James Warburg sent Roosevelt a copy of his book, *The Money Muddle*, which criticized the monetary policy of the New Deal, the president responded that Warburg ought to travel in a cheap car throughout the country, stay in hotels charging no more than $1.50 a night, and speak only with regular people (avoiding bankers and business executives). After this practical experience, according to Roosevelt, Warburg would be able to write a better book.[115] And because Roosevelt thought he was listening to and responding to the needs of the public, he had few qualms overriding the advice of experts.

Roosevelt's mistrustful attitude toward experts justified his preference for experimentation and his belief that "Good ideas might pop up from anywhere. 'You sometimes find something pretty good in the lunatic fringe,' Roosevelt once told his press conference: after all, America was remade by 'a whole lot of things which in my boyhood were considered lunatic fringe.'"[116] After interviewing Roosevelt in 1938, a *New York Times* journalist wrote, "He has come to doubt whether anybody really knows anything about economics, or can know enough, in a world where the elements of change work so incalculably to guarantee that any prescribed economic treatment will produce the effects intended."[117] Freidel writes, "in 1941 he looked back and commented to a group of teachers that he wished his schooling had been more practical. . . . He was rather skeptical of theory, remarking to the teachers that he had always claimed that there was no such thing as a proven system of economics: 'I took economics courses in college for four years, and everything I was taught was wrong. The economics of the beginning of this century are completely out of date. Why? Experience. . . . We are groping.'"[118] While other presidents might have suffered anxiety attacks having to make decisions in an erratic world where, according to Roosevelt, the laws of economics change every few years, he thought it was challenging. Groping for answers in an uncertain world was simply the human condition, and one might as well treat it as a game. Roosevelt knew he could not hit a home run every time he came up to the plate, but he was content to have a good batting average.

FDR was less of an intellectual than Hoover was. He did not read serious books of literature, history, or social analysis. He enjoyed fishing, playing poker with close friends, architectural design (he designed his own presidential library), and stamp collecting. Roosevelt kept informed by scanning about six newspapers during breakfast, maintaining a huge correspondence with a wide variety of friends, skimming official reports, and interacting with advisers and Congress members. He probably learned the most by verbal communication. For Roosevelt, useful information was not a comprehensive theory; it was a pertinent fact, a telling anecdote, a usable quote for his speeches. FDR best understood problems when he could think about them in terms of something concrete he knew, such as how a proposal would affect the sweater mill located on the outskirts of Poughkeepsie, near his boyhood home. "Whatever the sources of his information," according to Freidel, "Roosevelt demonstrated a remarkable breadth and detail of knowledge concerning the ramifications of both his administrative and political domains. Both at press conferences and meetings of his administrative councils, his range was often startling."[119] Burns wrote, "His working habits bespoke his mind. . . . [T]o an extraordinary extent he grasped an immediate specific situation in all its particulars and complexities. He knew, for example, the tangled political situations and multitude of personalities in each of the states; he could talk for hours about the housing, roads, people, and history of Hyde Park; he could describe knowledgeably the activities and problems of a host of businesses and industries; he could pull out of his head hundreds of specific prices, rents, wages; he could identify countless varieties of fish, birds, trees; he could not be stumped on geography."[120] If knowing the details is one of the prerequisites for being a successful president, Roosevelt was prepared.

Without an ideological road map to guide him, FDR's decision making was largely dependent on trial and error. Such experimentation was compatible with the times because there was little agreement about either the causes or the cures of the Depression. Roosevelt's commitment to experimentation in the 1932 campaign and during his first administration was acceptable because it justified a variety of New Deal actions and was favorably compared to the inactions of the Hoover administration. But Roosevelt's continued reliance on experimentation after the 1936 election, especially after the recession began in the autumn of 1937, became a liability. After five years in office, the president, it was thought, should know what had to be done. Continued experimentation now bred more anxiety than support: Would it lead to dictatorship? Would it inhibit business confidence?

Roosevelt understood that the plans of mice, men, and intellectuals often do not play out as originally conceived. They are subject to unforeseen complications and events. A leader had to be prepared for widely divergent contingencies. With advisers reflecting different viewpoints, Roosevelt was prepared to move in different directions. To illustrate, when in April 1933 reporters asked about his monetary policy, he replied: "It is a little bit like a football team that has a general plan . . . against the other side. Now, the captain and the quarterback of that team know pretty well what the next play is going to be and they know the general strategy of the team, but they cannot tell you what the play after the next play is going to be until the next play is run off."[121] This analogy reflects Roosevelt's comfort with the idea that some of his decisions would be successful while others would not. According to Frances Perkins, Roosevelt was also set free to experiment by "his feeling that nothing in human judgment is final. One may courageously take the step that seems right today because it can be modified tomorrow if it does not work well."[122] This belief must have eased Roosevelt's burden on the several occasions when he was told his decisions would determine the fate of western civilization.

FDR's mind and administrative procedures allowed him the flexibility to contemplate moving forward on a number of inconsistent paths. The unfolding political calculus would determine the path he would eventually choose. He had the patience to wait until the most advantageous choice revealed itself. While intellectuals, like Tugwell and Moley, complained about his illogical decisions, Roosevelt "had the politician's indifference to inconsistency." The president knew that "The public memory was short and he could change his mind without penalty if he had not made—as he seldom did—embarrassing public commitments."[123] Roosevelt's nonchalant acceptance of incompatible commitments could also fluster practical New Dealers like Marriner Eccles, the chairman of the Federal Reserve Board. On the afternoon of November 10, 1937, Roosevelt agreed with Eccles's Keynesian recommendation that federal spending should be increased to help the nation recover from the new recession; that evening, Secretary of the Treasury, Henry Morgenthau, a close confidant of the president, called for a balanced budget. Eccles later wrote, "The contradictions between the afternoon and evening positions made me wonder at this time whether the New Deal was merely a political slogan or if Roosevelt really knew what the New Deal was. . . . As I now reconsider the event, it seems clear that the President assented to two contradictory policies because he was really uncertain where he wanted to move."[124] Roosevelt's inconsistencies were also a result of his habit of trying to please whomever he was with by appearing to agree.

Periods of indecision in which he could not go on the offensive had an enervating effect on Roosevelt. McJimsey points out, "During periods of long frustration, while he waited for the opportunity to act, he could become lethargic and detached. He seemed to lose interest when he was not at the center and in control."[125] It was deciphering the winning political solution to policy puzzles that intrigued and delighted Roosevelt. No one has improved on Schlesinger's description of Roosevelt's "involved and inscrutable" process of making decisions: "His complex administrative sensibility, infinitely subtle and sensitive, was forever weighing questions of personal force, of political timing, of congressional concern, of partisan benefit, of public interest. Situations had to be permitted to develop, to crystallize, to clarify; the competing forces had to vindicate themselves in the actual pull and tug of conflict; public opinion had to face the question, consider it, pronounce upon it—only then, at the long, frazzled end, would the President's intuitions consolidate and precipitate a result."[126]

FDR revealed an aspect of his decision making in a meeting with Marriner Eccles in September 1935. When Eccles suggested a political maneuver to outsmart Senator Carter Glass, he noticed a heightened sense of presidential engagement: "The hint of a maneuver—of any kind and for any purpose—always brought a bright gleam of interest into Roosevelt's eyes. 'What's your idea?' he said."[127] When the president finally reached a decision, he was filled with childlike glee at launching a bombshell that would delight his supporters and disorient his enemies. Another adviser, Donald Richberg, suggests, "FDR did not claim to be an economist or a skilled lawyer. In fact, he would often listen patiently to the discussion of some question of economics or law and then, when the issue shifted to one of politics, he would interject with a sudden burst of energy: 'Now that's a question of politics and as to that I can claim to speak with authority.'"[128]

Richberg adds another insight which helps to explain both Roosevelt's decision making and his effectiveness as a political leader: "He had an extraordinary sense of what would influence public opinion. He had also a most exceptional ability to simplify issues for public statement. Part of this came from his habit, which was almost a necessity, of simplifying large issues for himself."[129]

The battle against the Depression was a multifront war, and Roosevelt felt politically protected because he could assert that the multiple programs of the New Deal had demonstrated that no one was forgotten by his benevolent administration. In his flexible and optimistic mind, compromise among competing forces was always possible. Deals could be negotiated between free traders and protectionists, budget balancers and big spenders, isolationists and internationalists, proponents of the New Nationalism and the New Freedom. Biographer Kenneth Davis argues that Roosevelt, in making his choices, "had a profound aversion to clear-cut irrevocable decisions and went to great lengths to avoid them, in his private as in his public life."[130] For Roosevelt, the less clear-cut the decision, the more opposing groups could be mollified.

Roosevelt could also be vindictive and irrational in his decision making. Though his vindictiveness was usually camouflaged by his conviviality, it was vividly displayed in his attempts to pack the Supreme Court in 1937 and to purge the Democratic party of anti–New Dealers in 1938. Roosevelt's irrationality was demonstrated by his growing belief that the economic recovery was being sabotaged by a big business conspiracy. From his perspective, he had saved business and the banks from ruin in 1933, and he was angered by the increasing opposition the business community and the banks were displaying by 1935. When the recession of 1937 began, Roosevelt and some of his leftist advisers interpreted it as a "capital strike" by selfish monopolists plotting to destroy the New Deal. Alan Brinkley writes, "He once went so far as to order the FBI (on the basis of an unsubstantiated letter from a hotel waiter in Chicago about a dinner table conversation among railroad executives he claimed to have overheard) to look into the possibility of criminal conspiracy. But Roosevelt never expressed such suspicions publicly."[131] This attitude relieved Roosevelt from any serious evaluations of whether his New Deal policies were hindering the recovery and also justified more antibusiness policies and rhetoric.

Was FDR mentally equipped to be a transformational leader? Burns and Dunn answer this question negatively: "He was as undisciplined intellectually as his followers were politically. . . . His judgments . . . were primarily instinctive rather than rational. . . . He was more of a broker of ideas than a creator of them, more a processor than an originator. Rather than organizing his goals and ideas into some priority order, in the mode of a transforming leader, he played by ear and boasted of it. He was following no set course, left, right, or center."[132]

This answer is overly negative. Although FDR was not guided by a grand design to construct a new regime, he was inspired by his belief in active government to bring about a more socially just system. Although his adherence to such traditional ideas as balancing the budget prevented him from exploiting the full potential of Keynesian economics, he was open to a number of new ideas that kept the New Deal on the offensive for over four years. What Roosevelt lacked in ideological zeal and consistency was compensated for by political skill and humanitarian concerns. He did think that farmers, workers, homeowners, and small investors were not being treated fairly under the old order and that new programs should be created to guarantee more secure lives for all Americans.

However, the evidence suggests that a more efficient decision-making system might have allowed Roosevelt to take advantage of the golden opportunities for regime change provided by the Depression. The weakness of his decision making was recognized by both supporters and opponents. In March 1935, Felix Frankfurter wrote a letter to Roosevelt complaining that "there isn't a lawyer in New York, with a sizable practice, who has not more dependable facilities and more systematic help in the preparation of the materials for his own action than has the President of the United States. . . . What I am talking about is provision for at least a fraction of the facilities available at 10 Downing Street."[133] In 1939, "Sam Rosenman had said that FDR still ran the United States as though it was the state of New York, wanting to do it on a personal contact basis—he had never really learned how to run his own office."[134] In a letter to Roosevelt in May 1934, Berle warned that "there are by actual count eighty-five administrators reporting directly to you. No man can do that and live. Make captains of tens and deal with eight."[135]

In December 1934, Walter Lippmann wrote in his column that it was ironic that New Dealers talked so much about planning when "the New

Deal never has had and does not now have any effective organ for planning its enormously ramified activities. It is focused on the mind of the president. It is surely beyond the capacity of any one mind to do all the planning, and experience has shown that in vital matters it has not been done."[136] The New Deal was too big and complex to be directed by the mind of Roosevelt alone, even if that mind may have been the most politically astute one in the twentieth century.

Conclusion

Studying six major advisers to FDR opens a window into the vast and complex enterprise of the New Deal. Each of these men brought strengths and weaknesses to his role. Raymond Moley was an excellent speechwriter who helped give Roosevelt's reconstructive vision verbal eloquence. Many of the political and policy goals of the New Deal were contained in his May 19, 1932, memo to Governor Roosevelt. Considering the variety of tasks he performed for FDR, he should have been offered a position in the White House, but that option was foreclosed by the jealousy of Louis Howe. Moley was doomed by his bureaucratic position under Cordell Hull and his attempts to impose policy consistency on the freewheeling Roosevelt. Rexford Tugwell helped Roosevelt understand the agriculture problem, but his outspoken commitment to national planning eventually made him a political liability. Adolf Berle gave Roosevelt a clearer picture of the structure of the corporate business world and how feelings of insecurity were causing the economy to persist in a downward spiral. Berle could envision social security, but his view of the growth potential of capitalism was stifled by the despair of the Depression.

Henry Morgenthau's vision combined fiscal orthodoxy with a strong social concern in public policy. Although not brilliant, Morgenthau offered his friend and neighbor loyal and diligent service. With an administration filled with policy makers anxious to spend billions to promote social justice, Roosevelt understood that it was necessary to have some advisers focusing on costs, and that was Morgenthau's role. For Morgenthau, fiscal irresponsibility threatened the viability of the New Deal Regime; fiscal responsibility would legitimize it.

Henry Wallace wanted to bring security to the farm sector by unifying farmers as a political force so that they could limit their production and raise prices for their products through a domestic allotment program. He believed that religion and science could be reconciled by American ingenuity to bring about balanced prosperity for both urban and rural areas.

In a pool of exceptionally bright advisers, Harry Hopkins emerged as the most successful because of his versatility, energy, loyalty, and administrative skills. After the frustrating inertia of the Hoover administration, Hopkins's ability to spend billions on work relief quickly served Roosevelt's political purposes. Hopkins was not able to convince Roosevelt to support his vision of a permanent federal program to guarantee publicly financed jobs for all those who could not find work in the private sector, but the president did demonstrate his confidence in Hopkins by assigning him important tasks during the 1930s and World War II.

Looking back on the advice Roosevelt received in the early 1930s from the perspective of the early twenty-first century, one is struck by the fact that none of his advisers foresaw the future accurately. Finding the keys to deal successfully with the Depression proved elusive. Hence, Roosevelt's strategy to never fully commit to one adviser, or to one school of thought, or to one policy, appears to be fairly rational.

6

Advising Reagan

By the time Ronald Reagan became president on January 20, 1981, the White House staff had changed significantly since the administration of Franklin Roosevelt. It had become larger, more specialized, and more bureaucratic, and it was usually under the central control of a chief of staff. These were trends that FDR would not have liked, but they reflected the rational responses of a series of chief executives who frequently felt overwhelmed by the pressures to provide political and policy leadership. Feeling under siege, both Democratic and Republican presidents responded by mobilizing resources under their direct control in the executive office of the president. The president's increasing reliance on the responsive competence of his White House staff, often recruited from the electoral campaign, meant that chief executives were relying less on their cabinet secretaries and the supposedly "neutrally competent" advice of departmental civil servants. The issue generated by this trend is whether the policies formulated by a more politicized and less expert set of advisers are effective in coping with major problems.

While the evolution of the White House had produced numerous changes, it did not alter the basic function of the advisory system, namely, how best to provide the president with the kind of information he needs to increase his chances for political success. The administrative challenge for each new president is still to recruit, structure, and interact with a set of advisers who will help him make decisions that will promote his political purposes. But because each person who occupies the Oval Office is different, there is no one best way to be president; some procedures have to be tailored to suit the personal needs of the new chief executive. The purpose of this chapter is to analyze how White House decision-making procedures were adapted to the needs of serving Ronald Reagan, an actor turned politician, whose rhetoric promised to end the liberal regime and create a conservative one.

The Reagan White House

To launch a successful presidency, Reagan's advisers believed they had to avoid the mistakes of the Carter administration. When Carter became president in 1977, he had set up a "spokes of the wheel" system in his White House and had eschewed using a chief of staff until the summer of 1979. Without the coordinating force of a chief of staff, the Carter administration lacked focus and often appeared to be in disarray. From the beginning, Carter overwhelmed Congress with legislation to deal with energy, welfare reform, government reorganization, tax stimulus, and tax reform. These multiple programs left Congress and the public unsure of what the strategic priorities of the Carter presidency were. Without central guidance, the administration was "characterized by vacillation, indecision, inconstancy, and confusion."[1]

In 1981, the Reagan White House (consisting of 350 people) and the executive office of the president (with about 1,700 people in ten agencies, including the Office of Management and Budget and the Council of Economic Advisers) would be about the same size as Carter's, but both White House staff and executive office agencies were run through the president's chief of staff. The need for a chief of staff reflected not only the negative experiences of the Carter years but the positive lessons of the Eisenhower administration. Reagan's advisers were aware of the trend for the White House staff to expand their influence at the expense of cabinet secretaries, but they initially hoped to restore the role of the cabinet in presidential decision making. The original plan, largely designed by Edwin Meese, was for the White House staff to serve both the president and his cabinet.[2]

Recognizing that Carter was never able to shake the negative reputation he acquired during his first six months in office, the new president's advisers were determined to define the administration's priorities, which were essentially Reagan's campaign promises, and to achieve early political success.

Their initial mantra was the need to hit the ground running, because "How we begin will significantly determine how we govern."[3] Although they believed that no president since Franklin Roosevelt had inherited a more difficult set of economic problems, this crisis also made it easier to focus on a legislative program to deal with the stagflation that had overwhelmed the Carter administration in its last two years. Reagan's advisers were determined to fortify his reputation by demonstrating his consistency, commitment, and resolve. While Carter had announced seven major economic programs in four years, Reagan and his planners foresaw the need for only one, albeit one with two goals: a supply-side tax cut to promote economic growth and a monetary policy to prevent inflation. In brief, Reagan would provide an image of steadfast leadership; he would not flip-flop like Carter did; he would set the right course to prosperity and would not deviate from it.

Like any president, Reagan had the kind of White House staff he wanted. It was composed of three types of advisers: conservatives, pragmatists, and practitioners in the field of public relations. (This categorization is not rigid; it does not mean that an adviser characterized as a conservative could not also have pragmatic inclinations.) Under Reagan, these three groups fought each other, but their conflicts were politically effective because each provided the president with vital services. The struggle among these staff members existed whether the White House was organized in the troika of the first administration or the more centralized system in the second. Among Reagan's advisers, conservatives were the most committed to regime change. These were also the most tightly knit group, bound together by ideology, by Adam Smith ties, and by an ideological commitment to Ronald Reagan. Conservatives such as Edwin Meese, William Clark, Martin Anderson, Edwin Harper, John Svahn, Gary Bauer, Jeane Kirkpatrick, and Peggy Noonan provided the energy and the ideological direction for the Reagan presidency. Their chief weakness was that they often lacked the federal government experience and the policy knowledge of their chief adversaries, the pragmatists, headed by James Baker. Consequently, although Reagan always kept a cluster of conservatives around him, he frequently selected pragmatists for the most important positions—especially the position of White House chief of staff. Nor were the conservatives as skilled as the pragmatists in the art of public relations, a fatal flaw in Reagan's highly image-conscious White House.

Conservatives oscillated between feelings of arrogant grandeur and despairing insecurity. At times they thought that their historical moment had come; they had put Reagan into the White House, and he would lead a revolution based on their eternal truths that would change the United States and the world. At other times they saw themselves as the helpless victims of a George Bush–James Baker cabal, aided by the liberal media, that was denying them the fruits of their victory by isolating and misinforming the president. Thus, the conservative James Watt, secretary of the interior, charged in 1983 that the pragmatists were not letting Reagan be Reagan. For conservatives, Reagan was not being his true self whenever he appointed a pragmatist to a key office (such as selecting George Shultz as secretary of state in 1982), signed a tax increase (in 1982, 1983, and 1984), transacted a legislative compromise with the Democrats (social security reform in 1983), or negotiated a diplomatic arrangement with Mikhail Gorbachev (the Intermediate Nuclear Force Treaty in 1987).

While the pragmatists and public relations experts argued that the Reagan administration had to accommodate to political realities, the conservatives advocated that the president should militantly pursue a broad range of economic, social, and foreign policy goals. It made no sense to hoard the president's popularity; it should be used to reverse the misguided policies that the United States had pursued since FDR's New Deal. Conservatives were convinced that the Great Communicator could circumvent Congress and the liberal media to mobilize an increasingly large majority (an electoral realignment) of the public to fulfill their agenda.[4] And they were in a hurry, especially after the nearly successful March 1981 assassination attempt. They thought that their views had been excluded and ridiculed (as Neanderthal) since the 1930s; they were more alienated and more anxious to change the America of the 1980s than were the pragmatists and, to their dismay, Reagan himself. The happy, accommodating Reagan agreed with the conservatives' dissatisfaction with the America of the 1980s, but he did not share their rage.

Movement conservatives' aspirations for a frontal assault on the liberal regime were often frustrated because they remained a minority within the administration; they could not attain allies, could not successfully manipulate the media, and could not enlist the full support of the president. Too many conservatives had a loyalty test (Were you with us in 1968 and especially in 1976?) that seemed to exclude potential allies. Conservative proposals and rhetoric were frequently untempered by concerns for political feasibility and public relations. In the second administration, Patrick Buchanan, the director of communications, strenuously objected to Donald Regan's aides' watering down Reagan's conservatism into what he called their "Constructive Republican Alternative Proposals (CRAP)." Buchanan conveyed what he thought about Deaver and public relations by labeling Deaver "Lord of the Chamber Pot." Buchanan satirized the spirit of compromise generated by the pragmatists and the public relations specialists by exclaiming, "Let's go up and compromise one for the Gipper."[5] Compromise outcomes were not considered victories by conservatives because they prolonged the existence of the liberal regime.

The conservative role and dilemma were best personified by the experiences of Edwin Meese. A dedicated conservative who served Governor Reagan in California as chief of staff in his second term and who played a major role in the 1980 campaign, Meese had expected to be named White House chief of staff. Instead, Michael Deaver, Stuart Spencer, and Nancy Reagan convinced Reagan that Meese lacked the organizational skill to run the White House. In Mrs. Reagan's eyes, Meese "was by far the most ideological member of the troika, a jump-off-the-cliff-with-the-flag-flying conservative. Some people are so rigid in their beliefs that they'd rather lose than win a partial victory, and I always felt that Meese was one of them."[6]

In the first Reagan administration, an original and innovative structure, the troika, was created in which Meese was named counselor to the president, James Baker was made chief of staff, and Michael Deaver was designated deputy chief of staff. During the transition, Meese and Baker negotiated an arrangement whereby the former was in charge of formulating policy and the latter handled operations. In their bargaining, Meese gained cabinet-level status for himself and control over the National Security Council (NSC) staff and the domestic policy staff. In February 1981, the president accepted Meese's recommendation to establish five cabinet councils: economic affairs, commerce and trade, human resources, natural resources, the environment, and food and agriculture. In 1982, two new councils were added: legal affairs and government management. By 1983, only three of these councils were meeting regularly. In the first term, according to Brownstein and Kirschten, "Only the economic affairs council met very frequently, and critics in the White House liked to gibe that councils held hundreds of meetings to reach only a handful of decisions."[7] When Donald Regan became chief of staff in 1985, he reduced the number of councils to two, economic policy and domestic policy.

Although Meese seemed to emerge with greater stature under these arrangements in 1981, Baker achieved control over the real levers of power. Because there is no clear demarcation between formulating and implementing policy, effective power usually shifts toward those with operational responsibility. According to Taylor Branch, "Baker had cheerfully given

Meese every position he wanted in return for one function: control of all the people and paper flowing to President Reagan. This secured Baker's position; in a bureaucracy like the White house, paper flow . . . is power, because it determines what the president knows about and therefore what he does."[8] Obviously, Baker's more sophisticated knowledge and experience in White House politics had helped him negotiate an arrangement that placed himself in a powerful position to reduce the influence of Meese in the first administration.

Meese's behavior also contributed to his limited role and diminished reputation. Although the lawyerly Meese was frequently designing organization charts, he was notoriously disorganized. Meese took on much more work than he could handle. A statement often heard in the White House—and repeated to the press—was that once Meese put a document in his bulging briefcase, it was lost forever. Whereas Baker's staff performed in a highly competent manner, Meese's top appointments—Richard Allen to be NSC adviser and Martin Anderson to head the Office of Policy Development—were generally considered "ineffectual," and both were quickly replaced.[9] Their poor performance, and especially Allen's involvement in a bribe scandal, reflected badly on Meese's judgment. One CEA official later wrote,

> As counselor to the president, Ed Meese was the most conspicuously
> mediocre man in American life. . . . Although he usually wore an Adam
> Smith tie, he confused Reaganomics with the interests of the last
> business group to visit his office, particularly if it was from California.
> Meese had a poor sense of priorities and was a terrible manager. He
> would often be speaking to some 4-H group at a time an important
> issue was being resolved. Memos would pile up on his in-box for
> months without being answered. His concept of management was
> to revise organization charts, issue executive orders, and arrange for
> presidential pep talks.[10]

According to Lou Cannon, Meese "idolized" Reagan and shared his ideas and optimism. But in serving as more of a cheerleader for the president than a counselor, Meese did not help Reagan or himself. Meese was often blamed when Reagan "garbled information or presented fantasies as facts." Cannon suggests, "Meese exaggerated Reagan's abilities as much as Darman and Stockman underrated them. In conversations with reporters and sometimes even with White House aides, he was given to rhapsodic appraisals that bordered on unintended parody." More seriously, Cannon charged, "The cabinet officers who struggled with Reagan to make him understand the realities of the deficit or the defense budget were infuriated by Meese's bland unwillingness to help them. By refusing to acknowledge that Reagan needed to be educated rather than exalted, Meese inevitably allowed moments crucial to the president's understanding to slip away from him."[11]

Meese's judgment came into question on a number of occasions. In August 1981, he failed to awaken Reagan and inform him that the U.S. Navy had shot down two Libyan planes. In January 1982, he talked Reagan into reversing a tax policy that had prohibited tax breaks for schools practicing segregation, a decision that caused an enormous amount of negative publicity and eventually had to be reversed. During the 1981–1982 recession, when hunger became an issue and the public relations staff was attempting to show how compassionate the president was, Meese suggested that some people went to soup kitchens voluntarily "because the food is free."[12] In the second administration, while serving as attorney general, Meese almost got himself indicted because of his involvement in the Wedtech scandal. No wonder Meese was known in the White House as a "roving mistake in search of a title."[13] In an administration dominated by public relations sensitivities, Meese was destined to experience trouble.

Nevertheless, there was never any public indication that Reagan was dissatisfied with Meese. Reagan demonstrated his support by appointing him attorney general and by accepting Meese's recommendations for the Supreme Court, including the ill-fated Robert Bork and Douglas Ginsburg. Meese resigned in the summer of 1988.

Whereas the conservatives were the most vociferous in proclaiming that Reagan was one of them, the pragmatists could point out that the president continually selected a pragmatist to head the White House as chief of staff: James Baker, Donald Regan,[14] Howard Baker, and Kenneth Duberstein. Each of these pragmatists helped Reagan focus on and achieve a limited number of strategic goals: the 1981 tax cut, the defense buildup, tax reform in 1986, the Intermediate Nuclear Force Treaty with the Soviet Union, and the election of George Bush in 1988. Although condemned by zealous conservatives for being philosophical spoilers, pragmatists claimed that their calculated finesse was largely responsible for the political successes of the Reagan presidency. The pragmatists also asserted that it was their restraining influence that may have prevented more loose-cannon types, exemplified by such conservative fanatics as John Poindexter and Oliver North, from causing lethal damage to the Reagan presidency. Moreover, the pragmatists stress that after the Iran-Contra scandal, when the administration was experiencing its greatest peril, Reagan turned to former Senator Howard Baker to help save his presidency. Reagan's selection of a pragmatist like Senator Baker, a villain to the right wing because of his support of the Panama Canal Treaty, indicated the president's understanding that he needed the kind of services pragmatists could provide.

Within Reagan's White House and administration, pragmatists supplied the Washington experience and the know-how to get things done. They understood that their lack of personal ties to Reagan left them vulnerable to attacks from movement conservatives and that they were frequently the ones who had to tell the president things he did not like to hear. The Reagan pragmatists were conservatives, but they were not engaged in a crusade; they were playing an endless game, the object of which was not all or nothing, but to win as often and as much as possible. They had played it before; it would go on whether they won or lost a particular phase. Compromise at the opportune moment was not forbidden; it demonstrated a sophisticated understanding of the political process. But by emphasizing their sophistication and their experience in previous administrations, they often enraged movement conservatives.

Conservatives believed that the pragmatists were too self-satisfied and were guilty of both overestimating their own abilities and underestimating Reagan's. Because pragmatists inferred that an unrestrained president would become his own worst enemy, they saw as their mission the need to "save Reagan from Reagan." Conservatives claimed that the positive use of the term *pragmatist* to describe their competitors reflected the liberal bias of both the media and academia. The conservative perspective on pragmatism was summarized by Dinesh D'Souza: "The problem with pragmatism as a philosophy, G. K. Chesterton once said, is that it doesn't work. The reason is that pragmatism supplies only the means, not the destination."[15] And the destination for conservatives was not high public approval ratings for Reagan or the passage of watered-down legislation; it was the creation of a full-fledged conservative regime.

Many pragmatists had experiences in the imperiled presidencies of Richard Nixon and Gerald Ford. From the outside, they had watched the burdens of the office overwhelm the Jimmy Carter presidency and reduce it to impotence and despair. They were determined to avoid the mistakes that had destroyed recent chief executives and to prove that the presidency, when skillfully managed, could be successfully run. These pragmatic attitudes were exemplified by James Baker and his chief assistant, Richard Darman.

In 1970, Texas Congress member George Bush asked his country club friend, James Baker, a successful corporate lawyer, to help run his Senate campaign. Bush lost that race to Lloyd Bentsen, but Baker discovered that politics was more exciting than corporate law. In 1975, Rogers Morton, secretary of commerce under President Ford, recruited Baker as an under-secretary. At Morton's suggestion, Ford chose Baker as his chief delegate hunter for the 1976 Republican party convention, and it was Baker who orchestrated Ford's narrow nomination victory over Governor Reagan. Ford was so impressed by Baker's skills that he named him chairman of his election campaign. In 1980, Baker ran the Bush campaign for the Republican nomination, which eventually placed the latter on the ticket with Reagan. Baker received the task of preparing Reagan for his debate with President Carter, and his successful performance of this job impressed Reagan, Mrs. Reagan, Michael Deaver, and Stuart Spencer. Hence, President-elect Reagan "opted for talent over ideology" in selecting Baker as his chief of staff, a decision that disappointed Meese and his conservative supporters.[16]

Richard Darman, who first worked for Baker in the Department of Commerce in 1975, believed that his boss was "ideally suited for coalition building." He described Baker as "an unusual combination of Princetonian and Texan [who] was both smooth and tough, moderate and conservative, broad-gauged and focused. He had a remarkable ability to earn people's confidence and respect almost immediately. And he used his, with skill and grace, to help people put away their lesser interests and find their way to constructive agreement."[17] The adeptness in achieving constructive agreements both within and outside an administration is certainly part of the job description for a chief of staff.

The locus for creating constructive agreements in the early years of the Reagan administration was not Meese's cabinet councils, but Baker's Legislative Strategy Group (LSG). The LSG was conceived by Darman and began meeting in late February to formulate strategy to advance Reagan's legislative program through Congress. It was chaired by Baker, and it met around a mahogany table located in his West Wing office. The other regular members were Meese (cochairman), Darman, who handled the paper flow, Donald Regan, secretary of the treasury, Kenneth Duberstein, assistant to the president for legislative affairs, Craig Fuller, assistant to the president for cabinet affairs, David Stockman, director of the Office of Management and Budget, Michael Deaver, deputy chief of staff, and David Gergen, assistant to the president for communications. The significance of the LSG was demonstrated by its various descriptions as the administration's Brains Trust, nerve center, and SWAT team.

The LSG became the most powerful unit in the administration for several reasons. First, because there are few issues that do not involve Congress, it was relatively easy for the LSG to expand its influence. Second, its small size and regular meetings meant that it could make rapid decisions. Third, as the president's program sailed through Congress in 1981, the LSG's political operations received rave reviews. Hedrick Smith reported, "In contrast to the Carter White House, Mr. Reagan's political team is widely praised as well-organized, purposeful, attentive and usually ahead of the Democrats in tactics."[18] Such positive evaluations helped elevate the status and power of Baker over Meese in the White House. However, Walter Isaacson pointed out in 1982, "What has made the LSG a lightning rod for the right is not its effectiveness in executing strategy but its success in moderating Reagan's policies."[19]

Baker assembled an excellent staff headed by Darman, and he quickly learned how to communicate with the president by using effective anecdotes to illustrate his points. In interviews with the press, Baker stressed that Reagan was the visionary leader, while his role as the "realist" was to advise the president as to what was politically feasible. As chief of staff, Baker was aware of the John Sears lesson (Sears was fired after the 1980 New Hampshire primary victory), which was that overestimating your own influence by underestimating Reagan's stubbornness and pushing too hard would backfire.[20] Baker let it be known that he was not in agreement with the entire Reagan program, but he was in charge of negotiating and implementing most of it. By advertising that he was not a fervent believer in the president's program, Baker was, in effect, announcing that he was a leader of a team that other moderate Republicans in the administration and in Congress, plus congressional Democrats, could do business with. Not being a true believer, Baker found it easier to forge compromises. Aided by Darman, Baker exhibited great skill at weaving coalitions across ideological lines. As a negotiator, he earned the respect of his opponents by demonstrating a detailed knowledge of their concerns and by being true to his word. He was not motivated by hate; nor did he deny the honor of those who held different positions. Baker believed that in the American game of politics, "only fools turn adversaries into enemies."[21] According to William Niskanen, a member of the CEA, Baker's political strategy was quite simple: "Do something for every element of your coalition. Don't alienate any group. Avoid policy proposals that might lose. Cut losses quickly. Focus on conditions between now and the next election."[22]

The fruits of Baker's negotiating labors included the 1981 budget and tax cuts, the Saudi arms sale in 1982, the tax increase in 1982, and especially the bipartisan social security compromise in 1983. However, Baker told a *Time* reporter in January 1985 that orchestrating Reagan's forty-nine-state victory in the 1984 election was his proudest accomplishment. Baker was as proud of his campaign triumph as James Farley was of his forty-six-state conquest in 1936.

But in engineering Reagan's electoral victory, Baker revealed both his skill and his prudence. "While he had few superiors in the craft of maneuver," according to Cannon, "his innate caution discouraged him from taking bold, strategic risks. . . . In 1984, it would prompt him to wage an almost issueless reelection campaign for Reagan and Bush."[23] Niskanen makes a similar point: "Maximizing votes . . . involves a different strategy than maximizing the president's policy agenda. . . . Baker would not risk the president's personal popularity for straight talk about the deficit, making the case for reform of social security and environmental legislation, stronger opposition to protectionist measures, or strengthening the Republicans in the House."[24] In brief, Baker placed a higher priority on achieving electoral victories and higher public approval ratings for Reagan than in taking higher risks to attain fundamentally conservative policy changes.

One of the factors that made Baker and Deaver natural allies was the former's skill in manipulating the press. As soon as Baker knew that he was going to be chief of staff, he began to cultivate the press by calling up journalists who had covered him in 1976 and during the 1980 campaign and letting them know that he would be available in the White House. Unlike Meese or Donald Regan, Baker understood that media relations is a necessary game of give-and-take. He always made sure that reporters came away from a Baker interview with juicy tidbits, even if they could not be attributed to Baker. He planted the image of Meese as "poppin' fresh — the Pillsbury doughboy," which helped undercut Meese's authority. When Baker wanted to change the president's mind about an issue, he might have an aide leak the notion that friends of Reagan feared he was hurting himself by being too rigid. Thus, the stage would be set for Baker, Deaver, and Mrs. Reagan to work on the president to change his mind on a particular issue and demonstrate his flexibility. Mrs. Reagan thought that Baker "was more inclined than Ronnie to compromise and make deals, but he was loyal, and he was certainly effective in helping get Ronnie's programs through Congress. He also cultivated the press assiduously—perhaps too much, because he leaked constantly."[25] In 1982, one reporter estimated that Baker saw twice as many newspeople as Deaver and Meese combined and that "many regular correspondents are agreed that Baker is the most adroit leaker in the White House."[26]

Perhaps the most adroit Machiavellian in the White House was Baker's assistant, Richard Darman. From the conservative point of view, Darman's background was as suspect as Baker's. The thirty-seven-year-old Darman was a Harvard MBA who had served under the moderate Republican, Elliot Richardson, in four cabinet departments in the Nixon and Ford administrations. As a mentor, "Richardson . . . taught Darman that running an organization meant developing the big ideas, make the decisions, mastering the details—nothing less than intellectual domination."[27] Within the White House, Darman quickly gained the reputation of being sharp-witted and sharp-elbowed.

Darman's memoirs reveal that he had different expectations for the Reagan presidency than conservatives did. While conservatives anticipated that Reagan would fulfill his visions, Darman thought that Reagan, reflecting both his years as president of the Screen Actors Guild and his adaptation to the American systems of checks and balances, would work toward promoting much-needed, moderately conservative reforms. In Darman's words, "On the basis of Reagan's record . . . , it seemed to me that, though he might talk like an ideologue, he might govern with a reasonable degree of moderation." Instead of a Reagan Revolution, Darman "saw the Reagan phenomenon as a potentially useful corrective" to the problems that had mounted during the 1970s. Darman hoped that the "Reagan presidency could reasonably be expected to produce: a healthier and more market-oriented economy, a stronger America in a still-dangerous world, and a renewed sense of national confidence. But, like a majority of other Americans who had voted for Reagan, I did not actually expect a hard-right revolution. Further, I had some doubts whether the incoming Reaganauts would even be able to get effective hold of government. . . . And it was unclear to me whether they had a working understanding of the governing culture for which their rhetoric had shown contempt. I suspected they did not."[28] Obviously, Darman and the conservatives were on a collision course.

Darman worked hard to induce the administration to follow his style of politics. He forged an alliance with Deaver and became a member of his communications strategy group. Darman became more knowledgeable about the wide array of issues facing the administration than any of

Reagan's advisers. A *New York Times* reporter, Frances X. Clines, called Darman "one of the Administration's most durable strategists and its unofficial Minister of Words in the Realpolitik of compromise." Clines suggested that Darman's "basic technique" was, "He tackles a problem first by mastering its special glossary, word by word, book by book. 'I've always tried to get myself to a position where, if possible, I could get to know as much or more than anyone else in the room on whatever was the issue of substance,' [Darman] says."[29] Darman described the role of the pragmatists on the LSG in these words: "As a group we were generally thought to have skills in the management of legislative strategy, public affairs, and policy development. Inevitably, we found ourselves managing the processes of compromise."[30]

Darman's role within the administration was reflected in several memos he wrote for a planning meeting at Camp David in February 1982. He alerted senior members of the White House that the legislative outlook for 1982 was not as promising as it had been the year before. The president's honeymoon was over; the Democrats still controlled the House; and the economy was in a recession, which was rejuvenating the opposition. Darman predicted that the administration would have to settle for fewer victories and more compromises in the 1982 legislative session. But Darman reminded his colleagues that there had been plenty of behind-the-scenes compromises in 1981: "In this regard, however, one should perhaps note that our big victories last year involved very substantial, though largely unnoticed compromises."[31]

In a second memo, Darman warned the senior staff about a potential vulnerability of the Reagan presidency, namely "The fairness issue." He recommended they develop a strategy "to counter the trend toward characterization of this administration as pro-rich, pro-bigness, do-nothing-for-the-little-guy, etc." Darman argued that these accusations might alienate "constituent groups whose support a Reagan administration ought to be consolidating, not losing: white ethnics, small businessmen, rural populists."[32] In short, Darman's political sensitivities would exert pressure to soften the sharp edges of Reagan's conservative policies.

But just when the Baker-Darman-Deaver axis appeared to achieve hegemony in the White House, Reagan proved that he was the chief executive who would make the final decision. In late 1983, Baker and Deaver negotiated an arrangement whereby Baker would replace William Clark as national security adviser, and Deaver would become chief of staff. However, the leading conservatives in the administration—Edwin Meese, William

Casey, William Clark, and Caspar Weinberger—were able to meet with the president and reverse the decision.[33] The conservatives hoped to place Jeanne Kirkpatrick in the NSC position, but Secretary of State George Shultz objected, and Robert McFarlane was selected.

The third faction in the Reagan White House was made up of those skilled in the art of public relations. Led by Michael Deaver, David Gergen, Larry Speakes, Richard Wirthlin, Richard Beal, and Roger Ailes, these people knew how to use Reagan's acting skills to maintain his popularity. The public relations practitioners used their expertise to make Reagan look good. They generally knew when and how to make him appear tough or compassionate, proud or humble, involved or uninvolved. Although Reagan started off in January 1981 with a comparatively low public approval rating of about 50 percent, which dipped to the mid-30s during the 1981–1982 recession and after the Iran-Contra scandal in late 1986, the president was far more popular than any Democrat, as evidenced by the 1984 landslide, and he finished his second term with a 65 percent approval rating. The least controversial aspect of the Reagan presidency is how effectively it utilized public relations.

There is a natural inclination to view public relations as a subordinate, tactical function in the White House. But one of the keys to interpreting the Reagan presidency is understanding that public relations was a strategic factor; it probably influenced more decisions than any other element in the administration. Reagan's public relations and pragmatic advisers agreed that recent history demonstrated that political success was dependent on the president's maintaining high public approval ratings. It is worth stressing that Reagan (and Mrs. Reagan) felt closer to Deaver, his public relations specialist, than to any of his policy advisers. One former Reagan aide was quoted as saying, "It was a Deaverized White House. . . . Everything was public relations. . . . Public relations was the reality."[34] Similarly, Larry Speakes, Reagan's deputy press secretary said, "Almost everything we do is still determined by whether we think it will get on the network news shows in the evening."[35]

All presidencies attempt to manage the news in order to influence public opinion, but the Reagan administration proved to be exceptionally successful at this. Whereas Kennedy had an attractive personality and the Nixon administration had sophisticated public relations techniques, Reagan had both. Reagan's media advisers had witnessed the debilitating consequences of the credibility gap in the Johnson and Nixon presidencies and the inept use of communication methods in the Ford and Carter administrations.

They felt that the chronic dilemma of the contemporary presidency is that its performance cannot match the public's expectations. The public confuses the president's prominence in the media with the president's power to resolve problems. Reagan's media advisers responded to this problem by developing methods that could satisfy many of the public's expectations symbolically rather than substantively. They also believed that the president could not lead the country if he could not communicate with it. In Mark Hertsgaard's words, "Both Deaver and Gergen recognized that to engineer mass consent in the modern media age, the government had to be able to present its version of reality to the public over and over again. Neutralizing the press, by limiting journalists' ability to report politically damaging stories, was necessary but not sufficient. The press had to be turned into a positive instrument of governance, a reliable and essentially non-intrusive transmitter of what the White House wanted the public to know."[36]

The public relations tactics used by the Reagan presidency included severely reducing the number of regular press conferences; presenting well-planned, coordinated themes of the day and/or week to repeatedly convey the president's message to the public; prepackaging attractive visuals; having members of the administration speak as one; and stage-managing Reagan's speeches to take advantage of his communication skills. This last strategy utilized Reagan's ability as an actor while camouflaging his lack of knowledge regarding policy.[37]

In Reagan's first administration, the man in charge of packaging the president was Michael Deaver. He first joined Reagan's team in California in 1967. When Governor Reagan's chief of staff, William Clark, was being driven crazy by phone calls from Mrs. Reagan, he assigned the task of responding to her requests to Deaver. Ironically, Deaver's relationship with Mrs. Reagan became his "ultimate chip" in the struggle for Reagan's mind. Whereas Deaver possessed the professional skills to be the choreographer in chief, Mrs. Reagan was "the supreme authority on her husband's needs as a performer."[38] Together, they saw the president more often than anyone else did; they became a team dedicated to Reagan's feeling comfortable and looking good in the eyes of the public. This meant that he could not be overworked; his public appearances had to be carefully orchestrated. Deaver and Mrs. Reagan believed that they had to compensate for Reagan's weaknesses by protecting him. For Mrs. Reagan, this guardian role became more manifest after the March 1981 assassination attempt. In her words, "I now understood that each day was a gift to be treasured, and that I had to be more involved in seeing that my husband was protected in every possible way."[39] While the failed assassination made the conservatives anxious to move ahead more quickly with their agenda to create a new regime, it made Mrs. Reagan more concerned about safeguarding her husband. A clash in priorities was inevitable.

Deaver and Mrs. Reagan felt that the president was sometimes ideologically rigid, naive, overly trusting of his subordinates, and too reluctant to fire anyone. They lobbied the president to soften his stance toward the Soviet Union, to slow down the increase in military spending, to pursue a diplomatic solution in Nicaragua, to cancel his trip to Bitburg, and to fire Edwin Meese, Raymond Donovan, William Clark, Helene Von Damm, Richard Allen, William Casey, and Donald Regan.[40] This is not to say that Reagan always agreed with their recommendations, nor does it imply that Mrs. Reagan and Deaver were closet liberals; but it does suggest the parallel interests of the pragmatists and the public relations specialists at the expense of the conservatives.

Deaver and Mrs. Reagan saw their role as protecting the popularity of Reagan from the sharp edges of his rhetoric and his conservative advisers. Deaver would explain to Mrs. Reagan that Richard Wirthlin's polls provided survey evidence that the president's performance ratings rose when the public saw him and Congress working together to resolve problems. Such cooperation was threatened by hard-line presidential speeches. Mrs. Reagan accepted this reasoning. A close friend of the Reagans was quoted as saying, "She was the force to say, 'This is too strident, this is too difficult for people to follow; it's politically not doable. . . . ' She often feels that many of these people are out to hurt the President, they're only in there for themselves. . . . When her own antennae go up, and she spots somebody trying to use Ronald Reagan for the benefit of his own philosophy, she'll fight like a tiger."[41] In brief, Mrs. Reagan was extremely sensitive about anyone's exploiting Reagan's popularity, an attitude that made her deeply suspicious of conservatives who were constantly exhorting the president to take bigger risks for their causes.

In response, conservatives argued that by trying to make Reagan look good and flexible, Deaver and Mrs. Reagan made him appear weak and malleable. By constraining his conservative instincts and isolating him from his conservative advisers, they were not allowing him to be the great president he was capable of being. The Hollywood-inspired feel-good type of conservatism advocated by the public relations people meant that presidential resources were used more to keep Reagan's ratings up than to implement the conservatives' policy agenda. Thus, Reagan did not steadfastly and unyieldingly press to balance the budget, end abortion, allow prayer in the classroom, and defeat communism in Central America and Cuba, as the hard-line conservatives wanted him to do.

The conflict among conservatives, pragmatists, and public relations practitioners caused pain and frustration for each group, but it caused Reagan minimal grief. Finding the squabbling among these groups unpleasant to contemplate, he typically denied its existence.[42] More importantly, the interaction among the three types of staff members provided Reagan with a blend of administrative capabilities that proved functional for Reagan's presidency. Thus, Reagan was able to appear to be a conviction politician, achieve a limited number of domestic and foreign policy goals, and maintain a fairly high approval rating. However, little of the liberal regime was destroyed.

Ronald Reagan's Decision-Making Style

Ronald Reagan's decision-making procedures, like FDR's, resonated positively with the American people. After the alleged flip-flopping of President Jimmy Carter, many citizens were pleased that Reagan had definite plans to deal with stagflation and foreign policy problems. What made Reagan's decision making appealing to the public was not how hard he worked, but how honestly committed he was to his conservative principles. Reagan was not a poll-driven politician; he was motivated by his convictions.

As a president practicing the politics of reconstruction, Ronald Reagan had one major advantage over Roosevelt—he had a clear-cut vision of his goals. Although it was difficult to summarize the New Deal in a sentence, the essence of the Reagan Revolution was to reduce the powers of the federal government, cut tax rates, promote patriotism and family values, and build up the military. Simplicity is compatible with focus. Reagan understood the importance of having a vision and articulating it in a consistent and eloquent manner. His challenge as a reconstruction leader was defined by Lou Cannon: "Reagan had goals, but no programs. He had ideas, without a practical conception of how to translate them into reality. He did not know how government functioned or the process by which it reached its objectives."[43] But this lack of knowledge was not an insurmountable problem for Reagan; he was happy to accept the help of both conservatives and pragmatists on his staff who knew how to build a more right-of-center America.

As with Roosevelt, Reagan's most important personality trait was his optimism. Cannon suggests, "Rexford Tugwell's description of Franklin Roosevelt as 'a man with fewer doubts than anyone I have ever known' is also a perfect description of Reagan. His optimism was unquenchable."[44] As an optimist, Reagan was prone to believe that there was a solution— usually a simple one—to any problem. As an ideologue, he was likely to assume that the solution was compatible with his conservatism. Reagan was optimistic about America, markets, religion, heroes, and the military; he was pessimistic about the federal government's ability to resolve problems. He had faith in his instincts and in his staff and therefore thought that there was no need to search for facts or agonize over alternative solutions. In his worldview, good intentions led to good results, and Reagan believed his intentions were governed by the highest morals. He was not likely to second-guess himself. This perspective was protected by his ability to screen out from his consciousness discordant facts that did not confirm his ideological expectations. Given the way his mind worked, Reagan was incapable of experiencing cognitive dissonance. When you don't experience cognitive dissonance, it impedes your capacity to learn. What you "know" is always confirmed; it is never challenged.

Reagan's serenity was bolstered by his religious beliefs. His life seemed to confirm his mother's religious faith that God has a positive plan for each of us. Like Voltaire's Candide, Reagan expected things to work out for the best, which helped him to be happy and self-confident. Because of his optimism, conservative ideology, and religious beliefs, the burdens of presidential decision making were rather light for Reagan.

Reagan was a conviction politician. Even those who ridiculed Reagan's convictions often conceded that they were honestly held. His beliefs were derived not from books but from his life experiences and from his mythical perceptions of American history. In Reagan's mind, "we the people" of the United States had discovered long ago the right values and correct answers to all the big questions. The eternal truths of individual liberty and limited government had been verified by our nation's history. Because these values were both morally correct and proven in their practical application, they could not be legitimately challenged, and no one could be more stubborn in their defense than Reagan. The contemporary problems of the nation were due to our having been seduced off the righteous path by leftist liberals who had overtaxed and overregulated the nation's citizens. The obvious solution was to return to the traditional values that had served us so well. Perhaps only those who combine a lack of historical knowledge with a strong commitment to a particular ideology can believe that the verities of history fully support their philosophical beliefs. In short, Reagan believed he knew how the world worked.

Because there were only a few simple truths and Reagan already knew them, he felt no need to engage in any rigorous intellectual activity. By avoiding details, Reagan could maintain his convictions and never have to confront the contradictions among them. He responded to charges that he was lazy by quipping, "It's true hard work probably never killed anybody, but I figure why take the chance." Most of the president's aides learned that he thought anecdotally, not analytically. For example, David Stockman, his budget director, wrote, "I soon learned that it made less sense to tell him that you were eligible for a 35-cents-a-meal lunch subsidy if your income was above 190% of the poverty line than to tell him, 'The kids of cabinet officers qualify.' He was not surprised by these revelations; they conformed to his *a priori* understanding of what outrages the federal government was capable of perpetrating."[45]

Reagan's photographic mind meant that he easily memorized the speeches written for him. In addition, he had inherited his father's ability to tell stories and to interject quips that could substitute for — and conceal — a lack of substantive knowledge. He was content to see the big picture, to point out the right direction, and leave the details to his subordinates. The explanation that the president was not a detail man became a mantra for Reaganites and implied that possessing detailed information was only for smaller minds and Jimmy Carter. In Meese's words, "Reagan, in contrast to Carter, was a big picture man. . . . Reagan did not immerse himself in details, but he had a true vision of what he wanted to accomplish, and how the various components of his policy fit together. It enabled him to govern with certainty and consistency."[46]

Reagan's intellectual passivity was legendary among those who knew him. Lou Cannon, who perhaps knew him best, wrote, "As a young man, he had failed to form the useful habit of subjecting his dearest assumptions to intellectual examination. In some respects, he was a prisoner of his gifts. He remembered what he had read without effort, which tempted him to regurgitate information and anecdotes rather than reflect upon ideas. His intuition was so sound that he relied on it too heavily, letting it lead him down paths where intuition should not go alone. Most of the time, President Reagan was intuitively keen but intellectually lazy."[47] A member of Reagan's staff told two journalists that, "Ronald Reagan is not a stupid person . . . but he was the least curious person that I have ever met."[48] But the most perceptive observation was made by David Broder: "Reagan, as everyone must know by now, is the living refutation of Frances Bacon's aphorism that 'knowledge is power.' He knows what he thinks and has the power of his own beliefs. But he treats knowledge as if it were dangerous to his convictions. Often it is."[49] Obviously, Reagan's success could not be attributed to Richard Neustadt's recommendation that a president should be his own political intelligence adviser, tenaciously seeking information that will give the necessary advantage in bargaining situations.

The chief organizational problem in managing the Reagan administration was conceptualized by Bert Rockman: "How can organizational structures, systems, and strategies be developed for a committed [to major policy changes] presidency and a detached president?"[50] The solution was to stress the president's public role, an orientation that enhanced the functions of the public relations staff. Reagan was more interested in presenting his policy proposal than in creating it. As a performer, he was delighted to use the bully pulpit; he believed in his message and never became bored with repeating it. Delivering inspiring speeches was what he felt he was born to do; presiding over meetings with bickering advisers was not comfortable for him. In 1984, Steven Weisman reported, "White House aides estimate that he spends 80 percent of his time selling programs and only 20 percent of his time actually shaping them."[51] As an actor, Reagan was uniquely capable of exploiting media trends both in the election campaigns and in governing. Whereas a president more knowledgeable about policy and more personally involved with the nitty-gritty details of resolving problems would have recognized the limitations of public relations activities, no one believed the illusion of public relations more readily than Reagan did. His principal role-relevant experience had been in Hollywood, where he had seen John Wayne become a war hero even though Wayne had never been in the military. In Reagan's mind, illusion created reality.

As is true of any president, there was a great deal of analysis and debate about Reagan's decision-making procedures. Liberals were upset that Reagan's disregard of facts was often treated as an enchanting idiosyncrasy. In 1986, presidential scholar James David Barber wrote, "Reagan's criterion of validity is theatrical rather than empirical."[52] Walter Williams angrily stressed, "His leadership and style of governance rested on unshakable principles, extreme optimism, hands-off management, and indifference to details, and it had no place for vigorous analysis that might challenge ideology."[53] Sidney Blumenthal believed that for Reagan, "facts don't determine the case; they don't make his beliefs true. Rather, his beliefs give life to the facts, which are tailored to have a moral. . . . He asks listeners to trust the tale, not necessarily the detail. If the facts belie his premises, then the facts are at fault."[54] Historian Lewis Gould added, "For [Reagan], the truth of an episode or illustration mattered less than its capacity to sway an audience. Much as a screenwriter 'adapted' a nonfiction story to be more compelling on screen, Reagan used tales of welfare queens or racial integration in place of policy analysis. While critics might point out a resulting inaccuracy, an untouched Reagan had moved on to another speech and another story."[55] While liberals complained that Reagan's decisions were based on myths and illusions, conservatives claimed they were derived from philosophical truths.

Those who were closer to Reagan, while stressing their affection for the man and admiration for his communication talents, nevertheless also paint an unflattering picture of his decision-making skills. When members of his staff were interviewed, they never claimed he was analytical, curious, or well-informed. Richard Reeves cites Donald Regan, the president's second chief of staff, as claiming, "Everyone there [the White House] thought he was smarter than the President."[56] "His mind was a trove of facts and anecdotes," Donald Regan wrote, "something like the morgue of one of his favorite magazines, *Readers' Digest*, and it was impossible to guess when or why he might access any one of these millions of bytes of data."[57] Secretary of State George Shultz provides two illustrations that reflect Reagan's carelessness with facts:

> On occasion I would try to correct the inaccurate chronology of a favorite story about something he had done earlier in his presidency. When he told me how the release of the Russian Pentecostals was linked to his subsequent lifting of the grain embargo against the Soviets imposed by Jimmy Carter, I pointed out that he had lifted that embargo shortly after taking office, over two years before the Soviets allowed the Pentecostals to emigrate. He nodded in agreement and kept right on telling the same story. More importantly, no matter how often I pointed out to him that he had indeed traded arms for hostages in the Iran-Contra affairs, he found that almost impossible to accept.[58]

In his biography of Reagan, Edmund Morris suggests a similar problem, namely, the rigidity of his views. "Once he made an emotional commitment to this or that policy or story, no amount of disproof would cause him to alter his belief in it. Exhaustive research by Scripps-Howard reporters in the late Fifties had established that one of his favorite Lenin quotes (The way to conquer capitalism is to debauch the currency) had actually been fabricated by John Maynard Keynes. Reagan stood corrected, but also stood by the quote, to the ultimate exasperation of Mikhail Gorbachev."[59]

As part of the conservative movement, Reagan had no problem being skeptical of experts. From his perspective, liberal experts had brought the nation to the verge of ruin in both domestic and foreign policy. He was especially dubious of economists and their propensity to make faulty predictions. Peggy Noonan quotes him as saying, "I majored in economics in college. And believe me, those fellows have a Phi Beta Kappa key on the end of their watch chains, and no watch! . . . The profession isn't up to the problems it has to analyze."[60] It should be noted that no economist entered his innermost circle of advisers despite the centrality of economic policy in Reagan's program. Cannon concludes, "Reagan had both the courage and the ignorance to ignore the collective wisdom of his experts and follow his own counsel when he was convinced he was on the right course."[61] And Reagan almost always felt he was following the right course.

Reagan may have resisted changing his mind, but he was able to accept compromise and to agree on policy changes. To prepare him for compromise, the pragmatists and the public relation experts on his staff, sometimes in cooperation with Mrs. Reagan, would subject the president to what they called "reality therapy." Republican congressional leaders would meet with Reagan and urge him to be more flexible in order to further his conservative agenda. According to Cannon, "He was enough of a true believer to demand consistency in himself, a trait that encouraged aides to invent arguments to persuade him that proposals in conflict with his advocacies actually advanced them. Thus, the Tax Equity and Fiscal Responsibility Act of 1982, a tax increase by any other name, became 'tax reform' in order to satisfy Reagan's self-imposed requirement of consistency."[62]

Reagan's staff understood that it was possible to change Reagan's mind by convincing him that he was not changing his mind. In Steven Weisman's words, "Their time-tested technique is to persuade the President that he is not reversing course even if that is precisely what they want him to do. Mr. Reagan truly does not believe that he changed policies significantly when he accepted a tax increase in late 1982, or when he dropped his efforts to delay construction of a natural gas pipeline from Siberia to Europe, or when he decided to withdraw American troops from Lebanon."[63] This subterfuge opened up Reagan to the charge that he was manipulated by his more moderate staff. But I believe that this aspect of Reagan's decision making helped him maintain his reputation as a conviction politician while providing the flexibility essential to making the compromises necessary for political success.

Those who worked under Reagan expressed astonishment at his passive administrative style. The president's secretary wrote, "He was never the initiator. He never even asked me to get Mac Baldridge or Bill Casey on the phone just because he hadn't heard from them in a while. He would make decisions as they were presented to him."[64] David Stockman recalled pre-inauguration meetings with Reagan: "We had a few informal sessions with the President-elect, during which he simply listened, nodded, and smiled. 'We have a great task ahead of us,' he would say, but he never finished the sentence. He gave no orders, no commands, asked for no information, expressed no urgency. That was startling to me."[65] Like the actor he had been, he was willing to have his schedule, movement, and speeches meticulously scripted. Larry Speakes, his press secretary, later wrote, "In a way Reagan belittled his own capacity as President. Where his schedule was concerned, Reagan should have asked, 'Why am I seeing all of these people?' Instead, he said, 'Each morning I get a piece of paper that tells me what I do all day long.'"[66]

Donald Regan was also surprised. As secretary of the treasury during the first administration, Regan was befuddled that the president never met with him privately to explain what goals he expected to accomplish. Because Regan was accustomed to management by objective—a method in which officials have in writing what is expected of them—he wondered how one could accomplish a task if this task was not defined. What Regan finally figured out was that as a member of the Reagan administration, one did not receive specific instructions from the president; instead, one had to read Reagan's speeches for policy guidelines. In Regan's words, "The President seemed to believe that his public statements were all the guidance his private advisers required. Ronald Reagan's promises *were* his policy. To him, in his extreme simplicity of character and belief, this was obvious. . . . Once I had grasped that principle, I understood that I was free to interpret his words and implement his intentions in my field of policy and action according to my best judgment."[67] The effect of Reagan's passive administrative style was to encourage subordinates to seek solutions of their own.

Reagan's ideas attracted the support of a number of talented people, and his administrative style encouraged them to work for his causes. There is no indication that Reagan's passive administrative style (laziness?) caused his subordinates to work less hard; on the contrary, it probably caused them to work harder. Terrel Bell, Reagan's first secretary of education, emphasizes how diligently he labored because he knew that conservatives like Meese were planning to eliminate his department. Bell suggests that Reagan "worked us hard so he could do his job and still be relaxed. . . . He had a laid-back style, but this did not mean he was not effective. Indeed, it enabled him to be effective."[68] The consequences of Reagan's management style are also implied in Stockman's words: "He [Reagan] conveyed the impression that since we all knew what needed to be done, we should simply get on with the job. Since I *did* know what to do, I took his quiet message of confidence to be a mandate. If the others weren't going to get his administration's act together, I would."[69] And no one toiled more zealously in 1981 to fulfill the conservative objectives of the Reagan administration than David Stockman. Reagan's detached style encouraged officials to take initiatives, to pick up the ball and run with it.

Reagan's administrative procedures induced the contending White House factions to fight one another rather than pressure the president. The competition for Reagan's approval was tough because the winners received a relatively free hand to make decisions in certain policy areas. Each group accused the other of "using" the president by taking advantage of his trusting disposition and his inattention to detail. What was often overlooked was how the competing staff groups were serving Reagan's interests. Whereas the hands-on management style of Carter resulted in his being blamed for much of what went wrong in his administration, Reagan seldom suffered for mistakes or controversial decisions made on his behalf. Aided by the Deaverized White House, blame was deflected to Stockman for cruel budget cuts, to Weinberger for the skyrocketing defense budget, and to James Watt for the lack of concern over the environment. Reagan's management style provided him with the ultimate plausible denial. It also minimized the need for Reagan to take sides in the conflicts among his staff, while it maximized the stakes in the struggles among the three groups.

Thus, Reagan's presidency oscillated between pragmatism and ideological purity, without suffering the negative consequences of flip-flopping as Carter's did. Although Reagan reversed himself on taxes, Panama, Taiwan, Lebanon, and the Soviet Union, he was able to maintain his image as a conviction politician. Reagan's staff provided him the opportunity to pursue conservative objectives by pragmatic skills and means. Frances Clines suggests that the "basic dynamic of the Reagan Administration" was to have pragmatists such as James Baker make the necessary "accommodations on a pressing issue while the President accepts them privately and continues a tougher grade of public rhetoric."[70]

While Reagan was a successful governor and president, there were serious flaws in his process of decision making. His reliance on 1-page memos, originally created by William Clark for Governor Reagan, which were composed of four paragraphs outlining the problem, providing basic facts, listing the options, and recommending a course of action, was a woefully inadequate way to deal with the complex issues a chief executive has to confront.[71] Even more importantly, the combination of Reagan's optimism and lack of attention to detail meant that he had no true way of measuring whether his policies were working. Because he saw no need for it, there was no reality testing. Reagan had an almost infinite capacity to live contentedly within his myth-dominated world. According to one of his aides, "You have to be careful with him. If you had nine bad items to tell him and one good one, he would latch on to the tenth favorable item and discount the other nine. The blind spots are very troubling."[72] According to Bruce Schulman, another staff aide "recalled the president's views on the [budget] deficit going through three stages: one, they won't occur; two, they'll be temporary; three, when they stick they serve a good purpose—they keep the liberals from creating new spending programs."[73] In Reagan's mind, unpleasant facts could be avoided; contradiction could be denied; anecdotes could overcome facts; movie illusions could substitute for history; unpleasant realities could be blamed on a hostile press. The simple truths that made Reagan a conviction politician could blind him to the facts that his tax cuts were not leading to balanced budgets, that the deregulation of the savings and loan industry was leading to a fiscal catastrophe, and that he was trading arms for hostages in the Middle East.

One of Reagan's favorite aphorisms was that he wanted his aides to provide solutions, not problems. This expectation, a function of his optimistic nature, is useful in explaining the major breakdown of Reagan's decision making in the Iran-Contra affair. In this case, most of the advice he received from the Departments of State and Defense concerned how difficult it would be to gain the release of the hostages. However, William Casey, Robert McFarlane, John Poindexter, and Oliver North provided a "solution" that appealed to the compassionate and staunchly anticommunist president. Their "neat idea" would free the hostages, forge a new strategic tie with moderates in Iran, and circumvent congressional prohibitions on aiding the Contras to overthrow the Sandinistas in Nicaragua. When Shultz and Weinberger criticized the pitfalls in this policy, Reagan allowed the locus of this decision making to become more secretive and continued the scheme until it self-destructed in late 1986.[74]

Was Reagan's decision-making style compatible with being a reconstruction president? Peggy Noonan answers this question negatively. From her perspective, Reagan was not a revolutionary because new ideas did not appeal to him; he was attracted to old-fashioned ones. When Reagan cited, as he often did, Tom Paine's liberal line that the United States had the opportunity to remake the world, Noonan claims that he did not mean it. (I think he did.) In her words, Reagan "was, in many ways, a pragmatist in full-throated pursuit of that least romantic of goals, the practical solution. He was temperamentally unsuited to a revolution. He believed in negotiation and compromise; he was inclined to split the difference."[75] Such a compromising attitude was not likely to destroy entrenched components of the liberal regime like social security, Medicare, or the Tennessee Valley Authority, but it certainly had the ability to remake the liberal regime into a more conservative one.

Cannon compares Reagan with FDR and claims that they shared strong convictions, a sense of direction, a lack of analytical skills, and an interest in "results rather than economic tidiness." However, the paradoxes of Reagan's decision making appear greater than Roosevelt's. Reagan, according to Cannon, "was at once the most malleable and least movable of men" while being "guided both by extraordinary vision and by remarkable ignorance."[76] Hence, Reagan's decision making had the potential for both big success and big failure.

Conclusion

Neither FDR nor Reagan felt overwhelmed by the burdens of being reconstruction presidents. They were both confident in their abilities as decision makers and skeptical of the prevailing wisdom, and thus both were prepared to make the choices necessary to repudiate the old regime and create a new one. Roosevelt and Reagan were comfortable with the paradox of American reform—namely, the successful reformer has to legitimate new ideas by proving how compatible they are with the traditional values of the American political culture. The religious beliefs of Roosevelt and Reagan played a dual role for these reconstructive presidents: they reassured the public of the moral commitments of these presidents' administrations; and they were politically advantageous in that they helped each president operate from the moral high ground in attacking the old regime and constructing the new one.

The Depression presented a greater array of problems and opportunities for Roosevelt than the malaise at the end of the 1970s did for Reagan. For Roosevelt, a liberal activist federal government was the solution; for Reagan, a liberal activist federal government was the problem. In performing the reconstructive role, Reagan, being more of a conviction president than was Roosevelt, had the advantage of possessing a clearer vision of the regime he wanted to create. Roosevelt had the benefit of being more skillful in the art of politics; he knew how to get things done. Roosevelt understood and was comfortable with the idea that under his administration, politics usually trumped ideology. Reagan, uninterested in how things got done, unknowingly allowed his pragmatic staff to dilute his conservative visions. While FDR enjoyed the planning of new programs, and especially the devising of political strategy necessary to get his programs enacted into law, Reagan took pleasure in making grand speeches proclaiming his conservative visions, which speeches were eventually followed—after the pragmatists in his administration had negotiated the compromises necessary to get a program passed—by a triumphant signing ceremony.

Roosevelt was more devious and vindictive than Reagan. James MacGregor Burns's charge that Roosevelt would "use the tricks of the fox to service the purposes of the lion" could not be legitimately leveled at Reagan. But on the other hand, no one would characterize Reagan's decision making as "infinitely subtle and sensitive," as Schlesinger describes Roosevelt's.

The pragmatic components of each president's administration had different consequences. Roosevelt's pragmatism had radical implications (but not necessarily radical results) because the depth and length of the Depression placed more aspects of the society, the economy, and the politics of the time into contention—that is, subject to proposals for significant change. Reagan's acceptance of pragmatic advice softened the edges of his conservative ideology, making his policies more accommodating to the liberal regime than one would have logically expected. Consequently, FDR's policies were frequently slightly left of center, and Reagan's were often slightly right of center, leaving radical supporters of each president repeatedly frustrated.

While Roosevelt's decision-making style represented more of a search for whatever policy might work, Reagan's style was designed to fulfill his conservative visions. Whereas FDR chose those to whom he gave access, access to Reagan was controlled by his staff. In the 1930s, no one claimed that presidential procedures operated in a manner that prevented Roosevelt from being Roosevelt. By constantly seeking detailed information regarding the political figures he had to deal with and the policies he might pursue to achieve his political ends, Roosevelt became the command center of the New Deal. As the New Deal expanded and became more and more complex, FDR undoubtedly tried to manage too much. Reagan, on the other hand, though a competitive man with a drive to succeed and a stubborn leader who continually championed his conservative program, was a passive official who rarely sought information and who was willing to turn the implementation of policy over to others and to be minutely managed and scripted by his staff. Hence, one of the great ironies is that while FDR endorsed the idea of "enlightened administration," he did not practice it in his White House, while Reagan believed there was no such phenomenon but depended on it in his White House.

The decision-making styles of FDR and Reagan were tilted against taking the big risks necessary to destroy major components of the old regime. To the dismay of their radical supporters, both presidents pursued the safer course of adding their policy preferences to the new governing arrangements. Hence FDR and Reagan were less successful in fulfilling the destructive role of reconstructive politics than their predecessors, Jefferson, Jackson, and Lincoln. The regimes initiated by FDR and Reagan, reflecting Skowronek's "waning of political time," were hybrid blends of the old and new and were not consistently liberal or conservative.

7

Core Policies of the New Deal

In practicing the politics of reconstruction, presidents will formulate a core set of public policies that reflects their political philosophy and what they are most dedicated to achieving. A new regime has a set of policy commitments that significantly differentiate it from its discredited predecessor and that will set the agenda for presidents engaged in the politics of articulation (i.e., LBJ's Great Society programs fulfilling many of the expectations and closing many of the gaps in the New Deal). In brief, a regime's core set of public policies will indicate its strategic priorities.

However, there is much controversy as to whether the zigzagging New Deal was constrained by priorities, which is expressed in the concepts of the first, second, and third New Deals, suggesting that the administration shifted gears and direction in 1933, 1935, and 1937. It was obviously more difficult for the Roosevelt administration than for the Reagan administration to decipher what its core policies were.

The Depression was much more severe than the malaise of the late 1970s. Roosevelt felt compelled to launch numerous policies on multiple fronts to bring about relief, recovery, and reform. He also had a wider variety of advisers operating in a less structured system than Reagan. Roosevelt was more prone to seek a broad range of advice and less likely to put all—or even most—of his eggs in one basket. Pursuing different contradictory policies did not bother Roosevelt. Inheriting the reform philosophy of the progressives reinforced FDR's belief in an active and compassionate federal government which would promote the people's interest, but it did not clarify what specifically should be done about the banking crisis, the farm problem, or the trusts.

Despite these obstacles, the New Deal, I believe, experimented and stumbled its way toward a set of core policies that we associate with the foundation and legacy of the liberal regime. The guiding light in this search for an essence was the need for security. Security would be provided by expanding the authority of the federal government. The Depression had painfully demonstrated that the Republican regime could not provide security for bank depositors, farmers, workers, homeowners, or investors. By providing security for important groups, the New Deal would institutionalize itself both economically and politically. To qualify as a core policy of the New Deal, a program would have to do more than provide security. It would have to epitomize the liberal regime by reflecting its philosophy, its electoral aspirations and obligations, and its long-term goals. A core policy, in brief, would have to demonstrate the strategic priorities of the regime. How the New Deal groped toward its core can be explained by examining its policies toward banking, farmers, business, labor, and social security.

Banking Policy

The United States was overbanked and undersupervised during the 1920s. In 1920, there were over 30,000 banks in the nation, many of them undercapitalized and located in rural towns. According to Helen Burns, "Bank supervision was divided between the federal and state governments. National banks were chartered by the federal government and were supervised by the Office of the Comptroller [located in the Treasury Department]. State banks were chartered by the various states and were regulated by the individual state banking authorities. In 1913, with the passage of the Federal Reserve Act, all national banks were required to become members of the Federal Reserve System. State banks meeting the membership requirements were permitted to elect membership in the system."[1] Because of the decline of the agricultural sector during the 1920s and the Depression, the number of banks had fallen to 18,734 by 1932. In response to the stock market crash in October 1929, congressional investigations publicized the scandalous activities of a number of prominent bankers who used depositors' funds to finance the speculative bubble that left so many people destitute.

After Roosevelt was elected in November 1932, and before he was inaugurated on March 4, 1933, the problems of the banking system accelerated, and there was fear of a total breakdown. In February 1933, several banks in Detroit collapsed, and the governor of Michigan felt compelled to declare an eight-day bank holiday. William Leuchtenburg writes, "By the end of the month [February], banks in every section of the country were in trouble. . . . People stood in long queues with satchels and paper bags to take gold and currency away from the banks to store in mattresses and old shoeboxes. It seemed safer to put your life's savings in the attic than to trust the greatest financial institutions in the country."[2] By March 4, thirty-eight states had closed their banks, and Richard Whitney announced that the New York Stock Exchange would not be open for business.

The *Kiplinger Washington Letter*, a newsletter circulated to business executives, saw a positive aspect of this banking crisis. It suggested that while people in Washington had been anticipating and dreading this panic, now that it was here, there was some feeling of relief because no longer was there hope that this problem would solve itself. The weaknesses of the banking system were now exposed; the federal government would have to do something.[3]

The hostility between President Hoover and President-elect Roosevelt prevented any cooperative effort to deal with the worsening banking situation. Nor could bankers overcome their divided interests and unite behind a program of reform. Some progressives and radicals wanted to take advantage of this crisis and nationalize the banks, but this was totally impractical because Roosevelt never intended to take such a radical step. Nevertheless, the breakdown was forcing the issue of what to do about the banks to the top of the New Deal's policy agenda. FDR did not particularly like bankers; he believed their greed had significantly contributed to the speculation in the stock market.

Roosevelt's point men in dealing with the banking crisis were Raymond Moley and William H. Woodin, the new secretary of the treasury. Both men had been working before the inauguration with Hoover's secretary of the treasury, Ogden Mills, with Arthur Ballantine, Hoover's undersecretary of the treasury, and with George Harrison, governor of the New York Federal Reserve Bank. Hoover's advisers had developed the idea of using the (nonlapsed) authority of a World War I piece of legislation, the 1917 Trading with the Enemy Act, to close the banks and then, after evaluating their liabilities and assets, to reopen the sound ones. However, because the 1917 law did not specifically authorize the president to close the banks, Hoover's advisers were not sure whether it could be used.[4] They also were not sure about how the reopened banks could be fortified with extra cash to prevent any further bank panics. According to McJimsey, "This problem Woodin solved by adopting a proposal to issue notes based on the assets of the banks. This currency would be Federal Reserve notes and be 'money that looks like money' [the Hoover people had been considering using scrip]."[5]

Time constraints compelled Woodin and Moley to accept most of the recommendations from Hoover's officials. When Woodin and Moley met with Roosevelt on the morning of his inauguration, they were apprehensive, first, about whether they had overstepped their authority in negotiating with the Hoover treasury officials, and second, whether FDR would accept their negotiated agreement. However, there was no need to worry because FDR was delighted with their successful negotiations, which gave him the opportunity to follow his inspiring inaugural address with decisive action. On March 6, at 1:00 A.M., the new president proclaimed a bank holiday and closed all the nation's banks under the authority of the Trading with the Enemy Act. On March 9, Roosevelt summoned Congress back into a special emergency session to validate his proclamation and to pass legislation supporting the reopening of the banks. Meanwhile, the president had ordered Woodin to have the Emergency Banking Act ready to submit to Congress by that date.

Congress convened at noon on March 9; at 3:00 P.M., the House and Senate were read a message from the president stressing the urgent need to pass the Emergency Banking Act. In his message, the president requested temporary executive authority over the banks in order to protect the depositors. Helen Burns writes, "Republican Bertrand Sell voiced the views of fellow Congressmen when he said: 'The house is burning down and the President of the United States says this is the way to put out the fire. And to me, at this time, there is only one answer to the question, that is to give the President what he says is necessary to meet the situation.'"[6] The bill passed the House by 4:00 P.M. and the Senate by 7:00 P.M. and was signed into law by the president at 8:30 P.M.

The Emergency Banking Act of 1933 legalized the action already taken by the president in closing the banks. It authorized the secretary of the treasury to examine bank records and decide which ones were qualified to reopen. For banks determined to be unsound, the comptroller of currency was permitted to install conservators who would have the authority to reorganize them. For banks that were basically solvent but temporarily in need of help, the new law authorized the Reconstruction Finance Corporation

(RFC) to invest in the preferred stock of these banks, which would help them reopen. The Federal Reserve was empowered to issue emergency currency to meet any future runs on the banks. Finally, the treasury secretary was authorized "to call in all privately held gold and gold certificates to be exchanged for paper currency,"[7] which he promptly did.

On Saturday, March 11, Roosevelt announced that the banks would begin reopening on Monday, March 13, and that he would explain what had been accomplished about the banking situation in a radio address—the first fireside chat—on Sunday night at 10:00 P.M. An estimated 60 million listeners heard the president explain the basics of the banking business and the reasons why he had proclaimed a banking holiday. He thanked Republican and Democratic Congress members for passing such urgently needed legislation so quickly, and he stressed that "nothing complex, or radical" had been done. Because of this reform legislation, he declared, "I can assure you that it is safer to keep your money in a reopened bank than under the mattress." However, Roosevelt warned that even this reformed banking system was dependent on the rational cooperation of the public: "Confidence and courage are the essentials of success in carrying out our plan. You people must have faith; you must not be stampeded by rumors or guesses. . . . We have provided the machinery to restore our financial system; it is up to you to support and make it work."[8] Implied in this statement was that if there was a run on the reopened banks, the fault would not be Roosevelt's.

But when the banks reopened, there was no panic. Instead, the Roosevelt magic prevailed, and deposits exceeded withdrawals. Two days later, on March 15, the stock market opened, and 3 million shares were traded as stock prices rose. Helen Burns reports, "Utilizing the powers granted by the Emergency Banking Act, the Treasury Department, the Office of the Comptroller of the Currency, the Federal Reserve System, and the state banking authorities joined together in the tremendous task of licensing those banks found to be sound. Banks having on hand rediscountable assets in amounts equal to their deposits began reopening on Monday, March 13. By March 15, banks controlling approximately 90 percent of the banking resources of the country had resumed business on an unrestricted basis."[9] In the autumn of 1933, 2,000 banks with combined deposits of nearly $8 billion were still closed, but with the RFC investing over a billion dollars in 6,000 banks, there was no longer a threat of a banking collapse. By January 1934, there were 14,440 commercial banks open for business, with $33 billion in deposits.[10]

In analyzing the Emergency Banking Act of 1933, scholars have stressed the ironic opportunism of FDR. Thus, Schlesinger writes, "The very moneychangers, whose flight from their high seats in the temple the president had so grandiloquently proclaimed in his inaugural address, were now swarming through the corridors of the Treasury."[11] Kenneth Davis points out, "Hoover's Treasury officials, the chief one being the archreactionary Ogden Mills, substantially wrote the first piece of New Deal legislation!"[12] Moley claims the unsung hero in this episode that saved capitalism in eight days was Treasury Secretary Woodin. The Brains Truster also emphasizes, "It cannot be emphasized too strongly that the policies which vanquished the bank crisis were thoroughly conservative policies. The sole departure from conservatism lay in the swiftness and boldness with which they were carried out."[13] But here Moley underestimates one of the characteristics that distinguished the New Deal from Hoover's presidency: FDR could move quickly; Hoover could not.

The passage of the Emergency Banking Act served FDR's political purposes very well. Although some progressives, like Tugwell, criticized the president for not taking advantage of the crisis to nationalize the banks, saving the banks demonstrated that he was not a dangerous radical. Instead, he exhibited the skills of an effective reformer who was not inhibited from using the ideas of his opponents to repair a flawed banking system. FDR was establishing his credentials as a political leader, one who, like General Grant, was constantly on the offensive, attacking the Depression.

The Banking Act of 1933, better known as the Glass-Steagall Act, also has weak New Deal roots. Its chief proponents were Senator Carter Glass and Congressman Henry B. Steagall. Glass considered himself the leading expert on banking policy and the Federal Reserve in Washington. He had first introduced his bill in 1931 and had unsuccessfully sought the support of President Hoover, but he had succeeded in getting his ideas included in the 1932 Democratic party platform. Glass was particularly concerned about legally separating commercial banking from securities selling because he considered the latter the root cause of many of the scandalous practices that had rattled public confidence in banking.

Passage of Glass's bill was both enhanced and complicated by the proposal to add to it a provision creating federal insurance of bank deposits. This increased the popularity of the legislation but was opposed by bankers, Glass, and Roosevelt. Many bankers believed that federal deposit insurance would force strong banks to subsidize weak ones. Glass and Roosevelt were opposed because numerous state attempts to protect depositors had all failed. But the proposal was popular in both the House and the Senate. Federal deposit insurance had been included in the original Federal Reserve Act in 1913, but had been dropped. In the 72nd Congress, the last one during the Hoover presidency, twenty-one bills had been introduced aimed at protecting depositors' money.[14] Representative Henry Steagall of Alabama, who championed the cause of small banks, supported it because he believed it would protect small unit banks. Federal deposit insurance was supported by Vice President John Nance Garner, Jesse Jones, and, surprisingly, Republican Senator Arthur Vandenberg from Michigan. On May 19, 1933, by prearrangement, Vice President Garner recognized Senator Vandenberg for the purpose of introducing an amendment to insure bank deposits up to $2,500, which was quickly accepted. Perhaps to relieve himself from responsibility if deposit insurance did not work, Roosevelt asked the conference committee to drop the Vandenberg Amendment, but it refused.

The Glass-Steagall Act passed the House on a vote of 262 to 19; it passed the Senate by a voice vote. When the president, bowing to public pressure, signed it into law on June 16, he quipped, "This bill had more lives than a cat."[15] The act increased the authority to impede speculation in securities, real estate, and commodities. To decrease what was considered a risky form of competition for deposits, the payment of interest on demand deposits by member banks was forbidden. John Steele Gordon adds, "The act also required banks to choose [within a year] whether they would be depository banks, taking deposits and making loans, or investment banks, which underwrite securities. The great House of Morgan, among many others, had to split into two separate entities, an investment bank known as Morgan Stanley and a depository bank still called J. P. Morgan and Company."[16]

The most important component of the Glass-Steagall Act created the Federal Deposit Insurance Corporation (FDIC). All banks that were in the Federal Reserve System were compelled to have their deposits insured by the FDIC, but nonmembers might be accepted by the corporation. Each member of the FDIC would have to contribute an amount equal to one-half of 1 percent of the total amount of deposits so certified. After considering several plans, FDIC coverage was raised to $5,000 for each depositor.[17]

Federal deposit insurance was successful. By June 1934, over 90 percent of the country's commercial banks had bought the insurance and subjected themselves to FDIC regulation. The extension of federal supervision over an increased number of state banks significantly reduced the number of bank closings. Because depositors' money was protected by the FDIC, there was no longer any incentive for runs on banks; thus, there was a drastic decline in bank failures. According to Leuchtenburg, "Fewer banks suspended during the rest of the decade than in even the best single year of the twenties."[18] Another success is claimed by Carter Galombe, who cites a Federal Reserve publication extolling the FDIC's positive role in promoting monetary policy: "From the individual's standpoint, deposit insurance provides protection, within limits, against the banking hazards of deposit ownership. But the major virtue of deposit insurance is for the Nation as a whole. By assuring the public, individuals, and business alike that cash in the form of bank deposits is insured up to a prescribed maximum, a major cause of instability in the Nation's money supply is removed."[19] A more secure money supply means a more secure economy, no longer subject to bank panics.

There is a delicious irony in the fact that the Glass-Steagall Act, generally considered one of the most successful pieces of New Deal legislation, was neither introduced nor supported by FDR during the first hundred days. Nevertheless, because of the Roosevelt magic, Glass's law, as amended by Senator Vandenberg, served Roosevelt's purposes. The banking crisis of March 4, which had seemed an insurmountable problem, was now solved by bills signed by the new president. "Fear had been conquered," according to Helen Burns, "but economic conditions had not improved substantially. Unemployment, overproduction, falling prices, credit contract, were among the problems remaining to be solved. The banking situation was intimately related to all of these."[20]

Farm Policy

Readers of today will perhaps be surprised that FDR was more committed to helping the farmer than any other group. Roosevelt liked farmers; he considered himself to be one since he owned farms in New York and Georgia. Roosevelt agreed with farm leaders and many Congress members that one of the major causes of the Depression was that the farm sector did not share in the prosperity of the 1920s. It naturally followed that a healthier farm economy would help bring about an economic recovery for the entire nation. FDR's social concern for the farmers was reinforced by knowledge that they represented a group that was disaffected with the Republican party and was therefore available to be added to his electoral coalition.

While it was clear that farm policy would play a major role in the New Deal, it was not obvious what specific agrarian policies FDR would endorse. Some Western Congress members were attracted to the old populist idea of inflating the currency, which would raise farm prices and reduce the farmer's debt burden. This solution had the appeal of being easy and nonbureaucratic and the disadvantage of being considered short-sighted and dangerous by many educated people. A second proposal, the McNary-Haugen Bill, called for the federal government to protect American farmers with a high tariff and to buy surplus crops and sell them (the derogatory word was "dump" them) in overseas markets. A third approach called for the federal government to determine the costs of production for farm products and then guarantee the farmers a profit. Implementing this policy would have created an administrative nightmare. The fourth approach was called the "domestic allotment" plan, and it was based on the federal government's paying farmers to curtail their production.

The key man who developed the domestic allotment idea was M. L. Wilson, a professor of economics at Montana State College. Schlesinger describes Wilson as "a gentle shaggy zealot, forty-eight years old, combining a farmer's passion for the soil with an ideologue's conviction that civilization rested on its agricultural base. The determination to save the republic by saving agriculture gave his advocacy of the new plan missionary zeal."[21] Wilson was able to sell his idea to Rexford Tugwell, the Brains Truster whose specialty was farm policy, and Tugwell then tried to convince Roosevelt of its merits. FDR most wanted a bill that farmers would agree on and could then be passed quickly. Secretary of Agriculture Henry Wallace wanted a bill passed before the spring planting in order to head off any increases in the surpluses that depressed farm prices. In February 1933, before Roosevelt was inaugurated, farm leaders traveled to the capital and met with Wallace, who guided them to support a major reform bill. In March, Wallace and his advisers worked frantically to develop a bill which they called the Agricultural Adjustment Act. Roosevelt accepted the bill and submitted it to Congress on March 16.

Despite the accusation from a Republican Congress member that this legislation was "bolshevistic," the bill passed the House quickly, but then ran into trouble from farm supporters in the Senate who wanted the legislation to do more. One proposed amendment, which failed, tried to replace the cost of production for parity as the bill's major objective. A second amendment, sponsored by Senator Elmer Thomas of Oklahoma in mid-April, called for inflating the currency and showed signs of being able to mobilize majority support. Many progressive senators believed that the Emergency Banking Act and the Economy Act, which had been passed in March, had increased deflationary pressures and were compounding the debt burdens for farmers. "Recognizing that the situation would soon be out of hand,"

Leuchtenburg notes, "Roosevelt decided to accept the Thomas proposal if it was rewritten to give the President discretionary powers rather than making any specific course of inflationary action mandatory. In its revised form, the Thomas amendment authorized the President to bring about inflation through remonetizing silver, printing greenbacks, or altering the gold content of the dollar. That night, hearing of Roosevelt's capitulation to the soft-money men, [Budget Director] Lewis Douglas cried: 'Well, this is the end of Western civilization.'"[22] It wasn't. And even though the president had offended his conservative advisers in accepting the Thomas amendment, he had assured passage of the bill and expanded his discretionary powers.

The Senate passed the bill, and the president signed it on May 12. It consisted of three parts: Title I was the Agricultural Adjustment Act; Title II was the Emergency Farm Mortgage Act; and Title III was based on the Thomas Amendment. The farm lobby, headed by the Farm Bureau Federation, was delighted, for they had been struggling for relief and reform for ten years. The focus of the AAA was to restore farm prices to parity—that is, to the relationship they had to industrial prices in the prosperous period from 1909 to 1914. To achieve this goal, farmers were to be paid by the Department of Agriculture to reduce their acreage in crops and livestock. The program was financed by a tax on food processors. In other words, it authorized the secretary of agriculture to set and collect a tax from agricultural processors and to use the revenue to recompense farmers who curtailed their production of seven basic commodities: wheat, corn, cotton, hogs, milk, rice, and tobacco. The law also relaxed antitrust restrictions in order to allow marketing agreements between farmers and processors of any agricultural commodity. It empowered "the secretary to mediate the terms of marketing contracts and to enforce them (if need be) by licensing firms in the industry."[23]

As is true of many New Deal pieces of legislation, the AAA cannot be classified as either liberal or conservative because it reflects FDR's skill in nuanced compromise:

> There was something old: a continuation of the Hoover administration's effort to stabilize the buying and selling of cotton, grain, and other commodities. There was something new: giving direct benefits or rental payments to farmers in exchange for voluntarily reducing acreage or crops. There was something so conventional as to be widely accepted: providing cheaper credit to farmers by

consolidating all government agencies lending to farmers and by refinancing farm mortgages at lower interest rates. There was something so controversial as to enflame major business interests: payment of the program not by general taxation but by levies on the processors of farm products. There was something so conservative as to win support of the big farmers' lobbying organizations: maintaining prices by reducing surplus crops of basic farm products and the setting of "parity" prices. And there was something that would become crucial in the passage of most New Deal measures: the inability of Congress to agree on key issues, followed by a wide delegation of authority to the president to make the necessary judgments.[24]

The boldness of this program prompted FDR to search for a conservative administrator. Wallace and Roosevelt first offered the job as head of the AAA to Bernard Baruch, but the financier, perhaps sensing difficulties in administering domestic allotment and definitely wanting a higher office, turned it down. Baruch recommended George Peek, who had worked under him on the War Industries Board and who was popular among farm groups for championing the McNary-Haugen bill, for the job. Peek's price for accepting the position was direct access to the president, which understandably bothered Peek's nominal boss, the secretary of agriculture.

While the Peek appointment may have assuaged agricultural interests and many Congress members, the sixty-year-old businessman alienated many New Dealers. He was still more committed to McNary-Haugenism than to domestic allotment. In Peek's view, "The elements of a sound policy . . . were a two-price system, a high tariff to save the American market for the American farmer, marketing agreements to control the flow of farm products into the home market, a government-sponsored export program to find markets at any price abroad for what could not be sold at the protected price at home—and no production controls. The idea of curtailing output was repugnant to Peek; it was the farmer's sin against the Holy Ghost."[25] Peek staffed the AAA with many of the people he had worked with before, but the New Dealers were successful in getting Jerome N. Frank, a protégé of Felix Frankfurter, appointed as general counsel.

The first dilemma the New Deal farm program faced was that because the AAA had been passed in midspring, the markets faced a glut of cotton and hogs. Wallace felt that the only solution, a painful one, was to pay farmers to plow up 10 million acres of cotton and kill 6 million piglets. This episode constituted the New Deal's first public relations fiasco; one can imagine how today's late-night comedians would have ridiculed the policy.[26] Nathan Miller reports, "Newspaper pictures of squealing piglets crowding the middle-western stockyards resulted in Wallace and Peek's being subjected to a flood of abuse, and the AAA received a black eye from which it never recovered. New Deal farm policy was denounced for trying to end want in the midst of plenty by doing away with plenty."[27]

The administration was successful in responding to the credit crisis that was causing the most misery and unrest in the rural areas. Three agencies were created to provide credit to farmers: "The Commodity Credit Corporation loaned money to farmers on the security of their crops. The Farm Credit Administration reorganized local agencies and supplied them with additional resources to form cooperatives and meet production costs. The federal land banks extended mortgage credit to farmers."[28] In late March 1933, the president consolidated the complex set of agricultural credit organizations into a new agency, the Farm Credit Administration, headed by Henry Morgenthau and his deputy, William Myers, a professor from Cornell. According to Blum, "The Farm Credit Administration undertook to refinance farm mortgages, in the process reducing the average interest they carried from 6 per cent to 4½ per cent. It also facilitated applications for intermediate and short-term agricultural credit. . . . In the first year of its life, the Federal Farm Credit Administration approved over 540,000 loans aggregating $1,356,000,000. In its first year and a half, it refinanced about 20 per cent of the total farm mortgage debt in the United States."[29] This program did not bring prosperity to the agrarian sector, but it did result in a dramatic decline in farm foreclosures.

In October 1933, Roosevelt was pressured by Senator John Bankhead of Alabama and other cotton state senators to provide an immediate loan on the 1933 cotton crop. The Southern senators requested a loan of 15 cents a pound, but FDR agreed to a loan of 10 cents a pound (at this time, the market price for cotton was less than this), which would be financed by the RFC. These loans would be available only to those cotton farmers who agreed to restrict their 1934 acreage by 40 percent. This specific deal evolved into the creation of the Commodity Credit Corporation, authorized to borrow from the RFC in order to bolster the price of farm commodities. The goal of the program was "to prevent storable crops that had already been harvested from reaching the market until prices had risen. . . . If prices rose, the farmer could repay the loan, redeem his crop, and sell it. If not, the government kept the crop, and the farmer kept his money."[30] By reducing the possibility of price collapses with crop loans, the New Deal had increased the economic security of the farmers. However, risk had been shifted from the farmer to the federal government, which was now threatened with footing the bill for mounting surpluses. Only World War II saved the New Deal from having to make some unpleasant choices to reduce agricultural surpluses.

The AAA was hampered by personality, policy, and cultural conflicts. While Peek defined his job as raising farm prices, there were reformers like Tugwell and urban intellectual lawyers working under Jerome Frank who wanted to do a lot more. Frank had recruited an all-star legal staff, which included such names as Lee Pressman, Nathan Witt, John Abt, Alger Hiss, Adlai Stevenson, George Ball, Thurmond Arnold, Abe Fortas, and Telford Taylor. Unfortunately, the first four names on this list had communist affiliations.[31] Lawyers in the AAA "were less interested in establishing a prosperous agriculture than in reforming rural society. . . . Specifically, they wanted to limit the profits of middlemen (the distributors and processors of agricultural commodities) in the interest of enlarging consumer demand. They would do this by licensing all buyers of agricultural products with agreements to set prices and by checking other marketing agreements to be sure they protected consumer interests."[32] To protect consumer interests, these lawyers began to argue that the AAA ought to be able to look into the books of food processors to determine whether unfair profits were being earned.

For Peek, "there were too many Ivy League men, too many intellectuals, too many radicals, too many Jews. Nor were things helped when . . . Lee Pressman, attending a meeting to work out a macaroni code, asked belligerently what the code would do for the macaroni growers."[33] When Peek tried to get Frank fired in November 1933, this galvanized Tugwell to orchestrate his enemy's ouster. Peek resigned on December 11 and was given a face-saving job as a special adviser on foreign trade. In 1935, he left the administration and became an ardent anti–New Dealer.[34]

Peek was replaced by Chester Davis, who, being more congenial than his former boss, believed he could tamp down the conflicts within the AAA. He was wrong. For a while it looked like the liberals had taken over the AAA, but within a year, there were complaints that the AAA was operating like a Republican law, not a New Deal one. It was aiding the large landowner, was not doing much for the small landowner, and was actually hurting sharecroppers. The 1930 census reported that there were over a million and a half sharecroppers; about 40 percent were Negro. The domestic allotment program was resulting in many Southern landlords pushing their tenants off the land and not sharing the payments with them.

Lash suggests, "The traditional Southern attitude was voiced by Senator 'Cotton Ed' Smith of South Carolina, who strode unannounced into Hiss's office. 'You're going to send money to my niggers, instead of me?' he asked and announced, 'I'll take care of them. . . . '"[35]

In January 1935, the liberals in the legal division decided to reinterpret a section of the law that said cotton growers "shall insofar as possible, maintain on this farm the normal number of tenants" and "shall permit all tenants to continue the occupancy of their houses." Culver and Hyde stress, "The vagueness of this clause—it didn't say whether the planter's obligation was legal or only moral, and a huge loophole was created by the 'insofar as possible' clause—made it useless as a legal weapon."[36] Nevertheless, Alger Hiss wrote a new interpretation of the law requiring landlords to maintain the same number of tenants. Frank knew that Davis would never accept this reinterpretation of the law because it would enrage powerful Southern legislators, so he waited until his boss was out of Washington and then announced the change by telegram to local offices. An incensed Chester Davis returned to the capital and obtained a free hand from a somewhat hesitant Wallace to deal with Frank's insubordination. In early February, Davis fired Frank, Lee Pressman, and several other lawyers, but for reasons that remain a mystery, not Alger Hiss. Tugwell was furious and threatened to resign. Roosevelt prevented that and appointed Tugwell to direct a new agency, the Resettlement Administration, designed to aid displaced farmers and tenants. FDR also found other jobs in his administration for Frank and Pressman.

These conflicts should not blind us from seeing the administrative capability and achievements of the AAA. The program was confronted with enlisting the participation of 6 million farmers spread out over one of the largest countries in the world. "To implement its novel policies with maximum speed," in Kennedy's words, "AAA turned to the network of Extension Service agents already in place in virtually every rural county in America. The county agents, in turn, arranged for the formation of local products-control committees in whom effective administrative authority over AAA programs came to reside."[37] M. L. Wilson supported the idea of using the Agricultural Extension Service of the Land Grant Colleges, but Tugwell was opposed because he felt it was too tied to the interests of the large farmers. But Wallace sided with Wilson on this issue. The organizational capability of the Extension Service was impressive: "Within a few days of the promulgation of the AAA, the Extension Service and its affiliates had sent out 22,100 agents in 956 counties to explain the AAA and persuade farmers of its virtues. Within less than a year and a half, over one million

AAA contracts had been signed."[38] By mid-1934, there were 4,000 county production control committees. Their job was to establish production quotas, to supervise acreage restrictions, and to distribute government payments.[39]

AAA officials wanted to keep their programs on a voluntary basis. They were sensitive to Republican charges that large bureaucracies would subject farmers to the kind of authoritarian controls in communist and fascist governments. Because farmers quickly realized that the higher the percentage of farmers who participated in the domestic allotment program, the more likely it was to be successful in reducing surpluses and raising prices, the local committees generated more pressure on nonparticipants than did AAA officials. Kennedy writes, "In two sectors—cotton and tobacco—the effort to induce voluntary compliance gave way in 1934 to compulsory, statutory measures, requested by a majority of the producers themselves. The Bankhead Cotton Control Act and its companion measure, the Kerr-Smith Tobacco Control Act, licensed thousands of individual growers and levied a punitive tax on crops produced in excess of stipulated quotas."[40] Liberals saw this as government responding to the needs of farmers, while conservatives viewed it as the expansion of an authoritarian bureaucracy.

The first AAA achieved moderate success. Production controls did stop the growth of farm surpluses that had dragged prices down. With prices rising, "Gross farm income rose from $6.4 billion in 1932 to $8.5 billion in 1934, and benefit payments totaling $577 million in 1933 and 1934 provided vitally needed cash for several million farmers."[41] Whatever further benefits the AAA could have provided for farmers were ended in January 1936 when the Supreme Court, in *United States v. Butler* declared that the tax on processors and production controls were unconstitutional.

When the National Industrial Recovery Act was declared unconstitutional in 1935, there were no major demands for its renewal. But farmers, faced with the prospect of no longer receiving government checks, pressured Congress to pass a substitute bill. Within eight weeks, in less time than it took Congress to pass the first AAA during the first hundred days, Congress passed the Soil Conservation and Domestic Allotment Act. With the nation increasingly concerned about dust storms caused by drought in the Great Plains from Canada to Texas, the new law championed soil conservation. It would pay farmers for planting soil-enriching grasses and legumes instead of soil-depleting commercial crops. The act was also compatible with Roosevelt's fundamental commitments to conservation and winning the farm vote.

In February 1938, Congress passed the second Agricultural Adjustment Act, which incorporated the 1936 soil conservation law. Burns and Dunn write, "Incorporating the ever-normal granary notion that Wallace had struggled for over the years, the bill: authorized the secretary of agriculture to fix marketing quotas when surpluses of export from commodities—notably corn, wheat, cotton, rice, and tobacco—threatened price stability; authorized acreage allotments to each farmer after two-thirds of the growers voted to approve the marketing quota in a referendum; and authorized the Commodity Credit Corporation to make loans to farmers on their surplus produce slightly below parity."[42] Both the 1936 and 1938 bills were financed by general tax revenues. The constitutionality of the second AAA was upheld by the Supreme Court in 1941 in *Wickard v. Filburn* as a legitimate exercise of Congress' power to regulate interstate commerce.

One way to evaluate the New Deal's agricultural policy is to look at the parity ratio over the years, because the major goal of the AAA was to raise farm prices to parity levels. According to Kennedy's figures, "The parity ratio . . . improved from 58 in 1932 to touch 93 in 1937, before slumping again to 81 by the eve of World War II."[43] Saloutos provides evidence that "Of the prices received for farm commodities, only one, that for beef cattle, had attained parity by August 1939. Corn was 59 percent of parity, cotton 66 percent, wheat 50, butterfat 59, hogs 60, chickens 93, and eggs 49."[44]

It is ironic that farmers, a group that prides itself on its rugged individualism, subjected themselves to bureaucratic controls in order to receive extensive benefits. Schlesinger points out, "With the New Deal and after, no sector of the economy received more systematic federal attention than agriculture; none more subsidy for research and development, more technical assistance, more public investment in education, in electrification and in infrastructure, more price stabilization, more export promotion, more credit and mortgage relief."[45] And despite all this help, the number of farms decreased while their size increased.

What depressed some New Dealers is that their programs and local committees did not promote a "planning consciousness" among their members. "What developed instead," according to Hamilton, "was a heightened 'interest-group consciousness' conducive to the growth of the Farm Bureau. . . . [The AAA] held its 'red hot' schoolhouse meetings, and . . . hundreds of thousands of farmers attended. Their universal concern at the meetings, however, was with prices and profits, not long-term adjustments or land use planning."[46] What was even more disillusioning for New Dealers is that many of these farmers began to shift their vote back to the Republicans in the 1938 and 1940 elections.

The National Industrial Recovery Act

The "intended" core policy of the first New Deal (1933–1935) was the National Industrial Recovery Act (NIRA). Ending the Depression was more dependent on producing jobs for the urban unemployed than on promoting higher prices for farmers. Various authors called the NIRA "the single most ambitious initiative for reconstruction [Roosevelt] sponsored," "the centerpiece of the New Deal's recovery package," "the signature New Deal creation," and "the mainspring of the first New Deal."[47] When Roosevelt signed the NIRA into law on June 16, 1933, he declared, "History will probably record the NIRA as the most important and far-reaching legislation ever enacted by the American Congress."[48] That is not the way history has evaluated the NIRA. Within a few years, the NIRA was looked on as a New Deal experiment that failed, an emergency proposal that created more problems than economic recovery, a plan of action that reflected FDR's initial political commitments and his lack of economic wisdom.

The NIRA had multiple roots. There were elements of Theodore Roosevelt's New Nationalism, the World War I War Industries Board run by Bernard Baruch, Mussolini's corporate state, the dream of national planning championed by visionaries like Rexford Tugwell, and the hopes of the trade associationalists led by Herbert Hoover and business leaders such as Gerard Swope, head of General Electric, and Harry Harriman, president of the United States Chamber of Commerce. Bernard Bellush writes, "In the 1920s, Hoover . . . initiated more than two hundred codes of fair practice, under which companies shared product and market information, anticipating many aspects of the New Deal's NRA [National Recovery Administration] codes."[49] As the Depression deepened after 1929, proponents of the trade association movement argued that their proposal for government-authorized industrial self-regulation would phase out destructive competition, which was deflating prices, and spur cooperative national planning. Such a cooperative program would require the suspension of antitrust laws—an idea that would antagonize the business-fearing progressives in Congress.

When the newly inaugurated President Roosevelt called Congress into a special session in March 1933, he had no bill prepared to reconstruct the industrial economy. In Roosevelt's mind, the Depression demonstrated the need for drastic changes, but discussions concerning reforms had not matured into an agreement centered around a specific proposal. Roosevelt was sympathetic to calls for planning made by his uncle, Frederic A. Delano, and Tugwell, but he thought that the time was not yet ripe for its political acceptance. Hence, the NIRA was the last significant reform developed by the administration during the first hundred days.

The NIRA emerged out of the fertile chaos of the early New Deal. Roosevelt had assigned Raymond Moley to collect and process proposals for industrial recovery in the hopes that his overworked Brains Truster could condense them into a single plan. Meanwhile, Commerce Under Secretary John Dickinson, Senator Robert Wagner from New York, and Labor Secretary Frances Perkins were also working on their separate proposals. What triggered decisive action by the administration was the increasing likelihood that Senator Hugo Black's thirty-hour bill would pass Congress and confront the president with a painful decision over whether to veto it. FDR watched the growing popularity of Black's bill with rising anxiety because he considered it unconstitutional and ineffective. Requiring a thirty-hour work week would allow business to lower wages and thus reduce purchasing power; it would also be ridiculous for the agricultural sector, in which planting and harvest time demanded longer hours of work. But Roosevelt's private criticisms were not able to block Black's bill—the Senate passed it on April 5—and so the president realized that he would have to kill the bill by substituting one of his own.

In late April, Moley accidentally met Hugh Johnson and suggested that Johnson review the various proposals for industrial regulation and draft a substitute for the thirty-hour bill. Johnson agreed to undertake this assignment, and Moley provided him with an office next to his own and a thick set of files. Within a day, Johnson composed a draft bill that was based on his experiences working for the War Industries Board, chaired by Bernard Baruch.[50]

While Johnson was working feverishly on his proposal, Under Secretary of Commerce John Dickinson was laboring on his own draft law. Dickinson had been an economist with the War Trade Board in 1917, and after the war, he had earned a Harvard law degree. Working in the Commerce Department had exposed him to business opposition to the antitrust laws, and meetings with planners in Agriculture, like Tugwell and Jerome Frank, had familiarized him with the arguments for industrial discipline and national planning. Dickinson was also in contact with Senator Wagner, and they soon agreed to cooperate on a common draft. Wagner was particularly interested in promoting a large public works program to stimulate employment.

Through the efforts of Secretary of Labor Frances Perkins, the Dickinson and Wagner groups were able to unite behind a single bill for industrial recovery. By early May, there were two bills competing for Roosevelt's endorsement: Johnson's bill called for a federal government licensing system and was supported by Moley, Lewis Douglas, and Donald Richberg. The Dickinson-Wagner draft was based on industrial self-government through trade associations. On May 10, the competing teams met in the Oval Office and presented their cases in a meeting that lasted two hours. Instead of making a choice, the president directed the participants to lock themselves in a room and reach a consensus. They then met in Lewis Douglas's office, and after hard bargaining, they reached an agreement. The contours of the reconciled bill were largely drawn by the efforts of Hugh Johnson, who "Infused the group with a crisis psychology that dismissed constitutional procedures as irrelevant and argued for a strong stroke of federal policy in the form of licensing and extensive presidential authority."[51] However, thanks to the commitment of Wagner and Perkins, Section 7(a) in Title I of the bill, which prohibited yellow dog contracts and guaranteed labor's right to organize and bargain collectively, remained in the bill. Obviously, the bill was designed to placate the interests of business and labor, a goal that Roosevelt's first New Deal believed was attainable.

Roosevelt accepted this bill and submitted it to Congress on May 17. On May 26, the measure passed the House with a 325-to-76 vote, but the bill ran into stiffer opposition in the Senate. Attempts to eliminate the licensing provisions and weaken Section 7(a) were defeated, but the antitrusters, led by progressive Senators William Borah and Burton Wheeler, did succeed "in adding an amendment providing that no code should 'permit combinations in restraint of trade, price fixing, or other monopolistic practices'; and with this gesture to the competitive tradition, the Senate passed the measure by a vote of 58 to 24."[52] The debate was summarized by Schlesinger: "Borah contended that the suspension of the antitrust acts would infallibly promote the concentration of wealth and power. Wagner replied that the urgent need was to outlaw sweatshops, long hours, and low wages, and that this could only be done by allowing business cooperation. The issue was quickly reduced to the question: Could industry be trusted to combine for fair standards for wages, hours, and working conditions without at the same time combining for pools and price-fixing."[53] The conference committee charged with reconciling the House and Senate versions of the NIRA eliminated Borah's amendment, which caused Senate progressives to vote against the bill. The NIRA passed the House and Senate and was signed into law on the last day of the first hundred days, June 16, 1933.

The NIRA was an emergency piece of legislation designed to operate for two years in order to revive and reform a debilitated business system. It authorized the chief executive to create the necessary administrative agencies. Ellis Hawley summarizes Title I of the legislation, which concerned the rules for constructing the fair practice codes:

> The President, under Section 3, might approve codes drawn up
> by trade or industrial groups providing that he found such codes
> to be equitable, truly representative, and not designed to promote
> monopolies or monopolistic practices. He might also make any
> necessary additions or deletions; and in an industry where no
> agreements could be reached, he might impose a code. The act,
> however, said little about the type of provisions that should be included
> in the codes. The only specific instructions, in fact, were those dealing
> with labor standards. Each code, according to Section 7, had to contain
> an acceptable provision for maximum hours, minimum wages, and
> desirable working conditions. In addition, it had to include a prescribed
> Section 7(a), which outlawed yellow dog contracts and guaranteed
> the right of laborers to organize and bargain collectively through
> representatives of their own choosing.[54]

The codes were exempted from the antitrust laws. Under Title II, Congress authorized a total of $3,300,000,000 that could be spent on public works projects. Title III provided the financing for public works.

Roosevelt was delighted with the NIRA. The bill contained provisions that pleased a variety of interests, and it reflected Roosevelt's moralistic view that if the nation would duplicate the cooperative efforts that had won the Great War, it could defeat the Great Depression. In his view, this law was providing the incentives and the means to overcome "selfish interests" through disciplined joint public and private activities. He hoped that the administrative arm of the NIRA, the National Recovery Administration (NRA), would provide the mechanism for a "cheap" solution to economic recovery, one that was not dependent on massive public expenditures. As he explained in a fireside chat on July 24, 1933, everyone would benefit, and no one would suffer if business acted correctly by paying their workers "reasonable wages" for "reasonable hours" of labor.[55]

The administrative strategy of the program was outlined in a speech by Donald Richberg, the general counsel of the NRA, in July 1933. Richberg suggested that the success of this "great adventure" "to find a democratic and truly American solution" to the problems that produced dictatorship in Europe would depend on the skill of business leaders to substitute "enlightened cooperation" for "cannibalistic" competition. But he warned that "unless industry is sufficiently socialized by its private owners and managers so that great essential industries are operated under public obligations appropriate to the public interest in them—the advance of political control over private industry is inevitable."[56] The threat that capitalism was being given one last chance to provide a more secure and socially just economy or else be subjected to more stringent political controls was not conducive to promoting business confidence.

The success of this program, now called the NRA, would largely depend on the skills of its administrative head. Not surprisingly, FDR appointed Hugh Johnson, the man who had largely designed the program, to direct the NRA. The fifty-one-year-old Johnson had valuable administrative experience: he had graduated from West Point; studied law at the University of California at Berkeley; helped construct the selective service system in World War I; worked with the War Industries Board, where he caught the eye of Baruch; and then resigned from the army in 1919 and became the general counsel of the Moline Plow Company, which was directed by George Peek (who was now leading the AAA). [57] According to David Kennedy, Johnson's "seamed and jowly face floridly testified to the rigors of the professional soldier's life as well as the ravages of drink. Melodramatic in his temperament, mercurial in his moods, ingeniously profane in his speech, Johnson could weep at the opera, vilify his enemies, chew out his underlings, and rhapsodize about the virtues of the NRA with equal flamboyance. On accepting his appointment in June 1933, he declared: 'It will be red fire at first and dead cats afterward'—one of the printable specimens of his sometimes mystifying inventive prose."[58]

Johnson had assumed that he would head both the NRA and the Public Works Administration (PWA), which had $3.3 billion to distribute. But Roosevelt was reluctant to concentrate that much power in any one administrator's control, and so he stunned Johnson by naming Secretary of the Interior Harold Ickes, as head of the PWA. Thereafter, New Dealers and scholars have fantasized whether both programs would have been more successful if the president had appointed Johnson to direct the PWA and Ickes to lead the NRA. Fearing another Teapot Dome scandal, Ickes was tightfisted with PWA money. In 1933, Ickes spent only about $110 million of PWA funds. "Under Ickes' obsessively prudent management," according to Kennedy, "PWA contributed nothing in 1933 to economic stimulus, rendering NRA effectively dead on arrival as a recovery measure."[59] But Ickes's administrative skills might have provided the NRA with the steady leadership it needed as a new experiment in business regulation. If the kinetic Johnson had headed the PWA, he might have challenged Harry Hopkins as a superspender, and the early New Deal would have received more Keynesian benefits.

As director of the NRA, Johnson was restricted by not being able to use PWA funds both to stimulate economic recovery and to encourage business to participate in and comply with codes of fair competition. Johnson was further handicapped by the legal advice he received from NRA lawyers that the NRA was unconstitutional. Hence, Johnson felt he had to rely on a combination of social compulsion and voluntary compliance to make the program work. "In this way," according to Schlesinger, "he could bypass the constitutional issue. NRA could not therefore be an agency of direction. It had to be a forum of bargaining. The licensing powers written so hopefully into the bill could not be invoked (and, indeed, never were)."[60] Thus the NRA had the responsibility to bring about an industrial recovery, but it did not have the legal authority to order any business to obey its guidelines.

By the end of June 1933, a cotton textile code outlawing child labor was negotiated, but no other major industry had submitted a code of fair business practices. An alarmed and desperate Johnson, anxious to demonstrate immediate progress to legitimize his beloved NRA, came up with the idea of the "blanket code," which was called the President's Reemployment Agreement (PRA). Under the PRA, the nation's 5 million employers were asked (that is, publicly pressured), pending the acceptance of a negotiated code, "to sign an agreement to observe minimum wage [$12 to $15 a week] and maximum hour [thirty-five to forty hours a week] standards, to abolish child labor, and to refrain from unnecessary price increases. In an inspired gesture, [Johnson] rewarded compliance with the emblem of the Blue Eagle, the Navaho Indian Thunderbird. 'We Do Our Part,' the emblem read."[61] On July 20, the day after another stock market crash, Johnson spoke on national radio, urging employers to wire their acceptance of the PRA. Within months, almost half the nation's employers signed the PRA, which covered about 16 million workers out of a total of about 25 million.

Johnson's public relations strategy was both romantic and ridiculous. It was inspired by the patriotic rallies of the Great War. Millions of Blue Eagle posters in stores and movies reminded citizens that Americans were fighting a war against industrial pirates, monopolistic price cutting, and chiselers. In early September 1933, 250,000 people marched up Fifth Avenue in New York City to demonstrate their support of the NRA while millions cheered from the sidelines—the largest parade in the city's history. Bellush writes, "Johnson used the rallies, parades, and four minute speakers to whip up public enthusiasm and convince millions of employers to sign the NRA pledges, in the expectation that this would automatically insure rising wages and millions of new jobs. . . . Carried away by his own enthusiasm, he predicted that the blanket agreement would insure the rehiring of five to six million workers in little more than a month. The next day, he ventured a more conservative estimate—that three million would be reemployed within a two month period."[62] When these optimistic predictions were not fulfilled, support for the NRA plummeted. Cynics claimed that its initials stood for the "National Run-Around." Because the NRA symbolized the New Deal in the public's mind after June 1933, its ineffectiveness and administrative chaos were a major setback for the legitimation of a liberal regime.

Realistically, the success of the NRA was not going to be determined by parades and Blue Eagle posters; it was going to be decided by the outcomes of its negotiating processes. Under NRA procedures, the bargaining over codes of fair practice would be dominated by business interests, an outcome that was acceptable to Johnson. Beneath Johnson's bombastic rhetoric and all the hoopla of Blue Eagle rallies, the NRA was a more passive agency than most people understood. In Schlesinger's words, "NRA's job was not to impose codes, but to accept them. Defining for Richberg the difference between AAA and NRA, Johnson wrote, 'AAA thinks that government should run business. NRA thinks that business should run itself under government supervision.'"[63]

Reflecting the power structure of the old order, business representatives in the trade associations had the resources to have their experts and ideas prevail in the negotiation of the codes. Labor and consumers did not. By utilizing the self-government system of regulation, according to Bellush, "a dominant place was automatically assured trade associations, for they were the best organized forces available. As a result, not only did officials of existing associations actively initiate a majority of the codes, but the code system became largely a direct offshoot of the trade association system. . . . Having been selected by trade associations, or in association-dominated elections, code-authority members were almost exclusively businessmen. Less than 10 percent of the code authorities had some labor representation, and little more than 1 percent had consumer spokesmen. The government members were themselves usually businessmen."[64] Hence, most of the two hundred deputy administrators in the NRA, who were supposed to represent the public interest in the code-writing process, were actually more likely to be sympathetic with business rather than labor or consumers.

Many students of the NRA believe that it made a major mistake in attempting to engage in "comprehensive" rather than "selective" administration of the many industries in the United States. If the NRA had concentrated its limited resources on the largest business, the so-called commanding heights of the economy, it might have been more successful. Instead, the NRA, which unlike the AAA had to create its administrative structure from nothing, attempted to manage a task that was probably more difficult than Prohibition. In its two years of existence, the NRA staff of about 4,500 "negotiated and approved 546 codes of fair competition and 185 supplemental codes, filling eighteen volumes and thirteen thousand pages, released some eleven thousand administrative orders interpreting the codes; and influenced the President to issue seventy executive orders dealing with rights, procedures, and privileges under the NRA."[65]

To flaunt how ridiculous the code-making authorities were, Leuchtenburg writes, "Code 450 regulated the Dog Food Industry, Code 427 the Curled Hair Manufacturing Industry and Horse Hair Dressing Industry, and Code 262 the Shoulder Pad Manufacturing Industry. In New York, I. 'Izzy' Herk, executive secretary of Code 348, brought order to the Burlesque Theatrical Industry by insisting that no production could feature more than four strips."[66] However, in a more serious vein, Schlesinger emphasizes, "By the beginning of 1935, 568 of over 700 codes had one form or another of a minimum-price provision. Of the many techniques for price defense, the most popular was the prohibition of sales below cost."[67] Johnson claimed this practice protected wages, but it also prevented price competition.

By the autumn of 1933, the evaluations of the NRA were turning negative. Progressives were publicizing the idea that the NRA was dominated by egocentric business interests who were taking advantage of the suspension of antitrust laws to engage in cartel activities. When Johnson launched a new "Buy Now" campaign to promote economic recovery, it failed; it only seemed to highlight that prices had risen faster than employment. The unemployed could not increase their purchases. Johnson was pressured into having public hearings on price complaints in the Commerce Building on January 9, 1934. "In over a thousand pages of testimony," according to Bellush, "witness after witness contended that the open-price provision written into many of the codes—which required the public posting throughout an industry of proposed price changes, generally with waiting periods before the new prices could go into effect—facilitated a decided trend toward monopolistic price fixing, insured uniformity of price quotations, and illustrated the true nature of self-government in industry."[68]

Johnson designated February 27 as a Field Day of Criticism, but the groundswell of complaints from labor, consumers, retail merchants, and small businessmen forced the NRA to extend the meetings for four days. To block a congressional investigation of monopolistic practices in the NRA by Senator Gerald Nye, Johnson agreed that the president would create a National Recovery Board in March, headed by the leftist seventy-seven-year-old trial lawyer, Clarence Darrow. When the board's reports were released to the public in May, they accused the NRA of engaging in monopolistic practices that hurt the small businessman and retarded economic recovery. An enraged Johnson and Richberg responded that Darrow's National Recovery Board was guilty of prejudice and partisanship.[69] Johnson was enduring the dead cats he had prophesied in June 1933.

Another dilemma for the administration of the NRA was labor. Johnson suggested at an early press conference that the NRA should not be used to unionize workers. But union leaders, who had lost membership during the 1920s and the first few years of the Depression, were determined to take advantage of Section 7(a). In their recruiting efforts, many labor leaders used the slogan, "The President wants you to join the union." Business leaders resisted the efforts of workers to unionize; the result was an increasing number of strikes. Another response of management to Section 7(a) was the creation of company unions as a means to meet the requirements of the law without strengthening labor's independent rights.[70]

In response to the increasing number of strikes, Johnson created the National Labor Board to manage the labor conflict. This board had seven members: three representing labor, three representing business, and, serving as chairman, the prolabor Senator Robert Wagner. In trying to promote the rights of workers, the National Labor Board developed progressively hostile relations with Johnson and Richberg. A major dispute concerned the issue of majority rule, that is, "a union designated by the majority of employees in a free election should become the recognized bargaining representative for all workers in the plant."[71] Both Johnson and Richberg accepted the idea of proportional representation, meaning that different unions, including company unions, could represent workers, despite the fact that proportional representation could be exploited as a union-busting maneuver.

Johnson also suggested that unions were no longer needed to protect workers and that strikes were counterproductive. Bellush notes, "Early on, Johnson and Richberg spoke out against the principle of majority rule in unionization, undermining the beneficial effects which labor leaders had wishfully anticipated from Section 7a's guarantees of the right to organize and bargain collectively. And acceptance of the company union by the NRA administrator and general counsel enabled management to evade those very provisions of the law which purportedly protected independent labor organizations."[72] The fact that Richberg, a lawyer that labor considered its representative at the general counsel of the NRA, sided with business on a number of key issues enraged a number of union officials.

By 1934, it was obvious that Johnson's leadership of the NRA was not promoting an economic recovery; was not maintaining business support; was alienating labor; and was generating endless disputes that required presidential decisions. Johnson's difficulties were amplified by his personal problems; he was an alcoholic who would occasionally disappear and engage in drinking binges, and he was having an affair with his assistant, Frances Robinson. Many New Dealers, including Tugwell, Perkins, and even Richberg, advised FDR to fire Johnson, but the president, perhaps reluctant to admit that he had made such a gigantic mistake, resisted what was inevitable for many months. The president finally ended the farce and received Johnson's resignation in September 1934.[73] In late October, Roosevelt created the National Emergency Council, headed by Richberg, to oversee the NRA. Reporters jumped to the conclusion that Richberg had become the "assistant president," a kiss-of-death title that irritated Roosevelt and some cabinet members.

Roosevelt had assumed that the NRA, designed to placate a variety of competing interests, informed by Industrial, Labor, and Consumer Advisory Boards, would be able to successfully negotiate the most sensitive political and economic problems in an administrative forum. But instead of erecting a mechanism that would permit tough decisions to be made and implemented, FDR forged a new battlefield where decisions could not be legitimated and thus provoked endless strife. Simply put, the NRA generated more problems than it solved. The NRA could not operate as planned because it was riddled with contradictions. For the historian Alonzo Hamby, the NRA was handicapped by an "identity crisis." "Was it simply government-sanctioned industrial self-organization subject to a few general rules, undertaken in the belief that a resurgent business sector would pull the economy to recovery? Was it an exercise in a state-managed economy that sought to provide equally for the interest of business, labor, and the larger public, defined as consumers? Ultimately, moreover, was not either alternative an affront to a deeply ingrained American ethic that valued business fragmentation and the free market?"[74] Lacking a political identity, much of what the NRA did—or even considered—could be attacked as being unauthorized.

The most notorious contradiction in the NIRA was created by clauses that exempted the proposed codes of fair competition from the antitrust laws, and by other clauses stating that no code should be implemented that would "permit monopolies or monopolistic practices," or that would eliminate, oppress, or discriminate against small enterprises. In brief, the NRA was licensed to cartelize but ordered not to engage in monopolistic practices. Cooperation among businesses was encouraged because it was good; monopolistic collusion was forbidden because it was bad.

Hawley traces the problems of the NIRA to the competing visions of national planners (Rex Tugwell), supporters of a business commonwealth (Hugh Johnson, Raymond Moley, and Gerard Swope), and antitrusters (Louis Brandeis, William Borah, and Gerald Nye). In Hawley's words, "The vision of enforcing competition, said the planners and business rationalizers, was outmoded, intellectually bankrupt and a proven failure. The vision of a business commonwealth, said the antitrusters and national planners, was only a mask for the proven evils of private monopoly. And the idea of democratic planning, said the antitrusters and business planners, was a contradiction in terms, a policy that could only result in the eventual destruction of political democracy, property rights, individual liberty, and the capitalist system."[75] With such a mixed and conflicting background, reinforced by rival pressure groups and political leaders, consistent administration by the NRA was impossible and thus roused great uncertainty.

That uncertainty about the ultimate purposes of the New Deal and where FDR's experimentation would eventually end up explains the growing business opposition to the NRA. After Roosevelt saved the banks in March 1933 and the economy began its slow recovery, first a few, then many business leaders exhibited growing anxieties about the role of the NRA. There were spreading fears that the NRA was paving the road to union domination, proving to be the initial step toward bureaucratic socialism, and creating a permanent system of government control of industry.[76] The new red tape and conflicting regulations were frustrating to almost all businesses, even the many who were benefiting from them. However, business representatives were deeply divided about the NRA. Richard Hofstadter reports, "A poll taken in 1935 [when the NIRA was being considered by Congress for renewal] showed Chamber of Commerce members were about three to one for continuing the NRA, while National Association of Manufacturers members opposed it three to one."[77] Small store owners demanded that the NRA block the efforts of chain stores to underprice them, which they considered a "monopolistic practice" designed to put them out of business, but which also aided consumers. Hawley notes, "Many of the business constraints . . . stemmed from the welter of conflicts within industries or between industries, conflicts between large units and small units, integrated firms and nonintegrated firms, chain stores and independents, manufacturers and distributors, new industries and declining ones, and so on *ad infinitum*. These conflicts had once been left to the marketplace, but now they were to be settled politically. . . . The Administration, moreover, was often caught in the middle."[78]

As a middle-way compromise program, the NRA was subject to attacks from all sides. Rosenof writes, "Adversaries ranged from those on the radical left, who denounced it as an institutionalization of the scarcity economics of capitalism; to those on the conservative right, who denounced it as an institutionalization of the scarcity economics of New Dealism. It was opposed by antimonopoly progressives, who saw in it a sanctification of trusts, and by conservatives, who insisted that it destroyed free market processes."[79] Farm leaders protested that the NRA was more successful raising industrial prices than the AAA was in boosting agricultural prices and thus was preventing farmers from achieving their goal of parity. A Keynesian like Marriner Eccles criticized the NRA for not providing the essential remedy for economic recovery, namely, a boost in consumer purchasing power. Instead, the NRA rendered a grim paradox: "Labor could get higher wages and no jobs; business could get higher prices and no markets."[80]

Perhaps the major contradiction about the NRA existed in FDR's head. "In his earlier career," according to Hawley, "he had tended to argue both sides of the question, and as President he still resisted consistency. On the one hand, he admired the principles of Louis Brandeis, was genuinely sympathetic with the problems of small business, and liked to talk about his Administration as a continuation of Wilson's New Freedom. Yet, at the same time, he liked to talk about Theodore Roosevelt's ideas of a 'partnership' between government and the better class of businessmen, and he could not get away from the notion that businessmen might gather around a conference table and schedule production so as to eliminate market gluts and stabilize employment."[81] In Roosevelt's mind, the abandonment of the NRA would mean the return of the chaos of overproduction and underemployment; he did not believe in market control or market rationality. But what FDR did not realize was that the NRA would never be able to provide security. Instead, it became the focal point of grievances for all those suffering from economic decisions and trends.

Despite all of the problems associated with the NRA, the president was still committed to its renewal. In February 1935, in a message to Congress largely written by Richberg, Roosevelt "recommended retention of Section 7a . . . , restriction of future price and production controls to protect small business, and the use of the antitrust laws against monopolies and price fixing."[82] Early in May, the United States Chamber of Commerce declared its opposition to the New Deal, and in late May, the Supreme Court, in *Schecter Poultry Corporation v. The United States*, unanimously proclaimed that Section 1 of the NIRA was unconstitutional. The *Schecter* decision liberated FDR from the authority-constricting role of defending a fatally flawed policy and prevented him from engaging in the robust politics of reconstruction.

One would have expected FDR to have suffered more political losses from the failure and collapse of the NRA. Instead, much of the blame fell on the shoulders of Johnson for his mercurial administration, on Richberg for betraying labor, and on businessmen for exploiting self-regulation to further their own selfish goals. In avoiding culpability for the NRA, FDR demonstrated the Teflon capabilities that we normally associate with Reagan's presidency, but that actually reflect one of the key advantages enjoyed by presidents practicing the politics of reconstruction.

In evaluating the NRA, one cannot write it off as a total failure because the results were more complex. Supporters of the NRA correctly claimed that it increased the rights and power of workers and abolished child labor—goals progressives had been pursuing since the early 1900s. They also suggest that the NRA did not bring about economic recovery but *did* "provide a psychological stimulant and help check the deflationary spiral that appeared so inexorable in the early months of 1933."[83] Each of the three groups that originally supported the program—the business commonwealth, the national economic planners, and the antitrusters—"tended to regard the NRA experience as confirmation of its own point of view, and the result was a heightening of mutual suspicion and a reluctance to be duped again."[84] Despite the efforts of reconstructive leaders to claim their proposals deserve universal support, their politics are polarizing and rarely bring about closure for the major issues of the day.

Finally, David Kennedy supplies the most perceptive criticism of the NRA by indicating that it "rested upon the assumption, widespread in the early New Deal years, that overproduction had caused the Depression and that in scarcity lay salvation. That premise precluded any serious search for economic growth, made stability the touchstone of policy, and underwrote the kinds of restrictionist practices traditionally associated with monopolies."[85] To raise prices, the strategy of the NRA was to limit production, a policy that would not promote employment.

The NRA was a false core policy; it could never fulfill New Deal objectives and be the successful centerpiece of a liberal regime. By killing the NRA, the Supreme Court not only alleviated the president from having to defend a policy that generated endless strife and had limited benefits, but it also expanded his authority to seek other avenues to achieve his goals. Roosevelt could now see with greater clarity that labor, not business, was his natural ally in creating a liberal regime. On July 5, 1935, FDR signed the National Labor Relations Act, a bill championed by Senator Wagner and designed to protect workers' rights, including majority rule for union representation.

Labor Policy

Roosevelt was not a consistent supporter of labor during the 1930s. Schlesinger explains FDR's behavior in terms of his background: "Reared in the somewhat paternalistic traditions of prewar progressivism and the social work ethos, Roosevelt thought instinctively in terms of government doing things for working people rather than giving the unions power to win their own victories."[86] Leuchtenburg points out, "while the details of agricultural policy fascinated him, the minutiae of collective bargaining vexed him. The president either could not or would not grasp the critical importance of the issue of employee representation. He told reporters irritatedly in May 1934 that workers could choose anyone they wished to represent them, including a union, the Ahkoond of Swat, or the Royal Geographic Society."[87] Roosevelt's top priority was economic recovery, not labor reform; his goal was to expand the number of jobs in order to increase purchasing power. Although he was angry that business leaders frequently neither recognized nor bargained in good faith with union representation, he was opposed to strikes because they would hinder the recovery.

In 1920, about 12 percent of the labor force was unionized; by 1933, less than 6 percent of U.S. workers (about 3 million) were members of unions.[88] Even during the prosperous 1920s, workers had little job security and were subject to the capriciousness of markets and the dictates of bosses. Thanks to the progressives, labor legislation had grown slowly to protect children, women, and the health of workers. A harbinger of more favorable attitudes toward unions was indicated in 1932, when Congress passed the Norris–La Guardia Act, and President Hoover reluctantly signed it. This law prohibited federal courts from issuing injunctions to enforce agreements—called yellow dog contracts—that employers pressured workers to sign, promising they would never join a union.[89] However, union leaders generally shared the prevailing assumption of minimal governmental intervention in the economy. They "believed that organization and collective bargaining, not laws, were the ways to improve labor conditions."[90] Considering how often unions had suffered at the hands of presidents, governors, and state and federal courts, it was almost impossible for labor leaders to envision that government could become an ally of workers. But the rise of the New Deal and a new set of more militant union leaders generated hope that a liberal regime could bring about "a living wage" for all workers (defined as sufficient remuneration to support working-class families), and "industrial democracy" (defined as the expansion of civil rights for workers in the private sector).[91]

The labor movement was also weakened by internal divisions. Since the 1880s, labor had been represented nationally by the American Federation of Labor (AFL). The AFL was largely guided by the philosophy of Samuel Gompers, a British immigrant who came to the United States when he was thirteen and was president of the AFL for almost twenty-eight years, until his death in 1924. Gompers and his successor, William Green, believed that unions should rely on collective bargaining with employers to achieve higher wages and better working conditions and should avoid ties with government and political parties. He also emphasized that workers ought to be organized by crafts—that is, as carpenters, plumbers, or electricians—as opposed to industrial unions, which organized all workers, whatever their craft, working in a single industry. According to Leuchtenburg, "Many of the Federation leaders, primarily skilled workers of northern European stock, displayed open contempt toward the new industrial unionists. Dan Tobin, head of the Teamsters, dismissed the factory workers as 'rubbish.' William Collins, the AFL representative in New York State confided: 'My wife can always tell from the smell of my clothes what breed of foreigners I've been hanging out with.'"[92] The craft union structure of the AFL and its condescending attitude toward the new immigrants meant that it was incapable of recruiting the semiskilled workers who labored in the mass-production industries.[93] Those semiskilled workers were now available for union mobilization thanks to the misery produced by the Depression and the hope generated by the New Deal.

In 1935, the best friend of labor in government was Senator Robert Wagner of New York. As the son of a German immigrant family, he had experienced poverty and had been initiated into politics by Tammany Hall. As a senator in the late 1930s, he would sometimes claim, with a smile, that Tammany was "the cradle of modern liberalism in America."[94] For Wagner, the best way to increase the purchasing power of workers, reduce gross disparities in income, promote the security of workers, and prevent another Depression was through the expansion of unions. He believed that the expansion of independent unions representing the interests of workers through collective bargaining with management would result in fewer strikes and a healthier economy.

With the help of his staff aide, Leon Keyserling, a Columbia University protégé of Rexford Tugwell, Wagner introduced a bill on February 21, 1935, designed to strengthen labor rights beyond what Section 7(a) of the NIRA had been able to accomplish. The National Labor Relations Act, or the Wagner Act as it was also called, "replaced the generalized statements of Section 7(a) with a comprehensive labor statute outlawing specific unfair labor practices such as company unions and other employer tactics which interfered with collective bargaining; provided for a permanent National Labor Relations Board with power comparable to that of the Federal Trade Commission to proceed on its own initiative against violators; and gave legal sanction to the right of an employee majority to choose collective-bargaining responsibilities for the whole group."[95] Although Wagner was sure his bill was constitutional, he was concerned that if his legislation was enacted into law, it would be seriously challenged in federal courts by the best lawyers big business could hire. The preamble of the Wagner Act stressed both how strikes influenced the flow of interstate commerce and how independent unions promoted the general welfare.

The Senate Labor Committee hearings on the Wagner bill in March and April attracted front-page coverage in the newspapers. Wagner's proposal was supported by union officials such as William Green and John L. Lewis, the president of the United Mine Workers (UMW), and vehemently opposed by the National Association of Manufacturers and the U.S. Chamber of Commerce. Business leaders and lawyers claimed that the bill was unconstitutional, that it was unfair because all restrictions were placed on business and none on unions, and that it promoted class conflict.[96] Some business leaders claimed the legislation "would out STALIN Stalin" and "end the fine spirit of cooperation . . . which has been growing through employee representation plans."[97] However, the Wagner bill was also opposed at the hearings by representatives of the Communist party, who condemned it as fascist.

The Senate Labor Committee endorsed the Wagner Act, and it easily won Senate approval by a vote of 63 to 12 on May 16. Although Wagner's bill went beyond the preferences of Roosevelt, who was still satisfied with labor's rights as outlined in Section 7(a), in response to the growing hostility of business and the leftist militancy of Congress, the president finally endorsed the legislation at a press conference on May 24. According to Freidel, "When he was told that President Green of the AFL had left his office saying he thought Roosevelt was in sympathy with and friendly to the purposes of the Wagner bill, Roosevelt remarked, 'Well, I think that is a fair statement.' In this almost offhand way, without the slightest expenditure of his lobbying strength upon Congress, Roosevelt linked himself with a measure that created the New Deal alliance with organized labor."[98] Three days later, on May 27, the Supreme Court delivered its Schecter Brothers decision, which unanimously declared the NIRA unconstitutional. The House of Representatives passed the Wagner bill without a roll call on June 19, and the president signed it into law on July 5.

With the passage of the National Labor Relations Act, union leaders could now aspire to be major players in the new liberal regime. The passage of the Wagner Act over the protests of business leaders reflected their declining influence in politics and policy making. For the first time in American history, workers had a powerful ally in the law and the federal government. The new labor legislation

> guaranteed workers the right to select their own union by majority vote, and to strike, boycott, and picket. And it enunciated a list of "unfair labor practices" by employers [but not unions], including the maintenance of company-dominated unions, the blacklisting of union activists, intimidation and firing of workers who sought to join an independent organization, and the employment of industrial spies. To determine the will of the workers, the new law established a National Labor Relations Board, which heard employee complaints, determined union jurisdiction, and conducted on-site elections. Whenever a majority of a company's workers voted for a union to represent them, management had a legal obligation to negotiate with that union over wages, hours, and working conditions.[99]

Within the AFL, there were those who supported industrial unionism, including John L. Lewis and Sidney Hillman, head of the Amalgamated Clothing Workers (ACW). With the passage of the National Labor Relations Act and the growing animosity between FDR and business, they believed this was labor's unique opportunity to expand union membership by millions of new members and forge a mutually beneficial political alliance with the New Deal. At the AFL convention in October 1935, Lewis advocated that the federation commit itself to unionizing mass production workers, but his proposal received only 38 percent of the delegate votes. The intensity of the conflict was demonstrated when Lewis punched "Big Bill" Hutcheson, president of the carpenters' union. Lewis and his supporters considered their defeat to be only a temporary setback, and within a few weeks, they created a Committee for Industrial Organization (CIO). In September 1936, the AFL suspended the CIO unions for violating their contracts with the federation. The CIO then renamed itself the Congress of Industrial Organizations and became a separate federation of industrial unions.[100]

Although business leaders felt no obligation to obey the Wagner Act because they were sure it would be declared unconstitutional by the Supreme Court, union officials, especially the militant organizers of the CIO, were galvanized by its passage and had high hopes of reelecting a more prolabor FDR in the 1936 elections. These conflicting views of business executives and union leaders produced alarming rates of labor strife. There were over 2,000 strikes in 1935–1936 and over 4,700 in 1937.[101] In the summer of 1936, Lewis and Roosevelt solidified their political alliance, and they campaigned together in the fall. Lewis created Labor's Nonpartisan League to mobilize support for FDR and prounion Democrats and eventually provided the huge sum of nearly $600,000 for the president's reelection.[102] FDR's landslide win in 1936 helped labor attain its greatest triumphs. In Dubofsky's words, "Between January and April 1937, trade unionism accomplished what it had failed to achieve during the previous half century. Organized labor conquered the two most significant outposts of the open shop in mass-production industry, wresting a collective bargaining contract from General Motors on February 11 and one from United States Steel three weeks later."[103] In 1937, unions enrolled more than 3 million members, nearly doubling their membership. Finally, in April 1937, in a 5-to-4 decision, the Supreme Court declared the Wagner Act constitutional in *National Labor Relations Board v. Jones and Laughlin Steel Corporation*. The role of unions in the American economy and the liberal regime was legitimized.

Labor's successes triggered some negative reactions, however, especially to the CIO tactic of sit-down strikes. At the end of 1936, workers at two General Motors plants in Flint, Michigan, instead of picketing outside of the plant, physically occupied the plant and stopped production for six weeks. General Motors was not able to enlist the support of either the Democratic governor of Michigan, Frank Murphy, or the president to force

the strikers to leave the premises. When, in February, General Motors ca-
pitulated and recognized the United Auto Workers, the strategy was widely
emulated. In 1937, about a half-million workers engaged in some five hundred sit-down strikes.[104] By then, most public officials, including FDR and
Governor Murphy, agreed that sit-down strikes were illegal because they
violated property rights. On April 7, 1937, the Senate denounced sit-down
strikes by a vote of 75 to 3.

When the CIO began to try to organize workers in the so-called little
steel companies in May 1937, it found its efforts were no longer supported
by local officials in Pennsylvania, Ohio, Indiana, and Illinois. After ten
workers were killed in South Chicago near the gates of Republic Steel,
Lewis asked for the president's help. But Roosevelt, seeking to find refuge
in a defensible political position, condemned the steel companies for not
engaging in collective bargaining and the CIO for its militant tactics by
proclaiming "a plague on both your houses." An enraged Lewis responded,
"It ill behooves one who has supped at labor's table . . . to curse with equal
fervor and fine impartiality both labor and its adversaries when they become locked in deadly embrace."[105] As a result of this conflict, Lewis tried
to deny Roosevelt the benefit of the labor vote in the 1940 presidential
election by supporting the Republican, Wendell Willkie, but the president
was able to maintain his working-class support and was elected for a third
time.

Between 1933 and 1940, union membership expanded from less than
3 million members to over 8 million, which was about 23 percent of the
nonagricultural work force. According to David Kennedy, "Union membership was heavily concentrated in the mature industries of manufacturing,
transportation, and mining and in the northeastern and Pacific Coast states,
especially those states where pro-labor governors presided. In the South, still
predominantly agricultural and still wedded to the idea that cheap labor was
its biggest competitive asset, only one worker in 10 belonged to a union as
the decade of the 1930s closed."[106] The seeds were being planted for the
eventual alienation of the South from the liberal regime.

The New Deal could not raise the status of labor—especially the
unions—without lowering the influence of business. While the major
thrust of the New Deal was to increase the role of labor so that it could
expand its purchasing power within the capitalist system and reward the
Democratic party with its votes, many business leaders and their Republican allies saw this as the first steps toward socialism. The growing hostility
of business toward FDR compelled him to replace his original vision of a

cooperative commonwealth with a more realistic concept of a conflicted concert of interests "in which the government made itself the protector of the nation's interests and invited those interests to bid for its favors."[107]

Social Security

The Depression was a period of exceptional insecurity. Who could feel safe when banks were collapsing, farm prices were dropping, mortgages were being foreclosed, and companies were laying off workers? The problems were especially severe for the estimated 6.6 million Americans who were over sixty-five. Kennedy points out, "For the great majority of workers, who lacked any pension coverage whatsoever, the very thought of 'retirement' was unthinkable. Most elderly laborers worked until they dropped or were fired, then threw themselves either on the mercy of their families or on the decidedly less tender mercies of a local welfare agency. Tens of thousands of elderly persons passed their final days in the 1920s in nearly thirteen hundred city and county supported 'old-age homes.'"[108] But the misery generated by the Depression and the hope activated by the New Deal created a fertile environment that inspired demands for new policies to meet the old problems of unemployment and old age.

The concept of social security was not new. Otto von Bismarck's government in Germany initiated sickness and maternity benefits for industrial workers in 1883, workers' compensation in 1884, and old age benefits in 1889. Facing the rise of the Social Democrats, Bismarck's goal was to gain the loyalty of German workers for a paternalistic state. A paternalistic state with a large bureaucracy was part of the German culture; it was not part of ours. Although the social insurance movement had spread to about fifty countries by the early 1930s, it was not able to take root in the United States because of our tradition of self-reliance and our lack of a labor party. Barry Karl describes the challenge for FDR: "A national ambivalence forced Roosevelt to shape his social security program into a form that would be widely acceptable. Americans had come to accept pensions for widows—usually women without careers whose livelihood ended if their husband died. Pensions for persons in low-paying public services, like school teaching, were also winning acceptance. But the idea that a man, employed throughout his life, should be compensated for having failed, as they would have seen it, to save for his later years . . . was not part of the traditional work ethic."[109] Creating a social security program that would be popular and compatible with our political culture and federal system would be a major test for FDR's political skills.

In Roosevelt's efforts to formulate a social security program, he would be aided by his secretary of labor, Frances Perkins, the first female cabinet member. When he offered her this job on February 22, 1933, Perkins stressed that she was committed to developing programs to aid the elderly and the unemployed. She was dedicated to promoting social justice because of her Christian religious beliefs, her education at Mount Holyoke College, her work at the Jane Addams Hull House, and her investigations, as a New York State official, of the 1911 fire at New York City's Triangle Shirtwaist Company, which killed 146 women workers. Kennedy claims, "the Triangle Fire episode shaped Frances Perkins' lifelong approach to such issues. It deepened her conviction that many employers, left to their own devices, could not be counted upon to deal squarely with their employees. It also reinforced her belief that enlightened middle class reformers could do more and better for the working classes through wise legislation than workers could do for themselves through union organization—and could do it more efficiently, without nasty industrial conflict and protracted social disruption."[110] In brief, Perkins carried the old progressive banner of reform into the New Deal.

The president's plan to devise a social security program was affected by a sixty-seven-year-old doctor in California, Dr. Francis Townsend. In 1934, Townsend proposed that the government pay a pension of $200 per month to all citizens over sixty who agreed to stop working and spend the entire amount that month. The pension would be financed by a 2 percent sales tax. Twenty-five million people signed petitions supporting the Townsend Plan. The plan generated a crusade that resembled a Protestant revival. "Townsend meetings," according to Leuchtenburg, "featured frequent denunciations of cigarettes, lipstick, necking, and other signs of urban depravity. Townsendites claimed as one of the main virtues of the plan that it would put young people to work and stop them from spending their time in profligate pursuit of sex and liquor."[111] The fiscal irresponsibility of the Townsend Plan is demonstrated by Schrieber and Shoven: "The $200 per month promised by the proposal in 1934 would be roughly equivalent to $3,900 per month in 1998 dollars. By comparison, the average monthly benefit for a retired worker receiving social security in 1998 was around $800 per month. The estimated annual cost of the Townsend Plan in 1934 would have been $24 billion if ten million people had taken advantage of it."[112] The Townsend Plan was harebrained, but it had public and congressional support because many people considered it an authentically American grassroots solution to the problems of recovery, unemployment, and retirement.

Roosevelt's vision of a social security program was based on several ideas. When he offered Frances Perkins the post of secretary of labor in February 1933, he made it clear to her that he was opposed to a dole. Perkins, who had worked under Roosevelt when he was governor of New York, assumed that her role was to be an occasional nag to remind the president to fulfill his social vision. At a later date, he once expressed that vision to her: "We are going to make a country in which no one is left out."[113] His ultimate vision was to provide citizens with "cradle to grave" protection from the hazards of life. In a message to Congress on June 8, 1934, he operationalized this idea by proclaiming that guarding the security of men, women, and children was his top priority, and by declaring his intentions to develop a program to protect citizens from the hazards of life—especially old age and unemployment. In conversations with Perkins, he made it clear that this new program should be largely based on the cooperation of the states and the federal government. He also emphasized that his future proposal would be financed by a contributory social insurance system and not through an increase in general taxation. Arthur Altmeyer, who would play a key role in the development of social security, explained Roosevelt's reasoning: "The President's desire to place chief reliance on a system of contributory social insurance was due as much to his belief that it was a financially safe system as to his belief that it provided protection as a matter of earned right. He felt that requiring the benefits to be financed entirely by contributions furnished a built-in safeguard."[114] In other words, his proposal, unlike the Townsend Plan, would be actuarially sound, and the recipients would not be receiving benefits for nothing—they would have earned them through years of contributions.

Now the challenge was to transform FDR's vision into a legislative proposal that could pass Congress. On June 29, 1934, the president issued Executive Order 6757 creating a Committee on Economic Security, a technical board, and an advisory council. The Committee on Economic Security was chaired by Frances Perkins and consisted of Henry Morgenthau, Homer Cummings, Henry Wallace, and Harry Hopkins. Arthur Altmeyer, who had a doctorate in economics from the University of Wisconsin and was serving as an assistant secretary under Perkins, was named chairman of the technical board, which was composed of government officials from various departments. Altmeyer recruited Professor Edwin Witte of the University of Wisconsin to be the executive director of the committee's staff. "The advisory council," in Altmeyer's words, "consisted of 23 persons, five of whom were labor leaders, five employers, and the rest persons interested in social welfare. The function of the advisory council, as the president conceived it to be, was to convey to the committee the views of interested individuals and groups outside of the government, but the council was not expected to make a formal report."[115]

The social security advisory mechanism was almost overwhelmed by conflict because the issues were so significant and the participants felt so strongly about their preferred solutions. Meetings were long and heated; deadlines were never met; and the Committee on Economic Security was just barely able to get its legislative recommendations to the president. The staff operating under Witte's supervision was split by what were called the Wisconsin and the Ohio models. Both Witte and Altmeyer were supporters of the Wisconsin model, which was based on pure insurance criteria. According to Schrieber and Shoven,

> With this approach, one insures against a specified risk by accumulating a contingency fund that can be used to cover the expense when the contingency insured against actually occurs. This underlying approach was at the heart of the design of the Wisconsin unemployment insurance program that was adopted in 1932. Under this plan, the benefits were financed through a state tax accumulated in individual employer accounts subject to specified reserve accounts. Each employer account covered only that employer's workers. So the employer who experienced little or no unemployment would not have to make contributions once the reserve limit was achieved. Those who experienced frequent unemployment would have to make constant contributions.[116]

Professors Barbara Armstrong of the law school of the University of California and J. Douglas Brown of Princeton University supported the Ohio model. "In their model, reserves would be pooled, not accumulated at the level of the individual employer. This approach to social insurance called for government subsidy in addition to individual premiums, for two reasons. The first was that such subsidies were necessary to provide 'adequate' benefits to meet unemployed workers' needs. The second was this insurance covered social ills caused by dysfunctions within the economy; these were beyond the control of individuals, and thus the financing of insurance should not be borne by the covered individual alone."[117] Obviously, the Ohio plan, if it were adopted, would have more redistribution of income consequences than the Wisconsin plan.

Within the committee, there were clashing visions between Perkins and Hopkins. Hopkins advocated that any citizen providing evidence of unemployment, old age, or ill health would receive benefits from the government financed by general tax revenues. Such a program, "by moving large sums of money from the rich minority, which paid federal taxes, to the poor majority, which did not, would redistribute income on a national scale."[118] When Hopkins and Perkins presented their arguments to the president, he rejected Hopkins's position because it was based on the dole.

Tugwell and Hopkins also objected to how old age insurance was going to be financed, namely, the payroll tax paid equally by worker and employer. The two advisers met with Roosevelt for two hours and argued that the payroll tax was essentially a sales tax, which was something the president had always opposed. But the president strongly supported the idea of worker contribution, for economic and political reasons.[119] It should be remembered that only 5 percent of the public paid an income tax in 1935.

According to FDR's executive order, the Committee on Economic Security was supposed to submit a written report to the president on December 1. But it wasn't until the afternoon of December 24 that Perkins and Hopkins, using a draft of the report, gave an oral summation of the committee's recommendations to the president. After a long discussion, Roosevelt accepted the recommendations and planned to present them to Congress by January 17, 1935. However, on the afternoon of January 16, he noticed a table in the old age insurance part of the proposal that disturbed him—namely, that in 1965, the old age insurance program would begin to run deficits that would have to be met with support from general tax revenues. Roosevelt summoned Perkins, who in turn called for Witte to come to the White House. At first Roosevelt believed that the conclusions expressed in the table were a mistake; when he was informed otherwise, he announced that the funding program would have to be changed and the proposal rewritten. Apparently, when Perkins and Hopkins had made their presentation to him on December 24, a busy Roosevelt had not understood how the committee had resolved the dilemma of how older workers, who would have only a limited number of years to contribute to the old age trust fund, could receive adequate benefits when they retired.

At the January 16 meeting, Perkins explained to Roosevelt, "If workers who reached retirement age in the early years of the program were to receive even a small benefit, they would have to be paid partly out of current taxes paid into the fund by employers and younger workers. Then when the younger workers reached retirement age the fund would not have enough money on hand to pay the benefits to which they were entitled. The money would have to come from the general tax revenues, but it probably would not cost the government any more than in the earlier years because as more and more workers qualified for old age insurance, fewer and fewer would need old age assistance."[120] Roosevelt rejected this idea because it violated his instructions that the program should function on sound insurance principles. "He suggested," according to Witte, "that this table be left out of the report and that the committee, instead of definitely recommending the particular tax rates and benefit schedules incorporated in the original bill, merely present these as one plan for meeting the problem which Congress might or might not accept."[121] After the bill was introduced to Congress on January 17, Morgenthau presented a plan for a self-supporting old age insurance system. As Martin explains, "The tax rate would start at 2 instead of 1 percent and rise to 6 in twelve years instead of 5 in twenty."[122] The Morgenthau amendment was accepted by Congress. This episode clearly demonstrates how dedicated Roosevelt was to a program that was contributory and self-financing.

In Roosevelt's message to Congress on social security on January 17, 1935, he never mentioned the Townsend Plan; instead he emphasized that his program, although new, was based on proven ideas and fiscally conservative procedures that would protect millions of Americans from the pain caused by economic insecurity. The crucial word in the speech was *sound*—he used it eight times. His proposal was based on a "sound idea" and "a sound ideal." "Most of the other advanced countries of the world have already adopted it and their experience affords the knowledge that social insurance can be made a sound and workable project." He also suggested that his proposal provided a mechanism that would offer relief, recovery, and reform at a reasonable cost. In Roosevelt's words, "No one can guarantee this country against the dangers of future depressions but we can reduce these dangers. We can eliminate many of the factors that cause economic depressions, and we can provide the means of mitigating their results. This plan for economic security is at once a measure of prevention and a method of alleviation. We pay now for the dreadful consequence of economic insecurity—and dearly. This plan presents a more equitable and infinitely less expensive means of meeting these costs."[123] No one was better than FDR in using conservative words—*sound, prudent, caution*—in support of liberal programs.

After the president submitted the bill to Congress on January 17, it was assigned to the House Ways and Means Committee. The committee held hearings from January 21 to February 12 and then reworked the language of the bill for two months. The title of the bill was changed from the

Economic Security Act to the Social Security Act. The committee accepted Morgenthau's proposal to raise the initial payroll tax, scheduled to begin on January 1, 1937, from 1 to 2 percent and then to raise the tax to 6 percent in twelve years rather than 5 percent in twenty years.

Southern Congress members were acutely sensitive about how social security would affect race relations in their segregated states. They were particularly opposed to a provision about old age insurance that required states to offer benefits that would provide, "when added to the income of the aged recipient, a reasonable subsistence compatible with decency and health." In Professor Witte's testimony before the Senate Finance Committee, he acknowledged that this provision was taken from Massachusetts and New York state laws because it "constituted a flexible standard related to varying circumstances throughout the country. However, Senator [Harry] Byrd [from Virginia] forced Dr. Witte to admit that in the final analysis this requirement meant that a federal official had the right to determine what constituted reasonable subsistence compatible with decency and health. The result was that the committee eliminated this clause from the bill."[124] Southern legislators were not going to allow federal officials to interfere in how the South discriminated against Negroes.

Republican Congress members generally opposed the social security bill. They believed that "recovery must precede reform" and that the imposition of payroll taxes in 1937, years before anyone would receive old age insurance benefits, would stifle the recovery. All of the Republicans on the Ways and Means Committee voted against the social security bill. Republicans argued that the bill was unconstitutional, that "it would impose a crushing burden upon industry and labor," and that it would "establish a bureaucracy in the field of insurance in competition with private business."[125] A Republican congressman from upstate New York, John Taber, declared, "Never in the history of the world has any measure been brought here so insidiously designed as to prevent business recovery, to enslave workers, and to prevent any possibility of the employers providing work for the people."[126] Social security was clearly a realigning issue between the Democrats and the Republicans.

On April 19, the House passed the social security bill by a vote of 371 to 33. On June 19, the Senate passed its version of the bill by a vote of 77 to 6. It took nearly two months for a conference committee to reconcile the differences, but on August 8, the committee's compromise bill passed the House; it passed the Senate the next day. On August 14, 1935, President Roosevelt signed the Social Security Act into law. In signing the law, FDR said, "We can never insure one hundred percent of the population against one hundred percent of the hazards and vicissitudes of life, but we have tried to frame a law which will give some measure of protection to the average citizen and to his family against the loss of a job and against poverty-ridden old age. This law, too, represents a cornerstone in a structure which is being built but is by no means complete."[127]

The Social Security Act created ten programs: old age insurance, unemployment insurance, old age assistance, aid to dependent children, maternal and child health aid, child welfare services, crippled children services, public health work, vocational rehabilitation, and pensions for the blind. Old age insurance initially covered about 26 million workers, or about 60 percent of the workforce. The first payroll deductions began in 1937, while the first distributions of benefits were scheduled for 1942. Congress revised the law so that the first distributions were paid in 1940. Workers and employers paid an equal tax on the first $3,000 of the workers' annual wages. Although old age insurance was solely a federal program, unemployment insurance was a cooperative program administered by the federal government and the states. It was financed by a federal tax on businesses employing eight or more workers. In 1936, the tax was set at 1 percent; it would rise to 2 percent in 1937, and 3 percent in subsequent years. Walter Trattner explains, "The law required employers to contribute to the federal treasury a certain percentage of their payroll for insurance purposes, but it also stipulated that 90 percent of that levy would be returned to those states that set up their own unemployment plans in accordance with standards approved by a federal Social Security Board created to administer the program. (Within two years, every state had set up an unemployment insurance system that met the requirements fixed by the board.)"[128]

Liberals, both in 1935 and in more recent times, have found much to criticize in the Social Security Act. To increase its chances of being enacted into law, health care was dropped from the original proposal. Because health problems are one of the major hazards in life, this was a major omission that conflicted with FDR's original vision. Many liberals also condemn the financing of retirement by payroll contributions rather than by income taxes because they believe that this is a regressive tax that prevents the system from being able to redistribute income. Liberals were particularly critical that over 9 million workers—especially many African Americans and farm laborers—were not originally covered by the retirement program. Even Frances Perkins lamented that the original concepts of social security "had been chiseled down to a conservative pattern."[129] Michael Katz argues, "By pointedly distinguishing social security from relief, they [New Deal policy makers] froze the distinction between social insurance and public assistance into federal policy, where it has been stuck ever since, and built a regressive system that reinforced economic inequalities. As salesmanship, their strategy was brilliant. For by dissociating social insurance from relief, they won public allegiance to welfare for the middle classes."[130]

These criticisms should not blind us to Roosevelt's achievement. He had circumvented nineteenth-century liberal traditions of individual self-reliance and local responsibility and created a national, compulsory program, with its own financing mechanism, that could—and would—be expanded. (For example, survivors' benefits were added to social security in 1939.) A program like social security, administered by a large federal bureaucracy, was unthinkable under the previous regime. FDR had formulated a welfare program that was popular with the public and (barely) acceptable to the Supreme Court. The significance of this change is explained by Walter Trattner: "For the first time in American history, funds to finance all or part of the needs of selected groups in the population became a major permanent item in the federal budget, one that has continued to grow each year. With the Social Security Act (and other New Deal programs), which introduced the idea of entitlement into national policy, the federal government assumed responsibility for the welfare of most, if not all, of its citizens."[131]

Finally, there is no better illustration of Roosevelt's political genius than his explanation of why he insisted workers pay payroll taxes. As Kennedy makes clear, FDR

> understood as clearly as any the inequity and economic dysfunctionality of the contributory payroll tax, but he understood equally those "legislative habits" and "prejudices" about which Perkins had reminded the Committee on Economic Security. "I guess you're right on the economics," Roosevelt explained to another critic . . . , "but those taxes were never a problem of economics. They are politics all the way through. We put those payroll contributions there so as to give the contributors a legal, moral, and political right to collect their pensions and their unemployment benefits. With those taxes in there, no damn politician can ever scrap my social program."[132]

And so far, no conservative president, such as Ronald Reagan or George W. Bush, has been able to alter social security in a conservative direction.

Conclusion

This chapter has tried to explain how the New Deal discovered and formulated its core policies. The common thread of many of FDR's policies was to provide security for those who had been wounded by the effects of the Depression: bankers, farmers, homeowners, and workers. The NIRA was the initial core policy, but it failed because it did not provide security for business, workers, and the Roosevelt administration. Its collapse constituted the end of the first New Deal, which was based on the idea of business-government cooperation. As the NIRA broke down and business withdrew its support from the New Deal, FDR felt the need to become the friend—but never the tool—of labor. Social security became the cornerstone of the New Deal for a number of reasons. As a national compulsory program, it provided a vivid contrast with the Republican regime, which wanted the poor cared for by local governments and private charity. Social security reflected the twentieth-century liberal philosophy that stressed that the federal government, guided by policy expertise and motivated by compassion, could promote the general welfare to a much greater degree than relying on competitive market outcomes. The social security program was also the actualization of what Roosevelt had said the country needed in his September 1932 Commonwealth Club speech, namely, enlightened administration. Unlike the Townsend Plan, social security was well planned, adequately financed, and efficiently administered, and it would eventually service millions with benefits. What also must have delighted FDR's partisan heart was that social security was the perfect realigning issue: the Republicans were opposed; the Democrats were for; and a heavy majority of voters supported the Democrats and the president in the 1936 election because of their support of social security.

8

Reagan's Core Policies

For Reagan, the core area of his reconstructive leadership was economic policy. Confident that he knew how the economic world worked, he wanted to lead the United States—which, in 1980, was suffering from a high misery index (a combination of the unemployment and inflation rates)—to a sustainable prosperity based on low tax rates, market rationality, the encouragement of entrepreneurial activities, and deregulation. Edwin Meese, perhaps the leading conservative in the administration, stressed that "since the economic agenda was the centerpiece of the Reagan program, an accurate understanding of what it meant in terms of taxes, budgets, deficits, and other outcomes is essential to any judgment of the President's place in history. The economic program was the first matter the administration tackled, and it dominated discussion of domestic politics for years. It was the most consistently attacked and most ardently defended of all the President's initiatives."[1] Reagan's economic performance was crucial to his political success because his election in 1980 was largely due to President Carter's inability to cure the stagflation of the late 1970s.

Reagan's Tax Policies

The Reagan presidency did not have to experiment to figure out what its core policies were. Because Reagan was a conviction politician, it was easier for him to select his legislative priorities than it had been for former presidents. While Carter had squandered his first hundred days (his honeymoon period) by overwhelming Congress with a barrage of legislative proposals, Reagan immediately established his strategic priorities: a three-year tax cut, budget reductions, and a major defense buildup. Believing that liberalism was a misguided ideology because it had led the nation into the dead end of the welfare state, his remedy was to renew the American Dream of individual freedom by utilizing supply-side tax cuts, budget reductions to reverse the growth of the welfare state, and a steep rise in defense expenditures that would allow the United States to vigorously defend its national interests against communism.

Reagan did not face as serious an economic crisis as FDR had in 1933, but with interest rates over 20 percent, an inflation rate of 13 percent, rising budget deficits, and fears of an impending recession, the American public was ready for a major change in economic policy. The question was whether the new president, with only a slim majority of Republicans in the Senate (53 to 47) and a minority in the House (192 to 243), would be able to obtain the congressional votes to enact his tax legislation.

A few days before the inauguration, Alan Greenspan, a top economic adviser during the transition, was quoted as saying, "The basic problem that faces the new administration is to lower rates on long-term bonds," because they reflect inflationary expectations. Greenspan predicted that if the administration could demonstrate that it was slowing the growth of federal expenditures and moving toward a balanced budget, "the markets will immediately lower the long-term inflation premium."[2]

David Stockman took on the job of moving the Reagan economic program into place as quickly as possible. The young, indefatigable Stockman gave up his congressional seat to accept Reagan's offer to be the director of the Office of Management and Budget. He entered the administration as a dedicated supply-sider but quickly became a fervent budget balancer. Stockman's grand doctrine (his term) was a minimalist state, relying on market rationality for progress and requiring the elimination of dozens of programs and the curtailing of social security and Medicare. Partly to his dismay, but appealing to his ambition and his ability to take advantage of opportunities, Stockman quickly saw that he was in a position to play a leading role in formulating Reagan's program. In Stockman's words, "I soon discovered that it would be up to me to design the Reagan Revolution. December [1980] brought hints, suggestions, and circumstantial evidence that the Californians—including the most crucial Californian—were neither equipped nor inclined to launch the kind of sweeping anti-statist revolution implied in the supply-side platform."[3]

Stockman blamed Edwin Meese for all the frantic activity, endless meetings, and lack of understanding about what it would take to launch the Reagan Revolution. He was also troubled by the few informal meetings he had with the president-elect in which Reagan generally listened, nodded, and smiled but neither issued orders nor requested information. Stockman stressed, "the President-elect . . . seemed so serene and passive. He conveyed the impression that since we all knew what needed to be done, we should simply get on with the job. Since I did know what to do, I took his quiet message of confidence to be a mandate. If the others weren't going to get his administration's act together, I would."[4] Consequently, he submitted a memo to Meese and James Baker on December 19, 1980, outlining a blueprint for commencing the economic recovery program within a few weeks of the inauguration. His action plan was accepted.

After the inauguration, Reagan's White House advisers, Edwin Meese as counselor, James Baker as chief of staff, and Michael Deaver as deputy chief of staff, worked together to make sure the president's time and resources were effectively focused on getting Congress to pass the economic program. After a series of failed presidencies, these advisers were also determined that Reagan achieve some early victories during his first few months in office and thus prove the ex-actor could govern as well as campaign. Stockman warned Reagan that the rising budget deficit, sluggish economic growth, and fears of inflation would split the budget balancers and supply-siders in the Republican party and erode the administration's ability to govern successfully. To avoid this calamity and to achieve major improvements before the November 1982 elections, Stockman advised Reagan to launch bold policies of supply-side tax cuts and major reductions in the budget within the first six months of his presidency. The key to holding the Reagan congressional coalition together was a budget cut that projected a balance by fiscal year 1984 because that would legitimize voting for a tax cut both by Republicans and Southern Democrats. Without the protection of a projected balanced budget, a vote for the largest tax reduction in United States history would look reckless because it would raise fears about inflation. The top goal was enactment of the three-year tax cut that was designed to spur economic growth, but the administration sought to make sure that a credible budget policy was passed first to calm concerns about inflation on Wall Street.[5]

In late January and early February 1981, Stockman engaged in weeks of feverish activity, transforming his grand doctrine into budget figures. In doing this, however, Stockman soon discovered that the economic program "was riddled with political contradictions." To reconcile these contradictions, there should have been tough meetings during which the trade-offs among Reagan's goals could have been clarified. But in the administration's haste to maintain its political advantages, there wasn't time for such meetings. The official most likely to see the urgency of such consultation, James Baker, was also the one most reluctant to call for it because of his association with George Bush's criticism during the Republican primaries that Reaganomics was based on "voodoo economics." Nor was Reagan likely to order such a debate because he never believed there was any incompatibility among his goals.

In the mad rush to project a balanced budget, Stockman created the magic asterisk. The asterisk was used as a temporary plug to fill in budget lines when actual cuts could not be specified. Officially, the asterisk meant "future savings to be identified." The magic referred to the elasticity of what dollar amounts the asterisk could signify; it could cover whatever it would take to reach a balanced budget by 1984. The asterisk eventually stretched to cover a gap of unspecified expenditure cuts of $44 billion. Stockman later claimed, "The circumstances of this accounting invention were slightly more innocent than what eventually materialized. I'd never believed we could review the entire $740 billion federal budget before February 18. So I contemplated two more budget-cut packages to be transmitted to Congress later."[6]

On February 18, within a month of being inaugurated, President Reagan presented his blueprint to change the direction of the United States in a nationally televised speech to Congress and in a widely distributed document, *America's New Beginning: A Program For Economic Recovery.* The administration was recommending the largest budget cuts ever proposed by a president because "The uncontrolled growth of government spending has been a primary cause of the sustained high rate of inflation experienced by the American economy."[7]

Using figures provided by the Office of Management and Budget (OMB), Reagan's economic program was proposing a $659.5 billion budget for fiscal year (FY) 1982 with a budget deficit of $45 billion. The president requested nondefense reductions totaling $41.4 billion in eighty-three major programs. He also asked for an additional $200 billion in cuts stretched out over the next three FYs that would decrease the federal government's share of the gross national product from 21 percent in FY 1981 to 19.3 percent in FY 1984. By FY 1984, on the basis of very optimistic forecasts, the administration predicted a balanced budget and modest surpluses there-after because revenues would be rising rapidly in response to the tax cut incentives. The budget reductions were designed to constrain the growth of federal spending rates from the 16 percent trend that prevailed during the last few years under Carter to about 7 percent over the next few years and to only about 5 percent by 1984. The defense program was projected to expand from one-quarter to one-third of total expenditures. To protect himself from Democratic accusations that his budget cuts were unfair, Reagan pledged in his speech, "We will continue to fulfill the obligations that spring from our national conscience. Those who, through no fault of their own, must depend on the rest of us, the poverty stricken, the disabled, the elderly, all those with true need, can rest assured that the social safety of programs they depend on are exempt from any cuts."[8] The protected social safety net programs, costing about $216 billion in FY 1982, were social security, Medicare, supplemental income for the blind, the aged, and the disabled, veterans' pensions, school lunch programs, Head Start, and summer youth jobs.

Although Reagan would have preferred that his tax cuts for individuals be retroactive to January 1, 1981, to raise more revenue, he proposed that tax rates be lowered by 10 percent on July 1, 1981; a second 10 percent on July 1, 1982; and the third 10 percent on July 1, 1983. The net effect would be a 5 percent cut in 1981 income taxes, a 15 percent in 1982 taxes, a 25 percent cut in 1983 taxes, and a 30 percent reduction in 1984 taxes. Marginal rates, ranging from 14 percent to 70 percent in 1980, would be lowered when fully implemented to a range between 10 percent and 50 percent. The Reagan tax bill also offered business faster depreciation tax write-offs (retroactive to January 1, 1981) in order to stimulate investment.

Stockman was disgusted to discover that there were members of the Reagan administration and not a few Republican Congress members who did not share his commitment to budget cutting. The budget director felt strongly, for example, that the federal government should not be spending $20 billion a year financing the repairing or building of local city streets, county roads, bridges, or mass transit systems. In his view, local improvements should be paid for by local taxes. But Drew Lewis, the secretary of transportation, was able to forge an alliance with conservative Senator Alfonse D'Amato and moderate Senator Arlen Specter to preserve most of these subsidies. Stockman later lamented, "In the end, the transportation sector of the pork barrel never even knew the Reagan Revolution had tilted at it."[9]

Stockman was also dismayed to find that although conservative Republican Congress members were demanding budget cuts, most of them had pet projects that they wished to protect. For Senator Orrin Hatch, it was the Job Corps, which had a major facility in Utah; for Senator Jesse Helms, it was the tobacco subsidy; for Senator Howard Baker, it was the Clinch River breeder reactor; for former astronaut Senator Jack Schmitt, it was the space program. Senator Schmitt told Stockman, "Technological progress is too important to be left to the free market." In response, Stockman later wrote, "Here was the premise of the Second Republic [Theodore Lowi's name for FDR's liberal regime] in a nutshell. Progress of *any* kind was too important to be left to capitalists. Only Washington could do it."[10] Even those espousing the ideas of the Reagan Revolution were susceptible to the enticements of the liberal regime. In brief, as Stockman desperately searched for places to cut the budget, he learned that each program was a sacred cow to some powerful figure. For Stockman, the dilemma was that in Washington, D.C., "sacred cows run in herds."[11]

As the number of real possibilities for cutting the budget diminished, the temptation to propose phony solutions increased. Both the administration and House Democrats rigged budget estimates and engaged in gimmick wars to escape from the dilemma of having to slice popular programs. One Democratic member of the House Budget Committee was quoted as saying, "It's our phony figures against Reagan's phony figures."[12]

After winning a budget vote in the House in March, several members of the Reagan administration thought that they had the momentum and opportunity to impose major reforms and cuts in social security. Both Reagan and Stockman viewed social security as an "intergenerational Ponzi game," where the workers of one generation were compelled to finance an increasing number of benefits to the retirees of the previous one. The structural dilemma of this arrangement was that the newer generations were producing fewer children while medical advances were extending the life span of the elderly, which meant that the ratio of workers to retirees was declining. Politicians exacerbated this problem by periodically adding benefits to the social security program and underestimating their costs. Disability benefits were added in the 1950s and early retirement (at age sixty-two with a 20 percent penalty in monthly benefits) was permitted in the 1960s. When automatic cost-of-living adjustments (COLAs) tied to the Consumer Price Index were added in 1972, expenditures accelerated. During the 1970s, old age and survivors' benefits soared by about 500 percent to $120 billion per year. Disability and Medicare costs went up even faster. By 1980, social security expenditures had risen to nearly $200 billion per year, but despite rising payroll taxes—including a major increase under Carter—the main trust fund was projected to go into deficit in 1983. The unfairness of the system was illustrated by the fact that although retirees in the next century were scheduled to receive far less in social security benefits than what they contributed, the average retired person in 1980 could look forward to receiving lifetime benefits five times as great as the total payroll taxes he or she had paid.[13]

According to Cannon, "Social security was always more tar baby than teflon for Reagan."[14] Stu Spencer (a campaign adviser) and James Baker considered social security to be Reagan's "Achilles heel" and urged him to avoid the issue as much as possible. During the 1980 campaign, following instructions, Reagan repeatedly promised to protect the financial foundation of social security and to preserve the benefits for retirees already receiving them. He refrained from making explicit commitments concerning future retirees. Reagan's advisers understood that his libertarian streak made him critical of the compulsory nature of the social security system and open to the notion of a voluntary plan that would permit workers to select their own investments.

For Stockman, "No single issue was as critical to the success of the Reagan Revolution as social security reform. Spending on that program alone consumed nearly $200 billion per year, just under one-third of the entire domestic budget. It was therefore impossible to suppose that we could cut enough out of the budget to make our equation balance without touching it."[15] The issue for Stockman was not whether to cut social security benefits, but when. To return social security to actuarial discipline, where workers received back what they had contributed plus interest, meant that so-called unearned benefits would have to be stripped away. Such cuts would serve the twin purposes of symbolizing the revolutionary change from a liberal regime to a market-oriented conservative one and of providing the substantive reductions that would give meaning to the magic asterisk and balance the budget.

In March, there were several attempts by Republican and Democratic Congress members to deal with the social security problem, but James Baker advised the president to reject the proposals because to accept them would place Reagan in the vulnerable position of appearing to renege on his campaign promise not to reduce social security benefits. Stockman, too, recommended the rejection of congressional suggestions because he felt their estimated savings were too small.

On April 10, Stockman and a group of White House advisers met with Richard Schweiker, the secretary of health and human services, in the Roosevelt Room to discuss the administration's stance on social security. The participants agreed they had to come up with between $75 and $100 billion in savings over the next five years in order to make the system solvent. Schweiker argued for an expansionist solution, a proposal to add federal, state, and local government employees to the social security system. Stockman, aided by his ideological ally, Martin Anderson, a White House domestic policy adviser, advocated a contractionist remedy that would reduce social security spending. The contractionist view prevailed. Schweiker was ordered by the White House to develop a number of options.

Within a few weeks, Schweiker and his department aides had come up with forty options presented in the obscure jargon of bureaucrats attempting to protect their interests. But Martin Anderson understood the complexities of social security, and Stockman had benefited from a crash tutorial on the subject from his staff. After much haggling, a one-hour meeting was set for 9:00 A.M. on May 11 at the White House, during which several proposals would be presented to the president. At the meeting, Reagan quickly rejected Schweiker's option to expand the payroll tax. Stockman then presented his proposal—also camouflaged in arcane terminology—for a stiff increase in the penalty for early retirement. Because about two-thirds of retirees were taking early retirement, Stockman's proposal was economically appealing because it would save billions; but it was politically treacherous because it would seriously decrease the monthly income of many citizens planning to retire at the age of sixty-two. After a round of debate, Schweiker agreed to support a penalty of 45 percent (more than doubling the current penalty of 20 percent) for those retiring at sixty-two. The practical effect of this reform would have sliced the monthly check for an early retiree from $469 to $310. Anderson strongly supported Stockman's proposal on ideological grounds; it was authentic Reaganism to steer social security away from unearned benefits. Anderson also knew that Reagan had disdain for Carter's 1977 rescue of social security, which had already demonstrated its deficiencies. Anderson encouraged the president to move quickly and decisively before his political advisers could dilute the reform proposal: "You'll be the first president in history to honestly and permanently fix social security. No one else has had the courage to do it."[16] The president took the bait so enthusiastically that he approved Stockman's package at the meeting, a rare occurrence.

Stockman was momentarily ecstatic; the president had agreed to social security budget cuts that would save $50 billion over the next five years. Not so James Baker and Richard Darman, who were caught off guard by this turn of events; together, they agreed that this unforeseen decision was politically lethal for Reagan and that they should distance him from it as quickly as possible. Although Baker could not unilaterally reverse a presidential decision, because he was in charge of White House operations, he could control how the decision was announced. Calling a meeting of the Legislative Strategy Group (LSG) for 2:00 P.M. that very afternoon to discuss how the presidentially approved plan would be publicized, he started the meeting by expressing his concern that this decision might interfere with the administration's top priority, namely, the economic program. Stockman protested that social security cuts were not a peripheral matter but a vital component in assuring a balanced budget. But when Darman asked whether the proposal had any support in Congress, Stockman and Schweiker had to concede that they had been so occupied working on options that they had not consulted with legislators. Baker decided that this proposal would not be proclaimed from the White House; it would be announced the next day from the Department of Health and Human Services and would be known as the Schweiker Plan. Both Schweiker and Stockman knew that this tactic would kill whatever chance the bill had; few Republican Congress members could be expected to fight for a controversial reform that the president was not willing to give his personal support.[17]

Schweiker made the announcement on May 12, which elicited this headline in the May 13 edition of the *Washington Post*: "Reagan Proposes 10% Cuts In Social Security Costs." Tip O'Neill called the proposal "despicable." The media were filled with stories of workers who had planned an early retirement in 1982 and were now blindsided by the severe penalty. Stockman argued that only a televised Reagan speech could save the situation, but Baker successfully urged a strategic retreat. When Democratic Senator Moynihan introduced a resolution defending social security, the LSG instructed Max Friedersdorf, the head of Reagan's congressional liaison staff, to negotiate a "face-saving" arrangement with Senators Baker and Dole. On May 20, the Senate voted 96 to 0 against any bill that would "precipitously and unfairly penalize early retirees."[18]

After a string of victories, the Reagan presidency had suffered its worst defeat. The resilient administration would recover quickly and enjoy other political triumphs in 1981, but the opportunity for an authentic Reagan

Revolution was now ended. As a defeated revolutionary Stockman would later lament, "The truth was, from that day forward, social security, the heart of the United States welfare state, was safely back in the world of actuaries who had kept its massive expansion quiet over the decades. The centerpiece of the American welfare state had now been overwhelmingly ratified and affirmed in the white heat of political confirmation."[19]

The Omnibus Budget Reconciliation Act of 1981 passed the House and Senate on July 31 and was signed into law by President Reagan on August 13, 1981. It cut expenditures for fiscal year 1982 by about $35 billion and over the 1982–1984 period by about $140 billion. More than two hundred program alterations were squeezed into a single piece of legislation, and few of the changes were subjected to separate votes. The big budget winner was the Department of Defense. Under Carter, the Pentagon had been allocated $180.7 billion for FY 1981; under Reagan, it received $199.7 billion for FY 1982. Military expenditures were projected to soar to $374.3 billion by 1986. Over the next five years, military spending authority was expected to reach $1.5 trillion.[20]

The big losers were social programs. Although the major middle-class entitlements, like social security and Medicare, were generally protected and continued to increase expenditures, two-thirds of the budget cuts came from the human services area. Eligibility for the food stamp program was tightened, reducing the rolls (22 million people received food stamps in 1981) by about 1 million and cutting its $12.6 billion allocation by $1.66 billion. About $1.5 billion was cut from programs costing $4.4 billion in 1981 by reducing subsidies for school meals, tightening eligibility for free or reduced-price meals, and curtailing supplemental feeding programs for women, infants, and children. Public service employment (300,000 jobs) under the Comprehensive Employment and Training Act (CETA) was ended. Expenditures for other CETA programs, including training, Job Corps, and summer youth jobs were reduced 20 percent. Additional unemployment benefits activated by national unemployment figures were terminated, and trade adjustment aid to workers was trimmed. Aid for Dependent Children payments were reduced for those who work. The 1981 $30 billion authorization for public housing and rental subsidies was slashed by $12 billion, cutting the number of planned new units from 254,000 to 154,000 and increasing the percentage of rent (from 25 percent to 30 percent) poor tenants had to pay. Medicaid grants to the states were cut by about a billion.[21]

The Reagan administration had scored a great victory, defeating the Democrats and paving the way for its top goal, the tax cut. But the president had spent much of his political capital and had been forced to make many more compromises to keep his congressional coalition together. Too much of the budget had been granted political protection; there was no way the budget could be balanced by 1984.

Helping to doom the effort to eliminate budget deficits was Reagan's personal commitment to cutting taxes. In terms of both rhetoric and behavior, Reagan demonstrated that significant reduction in tax rates was a strategic priority for him. From Stockman's perspective, however, the president's dedication to tax cuts was a problem because Reagan did not understand the tax code and its relationship to the budget. Given Reagan's economic beliefs and optimism, he never accepted the fact that cuts in taxes meant reductions in revenue.[22]

The problem for the administration in trying to pass the Economic Recovery Tax Act (ERTA) was that many Republican Congress members, including leaders like Howard Baker, Robert Dole, Pete Domenici, and Barber Conable, were not fully in support of the supply-side philosophy. Senator Baker was quoted labeling the tax cut "a riverboat gamble." Members of both parties feared that a tax cut would contribute to budget deficits, prevent the Federal Reserve from reducing interest rates, and fuel inflation. More experienced Congress members were skeptical about the administration's initial strategy of planning to pass two tax bills, the first being the simple tax cut bill introduced in February to deal with the economic emergency and the second being a more complex tax reform bill. When Treasury Secretary Donald Regan explained this strategy in February, Representative Rostenkowski, the new chairman of the Ways and Means Committee, interrupted and said: "Mr. Secretary, you know there might be only one train to Peoria this year. And if there is, everybody is going to want to get on it."[23] Rostenkowski's metaphor proved apt; many Congress members decided to get on board what they considered a gravy train.

In March, Rostenkowski announced that Reagan's tax bill was all but dead and that he would develop a Democratic substitute. As a new chairman, with ambitions to be Speaker of the House, Rostenkowski was anxious to be successful in his first shepherding of a tax bill. He was aware that the Republicans had more power on the floor of the House than in his Democratically stacked (2 to 1 majority) committee. Rostenkowski wanted to make sure that whatever bill emerged from his committee had enough Democratic and Republican support to win on the floor.

In April, Rostenkowski announced the details of his committee's alternative to the Reagan bill. The chairman's proposal called for a single-year tax cut, aimed more at the middle class (defined as citizens earning $20,000 to $50,000 a year), and an expansion of the Individual Retirement Account program (IRAs). According to tax expert John Witte, "This provision was supported by references to continuing concern over the national savings rate and by the argument that IRAs had become so widespread that it would be unfair if anyone were excluded from the program."[24] Over the next few weeks, the debate between the administration and Rostenkowski centered on the multiyear span of the tax reduction and on the issue of whether the reduction should be skewed (in favor of those who earn less than $50,000) or equal (each bracket receiving a 10 percent cut).

The bargaining situation changed drastically on May 7 as a result of the vote in the House on the administration's budget resolution, which demonstrated that the Republicans, with the aid of the Boll Weevils (a group of conservative Southern Democrats), could defeat the Democratic leadership on the floor. Rostenkowski recognized that he would have to make more compromises and began meeting with Senator Dole, the chairman of the Senate Finance Committee. The LSG met with the president on May 12 to discuss what changes would be needed to pass the bill. Donald Regan told the president that the administration's bill could not pass in its present, simple form and therefore compromises would have to be made. Baker and Darman were even more willing to compromise. "Their idea," according to Stockman, "was to achieve as much of the supply-side policy as you could without sacrificing the President's continuing capacity to succeed. As non-ideologues, they would have been happy to settle for a half loaf on the 30 percent rate cut—as long as it could be arranged so as to look like a 'win' for the President."[25]

Baker and Darman recommended that the administration negotiate with the Boll Weevils in order to get a better compromise from Rostenkowski. An acceptable deal with Rostenkowski was the best solution because it would avoid a bidding war and make it much easier to pass the tax cut in the House. Democratic Representative Kent Hance had lined up a number of Boll Weevils in support of delaying the first year's tax cut until 1982 and reducing its rate to 5 percent while adding reductions in estate taxes and savings incentives. As an ex-union leader, Reagan was not averse to accepting compromises in his original proposal, especially when most of these additions, or "ornaments" as they were called, to his simple bill were tax cuts that were compatible with his philosophy. He was willing to delay the tax cut if that would help gain votes for both the budget reconciliation bill and his tax bill. But the president was adamant that he would not accept anything less than a cut in tax rates of 25 percent over three years.[26]

Once Reagan specified his demands for a three-year 25 percent tax cut, Rostenkowski and his Democratic allies no longer wanted to negotiate with the administration; they wanted to fight. Reagan's advisers did not foresee that it would be better for Rostenkowski's political future to remain loyal to the Democratic party and lose to Reagan than to betray his party and accept most of the administration's bill. In early June, Rostenkowski did offer a two-year 15 percent tax cut plus ornaments, a proposal that was rejected by the president. The administration would now have to strike a deal with the Boll Weevils and then wage a bidding war against Rostenkowski's bill. By not reaching a compromise with Rostenkowski, the administration stumbled into a process that was driven by the need to buy votes in the House at the expense of rational tax and budget policy.

On June 4, Reagan announced that in place of his original proposal, he would support a substitute bipartisan bill to be introduced by Republican Barber Conable of New York and Democrat Kent Hance of Texas. This compromise bill would delay the first installment of the tax cut from July 1 to October 1, 1981, and reduce it from 10 percent to 5 percent. The Conable-Hance bill would also reduce tax losses by revising the depreciation (10–5–3) formula, but at the same time, it would increase IRA eligibility, lower gift and estate taxes, and reduce the rate on capital gains from 28 percent to 20 percent. The quest for a bipartisan compromise had now been replaced by a bidding war as each party tried to attain majority support for its legislation by adding ornaments.[27]

As a believer in the Reagan Revolution, Stockman was disillusioned to discover that "When it came to taxes, the GOP's idea of tax reform consisted of opening up loopholes in the IRS code. They preferred to pump up the welfare state from its back end by means of tax subsidies rather than direct expenditures."[28]

The Senate Finance Committee began meeting in late May, while the House Ways and Means Committee began markup sessions on June 10. Dole expressed reservations that the bidding war was overwhelming the usual legislative constraints that kept tax cuts within reason. For example, the Democrats were not blocking Republican efforts to help business; instead, they were matching and sometimes raising the bid. The policy environment was accurately described in June by the economics columnist Leonard Silk: "What started out as a simple, clean tax cut is becoming, with the Reagan Administration's collaboration, a Christmas tree bill that outglitters any of the past. With Republicans and Democrats vying for the privilege of providing tax breaks to assorted groups, the bill is becoming a masterpiece of fiscal graffiti—a bonanza perhaps most of all for tax law-yers, tax accountants and investment advisers."[29]

On Monday evening, July 27, the president addressed the nation in a television speech that Stockman characterized as "a masterpiece of propa-ganda." Reagan first played the role of a populist by stressing, "This is the first real tax cut for everyone in twenty years." But as a politician, he also pointed out that his bill contained benefits for select groups, such as farm-ers, small business owners, the savings industry, and small independent oil producers. Reagan enthusiastically endorsed indexing because "bracket creep is an insidious tax." He then compared the two bills with the aid of a graph that portrayed taxes under the Democratic proposal going down for two years but then rising during the third year, while under his legis-lation, taxes declined and stayed down. Reagan suggested that if citizens were planning to live longer than two years, they should support his bill. The president finished this well-delivered speech by advising the public to contact their representatives in support of his bipartisan legislation.[30]

They did—in record numbers. The vote in the House was scheduled for July 29, and shortly before the tally, O'Neill, the shaken Speaker of the House, said, "We are experiencing a telephone blitz like this nation has never seen. It's had a devastating effect."[31] What had appeared to be a close contest turned out to be a solid majority for the administration as the Conable–Hance II substitute for Rostenkowski's bill was passed by a vote of 238 to 195, with forty-eight Democrats abandoning their party's posi-tion, including thirty-one Boll Weevils. John Witte writes, "The final vote on the bill [again on July 29] was 323 to 107, allowing many more to claim a vote for tax reduction. On the same day, British Crown Prince Charles married Lady Diana Spencer, leading Speaker O'Neill to the cynical in-dictment: 'This has been quite a day for aristocracy: a royal wedding and a royal tax cut.'"[32] What O'Neill did not admit was how much of the Reagan tax cut philosophy was in the Democratic bill.

The slight differences between the House and Senate versions of the tax bill were ironed out by a conference committee in one day. ERTA was then passed by the Senate on August 3 by a vote of 67 to 8 and by the House on the following day by a vote of 282 to 95. It was signed into law by the president at his ranch in California on August 13.

ERTA was the largest tax cut in the history of the United States. It pro-vided a tax cut of over $37 billion in 1982, increasing to about $267 billion in 1986, for a total five-year revenue loss to the treasury of $750 billion. The rates on individual income taxes would be reduced by 5 percent on

October 1, 1981, 10 percent on July 1, 1982, and 10 percent on July 1, 1983. The top tax rate was sliced from 70 percent to 50 percent on January 1, 1982. For individuals, ERTA included marriage penalty relief, indexing (beginning in 1985 there would be annual adjustments in personal exemptions, zero bracket amounts, and income brackets to offset bracket creep caused by inflation), a drop in the capital gains rate from 28 percent to 20 percent, and wider margins on tax breaks for home sellers. Business received generous depreciation write-offs for buildings, equipment, and vehicles, investment tax credits ranging from 6 percent to 10 percent, and reductions in the corporate tax rates. Savings incentives were increased by authorizing banks and savings institutions to issue one-year savers' certificates and expanding the number of people eligible to participate in IRA programs. The threshold marking when estate taxes had to be paid was raised from $175,625 to $600,000, and tax-exempt gifts from parents to children or between spouses was raised from $3,000 to $10,000 per year. There were also numerous benefits for the oil industry and oil royalty owners. In brief, ERTA had two provisions that raised revenues and thirty that reduced them.[33]

ERTA was supported by a philosophy that held that it was good to riddle the tax code with tax expenditures (also known as tax loopholes) aimed at benefiting savers and investors. Supply-siders argued that the liberal regime's "income tax penalizes savers by taxing twice income earned and saved while taxing only once income earned and spent, and that the income tax taxes capital income twice—at both the corporate and the individual level. To redress this imbalance, conservatives often wanted to lower further the effective tax rate on capital income and supported the adoption of new tax expenditures favoring capital."[34] Because Reagan had publicly supported tax expenditures during the 1970s and even made the incredible argument that few loopholes benefit the wealthy, he did not object when business lobbyists like Charles Walker filled ERTA with tax breaks.[35] But C. Eugene Steuerle, a tax expert who worked in Reagan's Treasury Department, did object because he believed that the multitude of tax expenditures in ERTA violated rational tax principles. In Steuerle's words, "Unlike many previous subtle and hidden attempts to grant special favors, here was a wide open and readily acknowledged attempt to create zero or negative effective rates on an economy-wide scale. Many taxpayers began to believe that the government favored the purchase of shelters. . . . The government seemed to claim, at least temporarily, that what was good for the shelter market was good for the country."[36] It wasn't.

For Steuerle, the most significant component of ERTA was the requirement that the fourteen tax brackets, the personal exemption, and the

standard deduction be indexed, which meant annually adapted to the inflation rate after 1984. No longer would the perverse incentive exist where
the federal government would be rewarded with increased revenue because
of inflation. "By 1990," according to Steuerle, "the adjustment for inflation
alone was estimated to have reduced receipts by over $57 billion relative to
an unindexed tax code."[37] The irony here is that indexing was not part of
Reagan's initial tax bill; it was added by Congress.

The passage of ERTA did not produce the economic miracles predicted
by Reagan and his supply-side advisers. In September 1981, the economy
nosedived into a recession, unemployment rose to 10.7 percent in late
1982, revenue declined, and the budget deficit rose from $73.8 billion in
1980 to $207.8 billion in 1983. Public perceptions that the Reagan admin-
istration was promoting tax breaks for the rich and budget cuts for the poor
hurt both the president and the Republican party. In 1982, Reagan's public
approval ratings declined to about 35 percent, and the Republicans lost
26 House seats in the congressional elections. The public's fear of budget
deficits forced the administration to consider painful alternatives, such as
tax increases and cutting the growth in mandatory entitlement spending
for popular programs like social security and Medicare. The Reagan administration's response to the policy dilemma, in Steuerle's words, was not
a profile in courage:

> Leadership for the details of initiatives was seldom to be provided by
> the president and the White House. Real responsibility was to rest
> with the Republican Senate and with a commission [headed by Alan
> Greenspan] designed to deal with the possibility that the social security
> program might have insufficient funds to meet its obligations. Within
> the administration, political forces were split: some proclaiming the
> need for further tax cuts, and others working to try to reduce the
> deficit. The administration would waffle in its role. It did not want
> to take responsibility for any tax increases, but some of its members
> wanted deficit reduction that might include some tax increases.
> The president's public position was that he opposed all taxes, but
> he eventually accepted many increases. In this situation, the visible
> leadership role was often left to others.[38]

It was not part of Reagan's original design that he would feel compelled
to accept several tax increases in order to respond to the unexpected (for
him) soaring budget deficits. Jitters about soaring budget deficits and concerns about saving social security caused Congress to pass tax increases in

1982, 1983, and 1984, all of which were signed into law by Reagan. The most significant bill was the Tax Equity and Fiscal Responsibility act of 1982 (TEFRA), which was designed to raise $98.3 billion over three years and thus effectively regain one-fourth of the tax revenue lost in 1981. TEFRA was passed by Congress in August 1982 largely because of the political skills of Senator Robert Dole, who was then chairman of the Senate Finance Committee. This was the first significant tax increase enacted by Congress during an election year in peacetime since 1932. In July 1984, Congress passed and Reagan signed another bill, the Deficit Reduction act of 1984 (DEFRA), which raised taxes by closing sixteen loopholes. "Taken together," according to Brownlee and Steuerle, "TEFRA and DEFRA raised revenues on the average of $100 billion per year at 1990 levels of income. Increases this big had never been enacted except during major wars."[39] Obviously, there had been a retreat from the thinking that had supported ERTA in 1981.

After the debacle of trying to cut social security benefits in May 1981, and with forecasts indicating the social security trust fund would face a funding shortage in mid-1983, the Reagan administration decided to try a bipartisan approach in dealing with the problem. Reagan accepted a suggestion from Senator Howard Baker, the Republican majority leader, to create a task force composed of fifteen members, five each to be selected by Senator Baker, Speaker O'Neill, and the president. This task force would be given the responsibility of developing a plan to assure the financial safety of social security, which would then be submitted to Congress. Reagan signed an executive order on December 16, 1981, establishing the National Commission on Social Security Reform, with the conservative economist Alan Greenspan as its chairman, and set December 31, 1982, as the deadline for its report.

After months of public hearings in which expert witnesses testified, and additional months of negotiation among the fifteen members, the commission was divided by partisan and ideological divisions and was unable to agree on a set of recommendations within the allotted time. Greenspan had to ask the president for two extensions of time. Fearing a deadlock, and knowing that the public had doubts regarding Reagan's commitments to social security, the administration approached two Democratic members of the commission, Senator Daniel Patrick Moynihan and Robert Ball, to see if a compromise could be secretly negotiated. Ball had been chosen by O'Neill to be the chief negotiator for the Democrats because he was the most knowledgeable about the subject; he had worked for the Social

Security Administration for thirty years and served as its commissioner from 1962 to 1972. With the aid of Senator Robert Dole and Representative Barber Conable, and meeting secretly at James Baker's home, a small group of Democrats and Republicans hammered out a "consensus package" to recommend to Congress that was acceptable to the Speaker of the House, the Senate majority leader, the president, and twelve of the commission members. Three conservative legislators dissented.[40]

The commission recommended that the next COLA of benefits, scheduled for July 1983, be postponed until January 1984, and that all future COLAs be based on the calendar year rather than the fiscal one. A second recommendation would accelerate the scheduled payroll tax increases: "A rate set in law for 1985 would take effect in 1984, and part of the increase scheduled for 1990 would take effect in 1988."[41] Each of these recommendations would provide an extra $40 billion to the social security trust fund between 1983 and 1989. A third recommendation, which would yield an additional $30 billion by 1989, was that starting in 1984, the social security benefits of high-income persons would be taxed for the first time. There would also be tax increases on the self-employed. These recommendations, and several others I have not mentioned, would not raise enough revenue to cover the long-term deficit, but the remaining deficit should be met by a gradual increase in the age of normal retirement or with a hike in the tax rate.

When Congress received the commission's recommendations, it passed them and decided to gradually raise the normal age of retirement to sixty-seven by 2027. It also voted to continue allowing early retirement at sixty-two, but to gradually increase the reduction in benefits for early retirement from the current 20 percent to 30 percent by 2027.[42] On April 20, 1983, President Reagan signed the bill into law in front of three hundred guests and praised the bipartisan cooperation that had saved social security.[43]

Both sides had made major compromises: "Democrats accepted a six-month delay in the annual COLA and the increase in the retirement age, while Republicans accepted a faster-than-planned rise in payroll taxes and a substantial tax increase on the self-employed. The two sides closed the deal by subjecting up to half of social security benefits to income taxes for higher-income beneficiaries, a provision that allowed Democrats to say Republicans had passed a tax increase and Republicans to say Democrats had agreed to a benefit cut."[44] What angered conservatives is that the Reagan administration felt compelled to rescue a key institution of the liberal regime without a major effort to impose a conservative reform, such as allowing workers to place some of their contributions into private accounts.[45]

By the end of 1983, as the administration prepared for the president's 1984 state of the union address, a set of forces was launched that brought about major tax reform in 1986. In December 1983, Treasury Secretary Donald Regan, with the information that many corporations were able to avoid federal taxation by taking advantage of tax loopholes, tried to convince the president to advocate tax reform in his 1984 state of the union speech. The tax system needed to be fundamentally changed because it was too complex, too unfair, and too restrictive on economic growth.[46] James Baker and Richard Darman, the president's top pragmatic advisers, wanted Reagan to stress deficit reduction and were skeptical about the appeal of tax reform in the upcoming presidential election. But Baker and Darman were fearful that Walter Mondale, the likely Democratic presidential candidate, might focus his campaign on the unfairness of the tax code. Hence, early in 1984, Baker, mistakenly believing that Mondale might champion the Bradley-Gephardt tax bill, which would simplify the tax code and lower tax rates, suggested to Reagan that he direct the Treasury Department to develop comprehensive tax reform legislation. The president accepted Baker's advice, and in his 1984 state of the union address, he ordered Regan to conduct a study of tax reform and report back to him in December 1984. This maneuver essentially neutralized tax reform as an issue during the 1984 campaign. During the campaign, the focus was on the fact that Mondale wanted to raise taxes and Reagan did not.

The partisan side of Reagan was attracted to tax reform. Some of Reagan's political advisers believed that tax reform had the potential to be a realigning issue. That is, tax reform could broaden the appeal of the Republican party so that it could dominate both the presidency and Congress in much the same way that the social security issue gave the Democrats great advantages during the 1930s. Republican partisans believed that tax reform could serve as a "symbol of the GOP's metamorphosis from country-club conservatism to a new coalition reaching out to a broader spectrum of Americans: workers, Catholics, new immigrants and entrepreneurs as well as old-style Republicans."[47] But there were two fatal flaws in the strategy of the use of tax reform as a realigning issue: first, it was too complex an issue for most voters to understand; second, Reagan needed Democratic support, especially in the Democratically controlled House Ways and Means Committee, to pass the legislation. Moreover, a significant number of Republican Congress members opposed the bill because it raised taxes on corporations. To obtain the necessary Democratic votes required compromise, which allowed the Democrats to impose some of their own thinking on the bill. As Reagan's tax reform bill picked up bipartisan backing, its potential as a realigning issue evaporated.

After the 1984 election, the treasury presented its recommended tax reform bill (called Treasury I) to the president. Treasury I, skillfully prepared by the neutrally competent bureaucrats in the department, recommended the elimination of 38 of 105 tax expenditures. Early in 1985, Chief of Staff James Baker and Treasury Secretary Donald Regan switched jobs. In reviewing Treasury I, Treasury Secretary Baker and his deputy, Darman, decided that the proposal would have to be revised to make it more politically feasible before it could be introduced to Congress. This was done, and President Reagan presented his tax bill (known as Treasury II) to Congress in late May 1985. Unlike the situation in 1981, Reagan could not steamroll his opponents in 1985, but he was able to impose a major decision rule: any bill would have to be revenue neutral. That is, any new tax bill would have to raise the same amount of revenue as the existing tax law. According to tax policy expert John Witte, "Revenue neutrality had an important direct effect. It repressed the temptation to add revenue-losing tax breaks because it provided the committee chairs with a simple rule—for every break proposed, the proponent had to find an offsetting revenue gain."[48] Still, each house of Congress significantly modified the bill; the result was not simply a fulfillment of Reagan's vision. The Tax Reform Act (TRA) was finally passed by Congress and signed by President Reagan on October 22, 1986.

The philosophy underlying the TRA was that, in broadening the tax base by reducing the number of tax loopholes, the government could significantly lower tax rates. TRA's chief selling point was that it reduced the fourteen rate brackets to two rates of 15 and 28 percent, with a complicated surtax that placed some upper-middle-class families (with joint income between $71,900 and $149,250) in a 33 percent bracket. An estimated 80 percent of American families fell in the 15 percent bracket. Thus, as Michael Boskin pointed out, "The top marginal tax rate in the personal income tax will have gone from 70 percent in 1980 to 28 percent by 1988, an astounding reduction, making the top marginal tax rate in the United States lower than the bottom marginal tax rate in many countries."[49] By almost doubling the exemptions for self, spouse, and dependents, TRA removed approximately 6 million poor from the tax rolls. This provision was supported by Democrats for its fairness and by Republicans for being profamily. TRA eliminated the preferential treatment of capital gains income by raising the tax rate from 20 percent to the top individual rate of 28 percent. For many individuals, being able to take the standard deduction, which had been significantly raised, greatly simplified the filing of their tax returns. It was estimated that about 60 percent of all Americans paid slightly lower taxes (a few hundred dollars per year) because of this reform law, and another 25 percent paid what they had been paying before. The remaining 15 percent faced a relatively small tax increase.[50]

The TRA was an outstanding example of reform legislation because it overcame politicians' natural inclinations to reward special interests (especially those groups that provide generous campaign contributions) with tax breaks. According to Witte, "TRA dwarfs any of the three prior peacetime reform acts. . . . Seventy-two provisions tightened tax expenditures, including fourteen that involved complete repeal, a figure approximately equal to the total number of tax expenditures that had been repealed from 1913 to 1985. . . . The initial estimates of revenue gains from tightening and closing tax expenditures was $324 billion over five years."[51]

The most surprising feature of the TRA was that between 1986 and 1991, it shifted an estimated $120 billion of the tax burden from individuals to corporations. As explained by Boskin, "This occurs despite the fact that the basic corporate tax rate is being reduced from forty six percent to thirty four percent because of a very substantial increase in the corporate tax base, achieved through the elimination of the investment tax credit, much slower depreciation, and a stiff alternative minimum tax for corporations (to insure that no corporation that reports current profits to its shareholders will avoid paying taxes)."[52] The playing field for corporations may have been leveled by this tax reform, but it was now also more expensive to play.

The chief player in promoting the unlikely passage of the TRA was Ronald Reagan. He placed tax reform on the policy agenda by making it the symbol of his "Second American Revolution" in his 1985 state of the union address. Reagan had the chameleon-like capability of identifying with and appealing to those who thought that taxes were too complex, those who thought that taxes were unfair, those who thought that the rich were not paying their fair share, and those who thought that taxes impeded their chances to move up. One of his major public relations achievements was to plant the idea that the progressive income tax was elitist and that flatter rates were egalitarian because they provided more opportunities for more people to do better. Emphasizing this theme, Reagan claimed, "We are not lowering the top tax rate . . . so the rich will do better. We are lowering the top rate . . . so that every working American will have a better chance to get rich."[53] The president's tax reform was portrayed as profairness, profamily, and progrowth; it epitomized Reagan's conservative populism.

Reagan saved the bill in November 1985 when House Republicans were repelled by the modifications imposed by Dan Rostenkowski's Ways and Means Committee. He helped create an atmosphere in which no one wanted to appear responsible for killing the reform proposal. Witte suggests, "Reagan's support of tax reform amplified the unique political jockeying that the issue stimulated in both parties. In a bizarre political reversal of 1981, in deficit-plagued 1985 and 1986, tax reform acquired the same political momentum as wholesale tax reduction and loophole expansion had in 1981."[54] Steuerle explains, "Once it became clear that an administratively feasible system could be designed that would lower rates and eliminate shelters, remove the poor from tax rolls, and treat individuals with equal income more equally, no one wanted to be known as the person who stood in the way of this effort and caused it to fail."[55] In a major study of the passage of the TRA, two *Wall Street Journal* reporters concluded, "Reagan wanted to go down in history as the president who cut that top tax rate at least in half, from 70 percent to 35 percent or lower. If abandoning tax breaks and raising corporate taxes was the price he had to pay to achieve that goal, so be it."[56]

However, despite Reagan's enthusiastic speechmaking in support of the TRA, it is likely that he was not knowledgeable about the major provisions in his own proposal. In an interview after his 1985 state of the union address, the president revealed that he did not understand that his Treasury II proposal included a 36 percent increase in corporate taxes.[57] In Albert Hunt's words, "The president's ignorance of the specifics of his own proposal was startling; throughout, he misrepresented or misunderstood the measure's tax increase on business, but President Reagan's attachment to lower rates was real and his commitment to the concept of tax reform was even more powerful than his ignorance of the details. He never quite convinced the public, but his political persona and communication skills commanded such respect that they scared off a lot of potential opponents."[58]

The irony of the 1986 tax reform was that it was designed to close many of the loopholes in ERTA. Witte wryly concludes, "Ronald Reagan thus has the unique historical position of supporting both the largest tax reform and the largest anti-tax reform legislation in the history of the United States."[59]

Conclusion

Tax policy played a major role in the political success of President Reagan. The passage of ERTA in 1981 established Reagan's professional reputation as someone who could play and win in the major leagues. Reagan was more than an electoral phenomenon; his political leadership could formulate and achieve strategic priorities. The enactment of the TRA in 1986 constituted Reagan's major domestic policy success in the second term and helped him avoid the stigma of being considered a lame duck. Both of these tax laws can be viewed as steps toward Reagan's goal of creating a less intrusive federal government. But unlike the other two means of achieving this goal—budget cuts in domestic spending and the deregulation of industry—the tax proposals were able to attain wider support and more success.

Neither Reagan nor his two major tax bills was philosophically consistent. A major contradiction in Reagan's tax philosophy was that while he stressed that the taxing authority of the government must be used solely to provide revenues for legitimate government purposes, he also claimed that his tax proposal would provide multiple benefits for the American people. The irony of the 1986 tax reform was that it was designed to close many of the loopholes in ERTA, although it would be difficult to prove that Reagan understood that his 1981 bill had created many of these preferences and/or that his 1986 bill would eliminate many of them.

It should also be stressed that Reagan signed bills increasing taxes in 1982, 1983, and 1984. Nothing demonstrates better the skills of Reagan's public relations advisers and the ability of his administrative style to dissipate responsibility than the fact that despite his support of several bills raising taxes, he still maintained his reputation as a tax cutter and conviction politician.

Reagan achieved his success by focusing on reducing tax rates, which astutely served his political purposes throughout the decade. By championing tax cuts, Reagan was able to appeal to broad sectors of the American public as a conservative populist; substantiate his reputation as a conviction politician who fulfills his campaign promises; unite the Republican party; attract a sufficient number of Democratic Congress members to pass two major pieces of legislation; and dominate the domestic policy agenda for most of the 1980s. But the price of this political success was that the president ignored the revenue needs of the government and discarded the limited redistributive capabilities of the progressive income tax. Reagan also created a legacy that has led conservative Republicans to be as prone to fling tax breaks at problems as liberal Democrats were to throw money at maladies in the 1960s.[60]

In brief, tax policy probably contributed more to the political success of the Reagan presidency than any other substantive policy. Thus a paradox: the president with the simplest ideas achieved some of his major political victories in one of the most complex policy fields.

9

Legitimating the New Deal

In successfully pressing Congress to pass New Deal legislation, Franklin Roosevelt was denouncing the old conservative regime and creating a new liberal one. This liberal regime would have greater capabilities to tax, spend, regulate, and bureaucratize than the previous one. Were such developments a violation of American antistatist ideals? Were they a threat to democracy? Most Republicans answered yes to both questions. So did a majority of the Supreme Court for several years. FDR believed that American ingenuity could create an administrative state that conformed to our political traditions. The challenge for Roosevelt was to persuade the public that the bureaucratization of the American political system could provide security for them without endangering their liberty. Then, in order to legitimate and institutionalize his New Deal, the president would have to convince a majority of the Supreme Court that his reform programs did not violate the Constitution.

The hallmark of the administrative state, according to John Rohr, "is the expert agency tasked with important governing functions through loosely drawn statutes that empower unelected officials to undertake such important matters as preventing 'unfair competition,' granting licenses as the 'public interest, convenience or necessity' will indicate, maintaining a 'fair and orderly market,' and so forth. . . . The administrative state is in reality the welfare/warfare state we know so well."[1] The purpose of this chapter is to analyze how FDR defended the New Deal—which included the rise of the administrative state as an integral part of its program—from the attacks of the Republican party and the Supreme Court.

The New Deal Administrative State

Given the political culture of the United States, FDR's efforts to construct and legitimate an administrative state was an uphill battle. What Lipset labels the American creed can be summarized in five terms: liberty, egalitarianism, individualism, populism, and laissez-faire. He concludes, "The exceptional focus on law here as compared to Europe, derived from the Bill of Rights, has stressed rights against the state and other powers. America began and continues as the most anti-statist, legalistic, and rights-oriented nation."[2] Huntington argues, "all the varying elements in the American Creed unite in imposing limits on power and on the institutions of government. . . . The essence of liberalism is freedom from governmental control—the vindication of liberty against power, as Bernard Bailyn summed up the argument for the American Revolution."[3] Another historian of the American Revolution, Edward Morgan, adds, "Between 1776 and 1789, Americans replaced a government over them with a government under them. They have worried ever since about keeping it under."[4] The United States lacked monarchical and military traditions that became major facets of the administrative state in Europe. Would the rise of an administrative state mean the lowering of the status of citizens from participants to subjects? Could a nation programmed to cherish individual liberty learn to accept and trust a more bureaucratic federal government?

It should be recognized that FDR was not creating an administrative state from scratch; he was expanding and accelerating a trend that had already established a beachhead. By 1932, the last year of the Hoover administration, approximately 572,000 employees worked for the federal government. By the end of FDR's first term, the number of federal employees had ballooned to 829,000; by 1939, it reached 920,000.[5] When Henry Wallace became secretary of agriculture in March 1933, his department was administering sixty statutes.[6] Before Roosevelt came to power, there were already independent regulatory agencies regulating the railroads (the Interstate Commerce Commission, 1887), the banks (the Federal Reserve Board, 1913), and business (the Federal Trade Commission, 1914).

Despite all the rhetoric and mythology about laissez-faire, our earliest federal governments had experimented with the First and Second National

Banks, and state and national governments had subsidized the railroads. During World War I, numerous public corporations had been created to mobilize resources to win the war. Under Hoover, public corporations had been set up to help farmers and to fight the Depression. The largest and most important public corporation created under Hoover was the Reconstruction Finance Corporation.[7]

Nevertheless, as the United States responded to the needs of a more urban and industrial society, it developed its own variation of the modern state. In Ellis Hawley's words, "It lodged power not in a bureaucratic elite, but in patronage-based political parties, local government units, and a strong judicial system. Modern bureaucracy here had emerged primarily in the private sector, largely in connection with the rise of big business, rather than in the public. . . . The nation lacked the kind of autonomous administrative establishment to be found elsewhere, and it retained much that was hostile to the acquisition of one."[8] In brief, when FDR assumed office and was confronted with the political responsibility of fighting the Depression, he was handicapped by a lack of constitutional authority and executive resources that he could control.

The Depression provided the New Deal with several advantages in constructing an administrative state. First, it emasculated the Republican opposition and undermined the legitimacy of market controls. After the stock market crash and the revelations publicized by Senate investigations into stock manipulation on Wall Street, few believed anymore in the "magic of the marketplace." For a brief period, the nation's usual wariness about the expansion of federal power was suspended. New Dealers argued that nineteenth-century liberalism had served us well but that the Depression demonstrated that a new liberalism was needed to promote the progress of a more industrial and urban society. Further development would be much more dependent on national administrative skills and agencies. FDR took advantage of this window of opportunity to create sixty new federal agencies by 1935. His natural tendency was to circumvent existing agencies, probably filled with Republicans, and create new ones that he could pack with Democrats to deal with the problems of the Depression.

The second advantage enjoyed by the New Deal was FDR's ability to use his patronage powers to dominate the executive branch. Because the Democrats had not occupied the White House for twelve years, party members were especially hungry for public jobs. James Farley, the postmaster general, was in charge of filling 150,000 patronage jobs in 1933.[9] To maximize pressure on Democratic Congress members, the president decided to withhold patronage decisions until after the first hundred days' special session. This strategy was successful in getting Roosevelt's legislation passed, but it did mean, in Moley's phrase, "We stood in the city of Washington on March 4, like a handful of marauders in a hostile territory."[10]

Given the high unemployment rate in 1933, the pressure on Farley as the chief dispenser of public jobs was enormous. He estimated that he was able to find a job for only one applicant in twenty.[11] Roosevelt also proved skillful in balancing the needs of patronage, party, and program. Paul Van Riper explains, "The President . . . seldom disapproved congressional exemptions of newly created alphabetical agencies from the classified service. As these exemptions increased, the jobs proliferated and the appointive power of the President was accordingly greatly expanded."[12] Hence, the proportion of public employees covered by the Civil Service Commission declined from 80 percent under Hoover to about 60 percent under Roosevelt in 1936. It should be noted, however, that certain key agencies where skill and integrity were particularly essential, such as the TVA, the Farm Credit Administration, and the Social Security Administration, were placed under the merit system.[13]

What is remarkable about this period is that in practicing the spoils system, the Roosevelt administration, for the most part, avoided the corruption that is associated with that kind of politics. The New Deal was never hit by a Teapot Dome scandal, as was the Harding administration. In discussing this issue of corruption, Van Riper concludes, "The Home Owners' Loan Corporation . . . had to be reorganized after spoils policies had brought it almost to its knees. Far more damning were the widespread charges, many quite true, of local political corruption in the use of relief funds, relief jobs, and the moneys allocated for public works. However, considering the tremendous efforts involved and the short time in which most of the agencies had to organize and to spend their appropriations, fraud and corruption, while unquestionably present, were surprisingly negligible."[14] Because of its idealism, the New Deal generally recruited people who provided honest and dedicated administration.

The third advantage enjoyed by the New Deal was that it was in a position to recruit thousands of idealistic and talented people who were committed to constructing a new regime. With the Depression limiting job opportunities in the private sector, the combination of more jobs in the federal government along with the euphoric notion that it was now possible to accomplish great deeds was exhilarating. Roosevelt mobilized the reformist energies of the nation, which had been dormant during the 1920s.

Idealists rushed to Washington, D.C., in 1933 like gold seekers had sped to California in the 1850s. According to Leuchtenburg, "In the spring of 1933, Washington quickened to the feverish pace of the new mobilization. From state agricultural colleges and university campuses, from law faculties and social work schools, the young men flooded to Washington to take part in the new mobilization. Wholly apart from their beliefs or special competences, they imparted an enormous energy to the business of governing and impressed almost everyone with their contagious high spirits and their dedication."[15] They also frightened conservatives and Republicans.

The New Deal engaged in a new type of recruitment that Van Riper labeled "ideological patronage." He traced this innovation to a decision made by Governor Roosevelt during the 1932 campaign to put Moley in charge of policy and Farley in charge of politics. This separation of idea men from political organizers continued after FDR was elected president. Because Roosevelt thought that many of the men who served in the Wilson administration were too old and that businessmen tended to provide orthodox and self-serving recommendations, he increasingly turned to young lawyers and professors for policy advice. In Van Riper's words, "This phenomenon of the division of labor between the intellectuals and the politicians arose in part out of the tremendous pressures of the times, pressures which demanded extraordinary political and social inventiveness. The old-line politicians simply could not supply the ideas. Neither could the permanent civil service, for it had only rarely been encouraged to do the type of thinking needed in 1933."[16] Reforming the complex America of 1933 was going to take much more intellectual capital than had the three previous reconstructive periods: 1800, 1828, and 1860.

The New Deal's response to the Depression increased the numbers and the status of social workers. Although the number of jobs decreased during the Depression, the demand for social workers soared. Between 1930 and 1940, their numbers doubled from 30,000 to 60,000. The following social workers made significant contributions to the New Deal: Harry Hopkins, Frances Perkins, Molly Dawson (of the Women's Division of the Democratic National Committee), Aubrey Williams (director of the National Youth Administration), Katharine Lenroot and Martha Eliot (of the Children's Bureau), Jane Hoey (of the Social Security Administration), and Ellen Woodward (of the Federal Emergency Relief Administration and the Works Progress Administration). Walter Trattner concludes, "by the end of the decade, social work was not only an acknowledged obligation of the federal government and every city, village and hamlet in the nation, but its scope had greatly expanded. . . . Social work was no longer viewed as an emergency profession, but as an accepted part of the machinery of the state, an important everyday function in a modern industrial state."[17] The rise of social workers was a vital step in the construction of the welfare state because they provided both pressure for its expansion and the personnel to implement social policies.

Lawyers were more responsible for the behavior of the New Deal than social workers; indeed, many felt that the stereotypical New Dealer was a hotdog lawyer recruited by Felix Frankfurter, the Harvard Law School professor. New Deal history can be told through the lives of such prominent lawyers as Thurmond Arnold, Thomas Corcoran, Benjamin Cohen, William Douglas, Charles Fahy, Abe Fortas, Jerome Frank, Alger Hiss, Robert Jackson, James Landis, David Lilienthal, Samuel Rosenman, and Adlai Stevenson. In attempting to create a new regime, the New Deal required energized intellectuals to fight along multiple fronts, a need that liberal lawyers were more than happy to fulfill. FDR's policies were giving lawyers, especially Jewish and Irish lawyers, opportunities to do what they considered good deeds.

Obviously, not everyone was pleased by this influx into the nation's capital of young lawyers who claimed to have the answers to complex problems that had eluded older policy makers for decades. George Peek, the first head of the Agricultural Adjustment Administration (AAA), spoke for many pre–New Deal officials when he wrote: "They all claimed to be friends of somebody or other and mostly of Felix Frankfurter and Jerome Frank. They floated airily into offices, took desks, and asked for papers and found no end of things to be busy about. I never found out why they came, what they did or why they left."[18] Years later, the joke was told that they came to Washington to do good, and they stayed to make money.

For many New Deal lawyers, the Depression demonstrated that the old system no longer worked, and they felt eminently qualified by their educational success to solve the present economic problems and to devise reforms to ensure a better future. This attitude is reflected in the person of Jerome Frank, who was recommended for a position in the Department of Agriculture by Felix Frankfurter. In his letter to Rexford Tugwell, Frankfurter stressed that "you must recall . . . that he is widely read in the modern literature of economic and social thought, and has simply a fiendish appetite and capacity for work."[19] After becoming general counsel for the Department of Agriculture, Frank accumulated a staff of sixty lawyers, many of whom were recruited from Ivy League law schools. Frank outlined the qualities he desired in his lawyers in a 1933 speech to law school professors which was summarized by Peter Irons: "The ideal AAA lawyer would be . . . an idealist who shared Roosevelt's goal of giving 'the forgotten man a decent life, free of gnawing insecurity,' a goal which could be best achieved through 'an elaborate series of experiments which . . . will permit the profit system to be tried, for the first time, as a consciously directed means of promoting the general good.' Frank's ideal lawyer would also realize that 'experimentation is an imperative necessity' in a period of 'economic catastrophe.'"[20] One can guess the dismay of conservatives, most of whom believed in the positive consequences of capitalism as a sacred principle, hearing that Frank wanted lawyers to test whether the profit motive advanced the public interest.

Another New Deal lawyer worth examining is James Landis. Landis was born in Tokyo in 1899, the son of Presbyterian missionaries. He was the top student in his class at both Princeton and the Harvard Law School.[21] A brilliant student like Landis quickly caught the eye of Professor Frankfurter, who encouraged him to continue his legal studies and become a member of the law faculty. Beginning in 1925, Landis taught administrative law, wrote a casebook on labor law, and became the first professor of legislation at the Harvard Law School. In April 1933, Frankfurter lured Landis to Washington to work with Corcoran and Cohen on the Securities Act. Later in the year, Roosevelt appointed Landis to the Federal Trade Commission (FTC), which was initially charged with implementing the Securities Act. Landis again collaborated with Corcoran and Cohen in writing the Securities Exchange Act of 1934 and the Public Utility Holding Act of 1935. In 1934, FDR asked Landis to resign from the FTC and then appointed him to the Securities and Exchange Commission (SEC). When Joseph Kennedy resigned as chairman of the SEC in 1935, Landis succeeded him.

By the mid-1930s, Landis was experienced in the academic study of administrative law, the drafting of legislative proposals, and administering the law in the FTC and the SEC. He had learned a truth that many of his contemporaries were too tradition-bound to recognize, namely, that an industrialized society required the guidance of an administrative state. To publicize his insights, he wrote *The Administrative Process*. Landis argued that unregulated capitalism resulted in the Depression; the only feasible remedy was to expand regulatory capabilities of the federal government. Neither the Congress nor the courts had the necessary expertise to regulate the different sectors of our complex economy; only the executive branch had the required skills. In response to critics who charged that independent regulatory agencies violated the separation of powers doctrine because they exercised quasi-legislative, quasi-executive, and quasi-judicial functions and were therefore not restrained by checks and balances, Landis asserted that "the executive branch checked regulation through the appointment process, the legislature through enabling acts and control of appropriations, and the judiciary through review of agency decisions."[22] For Landis, the rise of the administrative state was not a threat to democracy because it provided a government the tools to be more responsive to human needs.

Landis expressed no fear that the growing need for expertise and efficiency would result in the proliferation of executive agencies. Such growth, in his view, was simply a natural and inevitable phenomenon. He was not worried about reducing the liberty of Wall Street wheelers and dealers, whose reckless and immoral behavior had contributed to the mass misery of the Depression. He did believe in the expertise of regulators and had faith in their professional integrity to uphold the public interest. Like so many New Deal lawyers, Landis believed in himself.

We should not forget that the most important New Deal lawyer trying to construct the American version of the administrative state was Franklin Roosevelt. In building this new edifice, the president did not have a blueprint; as was true of so much of the New Deal, he was improvising. Ellis Hawley suggests that in 1933, there were four competing models of the administrative state that influenced the New Deal. The first one was the "business-commonwealth," a partnership between government and business, with the latter the senior partner. Some viewed this corporate structure as reflecting fascist ideas imported from Europe, but Hawley suggests it had "firm roots in the American past" and support from progressive big business elites in the 1920s. Its appeal was based on the idea that it promised direct representation and "self-government." A second model was the "populist commonwealth," which was based on the idea of avoiding government bureaucracy and big business by "returning power to the people." This utopian vision believed that a reformist state could create a "people's money" by inflating the currency with silver-backed dollars and a "people's economy" by reinforcing the antimonopoly laws. The third model was based on the emergency form of the administrative state. Just as the Great War had called for a temporary departure from our typical governing arrangements, so should responding to the crisis of the Depression. The fourth formulation was the "brokered state," in which public administrators would reward favored interest groups. In this system, "We would be rescued from the intolerable features of the market economy through a politically brokered administrative expansion, which would allow groups in need of protection or enhanced economic power to acquire them. But the expansion would be such that power would remain in the hands of politicians and interest groups. We would be saved from bureaucratic statism."[23] Thus, even as the New Deal was creating an American version of the administrative state, it retained elements of antistatism.

During the first New Deal (1933–1935), programs were largely structured and justified by a blend of the emergency management and business commonwealth notions. FDR asked Congress to grant him emergency powers to fight the Depression that were analogous to the authority he would be given if the nation were invaded by a foreign enemy. "Once again," according to Hawley, "we had an array of new agencies, theoretically established for emergency purposes; and, as in the earlier case, these were set up outside the regular agencies of government, were reliant on a temporary 'nationalization' of private sector administrative resources rather than on a regular civil service, and were supposed to pass out of existence after this war had been won."[24] The other component was based on the idea that corporative institutions could eliminate unfair business practices and promote fair ones. These two models provided the guidelines to administer the major programs of the first New Deal — the National Industrial Recovery Act, the AAA, and the Federal Emergency Relief Act.

During the Second New Deal of 1935–1936, the evolution of the administrative state was affected by three developments. First, a series of adverse Supreme Court decisions undercut the legitimacy of the emergency concept and declared both the National Recovery Administration (NRA) and the AAA unconstitutional. Second, the New Deal lost its business support, became more partisan, moved to the left, and increased its ties to labor. And third, in Hawley's words, "new links were being forged between would-be administrative state-builders and those making gains in the political arena. Key groups of industrial relations specialists, social work and social science professionals, legal technicians, and resource-usage experts were now having considerable success in selling bureaucratic prescriptions — with appropriate roles, of course, for their specialties — to the labor movement and to reform-minded politicians and legislators."[25]

The key programs of this period were the Wagner Labor Relations Act, the Social Security Act, the creation of the Works Progress Administration, and new powers for the SEC and the Federal Reserve Board. By 1936, the New Deal regime had assumed a multitude of new social responsibilities and added the required bureaucratic agencies. However, as Hawley points out, "the new bureaucracy was still highly fragmented and particularized and still subject to the constraints of other forms of institutional power. It had . . . a 'hollow core,' a void where there should be a national planning agency and machinery for harmonizing agency goals with national ones; and it had to operate in an environment in which more of America's nineteenth-century state had survived and a good deal of power was still lodged with judges, party politicians, legislative committees, and local governmental units."[26] In other words, the new agencies operated as competing clusters of interest groups and not as a coordinated machine working together to build a liberal regime.

The Third New Deal (1937–1939) can be viewed as FDR's quest for mastery over the executive branch, the Supreme Court, and the Democratic party. Throughout his political career, Roosevelt was concerned and knowledgeable about administrative issues because he recognized that they could play a significant role in achieving his goals. When he became president in 1933, he had, under the Economy Act, the authority for several years to reorganize the federal bureaucracy subject to a congressional veto, but he used it sparingly because his attention was centered on passing legislation to deal with the Depression. Without a master plan, it is not surprising that the New Deal had an overlapping, jerry-built look by 1935. The irony for Roosevelt was that in expanding the executive branch and being accused of building a dictatorship, he had actually thrown together a rickety structure that was largely beyond his personal control. During his first term, he had created three cabinet-based instruments to coordinate the sprawling New Deal agencies: the Executive Council in July 1933, the National Emergency Council in November 1933, and the Industrial Emergency Committee in summer of 1934.[27] None of them was successful. After his victory in the 1936 elections, he told the press that the most vulnerable aspect of his first term was administration, but that the Republicans had not focused on that issue.

By 1935, Roosevelt was ready to seek the help of a new Brains Trust, namely, leading scholars in the field of public administration. In March 1936, after months of consultation, the president created the Committee on Administrative Management, more popularly known as the Brownlow Committee, which consisted of Louis Brownlow as chairman, Luther Gulick, and Charles Merriam. The committee was assisted by a professional staff of twenty-six experts under the supervision of Professor Joseph P. Harris. Roosevelt wanted the committee to understand that their job was to serve his political purposes; they were not to recommend anything that he could not support. This was not a problem because all the members of the committee were strong supporters of the New Deal. They believed that by increasing the managerial authority of the president, they were promoting democracy and a more socially just America. National security concerns also pervaded the committee's thinking, an unsurprising fact given the threats to and doubts about the viability of democracy during the 1930s. Polenberg points out, "The authors [Brownlow, Merriam and Gulick] rejected the totalitarian claim that democracy inevitably dissipated its energies in futile debate. The key to making democracy effective was vigorous executive leadership."[28] Brownlow later explained, "Not one of us harbored a doubt that our task amid the gathering world storm was to strengthen the presidency so that the President . . . might be better equipped not only to manage the affairs of the government but to defend the freedom of the American people."[29] The Brownlow Committee endorsed the political perspective of the New Deal.

Brownlow submitted his recommendations to Roosevelt on November 14, 1936. The president was pleased with the basic assumption of the report—that managerial direction of all executive agencies should be centered on the chief executive. But he raised two objections. First, the report recommended the creation of a White House secretariat under the supervision of an executive secretary. Today this sounds like a chief of staff, the position that President Eisenhower created in 1953 to run the White House staff. To Roosevelt, it sounded like a threat to his control over his personal staff; he made it perfectly clear that he alone would continue to supervise the White House staff. The recommendation was dropped. Second, Roosevelt complained that the president was not granted more control over the independent regulatory commissions. This was corrected on the final draft, which greatly pleased Roosevelt.[30] On January 19, 1937, Roosevelt submitted the Brownlow Committee report to Congress. It recommended that the president be strengthened in five ways:

> First, furnish six executive assistants to lighten the intolerable personal
> burden upon him. Second, reinvigorate the civil service by expanding
> the merit system and raising government salaries, and by replacing the
> ineffectual Civil Service Commission with an energetic administrator.
> Third, improve fiscal management by encouraging budget-planning,
> by restoring control of accounts to the Executive, and by providing
> Congress with an independent audit of all transactions. Fourth,
> establish the National Resources Planning Board as a permanent

central planning agency to coordinate government programs. Fifth, reorganize the government by creating two new cabinet posts and by bringing every executive agency, including independent regulatory commissions, under one of the twelve major departments.[31]

FDR began selling the merits of the Brownlow Committee in a long press conference on January 11, 1937. Demonstrating both his knowledge of and commitment to administrative reform, he emphasized that his proposal was consistent with American traditions of efficient management. Roosevelt was not trying to expand his political control; he was trying to obtain the authority to carry out the administrative responsibilities he already had under the Constitution. He had this advice for reporters: "I hope you will use the word management a great deal in any stories you may write. . . . The word management is a thoroughly clear American word. . . . If we say our wives are good managers, everybody understands what we mean. . . . What we are trying to do is to put good management into the government in exactly the same sense of the term."[32] Framing the issue in this way, who could object?

On January 12, Roosevelt submitted his special message, written by Luther Gulick, to Congress. In his message, the president declared that the present executive structure was "sadly out of date" and that the Brownlow Committee's recommendations provided practical and reasonable reforms to update the administrative system to meet present and future needs. To bring about greater efficiency and democratic accountability, it was necessary, according to Roosevelt, to "overhaul the 100 independent agencies, administrations, authorities, boards and commissions, and place them by Executive Order within one or the other of the 12 major executive departments." He struck a Hamiltonian note by declaring, "In these troubled years of world history, a self-government cannot long survive unless that government is an effective agency to serve mankind and carry out the will of the nation. A government without good management is a house builded on sand." Finally, he cited President Theodore Roosevelt in support of a controversial claim that was sure to be resisted by legislators in both parties, namely, that the task of reorganization was "essentially executive in its nature."[33]

FDR hoped that the combination of his landslide electoral victory and the support of the top scholars in public administration would mean that his legislative proposal for administrative reform would generate little controversy and pass easily. Instead, the bill provoked rabid opposition that prevented its passage for three years.

Initially, many Congress members resented the fact that the president had not consulted them; rather, he had presented them a completed package designed by academic experts (not their favorite people), which they were expected to pass quickly without change. Some legislators thought that Brownlow's recommendations were based on a distorted view of the Constitution. Brownlow's report talked about the president as the leader of his political party, the Congress, and the people, which was the New Deal's conception of the modern presidency, not the Constitution's. Some Congress members also suspected that the Brownlow argument—that the way to make the president accountable to Congress was to grant him almost exclusive control over the expanding bureaucracy—was dubious and reflected FDR's penchant for camouflaging his political objectives. In our system of checks and balances, the president is the chief executive; he is not the sole executive.

The result of increasing the president's executive power would be to decrease the executive power of Congress. Because a growing number of Congress members believed that the president had already expanded his legislative authority to dangerous levels at their expense, the stage was set for a long struggle. Furthermore, passage of the original bill would give Roosevelt a free hand to run the new and expanding powers of the administrative state, a scenario that scared almost everyone, even some New Deal Democrats who might trust Roosevelt but were apprehensive how future chief executives might exploit these extensive powers. And finally, under the neutral-sounding language of administrative reforms, this bill would, in Alonzo Hamby's words, "strengthen the presidency and institutionalize New Deal liberalism."[34] Under its provisions, two new departments would be added to the ten existing ones: Social Welfare and Public Works. This would signify the federal government's permanent, as opposed to temporary or emergency, commitment to these policies. Brownlow may have been comfortable with the New Deal vision that the country was going to be progressively run by talented public servants, but many in Congress were appalled by the notion.

Within a month, Roosevelt's attempt to reform the executive branch was overshadowed by his higher priority to reform the judiciary. His opponents immediately claimed to discern a conspiratorial plan to destroy democracy and bring about one-man rule. The bill to reform the judicial system was labeled "the court-packing scheme," while the proposal to reorganize the bureaucracy was called "the dictator bill." From then on, the reorganization bill labored under a dark cloud of suspicion that it harbored antidemocratic intrigues. But that fear is not what prevented passage of the bill for several years. What proved decisive in delaying the passage of the bill was that it lacked the ability to generate widespread support. Indeed, the bill did just the opposite; it had an uncanny facility to threaten interest group leaders and civil servants who had become comfortable working with each other.

Roosevelt, who was knowledgeable about bureaucratic politics and turf wars, tried to deal with the problem. For example, in his reform bills introduced in 1937 and 1938, the Army Corps of Engineers was specifically exempted from reorganization. Although nominally under the command of the president, the corps has always had closer relations to Congress because its river and harbor public works projects help legislators bring money and jobs into their districts.[35] Nevertheless, the corps and its supporters in the National Rivers and Harbors Congress were distressed that the creation of the National Resources Planning Board in the reorganization bill would erode the system of connections they had carefully cultivated. They knew how to play the game of obtaining financing for public works projects from Congress, but they would be faced with a mysteriously different set of procedures trying to convince a planning board to select and support their projects. Eventually, according to Polenberg, "Partisans of the Army Corps of Engineers saw to it that the Board could only recommend, not initiate, river development projects. The truncated National Resources Planning Board that emerged bore little resemblance to the planning agency envisioned by the Brownlow Committee."[36]

During the extensive congressional hearings over the reorganization bill, many different groups expressed their anxieties about the possibility that the president might rearrange their bureaucratic world. Otis Graham Jr. summarized these hearings: "The American Legion testified that it didn't want Veteran Affairs in the Department of Social Welfare, physicians didn't want the Public Health Service moved out of Treasury, social workers didn't want the Children's Bureau moved from Labor to Social Welfare, railway labor didn't want the Interstate Commerce Commission moved to Commerce. And the president's own bill was openly opposed by the secretaries of interior, agriculture, labor, the chairman of the National Labor Relations Board, of the U.S. Tariff Commission, of the Federal Trade Commission, the heads of the General Accounting Office and of the Bureau of Fisheries!"[37] The proposed reforms renewed the bitter, long-standing fight between the Departments of Agriculture and Interior over the location of the Forest Service. Interior had lost the Forest Service in 1905, but Harold Ickes was obsessed with getting it back and renaming his department the Department of Conservation. Henry Wallace, the secretary of the Department of Agriculture, refused to release the Forest Service. The result was an embarrassing public feud within the administration. Political reality dictated that the only way this bill would pass was if a number of powerful interest groups and agencies were guaranteed in the revised bill that their relationships would not be altered by the president's authority to reorganize. Ultimately, this is what happened.

The fallout from all this negative publicity wounded the administration but not Roosevelt personally. His popularity remained high even though support for the reorganization bill was low. "Polls taken in March 1938," according to Polenberg, "showed 20 percent in favor of reorganization, 35 percent opposed, 45 percent undecided. Nor can it be argued that those who expressed disapproval were all Republicans. Reorganization had less support among Roosevelt's admirers than any other New Deal measure."[38] This lack of public support can be partially explained by context; in 1938, the news was dominated by Hitler's triumphs, which raised fears about unchecked executive power. Demonstrating how far he had been forced on the defensive, the president issued the following public statement on March 31, 1938: "As you well know, I am as much opposed to American Dictatorship as you are, for three simple reasons: I have no inclination to be a dictator. I have none of the qualifications which would make me a successful dictator. I have too much historical background and too much knowledge of existing dictatorships to make me desire any form of dictatorship for a democracy like the United States of America."[39]

The polling data also reflected a dilemma for Roosevelt and the liberal regime he was constructing. The public was more willing to support what FDR was doing than how he was doing it. Roosevelt had been more successful in selling the goals of the welfare state than the bureaucratic means to provide one. Citizens wanted the fruits of the welfare state without enduring the bureaucratic costs.

A watered-down version of FDR's original reorganization bill, largely rewritten by legislators, finally passed Congress and was signed into law by the president on April 3, 1939. The Administrative Reorganization Act "did provide for [six] new presidential assistants and did allow the president to initiate reorganization plans that would go into effect if Congress did not vote to disapprove them. Under the act, Roosevelt was successful in implementing a series of plans that did establish an Executive Office of the President, bring the Bureau of the Budget and the National Resources Planning Board into it, and create a new administrative grouping of functionally related agencies, and transfer a number of units from one department to another."[40]

Passage of this law established the institutional basis of the modern presidency. Roosevelt gained resources and control over his immediate domain, the executive office of the president, but he did not obtain the control over the executive branch that he originally sought. No new departments were added; the independent regulatory agencies maintained their autonomy; and the president's authority to reorganize the bureaucracy and engage in centralized planning was limited. Hawley views this episode as a failed attempt to fill the hollow core of the American administrative state with professional managers and planners and thus establish mastery over the bureaucratic apparatus.[41] Without a strong planning and managerial facility, the political system would continue to produce public policies that were frequently incoherent—a situation that frustrated planners but pleased most Congress members. Skowronek claims that the compromises FDR was forced to accept denied him the authority to bring about greater consistency in the regime he was constructing. In his words, "The shadow form of the reorganization proposal that was passed . . . recognized the President as first among equals in tackling the problems of administrative management. But while Roosevelt got the institutional independence he needed to service the new regime, everyone else got the independence they needed to prevent him from controlling it."[42]

In summary, FDR had attempted to create a managerial state under the direction of the president; what he ended up producing was a continuation of what Karl calls "the uneasy state."

Republican Attacks on the New Deal

To understand the politics of reconstruction, one needs to examine not only the proponents of the new regime, but also its opponents. What critics of an emerging regime have to say can be illuminating in highlighting the changes that are occurring. The supporters of the old regime may have lost mass support but not their passionate allegiance to the way they feel the country ought to be governed.

During the 1930s, the Republican party was in an unenviable position. The party controlled both the presidency and Congress during the 1920s and, to a lesser degree, in the last two years of the Hoover administration, but it had been able neither to prevent the Depression nor to devise the means to lead the nation back to economic recovery. In this weakened condition, Republicans were facing FDR, arguably the most politically astute president in the twentieth century, who had the desire and the skill to wring every possible advantage from this context.

Most Republican leaders felt severely threatened by FDR and the New Deal. A party accustomed to governing since Lincoln, sure of its moral superiority over the Democrats, proud of its historic achievements, was now relegated to a humiliating, minority status. Schlesinger interprets the Republican confusion and rage in these words: "Depression and the New Deal had knocked the pinnings from under them; accustomed to security, they were adrift; accustomed to power, they were frightened as new forces boiled up from the lower depths. Everything they stood for seemed under mortal attack—and, worst of all, the man leading the barbaric onslaught was one of their own."[43] Because FDR and the New Deal were virtually synonymous, the demonization of him also stained the emerging liberal regime.

Their protest that the New Deal violated the American way of governing meant that Republican America was being changed. After FDR's first hundred days in 1933, Republican Congressman James Beck wrote to Herbert Hoover and lamented, "You have been much on my mind this session of Congress, which now seems to me to mark the end of our form of government. . . . I know you must view with grief, as I do, all that has happened."[44] Liberal Democrats would feel the same pain in the 1980s.

Republicans had a number of fundamental criticisms of the New Deal. First, conservative Republicans saw despotism lurking in the creation of the New Deal bureaucratic state. For conservative Republicans, New Deal proposals for planning, massive relief, and a managed economy were stepping stones toward a totalitarian state. Appealing to our national prejudices, Republicans claimed that these proposals were un-American, that they violated our political traditions, and that they were imported from Europe by New Deal intellectuals.[45] By 1935, ex-President Hoover charged that the New Deal was running out of letters of the alphabet for its new agencies. "'There are only four letters of the alphabet not now in use by the administration,' he charged. 'When we establish the Quick Loans Corporation for Xylophones, Yachts, and Zithers, the alphabet of our fathers will be exhausted.' But . . . he added ominously, 'the new Russian alphabet has thirty-four letters.'"[46]

Many Republicans blamed the authoritarian tendencies of the New Deal on the expanding influence of intellectuals. Businessmen and Republicans never tired of accusing intellectuals of dominating the Roosevelt administration, of imbuing it with a radical perspective, and of lacking the practical experience necessary for success in the real world. Kirkendall writes,

"At times, critics simply portrayed the Brains Trust or professors as the dominant group, while frequently the alarmed observers pointed to particular individuals, like Tugwell or Frankfurter, as the men of greatest power. Sometimes their brand of radicalism was not defined, but often such labels as 'communistic' and 'socialistic' were pinned on their philosophies."[47] Blaming intellectuals for the decisions of the New Deal was used more often in the early years of the administration when Republicans wanted to avoid direct assaults on FDR because of his personal popularity. But over time, as one supposed Rasputin after another (Moley, Richberg, Tugwell) declined in influence, the attacks converged on the president.

Second, Republicans claimed that New Deal attempts to reform capitalism with federal controls would inevitably degenerate into socialism. New Deal thinkers had to overcome stifling dogma during the 1930s that declared there was no middle ground between capitalism and socialism. Clyde Weed writes, "Such otherwise diverse thinkers as Harold Laski, Sydney Webb, Sidney Hook, and F. A. Hayek all reflected the widespread tendency to dismiss the possibility of a managed capitalist order. The existence of a 'middle way' seemed increasingly remote to a wide variety of observers during the period from 1930 through 1936 and Republican campaign appeals often reflected this."[48] To illustrate this tendency, Schlesinger cites Ogden Mills, Hoover's treasury secretary, and Hoover: "'We can have a free society or a socialistic one,' said Ogden Mills. 'We cannot have both. Our economic system cannot be half free and half socialistic. . . . There is no middle ground between governing and being governed, between tyranny and freedom.' Hoover was equally vehement. 'Even partial regimentation cannot be made to work,' he said, 'and still maintain live democratic institutions.' There was, he said, a borderline in the activities of free government. 'When the boundaries of Liberty are overstepped, America will cease to be American.'"[49]

Conservatives had a simple formula: the expansion of the federal bureaucracy meant the increasing regimentation of American life and the decline of individual liberties. New Dealers might claim they aimed at regulating only parts of the economy, but the initial thrust would naturally broaden to other aspects of life. It was impossible to contain federal regulation within the economic realm alone. Hoover explained this phenomenon in terms of an iron law of bureaucratic expansion. "'In all bureaucracies,' Hoover asserted, 'there are three implacable spirits—self-perpetuation, expansion, and an incessant demand for more power.' Wherever bureaucracy dominated, he said, the consequence was always the same, 'this host of government agents spread out over the land, limiting men's honest activities, conferring largesse and benefits, directing, interfering, disseminating propaganda, spying on, threatening the people and prosecuting for a new host of crimes.'"[50] From this perspective, any federal intervention into a new policy area—agriculture, banking, housing, the stock market—would inevitably lead to federal domination of that policy space. Republican Congressman John Taber, for example, "argued that if minimum wages and maximum hours were fixed by government, then all wages would be so fixed, and private enterprise would cease, and 'this . . . means . . . a totalitarian state.'"[51]

Third, Republicans accused the New Deal of being antibusiness, a policy that was inhibiting the recovery. The irony of the New Deal's emphasis on trying to supply more security for the bulk of the population was that it produced insecurity in the business and financial sectors. The uncertainty felt by these two related sectors was initially caused by their being blamed for causing the Depression and later by their becoming the targets of increased regulation and taxation. After the NRA experiment of business-government co-operation failed, business became alienated from Roosevelt, and he became more tied to labor. In 1934, big business created the Liberty League, and in 1935, it increased its campaign contributions to the Republican party in order to defeat FDR in the 1936 elections. When New Deal policies were not as successful as planned, business was rebuked again for sabotaging recovery by failing to invest—the alleged capital strike. Both Republican and business leaders thought that they were victims of a political dynamic whereby, when New Deal programs did not provide an impressive economic recovery, the resulting dissatisfaction was used to justify more radical reforms. They feared the business sector would be increasingly taxed to finance the welfare state, which would perpetuate FDR's political success at their expense. Businessmen were outraged that they were funding their economic and political decline under the new regime. Business could not be sure where New Deal experiments and visions would end up, but Republican orators were offering the most frightening projections. When Roosevelt condemned "economic royalists" in the 1936 campaign, was he criticizing a few bad apples, or was he preparing the public for an anticapitalist crusade?[52]

Fourth, Republicans charged that Roosevelt was creating a politicized administrative state that was more prone to serve the partisan purposes of the Democratic party than the public interest. The Republican claim and fear were that New Deal programs to help the farmer and the worker would result in Democratic party control of these groups. Although Roosevelt's relationship with the Tammany political machine in New York City was usually tense and wary, Republicans accused the president of attempting to build the first national political machine—in Senator Arthur Vandenberg's phrase, "to Tammanyize the whole United States."[53] When Republican Congress members lost elections in 1934 and 1936, they were likely to explain their defeat on the "relief vote."[54] From the Republican perspective, relief and public works funds administered by Hopkins and Ickes were surreptitiously distributed as campaign funds. In 1938, when newspapers reported that Hopkins declared the philosophy of the New Deal was to tax, spend, and elect (a statement Hopkins denied making), Republicans were both delighted and outraged to hear their darkest suspicions confirmed.

Perhaps the best way to analyze the Republican opposition to the New Deal is to look at Alfred Landon's 1936 campaign. Because we know that FDR was reelected by a landslide in 1936, with Landon winning only Vermont and Maine, it is easy to overlook the fact that the Republicans believed that they had a good chance to win in 1936. With Roosevelt having virtually united business against him, the GOP thought the contest might duplicate the election of 1896, when William McKinley, with the backing of business, defeated William Jennings Bryan. New Deal reforms had generated conflicts within the Democratic party between the North and the South, farmers and workers, intellectuals and party professionals, all of which led some Republicans to hope that the majority party would be handicapped by internal divisions. Republican strategists believed their key to victory was to overcome their historic split between conservative Eastern Republicans and progressive Western Republicans by nominating a moderate Western progressive. Such a candidate could win by carrying states in the Northeast, the Midwest, and the West. The man who seemed to fit this profile was Governor Alfred Landon, the "Kansas Coolidge," the only Republican governor elected in 1934.

Landon was a former Bull Mooser who had supported Teddy Roosevelt in 1912 but had since been a loyal Republican. Weed summarized Landon's political stance in these words: "long supportive of the administration's agricultural and conservation programs, he also endorsed the principle of social security, and favored labor's right to organize. . . . Fundamentally, a western progressive, Landon had gradually come to view that the New Deal increasingly reflected politicized responses to social problems, responses that retarded the achievement of its often laudable ends. He was sincerely convinced that constitutional government in the United States was imperiled by the possibility of a debased currency and by an increasing centralization of power that he felt had taken on dangerous momentum."[55]

Landon's beliefs blended the fears of conservative Republicans with the hopes of progressive Republicans.

The Republicans held their national party convention in Cleveland in June 1936, and Landon was nominated on the first ballot. Frank Knox, a Chicago publisher who had served as a Rough Rider under Teddy Roosevelt, was nominated for vice president. The party platform was hammered out between representatives of Landon's supporters and eastern Republican leaders. It supported such New Deal reforms as agricultural support, securities regulation, social security, and unemployment relief, but called for their administration in a "nonpartisan" manner. Nevertheless, the platform struck a virulent anti–New Deal note in its first line: "America is in peril." The country was in danger, not because of the Depression, but because of New Deal policies. Liberty was threatened because the New Deal "dishonored American traditions" by the president's usurping legislative power, flaunting the authority of the Supreme Court, and violating the rights reserved to the states and to the people. The Depression was prolonged because the administration's policies "bred fear and hesitation in commerce and industry, thus discouraging new enterprise." It condemned the administration for appealing to "class prejudice" and for being "guilty of frightful waste and extravagance" in "using public funds for partisan political purposes." The platform promised that a Republican presidency would return responsibility for relief administration to nonpolitical local agencies and to balance the budget immediately by cutting expenditures.[56]

In Landon's acceptance speech, he stressed that "the country is ripe for recovery" but that New Deal policies were blocking the confidence necessary for the economy to forge ahead. Landon argued that the New Deal deserved and had received a fair trial, but the record proved that its policies "did not fit together into any definite program of recovery. Many of them worked at cross purposes and defeated themselves." He added, "our growing debts and taxes are so enormous that, even if we tax to the utmost limits those who are best able to pay, the average taxpayer will still have to bear the major part. While spending billions of dollars of borrowed money may create a temporary appearance of prosperity, we and our children, as taxpayers, have yet to pay the bill."[57] His message was that although citizens might temporarily benefit from Roosevelt's policies, eventually they would have to pay off the rising national debt with higher taxes.

After he received the Republican nomination, Landon published a book entitled *America at the Crossroads*, which was designed to summarize the plain-spoken governor's ideas to the reading public. The prairie philosopher portrayed himself as a practical reformer, in contrast to the more radical Roosevelt, in this metaphor: "If the wind rips the roof off a house in our country, we don't tear down the walls . . . and abandon the whole structure." Landon described the 1936 election as "the crossroads where we must make a choice between the pig-in-the-poke policies of the present administration and those American institutions under which we have enjoyed more liberty and attained a higher standard of living than any other people in the world." It was not the Constitution that was retarding recovery, as many radical New Dealers were falsely claiming; it was Roosevelt's excessive expenditures, crippling taxation, stifling regulations, and uncertain monetary policy. The New Deal was providing politicized relief for the unemployed and patronage jobs in the bloated bureaucracy for its supporters, but it was not creating jobs in the private sector that would signify an authentic and sustainable recovery. Landon understood that Americans "not only want to safeguard our freedom, but we also want security and abundance of the good things of life. We are told, however, by defeatists that we cannot have both. We must, they say, choose between freedom and security." Landon promised both. Sounding like Reagan in the 1980s, Landon declared that once American enterprise was unshackled from governmental controls, "the energies of the . . . economic system will remedy the ravages of the depression and restore full activity and full employment."[58] The obvious hole in this argument was that business was unshackled before October 1929.

Landon was handicapped in the 1936 campaign because he "had to run carrying water on both shoulders, bearing the 'me too' weight of progressive Republicans and balancing it with reactionary nods and winks to the Old Guard."[59] The governor's initial moderate campaign strategy was immediately upstaged by his running mate's savage assault on Roosevelt. In contrast with the soft-pedaling Landon, "Frank Knox gave the voters what he thought they wanted to hear, a slashing frontal attack. 'We are not in a political campaign,' he stormed, 'we are in a crusade to save America' from 'fanatics, theorists and impractical experimenters.' In Denver, Knox described Roosevelt as 'a man drunk with power.' 'Be on your guard,' he warned. 'Silently in the night they are creeping up, seeking to impose upon us, before we realize it, a new and alien kind of government.'"[60] What makes these personal attacks so ironic is that four years later, FDR coopted Knox's support by appointing him secretary of the navy.

As the campaign heated up, Landon found himself slipping into the same vulnerable position Hoover had occupied in 1932; he was defending what a majority of the electorate found indefensible—components of the old regime. What Landon called the "American way" was really the "Republican way" of lower taxes and little regulation of business and financial markets. The threats to democracy and individual rights appeared to be driven by Republican fears that the rich would have to pay higher taxes to finance a welfare state, and corporate leaders would be legally obliged to negotiate with labor leaders. Although Landon protested that FDR's support of labor was motivated by partisan interest, it was impossible for the Republicans to avoid suspicion that their support of the business sector was not similarly inspired. When Landon saw he was going to lose, his rhetoric shifted to the right, and he sounded more like an old-guard Republican than a progressive Republican: "In Phoenix he declared that saving the American system of government was the fundamental issue of the campaign. The New Deal, he charged, in his most extreme statement of the campaign, 'violates the basic ideals of the American system. . . . No nation can continue half regimented and half free. If we are to preserve our American form of government, this administration must be defeated.'"[61] Landon may have been paraphrasing Lincoln, but he sounded like Hoover and would be similarly rejected.

FDR's Conflict with the Supreme Court

Because the Republicans had lost control of the presidency and Congress, and with the decline in prestige of business leaders, the most potent opposition to the New Deal, until the changes in 1937, was mounted by the federal courts. According to Peter Irons, "The real confrontation between New Dealers and their foes took place . . . in federal courtrooms dominated by Republican judges wedded to the states-rights and laissez-faire ideologies repudiated overwhelmingly by the voters in three successive elections between 1932 and 1936."[62] Because the constitutional foundations of both the declining Republican regime and the ascending liberal one were at stake, a major conflict could not be avoided. In this fight, there were few examples of FDR's fabled political skills and a surprising number of uncharacteristic mistakes. Nevertheless, he did succeed in getting most of the New Deal program legitimated by Supreme Court rulings, but he did so at the expense of his ability to pass additional reforms through Congress.

Roosevelt was aware that Republican-appointed judges dominated the federal courts and might attempt to block his programs. In his first inaugural address, perhaps more optimistically than realistically, Roosevelt declared, "Our Constitution is so simple and practical that it is possible always to meet extraordinary needs by changes in emphasis and arrangement without loss of essential form. That is why our constitutional system has proved itself the most superbly enduring political mechanism the modern world has produced."[63] At the beginning of his presidency, Roosevelt had attempted to replicate the "delightful" relations he claimed to have had as governor with New York State's highest court, but Chief Justice Hughes rejected his offer.[64] In November 1933, Roosevelt received a report from his attorney general, Homer Cummings, that of the 266 judges sitting on federal district courts and federal courts of appeal, only 28 percent were Democrats.[65] This knowledge, plus the growing awareness that opponents of the New Deal were seeking injunctions against allegedly unconstitutional laws, reinforced FDR's "hands-on approach" in selecting judges to nominate for the federal courts, and increased his concern to make more "policy-agenda appointments" of those who would be favorably disposed to liberal arguments. With three-fourths of lower federal court judges being Republican, it was not surprising that about sixteen hundred injunctions were issued blocking the enforcement of New Deal laws.[66]

As these cases worked their way up to the Supreme Court, it became obvious that a constitutional crisis was brewing. The goal of the New Deal was to legitimate the positive state, a far more activist federal government than what had been permitted before 1933. Liberals believed that the states had proved incapable of effectively responding to the massive problems of the Depression. They claimed the Depression had created a national emergency, analogous to being engaged in war, which legally justified Congress' delegating extraordinary authority to the president to administer solutions. And because no federal law had ever been declared unconstitutional because of excessive or improper delegation to the executive, New Deal lawyers thought they were on defensible terrain. Their major concern was with finding expandable clauses in the Constitution on which to base the kind of detailed intervention in market processes that the measures authorized. In practice, two such clauses were found. One was the clause authorizing taxation to provide for the "general welfare." The other, more important, one was that authorizing Congress "to regulate commerce . . . among the several States."[67] At the simplest level, the Depression was an economic crisis, and the commerce clause was the enumerated power in Article I most relevant for dealing with national economic problems. Supporters of the New Deal pointed out that probusiness conservatives had been successful in planting their pet provisions and interpretations in constitutional law, and now it was the liberals' turn. In 1934, John Hope Carter wrote, "The

New Dealers have no design against the Constitution, provided that it retains the elasticity of the original fabric. This elasticity has always been in evidence whenever a Philadelphia lawyer desired to drive a corporate caravan through it, but it has been remarkably rigid whenever the rights of the common man were up for consideration."[68]

FDR faced a major challenge in dealing with the Supreme Court. His chief obstacles were four conservative justices—George Sutherland, James McReynolds, Price Butler, and Willis Van Devanter—known as the Four Horsemen of the Apocalypse. The president's potential allies were Harlan Fiske Stone, Benjamin Cardozo, and Louis Brandeis. The swing voters were Charles Evans Hughes, who was appointed chief justice by President Hoover to replace the ailing William Howard Taft in 1930, and Owen Roberts. President Wilson had selected the liberal Brandeis and the conservative McReynolds, while Republican chief executives had appointed the other seven. Although the Hughes Court was exceptionally old, none of them retired between 1933 and 1936; FDR was the first president since James Monroe to be in office for four years and not have the opportunity to appoint a new justice to the Supreme Court.

The evolution of constitutional law strives for consistency, but with changes in society, politics, and personnel on the Court, it never achieves it. After the Civil War, probusiness justices had been successful in constructing a constitutional doctrine that promoted the capitalist development of the United States. John Rohr stresses, "By narrowly interpreting the constitutional power of Congress to regulate commerce among the states, the Court severely limited the scope of federal intervention in economic affairs. Conversely, by a broad interpretation of the due process clause in the Fourteenth Amendment, the Court restricted the power of the states to regulate their own economies."[69] Conservative judicial activists took the Fourteenth Amendment, which had been created in 1868 to protect the emancipated slaves in the South, and transformed it into a mechanism to shield corporations from public regulation. Much of what conservative jurists constructed—substantive due process, liberty of contract, dual federalism, and a restricted view of the commerce clause—became barriers to what first the progressives and later the New Dealers were trying to achieve.

Precedents were established in the following Court cases that supported the probusiness perspective. In *United States v. E. C. Knight*, 1895, the Supreme Court ruled that the Havenmeyer Sugar Trust, which controlled 98 percent of the nation's sugar refineries, was not violating the Sherman Antitrust Act because it was engaged in manufacturing, not commerce. In

Chief Justice Melville Fuller's majority opinion, the commerce that Congress could regulate was transportation across state lines, and not production, which was a local activity. He also ruled "that Congress had no power over enterprises whose effect on commerce was indirect, no matter how extensive, because the difference between 'direct' and 'indirect' was one of kind rather than degree."[70]

In *Lochner v. New York*, 1905, the Court ruled that a New York statute that limited the weekly and daily working hours of employees in the baking industry fell outside of the proper limits of the police power and was unconstitutional. Reflecting the laissez-faire philosophy, Justice Rufus Peckham's majority opinion condemned the state law as a "meddlesome interference" in the marketplace that violated an inalienable right—liberty of contract. The *Lochner* decision is also famous for Oliver Wendell Holmes's dissent, in which he admonished the majority that "the Fourteenth Amendment does not enact Herbert Spencer's *Social Statics*." Holmes was accusing the majority of basing their opinion on their social Darwinism ideology and not the text of the law.[71]

In *Hamner v. Dagenhart*, 1918, the Court, in a 5-to-4 decision, declared the Child Labor Act of 1916 unconstitutional. The majority (which included Van Devanter and McReynolds) ruled, "Congress could not ban the shipment in interstate commerce of goods produced by children because Congress was seeking to control intrastate activities."[72] In *Adkins v. Children's Hospital* (1923), the Court ruled that a 1918 congressional law establishing a District of Columbia board authorized to set minimum wages for women and children was unconstitutional. Felix Frankfurter, counsel for the plaintiff, argued that the law was an appropriate exercise of legislative power to protect public health, morals, and the general welfare in the nation's capital.[73] But in a 5–3 decision (Brandeis recused himself because his daughter was lobbying for similar laws), Sutherland declared that the federal law violated the liberty of contract guaranteed by (but not mentioned in) the due process clause of the Fifth Amendment. A major barrier to both federal and state efforts to regulate wages had been erected.[74]

These precedents were available for conservative justices to use against liberal state and federal legislation when FDR assumed office. But there was also uncertainty over whether anyone or any philosophy was going to be able to mobilize consistent majorities during this unprecedented crisis. Liberals won the first skirmish in January 1934, when the Court, in a 5–4 decision written by Chief Justice Hughes, upheld a Minnesota law postponing mortgage foreclosures. Two months later, in *Nebbia v. New York*, a

5–4 majority decided that a New York statute that established a board to set minimum and maximum retail prices for milk was constitutional. Leo Nebbia, a small businessman convicted of selling milk below the administered price, argued that the regulation deprived him of property without due process of law and therefore violated the Fourteenth Amendment. Citing the *Adkins* precedent, Nebbia's lawyers contended that the milk law should be declared unconstitutional, but their pleas received only the support of the four conservatives. The language of Owen Roberts's majority opinion encouraged New Dealers to hope that he might ally himself with the liberal faction in future cases. To the dismay of conservatives, Roberts suggested that neither property rights nor contract rights were absolute. He wrote, "The Fifth Amendment in the field of federal activity, and the Fourteenth, as respects state action, do not prohibit governmental regulation for the public welfare. They merely condition the exertion of the admitted power, by securing that the end shall be accomplished by methods consistent with due process. And the guarantee of due process . . . demands only that the law shall not be unreasonable, arbitrary, or capricious, and the means selected shall have a real and substantial relation to the object sought to be attained."[75]

The New Deal did badly in the Supreme Court in 1935. In January, the Court ruled, in *Panama Refining Co. et al. v. Ryan*, that Section 9(c) of the National Industrial Recovery Act, authorizing the president to prohibit the shipment in interstate and foreign commerce of petroleum produced or withdrawn from storage in excess of the quotas set by the individual states (this excess petroleum was known as "hot oil") was an unconstitutional delegation of legislative power to the executive.[76] This was the first federal law ever rejected by the Court on these grounds, but it would not be the last. In February, FDR's gold policy was accepted in a 5–4 decision. However, on May 6, a narrow majority of the Court declared the Railway Workers' Pension Act, enacted in June 1934, to be unconstitutional. Justice Roberts had joined the four conservatives and ruled that "The system of compulsory pensions is both a violation of due process . . . and an exercise of power not authorized under the commerce clause."[77] This decision appeared to doom the chances of social security, which was being considered by Congress at the time.

On May 27, the Supreme Court appeared to declare war on the New Deal by striking down three laws in three unanimous decisions. The Court invalidated both the Farm Mortgage Foreclosure Act of 1934 and the National Industrial Recovery Act (NIRA), and it ruled that the president did not have the authority to fire a member of an independent regulatory commission. FDR and his advisers were particularly incensed by the tone of Sutherland's opinion in *Humphrey's Executor v. the United States*, in which they detected a "touch of malice." According to Leuchtenburg, "The President and his circle thought that Sutherland had malevolently subjected Roosevelt to a public humiliation by making it appear that he had been willfully violating the Constitution by removing Humphrey from the Federal Trade Commission. Had the Court admitted it was modifying *Myers* [a decision granting the president extensive executive power written by Chief Justice Taft in 1926] and conceded that FDR might have been acting in good faith by being guided by that earlier opinion, the Court's ruling in *Humphrey* would not have aroused so much resentment."[78]

Headlines centered on the Court's unanimous decision in *Schecter Poultry Co. et al. v. United States*, which proclaimed NIRA, the centerpiece of the New Deal, unconstitutional. Hughes's opinion ruled that Congress had overstated its authority under the commerce clause and had unlawfully delegated legislative authority to the executive. Without citing the *E. C. Knight* 1895 case, Hughes used this reasoning:

> In determining how far the federal government may go in controlling intrastate transactions upon the ground that they "affect" interstate commerce, there is a necessary and well-established distinction between direct and indirect effects. . . . Where the effect of intrastate transactions upon interstate commerce is merely indirect, such transactions remain within the domain of State power. If the commerce clause were construed to reach all enterprises and transactions which could be said to have an indirect effect upon interstate commerce, the federal authority would embrace practically all the activities of the people, and the authority of the state over its domestic concerns would exist only by the sufferance of the federal government.[79]

Such a situation would destroy our federal system. Hence, in Robert Stern's words, "Only intrastate practices 'directly' affecting interstate commerce were subject to the federal power."[80] In a concurring opinion, signed by Stone, Cardozo condemned the appalling number of NRA codes as "delegation run riot."[81]

FDR should not have been surprised that he had lost the support of Louis Brandeis, a Wilsonian progressive. The seventy-eight-year-old justice had publicized his opposition to bigness, called for vigorous enforcement of antitrust legislation, and condemned the centralization of business and government. After the *Schecter* decision was announced, a visibly agitated Brandeis met with Corcoran and Cohen and told them: "This is the end of this business of centralization, and I want you to go back and tell the President that we're not going to let this government centralize everything. It's come to an end."[82]

Roosevelt was shocked both by these decisions and by the fact that the New Deal had been deserted by its hoped-for allies on the Court. He thought that the Court was disarming him in his war against the Depression. After being extensively briefed by Felix Frankfurter, FDR summoned reporters into his office on May 31, and for the next hour and a half, he criticized the *Schecter* decision. The president read a number of telegrams he had received from small businessmen expressing their fears about the renewal of cutthroat competition. He compared the *Schecter* decision to the infamous *Dred Scott* case in 1857, which had set the stage for the Civil War. "Of all the words the President spoke at the extraordinary conference," according to Leuchtenburg, "newspapermen singled out one sentence [with Roosevelt's permission] which headline writers emblazoned on late afternoon newspapers: 'We have been relegated to the horse-and-buggy definition of interstate commerce.'"[83] Roosevelt believed that something would have to be done in the near future to resolve this constitutional crisis, but he was undecided on what to do.

The conflict escalated in January 1936, when the Court, in a 6–3 decision, struck down another New Deal monument, the Agricultural Adjustment Act, in *United States v. Butler.* Roberts's opinion, in which he was joined by Hughes and the four conservatives, argued that the tax imposed on food processors, which was then used by the secretary of agriculture to subsidize the price of farm commodities for those farmers who agreed to cut production, was unconstitutional because it impinged on regulatory powers reserved to the states by the Tenth Amendment. One surprise in the *Butler* decision was that the Court unanimously accepted the Hamiltonian view "that the general welfare clause permitted Congress to tax and spend for the general welfare. The Court split on the issue of whether Congress could regulate agriculture through its general welfare power. The majority said it could not, and so the government lost its case."[84] In a stinging dissent, Stone, joined by Brandeis and Cardozo, suggested that the AAA could only be invalidated by a "tortured construction of the Constitution."[85] Stone's dissent was the opening salvo in the move by the Court to accept the liberal doctrine that it ought to practice judicial self-restraint in reviewing state and federal laws regulating the economy.

The unpredictability of the Hughes Court was exhibited in February 1936, when, in *Ashwander v. TVA*, it ruled in an 8–1 decision written by the chief justice, with only McReynolds dissenting, that "the TVA had the constitutional authority to compete with private power companies in the sale and distribution of electric power to customers."[86] In May 1936, a highly divided Court ruled in *Carter v. Carter Coal Co.* that the Bituminous Coal Conservation Act of 1935, the so-called little NRA for the coal industry, was unconstitutional. The law had two sections, one regulating labor affairs and the other fixing prices. With Roberts providing the decisive fifth vote for Sutherland's majority opinion, the Court invalidated the wages and hours provisions of the legislation "on the grounds (a) that they exceeded the scope of federal power under the commerce clause, and (b) that insofar as the act delegated to the majority of coal producers (rather than the government) the power to fix the hours and wages to be worked by other employees of other producers, it was 'clearly arbitrary' and therefore violated the due process clause of the Fifth Amendment."[87] The Court split in a 5–4 vote to declare the entire statute unconstitutional and 6–3 to strike down the law's labor provisions. The three liberals based their dissent, written by Cardozo, on a broad view of the commerce clause.

In June 1936, in *Morehead v. New York ex rel. Tipaldo*, the Court declared, in a 5–4 decision, that a New York state minimum wage law to protect women, originally drafted by Felix Frankfurter and Benjamin Cohen in 1933 to circumvent the *Adkins* precedent, was unconstitutional. The lawyer representing New York argued that its minimum wage law was a lawful exercise of state police power to protect the health and welfare of women workers. But Butler's majority opinion, joined by Roberts, "could find no meaningful difference between the New York and District of Columbia statutes. Both violated the liberty of contract safeguarding the equal rights of employer and employee to bargain over wages. The *Adkins* ruling and the reasoning on which it rested clearly showed that the state was without power by any form of legislation to prohibit, change, or nullify contracts between employers and adult women workers as to the amount of wages to be paid."[88] Butler's majority opinion evoked dissents from both Hughes and Stone. The latter wrote, "'There is grim irony in speaking of the freedom of contract of those who, because of economic necessity, give their services for less than is needful to keep body and soul together. . . . ' He added: 'The Fourteenth Amendment has no more embedded in the Constitution our preferences for some particular set of economic beliefs, than it has adopted, in the name of liberty, the system of theology we may approve.'"[89] Stone, like Holmes in his *Lochner* dissent, was accusing the majority of violating their judicial role by projecting their personal preferences into the words of the Fourteenth Amendment.

Liberals contended that the *Carter* and *Tipaldo* decisions had crippled both federal and state governments in dealing with economic problems. But these decisions had also brought upon the Court public criticism, including some from Republicans, such as ex-President Hoover. Indeed, the 1936 Republican party platform pledged to support a constitutional amendment to overturn the *Tipaldo* decision. By striking down a dozen New Deal laws, the Court had set the stage for a constitutional crisis.

The 1936 Democratic party platform expressed a hope that the New Deal's conflict with the Court could be reconciled; but if it could not, the party promised to seek a clarifying amendment. FDR, who was still unsure how he was going to deal with the Supreme Court and who probably believed that campaign discussions about curbing the Court would cost him votes, avoided the issue. However, by not addressing the question of Supreme Court reform during his 1936 election campaign, he could not honestly claim an electoral mandate to do so. Still, after winning the election by a landslide, the president was ready to retaliate against a Court that had rebuked his policies.

By the end of 1936, it was not irrational for Roosevelt to believe that the opposition of the Supreme Court posed a lethal threat to the success of the New Deal. The fruits of hard-earned legislative and electoral victories could easily be stolen by unelected and unaccountable judges. Because Roberts had retreated from his reasoning in the 1934 *Nebbia* decision and joined the Four Horsemen, it looked like the conservatives had the votes to strike down social security and the National Labor Relations Act, the crown jewels of the second New Deal. The conflict was morally charged by both the stakes and the intense feelings held by the two sides. From Roosevelt's perspective, he had been elected twice and therefore was defending democracy against the usurpation of judges representing the interests of a rejected philosophy. The inferred presence of "liberty of contract" in the Fifth and Fourteenth Amendments was as real to the conservative Justices as the literal absence of this phrase in the two amendments was for New Deal lawyers. From the conservative judges' point of view, they were defending a constitutional republic that was specifically designed by the Founding Fathers to withstand the onslaught of temporary democratic majorities.

After the 1936 electoral triumph, the president focused on reforming the Supreme Court by meeting regularly with Homer Cummings, the attorney general. FDR had been considering a variety of options with his advisers since the *Schecter* decision, but now it was necessary to select a plan of action. The choices included proposals to increase the size of the Supreme Court, to mandate a retirement age for judges, to curb or even eliminate the Court's power of judicial review, and to pass a constitutional amendment authorizing the expansion of federal powers.[90] Frankfurter and Corcoran recommended a constitutional amendment, but FDR rejected it because of his experience with the failure of the amendment forbidding child labor to gain the ratification of three-quarters of the states. Roosevelt finally agreed to a proposal "that if a federal judge who had served at least ten years did not resign six months after his seventieth birthday, the president could nominate another new judge to that court."[91] If passed, this law would have allowed FDR to nominate six new justices to the Supreme Court and forty-four to the lower federal courts. Roosevelt was sure that changing the size of the Court by statute was constitutional because it was the first Congress (not the Constitution) that had set the number of justices as six in 1789; in 1801, the number was reduced by Congress to five; in 1863, Congress increased the number to ten; only in 1869 was the number established as nine. He was also familiar with the fact that several British prime ministers had overcome political stalemates by threatening to enlarge the House of Lords. And he reacted with "puckish delight" when Cummings informed him that James McReynolds, while serving in the Wilson administration, had made a similar proposal regarding the number of judges on federal courts in 1913.[92] This proposal also satisfied Roosevelt because he believed the major obstacle blocking New Deal reforms was not the Constitution, but the way a majority of the Court was misinterpreting it.

After the January 20, 1937, inauguration, Roosevelt told Samuel Rosenman, "When the Chief Justice read me the oath and came to the words 'support the Constitution of the United States,' I felt like saying: 'Yes, but it's the Constitution as *I* understand it, flexible enough to meet any new problem of democracy—not the kind of Constitution your Court has raised up as a barrier to progress and democracy.'"[93]

At the end of January 1937, the president summoned Donald Richberg, Rosenman, and Stanley Reed (the solicitor general) to advise him how the Court reform bill could best be launched on February 5. These advisers were shocked that the president's draft message to Congress made no reference to the real and obvious justification for the legislation—that the Court was striking down New Deal legislation. They told FDR it was disingenuous to stress problems of crowded dockets and elderly justices who could not complete their work efficiently, but the president angrily dismissed their arguments.[94] On the morning of February 5, the president briefly informed Democratic congressional leaders about his proposal; an hour later, the press was briefed; at noon, the Judicial Procedures Reform Act was formally introduced in Congress. Almost immediately, the legislation became better known as the court-packing bill—an ominous sign.

Nevertheless, with overwhelming Democratic majorities in the House and Senate, the expectation was that FDR would successfully pressure Congress to pass his reform bill. But winning the election by such a wide margin seemed to have dulled his political sensitivity. The beginning of FDR's second administration was different from conditions in March 1933; there was less a sense of emergency in 1937, which meant the president would have to bargain more with Congress. Instead, blinded by his "post-election hubris," FDR anticipated "servile acquiescence from the Congress."[95] He did not see that there were few advantages for legislators to vote for this law and more incentives to vote against it. Roosevelt had not consulted members of Congress about the reform bill; it had been developed solely within the executive branch. Hence, many Congress members felt free to vote against it. Many of them had also been attacked by Republicans for being a rubber stamp for the president; now they had an opportunity to highlight their independence. It was an ill-boding sign for the fate of the legislation when House Judiciary Committee Chairman Hatton Sumners of Texas and Democratic Senator Burton Wheeler of Montana quickly announced their opposition. Even Republican Congress members were smart enough to act in a way not anticipated by Roosevelt—with a conspiracy of silence. Seeing that the Democrats were divided, they did not criticize the reform bill, reasoning that such a partisan attack might reunite the majority party.

FDR's court-packing proposal had inadvertently provided a rallying point for his opponents; indeed, it was more effective in unifying his enemies than uniting his allies.[96] For many people, this proposal transformed FDR from a popular leader to a dangerous one.[97] The pundit Walter Lippmann warned, "If the American people do not rise up and defeat this measure, then they have lost their instinct for liberty and their understanding of constitutional government."[98] On February 13, 1937, the well-known progressive Republican editor, William Allen White, wrote, "In a world challenging democracy, in a day when tyrants, appearing as demagogues, crying out against predatory wealth, have shattered Europe's democratic institutions, this Court message of the President's seems strangely like the first booming American sign of danger. Surely Mr. Roosevelt's mandate was to function as the President, not as *Der Fuerher.*"[99] Senator Carter Glass from Virginia, fearing that a Roosevelt-dominated Court would threaten white supremacy in the South, opposed the bill in a radio address.

Amidst this widespread criticism, Corcoran, Cohen, and Robert Jackson, an assistant attorney general who would later be appointed to the Supreme Court by FDR, finally persuaded the president that he ought to educate the public about the real reasons he was trying to enlarge the Court. On March 4, at a Democratic victory dinner celebrating the fourth anniversary of his first inauguration, Roosevelt used a non-Madisonian three-horse metaphor to characterize the present situation. If the three horses pull together as a team, the field can be plowed. He claimed the legislature and the executive were working together to fight the Depression, but the Supreme Court was acting like a superlegislature and obstructing progress.[100] On March 9, the president delivered a fireside chat urging the public to support the reform of the Supreme Court. He suggested that everyone reread the Constitution because, "Like the Bible, it ought to be read again and again." He complained, "In the last four years, the sound rule of giving statutes the benefits of all reasonable doubt has been cast aside. The court has been acting not as a judicial body, but as a policy-making body." Roosevelt condemned the Court for "reading into the Constitution words and implications which are not there, and which were never intended to be there." The president concluded that "to save the constitution from the Court and the Court from itself," it is essential "to infuse new blood into all our courts" with judges who will have "a present-day sense of the Constitution."[101] Surprisingly, the two speeches had little effect on public opinion.

Reflecting the prominence of this conflict, from February 3 to June 10, the Gallup Poll questioned national samples on eighteen separate occasions about Roosevelt's Court reform. Gregory Caldeira summarizes this polling data: "Support for FDR's proposal varied from a high of 46 percent immediately after his fireside chat to a low of 31 percent in the wake of Justice Van Devanter's resignation [May 18]. Over the entire period, support averaged 39 percent. Opposition to Court packing ranged from a low of 41 percent on 24 March to a high of 49 percent on 3 May."[102] These polling data suggest that although a majority of the American people liked Roosevelt, he was unable to lead them on this issue. Indeed, Caldeira's analysis shows that the Court's actions were more effective in influencing public opinion than FDR's.

In this chess match, FDR calculated that the Court would only hurt itself and bolster his case by declaring popular legislation unconstitutional.

He did not foresee that Chief Justice Hughes would be wily enough to undermine the foundations of his political strategy. But that is precisely what Hughes, a former governor of New York and Republican presidential candidate in 1916, did. Meeting with Brandeis, Van Devanter, and Senator Wheeler, Hughes produced a letter refuting the president's accusation that Wheeler presented to the Senate Judiciary Committee on March 22. According to Mason, "the Chief Justice's statistical analysis scotched the President's allegation that the Justices had fallen behind their docket. 'The Supreme Court is fully abreast of its work,' Hughes wrote. 'There is no congestion of cases upon our calendar. This gratifying condition has obtained for several years.' 'An increase in the number of Justices would not,' he said, 'promote the efficiency of the Court.'"[103] Hughes was responding to the president's congressional message about judicial efficiency and ignoring Roosevelt's complaints about judicial policy making in his two March speeches. The chief justice also suggested that he had not been able to consult with every member of the Court, but that because his letter was signed by Brandeis (a liberal) and Van Devanter (a conservative), he was confident it reflected the views of its members. That may not have been true because some justices were opposed to what they considered a lobbying effort by Hughes.[104] Obviously, Hughes could compete with FDR in political deviousness.

For reasons that are not clear, the Hughes Court in 1937 issued a series of decisions that legitimated the New Deal, thereby deflating the political pressure for FDR's reform bill and protecting the independence of the Supreme Court. On March 29, the Court upheld a Washington state minimum wage law in *West Coast Hotel v. Parrish*. Elsie Parrish was a maid who claimed her employer had paid her less than what she was entitled to ($216.19) under the terms of the Washington State minimum wage law passed in 1913. Counsel for the hotel argued that the *Adkins* and *Tipaldo* precedents confirmed that both federal and state minimum wage laws were unconstitutional. Because the Parrish case seemed indistinguishable from the *Tipaldo* one, which had been decided a year earlier, observers were surprised when the Court elected to hear the dispute. They were even more bewildered when Roberts deserted his conservative brethren—the "switch in time"—and supported Hughes's majority opinion. In language reflecting a more deferential attitude toward legislation dealing with economic regulation, Hughes argued that it was imperative to give the issue of minimum wage new consideration in light of the Depression. Sounding like a New Dealer, Hughes contended that the public interest is violated when workers are paid less than a living wage. He ruled that the minimum wage law was a legitimate use of the police power to protect the public and the wage earner. A business "affected with a public interest" could be regulated by the state.[105] In response to the conservative freedom of contract doctrine, Hughes pointed out, "The Constitution does not speak of freedom of contract. It speaks of liberty and prohibits the deprivation of liberty without due process of law. . . . But the liberty safeguarded is liberty in a social organization which requires the protection of law against the evils which menace the health, safety, morals and welfare of the people. . . . What can be closer to the public interest than the health of women and their protection from unscrupulous overreaching employers?"[106] Hughes's opinion specifically overruled *Adkins*, but, perhaps in an effort not to embarrass Roberts, did not nullify *Tipaldo*.

Speaking for the conservative bloc, which had just suffered their first defeat since 1935, Sutherland's dissent repeated his support for his 1923 *Adkins* doctrine that a minimum wage for women violated their constitutional right to freedom of contract. For him, it was still crystal clear that the due process clause in the Fifth and Fourteenth Amendments embraced freedom of contract. He also ridiculed the notion that the meaning of the Constitution could be altered by the Depression. Finally, Sutherland admonished the new liberal majority that the judicial role did not authorize justices to amend the Constitution through reinterpretations.[107]

Two weeks later, the Court upheld the constitutionality of the Wagner Act in *NLRB v. Jones and Laughlin* in another 5–4 decision written by Hughes. The case originated from a grievance to the National Labor Relations Board from ten workers who had been fired from the Jones and Laughlin Steel plant in Aliquippa, Pennsylvania, because of their union activities. The constitutionality of the Wagner Act was contingent on a broad interpretation of the commerce clause, which the Court had denied in its *Schecter* and *Carter* decisions.[108] "In *NLRB v. Jones and Laughlin*," according to McKenna, "a narrow majority adopted a broad interpretation of the commerce clause allowing Congress to regulate industrial labor relations and opening the way for further expansion of its authority in this field. . . . [Justice Hughes] discarded the old distinction between 'direct' and 'indirect' effects on commerce (accepted by Roberts in *Carter*), replacing it with Cardozo's contention in his *Carter* dissent, measuring the extent of the effect on interstate commerce."[109] Hughes emphasized that the steel company was located in a current of interstate commerce and could therefore be federally regulated because raw materials flowed from outside the state into the plant, where they were transformed into steel, which was then transported out of the state. Because of his commitment to continuity, Hughes did not feel the need to overturn the *Carter* decision, which he and Roberts had supported the year before, but most legal observers found the two decisions incompatible.

McReynold's dissent condemned the *Jones and Laughlin* ruling for reversing more than a century of legal precedents. He warned that the almost unlimited scope of the "stream of commerce" doctrine allowed the majority to eliminate the distinction between commerce and manufacturing and would inevitably threaten federalism by violating states' rights.[110]

On May 24, the Court upheld the constitutionality of social security in three cases. In *Steward Machine Company v. Davis*, Cardozo's majority opinion ruled that the law's cooperative federal-state unemployment compensation mechanism was a legitimate congressional power "to lay and collect taxes" and to provide for the general welfare. In *Helvering et al. v. Davis*, the majority agreed that social security's federal old age retirement benefits program did not violate Congress' authority to tax and spend for the general welfare. In *Carmichael v. Smith Coal and Coke Co.*, Stone's majority opinion upheld the Alabama Unemployment Compensation Act, which had been passed to finance the unemployment compensation sections of the Social Security Act. McKenna points out, "In its permissive, rather vague interpretation of the term 'general welfare,' *Steward* (and its companion case, *Helvering*) seemed to repudiate the *Butler* ruling's view that Congress, while exercising its power to tax for the general welfare, is required by the Tenth Amendment to eschew regulation of matters historically controlled by the states. The Court majority now held that providing for old-age security would help promote the general welfare."[111] In rejecting the old doctrine of dual federalism and approving the cooperation of the federal and state governments to administer the law, the Court was opening the road to a much more active public role in American life.

With each of these Court victories, the pressure on FDR to compromise on his reform proposal increased. The president refused to do this because he could not be sure how long Hughes and Roberts would continue to vote with the liberal faction. His opponents and some of his allies also suspected that another reason Roosevelt persisted in a strategy that appeared irrational was that he was determined to punish his enemies. This personal motivation, reflecting a part of his personality that was usually camouflaged by his congeniality, was now publicly revealed. McKenna paints this unflattering picture:

Seated before his desk, visitors asked him why he refused to compromise when he had the liberal majority he wanted on the bench. He replied that a five-to-four majority was not enough. He wanted a Court that would "cooperate" with him. To their utter amazement, he stated that a close relationship between the executive and the judiciary had to be established. He wanted six new Justices on the Court who would be "friendly" and "approachable," with whom he could confer from time to time on his "great plans for social and economic reforms."[112]

By refusing to compromise and seeking "mastery," FDR revealed that either he did not understand or did not believe in the separation of powers.

In mid-May, the president returned to the White House from a fishing vacation, escorted by a newly elected Congress member, Lyndon Johnson, who had just won an interim election during which he had openly supported FDR's Court reform bill. LBJ's victory encouraged FDR to continue fighting for his proposal despite the advice of Democratic congressional leaders. On May 18, Justice Van Devanter, convinced that his retirement pension was safe because of the passage of the judiciary retirement bill on March 1, informed the president of his intention to retire in June. This was not entirely good news for Roosevelt because several years before, he had promised the first opening on the Supreme Court to Senator Joseph Robinson of Arkansas, the Senate majority leader. Robinson had loyally served the New Deal in the Senate, but as a conservative Southerner, would he continue to do so on the Supreme Court? And after making age such an important factor in his original message, FDR had reason to fear that everyone would notice that Robinson was sixty-five years old.[113]

After a painful hesitation, the president met with Robinson on June 3 and confirmed that he would be the next nominee for the Court. Roosevelt also accepted Robinson's recommendation to authorize the senator to negotiate a compromise. Robinson focused on a proposal "that would empower the President to nominate a new Justice for every 75-year-old member of the Court, at a rate of one such appointment per year. This guaranteed Roosevelt at least two appointments in 1937 and one each in 1938, 1939, and 1940."[114] The majority leader's efforts to pass this compromise became more difficult when the Senate Judiciary Committee recommended rejection because it violated constitutional principles. The bill was brought to the floor of the Senate on July 2, in the middle of a hot, humid summer. Against an enraged opposition threatening a filibuster, the overweight Robinson vigorously defended the legislation over the next eleven days of debate. On July 14, Robinson was found dead in his apartment, the victim of a heart attack. Eight days later, the Senate buried FDR's Court reform bill by a vote of 70 to 20, the worst legislative defeat in his career.

It is not easy to summarize the outcome and meaning of FDR's struggle with the Supreme Court. The president cheerfully concluded that he had lost the battle to enlarge the Supreme Court but won the war because no New Deal legislation was declared unconstitutional after 1936. After not being able to appoint anyone to the Supreme Court in his first term, Roosevelt was able to name seven new justices between 1937 and 1941. By winning a series of presidential and congressional elections, New Dealers thought that they had earned the right to place their interpretations on the Constitution. This meant restricting the range of the due process clause in economic cases and expanding the scope of the commerce clause. By abandoning the concept of "liberty of contract," which promarket justices had read into the Fifth and Fourteenth Amendments, a major barrier preventing the government from regulating wages, hours, and labor conditions was removed.[115] The power to regulate interstate commerce was amplified to the power to regulate the national economy. "By the end of the decade [the 1930s]," according to Robert Stern, "every decision which had invalidated a congressional exercise of the commerce clause had been disapproved, or distinguished to death."[116] The dual federalism of the old was replaced by a cooperative federalism that would allow a more expansive role for the public sector in American development. The Court had legitimated a liberal regime armed with enhanced powers to promote economic security.

Roosevelt's victory was a costly one, however. The irony of FDR's winning the war in the court-packing episode is that he obtained the constitutional legitimacy of New Deal programs previously passed by Congress but exhausted the energy necessary to enact future reforms. By initially using a transparently devious strategy, FDR suffered a debilitating set of wounds: he squandered the capital of winning a landslide election; he exposed the devious and vindictive sides of his personality; he weakened his reputation for invincibility; he surrendered the moral high ground; he generated fear about the future aspirations of the New Deal; and he united his enemies into the conservative coalition that would hinder liberal legislation for several decades.

Conclusion

By 1935, Roosevelt was faced with the challenge of legitimizing an ambitious set of public enterprises in a nation that was traditionally opposed to a strong national government. The Brownlow Committee Report was contrived by FDR to justify the administrative state under the control of the president in much the same way that the Federalist Papers tried to make the case for the ratification of the new Constitution. Roosevelt claimed he was not requesting additional powers; he was asking for the managerial tools he needed to meet the executive responsibilities he already had under the Constitution. Improving the managerial authority of the president, according to him, was compatible with democracy because it helped the elected chief executive carry out the policy preferences of the nation. However autocratically the administrative state might operate in Europe, most New Dealers were convinced that it could function in a democratic fashion in the United States. In comparison to the authoritarian experiments going on in Europe, the American administrative state would be more decentralized and would rely more on self-regulation, wider participation, positive incentives, and voluntary responses. Roosevelt wanted citizens to see government not as a threatening intruder in their lives, but as an instrument of their desires as verified in elections. In brief, FDR had attempted to create an administrative state under the direction of the president; what he ended up producing was a partially legitimated state. Americans wanted the benefits of the welfare state but resented the required bureaucratic means and costs. With all the magic that FDR possessed, he was not able to sell his total package of reforms.

In response to FDR's politics and policies, Republicans raised a number of issues. They accused him of issuing demagogic and partisan appeals that divided Americans at a time when it was necessary to work together. By depending more on the administrative state, FDR was denounced for losing faith in the American people and relying on un-American doctrines to solve the nation's problems. For many Republicans, the fact that Roosevelt was rewarded for helping the unemployed through extensive relief efforts proved that politics, rather than compassion, was the real motivation of his behavior. And by the end of the decade, their allegations became more sinister. Because the failure of Roosevelt's economic policies was not blamed on him but on business, some Republicans charged that the New Deal had developed a vested interest in the continuation of the Depression. By not solving the problems of the Depression, the New Deal could perpetuate itself in power through its programs to tax, spend, bureaucratize, and elect Democrats.

When Republicans charged that FDR was creating a dictatorship, he responded that by developing a dynamic and responsive administration, he was preventing the causes of dictatorship. When Republicans claimed they were defending individual rights, Roosevelt countered that they were exploiting constitutional ideals to pander to rich and greedy interests. When Republicans accused the New Deal of violating citizenship rights, FDR replied that his policies were adding new rights to help citizens feel more secure in facing the hazards of life. The president understood that "Necessitous men are not free men." For Roosevelt and most New Dealers, providing security through federal programs was not a limitation of liberty, but an extension of it. Citizens receiving a social security or unemployment check were not regimented; they were given the means to continue living a dignified life.

In FDR's conflict with the Supreme Court, he finally succeeded in getting the judicial branch of government to accept the legitimacy of the New Deal in 1937. With Hughes and Roberts joining the three liberals, there was now a majority willing to allow Congress to employ a broad interpretation of the commerce clause to regulate the national economy for the general welfare. After 1936, the Supreme Court never declared another New Deal law unconstitutional. The next time the Court declared legislation unconstitutional on the grounds that it violated Congress' power to regulate interstate commerce was in 1995, when the William Rehnquist Court struck down a federal law banning guns in school zones in *United States v. Lopez.*[117]

10

Legitimating Reagan's Conservative Regime

While FDR legitimized the New Deal through its multiple efforts to combat the Depression, Reagan legitimized his conservative regime through its economic performance. The Reagan presidency failed to abolish most liberal programs and was not successful in passing Constitutional amendments outlawing abortion, allowing prayer in public schools, or requiring balanced budgets. Its support of deregulation contributed to the collapse of the savings and loan system, which eventually cost taxpayers several hundred billion dollars. But during the 1980s, the Reagan administration did succeed, partly by design, partly by compromise, partly by muddling through, in creating a policy regime that was capable of promoting long-term economic growth with low inflation. The malaise and stagflation of the 1970s were replaced in the 1980s by an adaptive economy that generated millions of new jobs and discredited the thesis that the United States was a declining superpower. To explain how this regime was built, I will examine the following topics: the 1981–1982 recession; economic growth; jobs; savings and investment; and monetary policy. I will also analyze how the Democrats attempted to undermine the moral foundations of Reagan's policies by claiming that his policies were unfair because they promoted inequality.

The 1981–1982 Recession

By design, Reagan was committed to large tax cuts, and much of his political success can be attributed to that fact. The Reagan administration predicted that the passage of the $750 billion tax cut in August 1981 would generate rational exuberance in financial markets. Supply-siders believed that even before the tax cuts took effect (5% in October 1981, 10% in July 1982, and 10% in July 1983), the depressed stock and bond markets would quickly react with brisk rallies. Instead, both the stock and bond markets declined in August and September 1981.[1] Rather than enjoying a burst of prosperity, Reagan found himself challenged by a recession.

A recession is usually defined as two consecutive quarters of declining gross domestic product (GDP). There had been a short recession in the first half of 1980, but the economic downturn that began in August 1981 proved to be more severe and to last longer. The 1981–1982 slump was the eighth recession the United States had suffered since the end of World War II. In the last quarter of 1982, factory utilization averaged only about 68 percent of capacity, the lowest figure on record since these measures were first compiled in 1948. High mortgage rates caused the number of housing starts to drop to 1,061,000, the fewest since 1946. There were over 25,000 business failures in 1982, the second-highest number since the Depression of 1933. In November 1982, more than 9 million Americans were unemployed, a number that would climb to a peak of 11.5 million in January 1983. While the seven postwar business cycles before 1982 averaged unemployment rates at the trough of 7.1 percent, the eighth one hit 10.8 percent at the end of 1982. About 2.3 million manufacturing jobs were lost in the recession, which fueled fears about the deindustrialization of the United States. The one encouraging statistic was that prices in 1982 rose only 3.9 percent, the smallest increase since 1972, when Nixon's wage and price controls were in effect.[2] The pathology of the recession was curing the disease of inflation.

After a decade of bad economic news in the 1970s, the length and depth of the 1981–1982 recession caused fear among economists about the future. They were concerned that even with a declining rate of inflation, interest rates remained high. Historically, the cost of borrowing money was usually about two to three points above the rate of inflation, but in 1982, interest rates were more than six points higher than the inflation rate. Many economists predicted that such high interest rates would restrict the recovery. Even more worrisome, some economists feared that they no longer understood how to cure the problems of the economy. A Yale economist lamented, "To those who follow developments in economics, the paralysis should come as no surprise, given the demise of the earlier Keynesian consensus. Economists are today a shellshocked army, barraged by criticism because of poor forecasts, confused because of divided intellectual leadership, unsure of which way to retreat."[3] Another economist wrote, "given the current state of the economy, an all-but-unthinkable question arises. Do we know how to prevent a deep recession from spiraling into a depression? It may be that the nation has arrived at a new spot on the economic map where the old remedies—or what we thought were remedies—have lost their power and the economic wise men have lost their magic."[4]

Reagan handled this trial by recession fairly well. When Murray Weidenbaum, the chairman of the Council of Economic Advisers (CEA), told Reagan in late July 1981 that a recession was about to begin, the normally amiable president reacted with a cold stare of disbelief.[5] By October, he admitted publicly that the economy was suffering from a "slight recession," but he predicted a fast recovery if Americans had the courage to "stay the course" and continue his policies. While supply-siders and Treasury Secretary Regan blamed the recession on Federal Reserve Board Chairman Paul Volcker's "excessive" tightening of the money supply, the president did not. He viewed the recession as stemming from the fact that his original supply-side proposal for cutting taxes by 10 percent for three successive years beginning on January 1, 1981, had been delayed and watered down. Reagan had unshakable beliefs that shielded him from doubts about the efficacy of his policies.

As economic conditions steadily worsened in 1982, Reagan consistently played the role of a cheerleader, encouraging citizens not to lose faith. He condemned the media for emphasizing "doom and gloom" stories, which he believed were delaying the recovery. In his 1982 *Economic Report* to Congress, Reagan declared, "I am convinced that our policies . . . are the appropriate response to our current difficulties and will provide the basis for a vigorous economic recovery this year. It is of the greatest importance that we avoid a return to the stop-and-go policies of the past. The private sector works best when the Federal Government intervenes least. The Federal Government's task is to construct a sound, stable, long-term framework in which the private sector is the key engine to growth, employment, and rising living standards."[6] In public speeches, Reagan pictured his administration as the "cleanup crew" tidying up the mess caused by a forty-year "non-stop binge" (a significant metaphor for the son of an alcoholic). This recession provided conclusive evidence that the economic policies of previous presidencies did not work. He exhorted Americans to increase their savings rate by two percentage points, which would add about $60 billion a year to the nation's capital pool to combat high interest rates and to finance investments, mortgages, and new jobs. In a national radio address in September 1982, he angrily condemned the Democrats for "the most cynical form of demagoguery" in suggesting that progress in lowering the rate of inflation was contributing to the rise in unemployment, a relationship that had been accepted by Reagan's recently appointed CEA chairman, Martin Feldstein. But Reagan vehemently denied that his policy was to fight inflation by increasing unemployment.[7]

In a nationally televised speech before the 1982 congressional elections, Reagan painted the best possible face on his policies. He stressed that when he came into office, the country faced five critical problems: high taxes, runaway government spending, inflation, high interest rates, and unemployment. Reagan claimed progress in dealing with the first four of these problems. As for his lack of success in raising employment, he pointed out that employment is always a lagging indicator during a recovery. He assured the nation that his policies were not based on "quick fixes" but on dealing with the "root causes" of our economic problems and that by taming inflation, which eventually led to unemployment when unabated, he was constructing a recovery that was "built to last."[8]

The recession helped the Democrats pick up 26 seats in the House of Representatives in the 1982 congressional election, thus ending Republican aspirations to control both chambers during the 1980s. Reagan's public approval ratings declined from a high of 67 percent in April 1981 to the mid-30s in early 1983. But exit polls in the 1982 elections indicated that voters were more likely to blame the Democrats, rather than Reagan, for economic problems.[9] The historian Alonzo Hamby suggests, "It was a measure of the depth of public dissatisfaction with Carter and the Democrats that Reagan was able to survive the worst economic trough since the Great Depression with little damage."[10] Lou Cannon wrote, "Later in his presidency, after Reagan had become a remote and disengaged monarch, first-term aides would recall the grim months of recession as if they were a golden age. They would remember Reagan scoffing at his critics and the polls and defiantly proclaiming that he would 'stay the course' with his economic program. 'The greatest show of his leadership was then,' said speechwriter Bentley Elliott."[11]

The irony of this episode is that the success of the Reagan administration's economic policies was not due to "staying the course," but to changing it significantly. Although Reagan had initially hoped that his fiscal and monetary policies would complement each other, with tax cuts promoting economic growth and a tight monetary policy lowering inflation, it turned out that stringent controls over the growth of the money supply overpowered the stimulative effects from the tax cuts and rising budget deficits. In early 1982, administration officials and supporters pressured Volcker to loosen the money supply; by that summer, Volcker had ended the monetarist experiment and was allowing the money supply to expand at a faster pace in order to lower interest rates. In August 1982, Reagan signed the Tax Equity and Fiscal Responsibility Act, which was designed to prevent soaring budget deficits by raising $98.3 billion over the next three years. It appears that an implicit compromise was negotiated: the administration accepted a tighter fiscal policy in exchange for the Fed's pursuing a looser monetary policy.

These changes in fiscal and monetary policy bore quick rewards. In August 1982, the stock market began the longest bull market in U.S. history. On August 17, the Dow Jones Index experienced its highest single-day increase in its history (38.81 points) to finish at 831.24, with a near-record trading volume of over 92 million shares.[12] Between July and October 1982, the Fed allowed the M1 money supply (currency in circulation and checking accounts) to grow by 15 percent. This growth in the money supply frightened strict monetarists like Milton Friedman and Beryl Sprinkel, who predicted that it would lead to rising inflation in 1983 and 1984. Instead, the economy grew strongly in those two years, and inflation remained under control.

In 1983, with a more accommodating monetary policy, the Reagan tax cuts were finally stimulating economic growth, but—more in line with a Keynesian perspective than a supply-side one—they were producing increases in consumption rather than in savings and investment. According to James Tobin, a Nobel laureate in economics, "By pure serendipity, the Administration carried out a classic well-timed Keynesian antirecession fiscal policy complementary to the countercyclical change in monetary policy in late 1982, when the Fed moved to rescue the economy from worsening unemployment."[13] Most of the public was not interested in the academic debate of whether the recovery was brought about by Keynesian or supply-side policies; what pleased them was that a long period of healthy economic growth had begun in 1983. And Reagan, because of his consistent conservative rhetoric camouflaging changing policies, reaped the political benefits of this prosperity. In Blumenthal's words, "By projecting an unchanging ideology throughout the economic crisis, he had been able to convince voters that his policies had not undergone any substantial revision and were actually the cause of the recovery. A majority of the voters gave him credit for the upturn. Between January and May 1983, he gained eleven points in the ABC–*Washington Post* poll. His interpretation of the recent past was prevailing—a triumph of ideology."[14]

Economic Growth

The economy began a long-lasting recovery from the recession in 1983, with the GDP increasing 3.6 percent in that year and a whopping 6.8 percent during the presidential election year of 1984. From 1983 to 1990, the economy grew at about 3.5 percent a year, and the GDP expanded by 32 percent. The Dow Jones industrial average went up 32.8 percent in Reagan's first term and 71 percent in his second. From 1982 to 1989, the Standard and Poor's Index of 500 stocks went up almost 300 percent. Reagan had fulfilled his 1980 campaign promise to rejuvenate the economy.

The most remarkable attribute of this period of economic growth was its durability. It lasted 92 months, which was more than twice the average length of expansions since 1945, and was exceeded only by the 106-month growth period from February 1961 to December 1969, which was partly fueled by the Vietnam War. A new and more resilient economy emerged in the 1980s, one which was able to grow despite fears raised by budget and trade deficits, by the 508-point drop in the Dow Jones Index in October 1987, and by all the technological changes that seemed to be accelerating.

Supply-siders exaggerated the success of Reagan's economic policies. They evaluated Reagan's performance by using data from 1983 to 1990, blaming the 1981–1982 recession on Carter and the 1991 recession on President Bush's decision to raise taxes. But productivity, which averaged almost 3 percent annually from 1948 to 1973, did not pick up in the 1980s, during which it averaged about 1.1 percent a year.[15] Nor did the tax cuts expand the capacity of the economy to grow beyond its natural potential of approximately 3 percent a year. As Charles Schultze points out, "After the deepest recession of the postwar period in 1982, the GNP [gross national product] did rise rapidly for some years, but this change reflected a period of aggregate demand catching up to potential GNP. The growth of potential GNP, and in particular, the growth of productivity—that is, output per worker—did not speed up during the 1980s."[16] In terms of annual GDP growth, Presidents Truman (5.9%), Kennedy/Johnson (4.9%), and Johnson (4.4%) had better records than Reagan (2.3% in his first term and 3.2% in his second).[17] What made Reagan's record look so good was comparisons to the last two years of the Carter presidency.

A number of factors should be credited for the Reagan growth period's longevity. The combined effects of a severe recession in 1981–1982 and increased competition from abroad compelled American businesses to grow leaner and more efficient. The oil shocks of 1973 and 1979, which sent energy prices soaring, had forced the business sector to make painful adjustments; in the 1980s, business was rewarded with lower energy costs. The private sector, which had also adjusted to many of the costly environmental regulations of the 1970s, felt freer in the 1980s to concentrate more on raising profits. While the adult population increased at an annual rate of 2.4 percent during the Carter administration, it slowed to 1.8 percent in the Reagan years. Thus, in the 1970s, the absorption of 20 million new and inexperienced workers—the big surge of the baby boom generation— probably acted as a drag on productivity. In the 1980s, these workers were more experienced and productive, and the economy had fewer new workers to assimilate.

What maintained living standards during the 1980s was the increase in the number of women working outside the home. While about half the female adult population worked in 1980, by 1988 about 57 percent did. With 50 million women in the labor force, the traditional family of the father as breadwinner and the mother as housewife was becoming a shrinking minority of American households.[18] These were changes being generated not by the counterculture of the 1960s (as alleged by the conservative movement), but by capitalism.

Most importantly, the United States was experiencing a rapid metamorphosis from a manufacturing economy to a more flexible information-based, service-providing economy created by computers, revolutions in shipping (UPS), just-in-time ordering, efficiency-minded reorganizations and plant closings, outsourcing, and the increasing use of temporary workers. The result was that corporations could better control their inventories, lower their overhead expenses, generate higher profits, and raise the value of their stocks. According to Joel Kurtzman, "In their efforts at greater efficiency, companies have jettisoned layers of middle management, reduced the number of production workers, and cut down the time it takes to bring new products to market. As a result, they are better positioned to deal with the upsets of a recession and able to design new products more quickly to suit the times."[19] In the 1980s, there was greater acceptance of the strategy that markets must be allowed to bring about change even though much of the change—considerably more than Reagan ever acknowledged—would cause pain to portions of society and the economy. But because this transformation bolstered American corporations to compete successfully in the global economy, more people benefited from the changes than suffered from them. In brief, public policy and private initiatives had a new formula and higher capability to prolong the growth stage of the business cycle.

Jobs

The political success of the Reagan presidency was largely dependent on the fact that the American economy produced over 18 million new jobs during the 1980s. In 1980, over 99 million Americans had jobs, while the unemployment rate stood at about 7 percent; by 1990, almost 118 million workers were employed, and the unemployment rate had dropped to 5.4 percent.[20] Apologists for Reagan skip over the point that 1.9 million jobs were lost between April 1981 and November 1982 and stress that in the 27 months after November 1982, 7.6 million jobs were produced. Reagan supporters also neglect to report that the economy produced more jobs in the 1970s than in the 1980s. In the administration's final *Economic Report*, the CEA declared, "this remarkable expansion has benefited all segments of the population. Although civilian employment has increased by more than 17 percent, Hispanic employment has grown by more than 45 percent, black employment by nearly 30 percent, and female employment by more than 20 percent."[21]

The United States' record in producing jobs during this period was impressive compared to Western Europe's. Until the late 1970s, unemployment rates in the United States were usually higher than in Western Europe. But by 1988, the unemployment rate in Western Europe was twice that in the United States, with Spain's rate at more than 20 percent, Italy's at more than 14 percent, and France's at 11 percent. Even in West Germany, Europe's strongest economy, the jobless rate in January 1988 was over 9 percent.[22] Paul Krugman points out, "the United States has been the great job engine of the advanced world, with a 38 percent increase in employment from 1973 to 1990, compared with 19 percent in Japan and only 8 percent in Europe."[23] From 1980 to 1995, the United States economy produced 24 million new jobs, while the European Union, with a one-third larger population than America, added less than 9 million.[24]

The success of American capitalism in producing more jobs than Western Europe destroyed the argument that the United States was a declining economic power. Clearly, American capitalism adapted more successfully to the requirements of competing in the global economy than did Europe's. Although European nations responded to economic changes by maintaining high wages (because of powerful unions), they were suffering from lack of job growth; on the other hand, the United States had much slower growth in real wages and a much higher rate of growth in the creation of new jobs. American families maintained their standard of living by placing more women in the workforce; in addition, more workers were absorbed into the labor force by their willingness to accept part-time and temporary jobs.[25] Unfortunately, many of these temporary or part-time jobs were at lower wage levels and did not include health care coverage.

While the economy was adding 18 million new jobs, Fortune 500 corporations were employing fewer workers (4 million fewer in 1991 than in 1981). Two-thirds of the manufacturing jobs lost in the 1981–1982 recession were never regained. The 1980s was the first decade in this century in which the number of Americans laboring in manufacturing declined. Yet during this period, productivity in manufacturing grew at a robust 3.1 percent a year, compared with 1 percent a year in nonmanufacturing jobs. Within the manufacturing sector, there was a shift from heavy industry to efficient high-tech industries like telecommunications.

These leaner and meaner corporations paid their executives higher salaries and earned the type of profits that encourage rising stock prices. But because factory jobs paid higher wages than service-sector jobs, the decrease in blue-collar employment limited the economic prospects of relatively uneducated workers. Unions were particularly hard hit by this phenomenon. The United Auto Workers lost nearly 40 percent of its membership between 1980 and 1992, dropping to about 850,000 from 1.4 million. During the same period, the United Steelworkers of America's union membership dropped from 1 million to 500,000, and the International Ladies Garment Workers Union membership fell from 350,000 to 150,000.[26]

The decline in manufacturing jobs was partially offset by Reagan's military buildup. As military spending rose from $157 billion in fiscal year 1981 to over $300 billion in fiscal year 1989, the number of people occupying jobs dependent on defense expenditures grew by 45 percent to a total of 3.2 million.[27] Between 1981 and 1989, the United States spent over $2.1 trillion on defense. Supporters of Reagan claim that these expenditures helped the United States win the cold war.

The big surge in jobs during the 1980s came in the service sector. Just as earlier in the century, when laborers pushed off the farm found employment with the railroads, the steel industry, the automobile manufacturers, and in highway construction, during the 1980s, new workers and displaced blue-collar laborers migrated to retailing, health care, restaurants, finance, and security occupations. According to Sylvia Nasar, "In the 80s, the services added a stunning 19 million new jobs, $800 billion worth of new technology, 16,000 new shopping malls, and three billion square feet of new office space (nearly as much again as existed in 1980)."[28] In the early part of the decade, most of these service jobs were low paying, but by the end of the 1980s and into the 1990s, salaries significantly improved. In the dawning information-age economy, about two-thirds of new service jobs were in the managerial and professional ranks.[29] However, although service jobs proliferated, their productivity gains were sluggish, averaging only about a third as high as the productivity increases of the manufacturing sector. By 1990, the bloated service sector was ripe for a major streamlining. Although there were few service job reductions during the 1981–1982 recession, in the 1990–1991 slump, 570,000 service jobs were lost.[30] This later recession hit the middle class particularly hard and prevented President George Bush from being reelected in 1992. But just as the adjustments to the 1981–1982 recession helped American factories compete successfully with those in Japan and Europe, the adaptation to the 1990–1991 downturn, which included finding new ways to use computers to give businesses a competitive edge, made the service sector more efficient and more capable of fueling steady economic growth in the years ahead.

Savings and Investment

The Reagan presidency had less success in increasing the propensity of Americans to save and invest than it did in providing jobs. Its disappointing record in encouraging higher rates of savings by lowering rates of taxation was not a potent political issue, but many economists were concerned about its long-range effects on competitiveness and standards of living. A nation that does not make sacrifices today, in terms of holding down consumption by augmenting savings and investment, will be less likely to enjoy a prosperous tomorrow. Fortunately for the administration's progrowth policy, however, the capital-short, consumption-driven U.S. economy was bailed out by an unforeseen boost in foreign investment, attracted to our low-inflation, high-interest safe haven.

In 1981, the Reagan administration's program for economic recovery stressed that in contrast to the inflationary, demand-led expansions of the past, the growth in the 1980s would be based on the supply side of the economy. Increases in savings and investment would allow the economy to flourish without anxiety about capacity-induced inflation pressures. Administration supply-siders like Norman Ture predicted that tax cuts would significantly increase gross private savings (which are composed of personal and business savings). Personal savings as a proportion of disposable personal income were projected to rise from an average of 5.4 percent in 1977–1980 to 7.9 percent in 1986. Business savings, which generally account for slightly more than two-thirds of total private savings, were forecasted to climb above the 17 percent GDP rate that had been maintained since 1956.[31]

These goals were not achieved. Personal savings, instead of rising to 8 percent of disposable income, fell and averaged only 4.5 percent during the 1980s. Gross national savings declined from 19.2 percent of GDP in 1980 to 15.6 percent in 1989.[32] From 1971 to 1980, the net national saving ratio averaged 8.9 percent of the GDP; from 1981 to 1988, it averaged only 3.7 percent.[33] Changes in the tax code did not cause the American people to give up their inclination to consume. Instead, we continued to be a buy-now, pay-later society. Consumer debt, as a proportion of personal income after taxes, climbed from 62.7 percent in 1970 to 74.9 percent in 1980 and reached 96.9 percent in 1990.[34] Increased consumption accounted for over two-thirds of the growth during the economic expansion from 1982 to 1990.[35] To the dismay of supply-siders, the evidence of the 1980s indicates that culture and demographics had a greater impact on saving rates than alterations in the tax code.

The decline in savings meant disappointing rates of private investment. According to a Harvard economist writing in 1993, "After allowance for replacement of buildings and machines that wore out or became obsolete, business investment in new productive facilities averaged 3.6 percent of U.S. national income in the 1960s and 3.7 percent in the 1970s. Since 1980, the average net investment rate has been just 2.6 percent."[36] From 1974 to 1980, gross investment averaged 18.8 percent of the GDP; from 1981 to 1991, it averaged 17 percent.[37] There was no supply-side revolution in the 1980s.

Economists believe that private investment equals the sum of three kinds of saving: private saving, government saving, and net inflows of capital from foreign nations. With private saving down and with the enormous federal budget deficits in the 1980s cutting into national savings, the United States became more dependent on foreign sources of capital. Between 1982 and 1989, foreigners increased the value of their U.S. government security holdings from $132.5 billion to $265.9 billion. During the same period, direct foreign investment in the United States expanded from $124.7 billion to $400.8 billion.[38] During the 1980s, the United States continued to be the leading source of foreign investment, and it also became the largest recipient of foreign investment. Although some scholars and political opponents of the Reagan presidency warned that these trends indicated that the United States was losing its independence and limiting future standards of living, the growing supply of foreign capital helped to reduce interest rates and increase investment capital. If foreign capital had not filled the gap caused by the lack of domestic savings, the budget deficits would have absorbed a much higher proportion of funds needed for business investment and led to much higher interest rates. And one of the keys to a long period of economic growth is avoiding higher interest rates.

Inflation and Monetary Policy

When Reagan assumed office in 1981, inflation appeared to be a chronic disease, a scourge that democratic governments lacked the understanding and discipline to handle successfully. By the time he left office, inflation was considered a manageable problem. Credit for taming inflation should be shared between the administration and Paul Volcker's Federal Reserve Board. During the decade, the consumer price index was reduced from 13.5 percent in 1980 to 4.1 percent in 1988. Inflation averaged about 3.6 percent between 1983 and 1989, which helped to lower interest rates. Because inflation has corrosive consequences on both the value of money and incentives to promote economic growth, lowering inflation rates was an essential ingredient in promoting long-term expansion. In the past, growth periods have been derailed by severe inflation that led to the Fed's imposing high interest rates. Cannon correctly argues, "The long period of low inflation had a stabilizing effect in the United States and was of enormous political benefit to Reagan. . . . The Reagan-Volcker legacy of treating inflation as Public Enemy No. 1 . . . may well prove the most enduring and popular of Reagan's conflicting economic legacies."[39]

The monetarist leg of the administration's economic recovery policy was based on the Fed's targeting the supply of money rather than interest rates. In 1981, Treasury Undersecretary Beryl Sprinkel suggested that M1 should decrease by one percentage point per year from 7 percent in 1981 to 3 percent in 1985. Despite these specific recommendations, the administration claimed to respect the autonomy of the Federal Reserve Board, which, as an independent regulatory agency, has the legal responsibility to regulate the money supply. The administration's initial anti-inflation strategy was based on Milton Friedman's theory, which assumed that there was a direct relationship between the quantity of money in the economy and the level of output. Hence, when the money supply decreased, there was a recession; when it expanded moderately, there was sustainable economic growth; and when it grew too fast, there was inflation. Obviously, the correct choice was to have the Fed provide a slow, steady increase in the supply of money; but this alternative, so easy to select in theory, proved impossible to implement in practice.

Monetary policy proved to be essential for Reagan's success in the 1980s, but not as originally planned by the administration. The key strategist in the battle against inflation was Paul Volcker, who had been appointed chairman of the Federal Reserve Board in 1979 by President Carter. Just as Reagan was attempting to restore confidence in the presidency, Volcker was trying to restore confidence in the Federal Reserve Board after its failure to control inflation in the late 1970s. During Volcker's Senate confirmation hearings, he labeled himself a "pragmatic monetarist," which signaled that he would not rigidly adhere to Friedman's doctrine. Volcker strongly believed that inflation was a growing menace threatening the health of the economy and that only a hard-nosed monetary policy could free us from its insidious effects. He saw that inflation had become deeply entrenched in our economic expectations and behavior. By the end of the 1970s, the inflationary process was feeding on itself and distorting economic incentives. In Volcker's words, "Too much of the energy of our citizens was directed toward seeking protection from future price increases and toward speculative activity, and too little toward production."[40] Unlike Reagan, he thought that only a prolonged and painful process would be successful in combating an inflationary system that had grown too large to be harnessed by moderate means.

With inflation appearing to be out of control, Volcker led the seven-person Federal Reserve Board into a Friedman-inspired monetary experiment in October 1979. Instead of trying to control interest rates, the Fed would set specific money supply goals and use its authority over bank reserves to achieve them. This shift in focus from interest rates to restricting the growth of the money supply was designed to signal markets that a new and far more serious effort was under way to combat inflation. The Fed's plan was to establish a target for M1 growth and then hit it by manipulating bank reserves. Bank reserves can be influenced by the activities of the Federal Open Market Committee (FOMC). The FOMC is composed of the seven members of the Federal Reserve Board and five of the twelve Federal Reserve Bank presidents. It always includes the president of the

Federal Reserve Bank of New York; the other members rotate. The FOMC determines open market policy—that is, it decides whether to buy or sell government securities (bills, notes, and bonds). FOMC directives to ease or to tighten the money supply are implemented by the Open Market Desk of the Federal Reserve Bank in New York. To stimulate monetary growth, the Federal Reserve buys government securities; conversely, to tighten the money supply, it sells government securities. As Albert Rees explains, "When the Federal Reserve buys securities, it pays for them by creating deposits for the sellers in the Federal Reserve Banks; these deposits serve as additions to reserves for commercial banks. The added reserves permit commercial banks as a group to expand their loans and deposits by a multiple of the new reserves; this multiple is the inverse of the reserve ratio. For example, if reserves of 10 percent are required against all deposits, an additional dollar of reserves could ultimately support $10 of additional deposits."[41] And when the Federal Reserve sells government securities, it has the opposite effect.

With inflationary expectations so embedded in pricing and wage behavior, and with politicians refusing to make the compromises necessary to prevent soaring budget deficits, Volcker knew it would take a long period of tight money to slow down inflation. Not operating in a campaign mode, Volcker never promised a quick or easy victory over inflation. As the Fed tightened the money supply and allowed interest rates to float, the economy slowed down and then went into a severe recession in the autumn of 1981. Historically high interest rates caused record-high business failures and rising unemployment rates. Volcker's cure for inflation seemed to be causing more pain than the disease. Inevitably, a wide variety of Congress members—House majority leader Jim Wright, Congressman Jack Kemp, Senator Ted Kennedy, and Senator Howard Baker—condemned the chairman. Although supply-siders criticized Volcker for tightening the money supply too much, some monetarists complained that Fed controls were producing erratically wide swings in the quantity of money. Within the Reagan administration, Volcker was reprimanded by Treasury Secretary Donald Regan and Treasury Undersecretary Beryl Sprinkel (a former student of Milton Friedman), who vaguely threatened the Fed by talking about administration studies that would reduce its independence. Yet Reagan generally supported the Federal Reserve Board.[42]

As inflation rates declined in 1982, Volcker acknowledged that stabilizing prices during the most severe recession in forty years was not a great victory. The real challenge was to promote a noninflationary recovery and sustained economic expansion. His goal was to use monetary policy to make the 1980s a "mirror image of the 1970s," reversing the debilitating trends of the past decade.[43]

In July 1982, after establishing its creditability as an inflation fighter, and seeing that Congress was about to pass a $98 billion tax increase that would lower future budget deficits, the Fed began to loosen the money supply by raising money targets. On July 19, 1982, the Fed lowered the discount rate from 12 to 11.5 percent, and the stock market began to recover. In October, Volcker supported further easing. The FOMC also announced that it was temporarily suspending money supply targeting. Kettl explains why: "More than $31 billion of special tax-free All-Savers certificates were about to come due and would suddenly pour into checking and saving accounts, and that sudden flood of money would cause the Fed to overshoot its target of M1. . . . Volcker announced the Fed's action as a temporary change: it would 'de-emphasize' . . . the most narrow measure of money (M1) and focus instead on broader measures (M2 and M3) that included savings accounts and certificates of deposit as well as cash and checking accounts."[44] Markets interpreted these changes as a harbinger of easier money; banks lowered their prime rate, and the stock market surged. Volcker had both initiated and ended Friedman's monetarist experiment and set the stage for a long period of noninflationary economic growth.

The 1980s were not kind to Milton Friedman's theory. After the Fed tightened the money supply in 1981 and 1982, it allowed M1 to grow by 11 percent in 1983 and 7 percent in 1984. James Alt reports, "For the 1980s as a whole, M1 growth [was] just under 8 percent per annum, two points higher than in the 1970s, while M2 growth averaged just over 8 percent, the same as it was in the 1970s."[45] Despite this growth in the money supply, inflation rates in the 1980s were considerably lower than in the 1970s. In the early 1980s, Milton Friedman forecast an increase in inflation, followed by a recession in 1984—predictions that were way off.[46] Benjamin Friedman (no relation to Milton) pointed out, "since 1980 the relationship between money growth and the growth of either income or prices in the United States has collapsed. . . . Further, because the mid-1980s brought both the fastest money growth of the postwar period and the greatest *dis*inflation, the correlation between money growth and price inflation calculated in the way recommended by Milton Friedman (using two-year averages to smooth out short-run irregularities, and a two year lag between the money growth and the inflation) is now *negative* for postwar samples including this decade."[47] Milton Friedman's theory was also wounded by the fact that with the government deregulating the banking system, it became more difficult, perhaps impossible, for the Fed to control the growth of the money supply. There were months when the Fed sought to restrict M_1, yet it expanded. At other times, the opposite occurred.

One reason that Friedman's theory did not work as predicted was that there was an unforeseen change in what is called the velocity of money. *Velocity* is the economist's concept that describes the relationship between the money supply and the GNP. As Kettl explains, "It is based on the willingness of consumers to hold or spend money. The same dollar is spent over and over again during any year; the faster consumers spend a given dollar, the more any given level of the money supply increases economic growth."[48] In the early 1980s, the Fed's money targets were generating less economic growth than what was predicted by monetarist models because beginning in the summer of 1981, the velocity of money unexpectedly slowed down. As inflation slackened, consumers were less inclined to spend their money quickly before prices climbed. As interest rates declined, this also slowed down velocity by lowering the opportunity costs of keeping assets in the form of currency and demand deposits. Niskanen argues, "The most probable reasons for the reduction in velocity were the increase in financial wealth and the combination of declining market interest rates and the higher rates on bank deposits allowed by deregulation, the latter conditions reducing the cost of holding assets in the form of bank deposits."[49]

Milton Friedman's theory concentrated on the slow, steady growth of the supply of money and did not consider interest rates and unemployment to be important. Because most of the public is affected by interest rates and unemployment and has no understanding of the quantity of money, it is not surprising that political support for Friedman's monetarism disintegrated during the early 1980s. After Volcker ended Friedman's monetarist experiment in 1982, Reagan reappointed him as chairman in 1983. Thus, Friedman experienced the reward of being awarded the Nobel Prize for Economics and the humiliation of having his theory prove unworkable when applied to national monetary policy.

The success of Volcker's pragmatic, discretionary monetary policy, as opposed to Friedman's automatic monetary policy, played an indispensable role in supporting Reagan's presidency. Volcker helped Reagan construct a vital component of a new policy regime that was able to promote economic growth less susceptible to inflation. Because the old system based on the Phillips curve, whereby the Fed allowed inflation to inch up in order to bring down unemployment, had broken down by the end of the 1970s, a new strategy was required in the 1980s. Instead of the Fed's using its controls over the money supply to balance levels of inflation and unemployment, the new system stressed the strategic importance of preventing inflation. The new strategy held that sustained economic growth was derived from an effective anti-inflationary policy, which meant hiking interest rates in response to the first signs of inflation. Given the rigidities of the budget and the frequent gridlock between the president and Congress, fiscal policy was playing a declining role in controlling inflation and in stabilizing the business cycle. With the federal government, private corporations, and individuals piling up debts and the increasing international mobility of private capital seeking higher interest rates, the role of monetary policy had grown rapidly and had become preeminent in promoting prosperity. By 1986, even a Keynesian economist could write, "the monetary policy of the Federal Reserve has become the dominant instrument of macroeconomic management. If any fine or coarse tuning of the economy is done, it's the Fed that calls the tune, through its control of money and interest rates. After all, chairman Volcker and his colleagues can make nine or ten moves a year. The budget makers in the executive and Congress can make only one, and in recent years their procedures, politics, and conflicts have become so complex that national economic prospects and strategies play little role in the outcome."[50] In brief, the chairman of the Federal Reserve had become the most important economic policy maker in the United States.

Volcker's success was dependent on some deviousness. He was probably less of a Friedmanite and more of a pragmatist than he appeared to be in 1979. By engaging in the experiment of targeting the money supply instead of interest rates, Volcker most likely knew what the results were going to be. When the Fed tightened the money supply by more than had been recommended by the Reagan administration, interest rates soared, businesses failed, and millions of workers lost their jobs. Volcker had launched a chain of predictable events that led to a recession, but he correctly, if disingenuously, claimed that he was targeting money aggregates, not throwing people out of work. With interest rates so high in 1981, Volcker could not announce that he planned to raise them higher without stimulating a political backlash that might threaten the very independence of the Fed. So he camouflaged his goal of raising interest rates to throttle inflation by restrictively targeting money aggregates.[51] Once the recession had killed inflation and Friedman's experiment, he could implement his preferred, pragmatic monetary policy of targeting interest rates. There were no specific rules to guide Fed decision making (as there are in Friedman's high-church monetarism), but there was a grim determination to prevent inflation from breaking loose again.

William Niskanen, a member of Reagan's CEA, asks and answers a question that may provide further insight into Volcker's motivation. Niskanen asks, why did the Fed limit the growth of the money supply more than the initial Reagan recommendations? He answers that just as Defense Secretary Weinberger decided to exploit the window of opportunity to finance a huge military buildup because he believed political support would soon fade, Volcker concluded that the Fed would have to subdue inflation quickly through a recession because there would not be enough political backing to sustain a multiyear struggle. In Niskanen's words, "My judgment is that Volcker believed that the consensus for monetary restraint was temporary and that the American political system would not tolerate the slow, steady reduction in money growth recommended by the initial Reagan guidance. He may have wanted to reduce inflation as rapidly as possible, despite the temporary adverse effects on the economy."[52]

The success of Volcker's policies causes some problems for Reagan's ideological supporters. First, Volcker was originally appointed chairman of the Federal Reserve by Carter, the personification of failed liberalism. After much debate within the Reagan administration, Volcker was reappointed in 1983, but he was replaced by Alan Greenspan in 1987. Second, Volcker's monetary policy, which was largely followed by his successor, was a national policy, formulated by a centralized political institution, that successfully muzzled inflation without inhibiting job creation and economic growth. The Federal Reserve's goal was to navigate an overheated economy to a soft landing, where growth remained positive, thus avoiding a hard landing, where the economy contracted. Such metaphors sounded suspiciously like the Keynesian concept of fine-tuning the business cycle that so offended conservatives in the 1960s. The Volcker-Greenspan success story weakens the conservative assertion that discretionary government policies cannot improve market outcomes. And finally, the record indicates that Volcker did more of the heavy lifting in fighting inflation than Reagan did. Although the president ran large budget deficits, Volcker bore the political heat of keeping interest rates fairly high. The self-serving conservative narrative is that Volcker's policies caused the recession and Reagan's policies brought about noninflationary economic growth. This chapter suggests that Reagan deserves credit for not attacking Volcker during the dark days of the 1981–1982 recession and for reappointing him in 1983, but that

Volcker was clearly the architect of the anti-inflationary strategy that has proven to be so essential for promoting a prolonged economic expansion.

Democratic Attacks on the Reagan Revolution

The role of an opposition party confronting the battering ram of a reconstructive president is frustrating. Because the Democrats controlled the House of Representatives throughout the 1980s and regained a majority of the Senate in the 1986 elections, they were not as weak as the Republicans were during the 1930s. Nevertheless, because a party largely defines itself in the United States by electing its presidential candidate, the Democrats were on the defensive throughout the decade. Writing in October 1980, James Q. Wilson described the Democratic party's precarious position: "the Democrats are simultaneously bereft of new ideas and forced to take responsibility for old ones."[53] Near the end of the Reagan presidency, one liberal evaluated the Democrats' opposition to Reagan in these bitter words: "Cowed by exaggerated impressions of Reagan's popularity, Congress, and the Democrats in particular, repeatedly shrank back from challenging Reagan's basic assumptions and directions. Indeed, throughout the Reagan era, the Democrats were a pathetic excuse for an opposition party—timid, divided, utterly lacking in passion, principle, and vision."[54] Kevin Phillips suggests that conservative speeches and TV ads during the 1980s had some success in portraying liberal Democrats "as a chicken-hearted, criminal-coddling, minority-pampering, taxpayer-subsidized rescue service for exotic wildlife and child pornography distributors."[55] In short, throughout the decade, the Republicans had a message (conservatism) and a messenger (Reagan), while the Democrats had neither.

In the early months of 1981, congressional Democrats were still shell-shocked from their defeat in the 1980 elections, ineffectively led by new party leaders, unsure of the validity of their party's ideas, in partial agreement with Republican proposals that taxes and the budget should be pared down, and fearful that the 1982 congressional elections could lead to further Republican gains. No wonder that the most used word to describe the Democrats was *disarray*. Democrats were divided over whether they should act as a majority party and recommend alternatives to the president's program, or respond like a minority party and try to delay and dilute the program's passage by publicizing its weaknesses. Barbara Kellerman notes, "the story of Reagan's success during his first nine months in office is also the story of a generally emasculated and disorganized opposition. The Democrats lacked a leader. Jimmy Carter vanished into the Georgia countryside; Robert Byrd, who was not . . . a strong leader even as head of the majority party, was even less consequential now that Senate Democrats were in the minority; and Tip O'Neill seemed to be out of his element as leader of an obstructionist opposition."[56]

As a result, the Democratic response to Reagan's thrust was frequently disorganized, sometimes supportive, occasionally obstructive, and almost always ineffective. These ambivalent orientations were reflected in the statements and behavior of congressional Democrats. In December 1980, Democratic Representative Henry Reuss said, "Our own prescriptions having proved ineffective, Democrats are likely to be charitable towards Republican economic policies, no matter how zany."[57] In February 1981, Representative David Obey of Wisconsin, a liberal Democrat, said, "I personally think it would be a political mistake if we don't give the administration an opportunity to test its views. There is a mandate for the administration to proceed with significant budget cuts and significant tax cuts."[58] In the spring, Senate Minority Leader Robert Byrd announced he was going to vote for the Reagan budget because he thought that the public wanted the president's program to be given the opportunity to work. In the House, where the Democrats had their best chance to thwart Reagan's initiatives, Tip O'Neill's behavior was especially ambivalent. On the one hand, O'Neill stressed the inequities in Reagan's proposals; on the other, he promised not to use his powers as the Speaker to prevent the president's program from reaching the floor of the House for a vote. According to Kellerman, "Since the generally accepted view was that delays would help opponents of the budget cuts, it was clear that by relinquishing control of the legislative schedule, O'Neill had given away one of his strongest cards. Later, one of his advisers sought to explain the Speaker's decision: "What the Democrats did . . . was to recognize the cataclysmic nature of the 1980 election results. The American public wanted this new president to be given a chance to try out his programs. We weren't going to come across as being 'obstructionists.'"[59] Moreover, during the April Easter recess, while the White House and Republican leaders were mobilizing their troops for upcoming votes, O'Neill and Dan Rostenkowski (the new chairman of the Ways and Means Committee) traveled to Australia and New Zealand. In short, the Democrats appeared to be paralyzed by the fear that the popular president would be able to frame them as obstructionists, thus placing the blame of continued economic troubles on them. Finally, as Kellerman points out, "the Democrats were not entirely averse to letting the president have his way because if Reaganomics proved to be a disaster, he and his party would take the blame."[60]

The Democratic dilemma in trying to block Reagan's program was captured in what House Majority Leader Jim Wright wrote in his diary in mid-June 1981: "His philosophical approach is superficial, overly simplistic and one-dimensional. What he preaches is pure economic pap, glossed over with uplifting homilies and inspirational chatter. Yet so far the guy is making it work. Appalled by what seems to me a lack of depth, I stand in awe nevertheless of his political skill. I am not sure that I have seen its equal."[61]

Reagan's legislative victories in 1981 were helped by the divisions within the Democratic party. Although the president energized and unified the Republican party, Democratic Congress members were dispirited and undisciplined and could not agree on any strategy to oppose Reagan. The one Democratic victory was its defense of social security. Reagan's domination of the policy agenda was indicated by the fact that even if the House had voted for the Democratic tax cut, the bill was still largely a copy of the Republican proposal. Most importantly, the Democrats had been defeated on issues that would place them on the defensive for the rest of the decade. By losing on the budget and the tax cut, the Democrats were severely restricted in their ability to propose new programs. As a conservative, Reagan did not need to recommend new legislation; liberal Democrats did.

After these electoral and congressional defeats in 1980 and 1981, and especially after Reagan trounced Walter Mondale in the 1984 presidential elections, Democrats recognized the need for candid self-criticism so that they could compete more effectively against the Reagan juggernaut. Many of them accepted the accusation that the party had degenerated into a squabbling collection of selfish interest groups that no longer had the ability to articulate the public interest. Theodore Lowi argued, "In its deterioration, pro-state liberalism became 'interest-group liberalism,' whereby its broad vision of using government to expand freedom was replaced by its embrace of a process in which corporate groups (of business, labor, agriculture, and other organized interests) were provided with direct and legitimate involvement in policymaking and in which group support became the primary basis of policy justification. Interest-group liberalism sees as both necessary and good that the policy agenda and the public interest be identified in terms of the organized interests in society."[62] But the growing economic and social problems of the 1970s demonstrated that trying to placate the leaders of a vast array of interest groups did not necessarily result in effective policies or electoral victories. By being viewed as too closely tied to special interests, the Democrats had allowed Reagan to be seen as the flag bearer for the public interest.

The challenge for the Democrats was to develop a new public philosophy that maintained its egalitarian commitments while promoting the prospects of individual opportunity and economic growth. FDR had transformed the progressive ideas of the early decades of the twentieth century into a liberalism to deal with the Depression. Now there was a need to update liberalism so that it could respond to the needs of America in the 1980s, which was more prosperous, middle-class, suburban, globally involved, and socially diversified than in the 1930s. By not renovating their philosophy to the changing conditions and problems of American society, the Democratic party and the liberal regime it had created were being rejected. Intellectuals within the Democratic party recognized the problem. Robert Kuttner stressed that somewhere in the late 1970s, "the New Deal formula . . . hit stall speed. The welfare state and the activism of government became something for 'them'—for ethnic and cultural minorities and the certified poor. In the liberal heyday, 1933–68, activist government was something for 'us.'"[63] Senator Daniel Patrick Moynihan lamented, "The Republicans simply left us behind. They became the party of ideas and we were left, in Lord Macauley's phrase, 'the Stupid Party.'"[64] Recognizing the need to revise the party's guiding ideas, however, did not mean that Democrats were going to be able to carry out this task. As Congresswoman Patricia Schroeder ruefully remarked in 1983, "There are three things the Democratic Party must do to win the White House. Unfortunately, no one knows what they are."[65]

Actually, there were a number of Democrats who knew what had to be done, but their proposals were not fully accepted. One major group of reformers were known as neoliberals. Senator Paul Tsongas, Senator Gary Hart, Representative Timothy Wirth, Representative Albert Gore, congressional staff aide Al From, and intellectuals like Charles Peters, editor of the *Washington Monthly*, and Michael Kinsley, a writer for the *New Republic*, attempted to revise liberalism so that it would be more appealing to a new generation of voters. Neoliberals advocated that the Democrats accept the efficiency of competitive markets, the long-term benefits of free trade, the need for a stronger defense, the limitations of centralized bureaucracies, the need to decrease the party's dependence on special interests (especially unions), and the obligation to change ineffective governmental programs.

In 1984, neoliberals were opposed to Walter Mondale's candidacy because they believed he personified special interest politics and would be easily defeated by President Reagan. Neoliberals asserted that to renew support for the Democrats "required embracing middle-class values and acknowledging that the widespread skepticism of government programs had a basis in fact. Thus, they argued, it was much more important to provide support to business and investors—'to worry about the health of the goose' rather than the distribution of golden eggs, said Tsongas—and they supported tax breaks for business incentives, for capital formation, and deregulation."[66] Neoliberals created the Democratic Leadership Council in 1985, but they had limited success in reforming the party in the 1980s because their ideas appeared to many liberal Democrats as a me-too surrender to Reagan's conservatism. Liberals outside this movement complained that one Republican party was enough; the nation did not need two.[67]

A second idea that temporarily strove to be the guiding light of the Democratic party was industrial policy. This proposal tried to be the answer to the loss of blue-collar manufacturing jobs known as deindustrialization and the alleged economic decline of the United States in competition with Japan and Western Europe. Industrial policy was touted by Robert Reich, who taught at Harvard's Kennedy School of Government, Ira Magaziner, a business consultant (who in the early 1990s would advise Hillary Clinton on a national health care program), and Felix Rohatyn, who had supervised New York City's financial rescue in the mid-1970s. The proponents of industrial policy wanted to redirect investment from "sunset" industries, such as steel, toward "sunrise" industries, such as computers. Their goal was "to develop businesses that could compete internationally in which the federal government helped workers displaced from failing industries train for new jobs, directed research and development funding to promising areas and undertook high-risk investments that private firms avoided. Separately, Rohatyn proposed that federal research and development funding and investments be provided through a revival of the Reconstruction Finance Corporation of the 1930s, to be run jointly—and, somehow, without political interference—by business, labor, and the government."[68]

Democrats like Mondale and Kennedy hoped that industrial policy would become the means to provide both economic growth and distributive justice. However, the industrial policy balloon was popped in 1984 when it was ridiculed by liberal economists like Nobel laureates Paul Samuelson and James Tobin. Charles Schultze, Lyndon Johnson's budget director and Carter's chairman of the Council of Economic Advisors, wrote a devastating critique: "America is *not* de-industrializing. Japan does *not* owe its industrial success to its industrial policy. Government is *not* able to devise a 'winning' industrial structure. Finally, it is *not* possible in the American political system to pick and choose among industrial firms and regions in the substantive, efficiency-driven way envisaged by advocates of industrial policy."[69] And with the economy booming in 1984, political support for industrial policy evaporated.

What did not evaporate was the Democrats' commitment to the idea of fairness. For most liberal Democrats, Reagan's supply-side tax cuts were another version of the Republican propensity for trickle-down economics and top-down policies that aid the already privileged and ignore the problems of the poor. Most modern liberals conceded that competitive markets are efficient, but they claim that governmental interference is often necessary to ensure social justice. American conservatives value individual freedom far more than equality. A clash of visions occurs because liberal Democrats believe that equality and liberty can be reconciled, but conservative Republicans do not. Whereas liberals claim that by extending equality, freedom is also expanded, conservatives assert that attempts to augment equality constitute lethal threats to individual freedom. The Democratic argument is summarized by the Keynesian economist, John Kenneth Galbraith:

> Taxes on the affluent do reduce the freedom of those so taxed to spend their own money. . . . But welfare payments, unemployment compensation, and old-age pensions serve even more specifically to increase the liberty of their recipients. That is because the difference for liberty between considerable income and a little less income can be slight; in contrast, the effect on liberty of the difference between no income and some income is always . . . very great. It is the unfortunate habit of those who speak of the effect of government on freedom that they confine their concern to the loss of freedom for the affluent.[70]

Evidence accumulated during the 1980s and 1990s that income and wealth inequality was growing in the United States, a trend that outraged liberal Democrats. Republican dismissal of this evidence is reminiscent of tobacco companies' denials that smoking constitutes a health threat. But Democratic accusations that Reagan's tax and budget policies were the major cause of increasing inequality are also inaccurate. America was becoming more unequal before Reagan came into office, and the inequality trend has continued since he left office.

After World War II, Simon Kuznets argued that inequality in income increased as nations developed economically and decreased after they industrialized. Data from the United States supported Kuznets's theory.

During the 1950s and 1960s, income growth was equalizing, as the average adjusted family income of the lowest two quintiles of households increased faster than that of the other three. But in the 1970s, this equalizing trend began to slow down. For example, between 1950 and 1960, family income of the lowest quintile increased by 117 percent, while that of the highest quintile increased by 51.4 percent. However, between 1970 and 1980, the lowest quintile raised its income by 7.9 percent while the highest quintile's income went up by 10.3 percent.[71]

In 1991, a Census Bureau study of 24,000 households chosen to be representative of the nation's 92 million households concluded that the wealth of the most affluent Americans increased substantially during the 1980s while the net worth of other citizens barely kept pace with inflation. The Census Bureau defines wealth, or net worth, as the value of savings and checking accounts, real estate, stocks and bonds and other assets, minus debts. Wealth is more concentrated than income because it reflects not a single year's income, but the lifetime accumulation of assets. After adjusting for inflation, wealth of the richest fifth of all households increased 14 percent from 1984 to 1988, while the remaining four-fifths of households did not experience any significant change in net worth.[72]

In 1970, the richest 1 percent of households possessed about 20 percent of the nation's wealth. Data from a 1995 Federal Reserve study showed that the wealthiest 1 percent of households—with net worth of at least $2.3 million each—now owned nearly 40 percent of the nation's wealth.[73] In 1996, a University of Michigan study found that the most affluent 10 percent of American households held 61 percent of the country's wealth in 1989 and over 66 percent in 1994.[74] A 1996 Census Bureau report concluded that from 1968 to 1994, the share of the nation's aggregate income earned by the top 20 percent of households increased to 46.9 percent from 40.5 percent. During the same period, the proportion of income attained by the other quintiles decreased or remained stationary. While the average income of households in the bottom 20 percent of earners rose from $7,702 to $7,762, the average in the top 5 percent of earners surged from $111,189 to $183,044.[75]

Apparently, the opportunity to become richer has expanded in recent decades. In 1980, there were 4,414 millionaires in the United States; by 1987, there were 34,944, and by 1994, there were about 65,000.[76] In 1982, there were 21 billionaires in the nation; by 1991, there were 71.[77] The top 1 percent of households own a lopsided proportion of many types of assets: 49 percent of publicly held stock; 62 percent of business assets; 78 percent of bonds and trusts; and 45 percent of nonresidential real estate. Controlling these assets has meant that these affluent households have attracted three-fourths of the gain in pretax income from 1977 to 1989. Sylvia Nasar concludes, "By 1989, the top one percent (834,000 households with about $5.7 trillion of net worth) was worth more than the bottom 90 percent of Americans (84 million households with about $4.8 trillion in net worth)."[78] Lester Thurow adds, "By the early 1990s, the share of the wealth (more than 40 percent) held by the top one percent of the population was essentially double what it had been in the mid-1970s and back to where it was in the late 1920s, before the introduction of progressive taxation."[79] In terms of growing income inequality, we appear to be headed back to the future.

There is no agreement and much controversy concerning why inequality has been expanding in the United States. The usual suspects include declining wages for unskilled workers as automation spreads; the shift in the economy from manufacturing jobs to service jobs; the decline in the numbers of workers who are unionized; the increasing use of part-time workers; global competition; the rapid expansion in the 1980s of the stock and bond markets; and the low tax rates on the affluent during the 1980s. Whatever the causes, "United States wage distribution is more unequal than in other countries, and we do less in terms of tax and transfer policy to cushion the disparities."[80]

Comparative data suggest that "rather than being an egalitarian society, the United States has become the most economically stratified of the industrial nations."[81] We have more poor and more rich than other industrialized nations. America's chief executive officers (CEOs) are paid two to three times more than Germany's or Japan's. George Will writes, "In Japan, the compensation of major CEOs is 17 times that of the average worker; in France and Germany, 23–25 times; in Britain 35 times; in America, between 85 and 100 times. The American CEO-worker disparity doubled during the 1980s—while the top income tax rate was cut and workers' tax burden increased because of social security taxes."[82]

Because Reagan was not elected to bring about more equality, the growth of inequality during the 1980s did not create a lethal problem for him. Although his more pragmatic advisors, along with his public relations team, understood that the president might be vulnerable to Democratic accusations that his policies stimulated inequality and were therefore unfair, they reasoned correctly that even as evidence mounted that inequality was increasing, they could neutralize the publicity of such disparity as long as the economy continued to grow.

Still, given the equalitarian heritage of the United States, one might have predicted that such inequalitarian trends would have caused the administration more political problems than it did. Certainly the Democrats hoped that it would. They continually blasted the Reagan presidency for its tax policies, which benefited the rich, and its budget cuts, which hurt the poor. They condemned it for its "moral meanness" in its disregard for African American civil rights and for its lack of concern in promoting the equal rights of women. The Democrats also attacked the Reagan administration for trying to cut Medicare while proposing high increases in the defense budget, and for posing as the champion of family values while slashing programs that benefited education, child nutrition, health, and job training.

Lane Kirkland, the president of the AFL-CIO, described Reagan's policy in 1981 as "economic Darwinism, that is, the survival of the richest."[83] House Speaker Tip O'Neill proclaimed, "This has been a program of the rich, by the rich, and for the rich."[84] During the 1984 presidential election, Democratic party advertisements maintained: "It isn't fair. It's Republican." Hodding Carter, a political appointee in the Carter administration, responded to Reagan's 1982 proposals to shift policy responsibilities for the poor from the federal government to the states by writing, "Rather than nurturing a more perfect union, they would instead produce a confederacy of inequality, in which the obligations of shared national community are submerged in the rush by states and individuals to beggar their neighbors."[85] A Democratic Congress member charged that "the President, by expressing no sympathy for the disadvantaged yet cutting tax rates for the affluent by nearly two thirds, followed a career path that was the reverse image of Franklin D. Roosevelt's: while FDR was born rich and grew to be a tribune for the underdog, Mr. Reagan was born poor and grew up to champion the rich."[86] What Reagan extolled as encouragement for individuals to take advantage of the expanding opportunities in a dynamic economy were condemned by the Democrats as appeals to avarice. For Democrats, vain and arrogant millionaires like Charles Keating, Michael Milken, Leona Helmsley, and Donald Trump personified the "go for it" greed of the 1980s.

Carter or Mondale might have been perceived as being more concerned about the poor than Reagan, but they were also seen as ineffective political leaders. After the failures of the 1970s, few believed that liberal sensitivities about poverty could be transformed into competent policies to help the poor. Nor could the Democrats receive credit for their rhetoric about social justice when much of their motivation appeared to be electoral payoffs to special interests. By election day of 1984, according to Cavanagh and

Sundquist, "The Democratic Party was seen not as the traditional defender of the middle class but as tax collector for the welfare state, the Republican Party not as the tool of Wall Street and the rich but as the instrument to bring about widespread economic growth and opportunity."[87] For many Americans, the limited improvements made under Reaganomics appeared better than the painful losses suffered under Carter. And for the many who had not yet received increases in real income, the long period of growth nurtured hopes that they would eventually share in the prosperity.

The Democratic party's dilemma was painfully revealed in its own studies in 1985, which showed that white middle-class and white working-class voters equated the word *fairness* with giveaways to blacks. The studies demonstrated how difficult it would be for the party to construct messages that would regain the support of disaffected white middle- and working-class voters without alienating blacks.[88] With the increasing emphasis on affirmative action, civil rights now meant preferential treatment for minorities and women rather than equality under the law. The result was less support for civil rights among whites, especially white working-class men. Peter Applebaum reports, "*New York Times* polls indicate significant slippage in support for any preferential employment practices. When respondents were asked in May 1985 if they favored preferences in hiring or promotion for blacks in areas where there had been discrimination in the past, 42 percent said 'yes' and 46 percent said 'no.' Asked the same question in December 1990, 32 percent said 'yes' and 52 percent said 'no.'"[89]

The Reagan administration countered Democratic attacks on the basis of the growing inequality issue with conventional conservative arguments, effective use of White House public-relations capabilities, and utilization of Reagan's political skills. The conservative case against the liberal welfare state can be analyzed by using Albert O. Hirschman's book, *The Rhetoric of Reaction.* Hirschman claims that conservatives use three basic rhetorical arguments to criticize and ridicule attempts to promote equality. In his words, "According to the *perversity* thesis, any purposive action to improve some feature of the political, social, or economic order only serves to exacerbate the condition one wishes to remedy. The *futility* thesis holds that attempts at social transformation will be unavailing, that they will simply fail to 'make a dent.' Finally, the *jeopardy* thesis argues that the cost of proposed changes or reform is too high as it endangers some previous, precious accomplishment."[90]

The futility argument, backed up by the jeopardy thesis, is stressed by market economists. For them, the laws of supply and demand are immutable. It is as pointless to try to alter the natural outcome of markets as it would be to order a change in the tides. All nations have unequal wealth and income distribution, and it is foolhardy to criticize any degree of market-determined inequality where inequality is the natural order of things. On top of that, any attempt to bring about greater equality is likely to jeopardize freedom. The jeopardy thesis is best articulated in the books of Friedrich Hayek and Milton Friedman.[91]

Hirschman claims the argument conservatives most often use to delegitimize efforts to foster equality is the "perversity" contention. Liberal reformers are "world worseners" because the results of their attempts to improve conditions inevitably backfire. Any liberal attempt to reduce unemployment actually increases it; liberal efforts to help families with dependent children encourage mothers on welfare to have more children, thus creating their own prison of poverty. In *Losing Ground*, the conservative author Charles Murray argues, "We [the United States] tried to provide more for the poor and produced more poor instead. We tried to remove the barriers to escape poverty and inadvertently built a trap."[92] White House Counselor Edwin Meese stressed in a 1984 speech, "the broken families, dependent mothers and fatherless children that were spawned by a decade of aimless spending are the real victims of a well-meaning but misguided system of government aid and regulations."[93] In brief, while conservatives might occasionally concede that liberal policies are well intentioned, they generally argue that such efforts produce negative consequences.

The perversity thesis postulates that a liberal activist government generates more problems than solutions. Waligorski explains the conservative position by writing, "If equalization policies, whether affirmative action or minimum wage laws, necessarily fail to attain their end but cause inequality, then refusal to intervene, while seemingly anti-egalitarian, is in fact egalitarian because it forces people onto the market which rewards them according to their contribution to the welfare of others, thereby producing whatever equality is possible."[94] Milton and Rose Friedman add, "a society that puts freedom first will, as a happy by-product, end up with both greater freedom and greater equality."[95] Hence, in the ultimate irony, conservatives have argued that their emphasis on freedom will eventually produce more equality than liberalism.

Reagan's White House public relations machine was also utilized to ward off Democratic attacks. The bluntest responses came from conservatives, like Meese, who considered Democratic concerns about inequality to be a bogus issue. Conservatives claimed that liberals were demagogues and engaged in the politics of envy; they ridiculed the idea that poor people are poor because rich people are rich. David Stockman, the director of the Office of Management and Budget, was particularly active in defending the administration against Democratic charges of unfairness. For Stockman, the active pursuit of equality inevitably brought about a tyrannical state and an inefficient economy. In his words, "I don't accept that equality is a moral principle. . . . That's the overlay, the idea around the welfare state. A safety net is different—it's the minimum to which you'll allow anyone to fall. To go beyond that and seek to level incomes is morally wrong and practically destructive."[96]

At a more profound level, the Reagan administration was trying to change the policy context by substituting its conservative public philosophy for welfare state liberalism. Whereas the New Deal and the Great Society had tried to make the public aware of what government could do *for* them, the Reagan administration was attempting to make citizens fear what the government could do *to* them. The administration used the jeopardy argument to play on the taxpayer's fear of higher taxes, the businessman's fear of stifling regulations, the white male worker's fear of affirmative action, and the fear of religious groups of an expanding secular state. Democratic Senator Daniel Patrick Moynihan complained, "There is a movement to turn Republicans into Populists, a party of the people arrayed against the party of the state."[97] Judging by the presidential elections of the 1980s, this Republican strategy had considerable success.

Reagan's public relations specialists, such as Michael Deaver and David Gergen, and his politically sensitive advisers, led by James Baker and Richard Darman, made sure the administration could respond to Democratic attacks with facts and figures. In the spring of 1983, the White House compiled a 286-page briefing book to aid officials in defending the Reagan presidency against charges of unfairness.[98] The president and his spokesmen continually stressed that their budget cuts had not destroyed the social safety net that protected the old, sick, poor, and disabled. Moreover, the administration's tax cuts in 1981 and 1986 were fair because they removed 6 million poor families from the tax rolls and resulted in the rich paying a higher proportion of the nation's taxes at the end of the decade than at the beginning. Reagan's supporters also argued that in a dynamic capitalist society, income inequality statistics of quintiles were meaningless. According to Paul Craig Roberts, a supply-sider who served in Reagan's Treasury Department, "The reason is the extremely high rate of income mobility in the United States. The poor and the rich will always be with us, but they are not the same people from year to year. The poor move up over time and the rich fall off their high peaks."⁹⁹ For example, only 171 of the original 400 richest Americans listed in *Forbes* magazine in 1982 were again listed in the magazine's 1991 issue. For conservatives, it was about as significant to analyze income inequality statistics as it was to probe which soap bubbles rose to the top in a washing machine.

But the Reagan White House believed that its strongest defense against charges of unfairness was that its policies had ended the stagflation of the 1970s and were providing sustainable economic growth. Economic expansion fueled opportunities for investors to increase their wealth on Wall Street and for workers to improve themselves in the job market. Conservatives characterized the 1980s as a decade in which both the poor and the rich got richer. After the 1981–1982 recession (labeled the Carter recession by Reagan's supporters), the White House was constantly publicizing statistics that proved that Reaganomics was producing more growth and jobs than the policies of our European and Japanese allies. The Reagan growth period lasted ninety-two months, until July 1990, which was more than twice the average period of expansion since 1945. Between 1982 and 1990, real disposable income per capita increased by 18 percent, and the economy added 18.4 million jobs.[100] Reagan believed that the poor would be better off with a soaring economy than with an expanding bureaucracy. When a Census Bureau report indicated a drop in the poverty rate in 1984, Reagan announced, "I believe these numbers are further proof that the greatest enemy of poverty is the free enterprise system. The success of 1984 does not mean that the battle against poverty in this country is over; it does mean that America, after a difficult decade, is once again headed in the right direction."[101]

In explaining Reagan's landslide victory over Mondale in the 1984 elections, Richard Wirthlin, the president's pollster, indicated that economic prosperity had shielded the administration from Democratic fairness assaults. In Wirthlin's words, "Growth is the best alternative we can offer to the Democrats' state welfarisms."[102] Given the policy context of the 1980s and 1990s, the Republicans had immunized themselves from accusations of unfairness as long as they were producing economic growth. However, during periods of economic contraction, such as 1981–1982 and 1990–1991, Democratic attacks were more likely to draw blood—and voters.

The administration's stress on promoting growth was analogous to the conservative's emphasis on liberty. Economic expansion would bring higher standards of living for almost everyone. To express this idea, Reagan often borrowed President Kennedy's maxim that a rising tide lifts all boats.

Hence, a focus on economic growth would produce more equality in the long run than if there were more emphasis on liberal distributive policies.[103]

The most effective asset the Republicans had to neutralize the inequality issue was Ronald Reagan. Born poor in the Midwest, moving west to become a rich movie star, and then achieving the presidency, Reagan was the personification of the American dream. Deaver made sure the president was frequently pictured promoting charities, education, the Special Olympics, and so on.[104] Reagan presented a softer and gentler image than most other conservatives. As an inclusive political leader, Reagan was proud of his past affiliation in the Democratic party, and he used it effectively to invite Democrats to join him in the new Republican party. Although Democrats were trying to portray Reagan as a tool of the rich, Reagan was declaring, "The secret is that when the left took over the Democratic Party, we took over the Republican Party. We made the Republican Party into the party of the working people, the family, the neighborhood, the defense of freedom, and, yes, the American flag and the Pledge of Allegiance to one nation under God. So, you see, the party that so many of us grew up with still exists except that today it's called the Republican Party, and I'm asking all of you to come home and join me."[105]

Because Reagan did not intend to have his policies bring about more inequality, it was sufficient for him to believe that it was not happening. But Reagan's budget, tax, and antiregulatory policies did nothing to thwart the inequality trends that preceded his administration, and they may have accelerated wealth disparities. For the first time since the New Deal, the federal government ceased attempting to constrain the propensity of capitalism to generate inequality. Nevertheless, Reagan was able to avoid being wounded by the fairness issue by framing himself as a conservative populist. The president was also successful in delegitimizing most Democratic party proposals to deal with inequality by labeling them not as sincere efforts to remedy social injustice, but as selfish attempts by liberal elitists to reward special interests and federal bureaucrats.

The combination of Carter's political failures in the 1970s and Reagan's political success in the 1980s meant it would become more difficult to propose policies to aid the poor and promote equality. Reagan helped create an atmosphere in which it was easier for the public to approve increased funding for the military, the police, and prisons rather than education, health, or housing. His political success and his insensitivity to equality arguments created a model for today's politicians that may delay endeavors to deal with growing inequality problems. New York's Democratic governor, Mario Cuomo, voiced a telling criticism when he said, "At his worst, Reagan made the denial of compassion respectable."[106] By the end of his presidency, nearly one in five children was living in poverty, but with the exception of Jesse Jackson, no serious presidential candidate would take the risk of trying to change this situation with a major new initiative.

It is certainly reasonable to subject social welfare policies, like any other proposals, to serious scrutiny as to whether they will achieve their objectives within a reasonable cost. It is less reasonable—and perhaps immoral—to erect new barriers to promoting a more socially just society by denying the success of previous policies and automatically maligning new projects for being motivated by selfish purposes. In evaluating the Reagan presidency on this issue of equality, David Broder wrote, "History will not deal kindly with his administration's deliberate efforts to slow down or reverse the two previous decades of steady progress in reducing poverty and discrimination. . . . [Reagan] was neither heartless nor biased personally, but he was deaf to calls for justice. The Great Communicator used all his rhetorical tools to advance the causes he cared about; unfortunately, justice was not one of them."[107]

Conclusion

Emerging from the uncertainty and despair of the 1970s, the United States in the 1980s constructed a new framework for economic growth. This new regime had less confidence in what government could accomplish and more faith in the efficiency of markets. By the end of the 1980s, the economy resembled the mirror image of the end of the 1970s: corporate profits were strong, unemployment low, jobs multiplying, inflation negligible, and the stock market flourishing. The revolution in computer technology caused painful adjustments, but eventually made both the manufacturing and service sectors more efficient. "After years of travail," according to Louis Uchitelle, "this country has finally fielded the right formula for generating wealth and prosperity in the highly competitive global economy. . . . The essence of the American formula . . . is this: Business must be free to innovate, restructure, relocate. These are necessary ingredients for baking an ever larger pie, however distasteful the downsizing and wage inequality that are part of the process."[108]

President Reagan made major contributions to the creation of this policy regime. His tax cuts for both individuals and corporations stimulated the prosperity that, except for a short, mild recession in 1990–1991 and 2001, has continued into the twenty-first century. However, this framework for economic growth was not simply a function of fulfilling Reagan's original vision in 1980. Contrary to Reagan's speeches and conservative myth spinners, the president's success was not based on "staying the course"; rather, it derived from his skill in shifting policy directions while maintaining rhetorical consistency. By 1982, it was apparent that there was a fundamental incompatibility between Reagan's fiscal and monetary policies. An implicit compromise was arranged whereby the administration accepted a tighter fiscal policy by acquiescing to tax increases, and Paul Volcker's Fed agreed to implement a looser monetary policy. Volcker ended Friedman's experiment in 1982, was reappointed chairman in 1983 by Reagan, and then skillfully directed monetary policy to constrain inflation. Low levels of inflation were an essential ingredient in prolonging the growth stage of the business cycle. Ironically, then, Reagan's success was partly dependent on the skill and courage of a pragmatic bureaucrat originally appointed by President Carter.

Reagan's economic achievements are clouded, at least in the eyes of liberals, by the fact that indices of inequality have increased since the 1970s. These changes are altering the nature of the United States from one of the most equalitarian industrialized nations to one of the least. The evidence indicates that the policies of the Reagan administration were not the origin of the growing inequality, but it does suggest that they contributed to that trend. More importantly, Reagan's policies did nothing to inhibit inequality, and his administration attempted to delegitimize any governmental endeavors to promote equality. By adding barriers to the already Herculean task of initiating policies to help the poor, Reagan served his partisan purposes but not necessarily the nation's good. The claims of Reagan's supporters that he was a great moral leader can be seriously challenged because he contributed to poisoning the policy milieu against proposals to bring about a socially just nation.

In a country that has traditionally prided itself on its early and continuing commitment to equality, one would have expected the inequalitarian trends that began in the 1970s and accelerated in the 1980s to have caused more political problems for the Reagan presidency. Increasing inequality means a narrowing of opportunity for those hoping to share in the American dream. The unique and sustaining myth of the American dream is that it is achievable by the many and not by just the select few. As conservatives have tried to expand their electoral popularity, they have argued that their ideology of emphasizing freedom will eventually produce more equality than liberalism will. The statistical trends of the 1980s do not support their contention. Their policy of relying on competitive markets produced powerful incentives for efficiency and economic growth, but not equality.

11

FDR's Reconstructive Party Leadership

To fulfill their historic roles, reconstructive presidents have to demonstrate the skills of outstanding party leaders.[1] They must obtain their party's nomination, win the general election, mobilize majority support for their core legislative programs in Congress, and legitimate their policy changes by being reelected. The representatives of the old regime must be rejected in elections; the representatives of the new regime must be supported by an expanded electoral coalition. To bring about regime change, the president has to combine and mobilize several streams of discontent into an electoral coalition capable of winning a series of congressional elections. A new regime is not constructed in a day or in one hundred days; it requires multiple legislative successes over several years to build a new governing structure. As leader of his party, a reconstructive president is faced with the challenges of expanding its electoral base, maintaining party unity during a period of rapid change, and responding to new issues with innovative policies. While reconstructive executives operate in a context (opposition to a vulnerable regime) that grants them the broadest authority to proclaim new messages and policies, they must not appear dangerously radical to the electorate. A reconstructive president has to be careful not to scare more voters than he attracts with his visions of a new regime. The time-tested strategy to soothe the electorate in this situation is to convince it that his proposals are more compatible with our political traditions than the politics and policies of the present regime. The new programs will not destroy that which is precious in our heritage; it will only demolish the components of the old regime that have been retarding the progress Americans consider their birthright.

The purpose of this chapter and the next is to compare FDR and Ronald Reagan as party leaders. Roosevelt transformed the Democratic party from a minority party to a majority party geared to winning presidential and congressional elections and passing New Deal legislation. He also converted the party's philosophy from Jeffersonian liberalism to a positive-state liberalism that resonated favorably with the millions of citizens who needed help from the federal government during the Depression. Without the benefit of a critical election victory that would have given the Republicans control of Congress, Reagan was able to unify the Republican party under a conservative banner dedicated to lowering tax rates, deregulating the economy, building up the military, and championing traditional values. With the Democrats controlling a majority of the seats in the House of Representatives throughout the 1980s, Reagan was not able to destroy the liberal regime, but he did slow its growth and construct a conservative edifice that proved popular with a wide variety of voters.

FDR as Party Leader

The challenge for Franklin Roosevelt was to raise the status of the Democratic party from a minority party to a majority party that could successfully govern. Beginning with the Civil War and the leadership of Abraham Lincoln, the Republican party had dominated the political system. John Allswang points out, "Between the election of Lincoln and that of 1932, the Republicans won 14 of 19 presidential elections, controlled the Senate 62 out of 72 years, and the House 46 out of 72 years. From 1861–1875, again from 1897–1911, and again from 1921–31, they held control of both houses of Congress and the presidency."[2] The Republicans clearly had a message that was frequently endorsed by voters. Their party was rejuvenated by the election of 1896, when the electorate supported William McKinley and his urban-industrial program against the agrarian, prosilver visions of the Democratic candidate, William Jennings Bryan. In that critical election, the Republicans established themselves as the voice of the rising cities. In Carl Degler's words, "Not only was it the party of respectability, wealth, and the Union; it was also the party of progress, prosperity, and national authority. As such, it could and did enlist the support of industrial workers and immigrants as well as merchants and millionaires."[3]

But lurking within the Republican party's success were three factors that would eventually erode its majority support. First, there were a number of progressive reformers within the party, men like Teddy Roosevelt from New York and Robert M. LaFollette from Wisconsin, who advocated that the Republicans loosen their ties to big business and use federal authority to promote a broader concept of the public interest to include small business, workers, and farmers. The ideological split in the Republican party caused a fratricidal split between President William Howard Taft and Teddy Roosevelt that allowed Woodrow Wilson, the Democratic candidate, to be elected president in 1912. LaFollette ran as a progressive third-party candidate in 1924, but this futile effort did not prevent President Calvin Coolidge from being reelected with 54 percent of the vote. Thus, there were progressive Republican voters and legislators who were potential supporters for FDR's candidacy and progressive program.

Second, the nativism and the moral streak in the Republican party hindered efforts to attract the votes of the 24 million immigrants who migrated to the United States between 1890 and 1920. While urban Democratic machines were providing services for the immigrants in return for their votes, Republicans hoped that the prosperity of the 1920s would eventually filter down to the rapidly expanding city populations. Meanwhile, the major issue in the cultural wars of the 1920s was Prohibition, enshrined in the Constitution by the Eighteenth Amendment, which alienated everyone from urban immigrants to rural Protestants. The passage of this amendment at the end of the Great War "was a classic success of a committed minority. But its support was as much on cultural grounds as moral ones—it was, to its proponents, another way of establishing the hegemony of traditional American values, and traditional Americans, over new values and new people. And to the immigrants, Prohibition was not simply the denial of their right to drink, it was something willfully and maliciously foisted on them by old stock Americans."[4]

By nominating Al Smith, the son of an Irish immigrant, in 1928, the Democrats were rejecting Bryan's influence and making a successful bid to attract the growing urban vote. While John W. Davis had received only about 8.4 million votes in 1924, Smith in 1928 earned over 15 million (40.8 percent of the popular vote). In comparing the vote of the twelve largest cities over a series of elections, Degler stresses, "the striking thing about Smith's candidacy was that it attracted the big city vote away from the Republicans for the first time since the 1890s. . . . If the votes of all twelve cities are added together, Smith secured 38,000 more votes than Hoover;

in 1920, the Republicans had carried the same cities by 1,638,000 votes."[5] Thus, the Republicans were losing their urban base *before* the Depression.

The third factor concerned how dependent the Republicans were on continuing prosperity. With the Republicans being considered the party of business and with Hoover being a former secretary of commerce, an economic collapse would undermine one of the key rationales for their public support. If their probusiness policies could no longer provide jobs for workers, profitable prices for farmers, and security for bank depositors, the party would be deserted by many of its former partisans and lose its ability to attract new voters. In brief, when Herbert Hoover defeated Al Smith by over 6 million votes in 1928 (Hoover won over 58 percent of the popular vote), Republican hegemony was less secure than most observers could see.

The Democratic party in the late 1920s was woefully unprepared to lead a crusade for federal reforms. Its Founding Father was Thomas Jefferson, which meant, according to Milkis, "a commitment to individual autonomy, states' rights, and a limited role for the national government."[6] To many Republican progressives, the Democratic party appeared to be an unholy alliance of corrupt Northern urban machines and racist Southern organizations. The reform energies that President Wilson had mobilized had dissipated because of disillusionment with the outcome of the Great War. What little national party machinery existed was controlled by John J. Raskob, a wealthy businessman who had worked for the DuPont corporation. Smith had appointed Raskob national party chairman in 1928, and because he was funding the party headquarters, he remained in that position until 1932. According to Leuchtenburg, "An arch reactionary and a leader of the wets, Raskob muted the economic issues of the depression by insisting that prohibition was the greatest question before the country. He mobilized all the resources of the national party organization against Roosevelt's bid for the nomination."[7] Under Raskob's influence, the party was associated with big business and had little chance to recover the Protestant rural voters who had deserted Smith in 1928 or to take advantage of the economic issues generated by the Depression in 1932.

FDR obviously had the skills to be a great party leader. After his struggles with polio, he made his political comeback at the Democratic convention in 1924 by delivering the nominating speech for Al Smith. After John W. Davis's humiliating loss to President Coolidge, Roosevelt, with help from Louis Howe, sent a letter to three thousand Democrats throughout the nation, setting out his recommendations for party reform and seeking their suggestions. In 1928, FDR again gave the nominating speech for the "Happy Warrior" and was persuaded, after much pressure by Smith, to run for governor of New York. While Smith failed to carry New York as the presidential candidate, FDR was elected by a narrow margin of 25,000 votes. In 1930, however, Roosevelt was reelected by a landslide of 725,000 votes, doubling Smith's highest margin in 1922. Roosevelt was now the front-runner to win the Democratic nomination for president in 1932.

As governor and later president, FDR demonstrated the ability to project broad appeal to both urban and rural voters. What had been an insurmountable gap for Smith was easily bridged by FDR. After becoming governor, and in defeating Smith for the Democratic nomination in 1932, Roosevelt was able to avoid the stigma of appearing anti-Catholic and retain the support of Catholic voters. Publicizing his second home in Warm Springs, Georgia, Roosevelt was a popular figure in the South. His skills as a harmonizer and reconciler were derived from his wide range of acquaintances and experiences. The kinds of appeals and deals necessary to assuage downstate urban residents and upstate rural citizens were not anathema to him; they were a puzzle he loved to solve. The same facility that allowed him to be comfortable with policy inconsistencies also encouraged him to pursue strange political alliances. FDR could court free traders and protectionists, African Americans in the North and racists in the South, Republican progressives in the West and urban machines in the Northeast. He believed he could charm leaders of farmers and labor and provide effective policies for their followers. Although FDR never hid that he was a patrician from Hyde Park, he had the facility to make millions think that he understood their problems and was going to do something about them.

Roosevelt perceived that the Depression not only wounded the Republican party, but could also unify the Democrats under the progressive banner—which was his flag. Being tied to the old regime, Republicans, and especially Hoover, could not reinvent themselves in 1932, or even 1936, by rolling out new, innovative programs to deal with the massive suffering resulting from economic collapse. Because FDR had no bonds with the unraveling regime, he could offer the voters a progressive New Deal. Although he was advised by Democratic party leaders and Louis Howe that there was no need to campaign hard because his victory over Hoover was assured, FDR was determined to win big. He wanted the Democratic party's electoral success to be viewed as his *personal* success so that his governing goals could be enacted into law.[8] Roosevelt's future policy objectives were dependent on extending his personal control over the Democratic party.

As Burner explains, "The role of the Roosevelt candidacy in the rebirth of the Democratic party is, therefore, of a double nature; for FDR gave the Democracy both a degree of harmony and a progressive cast. Both achievements owe much to his special temperament—inductive, experimental, even opportunistic rather than philosophically reformist—relishing the plasticity of the social and political materials in which he worked."[9]

Roosevelt's success as a reconstructive president was dependent on his ability to transform the Democratic party. He believed that a "strong party had to be built around a clear philosophy and program of governance."[10] FDR wanted to create a party system in which the Democrats would champion a liberal philosophy and the Republicans would advocate a conservative orientation to public policy. With both parties guided by their own political philosophy, it would be easier for each to enact their programs if they received majority support from the electorate. Such a party system would simplify voting decisions for the electorate and would bring about more party accountability to American voters. Parties that failed to fulfill their campaign promises would be punished in the next election.

Roosevelt's efforts to transform the Democratic party have been extensively studied by Sidney Milkis. Milkis argues that Roosevelt was influenced by the progressive fear that by the beginning of the twentieth century, modernization had rendered some of Jefferson's ideas obsolete. According to Milkis,

> With the consolidation of private power in the hands of giant trusts, a constitutional program providing for societal domination of the state was now a recipe for economic oligarchy. Just as Jefferson defined the task of party leadership as rallying public opinion against the state, Roosevelt sought to transfer the American people's allegiance from private interests to public authority. As such, the New Deal Democratic party was organized during the 1930s as a "government party," one based on a program to build a "modern" state, which Roosevelt and his Brain Trust saw as an indispensable element in restoring economic and political democracy to the United States.[11]

That was FDR's philosophical goal. Organizationally, he was trying to alter a decentralized party, responsible to local electorates, into a mechanism responsive to the directions of the national party leader—the president. This meant that when a president led his party to an electoral victory, congressional members of his party should be loyal and disciplined in supporting his legislative program. As FDR expanded the powers of the presidency, "it preempted party leaders in many of their limited, but significant duties: providing a link to interest groups, staffing the executive departments, contributing to policy development, and organizing campaign support."[12] Roosevelt increasingly thought that the development of rational policy to deal with the complex problems of modern society required reduced roles for both Congress and the majority political party and augmented authority for experts in the executive branch. Hence, FDR's visions conflicted with the constitutional principles of separation of powers and checks and balances, and the Jeffersonian tradition of decentralized parties.[13]

Roosevelt's attempt to transform the Democratic party was enhanced by his electoral success, both his own and that of those who rode his extensive coattails aiding the Democrats to win elections in congressional and state contests. "Campaigning, for him," according to Moley, "was unadulterated joy."[14] The New Deal can be considered the first example of what has been called "the permanent campaign"; FDR was constantly and joyously selling himself and his programs in electoral campaigns, press conferences twice a week, and occasional fireside chats. Citizens flocked to hear him in person; they loved to hear him on radio. Ironically, his upper-class accent soothed the poor and irritated the rich because of its liberal message. Roosevelt campaigned against the Depression, the icy indifference of Hoover, the irresponsibility of speculators, and the greed of "economic royalists." He campaigned for the welfare state and made most citizens believe that they would be the beneficiaries of its newly created capabilities. Before the 1934 congressional elections, he defended the New Deal by asking a question in a fireside chat that Reagan would later use against Carter: "The simplest way for each of you to judge recovery lies in the plain facts of your individual situation. Are you better off than you were last year? Are your debts less burdensome? Is your bank account more secure? Are your working conditions better? Is your faith in your own individual future more firmly grounded?"[15] Evidently, voters responded positively to these questions.

Roosevelt and his advisers saw that the crisis of the Depression provided an unprecedented opportunity to reconstruct America. Playing the role of a statesman educating the public about the distributive benefits of New Deal policies was a role that the aristocratic FDR thought that he was born to perform. Milkis writes, "Close associates such as Felix Frankfurter were constantly urging the president, when in the midst of political controversy, to use the radio—to 'take the country to school,' giving the people a 'full dress explanation and analysis,' as only he was capable. This was a role Roosevelt relished."[16] The president recognized that if he was going to be successful in institutionalizing the New Deal as something significantly more than an emergency response to the Depression, he would have to use the bully pulpit of his office to legitimate his liberal regime.

Roosevelt faced a number of political challenges as he attempted to build and maintain a majority coalition during a time of great turmoil. The Depression spawned an atmosphere of ideological polarization unparalleled in the history of the United States. Sundquist writes, "If the country's activists were enraged by the fact of human suffering, its conservatives were no less incensed by the nature of the remedies proposed—as well as by the heightened rhetoric of Roosevelt's reelection campaign [in 1936] which at times could be as polarizing as Hoover's."[17] In this politically charged environment, FDR tried to head the contending progressive forces and get them to avoid internecine conflicts and support politically feasible solutions to the terrible problems of the day. There was always a danger, however, that "Roosevelt's dream of advancing liberalism by forging a new electoral union of forward-thinking Democrats and progressive Republicans threatened to degenerate into a nightmare in which the various progressive forces in the country might so fragment as to lose all capacity for common political action."[18]

There were progressives who doubted whether FDR could transform the Democratic party. Intellectuals like John Dewey and Paul Douglas thought that neither party could provide desperately needed reforms, and therefore they created the League for Independent Action in 1929. The dream of these intellectuals was to form a progressive third party. They thought that the Democratic party could never become an instrument of reform because of its reliance on reactionary Southerners and corrupt urban machines. In 1932, Paul Douglas warned, "It is a sobering thought that twenty years ago many Progressives were pinning similar hopes on Woodrow Wilson, who, with all respect to Governor Roosevelt, was a far keener thinker and a more determined fighter. . . . Yet, after eight years, Wilson retired with the Democratic party as cancerous as ever in its composition and as conservative in its policies. If such was the fate of Wilson, how can we hope for better things from Franklin Roosevelt."[19] In this evaluation, Douglas obviously underestimated the political skills and progressive commitments of FDR. By transforming the Democratic party into a more liberal organization, Roosevelt was able to inhibit a major third-party challenge from Governor Floyd Olsen in Minnesota, Robert and Phillip LaFollette in Wisconsin, and Huey Long in Louisiana. Roosevelt's success in draining support from the radical left can be measured in the decrease of the socialist Norman

Thomas's vote for president from almost 900,000 in 1932 to 200,000 in 1936. To use a contemporary metaphor, FDR cut off the air supply of competing politicians.

FDR's political success generated major political challenges to the New Deal. His ability to mobilize voters also meant that he became the target of their pressures. Patterson stresses, "Union men, Negroes, farmers, underprivileged ethnic groups—all viewed the New Deal as their friend. They had been the heart of Roosevelt's increased popular support in 1936 and had shifted the majority strength of the Democratic party from its old southern enclave in the 1920s to a northern urban base by 1937. From this point they became increasingly insistent, and they clamored for more federal aid at the same time the old party wheelhorses were demanding that it be curtailed."[20]

Despite all the New Deal had done for the farmers, they began to desert the Democrats in the 1938 congressional elections and migrate back to their Republican roots. Farmers liked price support policies but chafed under production controls. While New Deal policies helped many farmers avoid foreclosures and improved the prices for their products, there was growing resentment toward the federal government, sometimes expressed in the question, What have you done for me lately? According to Allswang, farmers "resented the money going to labor and urban people generally, often for cultural and ideological reasons rather than purely economic ones. Thus, the Democrats' honeymoon with most farmers [especially with farmers who owned more than 500 acres] was not a long one."[21] Roosevelt's goal of a grand alliance between farmers and workers was not consummated.

African Americans who thought that they had paid their debts to Abraham Lincoln were switching their votes to the Democrats and now wanted to be rewarded. Because they were suffering terribly from the Depression, they pressured the administration to guarantee that they would receive full benefits from the relief agencies and not be subject to discrimination. By 1936, there was a group of over thirty Negro officials from a number of federal agencies, called the Black Cabinet, which often met at the home of Mary McLeod Bethune, the director of the National Youth Administration's Division of Negro Affairs, to discuss how the New Deal should respond to the particular problems of their race. African Americans were particularly concerned about obtaining the president's support in getting antilynching legislation passed by the Congress, but in deference to the clout of Southern Democrats and against the moral objections of Eleanor Roosevelt, FDR never gave his full blessing to the proposal. Indeed, because of political reasons, helping African Americans never became a priority for FDR. Nevertheless, a harbinger of the future occurred in the House election of 1934 in Chicago, when the Negro Democrat Arthur W. Mitchell defeated the Negro Republican incumbent Oscar DePriest and became the first African American Democrat ever elected to Congress.

As the party leader, the biggest challenge facing FDR was the South. The dilemma for Roosevelt was that this region of the eleven former Confederate states was an anchor, a social base, and "a potential drag on any effort to innovate."[22] It contained the Democratic party's most reliable voters and its most skeptical set of leaders concerning the direction of the New Deal. With FDR expanding the number of voters supporting the Democratic party, the traditional importance of the South was diluted. In 1936, Roosevelt was able to end the Solid South's ability to veto the party's nominees for president and vice president at the national party convention by abolishing the rule that required candidates to receive two-thirds of the delegate votes in order to receive the party's nomination. This rule, originally adopted in 1832 when Andrew Jackson was president, had paralyzed the party in 1924 when neither Al Smith nor William McAdoo could muster majority support at the convention, and it took 103 ballots before the party nominated the lackluster candidacy of John W. Davis. The rule also caused Roosevelt a great deal of stress in 1932 when it delayed his nomination until the fourth ballot. From now on, Democratic candidates would obtain the party nomination by winning the votes of only a majority of the delegates to the party convention.

In Congress, FDR relied on Southern votes to pass his domestic programs and to support his reciprocal trade agreements and military rearmament policies. But the president also wanted "to reshape the political and economic culture of the South, to rouse it from the slumber of tradition and nudge it into the modern, industrial era."[23] In 1938, he publicly proclaimed that the South was the nation's number one economic problem. Southern leaders were not sure that FDR could help the region without destroying its autonomy and traditions. As Allswang explains, "The rapid expansion of the federal power, and of the executive, violated traditional southern localism and stress on the legislative branch. Senator [Josiah] Bailey of North Carolina wrote to Senator [Harry] Byrd of Virginia in the fall of 1937, that 'what we have to do is to preserve, if we can, the Democratic Party against his efforts to make it the Roosevelt party.'"[24] Because Roosevelt's New Deal would permeate the South with federal authority, it threatened local elites. According to George Tindall, "the New Deal jeopardized a power that rested on the control of property, labor, credit, and local government. Relief projects reduced dependency; labor standards raised wages; farm programs upset landlord-tenant relationships; government credit bypassed bankers; new federal programs skirted county commissioners and even state agencies."[25]

In brief, Southern politicians were pleased with the federal aid their region received but were apprehensive about its accompanying federal controls. From the Southern Democratic perspective, the New Deal was evolving in a way that threatened vital regional interests: "relief moneys went too much to the cities; the labor legislation, and especially minimum wage-maximum hours, undercut the south's advantage of having cheaper labor costs and threatened the stability of southern business. Moreover, the New Deal was a social threat, particularly in terms of race; both specific legislation and New Deal commitments, and the general trend of the administration, seemed threatening to the system of racial segregation on which southern society was built."[26] The fear that the New Deal was beginning a second period of reconstruction drove a number of Southern Democrats to oppose FDR's efforts to enlarge the Supreme Court in 1937 and to form a conservative coalition with the Republicans.

Ironically, the weakness of the Republican opposition in the 75th Congress (1937–1938) motivated Southern Democrats to create the conservative coalition and triggered FDR's response to purge conservative Democrats in the 1938 primaries. After Roosevelt's landslide victory in the 1936 elections, he expected legislative victories. Instead, he was stunned by a series of defeats for his proposals to reform the Supreme Court and increase presidential authority over the executive branch. In December 1937, leaders of the conservative coalition (Democratic Senators Josiah Bailey of North Carolina, Harry Byrd of Virginia, and Millard Tydings of Maryland; Republican Senators Arthur Vandenburg of Michigan, and Warren Austin of Vermont) published a declaration of principles maligning New Deal reforms as radical violations of the nation's constitutional traditions. Milkis writes, "In part, this statement called for a return to normalcy, advocating conservative positions on taxes, labor, and relief. But the conservative coalition's manifesto was not presented as merely a limited disagreement with the New Deal at the level of policy; rather the connection of conservative policies to the defense of traditional constitutional democracy suggested that a crisis of regime was at hand."[27] The conservative coalition hoped to unite and stop the march of the New Deal under the halo of limited constitutional government.

During his first term, FDR had upheld the political tradition that presidents should not interfere in their party's local primaries. Both Presidents Taft and Wilson had tried to influence local primaries without success. Milkis suggests, "Underlying this commitment to decentralized party politics was the constitutional principle of division and separation of powers. Arguably, a president's interference in primary campaigns reflected an unhealthy desire to control Congress, to defeat those members of his party who disagreed with him and secure the election of others who agreed with him, thus undermining the independence of the legislature necessary to uphold American constitutional government."[28] By 1938, Roosevelt felt compelled by the successes of the conservative coalition and concerns for his reforms to break yet another precedent and launch a purge of Democratic Congress members.

FDR was motivated to initiate this high-risk strategy of eliminating conservative Democrats for a number of reasons. First, he was personally outraged that so many Democratic Congress members had deserted him over the issue of reforming the Supreme Court. Lingering resentment from that stinging defeat made him yearn for a moment of sweet revenge. Second, he felt betrayed that many Democrats masqueraded as New Dealers in order to feed off his popularity during elections and then felt free to block his programs. Third, Roosevelt was frustrated that the conservative coalition was winning legislative victories despite the public's support for him and his New Deal policies. Fourth, in December 1937, Harry Hopkins organized an advisory committee of liberals called the "elimination committee," which included Tom Corcoran, Harold Ickes, and the president's son and secretary, James Roosevelt, to look into the possibility of punishing conservative Democrats and securing New Deal domination of the 1940 Democratic convention.[29] Finally, part of FDR's motivation for the purge was his fear that his New Deal legacy might be undone in the 1940 election, just as Wilson's was in the 1920 contest. Roosevelt was determined that the Democratic presidential candidate in 1940 would be a liberal like himself, who could win and continue expanding the New Deal.

After Democratic Senator Claude Pepper, with the aid of FDR's public endorsement, defeated his anti–New Deal opponent in the Florida primary on May 3, the president thought that the time was favorable for more extensive interventions. To explain and justify that change, Roosevelt asked Corcoran and Ben Cohen to draft a fireside chat that would be delivered on June 24. However, Roosevelt dictated the key lines in the speech, pointing out the distinction between liberalism and conservatism and stressing his obligations not as president but as the leader of the liberal party, to carry out what the Democrats had promised to do in the 1936 elections—and what the public had overwhelmingly endorsed.[30] In Roosevelt's mind, this meant he had the right to voice his support or opposition in the few Democratic primaries where there was a clear issue between pro– and anti–New Deal candidates.

Roosevelt's attempt to gain more centralized control over the Democratic party was opposed by James Farley, the postmaster general and chairman of the Democratic National Committee, on the grounds that it violated political traditions and would probably not work. Farley's opposition was also personally motivated by his anger at being replaced as top political adviser by New Dealers like Hopkins. Farley also had ambitions to be the Democratic nominee for president in 1940, which he feared would be opposed by liberal New Dealers.

Although FDR viewed his party reform as promoting democratic accountability, he was appalled when the press called it a purge. That his proposal to reform the federal courts had become known as the court-packing scheme, his executive reorganization bill had been termed the dictator bill, and now his plan to transform the Democratic party was branded a purge indicated that FDR in his second term was losing control over the labeling of his actions. It was not going to help the president mobilize public effort to liberalize his party when the word to describe it was *purge*—the same word used to depict the efforts of Hitler and Stalin to control their parties.[31] A dissident purged by European dictators was dead; a dissident opposed by FDR faced a tougher primary election.

The administration's efforts were more successful in helping the renomination of pro–New Deal incumbents than it was in eliminating anti–New Deal Democrats. One of his few successes, personally orchestrated by Corcoran, was bringing about the defeat of Representative John H. O'Connor in New York City. As chairman of the Rules Committee, O'Connor had joined with Southern Democrats and Republicans in blocking New Deal legislation, like the Fair Labor Standards Act, from reaching the floor of the House for a vote. However, when FDR's open support aided Senate Majority Leader Alben Barkley in defeating Governor A. B. "Happy" Chandler by 50,000 votes in Kentucky, there were allegations of WPA interference in favor of the pro–New Deal legislator. Senator Barkley's victory was a costly one because it raised anxieties among Southern Democrats and Republicans that Hopkins was constructing a national political machine.

In a campaign swing through the South in August, FDR attacked Senators Walter George from Georgia, "Cotton" Ed Smith from South

Carolina, and Millard Tydings from Maryland. In Barnsville, Georgia, the president endorsed Senator George's opponent because the incumbent was not supporting the liberal policies that would develop the South. According to Milkis, "Roosevelt felt that the deep South would not have to be conceded by a liberalized Democratic party. . . . He believed that the people in the South could be persuaded of the advantage of a liberal Democratic party if the race issue and the reconstruction era could be forgotten amid a chorus of demands for economic justice — demands that would be important to the majority of whites as well as blacks."[32] Roosevelt claimed to be a Southerner on the basis of his second home in Warm Springs, Georgia, but he badly misread the temper of white voters in the region. His notion that the New Deal could circumvent the race issue is one of the few cases where FDR was incredibly naive. The president's efforts were overwhelmed by the well-entrenched incumbents; all three were renominated in the primaries.

Although the results of FDR's efforts to help his friends and punish his enemies in 1938 were mixed, the public image was one of failure. Instead of overcoming the liberal-conservative split within the Democratic party, he had widened it. Southern Democrats now had more reasons to distrust the president and seek further support from Republicans to block the advance of the New Deal. Milkis summarizes the episode by writing, "In the final analysis, Roosevelt's program to make the Democratic party a more consistent instrument of liberalism was generally viewed by representatives and the public as an irresponsible attempt to fashion a rubber stamp Congress. . . . FDR had 'demonstrated in the most public way,' *New York Times* columnist Arthur Krock claimed, 'that the American system and tradition are still stronger than he is.'"[33] In the struggle between the president's new federal machine and the traditional local organizations, the latter had won. Roosevelt failed to achieve the mastery he sought over the Democratic party and had to settle for a reluctant reconciliation with the Southern members of his party.

Part of the reluctant reconciliation was the passing by Congress and the signing by the president of an Act to Prevent Pernicious Political Activities, better known as the Hatch Act, in August 1939. As a result of WPA interference in the Barkley-Chandler primary, a Senate investigation, and the purge, Congress was alarmed at Roosevelt's attempts to exploit his executive authority to influence local elections. The Hatch Act, according to Paul Van Riper, "basically applied the restrictions on political activity effective for classified employees to unclassified employees other than those in top policy determining posts. In addition, the act strengthened existing regulations by further extending the definition of prohibited political activities to include those especially related to the administration of public welfare and relief. The penal provisions against pernicious political activity were reinforced by fines and imprisonment."[34] In the Hatch Act of 1940, prohibitions against partisan behavior were broadened to include state and local workers paid in full or in part by federal funds. One measurable effect of the Hatch Acts was that while approximately half of the 1,100 delegates at the 1936 Democratic convention held federal jobs, at the 1940 meeting, the only federal officials attending were Congress members and cabinet officers.[35] The significance of the two Hatch Acts is that the conservative coalition thwarted any temptation FDR might have had—planned or unplanned—to Tammanyize the national electoral system.

The FDR Electoral Coalition

While FDR was trying to transform the Democratic party into a liberal party, he was also trying to realign the electorate from one that normally voted Republican to one that usually voted Democratic. He hoped that the election of 1932 would be what scholars label a critical election, a turning point like the elections of 1800, 1828, 1860, and 1896, which ushered in new majority parties that provided significant changes in public policy. According to Brady and Stewart,

> Unlike the realignments of the 1850s and 1890s, the political evolution known as the New Deal was the product of a single event—the Great Depression. The underlying issue dimension that separated and distinguished the parties was the question of whether the government would actively deal with national economic problems. Hoover and the Republican party rejected strong government activity. The Democrats, while not entirely clear on which direction to move, had adopted an activist stance by 1932. Unlike the previous types of realignment, the New Deal realignment did not polarize the country along regional (North-South) or urban-rural lines.[36]

President Hoover played his ill-fated role in the realignment drama as the personification of the losing side. He may have had some progressive beliefs, but in 1932, Hoover clearly campaigned as a conservative, futilely defending a regime that needed major changes. Roosevelt may have used some conservative rhetoric in 1932, the most notorious being his promise to cut Hoover's budget by 25 percent, but his commitment to delivering a

New Deal for the American people was decidedly liberal. Voters in 1932 could not know what the New Deal would be like, but they did recognize that the Republican regime had not been able to prevent the Depression or find the means to lead us out of it. Hence, they voted against Hoover and gave FDR and his party the opportunity to bring about a realignment based on their governing success.

FDR played a vital role in the realignment because, in Barbara Sinclair's words, "in our system, only a president with his 'bully pulpit' can produce in the voters' minds an identification between policies and his party. In the case of the New Deal, much of the major legislation was developed in the executive branch. . . . Thus, it was Roosevelt who made the Democratic party the party of the new agenda in the eyes of the electorate."[37] By championing that new policy agenda, Roosevelt was able to mobilize and convert millions of voters into supporting the Democratic party. Between 1928 and 1936, the Democratic presidential vote soared from 15.0 to 27.8 million, while the Republican vote dwindled from 21.4 to 16.7 million. FDR was able to hold the Southern states, winning every state south and west of Pennsylvania in 1932, then carry every state but Vermont and Maine in 1936. His political skills allowed him to take advantage of both the "ethnic/ religious/cultural forces" that had emerged at the end of the 1920s and the class-based cleavages that originated in reaction to his prolabor policies in the second New Deal. In 1936, the electorate endorsed FDR's New Deal by reelecting him with 60.8 percent of the vote.[38]

FDR's leadership also changed the nature of the Democratic party in Congress. From 1925 to 1930, about two-thirds of Democratic House members were from the South, and the Democrats were usually the minority party, occupying less than one-third of the seats in the other regions. In 1930, the Democrats picked up 53 House seats; in 1932, Roosevelt's coattails helped the Democrats add 97 seats; in 1934, 9 seats; and in 1936, 11 seats. The Democrats controlled both houses of Congress throughout FDR's twelve years as president. In the 75th Congress (1937–1938), there were only 89 Republicans in the House and 16 Republicans in the Senate. Brady and Stewart used census data to show that "during the New Deal era (1932–1938) the Democrats made their greatest gains in industrial, urban, and blue-collar districts. . . . That is, within urban, labor, industrial districts, the Democrats went from about one third of the seats to about two-thirds."[39] Consequently, the influence of Southern Democrats declined (they now occupied less than 40 percent of the Democratic seats) while the proportion of House Democrats representing urban districts increased from 29 percent in 1931 to 46 percent in 1937. Beginning with the 74th Congress (1935–1936), Democratic majorities pressured Roosevelt from the left for more relief and reform.

The reform thrust of the New Deal was ended by the Congressional elections of 1938. Because of Roosevelt's defeats in trying to enlarge the Supreme Court and purge conservative Democrats and the rising unemployment due to the "Roosevelt recession" in 1937–1938, the Republicans enlarged their congressional representation for the first time since the 1928 elections. In 1938, the Republicans gained 81 seats in the House and 8 in the Senate. While more than 20 percent of Democratic incumbents in the House were defeated, no Republican incumbents lost their seats. In the House elections, Republicans picked up 45 seats from the Midwest and 27 from the Northeast. However, the Democrats still outnumbered the Republicans 69–23 in the Senate and 263 to 169 in the 76th Congress (1939–1940). And even after the Democratic losses in 1938, Roosevelt knew "he was the first two-term president since James Monroe who had not lost control of Congress before the end of his second term."[40]

A vivid illustration of the effects of FDR's leadership is provided in a public opinion poll Elmo Roper did for *Fortune* magazine in the spring of 1940. After more than seven years in office, after being targeted by numerous Republican accusations, and despite widespread public opposition to FDR's breaking the two-term tradition, the president was still the most popular presidential candidate among Democrats. Almost 36 percent of Democrats wanted him to be the party nominee again in 1940; his closest rival was Vice President John Nance Garner, who had the support of only 5.6 percent of Democratic voters. Among Republicans, Thomas Dewey was the most popular, with the support of almost 15 percent of party members. However, Roosevelt was more popular than all six of the Republican candidates listed in the survey combined. The Democratic party also had a 2-to-1 advantage over the Republicans in terms of having "the most real interest in the people as a whole."[41] In brief, FDR's party leadership during the 1930s did not allow any competitor's star—in either party—to shine as brightly as his own.

Conclusion

As a party leader, FDR successfully engaged in the politics of reconstruction by transforming the Democrats into a party of protest against the old regime as well as a party that could govern. He had the experience and political skills to take advantage of the cultural discontent frustrating the immigrant population from the 1920s and the economic misery caused by the Depression in the 1930s. The Depression was generating desperate cries for help from a variety of groups—cries to which the old regime could not respond. Roosevelt created a liberal regime that could and did respond. His New Deal became institutionalized because he created an electoral coalition that could win presidential and congressional elections and then pass legislation that provided sufficient measures of relief, recovery, and reform to maintain majority support. The New Deal was launched by the Depression, but Roosevelt had ambitions for his project to be much more than just a temporary emergency response to an economic catastrophe. He envisioned the New Deal as a governing arrangement that could prevent future Depressions by providing economic security for farmers, workers, homeowners, investors, and the elderly. In Roosevelt's mind, expanding economic security was also promoting social justice and equality that constituted a modern updating of our political tradition.

Providing economic security would also be good politics. FDR's political instrument to carry out this task was the Democratic party, which he tried to transform from a decentralized party responsible to local interests into a more centralized party responsible to a president that had been elected by a majority of the voters. Thus, Roosevelt created an electoral coalition consisting of white voters in the South and African Americans in the North, plus labor, ethnics, farmers, liberal intellectuals, and civil servants. This coalition was capable of winning elections, but it contained contradictions, including the white South and African Americans, which would eventually cause major problems. Roosevelt's new Democratic party, in Sundquist's words, "was issue-oriented, working-class based, even more urban-centered than before, activist, liberal, and wholly devoted to Rooseveltian leadership."[42]

Finally, while most scholars agree that FDR was a successful party leader, there are two criticisms of his party leadership that we should mention. James MacGregor Burns criticizes FDR for being too accepting of existing political forces and not being committed enough to changing them. As a brilliant tactician, Roosevelt could exercise a broker style of leadership that could respond successfully to the great variety of demands made on his administration. This kind of leadership can win elections and get watered-down legislation passed. Roosevelt could improvise brilliantly, but he lacked the unifying vision necessary for a transformative style of leadership, which requires a long-term commitment. Burns is frustrated because he believes the Depression offered a rare opportunity for a president to exercise a transformative leadership that FDR did not fully exploit.[43]

The second criticism comes from Raymond Moley, an original member of the Brains Trust. Moley describes a psychological process whereby FDR originally worked hard to learn how to be the progressive voice of the people, and then, after being elected and treated deferentially in the presidency, self-righteously believed he became that voice. Moley condemned FDR for failing to learn the lesson of Woodrow Wilson: "that the more a leader becomes obsessed with the idea that he speaks the people's will, the less able he is to divine that will."[44] It is an occupational hazard of occupying the Oval Office that in trying to hear the people's voices, the president will come to hear only his own. Moley believed that the disappointments of the second term were caused by Roosevelt's assuming that his landslide election proved he personified the will of the majority and that his motives were pure and his opponents' were selfish. Those attitudes are not conducive to rational political decision making.

12

Reagan's Reconstructive Party Leadership

Ronald Reagan was well suited to perform the role of a reconstructive party leader. As an actor, he relished performing the dramatic rituals—acceptance speeches at the Republican party national convention, the inaugural address, the state of the union addresses—that provide precious opportunities for the president to influence the public. As a former spokesman for General Electric, he knew how to reach and charm smaller audiences. As a former Democrat, he was skillful in persuading Democrats to take the difficult step of converting to Republican voters. And like FDR, Reagan was never embarrassed about the compromises and inconsistencies a party leader has to practice in order to win presidential elections. Once elected, the self-confident Reagan was sure that he would be able to fulfill his noble visions. Even without the benefit of a critical election victory that would have given the Republicans control of Congress, Reagan was able to unify the Republican party under a conservative banner dedicated to lowering tax rates, deregulating the economy, building up the military, and championing traditional values. With the Democrats controlling a majority of the seats in the House of Representatives throughout the 1980s, Reagan was not able to destroy the liberal regime, but he did slow its growth and construct a conservative edifice that proved popular with a wide variety of voters.

Reagan as Party Leader

Up until Reagan decisively beat President Carter in 1980, the FDR election coalition had been successful. When President Lyndon Johnson crushed Senator Barry Goldwater in the 1964 elections by almost 16 million votes, it appeared that liberalism was rejuvenated and conservatism was dead. Four years later, however, Johnson felt compelled to withdraw from the race, and Richard Nixon defeated Vice President Hubert Humphrey by a small margin. In 1972, leftist Democrats nominated Senator George McGovern, who was subsequently buried in an avalanche of votes (60.7 percent) for President Nixon. But even with the lopsided Republican victory, the Democrats maintained their majority control over Congress. Nixon's involvement in the Watergate scandal ruined any opportunity the Republicans had to develop the potential for an emerging Republican majority in the electorate. In 1976, a Southern moderate from Georgia, Jimmy Carter, earned the Democratic nomination and barely defeated President Gerald Ford. With Carter in the White House and Democrats controlling Congress, the party had one more chance to govern effectively and renew its mass appeal among the electorate. Carter failed miserably as a party leader, alienating millions of voters, who felt free to vote for a risky Republican in 1980.

By the 1970s, New Deal liberalism was largely a spent force. As both a partisan and public philosophy, it had guided Democratic politicians after World War II to promote policies that advanced economic growth, social mobility, and progress in social justice for minorities. But with the United States far more affluent than it had been in the 1930s, there was a need to update liberalism so that it could reflect the conditions of the 1970s and justify a new policy agenda. The new liberalism that emerged was not easy to define, but Everett Carl Ladd suggests,

> it places less emphasis upon economic well-being and security and is less materialistic [than the old liberalism]. It emphasizes civil liberties and civil rights. . . . It is less attentive to the demand for economic growth, stressing environmental costs of such growth. . . . The new liberalism shares the equalitarian commitments and flavors of the old . . . ; but its equalitarianism is more sensitized to the needs of the deprived (often ethnic) minorities. The new liberalism is attracted to the socially and culturally avant-garde, to experimentation and change in life styles, personal values and ethical or normative codes.[1]

When this renovated liberalism was offered to the American voter by George McGovern in 1972, it was overwhelmingly rejected. The Democratic party was stymied by its residual commitments to an obsolete liberalism and its inability to create a more relevant and viable new one.

By the mid- and late 1970s, the economic shocks of rising oil prices and stagflation, combined with the cultural conflicts concerning abortion, the Equal Rights Amendment, the rising crime rates, and prayer in the schools, began to exert enormous strains on the Democratic party. Many voters who had identified themselves as Democrats because they thought that the party best represented their interests began to have second thoughts, became alienated, and were eventually responsive to the persuasive rhetoric of Reagan. Blue-collar workers, whose jobs were threatened as companies increasingly manufactured their products in countries with cheaper labor, often thought that Democratic party leaders were more sensitive to minority needs than to theirs. White Southerners felt that Northern liberals had taken over their party and were championing the African American cause at their expense. White men perceived affirmative action programs as a threat to their future. The middle class felt imperiled by inflation, which lowered the value of the dollar and raised the amount they had to pay in income taxes. Citizens who were imbued with patriotic feelings were incensed by the war in Vietnam and the Iranian kidnapping of American embassy personnel. Religious fundamentalists felt endangered by secular humanist control of the public schools and liberal domination over the media. The optimism of the 1950s and the first half of the 1960s turned pessimistic in the 1970s. The pleasantly challenging issue of what to do with our economic abundance was transformed into dismal disputes over economic decline, coping with scarcity, and living within limits. Liberalism was losing its capability of generating mass appeal.[2]

The opposite was true of conservatism. Republicans and conservatives rebounded from the Goldwater debacle in 1964 and Nixon's Watergate scandal in 1972. Paul Allen Beck stresses that the rehabilitation of the Republican party owes a lot to William Brock, who became Republican National Committee (RNC) chairman in 1977. Brock focused his efforts on making the RNC "into a powerful fund-raiser and campaign resource for Republican candidates." Between 1977 and 1980, the RNC raised over $110 million, while the Democratic National Committee collected a little more than $26 million. Beck concludes, "By the 1980s, the Republican National Committee was a potent force for the recruitment of good candidates for a variety of offices, the professionalization of their campaigns, and the building of stronger grass-roots Republican organizations. . . . These efforts enabled the GOP to be an 'overachiever,' gaining more votes than its electoral base alone would have produced, and constituted an important investment in the future."[3] That investment paid dividends in the 1980s.

Republicans also recognized that they would have to repackage their conservative ideology if they were going to market it successfully to the electorate. Before Reagan, Republicans were advocating balanced budgets and fiscal austerity. Even Goldwater had opposed Kennedy's tax cut proposal in 1963 because he believed it would increase the budget deficit. Dinesh D'Souza suggests that there is little wonder that voters supported Democratic candidates' playing the role of Santa Claus by offering the public generous spending programs, while the Republicans followed a "Scrooge strategy," sometimes cutting benefits and raising taxes to fund Democratic programs.[4]

The major reason for the Republican party's success in the 1980s was its alliance with the New Right. According to Sundquist,

> The New Right is composed of the groups, organized or unorganized, who have been spawned by the crosscutting social and moral issues that arose in the 1960s—right-to-life organizations that sprang up after the Supreme Court's 1973 abortion decision, religious groups mobilized to protest the same court's decision barring organized prayer from public school classrooms, organizations formed to oppose gun control in any form, neighborhood groups opposed to bussing for purposes of school integration, inheritors of the anti–civil rights forces of the 1960s who resented what was perceived as government favoritism toward minorities, and so on.[5]

While espousing traditional values, New Right organizations were skillful in using the most modern communications techniques to locate and activate their supporters. These groups, particularly numerous in the South and West, provided the Republican party with votes, a growing stream of campaign contributions, and the zealous energy that comes from moral outrage. New Right leaders and Reagan were effective in mobilizing the multiple streams of discontent into a populous revolt against a common enemy, the liberal establishment, and for a common solution, electing Reagan president.

When Reagan and his conservative supporters took over the Republican party in 1980, most of its members were ecstatic. The party could finally display its true colors and proudly express its conservative beliefs; its presidential candidate could proclaim antigovernment sentiments with an eloquence that appealed to a wide variety of voters. From Reagan's point of view, the Democrats were the party of special interests who lacked any concept of the public interest. By emphasizing the shared values that had made America great, the Republicans were now the party of liberty and virtue.[6] Reagan was ready to follow in the footsteps of Jefferson, Jackson, Lincoln, and FDR and play the role of a reconstructive party leader.

According to James Q. Wilson, in the 1980 presidential campaign, for the first time since Teddy Roosevelt, it was the Republican party which promised fundamental change. In the past, the Republicans had represented "normalcy," business, and "the party of resistance [to liberal policies] alternating with periods of reluctant 'me-too-ism.' Under Eisenhower, it was the party of consensus and national unity. Under Goldwater, the challenge [to Democratic orthodoxy] was poorly developed, linked to the fortunes of a half-hearted and impolitic candidate, and widely regarded as expressing the deviant sentiments of an unimportant minority." However, with Reagan heading the ticket, the Republicans had "acquired a skillful spokesman, a vast (though quarrelsome) organizational network, the leading position in the public opinion polls, and—most importantly—an alternative vision of what American government and American society ought to be like."[7] The Democrats now appeared to be the party of timeworn proposals that did not work, while the Republicans were the party of new ideas that deserved an opportunity to be tested.

In the campaign against President Carter, Reagan built on the electoral achievements of Governor George Wallace and Richard Nixon. Both Wallace and Nixon had demonstrated that there were many disaffected Democrats who would respond to conservative messages. The Reagan campaign thus targeted white Southerners, blue-collar ethnics, evangelic Christians, and Roman Catholics. African Americans were ignored, as they had been since Goldwater's 1964 campaign. Carter and liberal Democrats were blamed for virtually every domestic and foreign problem. Carter was portrayed as a lethally weak leader, whose ineptitude had brought about double-digit inflation and the Iranian takeover of the U.S. embassy. Reagan was pictured as a decisive leader, whose simple solutions to reduce taxes, deregulate the economy, and increase military spending would end America's period of self-doubt. A key question was whether Reagan could overcome the contradiction of promising a massive three-year tax cut and a large military buildup without ballooning the budget deficit, which was believed to be fueling inflation. Reagan succeeded in escaping from this trap by using the elixir of supply-side economics, which predicted that its tax reductions would result in record-breaking economic growth. This growth would increase tax revenues and balance the budget by 1983.

In the 1980 elections, Reagan received 50.7 percent of the popular vote to Carter's 41 percent (John Anderson got about 6 percent). Reagan had earned 8.4 million more votes than the president. With Carter winning in only five states and the District of Columbia, Reagan won by an overwhelming margin of electoral college votes, 498–49. While Carter carried ten of eleven Southern states against President Ford in 1976, he won only in Georgia (his home state) in 1980. Carter received about 82 percent of the black vote, but there was a lower turnout of black voters than in 1976. Indeed, virtually every Democratic constituency had a lower voting turnout in 1980 than in 1976, which partially explains why Carter collected 5.3 million fewer votes against Reagan than against Ford. Exit polls indicated that 38 percent of Reagan's supporters were voting against Carter and only 11 percent for his conservative policies. Of those who voted for Reagan, 59 percent selected inflation as a determining issue. In congressional elections, the Republicans gained 33 seats, but the Democrats maintained control of the House of Representatives. The Republicans did gain majority control of the Senate for the first time since 1952 by picking up 12 seats.[8]

Four years later, President Reagan was challenged for reelection by Carter's vice president, Walter Mondale. In order to obtain the Democratic nomination, Mondale had to withstand the efforts of Senator Gary Hart, who claimed he could rejuvenate the party with his new ideas, and by Jesse Jackson, who declared that he represented the "rainbow coalition" of American diversity. Seldom in American history has a presidential candidate appeared more destined for humiliating defeat than the former Democratic senator from Minnesota. He was weighed down by the negative baggage of being labeled a tax-and-spend liberal who was overly beholden to special interests, particularly labor. He was also tied to the failures of the Carter administration—a relationship that Reagan's campaign message never let the voters forget.

The dilemmas that faced Mondale reflected the advantages of the Reagan-led Republican party. Democrats desperately need the black vote to win presidential elections; Republicans do not. African Americans were the one group in the FDR electoral coalition whose loyalty was not declining; they were the most likely to vote for Democratic candidates. Running in Democratic primaries, Jesse Jackson could mobilize more than 1.3 million new African American voters in the South, but he would also trigger a backlash of over 3 million new Southern white voters. As Jeremy Mayer points out, "Jackson's prominence played right into Republican plans to demonize the Democrats as captives of special interests."[9] The quandary for Mondale's campaign strategists was to formulate a message that would attract Northern working-class and Southern white voters without alienating blacks. Mondale hoped that by emphasizing issues of fairness, he could expand his support, but polls "found that many white voters saw fairness as a code word for handouts to undeserving blacks."[10] Mondale, despite his conflicts with Jackson, did earn about 90 percent of the African American vote in the 1984 election.

In both 1980 and 1984, Reagan was able to win large majorities of the white vote while generally avoiding the stigma of being considered a racist. The evidence concerning Reagan's racial attitudes is ambivalent. Lou Cannon writes, "I do not believe that Reagan was racially prejudiced in the normal meaning of the term. He had been taught by his parents that racial intolerance was abhorrent, and the many people I interviewed who knew him as a young man were unanimous in believing that he absorbed these lessons."[11] In Reagan's autobiography, he tells the story of inviting two of his black teammates from the Eureka College football team to stay at his home when they were refused admission at a hotel. One of these African Americans was William Franklin Burghardt, who remained friends with Reagan until his death in 1981.

In Reagan's own mind, he was not prejudiced; indeed, he saw himself as an unrecognized civil rights supporter. When questioned about his racial attitudes, he often became indignant and responded with anecdotes about his black teammates' being welcomed in his home and his support for Jackie Robinson's integrating baseball in 1947. However, he never supported the major civil rights laws of the 1960s because he claimed they were unconstitutional. Nor did his early political speeches ever reveal any knowledge, concern, or sensitivity about the shameful treatment of African Americans. In his 1968 campaign to gain the Republican nomination, he refused to condemn George Wallace's segregationist policies. In his 1980 presidential debate with President Carter, as noted by Mayer, Reagan made "a revealing gaffe, speaking of a time 'when this country didn't even know it had a racial problem.' As Jimmy Carter quickly pointed out, for the victims of racial oppression, there was no such halcyon era. . . . Reagan relentlessly used his private opposition to racial discrimination to mask his consistent failure to endorse public efforts to fight it."[12] For Reagan, the cure of using federal law to prevent Southern whites from discriminating against blacks was worse than the disease.

In 1976, while campaigning against President Ford in Republican primaries, Reagan frequently talked about a "welfare queen" in Chicago who was fraudulently using multiple names and addresses to steal money from the welfare system. Reagan never mentioned her name, which was Linda Taylor, or her race, which was African American, but few Democrats doubted that his frequent mentioning of this case in his speeches was a blatant appeal to racial stereotyping. Mayer adds, "Even after reporters pointed out the many errors and exaggerations in his welfare queen story, Reagan continued to tell his erroneous version, which was quite a crowd pleaser."[13]

In 1980, Reagan initiated his general election campaign in Neshoba, Mississippi, the place where three civil rights workers were brutally murdered in 1964. Despite being warned by several of his advisers to cancel his speech there because of the message it would convey, Reagan stubbornly insisted on delivering his talk on states' rights—"perhaps the hoariest of all southern code words. To promote states' rights in a county where men were murdered for advocating federal intervention carried a powerful message."[14] Such messages antagonized blacks but helped Reagan win an overwhelming majority of the Southern white vote in 1980 and 1984.

Reagan was running for reelection in 1984 under ideal conditions: peace, prosperity, and personal popularity. Perhaps because Reagan was more popular than his conservative policy positions, the president's campaign advisers, headed by James Baker, decided he could win by the largest margin by running an "issueless campaign." According to Cannon, "It was difficult for Reagan to be an 'issues candidate' in 1984 because he had failed to carry out his 1980 promise to balance the federal budget. . . . The combination of a continuing commitment to low taxes and high military spending made it impossible to pay even for existing programs, let alone new ones."[15]

In contrast to 1980, when Reagan's advisers were hesitant about using the most modern marketing techniques because they feared to do so would accentuate the candidate's ties to Hollywood, in 1984, the president's advertising was designed by a set of Madison Avenue experts called the Tuesday Group, who produced highly professional ads. As Lemann explains, based on successful campaigns for Pepsi-Cola and McDonald's, "the commercials used poignant music and soft sun-dappled scenes of life in a California small town as a way of conveying what Reagan had done for America."[16] America was back from the gloom of the Carter years; traditional values were restored; the nation was standing tall and proud. Although many conservatives were disturbed by Baker's issueless campaign because they believed there was so much more of the liberal regime to target and so much left to do in building a conservative one, Reagan was pleased by the lyrical commercials. In Cannon's words, "He was a salesman, and he valued the work that salesmen did. At the first White House meeting of his campaign advertisers . . . , Reagan poked his head in the door and said to them, 'Since you're the ones who are selling the soap, I thought you'd like to see the bar.'"[17] Reagan was both modest and self-centered.

As expected, Reagan trounced Mondale in the 1984 elections. He attracted almost 10.5 million more votes in 1984 than he did in 1980. Reagan received 58.8 percent of the popular vote and won the electoral college votes of forty-nine states. Mondale earned the electoral votes of only Minnesota, his home state, and Washington, D.C., which is overwhelmingly African American. Selecting Congresswoman Geraldine Ferraro as Mondale's running mate had little effect; Reagan won 56 percent of the female vote, six points less than his male total. In congressional elections, the Democrats lost 14 seats in the House, but maintained a majority of 253 to 182. In the Senate, the Republicans retained their majority but lost three seats. The electorate had obviously rewarded Reagan with a great personal victory; a large majority of voters had approved of his performance. However, because he had conducted an issueless campaign, many experts concluded that the president had "won a landslide without a mandate."[18]

Reagan's electoral success bolstered his role as party leader. As candidate and president, he had the skill to unite economic and social conservatives, which was the formula for the Republicans to replace the Democrats as the majority party. Under Reagan's leadership, Republican moderates were marginalized without the trauma of a party purge. Even a liberal critic like Garry Wills could marvel, "Every faction in the party can look to Reagan as their leader — the religious right, the tax cutters, the anti-regulators, the budget balancers, the defense spenders."[19] Milkis adds, "Reagan seemed to represent the forceful change to the New Deal that ardent conservatives had long awaited. Much more than Nixon, he presented himself in word and policy as the founder and first magistrate of a conservative political dynasty — as the Republican FDR."[20]

Just as FDR's presidency changed the public image of the Democratic party, so Reagan's leadership altered the perceptions of the Republican party. The Republicans were now seen as the party of economic growth, individual opportunity, military power, and social conservatism. According to Cavanagh and Sundquist, "The Republican party is no longer the party of austerity, the party of balanced budgets and tight money that, in its obsession with inflation, produced recessions under Presidents Eisenhower, Nixon and Ford. Its adoption of supply-side economics has given it a new rhetoric of growth and opportunity, and its policies have given priority to tax reduction for both individuals and corporations with an almost casual disregard for deficits far larger than those for which it used to castigate the Democrats."[21] The Republicans had finally buried the memory of Herbert Hoover—but not necessarily many of his ideas.

The Reagan Electoral Coalition

Because of the growing sophistication of polling methods, social scientists can measure the changes in electoral behavior more accurately in the Reagan era than in the FDR period. In the 1980s, we have a clearer picture of the voting habits of different groups within the electorate. But increased accuracy does not mean reduced controversy over interpretations of the electoral changes; indeed, as we shall see, the opposite is true.

One trend that is not subject to debate is that after Lyndon Johnson's landslide victory over Goldwater in 1964, the Republicans had a significant advantage in presidential elections. After George H. W. Bush's victory over Dukakis in 1988, Ladd wrote, "In the last six presidential elections—1968 to 1988—the Republicans garnered 53 percent of all the ballots cast, the Democrats just 43 percent. Only one previous extended set of elections was decided more decisively: the five from 1932 through 1948, when the Democrats won 55 percent of the vote to the Republicans' 43 percent."[22] These figures indicate that the FDR coalition was eroding and the electoral appeal of liberalism was declining. The Reagan coalition was being constructed; the electoral appeal of conservatism was expanding.

CBS/*New York Times* exit polls provide us with an excellent portrait of the Reagan electoral coalition.[23] Reagan won huge support from self-identified Republican voters, 86 percent in 1980 (in a three-way race) and 92 percent in 1984, while collecting a majority of votes from self-identified independents, 55 percent in 1980 and 63 percent in 1984, and attracting about a quarter of the vote from self-identified Democrats in 1980 and 1984. He was particularly popular with men, winning 55 percent of the male vote in 1980 and 62 percent in 1984. Among white voters, Reagan received 56 percent of the vote in 1980 and 64 percent in 1984. He was even more favored by Southern whites, gaining 61 percent of their vote in 1980 (against Carter, a Southern president) and 71 percent in 1984. White Protestants, a long-term Republican constituency, overwhelmingly endorsed Reagan, giving him 63 percent of their vote in 1980 and 72 percent in 1983. As for Catholics, an important constituency in the FDR coalition, Reagan captured 50 percent of their vote (to Carter's 42 percent) in 1980 and increased that to 54 percent in 1984. Reagan was even competitive among union household voters, earning 44 percent of their vote in 1980 and 46 percent in 1984. What was frightening to Democrats was that Reagan did so well with voters under thirty, gaining 43 percent of this group in 1980, one point less than Carter, and 59 percent in 1984. Reagan, the oldest man ever to run for the presidency, was the first Republican candidate in over fifty years to attract more younger voters than his Democratic opponent.[24] With young voters becoming alienated from the Democrats, was the Democratic party condemned to minority status for the foreseeable future?

Although the changes in voting behavior provided encouraging news for the long-suffering Republican party, it also presented a puzzle to political scientists. Was this the long-awaited and overdue electoral realignment? Walter Dean Burnham tries to answer this question by describing the basic characteristics of previous realignments: "Traditional realignments, in whichever partisan direction, . . . or over whatever issues, uniformly entailed the . . . control *by a single party* of all branches of the federal government and (usually) a preponderant majority of state legislative seats. . . . As well, all of them were marked either by very high turnout rates or (as in 1828 or the 1930s) by sharply increased levels of participation from very low bases in the preceding era."[25] What occurred during the 1980s is not compatible with this model of realignment. Electoral turnouts continued to be low during the 1980s; only 53 percent of eligible voters participated in the 1984 elections. The Democrats continued to control a majority of the state governments during the 1980s. Most significantly, the Democrats controlled the House of Representatives throughout the 1980s and regained control of the Senate in the 1986 elections. The Republicans did not achieve control of the Congress until the 1994 elections when, led by Newt Gingrich, they gained 53 seats in the House and 8 in the Senate and dominated both houses for the first time in forty years. Students of electoral politics generally agreed that significant changes were taking place, but they were not duplicating the Roosevelt realignment. In the 1980s, there was no critical election such as in 1932, when, with FDR heading the ticket, the Democrats had picked up 97 House seats. Reagan was popular, but he did not have the long coattails of a Roosevelt. Although the New Deal was strengthened by voters in the 1934 elections by gaining 9 seats, the Reagan Revolution was reprimanded in 1982 by losing 26 House seats. Hence, the New Deal was able to achieve major victories in 1935 (social security, the National Labor Relations Act), while the Reagan administration was forced to tread water in 1983.

Some political observers questioned whether a Roosevelt realignment was possible with the decline of party identification among the public and the rise of candidate-centered elections. At one time, party identification had been compared to religious affiliation because once someone defined him- or herself as being a Democrat or Republican, that identification tended to be durable and influential. By the 1970s, however, party identification was weaker than in the 1950s. The electorate had fewer strong partisans and more independents than before, and voters were more likely to defect or to split their tickets, choosing to vote for or against specific issues or candidates rather than adhering to the party line.[26] In both the 1980 and 1984 elections, for example, over 20 percent of those who voted for Reagan then split their ticket and supported Democratic candidates for Congress.[27]

There is a unique aspect to the policy realignment in the 1980s, namely, it seems to be a replay of the issues that dominated the 1930s. Cavanagh and Sundquist point out,

> The line of cleavage established in the 1930s has not been superseded by a new one cutting across the electorate in a different direction, carved by a fresh and powerful issue that arose to dominate political discussion—as the issue of slavery did in the 1850s, free silver in the 1890s, and relief of Depression hardship in the 1930s. The quarrel between the parties in 1984 centered on the same set of issues that impelled the New Deal realignment: What is the proper role of government? How big, how active, and how expensive should it be? How much should the haves be taxed for the benefit of the have-nots? How activist should the government be in redistributing wealth and income and opportunity from the more to the less favored and protecting citizens against the hazards of life.[28]

In the second round of this epic struggle, the advantage had shifted to the Republicans. Hoover's rhetoric was now declared by Reagan with eloquence and humor to an audience that was not drowning in the despair of the Depression. Because of the post–World War II prosperity, there was now a much larger proportion of haves to have-nots than there were in the 1930s. Unlike the 1930s, the vast numbers who made up the working population were now paying income taxes and were more likely to view themselves as the victims of taxes than as the beneficiaries of a new government program. In the New Deal, the few were being taxed to benefit the many; by the late 1970s, Republican rhetoric was exploiting the idea that the many were being taxed for the benefit of the few.

As a reconstructive party leader, Reagan was attempting to change not just the behavior of the voters but also the attitudes of the electorate. The evidence suggests that he was most successful in persuading voters to support *him*, less successful in mustering support for Republican Congress members, and least successful in getting the public to accept his conservative approach to major problems. Reagan won two presidential elections by large margins, but he was not capable of convincing the bulk of the public to end its New Deal propensity to see government as the appropriate response to many of its problems and instead to accept the conservative philosophy that the government was the source of so many of its problems.

There were many reasons to vote for Reagan other than his conservative philosophy. For example, in 1980, many independents and Democrats voted *against* Carter by casting their ballots for Reagan. In 1984, many voters thought that Reagan had earned their support by his performance in the White House; he deserved a second term because he was providing peace and prosperity. After analyzing the 1984 voting statistics, Warren Miller concludes, "the most dominant 'reason' for the growth of Republican strength appears to have resided in perceptions of personal attributes of Ronald Reagan, who, in this sector of the electorate, was ever more visible as a competent, moral, knowledgeable, inspiring leader."[29] In brief, Reagan was more popular than his party and his philosophy.

In the 1984 elections, the plurality of voters favored the Democrats over the Republicans "by 46 to 36 percent as the party more 'concerned with the needs and problems of people like yourself,' by 43 to 34 percent in running 'a government that is fair to all people,' and by a wide 54 to 24 percent when it comes to preserving social security and Medicare." The fairness issue was clearly Mondale's most potent weapon in 1984, but "it was overshadowed by approval of the Reagan administration's economic performance: the economy was considered a priority issue by 40 percent of the voters, exactly double the share concerned about fairness toward the poor."[30] However, these data do indicate the vulnerability of the Republican party and Reagan's conservative philosophy on the fairness issue.

There was less resistance to Reagan's conservatism than there was ambivalence toward it. Throughout the 1980s, despite Reagan's use of the bully pulpit condemning the vices of government and the virtues of private enterprise, the public continued "to view government as a persisting mix of the helpful and the harmful."[31] "The modal voter," according to Cavanagh and Sundquist, looks both ways on almost any issue: in favor of a strong defense but against militarism; for a tough stance against communism but against another Vietnam; for helping the deserving poor but not the undeserving; for increased spending for education, health and a variety of other services but against increased taxes; for economic development but without damage to the environment; for cutting budgets but not services; for the right to abortion in some circumstances but against complete freedom of choice; for progress by blacks but not at the expense of whites; for regulating the economy but not stifling enterprise with regulatory burdens.[32]

New Deal visions of how government should help citizens deal with their problems and conservative visions of how expensive and inefficient government can be exist side by side in the public's mind. After the Carter failures, Reagan exploited the public's skepticism of government, but he was not able to dislodge the public's reliance on the state to help it deal with problems. As Gary Jacobson wryly observes, "Americans clearly dislike intrusive, expensive 'big government;' they also clearly appreciate most of the programs that comprise it."[33] Reagan straddled the public's ambivalence to the welfare state and maintained his personal popularity by rhetorically condemning big government but not eliminating the policies that constitute the modern state. Voters reflected their ambivalence by supporting divided government (where one party controls the executive and the other dominates the legislature) throughout most of the 1980s and the 1990s. The result was a hybrid regime that was a mixture of liberal and conservative visions.

Conclusion

As a party leader, Reagan successfully engaged in the politics of reconstruction by transforming the Republicans into a party that could channel a number of economic and cultural discontents against liberalism as well as a party that could govern. By the end of the 1970s, the Democrats were handicapped by their pessimism, while the Republicans were energized by their optimism. While Carter was trying to teach Americans that we had entered an age of limits, Reagan assured the public that there were still boundless opportunities ahead. During the 1980s, the Democratic party was doubtful and insecure about its ideological direction while the Republicans, under the leadership of Reagan, were more confident about how and where they wanted to lead the nation. Reagan succeeded in expanding the appeal of conservatism and decreasing the attractiveness of liberalism. During his administration, more citizens defined themselves as conservative than liberal; most Republican politicians proudly claimed to be promoting conservatism; and many Democratic office seekers tried to avoid being labeled liberal.

By dealing successfully with stagflation, a problem that appeared insoluble in 1980, the Reagan administration provided economic growth with low inflation—an accomplishment that helped Reagan get reelected in 1984 by a landslide. By forging an alliance with the New Right, Reagan helped the Republicans become a truly national party that could maintain its traditional business and Protestant support, compete successfully in the South, and respectfully bid for working-class votes. There were obvious inconsistencies and conflicts in Reagan's electoral coalition between those who wanted to restrain the federal government in order to expand economic freedom and those who wanted to use public authority to enforce morality, but the verbally nimble Reagan easily maintained the loyalty of both groups.

Although strictly speaking there was never a critical election during the 1980s that catapulted the Republican party from minority to majority status, Reagan's leadership did help to bring about a decrease in Democratic identification from 41 percent of the electorate in 1980 to 36 percent in 1988, and increase Republican identification from 23 percent to 28 percent. Abramovitz points out, "The eight-percentage-point gap between Democratic and Republican identifiers in 1988 was the smallest in the 36-year history of the national election studies."[34] With this change, the Democrats were no longer close to winning elections by simply mobilizing their base; they now faced the tougher task of finding a way to broaden their appeal in order to attract the votes of independents and Republicans.

Reagan's politics and policies produced a more conservative Republican party and a more liberal Democratic party. Ironically, this polarization was one of FDR's goals; Reagan achieved it without the traumatic use of a purge. In the 1980s, the New Deal issues concerning the proper role of government in promoting economic security were still prominent in the party conflict, but now the Republicans had the advantage of public debates for three reasons. First, with the greater distrust of government after the failures of the 1970s, a smaller proportion of the public believed that government programs provided solutions. Second, many whites believed that liberal programs were financed by their taxes to appease undeserving minorities. Third, in round two of this ideological war, the conservative side was no longer articulated by a Herbert Hoover bearing the burden of the Depression; it was eloquently broadcast by a confident Reagan. There was truth in Tip O'Neill's partisan barb that Reagan was Hoover with a smile. But in the context of the mid-1980s, Reagan's message was bolstered by prosperity, and it resonated favorably with Americans who believed that economic growth and rising stock prices would help them fulfill the material component of the American Dream.

The results of Reagan's party leadership were spectacular for himself, impressive for his party, and mixed in terms of altering the belief systems of the voters. A majority of voters were willing to vote for Reagan in 1980 and 1984, but they remained as ambivalent and divided about the role of government at the end of the decade as they were at the beginning. Because Reagan was effective in making citizens more conscious of themselves as taxpayers than as beneficiaries of public policies, it was easy for him to sell the advantages of tax cuts. What he could not peddle was any significant retreat from liberal policies. He could not dislodge the New Deal concerns for economic security that have been embedded in the minds of so many voters. Given the popularity of many liberal policies, such as social security, unemployment insurance, Medicare, and environmental protection, if Reagan had militantly pursued the logic of his philosophy and attempted to eliminate New Deal and Great Society programs, his popularity would have plummeted. The pragmatists and public relations experts on Reagan's staff made sure it was never seriously attempted.

The public's ambivalence toward the welfare state was reflected in the fact that by the end of the 1980s, a majority of the public supported divided government, in which one party controlled the executive branch and the other dominated the legislature. Both New Deal visions about the need for economic security and conservative visions about the desire for economic freedom continue to exist in the minds of voters, lending support to the hybrid regime that exists today. Such ambivalence suggests that a replay of liberal and conservative conceptions of the public interest will continue.

Conclusion

Reconstructive presidents, such as Jefferson, Jackson, Lincoln, FDR, and Reagan, are key actors in American political development because they have received the widest warrants of authority to repudiate the old regime and to create a new one. I have defined a regime as a temporary institutional arrangement, guided by a political philosophy and supported by an electoral coalition that dominates the policy agenda for a period of time. The U.S. Constitution is flexible enough to allow a succession of regimes to develop, disintegrate, and be reconstructed without the violence of revolutions. Because they created regimes, Roosevelt and Reagan have had more significant and prolonged impacts than any other presidents of the twentieth century.[1] We are still living in a period in which the age of Roosevelt competes with—and in some ways is being replaced by—the age of Reagan.

While Skowronek suggests that the increasing number of entrenched institutions and interests in the past one hundred years reduced the ability of reconstructive presidents to bring about fundamental reforms, I argue that they will continue to play a major role in bringing about regime changes. It is true that it has become more difficult for reconstructive presidents to destroy components of the old regime, which means that aspects of the old order will persist in the new one. Hence, the revised role of reconstructive leaders is to do more denouncing of the old regime rather than destroying its different elements. But the most ambitious politicians still compete to reside in the White House; and presidential campaigns still require candidates to gauge where we are as a nation and whether we should remain on the same path (extend the existing regime) or veer in a different direction (create a new regime). Reconstructive presidents still have the authority and power to create the new bursts of reform energy needed to overcome the drag of tired regimes and to perceive the better life that can be achieved by a new, dynamic regime.

Skowronek points out that presidents like Herbert Hoover and Jimmy Carter, who come into office affiliated with a vulnerable regime, will engage in the politics of disjunction. Operating in this context, presidents are destined to see their prodigious efforts fail because they can neither completely support the rectitude of the existing regime nor effectively repudiate it. With the social base of the old regime eroding, and unable to attract new support, these chief executives are in a no-win situation. Their attempts to legitimize their authority by claiming outstanding administrative skills has a lethal tendency to boomerang on them as they become the personalized symbols of the failed regime. In Burnham's words, "Repudiation of the last President in this sequence [the cycle of political time] will go far beyond the personal level; it will involve rejection of the Old Order itself."[2] Presidents practicing the politics of disjunction inevitably become portrayed as the problem and forfeit the possibility of being viewed as the solution. In acknowledging the need for reform, Hoover and Carter alienated old supporters, failed to attract new ones, helped to delegitimate their regimes, and paved the way for their reconstructive successors.

In Chapters 2 and 3, I tell the story of how the Republican regime was overpowered by the Depression in the 1930s and how the liberal Democratic regime was eroded by the problems and frustrations of the 1970s. Neither Hoover nor Carter was able to save his regime or prevent the election of a leader dedicated to creating a new one. The destiny of disjunctive politics to bring about failure for its practitioners is reflected in the tragic fates of Hoover and Carter. Despite Hoover's outstanding record as a humanitarian, FDR was able to label him as an icy, uncaring man who was not willing to help the victims of the Depression. Despite Carter's intense religious commitment, he was deserted by many religiously motivated voters in 1980, who shifted their support to a candidate who believed in astrology.

Roosevelt was born on a luxurious Hudson River estate and educated at Groton, Harvard, and Columbia, whereas Reagan was born above a bakery in Tampico, Illinois, and educated at Eureka College; they obviously had very different backgrounds. Nevertheless, a number of interesting comparisons can be made. Both FDR and Reagan were close to their mothers and grew up to be secure, optimistic adults. Each had lots of acquaintances but few intimate friends. Both men had simple religious beliefs and saw themselves as leaders motivated by moral concerns. Each of them was considered lucky by contemporaries, although Roosevelt suffered from the paralysis of polio and Reagan was raised by an alcoholic father and was seriously wounded in the third month of his presidency. Both men were resilient, which is essential for the success of a reconstructive leader. Both FDR and Reagan had a propensity to overestimate their ability to "reconcile the irreconcilable," a characteristic that helped them construct electoral coalitions. The intelligence of both men was questioned, FDR's by Walter Lippmann, Reagan's by *Doonesbury*. In performing the reconstructive role, FDR felt confident because he believed he had the wisdom to find the best political solution; Reagan was confident because he believed his conservative ideology provided the correct answer. Both men attempted to change what Americans thought about the legitimate role of government. FDR tried to convince the public that the Depression demonstrated the limitations of unregulated capitalism and that the country ought to rely more on the modern liberal idea that experts in the administrative state could formulate rational solutions to many of the nation's problems without endangering democracy. Reagan tried to educate citizens that the rise of the positive state was the road to totalitarianism; he urged Americans to roll back the growth of the state and shift their support to the magic of the marketplace, which would provide prosperity and preserve freedom. For Reagan, FDR's concept of—and belief in—enlightened public administration was probably inconceivable.

All presidents need help to perform their multirole job, but this is particularly true for reconstructive leaders. They need advisers who can point out the vulnerable components of the old regime, help their chief executive imagine a better America, and suggest the key policies that are both feasible and will have a major effect in creating the foundations of the new regime. FDR was exceptionally skillful in attracting a variety of advisers with adventurous minds who would keep him on the political offensive through most of the 1930s. Although the range of people FDR consulted was breathtaking, I examine the contributions of only six of his many advisers: Raymond Moley, Rexford Tugwell, and Adolf Berle (the Brains Trust); and Henry Morgenthau, Henry Wallace, and Harry Hopkins. Even within this small group, there were great differences of opinion concerning the best way to bring about relief, recovery, reform, and realignment. FDR created an advisory system that provided him with multiple options, but his procedures meant New Dealers spent considerable time fighting one another to win the president's support. Roosevelt was notoriously promiscuous in seeking advice, transferring his reliance from one favorite to another. At different times, his top advisers included Moley, Lewis Douglas, Donald Richberg, Thomas Corcoran, and especially Hopkins. As the "speediest spender" in the administration, Hopkins helped to convey a favorable contrast with the Hoover presidency: the New Deal was both activist and compassionate.

Blessed with the unfailing wisdom of hindsight, we can see that one option that neither FDR nor his advisers seriously considered was the rejuvenation of capitalism. Most New Deal policies talked about restricting production instead of increasing it. Adolf Berle was Roosevelt's most knowledgeable economic adviser, and in the Commonwealth Club speech of September 1932, which Berle wrote for the candidate, it was stressed that our industrial plant was already built and that the present challenge was to administer what we were producing in a more equitable way. The normally optimistic FDR was not sanguine about the dynamic qualities of capitalism until World War II. This blind spot prevented him from being able to restore business confidence in the 1930s.

FDR was clearly the command center of the New Deal. No one could claim that any advisers were preventing Roosevelt from being Roosevelt. He considered himself to be the quarterback—the leader who called the plays and was the star of the team. He immersed himself in the details of both policy and politics, but he knew that he was particularly gifted in the game of politics. As a practical politician, one who had witnessed the machinations of Tammany Hall in New York, he understood that politics frequently trumped ideology. As a progressive, he wanted to outdo the achievements of Theodore Roosevelt and Woodrow Wilson, and he recognized that the severity of the Depression offered him the grandest opportunity to accomplish that. FDR did not consider these orientations—practical politician and progressive reformer—to be conflicting; indeed, he believed they were both essential for presidential success. In James MacGregor Burns's words, "He would use the tricks of the fox to serve the purposes of the lion."[3] In brief, Roosevelt was comfortable using Machiavellian means to obtain liberal policies promoting social justice—and electoral victories.

The Reagan White House was designed to avoid the mistakes of the Carter presidency: it had a chief of staff who helped the new president focus on his strategic priorities: tax cuts, budget reductions, and a defense buildup. Reagan had the most successful initial year in office since FDR's first hundred days. But even though Reagan's advisers were all conservative, there was still a considerable amount of strife among them. I classified Reagan's advisers into three groups: conservatives, who provided the administration with energy and ideological direction; pragmatists, who supplied the administration with experience and the knowledge of how to get things done in Washington; and public relations practitioners, who furnished strategies on how to maintain high public approval ratings for the president.

As chief of staff in Reagan's first administration, James Baker was the leader of the pragmatic faction. He emphasized that Reagan was the visionary leader, while his task was to be a realist by instructing the president about what was politically feasible. Baker and his public relations allies such as Michael Deaver were more concerned with achieving electoral victories and higher public approval ratings for Reagan than in taking higher risks to attain a greater variety of major conservative policy changes. Most pragmatists were content that the Reagan administration had corrected some of the problems of the 1970s by establishing more market-oriented policies and by slowing down the growth of federal expenditures. The pragmatists in Reagan's administration were the personification of Skowronek's concept of the waning of political time. By stressing what could be realistically accomplished and the need for compromise, they guided Reagan toward implicitly accepting much of the liberal regime. Baker was viewed as a villain by conservatives, however, because they believed that he watered down the president's visions and was not letting Reagan be Reagan. For many conservatives, the true Reagan would lead a revolution: liberal programs would be abolished rather than having their appropriations reduced one year, then incrementally increased the next.

Reconstructive presidents create a key set of policies that manifest their philosophy and commitments. Given the experimental and changing nature of FDR's politics, which is sometimes expressed in the concepts of the first, second, and third New Deals, not everyone will agree that it was disciplined by strategic priorities. Nevertheless, I argue that the New Deal stumbled its way toward a set of governmental programs with an overriding purpose. Although many conservatives condemn the New Deal for its commitment to equality, the guiding light for the liberal regime was security. As the New Dealers saw it, the Depression exposed the fact that competitive markets could not supply security to farmers, bank depositors, workers, and elderly citizens; thus, it was now the new duty of the federal government to increase its size and authority to protect citizens from the hazards of modern life.

In Roosevelt's second inaugural address, after declaring himself dissatisfied with "one-third of a nation ill-housed, ill-clad, and ill-nourished," he professed a liberal standard of performance: "The test of our progress is not whether we add more to the abundance of those who have much, it is whether we provide enough for those who have too little."[4] By providing security for important sectors of society, Roosevelt hoped his policies would prevent another Depression (they did) and institutionalize a liberal regime economically and politically (they did until the late 1970s).

For many reasons, the most potent core policy developed by FDR was Social Security: it was popular as well as opposed by Republicans; it created a new constituency of retired citizens who remained loyal to the Democratic party for many years; it had its own financing mechanism; and it was expandable.

Although there is debate over whether the New Deal had a set of core policies, there is a general consensus that Reagan's domestic priority was cutting taxes. Although FDR claimed he did not believe in cure-alls, Reagan did: the positive effects of reducing taxes. It is amazing how much mileage Reagan derived from his simple idea that taxes were too high. That conviction helped transform him from an ardent New Dealer to a committed conservative; it unified the Republican party; by promising tax reductions to everyone, it broadened Reagan's appeal to the public as a conservative populist; in fulfilling that promise, it corroborated his reputation as a conviction politician; it promoted an outstanding period of economic growth after 1982; it carried with it Reagan's expectation that decreased taxes would compel the federal government to decrease its size; and it kept the Democrats on the defensive throughout the 1980s. One of Reagan's major conservative achievements was to convince many Americans that the progressive income tax was not promoting equality; by taxing success at higher rates, it was blocking the social mobility necessary for the fulfillment of the American Dream. Reagan and many of his advisers hoped that the administration's tax policy would expand the allure of the Republican party in the same manner as the Social Security issue helped the Democrats in the 1930s.

The cost of Reagan's political success arising from his tax policy, however, was that he was never able to balance the budget, the nation was burdened with a major increase in the national debt, and the tax system had its limited redistributive capability curtailed even more. As David Stockman lamented, Reagan did not understand the relationship between the tax code and the budget. The president "could not grasp that to fiddle significantly with the former was to change the numbers in the latter—and for the worse."[5] Given Reagan's economic beliefs and optimism, he never accepted the fact that cuts in taxes meant reductions in revenue. He also created a knee-jerk propensity for Republicans to toss tax breaks at problems in much the same way as liberal Democrats were prone to throw money at problems in the 1960s. Finally, neither Reagan nor most Republican politicians were able to acknowledge the reality that tax cuts were not producing balanced budgets, a smaller federal government, or increases in the propensity of Americans to save.

The embryo of an administrative state was emerging under Hoover's Republican regime, but it was like an uninvited guest at a dinner party, a presence the Republicans preferred to ignore. FDR wanted to recognize the guest as one of the family who was performing essential services. For him and many New Dealers, the administrative state was a necessary and proper addition to the American political system. As societies became more complex, their governments had to increase their administrative capabilities in order to promote the general welfare. The Depression demonstrated that we could not depend on business leaders and markets to provide prosperity; we needed the enlightened and compassionate administration of a more centralized government. This transformation from a regime that mainly aided large corporations to one that took a broader and more balanced view of the public interest was not a threat to American political traditions.

As explained by Roosevelt in his second inaugural speech, government is "the instrument of our united purpose to solve for the individual the ever-rising problems of a complex civilization." Government had the "innate capacity" to protect Americans from disasters while citizens still retained their voting rights. The rise of the positive state was not a threat to democracy; it was simply "a new chapter in our book of self-government."[6] Roosevelt was trying to convince Americans to overcome their traditional distrust of centralized government and view it as the agent of their preferences, as certified in free elections. Despite FDR's skills as a communicator, he achieved only a partially legitimated state.[7] Americans wanted the benefits of the welfare state, but they were uneasy about the bureaucratic costs. Most Americans did not want the federal government to dominate the capitalist economy; nor did they want a completely unregulated private sector.

Republicans were understandably bitter about FDR's policies and politics. He had dislodged them from their role as a majority party that ruled to a humiliating minority status that whined on the sidelines; he blamed their policies for the Depression; and he was urging progressive Republicans to join his party so that future elections would be more clear-cut contests between liberal Democrats and conservative Republicans. Republicans argued that by touting the role of an expanding bureaucracy as the solution to our economic problems, he was shattering the business confidence that we needed to depend on for an authentic recovery. They believed that New Deal policies to reform capitalism were un-American and would inevitably lead to totalitarianism. They dogmatically asserted that the growth of the federal bureaucracy automatically brought about the regimentation of American life.

For Republicans, federal intervention into a new policy area meant the eventual federal domination of that policy space. New Deal efforts to provide relief, jobs, and shelter for the victims of the Depression were interpreted as attempts to "Tammanyize" the nation for partisan purposes. In their view, FDR was not providing enlightened administration; he was creating a politicized administrative state that would help Democrats win elections but inhibit economic recovery. By elevating both his own personal status and that of his office (whereby he created what is now known as the modern presidency), Republicans charged that he was lowering the role of legislators, judges, and citizens to subjects. Although FDR argued that he was preventing dictatorship by showing that our democratic government could respond effectively to citizen needs, Republicans retorted that by centralizing authority in his hands, he was violating the separation of powers doctrine that was the foundation of American democracy.

Although FDR clearly beat the Republicans until the 1938 elections, his interaction with the Supreme Court was more complex. Since Roosevelt was not able to place any new justices on the Court during his first term, the Court was the last bastion of the Republican regime's values. In 1935 and 1936, the justices grimly accepted the role of conservative judicial activists determined to block the creation of a liberal regime by declaring the Agricultural Adjustment Act and the National Industrial Recovery Act unconstitutional. At the end of 1936, despite FDR's landslide reelection, it looked like the Court was ready to strike down Social Security, the National Labor Relations Act, and the Tennessee Valley Authority, which would essentially destroy the New Deal. FDR proposed to enlarge the number of justices on the Supreme Court from nine to fifteen. The usually politically astute president stumbled badly in this case by declaring he was trying to help the elderly justices with their workload, when everyone understood he was angry at their decisions and wanted to pack the Court so that it would accept the constitutionality of New Deal legislation.

Roosevelt lost the battle to enlarge the Court when the Senate voted against him, but he won the war when Justice Owen Roberts switched his vote, thus making it possible for New Deal legislation to muster majority support. The Supreme Court now accepted the legitimacy of the New Deal and switched its agenda to protecting the rights of minorities, a subject area that Roosevelt had been reluctant to engage in because it would alienate his white Southern constituents. Ironically, the future success of liberal judges in expanding the rights of minorities, women, homosexuals, and suspected criminals would be a major cause for splitting the FDR electoral coalition, thereby helping the New Right attract support in the 1970s and 1980s.

Although FDR legitimated the New Deal largely through multiple activities, Reagan accomplished the same task by solving the problem of stagflation. In the contest between society's propensity to generate problems and government's effort to cure them, this was a rare victory. Reagan's tax policies, combined with Paul Volcker's monetary policy as chairman of the Federal Reserve, provided a long period of economic growth, 18 million new jobs, and low inflation. A key component of the new conservative regime was treating inflation, not unemployment, as economic enemy number one. According to George Will, when Reagan became president in 1981, "prudent people were worried that inflation was the systemic disease of democracies. That is, democracies could not resist deficit spending, and would use inflation as slow motion repudiation of their deficits. Furthermore, democracies, with low pain thresholds could not endure the pain involved in wringing inflation from the system."[8] But the Reagan-Volcker policy of the 1980s showed that if you could prevent inflation, the nation would reap the benefit of a longer phase of economic growth in the business cycle. In short, confronting inflation was as important for Reagan's success as dealing with unemployment was for FDR's.

Reagan's visions were only partially successful and certainly did not produce what his most exuberant supporters labeled the "Reagan Revolution." When Reagan and his supply-side supporters came to power, they euphorically expected that their tax cuts would both stimulate the economy and shrink the federal government by reducing its funding. Once their candidate was in office, however, confronting a Democratically controlled House throughout the 1980s, it was more politically feasible to cut taxes than to slash expenditures. In 1980, federal taxes constituted 19 percent, and federal expenditures 21.4 percent, of the gross domestic product. By 1989, taxes constituted a slightly lower 18.5 percent, while expenditures remained at 21.4 percent of a considerably larger gross domestic product.[9] Despite Reagan's rhetoric opposing big government, he eliminated few programs and succeeded only in slowing down the growth of federal spending (adjusted for inflation) from about 4 percent a year during the Carter years (1979–1981) to about 2.5 percent during the 1980s.[10] One could plausibly argue that the Reagan Revolution legitimized itself to many citizens by demonstrating that it was not a revolution. Reagan inherited an inflation-battered economy from Carter and bequeathed a deficit-burdened economy to his successor, George Bush.

The evidence also suggests that cuts in tax rates did not bring about supply-side miracles. What seemed so clear to Reagan—namely, that lowering tax rates would dramatically increase the savings rate—turns out not to be true in the real world.[11] Consequently, the United States became more dependent on foreign capital during the 1980s and experienced a decline in status from a creditor to a debtor nation.

A reconstructive leader has to have the political skills to mobilize several streams of grievances into an electoral coalition capable of winning a series of elections. Coming from the diversified state of New York, and owning a home in Warm Springs, Georgia, Roosevelt had the experience and talent to exploit the cultural frustrations of the emerging immigrant population and the economic torments caused by the Depression. As an educator, FDR strove to convert his party's philosophy from Jeffersonian liberalism, which stressed limited government and states' rights, to a more positive liberalism, which emphasized the capabilities of the federal government to provide beneficial services. As a party leader, Roosevelt tried to change his decentralized organization, accountable to local interests, into a mechanism more obligated to the president. As a visionary politician, Roosevelt saw that the Depression not only weakened the Republican party, but also provided a rare opportunity to reconstruct America. He was determined that the New Deal be more significant than just a temporary, emergency response to the Depression. Roosevelt wanted his reforms institutionalized so that they could prevent future collapses and promote a more socially just America by expanding economic security.

To the surprise of Democrats, who continually underestimated Reagan, the ex-actor was an excellent party leader. Unlike the Republicans in the 1930s, who demonized FDR, the Democrats in the 1980s ridiculed

Reagan. Neither strategy worked. Democrats were so prone to attribute Reagan's success to his communication skills, to his public relations staff, and to pure luck that they did not recognize his political talents or comprehend that he was articulating a message that was attracting many of their constituents. Reagan was effective in portraying the Democrats as a party of quarreling special interests who lacked any concept of the public interest. The Democrats were shocked and unprepared when Reagan, allied with the New Right, was able to mobilize multiple streams of discontent into a populous revolt against the liberal establishment. Reagan's leadership unified the Republicans into a national party that held its traditional business and Protestant support, competed successfully in the South, and attracted a significant proportion of working-class votes. The Republicans, overcoming the negative reputations of Hoover and Goldwater, were now viewed as the party of prosperity, opportunity, optimism, national security, and traditional values.

Reagan also succeeded in making the Republicans more consistently conservative and the Democrats more consistently liberal, which, oddly enough, was one of FDR's unfulfilled goals. However, although Reagan won two presidential elections by landslides, he was never able to lead the Republicans to majority control in the House of Representatives. Democrats were on the defensive throughout the 1980s, but they did have the votes to preserve most of the programs associated with the liberal regime.

Finally, although Reagan was persuasive in making Americans identify themselves as taxpayers rather than as beneficiaries of public policies, he was less effective in dislodging their dependence on federal programs. Scholars of public opinion have long noted that the American public is frequently ideologically conservative but operationally liberal, which means that although Americans express fears about big government and high taxes, they also want to expand — not simply maintain or cut — programs such as Social Security and Medicare, as well as those that protect the environment.[12]

When both FDR and Reagan entered office, they were confronted with baffling problems that overwhelmed their predecessors and fatally wounded the existing regime. But they were also assuming power in a context that gave them the rare opportunity to circumvent the usual constraints of our political system and produce major changes in the nation's policies and politics. Roosevelt and Reagan are important presidents, worthy of intense study, because they and their advisers had visions about how America should overcome its present crisis and create the type of regime that could promote progress for the foreseeable future. For FDR, the Republican regime that relied on private market solutions and discouraged the federal government from intervening was the problem; the solution was an activist, compassionate, and expert-led set of federal programs that would provide economic security. For Reagan, the federal government was not the solution; it was the problem. The solution was to rely more on competitive markets by cutting tax rates, deregulating the economy, and reducing the role of government to its basic functions.

FDR's presidency tended to overestimate the capabilities of the federal government and underestimate the potential of private enterprise; the opposite was true for Reagan's. FDR's New Deal and LBJ's Great Society are entrenched in legislation, budget lines, and Social Security trust funds. Reagan's conservative regime is entrenched in the tax code. Each of the regimes generated disturbing questions. Was a liberal regime capable of developing a rational administrative state that would not threaten democracy and inhibit economic growth? Would not a conservative regime's reliance on tax cuts result in increasing concentrations of income and wealth? Conservatives claimed that the underlying strategy of the New Deal was to tax, to spend, and to elect. Democrats countered that the operative strategy of the Reagan Revolution was to spend, to borrow, and to elect.

A reconstructive president's influence transcends his time in office. Because of his mythical status as the father of a regime, his visions guide the behavior of subsequent presidents and legislators. The fulfillment of FDR's New Deal could be felt when Lyndon Johnson's Great Society championed Medicare, Medicaid, and the war on poverty; Reagan's influence could be seen in Newt Gingrich's Contract with America victory in the 1994 congressional elections, which set the stage for a conservative-inspired welfare reform that President Clinton felt compelled to sign in 1996. In brief, our policies and politics are still profoundly affected by the clashing visions of FDR and Reagan concerning the appropriate roles of the public and private sectors.

NOTES

Chapter 1. Reconstructive Presidents as Principal Agents of Regime Change

1. Stephen Skowronek, "Response," *Polity* 37 (Spring 1995): 518.

2. Citing Abraham Lincoln, Stephen Skowronek, *The Politics Presidents Make: Leadership from John Adams to George Bush* (Cambridge, Mass.: Belknap Press of Harvard Unversity Press, 1993), 198.

3. Ibid., 52.

4. Joseph Ellis, *Founding Brothers: The Revolutionary Generation* (New York: Alfred A. Knopf, 2000).

5. Skowronek, *Politics*, 9–10.

6. Eldon J. Eisenach, "Reconstituting the Study of American Political Thought in a Regime-Change Perspective," *Studies in American Political Development* 4 (1990): 224.

7. Karren Orren and Stephen Skowronek, "Regimes and Regime Building in American Government: A Review of Literature on the 1940s," *Political Science Quarterly* 113 (Winter 1998–1999): 697.

8. Ibid., 696.

9. John Karaagic, *Between Promise and Policy: Ronald Reagan and Conservative Reformism* (Lanham, Md.: Lexington Books, 2000), 260.

10. Skowronek, *Politics*, xiv.

11. John W. Kingdon, *Agendas, Alternatives and Public Policies*, 2nd ed. (New York: Harper and Collins, 1995), 23, 69.

12. James MacGregor Burns, *Roosevelt: The Lion and the Fox* (New York: Harcourt, Brace, 1956), 197.

13. Terry Moe, "The Politicized Presidency," in *The New Directions in American Politics*, ed. John E. Chubb and Paul E. Peterson (Washington, D.C.: Brookings Institution, 1985), 242.

14. Allan J. Lichtman, "Critical Election Theory and the Reality of American Presidential Politics, 1916–1940," *American Historical Review* 81 (April 1976): 343.

Chapter 2. The Collapse of the Republican Regime

1. Stephen Skowronek, *The Politics Presidents Make: Leadership from John Adams to George Bush* (Cambridge, Mass.: Belknap Press of Harvard University Press, 1993), 39.

2. Ibid., 40.

3. Ibid.

4. Eugene White, "The Stock Market Boom and Crash of 1929 Revisited," *Journal of Economic Perspectives* (Spring 1990): 69; Carolyn Webber and Aaron Wildavsky, *A History of Taxation and Expenditure in the Western World* (New York: Simon and Schuster, 1986), 446; John Steele Gordon, *The Great Game: The Emergence of Wall Street as a World Power* (New York: Simon and Schuster, 1998), 224.

5. Michael Parrish, *Anxious Decades: American Prosperity and Depression, 1920–1941* (New York: W. W. Norton, 1992), 57.

6. Arthur M. Schlesinger Jr., *The Crisis of the Old Order, 1919–1933* (Boston: Houghton Mifflin, 1957), 69.

7. John Steele Gordon, *An Empire of Wealth: The Epic History of American Economic Power* (New York: Harper Collins, 2004), 307.

8. Parrish, *Anxious Decades*, 34, 37.

9. Gordon, *Great Game*, 224; Parrish, *Anxious Decades*, 40.

10. Cited by Parrish, *Anxious Decades*, 78–81.

11. Lendel Calder, *Financing the American Dream: A Cultural History of Consumer Credit* (Princeton, N.J.: Princeton University Press, 1999), 18; Gordon, *Great Game*, 226.

12. Parrish, *Anxious Decades*, x.

13. John M. Rothgeb Jr., *United States Trade Policy: Balancing Economic Dreams and Political Realities* (Washington, D.C.: Congressional Quarterly Press, 2001), 33.

14. David Hamilton, *From New Day to New Deal: American Farm Policy from Hoover to Roosevelt, 1928–1933* (Chapel Hill: University of North Carolina Press, 1991), 46.

15. Parrish, *Anxious Decades*, 87.

16. Robert S. McElvaine, *The Great Depression: America, 1929–1941* (New York: Times Books, 1984), 37.

17. Ibid., 39.

18. Parrish, *Anxious Decades*, 81.

19. Mitchell Zuckoff, *Ponzi's Scheme: The True Story of a Financial Legend* (New York: Random House, 2005).

20. William E. Leuchtenburg, *The Perils of Prosperity, 1914–1932* (Chicago: University of Chicago Press, 1958), 184.

21. Parrish, *Anxious Decades*, 228.

22. Ibid., 231.

23. McElvaine, *Great Depression*, 43–44.

24. Maury Klein, *Rainbow's End: The Crash of 1929* (New York: Oxford University Press, 2001), 159, 183.

25. Gordon, *Empire*, 312.

26. Klein, *Rainbow's End*, 62–63.

27. Donald Kettl, *Leadership at the Fed* (New Haven, Conn.: Yale University Press, 1986), 35.

28. Klein, *Rainbow's End*, 227.

29. White, "Stock Market Boom," 74.

30. Kettl, *Leadership*, 35–36.

31. Klein, *Rainbow's End*, 194.

32. Ibid., 205.

33. Ibid., 213–14. See also David M. Kennedy, *Freedom from Fear: The American People in Depression and War, 1929–1945* (New York: Oxford University Press, 1999), 37.

34. Cited by Klein, *Rainbow's End*, 226.

35. George D. Green, "Great Depression," in *Franklin D. Roosevelt: His Life and Times: An Encyclopedic View*, ed. Otis L. Grahm Jr. and Meghan Robinson Wander (Boston: Da Capo Press, 1985), 164.

36. Clyde Weed, *The Nemesis of Reform: The Republican Party during the New Deal* (New York: Columbia University Press, 1994), 18. See also Bernard M. Baruch, *Baruch: The Public Years* (New York: Holt, Rinehart and Winston, 1960), 217.

37. McElvaine, *Great Depression*, 321.

38. Hamilton, *New Day*, 67; Kennedy, *Freedom*, 162–63; Jeremy Atack and Peter Passell, *A New View of American History from Colonial Times to 1940*, 2nd ed. (New York: W. W. Norton, 1994), 629; McElvaine, *Great Depression*, 75.

39. Alan Meltzer, *A History of the Federal Reserve*, vol. 1, 1913–51 (Chicago: University of Chicago Press, 2003), 271.

40. Merle Fainsod and Lincoln Gordon, *Government and the Economy*, rev. ed. (New York: W. W. Norton, 1948), 13; McElvaine, *Great Depression*, 174.

41. Cited by William E. Leuchtenburg, *Franklin D. Roosevelt and the New Deal: 1932–1940* (New York: Harper and Row, 1963), 26.

42. J. M. Kenworthy, "The Way Back to Prosperity," *Current History* 36 (April 1932): 129.

43. Kennedy, *Freedom*, 174.

44. George McJimsey, *The Presidency of Franklin Delano Roosevelt* (Lawrence: University Press of Kansas, 2000), 2.

45. William E. Leuchtenburg, "The New Deal and the Analogue of War," in *Change and Continuity in Twentieth Century America*, ed. John Braeman, Robert Bremmer, and Everett Walters (Columbus: Ohio State University Press, 1964), 81–82.

46. Cited by William E. Leuchtenburg, "FDR: The First Modern Presidency," in *Leadership in the Modern Presidency* (Cambridge, Mass.: Harvard University Press, 1988), 12.

47. Cited by Arthur Schlesinger Jr., *The Coming of the New Deal* (Boston: Houghton Mifflin, 1959), 3.

48. Walter Lippmann, *New York Herald Tribune*, July 19, 1932.

49. Martin L. Fausold, *The Presidency of Herbert C. Hoover* (Lawrence: University Press of Kansas, 1985), 2–11.

50. Weed, *Nemesis*, 18.

51. Cited by Parrish, *Anxious Decades*, 208.

52. Ellis Hawley, "The Constitution of the Hoover and Franklin Roosevelt Presidencies during the Depression Era," in *The Constitution and the American Presidency*, ed. Martin L. Fausold and Allan Shank (Albany: State University of New York Press, 1991), 88.

53. David Burner, *Herbert Hoover: A Public Life* (New York: Knopf, 1979), 260.

54. Herbert Stein, *The Fiscal Revolution in America* (Chicago: University of Chicago Press, 1969), 7–8.

55. Skowronek, *Politics*, 268.

56. Burner, *Herbert Hoover*, 274. See also Ellis W. Hawley, "Herbert Hoover, The Commerce Secretariate and the Vision of an Associative State, 1921–1928," *Journal of American History* 61 (June 1974), 117.

57. Schlesinger, *Crisis*, 163.

58. Parrish, *Anxious Decades*, 249.

59. Fainsod and Gordon, *Government and the Economy*, 91.

60. Walter I. Trattner, *From Poor Law to Welfare State: A History of Social Welfare in America*, 6th ed. (New York: Free Press, 1999), 277.

61. Michael B. Katz, *In the Shadow of the Poorhouse: A Social History of Welfare in America* (New York: Basic Books, 1966), 222.

62. Parrish, *Anxious Decades*, 250–51.

63. Arthur M. Schlesinger Jr., *The Cycles of American History* (Boston: Houghton Mifflin, 1986), 338. See also Fausold, *Presidency*, 163.

64. Stein, *Fiscal Revolution*, 31–32.

65. Hamilton, *New Day*, 282. See also Carl Degler, "The Ordeal of Herbert Hoover," *Yale Review* 52 (Summer 1963): 573; John F. Witte, *The Politics and Development of the Federal Income Tax* (Madison: University of Wisconsin Press, 1985), 96; and James D. Savage, *Balanced Budgets and American Politics* (Ithaca, N.Y.: Cornell University Press, 1988), 169.

66. Stein, *Fiscal Revolution*, 14.

67. Kennedy, *Freedom*, 55.

68. Klein, *Rainbow's End*, 245.

69. Leuchtenburg, *Franklin D. Roosevelt*, 19.

70. Cited by Schlesinger, *Crisis*, 459.

71. Barry Karl, *The Uneasy State: The United States from 1915 to 1945* (Chicago: University of Chicago Press, 1983), 99.

72. Cited by Burner, *Herbert Hoover*, 268.

73. James L. Sundquist, *Dynamics of the Party System* (Washington, D.C.: Brookings Institution, 1973), 204.

74. Schlesinger, *Crisis*, 246.

Chapter 3. Erosion of the Liberal Regime

1. Peggy Noonan, *What I Saw at the Revolution: A Political Life in the Reagan Era* (New York: Random House, 1990), 270. See also Theodore Lowi, "An Aligning Election and a Presidential Plebiscite," in *Election of 1984*, ed. Michael Nelson (Washington, D.C.: Congressional Quarterly Press, 1985), 279.

2. Michael Foley, "The Presidential Leadership and the Presidency," in *The Reagan Years*, ed. Joseph Hogan (New York: Manchester University Press), 42.

3. Council of Economic Advisers, *Economic Report of the President* (Washington, D.C.: U.S. Government Printing Office, 1989), 39. See also Herbert Stein, *Presidential Economics: The Making of Economic Policy from Roosevelt to Reagan and Beyond* (New York: Simon and Schuster, 1984), 219; Michael J. Boskin, *Reagan and the Economy: The Successes, Failures, and Unfinished Agenda* (San Francisco: Institute for Contemporary Studies, 1987), 13.

4. Boskin, *Reagan and the Economy*, 13.

5. James E. Alt, "Leaning into the Wind or Ducking out of the Storm? U.S. Monetary Policy in the 1980s," in *Politics and Economics in the Eighties*, ed. Alberto Alesina and Geoffrey Carliner (Chicago: University of Chicago Press, 1991), 66. See also Charles L. Schultze, *Memos to the President* (Washington, D.C.: Brookings Institution, 1992), 140.

6. James T. Patterson, *Restless Giant: The United States from Watergate to Bush v. Gore* (New York: Oxford University Press, 2005), 66.

7. Boskin, *Reagan and the Economy*, 139.

8. Kenneth Bacon, *Wall Street Journal*, January 22, 1981.

9. Stein, *Presidential Economics*, 221.

10. Steven M. Gillon, *The Democrat's Dilemma: Walter F. Mondale and the Liberal Legacy* (New York: Columbia University Press, 1992), 199.

11. Ibid., 135, 148.

12. Ibid., 295.

13. Stephen Skowronek, *The Politics Presidents Make: Leadership from John Adams to George Bush* (Cambridge, Mass.: Belknap Press of Harvard University Press, 1993), 116.

14. Alonzo Hamby, *Liberalism and Its Challengers: From FDR to Bush*, 2nd ed. (New York: Oxford University Press, 1992), 386. See also Gillon, *Democrat's Dilemma*, 297.

15. E. J. Dionne, *Why Americans Hate Politics* (New York: Simon and Schuster, 1991), 144.

16. Charles O. Jones, *Separate but Equal Branches: Congress and the Presidency* (Chatham, N.J.: Chatham House, 1995), 44.

17. Lowi, "Aligning Election," 278.

18. Skowronek, *Politics*, 121–22.

19. Sidney Milkis, *The President and the Parties: The Transformation of the American Party System since the New Deal* (New York: Oxford University Press, 1993), 133.

20. Gillon, *Democrat's Dilemma*, 170, 180.

21. Erwin C. Hargrove, *Jimmy Carter as President: Leadership and the Politics of the Public Good* (Baton Rouge: Louisiana State University Press, 1988), 5.

22. James Sterling Young, foreword to ibid., xx.

23. Hargrove, *Jimmy Carter*, 164.

24. Sidney M. Milkis and Michael Nelson, *The American Presidency: Origins and Development, 1776–1990* (Washington, D.C.: Congressional Quarterly Press, 1990), 237. See also Hamby, *Liberalism*, 354.

25. John P. Burke, *The Institutional Presidency* (Baltimore, Md.: Johns Hopkins University Press, 1992), 119.

26. Zbigniew Brzezinski, *Power and Principle: Memoirs of the National Security Adviser, 1977–1981* (New York: Farrar Straus Giroux, 1985), 71.

27. Interview with Stuart Eizenstat, White Burkett Miller Center of Public Affairs, University of Virginia, Project on the Carter Presidency, vol. XIII, January 29–30, 1982, 58, Jimmy Carter Library (hereafter cited as PCP). See also Burke, *Institutional Presidency*, 120, 122, 130.

28. Emmet John Hughes, "The Presidency vs. Jimmy Carter," *Fortune* 98 (December 4, 1978), 52. See also Colin Cambell, "The White House and Cabinet under the 'Let's Deal' Presidency," in *The Bush Presidency: First Appraisals*, ed. Colin Cambell and Bert Rockman (Chatham, N.J.: Chatham House, 1991), 92.

29. Hargrove, *Jimmy Carter*, 190. See also James Fallows, "The Passionless Presidency, Part I," *Atlantic Monthly*, May 1979, 42–43.

30. Stephen Hess, *Organizing the Presidency*, 2nd ed. (Washington, D.C.: Brookings Institution, 1988), 145. See also James Fallows, "For Old Times Sake," *New York Review of Books*, December 16, 1982, 9.

31. Dionne, *Why Americans Hate Politics*, 119.

32. Gary H. Reichard, "Early Returns: Assessing Jimmy Carter," *Presidential Studies Quarterly* 20 (Summer 1990): 616.

33. James David Barber, *The Presidential Character: Predicting Performance in the White House*, 4th ed. (Englewood Cliffs, N.J.: Prentice-Hall, 1992), 432.

34. Jones, *Separate but Equal*, 153.

35. Hargrove, *Jimmy Carter*, 188.

36. Interview with Landon Butler, part of the Hamilton Jordan interview, PCP, vol. VI, November 6, 1981, 36.

37. Robert Strong, "Recapturing Leadership: The Carter Administration and the Crisis of Confidence," *Presidential Studies Quarterly* 16 (Fall 1986): 643. See also Hargrove, *Jimmy Carter,* 173–74.

38. Thomas P. O'Neill with William Novak, *Man of the House: The Life and Political Memoirs of Speaker "Tip" O'Neill* (New York: Random House, 1987), 297, 308. See also Paul Quirk, "Presidential Competence," in *The Presidency and the Political System*, ed. Michael Nelson (Washington, D.C.: Congressional Quarterly Press, 1990), 135–36.

39. Interview with Hamilton Jordan, PCP, vol. VI, November 6, 1981, 27. See also Jones, *Separate but Equal,* 189.

40. Interview with Stuart Eizenstat, PCP, 63, 102.

41. Cited by Gillon, *Democrat's Dilemma,* 207.

42. Ibid., 255.

43. Hargrove, *Jimmy Carter,* 187.

44. Ibid., 107, 80.

45. Interview with Stuart Eizenstat, PCP, 88. See also Burton I. Kaufman, *The Presidency of James Earl Carter, Jr.* (Lawrence: University Press of Kansas, 1993), 100.

46. Dionne, *Why Americans Hate Politics,* 141.

47. Richard Neustadt, *Presidential Power and the Modern Presidents: The Politics of Leadership from Roosevelt to Reagan* (New York: Free Press, 1990), 208. See also Bert Rockman, *The Leadership Question: The Presidency and the American System* (New York: Praeger, 1985), 186.

48. Kaufman, *Presidency of James Earl Carter, Jr.,* 143–44.

49. Gillon, *Democrat's Dilemma,* 261.

50. Ibid., 264; Steven F. Hayward, *The Age of Reagan: The Fall of the Old Liberal Order* (Roseville, Calif.: Primo Publishing, 2001), 574–84.

51. James L. Sundquist, "The Crisis of Competence in Our National Government," *Political Science Quarterly* 95 (Summer 1980): 183–208.

52. Foley, "Presidential Leadership," 28.

53. James A. Baker III, *The Politics of Diplomacy* (New York: G. P. Putnam, 1995), 261.

54. Skowronek, *Politics,* 366.

55. Bruce Schulman, "Slouching toward the Supply-Side: Jimmy Carter and the New American Political Economy," in *The Carter Presidency: Policy Choices in the Post–New Deal Era*, ed. Gary Fink and Hugh Davis Graham (Lawrence: University Press of Kansas, 1998), 52, 54, 64, 66.

Chapter 4. The Life, Personality, and Political Philosophy of Franklin Roosevelt and Ronald Reagan

1. William Leuchtenburg, "FDR: The First Modern President," in *Leadership in the Modern Presidency*, ed. Fred I. Greenstein (Cambridge, Mass.: Harvard University Press, 1988), 26.

2. Frank Freidel, *Franklin D. Roosevelt: A Rendezvous with Destiny* (Boston: Little, Brown, 1990), 8.

3. Jerome Mileur, "The Boss: Franklin Roosevelt, the Democratic Party, and the Reconstruction of American Politics," in *The New Deal and the Triumph of Liberalism*, ed. Sidney M. Milkis and Jerome Mileur (Amherst: University of Massachusetts Press, 2002), 125.

4. Freidel, *Franklin D. Roosevelt,* 20.

5. Geoffrey Ward, *A First-Class Temperament: The Emergence of Franklin Roosevelt* (New York: Harper and Row, 1989), 166. See also James MacGregor Burns and Susan

Dunn, *The Three Roosevelts: Patrician Leaders Who Transformed America* (New York: Atlantic Monthly Press, 2001), 136.

6. Alfred B. Rollins Jr., *Roosevelt and Howe* (New York: Alfred A. Knopf, 1962).

7. Arthur M. Schlesinger Jr., *The Crisis of the Old Order, 1919–1933* (Boston: Houghton Mifflin Company, 1957), 340.

8. Ward, *First-Class Temperament,* 231.

9. Schlesinger, *Crisis,* 345–46.

10. Freidel, *Franklin D. Roosevelt,* 26–31.

11. Ibid., 25–26.

12. Conrad Black: *Franklin Delano Roosevelt: Champion of Freedom* (New York: Public Affairs Press, 2003), 127–28.

13. Ward, *First-Class Temperament,* 576–704.

14. Ted Morgan, *FDR: A Biography* (New York: Simon and Schuster, 1985), 257–58.

15. James MacGregor Burns, *Roosevelt: The Lion and the Fox* (New York: Harcourt, Brace and Company, 1956), 88–89.

16. Ward, *First-Class Temperament,* 607. See also Garry Wills, *Certain Trumpets: The Call of Leaders* (New York: Simon and Schuster, 1994), 26–30.

17. Paul K. Conkin, *FDR and the Origins of the Welfare State* (New York: Thomas Y. Crowell, 1967), 6.

18. Freidel, *Franklin D. Roosevelt,* 53–54.

19. Black, *Franklin Delano Roosevelt,* 207.

20. Cited by Arthur M. Schlesinger Jr., *The Coming of the New Deal* (Boston: Houghton Mifflin Company, 1959), 586.

21. Kenneth Davis, "FDR as a Biographer's Problem," *American Scholar* 53 (Winter 1983–1984): 107.

22. Ibid., 104.

23. Freidel, *Franklin D. Roosevelt,* 67–68.

24. Schlesinger, *Coming of the New Deal,* 586.

25. Davis, "FDR as a Biographer's Problem," 107.

26. William E. Leuchtenburg, *Franklin D. Roosevelt and the New Deal* (New York: Harper and Row, 1963), 167–68.

27. Robert E. Sherwood, *Roosevelt and Hopkins: An Intimate History* (New York: Grosset and Dunlop, 1950), 9.

28. Leuchtenburg, "FDR," 8.

29. Burns, *The Lion and the Fox,* 244.

30. Ibid., 237–38.

31. Cited by Schlesinger, *Crisis,* 483–84.

32. Arthur Schlesinger Jr., *The Politics of Upheaval* (Boston: Houghton Mifflin Company, 1960), 651.

33. Ibid., 620.

34. David Kennedy, *Freedom from Fear: The American People in Depression and War, 1929–1945* (New York: Oxford University Press, 1999), 118.

35. Schlesinger, *Crisis,* 538. For what was not forecast, see Leuchtenburg, *Franklin D. Roosevelt,* 12.

36. Franklin D. Roosevelt, *The Public Papers and Addresses of Franklin D. Roosevelt,* ed. Samuel I. Rosenman, 13 vols. (New York: Harper and Brothers, 1950), 1:624–27.

37. Ibid., 632.

38. Ibid., 639–47.

39. Ibid., 657.

40. Kennedy, *Freedom from Fear,* 245–46.

41. Clinton L. Rossiter, "The Political Philosophy of FDR: A Challenge to Scholarship," *Review of Politics* 11 (January 1949): 90.

42. George McJimsey, *The Presidency of Franklin Delano Roosevelt* (Lawrence: University Press of Kansas, 2000), 24.

43. Sidney M. Milkis, *The President and the Parties: The Transformation of the American Party System since the New Deal* (New York: Oxford University Press, 1993), 41.

44. Roosevelt, *Public Papers,* 1:752.

45. Jules Tygiel, *Ronald Reagan and the Triumph of American Conservatism* (San Francisco: Pearson and Longman, 2005), 8.

46. Ibid., 20.

47. Ibid., 24.

48. Ibid., 34.

49. Ibid., 45.

50. Ibid., 50.

51. Garry Wills, *Reagan's America: Innocents at Home* (Garden City, N.Y.: Doubleday, 1987), 215.

52. Lyn Nofziger, *Nofziger* (Washington, D.C.: Regnery Gateway, 1992), 303.

53. Tygiel, *Ronald Reagan,* 70–71.

54. Ibid., 75.

55. Ibid., 96. See also Matthew Dallek, *The Right Moment: Ronald Reagan's First Victory and the Decisive Turning Point in American Politics* (New York: Free Press, 2000).

56. Lou Cannon, *Governor Reagan: His Rise to Power* (New York: Public Affairs, 2003), 359.

57. Charles D. Hobbs, "How Ronald Reagan Governed California," *National Review,* January 17, 1975, 28–42.

58. James W. Ceaser, "The Reagan Presidency and American Public Opinion," in *The Reagan Legacy,* ed. Charles Jones (Chatham, N.J.: Chatham House, 1988), 183.

59. Garry Wills, "Mr. Magoo Remembers," *New York Review of Books,* December 20, 1990, 4.

60. *Houston Chronicle,* June 6, 2004.

61. Martin Anderson, *Revolution* (New York: Harcourt Brace Jovanovich, 1988), 288.

62. Michael Deaver, *Behind the Scenes* (New York: William Morrow, 1987), 40.

63. Lou Cannon, *President Reagan: The Role of a Lifetime* (New York: Simon and Schuster, 1991), 401.

64. Donald Regan, *For the Record: From Wall Street to Washington* (New York: Harcourt Brace Jovanovich, 1988), 3–5, 70–71, 73–74, 90, 93, 290, 359, 367–70.

65. Edmund Morris, "The Unknowable: Ronald Reagan's Amazing, Mysterious Life," *New Yorker,* June 28, 2004, 50.

66. Tygiel, *Ronald Reagan,* 98.

67. James Patterson, *Restless Giant: The United States from Watergate to Bush v. Gore* (New York: Oxford University Press, 2005), 147.

68. Steven F. Hayward, *The Age of Reagan: The Fall of the Old Liberal Order* (Roseville, California: Prima Publishing, 2001), 622; Richard Reeves, *President Reagan: The Triumph of Imagination* (New York: Simon and Schuster, 2005), 280.

69. Wills, *Reagan's America*, 123.

70. Reeves, *President Reagan*, 33.

71. Ibid., xii.

72. Andrew Busch, *Ronald Reagan and the Politics of Freedom* (Lanham, Md.: Rowman and Littlefield, 2001), xviii.

73. Cited by Dinesh D'Souza, *Ronald Reagan: How an Ordinary Man Became an Extraordinary Leader* (New York: Free Press, 1997), 65.

74. Cited by ibid., 53.

75. Cited by Tygiel, *Ronald Reagan*, 114.

76. Cited by Hayward, *Age of Reagan*, xv.

77. Cited by Michael Schaller, *Right Turn: American Life in the Reagan-Bush Era: 1980–1992* (New York: Oxford University Press, 2007), 12.

78. Kiron K. Skinner, Annelise Anderson, and Martin Anderson, eds., *Reagan: A Life in Letters* (New York: Free Press, 2003), 343.

79. Kiron K. Skinner, Annelise Anderson, and Martin Anderson, eds., *Reagan in His Own Hand* (New York: Free Press, 2001), 228.

80. *New York Times*, May 29, 1985.

81. Skinner et al., *Reagan in His Own Hand*, 274, 279.

82. Ronald Reagan, *An American Life* (New York: Simon and Schuster, 1990), 231.

83. Skinner et al., *Reagan: A Life in Letters*, 318.

84. D'Souza, *Ronald Reagan*, 69.

85. Hugh Heclo, "Ronald Reagan and the American Public Philosophy," in *The Reagan Presidency: Pragmatic Conservatism and its Legacies*, ed. W. Elliot Brownlee and Hugh Davis Graham (Lawrence: University Press of Kansas, 2003), 21.

86. Tygiel, *Ronald Reagan*, 114–15.

87. Mary Stuckey, *The President as Interpreter-in-Chief* (Chatham, N.J.: Chatham House, 1991), 117; Robert E. Denton Jr., *The Primetime Presidency of Ronald Reagan* (New York: Praeger, 1988), 65–66; Roderick Hart, *Verbal Style and the Presidency* (Orlando, Fla.: Academic Press, 1984), 215–28.

88. Wills, *Reagan's America*, 284.

89. D'Souza, *Ronald Reagan*, 59.

90. Ronald Reagan, *Speaking My Mind: Selected Speeches* (New York: Simon and Schuster, 1989), 22–27.

91. William Muir, *The Bully Pulpit: The Presidential Leadership of Ronald Reagan* (San Francisco: ICS Press, 1992), 18.

Chapter 5. Advising FDR

1. Arthur M. Schlesinger Jr., *The Coming of the New Deal* (Boston: Houghton Mifflin, 1959), 18.

2. Thomas S. Langston, *Ideologues and Presidents: From the New Deal to the Reagan Revolution* (Baltimore, Md.: Johns Hopkins University Press, 1992), 28.

3. Beatrice Bishop Berle and Travis Beal Jacobs, eds., *Navigating the Rapids: From the Papers of Adolf A. Berle*, introduction by Max Ascoli (New York: Harcourt Brace Jovanovich, 1973), 81.

4. Raymond Moley, *After Seven Years* (New York: Harper and Brothers, 1939), 4.

5. Raymond Moley with Elliott A. Rosen, *The First New Deal* (New York: Harcourt, Brace and World, 1966), 14.

6. Kenneth S. Davis, *FDR: The New York Years, 1928–1933* (New York: Random House, 1979), 265–66.

7. Moley, *First New Deal*, 225.

8. Moley, *After Seven Years*, 184.

9. Cited in Elliot A. Rosen, "Roosevelt and the Brains Trust: An Historiographical Overview," *Political Science Quarterly* 87 (December 1972): 544.

10. Ibid., 538.

11. Ibid., 538; Moley, *First New Deal*, 224.

12. Moley, *First New Deal*, 289.

13. Moley, *After Seven Years*, 166–67.

14. Schlesinger, *Coming*, 181.

15. Moley, *After Seven Years*, 176–78.

16. Ibid., 189.

17. Ibid., 289; Schlesinger, *Coming*, 468.

18. Moley, *First New Deal*, 346.

19. Rexford G. Tugwell, *The Brains Trust* (New York: Viking Press, 1968), 154.

20. Moley, *After Seven Years*, 342; Moley, *First New Deal*, 340; George E. Reedy, *The Twilight of the Presidency* (New York: World Publishing, 1970).

21. Reported in the *New York Sun*, July 1, 1936.

22. Moley, *First New Deal*, 356.

23. Tugwell, *Brains Trust*, 309.

24. Donald R. Richberg, *My Hero: The Indiscreet Memoirs of an Eventful but Unheroic Life* (New York: G. P. Putnam's Sons, 1954), 156; Bernard Sternsher, *Rexford Tugwell and the New Deal* (New Brunswick: Rutgers University Press, 1964), 330.

25. Sternsher, *Rexford Tugwell*, 391.

26. Michael V. Namorato, *Rexford G. Tugwell: A Biography* (New York: Praeger, 1988), 14.

27. Tugwell, *Brains Trust*, 216.

28. Rexford G. Tugwell, *In Search of Roosevelt* (Cambridge, Mass.: Harvard University Press, 1972), 100.

29. Tugwell, *Brains Trust*, 172.

30. Namorato, *Rexford G. Tugwell*, 52.

31. Tugwell, *Brains Trust*, 174.

32. Paul K. Conkin, *FDR and the Origins of the Welfare State* (New York: Thomas Y. Crowell, 1967), 38.

33. Rexford G. Tugwell, "The Progressive Tradition," *Atlantic Monthly*, April 1935, 414, 416.

34. Tugwell, *Brains Trust*, 264.

35. Ibid., 44.

36. Moley, *First New Deal*, 357.

37. Tugwell, *Brains Trust*, 47, 410.

38. Tugwell, *In Search of Roosevelt*, 210.

39. Rosen, "Roosevelt and the Brains Trust," 556.

40. Schlesinger, *Coming*, 550.

41. Rexford G. Tugwell, *Roosevelt's Revolution: The First Year — A Personal Perspective* (New York: Macmillan, 1977), 276.

42. Ted Morgan, *FDR: A Biography* (New York: Simon and Schuster, 1985), 345.

43. James MacGregor Burns, *Roosevelt: The Lion and the Fox* (New York: Harcourt, Brace, 1956), 154.

44. Berle and Jacobs, *Navigating*, 45.

45. Ibid., 31.

46. Franklin D. Roosevelt, *The Public Papers of Franklin D. Roosevelt*, ed. Samuel I. Rosenman, vol. 1, *The Genesis of the New Deal, 1928–1932* (New York: Random House, 1938), "Campaign Address on Progressive Government at the Commonwealth Club, San Francisco, California, September 23, 1932," 742–57.

47. Sidney M. Milkis, "FDR, the Economic Constitutional Order, and the New Politics of Presidential Leadership," in *The New Deal and the Triumph of Liberalism*, ed. Sidney M. Milkis and Jerome M. Mileur (Amherst: University of Massachusetts Press, 2002), 35.

48. Schlesinger, *Coming*, 243.

49. Ibid., 122.

50. Grace Tully, *FDR: My Boss* (New York: Charles Scribner and Sons, 1949), 192.

51. John Morton Blum, *Roosevelt and Morgenthau* (Boston: Houghton and Mifflin, 1970), 250.

52. Cited in Julian E. Zelizer, "The Forgotten Legacy of the New Deal: Fiscal Conservatism and the Roosevelt Administration, 1933–1938," *Presidential Studies Quarterly* 30 (June 2000): 337.

53. Ibid., 355.

54. Robert Paul Browder and Thomas G. Smith, *Independent: A Biography of Lewis W. Douglas* (New York: Alfred A. Knopf, 1986), 116.

55. Ibid., 91.

56. Ibid., 106.

57. Lewis Douglas memo to President, December 30, 1933, President's Secretary Files, FDR Library.

58. Zelizer, "Forgotten Legacy," 355.

59. Tugwell, *Brains Trust*, 72; Harold L. Ickes, *The Secret Diary of Harold L. Ickes*, vol. I, *The First Thousand Days, 1933–1936* (New York: Simon and Schuster, 1953), 239.

60. Blum, *Roosevelt and Morgenthau*, xv.

61. John Morton Blum, *From the Morgenthau Diaries: Years of Crisis, 1928–1938* (Boston: Houghton Mifflin, 1959), 254.

62. Ibid., 151.

63. Zelizer, "Forgotten Legacy," 352–53.

64. Blum, *From the Morgenthau Diaries*, 419–24; Zelizer, "Forgotten Legacy," 354.

65. Blum, *From the Morgenthau Diaries*, 424–25.

66. Zelizer, "Forgotten Legacy," 341.

67. David M. Kennedy, *Freedom from Fear: The American People in Depression and War, 1929–1945* (New York: Oxford University Press, 1999), 205.

68. John C. Culver and John Hyde, *American Dreamer: The Life and Times of Henry A. Wallace* (New York: W. W. Norton, 2000), 120.

69. Schlesinger, *Coming*, 30.

70. Culver and Hyde, *American Dreamer*, 119.

71. Ibid., 51.

72. Schlesinger, *Coming*, 236.

73. Stanley High, "Will It Be Wallace?" *Saturday Evening Post*, July 3, 1937, 85.

74. Culver and Hyde, *American Dreamer*, 191.

75. Ibid., 127–28.

76. Tully, *FDR*, 187.

77. Schlesinger, *Coming*, 35.

78. Culver and Hyde, *American Dreamer*, 204.

79. Ibid., 150.

80. Ibid., 153.

81. Cited by ibid., 326.

82. Cited by ibid., 337.

83. *Time*, December 19, 1938, 13.

84. Culver and Hyde, *American Dreamer*, 149.

85. June Hopkins, *Harry Hopkins: Sudden Hero, Brash Reformer* (New York: St. Martin's Press, 1999), 9.

86. Kennedy, *Freedom from Fear*, 161.

87. Schlesinger, *Coming*, 266.

88. Hopkins, *Harry Hopkins*, 157.

89. Cited by ibid., 164.

90. Ibid., 176.

91. Ibid., 1.

92. Ibid., 4, 20. See also Robert E. Sherwood, *Roosevelt and Hopkins: An Intimate History* (New York: Grosset and Dunlop, 1950), 21.

93. Hopkins, *Harry Hopkins*, 203.

94. June Hopkins, "The Road Not Taken: Harry Hopkins and New Deal Work Relief," *Presidential Studies Quarterly* 25 (June 1999): 311.

95. Nathan Miller, *FDR: An Intimate History* (New York: Doubleday, 1983), 338.

96. T. H. Watkins, *The Hungry Years: A Narrative History of the Great Depression in America* (New York: Henry Holt, 1999), 275.

97. Schlesinger, *Coming*, 475.

98. Sherwood, *Roosevelt and Hopkins*, 102–3.

99. Ibid., 44. See also "Harry Hopkins," *Fortune* 12 (July 1935): 59.

100. Kenneth S. Davis, *FDR: The New Deal Years* (New York: Random House, 1986), 80.

101. Moley, *First New Deal*, 271.

102. Frances Perkins, *The Roosevelt I Knew* (New York: Harper and Row, 1964), 191.

103. Geoffrey T. Hellman, "Profiles," *New Yorker*, August 7, 1943, 27.

104. Arthur Schlesinger Jr., "Getting FDR's Ear," *New York Review of Books*, February 16, 1989, 22.

105. Sherwood, *Roosevelt and Hopkins*, 5.

106. Ibid., 2–3.

107. George McJimsey, *The Presidency of Franklin Delano Roosevelt* (Lawrence: University Press of Kansas, 2000), 123.

108. Schlesinger, *Coming*, 528.

109. Burns, *Roosevelt*, 477.

110. Stephen Skowronek, *The Politics Presidents Make: Leadership from John Adams to George Bush* (Cambridge, Mass.: Belknap Press of Harvard University Press, 1993), 299.

111. Richard Hofstadter, *The American Political Tradition* (New York: Vintage Books, 1960), 315; Kennedy, *Freedom from Fear*, 113; Burns, *Roosevelt*, 155, 238; Arthur M. Schlesinger Jr., *The Politics of Upheaval* (Boston: Houghton Mifflin, 1960), 654.

112. Skowronek, *Politics*, 298.

113. Schlesinger, *Politics*, 649–50.

114. Burns, *Roosevelt*, 245.

115. FDR letter to James P. Warburg, May 23, 1934, President's Personal Files 540, FDR Library.

116. Schlesinger, *Coming*, 526–27.

117. Anne O'Hare McCormick, "As He Sees Himself," *New York Times Magazine*, October 16, 1938, 19.

118. Frank Freidel, *Franklin D. Roosevelt: A Rendezvous with Destiny* (Boston: Little, Brown, 1990), 17.

119. Ibid., 125. See also McJimsey, *Presidency*, 124; Perkins, *The Roosevelt I Knew*, 97.

120. Burns, *Roosevelt*, 334.

121. FDR press conference, April 19, 1933, in *Complete Presidential Press Conferences of Franklin D. Roosevelt* (Boston: Da Capo Press, 1972), 1:156.

122. Perkins, *The Roosevelt I Knew*, 164.

123. Tugwell, *In Search of Roosevelt*, 248.

124. Marriner Eccles, *Beckoning Frontiers: Public and Personal Recollections*, ed. Sydney Hyman (New York: Alfred A. Knopf, 1951), 304.

125. McJimsey, *Presidency*, 128.

126. Schlesinger, *Coming*, 528.

127. Eccles, *Beckoning Frontiers*, 237.

128. Richberg, *My Hero*, 293.

129. Ibid.

130. Kenneth S. Davis, "FDR as a Biographer's Problem," *American Scholar* 53 (Winter 1983–1984), 105.

131. Alan Brinkley, *The End of Reform* (New York: Vintage Books, 1996), 56. See also Ellis W. Hawley, *The New Deal and the Problem of Monopoly* (Princeton, N.J.: Princeton University Press, 1966), 389.

132. James MacGregor Burns and Susan Dunn, *The Three Roosevelts: Patrician Leaders Who Transformed America* (New York: Atlantic Monthly Press, 2001), 288.

133. Felix Frankfurter letter to FDR, March 19, 1935, Joseph Lash Papers, Box 63, FDR Library.

134. Cited by Morgan, *FDR*, 508.

135. Adolph Berle letter to FDR, May 18, 1934, Adolph Berle Papers, Box 10, FDR Library.

136. Walter Lippmann, *Herald Tribune*, December 18, 1934.

Chapter 6. Advising Reagan

1. Richard Beal, Final Report of the Initial Actions Project, January 29, 1981, 17, Ronald Reagan Library.

2. Richard Darman, Talking Points for Presentation on White House Office, n.d., Box 5, Ronald Reagan Library.

3. Beal, Initial Actions Project, 1.

4. Peggy Noonan, *What I Saw at the Revolution: A Political Life in the Reagan Era* (New York: Random House, 1990), 240.

5. Ibid., 213. Richard Reeves, *President Reagan: The Triumph of Imagination* (New York: Simon and Schuster, 2005), 428.

6. Nancy Reagan with William Novak, *My Turn: The Memoirs of Nancy Reagan* (New York: Random House, 1990), 240–41.

7. Ronald Brownstein and Dick Kirschten, "Cabinet Power," *National Journal,* June 28, 1986, 1583. John P. Burke, *The Institutional Presidency,* 2nd ed. (Baltimore, Md.: Johns Hopkins Press, 2000), 144, 150.

8. Taylor Branch, "James A. Baker III, Politician," *Texas Monthly,* May 1982, 258.

9. Dick Kirschten, "Decision Making in the White House," *National Journal,* April 3, 1982, 585; *New York Times,* October 4, 1981; "The President's Men," *Time,* December 14, 1981, 18.

10. William Niskanen, *Reaganomics: An Insider's Account of the Policies and the People* (New York: Oxford University Press, 1988), 301.

11. Lou Cannon, *President Reagan: The Role of a Lifetime* (New York: Simon and Schuster, 1991), 66, 160–61.

12. *New York Times,* April 15, 1985.

13. Branch, "James A. Baker III," 264.

14. Donald Regan is one of the most difficult staff aides to classify. He had no personal ties to Reagan and was not a movement conservative. In an interview (*New York Times Magazine,* January 5, 1986, 31), he defined himself as "a pragmatist but definitely on the conservative side." However, he had no previous Washington experience, and he possessed few skills in public relations. And he certainly failed to make the key alliance with Nancy Reagan.

15. Dinesh D'Souza, *Ronald Reagan: How an Ordinary Man Became an Extraordinary Leader* (New York: Free Press, 1997), 242.

16. Frances X. Clines, "James Baker: Calling Reagan's Re-Election Moves," *New York Times Magazine,* May 20, 1984, 53.

17. Richard Darman, *Who's in Control? Polar Politics and the Sensible Center* (New York: Simon and Schuster, 1996), 37.

18. Hedrick Smith, "Taking Charge of Congress," *New York Times Magazine,* August 9, 1981, 17; Dick Kirschten, "Reagan's Legislative Strategy Team," *National Journal,* June 26, 1982, 1127–30.

19. Walter Isaacson, *Time,* August 23, 1982, 23.

20. Branch, "James A. Baker III," 256.

21. Clines, "James Baker," 60.

22. Niskanen, *Reaganomics,* 300.

23. Cannon, *President Reagan,* 262.

24. Niskanen, *Reaganomics,* 300.

25. Nancy Reagan, *My Turn,* 241.

26. Branch, "James A. Baker III," 249. For reporters' negative views toward Meese, see Jane Mayer and Doyle McManus, *Landslide: The Unmaking of the President, 1984–1988* (Boston: Houghton Mifflin, 1988), 324.

27. Bob Woodward, *Washington Post,* October 6, 1992.

28. Darman, *Who's in Control?* 32, 39.

29. Frances X. Clines, "Reagan's Master of Compromise," *New York Times Magazine,* February 16, 1986, 35, 38.

30. Darman, *Who's in Control?* 84.

31. Richard Darman Papers, "Legislative Outlook," Briefing Book for Long Range Planning Meeting, Camp David, February 5, 1982, Ronald Reagan Library.

32. Richard Darman Papers, Darman memo for Deaver Group, January 8, 1982, Briefing Book for Long Range Planning Meeting, Camp David, February 5, 1982, Ronald Reagan Library.

33. Helen Von Damm, *At Reagan's Side: Twenty Years in the Political Mainstream* (New York: Doubleday, 1989), 292–94.

34. *New York Times*, April 21, 1988.

35. *Houston Chronicle*, April 15, 1984.

36. Mark Hertsgaard, *On Bended Knee: The Press and the Reagan Presidency* (New York: Farrar Straus Giroux, 1988), 19–20, 45.

37. Ibid., 5, 32, 34, 37.

38. Garry Wills, *New York Review of Books*, June 16, 1988, 4.

39. Nancy Reagan, *My Turn*, 17.

40. *New York Times*, February 3, 1988.

41. Ibid.

42. Hugh Sidey, "A Conversation with Ronald Reagan," *Time*, August 5, 1985, 22.

43. Cannon, *President Reagan*, 119.

44. Ibid., 179.

45. David Stockman, *The Triumph of Politics: Why the Reagan Revolution Failed* (New York: Harper and Row, 1986), 90.

46. Edwin Meese, *With Reagan: The Inside Story* (Washington, D.C.: Regnery Gateway, 1992), 22.

47. Cannon, *President Reagan*, 372.

48. Quoted in Bob Schieffer and Gary Paul Gates, *The Acting President* (New York: E. P. Dutton, 1989), 90.

49. David Broder, *Houston Chronicle*, September 2, 1985.

50. Bert Rockman, "The Style and Organization of the Reagan Presidency," in *The Reagan Legacy*, ed. Charles O. Jones (Chatham, N.J.: Chatham House, 1988), 8. See also Donald T. Regan, *For the Record: From Wall Street to Washington* (New York: Harcourt Brace Jovanovich, 1988), 267.

51. Steven R. Weisman, "Can the Magic Prevail?" *New York Times Magazine*, April 19, 1984, 46.

52. James David Barber, *Time*, July 7, 1986, 14.

53. Walter Williams, *Mismanaging America: The Rise of the Anti-Analytic Presidency* (Lawrence: University Press of Kansas, 1990), 64.

54. Sidney Blumenthal, *The Rise of the Counter-Establishment: From Conservative Ideology to Political Power* (New York: Harper and Row, 1986), 241.

55. Lewis Gould, *Grand Old Party: A History of the Republicans* (New York: Random House, 2003), 407.

56. Reeves, *President Reagan*, xv.

57. Regan, *For the Record*, 249.

58. George Shultz, *Turmoil and Triumph: My Years as Secretary of State* (New York: Charles Scribner's Sons, 1993), 1133.

59. Edmund Morris, *Dutch: A Memoir of Ronald Reagan* (New York: Random House, 1999), 394.

60. Noonan, *What I Saw*, 145.

61. Cannon, *President Reagan*, 631.

62. Ibid., 185–86. See also: M. Stephen Weatherford and Lorraine M. McDonnell,

"Ideology and Economic Policy," in *Looking Back on the Reagan Presidency*, ed. Larry Berman (Baltimore, Md.: Johns Hopkins University Press, 1990), 127.

63. Weisman, "Can the Magic Prevail?" 52. See also Hedley Donovan, *Roosevelt to Reagan: A Reporter's Encounters with Nine Presidents* (New York: Harper and Row, 1985), 209.

64. Von Damm, *At Reagan's Side*, 188.

65. Stockman, *Triumph*, 76.

66. Larry Speakes with Robert Pack, *Speaking Out: The Reagan Presidency from Inside the White House* (New York: Charles Scribner's Sons, 1988), 306.

67. Regan, *For the Record*, 142–46.

68. Terrel H. Bell, *The Thirteenth Man: A Reagan Cabinet Memoir* (New York: Free Press, 1988), 32.

69. Stockman, *Triumph*, 76.

70. Clines, "James Baker," 58. See also Peter Robertson, *How Reagan Changed My Life* (New York: Regan Books, 2003), 215–16.

71. D'Souza, *Ronald Reagan*, 65.

72. *Time*, December 13, 1982, 14.

73. Bruce Schulman, *The Seventies: The Great Shift in American Culture, Society, and Politics* (New York: Free Press, 2001), 238.

74. Mayer and McManus, *Landslide*, 189–271.

75. Noonan, *What I Saw*, 268.

76. Cannon, *President Reagan*, 55, 135, 290.

Chapter 7. Core Policies of the New Deal

1. Helen M. Burns, *The American Banking Community and the New Deal Banking Reforms, 1933–1935* (Westport, Conn.: Greenwood Press, 1974), 3–4.

2. William E. Leuchtenburg, *Franklin D. Roosevelt and the New Deal, 1932–1940* (New York: Harper and Row, 1963), 39.

3. *Kiplinger Washington Letter*, February 25, 1933, 1.

4. Raymond Moley, *The First New Deal* (New York: Harcourt, Brace and World, 1966), 157.

5. George McJimsey, *The Presidency of Franklin Delano Roosevelt* (Lawrence: University Press of Kansas, 2000), 36.

6. Burns, *American Banking Community*, 48.

7. T. H. Watkins, *The Hungry Years: A Narrative History of the Great Depression in America* (New York: Henry Holt, 1999), 51.

8. Franklin D. Roosevelt, *The Public Papers and Addresses of Franklin D. Roosevelt*, vol. 2, *The Year of Crisis, 1933* (New York: Random House, 1938), 61–65.

9. Burns, *American Banking Community*, 116.

10. Moley, *First New Deal*, 197–99.

11. Arthur M. Schlesinger Jr., *The Coming of the New Deal* (Boston: Houghton Mifflin Company, 1959), 5.

12. Kenneth Davis, *FDR: The New Deal Years* (New York: Random House, 1986), 51.

13. Raymond Moley, *After Seven Years* (New York: Harper and Brothers, 1939), 155.

14. Carter Galombe, "The Deposit Insurance Legislation of 1933," *Political Science Quarterly* 75 (June 1960): 181.

15. Moley, *First New Deal*, 316.

16. John Steele Gordon, *The Great Game* (New York: Simon and Schuster, 1999), 237.

17. Galombe, "Deposit Insurance Legislation," 193.

18. Leuchtenburg, *Franklin D. Roosevelt*, 60.

19. Galombe, "Deposit Insurance Legislation," 195.

20. Burns, *American Banking Community*, 115–16.

21. Schlesinger, *Coming*, 36.

22. Leuchtenburg, *Franklin D. Roosevelt*, 50.

23. John Mark Hansen, *Gaining Access: Congress and the Farm Lobby, 1919–1981* (Chicago: University of Chicago Press, 1991), 78.

24. James MacGregor Burns and Susan Dunn, *The Three Roosevelts: Patrician Leaders Who Transformed America* (New York: Atlantic Monthly Press, 2001), 262.

25. Schlesinger, *Coming*, 47.

26. David M. Kennedy, *Freedom from Fear: The American People in Depression and War, 1929–1945* (New York: Oxford University Press, 1999), 205.

27. Nathan Miller, *FDR: An Intimate History* (New York: Doubleday, 1983), 332.

28. McJimsey, *Presidency*, 55.

29. John Morton Blum, *From the Morgenthau Diaries: Years of Crisis, 1928–1938* (Boston: Houghton Mifflin, 1965), 30.

30. Kennedy, *Freedom from Fear*, 204. See also Frank Freidel, *Franklin D. Roosevelt: A Rendezvous with Destiny* (Boston: Little, Brown, 1990), 132.

31. Miller, *FDR*, 333.

32. McJimsey, *Presidency*, 57–58.

33. Schlesinger, *Coming*, 50.

34. John C. Culver and John Hyde, *American Dreamer: The Life and Times of Henry A. Wallace* (New York: W. W. Norton, 2000), 126–27.

35. Joseph P. Lash, *Dealers and Dreamers: A New Look at the New Deal* (New York: Doubleday, 1988), 222.

36. Culver and Hyde, *American Dreamer*, 155.

37. Kennedy, *Freedom from Fear*, 206.

38. Conrad Black, *Franklin Delano Roosevelt: Champion of Freedom* (New York: Public Affairs, 2003), 307.

39. Jeremy Atack and Peter Passel, *A New American History from Colonial Times to 1940*, 2nd ed. (New York: W. W. Norton, 1994), 671.

40. Kennedy, *Freedom from Fear*, 206.

41. David E. Hamilton, *From New Day to New Deal: American Farm Policy from Hoover to Roosevelt, 1928–1933* (Chapel Hill: University of North Carolina Pres, 1991), 247.

42. Burns and Dunn, *Three Roosevelts*, 371.

43. Kennedy, *Freedom from Fear*, 207.

44. Theodore Saloutos, "New Deal Agricultural Policy: An Evaluation," *Journal of American History* 61 (September 1974): 397.

45. Arthur M. Schlesinger Jr., *The Cycles of American History* (Boston: Houghton Mifflin, 1986), 239.

46. Hamilton, *From New Day*, 247–48.

47. Stephen Skowronek, *The Politics Presidents Make: Leadership from John Adams to George Bush* (Cambridge, Mass.: Belknap Press of Harvard University Press, 1993), 305; Alonzo L. Hamby, *For the Survival of Democracy* (New York: Free Press, 2004), 160; Kennedy, *Freedom from Fear*, 177; Richard Hofstadter, *The American Political Tradition* (New York: Vintage Books, 1960), 333.

48. Cited by Bernard Bellush, *The Failure of the NRA* (New York: W. W. Norton, 1975), 1.

49. Ibid., 4.

50. McJimsey, *Presidency*, 46.

51. Ibid., 46.

52. Ellis W. Hawley, *The New Deal and the Problem of Monopoly: A Study in Economic Ambivalence* (Princeton, N.J.: Princeton University Press, 1966), 30.

53. Schlesinger, *Coming*, 100.

54. Hawley, *New Deal*, 31.

55. FDR Fireside Chat, July 24, 1933, *The Essential Franklin Delano Roosevelt* (New York: Gramercy Books, 1995), 64–65.

56. Address of Donald Richberg at Luncheon of the Merchants' Association of New York, July 6, 1933, at Hotel Astor, FDR Library.

57. Hamby, *For the Survival*, 144.

58. Kennedy, *Freedom from Fear*, 177.

59. Ibid., 178–99.

60. Schlesinger, *Coming*, 108–9.

61. Lash, *Dealers and Dreamers*, 126.

62. Bellush, *Failure*, 51.

63. Schlesinger, *Coming*, 110.

64. Bellush, *Failure*, 45, 47.

65. Ibid., 35.

66. Leuchtenburg, *Franklin D. Roosevelt*, 68.

67. Schlesinger, *Coming*, 125.

68. Bellush, *Failure*, 68–69.

69. Ibid., 147.

70. Schlesinger, *Coming*, 145.

71. Hawley, *New Deal*, 91.

72. Bellush, *Failure*, 87.

73. Hawley, *New Deal*, 105–6.

74. Hamby, *For the Survival*, 165.

75. Hawley, *New Deal*, 51.

76. Ibid., 69.

77. Hofstadter, *American Political Tradition*, 333.

78. Hawley, *New Deal*, 69–70.

79. Theodore Rosenof, *Dogma, Depression and the New Deal* (Port Washington, N.Y.: Kennikat Press, 1975), 91.

80. Marriner S. Eccles, *Beckoning Frontiers: Public and Personal Recollections*, ed. Sidney Hyman (New York: Alfred A. Knopf, 1951), 126.

81. Hawley, *New Deal*, 123.

82. Bellush, *Failure*, 165.

83. Hawley, *New Deal*, 132.

84. Ibid., 145.

85. Kennedy, *Freedom from Fear*, 189.

86. Schlesinger, *Coming*, 402.

87. Leuchtenburg, *Franklin D. Roosevelt*, 108.

88. Schlesinger, *Coming*, 385.

89. Davis, *FDR*, 120.

90. Elisabeth Brandeis, "Organized Labor and Protective Labor Legislation," in *Labor and the New Deal*, ed. Milton Derber and Edwin Young (Madison: University of Wisconsin Press, 1961), 196.

91. Nelson Lichtenstein, *State of the Union: A Century of American Labor* (Princeton, N.J.: Princeton University Press, 2002), 5–6, 30.

92. Leuchtenburg, *Franklin D. Roosevelt*, 109.

93. Lichtenstein, *State of the Union*, 39.

94. Lash, *Dealers and Dreamers*, 425.

95. Bellush, *Failure*, 170–71.

96. R. W. Fleming, "The Significance of the Wagner Act," in *Labor and the New Deal*, ed. Milton Derber and Edwin Young (Madison: University of Wisconsin Press, 1961), 130.

97. James A. Morone, *The Democratic Wish: Popular Participation and the Limits of American Government* (New York: Basic Books, 1990), 172.

98. Frank Freidel, *Franklin D. Roosevelt: A Rendezvous with Destiny* (Boston: Little, Brown, 1990), 159.

99. Lichtenstein, *State of the Union*, 36–37.

100. Robert S. McElvane, *The Great Depression: America, 1929–1941* (New York: Times Books, 1993), 289–90.

101. Morone, *Democratic Wish*, 175; Melvyn Dubofsky, *The State of Labor in Modern America* (Chapel Hill: University of North Carolina Press, 1994), 132–33.

102. Dubofsky, *State of Labor*, 135.

103. Ibid.

104. Morone, *Democratic Wish*, 177.

105. Cited by Leuchtenburg, *Franklin D. Roosevelt*, 243.

106. Kennedy, *Freedom from Fear*, 320.

107. McJimsey, *Presidency*, 82–83.

108. Kennedy, *Freedom from Fear*, 261.

109. Barry D. Karl, *The Uneasy State: The United States from 1915 to 1945* (Chicago: University of Chicago Press, 1983), 141.

110. Kennedy, *Freedom from Fear*, 259–60.

111. Leuchtenburg, *Franklin D. Roosevelt*, 105.

112. Sylvester I. Schrieber and John B. Shoven, *The Real Deal* (New Haven, Conn.: Yale University Press, 1999), 24.

113. Frances Perkins, *The Roosevelt I Knew* (New York: Harper and Row, 1964), 113.

114. Arthur J. Altmeyer, *The Formative Years of Social Security* (Madison: University of Wisconsin Press, 1966), 11.

115. Ibid., 8.

116. Schrieber and Shoven, *Real Deal*, 28.

117. Ibid., 29.

118. George Martin, *Madam Secretary: Frances Perkins* (Boston: Houghton Mifflin, 1976), 345.

119. Lash, *Dealers and Dreamers*, 245–46.

120. Martin, *Madam Secretary*, 353.

121. Edwin E. Witte, *The Development of the Social Security Act* (Madison: University of Wisconsin Press, 1963), 74.

122. Martin, *Madam Secretary*, 354.

123. FDR's Message to Congress on Social Security, January 17, 1935, *Essential Franklin Delano Roosevelt*, 90–93.

124. Altmeyer, *The Formative Years*, 35–36.

125. Ibid., 37.

126. Ibid., 37–38.

127. "Presidential Statement upon Signing the Social Security Act, August 14, 1935," *The Public Papers and Addresses of Franklin D. Roosevelt*, vol. 4, 1935, 324.

128. Walter I. Trattner, *From Poor Laws to Welfare State: A History of Social Welfare in America*, 6th ed. (New York: Free Press, 1999), 290.

129. Cited by Kennedy, *Freedom from Fear*, 296.

130. Michael Katz, *In the Shadow of the Poorhouse: A Social History of Welfare in America* (New York: Basic Books, 1996), 242–43.

131. Trattner, *From Poor Laws*, 294.

132. Kennedy, *Freedom from Fear*, 267.

Chapter 8. Reagan's Core Policies

1. Edwin Meese, *With Reagan: The Inside Story* (Washington, D.C.: Regnery Gateway, 1992), 148.

2. Alan Greenspan, *Wall Street Journal*, January 16, 1981.

3. David Stockman, *Triumph of Politics: Why the Reagan Revolution Failed* (New York: Harper and Row, 1986), 75.

4. Ibid., 76.

5. Ibid., 71–74; Lou Cannon, *President Reagan: The Role of a Lifetime* (New York: Simon and Schuster, 1991), 107; Laurence I. Barrett, *Gambling with History: Reagan in the White House* (New York: Doubleday, 1983), 134–35.

6. Stockman, *Triumph*, 124.

7. *America's New Beginning: A Program for Economic Recovery*, published by the White House, February 18, 1981, 10.

8. *New York Times*, February 19, 1981.

9. Stockman, *Triumph*, 38.

10. Ibid., 151.

11. Ibid., 147.

12. Dennis Farney, *Wall Street Journal*, April 6, 1981. See also Walter Williams, *Managing America: The Rise of the Anti-Analytic Presidency* (Lawrence: University Press of Kansas, 1990), 78.

13. Cannon, *President Reagan*, 243; Barrett, *Gambling*, 155.

14. Cannon, *President Reagan*, 243.

15. Stockman, *Triumph*, 181.

16. Cited by Stockman, *Triumph*, 188.

17. Ibid., 187–90; Cannon, *President Reagan*, 250–51.

18. Stockman, *Triumph*, 192.

19. Ibid., 193.

20. James Pfiffner, "The Reagan Budget Juggernaut," in *The President and Economic Policy*, ed. James Pfiffner (Philadelphia: Institute for the Study of Human Issues, 1986), 124.

21. Ibid., 128. See also Dennis S. Ippolito, *Uncertain Legacies: Federal Budget Policy from Roosevelt through Reagan* (Charlottesville: University Press of Virginia, 1990), 221.

22. Stockman, *Triumph*, 234.

23. Steven R. Weisman, "Reaganomics and the President's Men," *New York Times Magazine*, October 24, 1982, 85.

24. John F. Witte, *Politics and Development of the Federal Income Tax* (Madison: University of Wisconsin Press, 1985), 223.

25. Stockman, *Triumph*, 235.

26. Ibid., 239.

27. Witte, *Politics*, 223.

28. Stockman, *Triumph*, 231.

29. Leonard Silk, *New York Times*, June 12, 1981.

30. Stockman, *Triumph*, 263. See also Witte, *Politics*, 229.

31. "Tax Cut Passed by Solid Margin in House, Senate," *Congressional Quarterly Weekly Report* 39 (August 1, 1981): 1374.

32. Witte, *Politics*, 230.

33. Ibid., 230; *New York Times*, August 2, 1981.

34. W. Elliot Brownlee and C. Eugene Steuerle, "Taxation," in *The Reagan Presidency: Pragmatic Conservatism and its Legacies*, ed. W. Elliot Brownlee and Hugh Davis Graham (Lawrence: University Press of Kansas, 2003), 159.

35. Ibid., 158.

36. C. Eugene Steuerle, *The Tax Decade: How Taxes Came to Dominate the Public Agenda* (Washington, D.C.: Urban Institute Press, 1992), 50.

37. Ibid., 43.

38. Ibid., 58.

39. Brownlee and Steuerle, "Taxation," 168.

40. Martha Derthick and Steven M. Teles, "Riding the Third Rail: Social Security Reform," in *The Reagan Presidency: Pragmatic Conservatism and its Legacies*, ed. W. Elliot Brownlee and Hugh Davis Graham (Lawrence: University Press of Kansas, 2003), 198–99.

41. Ibid., 199.

42. Ibid., 201.

43. Paul Light, *Artful Work: The Politics of Social Security Reform* (New York: Random House, 1985), 228.

44. Paul Light, *New York Times*, March 5, 2005.

45. John Lofton, "Social Security Farce Continues," *Washington Times*, April 22, 1983.

46. Brownlee and Steuerle, "Taxation," 167.

47. *Wall Street Journal*, May 23, 1985. See also Hedrick Smith, *The Power Game: How Washington Works* (New York: Random House, 1988), 552.

48. John F. Witte, "The 1986 Tax Reform: A New Era in Politics?" *American Politics Quarterly* 19 (October 1991): 445.

49. Michael J. Boskin, *Reagan and the Economy: The Success, Failures, and Unfinished Agenda* (San Francisco: Institute for Contemporary Studies, 1987), 158.

50. *New York Times*, September 18, 1986. See also Ronald F. King, "Introduction: Tax Reform and American Politics," *American Politics Quarterly* 19 (October 1991): 417–25.

51. Witte, "1986 Tax Reform," 444.

52. Boskin, *Reagan and the Economy*, 122.

53. *New York Times,* June 30, 1985.

54. Witte, "1986 Tax Reform," 447.

55. Steuerle, *Tax Decade,* 121.

56. Jeffrey H. Birnbaum and Allan S. Murray, *Showdown at Gucci Gulch: Lawmakers, Lobbyists and the Unlikely Triumph of Tax Reform* (New York: Vintage Books, 1988), 286.

57. Ibid., 73. See also Timothy J. Conlan, Margaret T. Wrightson, and David R. Beam, *Taxing Choices* (Washington, D.C.: CQ Press, 1990), 71.

58. Albert Hunt, "Introduction," in Birnbaum and Murray, *Showdown at Gucci Gulch,* xiv.

59. Witte, "1986 Tax Reform," 443.

60. Dennis S. Ippolito, "Tax Policy and Spending Policy," *American Politics Quarterly* 19 (October 1991): 43.

Chapter 9. Legitimating the New Deal

1. John A. Rohr, *To Run a Constitution: The Legitimacy of the Administrative State* (Lawrence: University Press of Kansas, 1986), xi.

2. Seymour Martin Lipset, *American Exceptionalism: A Double-Edged Sword* (New York: W. W. Norton, 1996), 20.

3. Samuel P. Huntington, *American Politics: The Promise of Disharmony* (Cambridge, Mass.: Belknap Press of Harvard University Press, 1981), 20.

4. Edward Morgan, *New York Review of Books,* November 18, 1999, 39.

5. Richard J. Stillman, *The American Bureaucracy: The Core of Modern Government* (Chicago: Nelson-Hall, 1996), 62; George Wolfskill and John A. Hudson, *All but the People: Franklin D. Roosevelt and His Critics* (Toronto: Macmillan, 1969), 267.

6. Paul H. Appleby, *Big Democracy* (New York: Alfred A. Knopf, 1945), 12.

7. Merle Fainsod and Lincoln Gordon, *Government and the American Economy,* rev. ed. (New York: W. W. Norton, 1948), 686.

8. Ellis Hawley, "The New Deal State and the Anti-Bureaucratic Tradition," in *The New Deal and Its Legacy,* ed. Robert Eden (Westport, Conn.: Greenwood Press, 1989), 78–79.

9. Jerome M. Mileur, "The Boss: Franklin Roosevelt, the Democratic Party, and the Reconstitution of American Politics," in *The New Deal and the Triumph of Liberalism,* ed. Sidney M. Milkis and Jerome M. Mileur (Amherst: University of Massachusetts Press, 2002), 128.

10. Raymond Moley, *After Seven Years* (New York: Harper and Brothers, 1939), 128.

11. Paul Van Riper, *History of the United States Civil Service* (Evanston, Ill.: Row, Peterson, 1958), 317.

12. Ibid., 320.

13. Ibid., 320, 323.

14. Ibid., 321; Raymond Moley with Elliot A. Rosen, *The First New Deal* (New York: Harcourt, Brace and World, 1966), 9.

15. William E. Leuchtenburg, *Franklin D. Roosevelt and the New Deal: 1932–1940* (New York: Harper and Row, 1963), 63; Frank Freidel, *Franklin D. Roosevelt: A Rendezvous with Destiny* (Boston: Little, Brown, 1990), 121.

16. Van Riper, *History,* 325–26.

17. Walter I. Trattner, *From Poor Law to Welfare State: A History of Social Welfare in America,* 6th ed. (New York: Free Press, 1999), 298–99.

18. Cited by Leuchtenburg, *Franklin D. Roosevelt,* 64.

19. Cited by Peter H. Irons, *The New Deal Lawyers* (Princeton, N.J.: Princeton University Press, 1982), 121.

20. Ibid., 123.

21. Thomas K. McCraw, *Prophets of Regulation* (Cambridge, Mass.: Belknap Press of Harvard University Press, 1984), 156.

22. Ibid., 215.

23. Hawley, "New Deal State," 80–81.

24. Ibid., 82.

25. Ibid., 85.

26. Ibid., 85–86.

27. Peri Arnold, *Making the Managerial Presidency: Comprehensive Reorganization Planning, 1905–1996*, 2nd rev. ed. (Lawrence: University Press of Kansas, 1998), 89–90.

28. Richard Polenberg, *Reorganizing Roosevelt's Government, 1936–1939: The Controversy over Executive Reorganization* (Cambridge, Mass.: Harvard University Press, 1966), 21.

29. Louis Brownlow, *A Passion for Anonymity* (Chicago: University of Chicago Press, 1958), 371.

30. Polenberg, *Reorganizing Roosevelt's Government*, 20–21.

31. Ibid., 21.

32. Ibid., 28.

33. Rohr, *To Run a Constitution*, 211–14.

34. Alonzo L. Hamby, *For the Survival of Democracy: Franklin Roosevelt and the World Crisis of the 1930s* (New York: Free Press, 2004), 342.

35. David B. Truman, *The Governmental Process* (New York: Alfred A. Knopf, 1960), 410.

36. Polenberg, *Reorganizing Roosevelt's Government*, 135.

37. Otis Graham Jr., *Toward a Planned Society: From Roosevelt to Nixon* (New York: Oxford University Press, 1976), 62.

38. Polenberg, *Reorganizing Roosevelt's Government*, 147–48.

39. Ibid., 159; Barry D. Karl, *The Uneasy State: The United States from 1915 to 1945* (Chicago: University of Chicago Press, 1983), 187.

40. Ellis Hawley, "The Constitution of the Hoover and Franklin Roosevelt Presidency during the Depression Era," in *The Constitution and the American Presidency*, ed. Martin L. Fausold and Alan Shank (Albany: State University of New York Press, 1991), 103.

41. Hawley, "New Deal State," 87.

42. Stephen Skowronek, *The Politics Presidents Make: Leadership from John Adams to George Bush* (Cambridge, Mass.: Belknap Press of Harvard University Press, 1993), 319.

43. Arthur M. Schlesinger Jr., *The Coming of the New Deal* (Boston: Houghton Mifflin, 1959), 568.

44. Clyde P. Weed, *The Nemesis of Reform: The Republican Party during the New Deal* (New York: Columbia University Press, 1994), 140.

45. Wolfskill and Hudson, *All but the People*, 337.

46. Cited by ibid., 239.

47. Richard S. Kirkendall, "FDR and the Service Intellectual," *Journal of American History* 49 (December 1962): 463.

48. Weed, *Nemesis of Reform*, 83.

49. Schlesinger, *Coming*, 479.

50. Cited by Wolfskill and Hudson, *All but the People*, 335.

51. Cited by Theodore Rosenof, *Dogma, Depression and the New Deal* (Port Washington, N.Y.: Kennikat Press, 1975), 106.

52. James MacGregor Burns, *Roosevelt: The Lion and the Fox* (New York: Harcourt, Brace, 1956), 238–40; Conrad Black, *Franklin Delano Roosevelt: Champion of Freedom* (New York: Public Affairs, 2003), 420; Weed, *Nemesis of Reform*, 74–76.

53. Cited by Weed, *Nemesis of Reform*, 47.

54. Ibid., 46.

55. Ibid., 101.

56. Arthur M. Schlesinger Jr., ed., *History of American Presidential Elections: 1789–1968* (New York: Chelsea House Publisher, 1971), 3:2856–62; Weed, *Nemesis of Reform*, 98.

57. Aaron Singer, ed., *Campaign Speeches of American Presidential Candidates: 1928–1972* (New York: Frederick Ungar, 1976), 138–40.

58. Alfred M. Landon, *America at the Crossroads* (Port Washington, N.Y.: Kennikat Press, 1971), 18, 20, 21, 33, 64.

59. Milton Plesur, "The Republican Comeback of 1938," *Review of Politics* 24 (October 1962): 526.

60. Cited by Wolfskill and Hudson, *All but the People*, 248.

61. Ibid., 248–49; Weed, *Nemesis of Reform*, 110–11.

62. Irons, *New Deal Lawyers*, 3.

63. Franklin Delano Roosevelt, *The Essential Franklin Delano Roosevelt*, ed. John Gabriel Hunt (New York: Gramercy Books, 1995), 34.

64. Burns, *Roosevelt*, 231.

65. Marian C. McKenna, *Franklin Roosevelt and the Great Constitutional War: The Court Packing Crisis of 1937* (New York: Fordham University Press, 2002), 146.

66. Sheldon Goldman, *Picking Federal Judges: Lower Court Selection from Roosevelt to Reagan* (New Haven, Conn.: Yale University Press, 1997), 17, 62, 63.

67. Hawley, "Constitution," 93.

68. John Hope Carter, *New Dealers* (New York: Simon and Schuster, 1934), 392.

69. Rohr, *To Run a Constitution*, 115.

70. Alpheus T. Mason, *The Supreme Court from Taft to Warren* (Baton Rouge: Louisiana State University Press, 1958), 221. See also William E. Leuchtenburg, *The Supreme Court Reborn: The Constitutional Revolution in the Age of Roosevelt* (New York: Oxford University Press, 1995), 215–16. My colleague, Robert Carp, pointed out that there were also liberal precedents supporting a broader view of the commerce clause, such as *Champion v. Ames*, 1903, and *Houston, East and West Texas Ry v. U.S.*, 1914.

71. G. Edward White, *The Constitution and the New Deal* (Cambridge, Mass.: Harvard University Press, 2000), 241–42.

72. Leuchtenburg, *Supreme Court*, 214.

73. McKenna, *Franklin Roosevelt*, 210.

74. Leuchtenburg, *Supreme Court*, 165; Robert Stern, "The Commerce Clause and the National Economy, 1933–1946," *Harvard Law Review* 47 (June 1946): 884.

75. Cited by Barry Cushman, *Rethinking the New Deal Court: The Structure of a Constitutional Revolution* (New York: Oxford University Press, 1998), 79.

76. McKenna, *Franklin Roosevelt*, 37–44.

77. Ibid., 67.

78. Leuchtenburg, *Supreme Court*, 78.

79. Cited by Mason, *Supreme Court*, 85–86.

80. Stern, "Commerce Clause," 662.

81. Cited by McKenna, *Franklin Roosevelt*, 102.

82. McKenna, *Franklin Roosevelt*, 103–4.

83. Leuchtenburg, *Supreme Court*, 8.

84. Rohr, *To Run a Constitution*, 126.

85. Irons, *New Deal Lawyers*, 195.

86. McKenna, *Franklin Roosevelt*, 189.

87. Cushman, *Rethinking*, 93.

88. McKenna, *Franklin Roosevelt*, 410.

89. Ibid., 412–13.

90. Michael Nelson, "The President and the Court: Reinterpreting the Court-Packing Episode of 1937," *Political Science Quarterly* 103 (Summer 1988): 273.

91. Michael E. Parrish, *Anxious Decades: America in Prosperity and Depression* (New York: W. W. Norton, 1992), 309.

92. Leuchtenburg, *Franklin D. Roosevelt*, 232.

93. Freidel, *Franklin D. Roosevelt*, 226.

94. McKenna, *Franklin Roosevelt*, 273–76.

95. Ted Morgan, *FDR: A Biography* (New York: Simon and Schuster, 1985), 478.

96. Leuchtenburg, *Supreme Court*, 156.

97. Karl, *Uneasy State*, 150.

98. Cited by Wolfskill and Hudson, *All but the People*, 263.

99. Cited by McKenna, *Franklin Roosevelt*, 308.

100. McKenna, *Franklin Roosevelt*, 345.

101. Roosevelt, *Essential Franklin Delano Roosevelt*, 133–41.

102. Gregory A. Caldeira, "Public Opinion and the Supreme Court: FDR's Court-Packing Plan," *American Political Science Review* 81 (December 1987): 1146.

103. Mason, *Supreme Court*, 96.

104. Ibid., 97.

105. Cushman, *Rethinking*, 85.

106. Cited by McKenna, *Franklin Roosevelt*, 415. See also Irons, *New Deal Lawyers*, 279.

107. McKenna, *Franklin Roosevelt*, 416.

108. David M. Kennedy, *Freedom from Fear: The American People in Depression and War, 1929–1945* (New York: Oxford University Press, 1999), 335–36.

109. McKenna, *Franklin Roosevelt*, 427.

110. Melvyn Dubofsky, *The State and Labor in Modern America* (Chapel Hill: University of North Carolina Press, 1994), 145.

111. McKenna, *Franklin Roosevelt*, 434.

112. Ibid., 445–46.

113. Leuchtenburg, *Supreme Court*, 145.

114. Nelson, "The President and the Court," 287.

115. Vincent M. Barnett, "The Supreme Court and the Capacity to Govern," *Political Science Quarterly* 63 (September 1948): 358.

116. Stern, "Commerce Clause," 945–46.

117. Jeffrey Rosen, "The Unregulated Offensive," *New York Times Magazine*, April 17, 2005, 44.

Chapter 10. Legitimating Reagan's Conservative Regime

1. John Brooks, "The Supply Side," *New Yorker*, April 19, 1982, 11.

2. *Time*, January 31, 1983; Alfred Malabre, *Wall Street Journal*, January 17, 1983; Charles L. Schultze, *Memos to the President: A Guide through Macroeconomics for the Busy Policymaker* (Washington, D.C.: Brookings Institution, 1992), 21; Lou Cannon, *President Reagan: The Role of a Lifetime* (New York: Simon and Schuster, 1991), 232.

3. William D. Nordhaus, *New York Times*, December 26, 1982.

4. Benjamin Stein, "A Scenario for a Depression?" *New York Times Magazine*, February 28, 1982, 36. See also Robert Heilbroner, "Does Capitalism Have a Future?" *New York Times Magazine*, August 5, 1982, 20.

5. Sidney Blumenthal, "Letter from Washington," *New Yorker*, 30.

6. *Economic Report of the President, January 1982* (Washington, D.C.: U.S. Government Printing Office, 1982), 9–10.

7. Steven Weisman, *New York Times*, September 26, 1982; *Public Papers of the Presidents of the United States, Ronald Reagan, 1982* (Washington, D.C.: U.S. Government Printing Office, 1983), 27, 28, 53.

8. *New York Times*, October 14, 1982.

9. Mark Peffey and J. T. Williams, "Attributing Presidential Responsibility for National Economic Problems," *American Politics Quarterly* 13 (October 1985): 414.

10. Alonzo L. Hamby, *Liberalism and Its Challengers: From FDR to Bush*, 2nd ed. (New York: Oxford University Press, 1992), 368.

11. Cannon, *President Reagan*, 275.

12. Alexander Haines, *New York Times*, August 18, 1982.

13. Quoted in Leonard Silk, *New York Times*, May 26, 1984.

14. Sidney Blumenthal, *The Rise of the Counter-Establishment: From Conservative Ideology to Political Power* (New York: Harper and Row, 1986), 277.

15. Peter Passell, *New York Times*, August 24, 1996.

16. Schultze, *Memos to the President*, 220.

17. *Barron's*, August 12, 1996, 30.

18. Karen Arenson, *New York Times*, April 8, 1984; Peter Kilborn, *New York Times*, September 4, 1988.

19. Joel Kurtzman, *New York Times*, August 12, 1990.

20. *Economic Report of the President, January 1991* (Washington, D.C.: Government Printing Office, 1991), 322.

21. *Economic Report of the President, January 1989* (Washington, D.C.: Government Printing Office, 1989), 7.

22. Steven Greenhouse, *New York Times*, January 25, 1988.

23. Paul Krugman, *Peddling Prosperity: Economic Sense and Nonsense in the Age of Diminished Expectations* (New York: W. W. Norton, 1994), 262.

24. John Tagliabue, *New York Times*, June 20, 1996.

25. Barbara Presley Noble, *New York Times*, May 8, 1994; Robert Kuttner, *Everything for Sale: The Virtues and Limits of Markets* (New York: Alfred A. Knopf, 1997), 106.

26. E. J. Dionne, *Houston Chronicle*, November 29, 1993.

27. Robert Pear, *New York Times*, October 1, 1987.

28. Sylvia Nasar, *New York Times*, January 2, 1992. See also Louis Uchitelle, *New York Times*, March 22, 1994.

29. Sylvia Nasar, *New York Times*, October 17, 1994.

30. Louis Uchitelle, *New York Times,* January 8, 1992.

31. *America's New Beginning: A Program for Economic Recovery,* published by the White House, February 18, 1981, 10. See also Edward Cowan, *New York Times,* May 3, 1981.

32. Schultze, *Memos to the President,* 259; Krugman, *Peddling Prosperity,* 158.

33. Andrew Dean, Martin Durand, John Fallon, and Peter Hoeller, "Saving Trends and Behavior in OECD Countries," *OECD Economic Studies* 14 (Spring 1990): 9.

34. Leonard Silk, *New York Times,* November 29, 1991.

35. Keith Bradsher, *New York Times,* June 17, 1994.

36. Benjamin M. Friedman, "The Clinton Budget: Will It Do?" *New York Review of Books,* July 15, 1993, 37.

37. Krugman, *Peddling Prosperity,* 158.

38. *Economic Report of the President, January 1991,* 401.

39. Cannon, *President Reagan,* 278.

40. *New York Times,* February 11, 1982.

41. Albert Rees, *Striking a Balance: Making National Economic Policy* (Chicago: University of Chicago Press, 1984), 71.

42. Paul Volcker, *Changing Fortunes: The World's Money and the Threat to American Leadership* (New York: Random House, 1992), 175.

43. Quoted in Kenneth Bacon, *Wall Street Journal,* April 19, 1982.

44. Donald F. Kettl, *Leadership at the Fed* (New Haven, Conn.: Yale University Press, 1986), 183.

45. James E. Alt, "Leaning into the Wind or Ducking out of the Storm? U.S. Monetary Policy in the 1980s," in *Politics and Economics in the Eighties,* ed. Alberto Alesina and Geoffrey Carliner (Chicago: University of Chicago Press, 1991), 46.

46. Alfred L. Malabre, *Lost Prophets: An Insider's History of the Modern Economists* (Cambridge, Mass.: Harvard Business School Press, 1994), 163.

47. Benjamin Friedman, "Comment," in Alesina and Carliner, *Politics and Economics,* 82–83.

48. Kettl, *Leadership at the Fed,* 147.

49. William Niskanen, *Reaganomics: An Insider's Account of the Policies and the People* (New York: Oxford University Press, 1988), 315.

50. James Tobin, "How to Think about the Deficit," *New York Review of Books,* September 25, 1986, 44.

51. Kettl, *Leadership at the Fed,* 177; Peter Kilborn, *New York Times,* June 3, 1987; and Krugman, *Peddling Prosperity,* 173.

52. Niskanen, *Reaganomics,* 168–69.

53. James Q. Wilson, "Reagan and the Republican Revival," *Commentary* 70 (October 1980): 25.

54. Mark Hertsgaard, *On Bended Knee: The Press and the Reagan Presidency* (New York: Farrar Straus Giroux, 1988), 346.

55. Kevin Phillips, *Houston Chronicle,* September 29, 1991.

56. Barbara Kellerman, *The Political Presidency* (New York: Oxford University Press, 1984), 229.

57. *New York Times,* December 14, 1980.

58. Quoted in Norman Miller, *Wall Street Journal,* February 26, 1981.

59. Kellerman, *Political Presidency,* 232, 244.

60. Ibid., 245.

61. Quoted by Richard Reeves, *President Reagan: The Triumph of Imagination* (New York: Simon and Schuster, 2005), 71.

62. Theodore J. Lowi, "Ronald Reagan — Revolutionary?" in *The Reagan Presidency and the Governing of America*, ed. Lester M. Salamon and Michael S. Lund (Washington, D.C.: Urban Institute Press, 1985), 30.

63. Robert Kuttner, "Reaganism, Liberalism, and the Democrats," in *The Reagan Legacy*, ed. Sidney Blumenthal and Thomas Byrne Edsall (New York: Pantheon Books, 1988), 110–11.

64. Quoted by John Kenneth White, *The New Politics of Old Values*, 2nd ed. (Hanover, N.H.: University Press of New England, 1990), 139.

65. Quoted in White, *New Politics*, 74.

66. John Ehrman, *The Eighties: America in the Age of Reagan* (New Haven, Conn.: Yale University Press, 2005), 76.

67. Kenneth S. Bacr, *Reinventing Democrats* (Lawrence: University Press of Kansas, 2000), 128.

68. Ehrman, *Eighties*, 41, 57. See also Sidney Blumenthal, "Drafting a Democratic Industrial Plan," *New York Times Magazine*, August 28, 1983, 31–53.

69. Quoted by Simon Lazarus and Robert E. Litan, "The Democrats' Coming Civil War over Industrial Policy," *Atlantic Monthly*, September 1984, 94.

70. John Kenneth Galbraith, "The Conservative Onslaught," *New York Review of Books*, January 27, 1981, 31.

71. Committee on Ways and Means, U.S. House of Representatives, "Overview of Entitlement Programs," 1991 Greenbook, 102nd Congress, 1st session, May 7, 1991, 1261–62.

72. Robert Pear, *New York Times*, January 11, 1991.

73. Andrew Hacker, "The Rich: Who They Are," *New York Times Magazine*, November 19, 1995, 70. See also Keith Bradsher, *New York Times*, April 17, 1995; Edward N. Wolff, *Top Heavy: A Study of Increasing Inequality of Wealth in America* (New York: Twentieth Century Fund Press, 1995), 7.

74. Keith Bradsher, *New York Times*, June 22, 1996.

75. Steven Holmes, *New York Times*, June 20, 1996.

76. Michael Lewis, "The Rich," *New York Times Magazine*, November 19, 1995.

77. Sylvia Nasar, *New York Times*, August 16, 1992.

78. Sylvia Nasar, *New York Times*, April 21, 1992. See also Sylvia Nasar, *New York Times*, March 5, 1992.

79. Lester Thurow, "The Rich: Why Their World Might Crumble," *New York Times Magazine*, November 19, 1995, 78.

80. Keith Bradsher, *New York Times*, April 17, 1995. See also Wolff, *Top Heavy*, 21–31.

81. Keith Bradsher, *New York Times*, April 17, 1995.

82. George Will, *Houston Chronicle*, September 5, 1991.

83. *Time*, September 14, 1981, 14.

84. Quoted by Robert Pear, *New York Times*, July 25, 1983.

85. Hodding Carter, *Wall Street Journal*, February 11, 1982.

86. Mark Green, *New York Times*, January 22, 1988.

87. Thomas E. Cavanagh and James L. Sundquist, "The New Two Party System," in *The New Direction in American Politics*, ed. John E. Chubb and Paul E. Peterson (Washington, D.C.: Brookings Institution, 1985), 37.

88. Paul Taylor, *Washington Post*, November 23, 1985; Paul Taylor, *Washington Post*, December 14, 1985.

89. Peter Applebaum, *New York Times*, April 3, 1991.

90. Albert O. Hirschman, *The Rhetoric of Reaction: Perversity, Futility, and Jeopardy* (Cambridge, Mass: Belknap Press of Harvard University Press, 1991), 7.

91. Friedrich A. Hayek, *The Road to Serfdom* (Chicago: University of Chicago Press, 1976); Milton Friedman, *Capitalism and Freedom* (Chicago: University of Chicago Press, 1962).

92. Charles Murray, *Losing Ground: America's Social Policy, 1950–1980* (New York: Basic Books, 1984), 9.

93. Edwin Meese quoted by Frances X. Clines, *New York Times*, December 16, 1983.

94. Conrad Waligorski, "The Economic Justification of Inequality," paper presented at the Southwest Social Science Convention, Dallas, March 1995, 14.

95. Milton Friedman and Rose Friedman, *Free to Choose: A Personal Statement* (New York: Avon, 1979), 139.

96. Quoted by Blumenthal, *Rise of the Counter-Establishment*, 222.

97. White, *New Politics*, 53.

98. Niskanen, *Reaganomics*, 279.

99. Paul Craig Roberts, *Houston Chronicle*, June 8, 1992.

100. Robert L. Bartley, *The Seven Fat Years: And How to Do It Again* (New York: Free Press, 1992), 135–49; Lawrence Lindsey, *The Growth Experiment: How the New Tax Policy Is Transforming the U.S. Economy* (New York: Basic Books, 1990), 53–91.

101. Cited by Robert Pear, *New York Times*, August 28, 1985.

102. Quoted in White, *New Politics*, 70.

103. Kate Walsh O'Beirne, *Houston Chronicle*, September 9, 1988.

104. Michael K. Deaver, *Behind the Scenes* (New York: William Morrow, 1987). See also Francis X. Clines, *New York Times*, December 13, 1983.

105. Mickey Kaus, *The End of Equality* (New York: Basic Books, 1992), vi.

106. Cannon, *President Reagan*, 24.

107. David Broder, *Houston Chronicle*, January 15, 1989.

108. Louis Uchitelle, *New York Times*, April 27, 1997.

Chapter 11. FDR's Reconstructive Party Leadership

1. Stephen Skowronek, *The Politics Presidents Make: Leadership from John Adams to George Bush* (Cambridge, Mass.: Belknap Press of Harvard University Press, 1993), 38.

2. John M. Allswang, *The New Deal and American Politics: A Study in Political Change* (New York: John Wiley, 1978), 1.

3. Carl Degler, "American Political Parties and the Rise of the City: An Interpretation," *Journal of American History* 51 (June 1964): 49.

4. Allswang, *New Deal*, 4.

5. Degler, "American Political Parties," 52–53.

6. Sidney Milkis, "New Deal Party Politics, Administrative Reform, and the Transformation of the American Constitution," in *The New Deal and Its Legacy: Critique and Reappraisal*, ed. Robert Eden (New York: Greenwood Press, 1989), 127.

7. William E. Leuchtenburg, *Franklin D. Roosevelt and the New Deal: 1932–1940* (New York: Harper and Row, 1963), 5.

8. Rexford G. Tugwell, *The Brains Trust* (New York: Viking Press, 1968), 503–4.

9. David Burner, *The Politics of Provincialism: The Democratic Party in Transition, 1928–1936* (New York: Knopf, 1968), 246.

10. Jerome Mileur, "The 'Boss': FDR, the Democratic Party, and the Reconstitution of American Politics," in *The New Deal and the Triumph of Liberalism*, ed. Sidney Milkis and Jerome Mileur (Amherst: University of Massachusetts Press, 2002), 105, 107.

11. Sidney Milkis, *The President and the Parties: The Transformation of the American Party System since the New Deal* (New York: Oxford University Press, 1993), 103.

12. Milkis, "New Deal Party Politics," 142.

13. Sidney Milkis, "FDR and the Transformation of Partisan Politics," *Political Science Quarterly* 100 (Autumn 1985): 484; Paul K. Conkin, *FDR and the Origins of the Welfare State* (New York: Thomas Y. Crowell, 1967), 95.

14. Raymond Moley, *After Seven Years* (New York: Harper and Brothers, 1939), 52.

15. Cited in Arthur M. Schlesinger Jr., *The Coming of the New Deal* (Boston: Houghton Mifflin, 1959), 503.

16. Milkis, "New Deal Party Politics," 134.

17. James Sundquist, *Dynamics of the Party System* (Washington, D.C.: Brookings Institution, 1973), 213.

18. David M. Kennedy, *Freedom from Fear: The American People in Depression and War, 1919–1945* (New York: Oxford University Press, 1999), 219.

19. Cited by Milkis, *The President and the Parties*, 49.

20. James T. Patterson, *Congressional Conservatism and the New Deal: The Growth of the Conservative Coalition in Congress, 1933–1939* (Lexington: University of Kentucky Press, 1967), 133.

21. Allswang, *New Deal*, 50–51.

22. Kennedy, *Freedom from Fear*, 127.

23. Ibid., 128.

24. Allswang, *New Deal*, 119.

25. George B. Tindall, "The South," in *Franklin D. Roosevelt, His Life and Times: An Encyclopedic View*, ed. Otis L. Graham Jr. and Meghan Robinson Wander (Boston: Da Capo Press, 1985), 393.

26. Allswang, *New Deal*, 120.

27. Milkis, *The President and the Parties*, 80.

28. Ibid., 77–78.

29. Milton Plesur, "The Republican Comeback of 1938," *Review of Politics* 24 (October 1962): 540–41; Joseph P. Lasch, *Dealers and Dreamers: A New Look at the New Deal* (New York: Doubleday, 1988), 353; James MacGregor Burns and Susan Dunn, *The Three Roosevelts: Patrician Leaders Who Transformed America* (New York: Atlantic Monthly Press, 2001), 387–88.

30. Milkis, *The President and the Parties*, 85.

31. Milkis, "FDR and the Transformation of Partisan Politics," 485–86.

32. Ibid., 490.

33. Milkis, *The President and the Parties*, 96.

34. Paul Van Riper, *History of the United States Civil Service* (Evanston, Ill.: Row, Peterson, 1958), 340–41.

35. Milkis, "FDR and the Transformation of Partisan Politics," 495.

36. David Brady with Joseph Stewart Jr., "Congressional Party Realignment and Transformations of Public Policy in Three Realignment Eras," *American Journal of Political Science* 16 (May 1982): 352.

37. Barbara Deckard Sinclair, "Party Realignment and the Transformation of the Political Agenda: The House of Representatives, 1925–1938," *American Political Science Review* 71 (September 1977): 952.

38. Sundquist, *Dynamics*, 314; Allswang, *New Deal*, 30, 64; Robert Erikson and Kent Tedin, "The 1928–1936 Partisan Realignment: The Case for the Conversion Hypothesis," *American Political Science Review* 75 (September 1981): 951–62.

39. Brady and Stewart, "Congressional Party Realignment," 354; Sinclair, "Party Realignment," 941; Clyde P. Weed, *The Nemesis of Reform: The Republican Party during the New Deal* (New York: Columbia University Press, 1994), 174.

40. Ted Morgan, *FDR: A Biography* (New York: Simon and Schuster, 1985), 496; Frank Freidel, *Franklin D. Roosevelt: A Rendezvous with Destiny* (Boston: Little, Brown, 1990), 287; Weed, *Nemesis*, 201; Jamie Carson, "Electoral and Partisan Forces in the Roosevelt Era: The U.S. Congressional Elections of 1938," *Congress and the Presidency* 28 (Autumn 2001): 161–64.

41. "The *Fortune* Survey," *Fortune*, May 1940, 76–77, 168.

42. Sundquist, *Dynamics*, 227.

43. James MacGregor Burns, *Roosevelt: The Lion and the Fox* (New York: Harcourt, Brace, 1956), 404, 403, 380.

44. Moley, *After Seven Years*, 360, 363.

Chapter 12. Reagan's Reconstructive Party Leadership

1. Everett Carll Ladd with Charles D. Hadley, *Transformation of the American Party System: Political Coalitions from the New Deal to the 1970s* (New York: W. W. Norton, 1975), 340.

2. For an excellent description of how three Catholic families evolved from loyal Democrats to loyal Republicans, see Samuel G. Freedman, *The Inheritance: How Three Families and America Moved from Roosevelt to Reagan and Beyond* (New York: Simon and Schuster, 1996).

3. Paul Allen Beck, "Incomplete Realignment: The Reagan Legacy for Parties and Elections," in *The Reagan Legacy: Promise and Performance*, ed. Charles E. Jones (Chatham, N.J.: Chatham House, 1988), 156.

4. Dinesh D'Souza, *Ronald Reagan: How an Ordinary Man Became an Extraordinary Leader* (New York: Free Press, 1997), 80. See also Charles W. Dunn and J. David Woodard, "Ideological Images for a Television Age: Ronald Reagan as Party Leader," in *The Reagan Presidency: An Incomplete Revolution?* ed. Dilys Hill, Raymond Moore, and Phil Williams (New York: St. Martin's Press, 1990), 118.

5. James L. Sundquist, *Dynamics of the Party System* (Washington, D.C.: Brookings Institution, 183), 413. See also Benjamin Ginsberg and Martin Shefter, "A Critical Realignment? The New Politics, the Reconstituted Right, and the Election of 1984," in *The Elections of 1984*, ed. Michael Nelson (Washington, D.C.: Congressional Quarterly Press, 1985), 1–26.

6. D'Souza, *Ronald Reagan*, 81, 253.

7. James Q. Wilson, "Reagan and the Republican Revival," *Commentary* 70 (October 1980): 25.

8. Beck, "Incomplete Realignment," 154; Burton I. Kaufman, *The Presidency of James Earl Carter, Jr.* (Lawrence: University Press of Kansas, 1993), 206; Edward Cowens, *New York Times*, November 6, 1980.

9. Jeremy Mayer, *Running on Race: Racial Politics in Presidential Campaigns, 1960–2000* (New York: Random House, 2002), 187, 194.

10. Ibid., 199.

11. Lou Cannon, *President Reagan: The Role of a Lifetime* (New York: Simon and Schuster, 1991), 519.

12. Mayer, *Running on Race*, 152.

13. Ibid., 154; Cannon, *President Reagan*, 518.

14. Mayer, *Running on Race*, 168.

15. Cannon, *President Reagan*, 515.

16. Nicholas Lemann, "Implications: What Americans Wanted," in *The Elections of 1984*, ed. Michael Nelson (Washington, D.C.: Congressional Quarterly Press, 1985), 266.

17. Cannon, *President Reagan*, 513.

18. Ibid., 515.

19. Garry Wills, "It's His Party," *New York Times Magazine*, August 11, 1996, 30.

20. Sidney M. Milkis, *The President and the Parties: The Transformation of the American Party System since the New Deal* (New York: Oxford University Press, 1993), 261.

21. Thomas E. Cavanagh and James L. Sundquist, "The New Two-Party System," in *The New Directions in American Politics*, ed. John E. Chubb and Paul E. Peterson (Washington, D.C.: Brookings Institution, 1985), 37.

22. Everett Carll Ladd, "The 1988 Election: Continuation of the Post-New Deal System," *Political Science Quarterly* 104 (Spring 1989): 7.

23. News of the Week, *New York Times*, November 12, 2000.

24. Beck, "Incomplete Realignment," 166.

25. Walter Dean Burnham, "The Reagan Heritage," in *The Elections of 1988: Reports and Interpretations*, ed. Gerald M. Pomper (Chatham, N.J.: Chatham House, 1989), 16.

26. Cavanagh and Sundquist, "New Two-Party System," 40.

27. News of the Week, *New York Times*, November 12, 2000.

28. Cavanagh and Sundquist, "New Two-Party System," 36.

29. Warren Miller, "A New Context for Presidential Politics: The Reagan Legacy," *Political Behavior* 9, no. 2 (1987): 100.

30. Cavanagh and Sundquist, "New Two-Party System," 36.

31. Richard Reeves, "America's Choice: What It Means," *New York Times Magazine*, November 4, 1984, 31.

32. Cavanagh and Sundquist, "New Two-Party System," 65.

33. Gary C. Jacobson, "Meager Patrimony: The Reagan Era and Republican Representation in Congress," in *Looking Back on the Reagan Presidency*, ed. Larry Berman (Baltimore, Md.: Johns Hopkins University Press, 1990), 297.

34. Alan I. Abramovitz, "Issue Evolution Reconsidered: Racial Attitudes and Partisanship in the U.S. Electorate," *American Journal of Political Science* 38 (February 1994): 6.

Conclusion

1. Jules Tygiel, *Ronald Reagan and the Triumph of American Conservatism* (San Francisco: Pearson and Longman, 2005), 191–92.

2. Walter Dean Burnham, "The Reagan Heritage," in *The Election of 1988*, ed. Gerald M. Pomper (Chatham, N.J.: Chatham House, 1989), 2.

3. James MacGregor Burns, *Roosevelt: The Lion and the Fox* (New York: Harcourt, Brace, 1956), 477.

4. John Gabriel Hunt, ed., *The Essential Franklin Delano Roosevelt* (New York: Gramercy Books, 1995), 131.

5. David A. Stockman, *The Triumph of Politics: Why the Reagan Revolution Failed* (New York: Harper and Row, 1986), 234.

6. Hunt, *Essential Franklin Delano Roosevelt*, 127–33.

7. Barry D. Karl, *The Uneasy State: The United States from 1915 to 1945* (Chicago: University of Chicago Press, 1983).

8. George Will, *Houston Chronicle*, May 23, 1999.

9. Fiscal Year 1991, *Historical Tables* (Washington, D.C.: United States Government Printing Office, 1998), 21–22.

10. David Wessel and Gerald F. Seib, *Wall Street Journal*, June 7, 2004. See also Andrew E. Busch, *Ronald Reagan and the Politics of Freedom* (Lanham, Md.: Rowman and Littlefield, 2001), 90.

11. Nicholas Confessore, "Breaking the Code: The Slow Motion Tax Revolution: How Bush Could Do What Reagan Couldn't," *New York Times Magazine*, January 16, 2005, 38.

12. Lloyd Free and Hadley Cantril, *The Political Beliefs of Americans* (New York: Simon and Schuster, 1967); Robert S. Erikson and Kent L. Tedin, *American Public Opinion: Its Origins, Content and Impact*, 6th ed. (New York: Longman Publishers, 2003), 83–84.

INDEX

Abramovitz, Alan I., 354
Abt, John, 190
Acheson, Dean, 119, 121
Adkins v. Children's Hospital, 271, 272, 275, 280, 281
Administrative Reorganization Act, 260–261, 333
Administrative state
  compatibility with American ideals, 247, 285
  criticism of, 262, 264–265, 285–286
  executive powers, 256–261, 326–327, 363
  expert agencies, 246–247
  historical evolution, 247–248
  models, 253–254
  New Deal, 248–250, 253–261, 262, 285, 362–363
  rationale, 252–253, 285
  Reagan's attacks on, 97
  See also Bureaucracy; Regulatory agencies
Advertising industry, 21–22
Advisers
  of Carter, 53–54, 56–57, 60, 62, 63
  competition and conflicts among, 15, 54
  core ideas, 15
  factions, 15
  of Hoover, 33
  managing, 15–16, 150–151
  motivations, 14–15
  See also White House staff
Advisers, Reagan
  blamed for administration failures, 173
  chiefs of staff, 151, 152, 154, 156, 225, 242, 359–360
  comparison to FDR's advisers, 2, 358–360
  conflicts among, 91, 152, 153–154, 156, 161, 162–163, 165–166, 173, 360
  conservatives, 152–156, 157, 162–163, 165, 166, 360
  core ideas, 15

  economic, 224
  goals, 151–152
  Legislative Strategy Group, 158–159, 162, 231, 234
  Nancy Reagan's relations with, 86, 154, 160–161, 163, 164–165, 382n14
  relations with Reagan, 2, 91, 168, 171–173, 225
  responses to Democratic attacks, 315–317
  troika, 154–155, 225
  See also Pragmatists (Reagan advisers); Public relations practitioners; *and individual names*
Advisers, Roosevelt, 358–359
  Brains Trust, 75, 102, 103–104, 112, 262–263
  comparison to Reagan's advisers, 2, 358–360
  competition encouraged by FDR, 106, 140
  conflicts among, 101–102, 108, 109, 113, 124–125, 131, 148
  core ideas, 15, 101–102
  during 1932 campaign, 102, 103–104, 112–113, 250
  intellectuals, 250, 251, 255–258, 262–263
  political commitment, 113
  politicians, 250
  public administration scholars, 255–258
  relations with FDR, 2, 105–106, 112, 123, 137–138, 140, 142–143, 359
  roles, 103–104
  selection, 102, 140
  social workers, 250
  speechwriters, 76, 81, 103, 106, 108, 113, 116–118, 127
  spenders (consumptionists), 124–125, 126
  staff organization, 147
  See also individual names
Affirmative action, 314, 315, 342

AFL. *See* American Federation of Labor
AFL-CIO, 313
African Americans
   in Congress, 330
   Democratic voters, 329–330, 345–346
   ignored by Republican Party, 344
   preferential employment practices, 314,
      315, 342
   racial segregation, 331, 346
   Reagan's racial attitudes, 346–347
   in Roosevelt administration, 329
   Southern tenant farmers and
      sharecroppers, 131, 190–191
   support of FDR, 325, 329–330
   voter registration, 49
Agencies. *See* Regulatory agencies
Agrarian economies, 29, 115
Agrarian reformers, 131
Agricultural Adjustment Act of 1933,
      186–188, 192, 254, 274
Agricultural Adjustment Act of 1938,
      192–193
Agricultural Adjustment Administration
      (AAA)
   administrators, 131, 188–189, 190
   legal division, 190, 191, 251–252
   problems, 190–192
   production control committees, 191–192
   staff, 131, 188, 190
   successes, 192
Agricultural Export Corporation, 23
Agricultural extension agents, 191–192
Agricultural Marketing Act, 34–35
Agriculture
   credit, 189–190
   domestic allotment plan, 127, 129, 186,
      188, 190–192
   exports during World War I, 22
   FDR's interest, 77, 185
   marketing quotas, 193
   New Deal policies, 185–193, 329
   parity concept, 22–23, 186, 187, 193, 205
   prices, 28, 34–35, 127, 193, 205
   problems in 1920s, 22, 34, 110, 185
   production restrictions, 187, 188–189,
      191–192, 329
   soil conservation, 192
   Wallace's policies, 129–130
   See also Farmers
Agriculture, Department of
   Forest Service, 259–260

   in Harding and Coolidge administrations,
      126, 127
   New Deal policies, 132
   pragmatic agrarians vs. social
      reformers, 131
   responsibilities, 247
   Tugwell's position, 109
   Wallace as secretary, 127, 128–132, 148,
      186, 189, 191, 193, 247, 260
Ailes, Roger, 163
Alabama Unemployment Compensation
      Act, 282
Allen, Richard, 155, 165
Allswang, John W., 322, 329, 330
Alt, James E., 46, 301
Altmeyer, Arthur J., 215–216
American Dream myth, 224, 318, 320,
      355, 361
American exceptionalism, 96–97
American Federation of Labor (AFL), 208,
      210–211
American Revolution, 247
*America's New Beginning: A Program for
      Economic Recovery*, 226–227
Anderson, John, 90, 345
Anderson, Martin, 91, 152, 155, 230
Antitrust policies, 87, 104, 106, 111,
      270–271
Applebaum, Peter, 314
Armstrong, Barbara, 216
Army Corps of Engineers, 259
Arnold, Thurmond, 190, 251
Articulation, politics of, 4
Ashwander v. TVA, 275
Austin, Warren, 331
Automobile industry, 21, 22, 211–212

Babson, Roger, 27
Bailey, Josiah, 330, 331
Bailyn, Bernard, 247
Baker, Howard, 156, 157, 228, 231, 233,
      239, 300
Baker, James, 157–161
   career, 158
   on Carter, 64
   as chief of staff, 154, 156, 158, 225,
      226, 360
   conflicts with other Reagan advisers, 153,
      162–163
   economic policies, 241
   media relations, 160, 161

political advice, 160, 241, 347
pragmatism, 152, 173, 234, 360
relationship with Reagan, 159
responses to Democratic attacks, 316
on social security, 229, 231
social security reform commission
   and, 240
as treasury secretary, 242
Ball, George, 190
Ball, Robert, 239–240
Ballentine, Arthur, 180
Bankhead, John, 189
Bankhead Cotton Control Act, 192
Banking Act of 1933 (Glass-Steagall Act),
   183–185
Banking policy
   deregulation, 302
   of Hoover, 37, 180–181, 183
   New Deal legislation, 181–185
Banks
   deposit insurance, 183–185
   discount rates, 21, 25
   failures, 29, 179, 180, 185
   problems in Depression, 179–180
   regulation, 116, 179, 183–185
Barber, James David, 169
Barkley, Alben, 333
Barton, Bruce, 21–22
Baruch, Bernard, 27, 109, 125, 188, 194,
   195, 198
Beal, Richard, 163
Beck, James, 262
Beck, Paul Allen, 342–343
Bell, Griffin, 53, 54
Bell, Terrel, 172–173
Bellush, Bernard, 194, 199–200, 201, 202
Berle, Adolf A., Jr., 114–118
   background, 114
   on causes of Depression, 115
   influence on New Deal policies, 118
   personality, 114
   policy recommendations, 113, 115–
   116, 359
   relationship with FDR, 118, 148
   speeches written by, 81
   on White House staff organization, 147
Bethune, Mary McLeod, 329
Bismarck, Otto von, 213
Bituminous Coal Conservation Act of
   1935, 275
Black, Hugo, 195

Black Cabinet, 329
Blum, John Morton, 120, 125–126, 189
Blumenthal, Michael, 60
Blumenthal, Sidney, 169, 291–292
Borah, William, 130, 196, 204
Boskin, Michael J., 46, 242, 243
Bosworth, Barry, 60
Brady, David, 335, 336
Brains Trust, 75, 102, 103–104, 112,
   262–263. *See also* Advisers,
   Roosevelt
Branch, Taylor, 154–155
Brandeis, Louis
   antitrust policies, 101, 104, 204, 205, 273
   Berle and, 114
   on Supreme Court, 270, 271, 273–
   274, 280
Brinkley, Alan, 146–147
Brock, William, 342–343
Broder, David, 168–169, 319
Brokered state, 253–254
Brown, J. Douglas, 216
Brownlee, W. Elliot, 239
Brownlow, Louis, 255
Brownlow Committee (Committee
   on Administrative Management),
   255–258, 285
Brownstein, Ronald, 154
Bryan, William Jennings, 24, 265, 322, 323
Brzezinski, Zbigniew, 53, 54
Buchanan, Patrick, 153–154
Budgets. *See* Federal budgets
Bureaucracy
   criticism of, 263–264, 363
   Hoover's view, 34, 263–264
   New Deal, 254–255
   private-sector, 248
   Reagan's view, 94
   See also Administrative state; Regulatory
   agencies
Bureau of Labor Statistics, 23
Bureau of the Budget, 120, 260
Burghardt, William Franklin, 346
Burke, John P., 53F
Burner, David, 33, 34, 38
Burnham, Walter Dean, 350, 357
Burns, Helen M., 179, 181, 182, 185
Burns, James MacGregor, 13, 62, 72, 77,
   114, 140, 142, 143–144, 147, 176,
   192–193, 338, 359
Busch, Andrew, 93

Bush, George H. W.
  Baker and, 158
  election campaign (1988), 349
  presidential primaries (1980), 90,
    158, 226
  re-election defeat, 296
  Senate campaign, 158
  as vice president, 153, 158
Business
  antitrust policies, 104, 106, 111, 270–271
  industry concentration, 115, 116, 120
  liberty of contract, 271, 275, 276, 281, 284
  National Association of Manufacturers,
    204, 209
  National Recovery Administration and,
    201, 203, 204–205
  opposition to New Deal, 146, 204–205,
    206, 212–213, 264
  political influence, 210, 237
  regulation, 104, 105, 110–111
  relationship with government, 33–34,
    106, 117, 205
  Supreme Court decisions favoring,
    270–271
  trade association movement, 194, 200
  See also Corporations
Business commonwealth, 204, 206, 253, 254
Butler, Price, 270, 275
Butler, United States v., 193, 274, 282
Byrd, Harry, 219, 330, 331
Byrd, Robert, 306

Caddell, Patrick, 54, 62
Caldeira, Gregory, 279
Calder, Lendel, 22
Califano, Joseph, 63
California Welfare Reform Act
    (CWRA), 89
Cannon, Lou, 91, 155–156, 160, 166–167, 168,
    171, 175, 229, 290, 298, 346, 347–349
Capital markets
  foreign investors, 297–298, 365
  lack of regulation, 24
  See also Stock market
Cardozo, Benjamin, 270, 273, 274, 275,
    281, 282
Carmichael v. Smith Coal and Coke Co., 282
Carter, Hodding, 313
Carter, Jimmy
  administrative focus, 52, 56, 357
  advisers, 53–54, 56–57, 60, 62, 63
  background, 50

  comparison to Hoover, 54, 63
  Crisis of Confidence speech, 62–63
  defense spending, 232
  deregulation policies, 10
  economic policies, 50, 52, 59–61, 152
  election campaign (1976), 50–51, 59–60,
    341, 345
  election campaign (1980), 56, 58–59, 61,
    63–64, 90, 344, 352
  failures, 44, 50, 57, 61–62, 64, 90
  foreign policy, 51, 52, 59
  Iranian hostage crisis, 59, 63, 64, 90,
    342, 344
  leadership style, 54–55, 64–65
  management style, 53–57
  outsider status, 50, 51, 53
  party leadership, 57–58
  payroll tax increase, 229, 230
  political philosophy, 50–51, 55
  political skills, 50, 54, 55, 56
  politics of disjunction and, 357
  public approval ratings, 59, 63
  Reagan's presidency as reaction to, 44,
    64, 89–90
  relations with Congress, 51, 57
  religious beliefs, 50, 51–52
  staff organization, 53–54, 56, 63, 151
  voters, 349, 350
Carter, John Hope, 269–270
Carter v. Carter Coal Co., 275, 276, 281, 282
Casey, William, 162–163, 165
Catholic voters, 325, 344, 349
Cavanagh, Thomas E., 313–314, 348–349,
    351, 352–353
CEA. *See* Council of Economic Advisers
Chandler, A. B. "Happy," 333
Chase, Stuart, 21
Chiefs of staff
  Carter White House, 56, 63
  Reagan White House, 151, 152, 154,
    156, 225, 242, 359–360
  role, 150, 256
Child labor, 199, 206, 271
Child Labor Act of 1916, 271
Churchill, Winston, 133
CIO. *See* Congress of Industrial
  Organizations
Civil rights, 47, 48–49, 314
Civil Service Commission, 249, 256
Civil Works Administration (CWA), 84,
    133, 138
Clark, William, 152, 162–163, 164, 165, 173

Clines, Francis X., 162, 173
Clinton, Bill, 367
Coal industry, 275
Cohen, Benjamin, 113, 124, 251, 252, 274, 275, 279
Collins, William, 208
Commerce, Department of
    Hoover as secretary, 32, 127
    Hopkins as secretary, 133, 136
    Wallace as secretary, 127
Committee on Administrative Management (Brownlow Committee), 255–258, 285
Committee on Economic Security, 215, 216–218
Commodity Credit Corporation, 189–190, 193
Commonwealth Club speech (FDR), 81–82, 116–118, 222, 359
Communism
    fears of, 31
    New Deal staff with ties to, 190
    red scare, 85
Communists, criticism of Wagner bill, 209
Conable, Barber, 233, 235, 240
Congress
    administrative reform proposals, 257–261
    African American members, 330
    agricultural bills, 23, 34–35, 127, 186–188, 192–193
    banking legislation, 181–185
    court-packing plan and, 278–280, 283–284
    Democratic control in 1930s, 336
    Democratic control in 1980s, 305, 345, 348, 350
    elections (1934), 265, 327, 350
    elections (1936), 265
    elections (1938), 331, 337
    elections (1940), 332–334
    elections (1982), 238, 290, 350
    elections (1984), 348
    emergency session (1933), 181, 194–195, 196, 249
    executive power, 258
    interstate commerce regulation, 193, 269, 270–271, 273, 281, 284
    labor legislation, 207, 209–210
    pork barrel spending, 227–228
    Reagan's tax cuts, 233–237
    relations with Carter, 51, 57
    relations with FDR, 278
    Republican control in 1990s, 350

Smoot-Hawley tariff, 35–36, 39–40
Social Security Act, 218–219
social security reform proposals, 229
Southern Democrats, 234, 235, 236, 330, 333
tax reform, 241–242
Congress of Industrial Organizations (CIO), 211–212
Conkin, Paul K., 73, 111
Conservatism
    freedom valued more than equality, 310, 315, 320
    New Right, 343, 354, 364
    in 1970s, 342–343
    of Reagan, 87–88, 93–99, 100, 167, 243, 245
    of Roosevelt, 77, 78
Conservatives
    criticism of New Deal, 135, 263–264, 331
    criticism of welfare state, 314–316
    in Democratic Party, 331, 332–334, 335
    pork barrel spending, 227–228
    Reagan advisers, 152–156, 157, 162–163, 165, 166, 360
    Supreme Court justices, 270, 274, 281
Constitution
    commerce clause, 193, 269, 270–271, 273, 275, 281, 284
    general welfare clause, 269, 274, 282
    New Deal issues, 268–270, 271–276, 284
    regime changes under, 7, 9, 12
Constitutional amendments
    Fifth, 271, 272, 275, 276, 281, 284
    Tenth, 274, 282
    Fourteenth, 270, 272, 275–276, 281, 284
    Eighteenth, 323
Consumer Price Index (CPI), 46, 60, 298. *See also* Inflation
Consumption, 21–22, 23, 47, 297
Contract with America, 367
Coolidge, Calvin
    cabinet, 127
    economic policies, 20, 33
    election, 19, 73
    re-election, 323, 324
    vetoes of McNary-Haugen bill, 23, 127
    as vice president, 71
Corcoran, Thomas, 251, 252, 274
    economic policies, 124
    Moley on, 106
    political activities, 332, 333
    relationship with FDR, 113, 138
    Supreme Court reforms, 277, 279

Corporations
  contributions to Republican Party, 264
  economic power, 23, 110, 114, 115
  efficiency gains, 293, 295
  executive compensation, 295, 312
  FDR's view of, 79, 106
  investment rates, 297
  profits, 295
  public esteem of leaders, 28
  stocks, 24
  taxes, 227, 237, 241, 243, 244
  See also Business
Corruption, 249
Council of Economic Advisers (CEA), 155,
  289, 290, 304, 309
Council on Wages and Price Stability
  (COWPS), 60–61
Court-packing plan. *See* Supreme Court,
  FDR's court-packing plan
Courts, federal, 268–269. *See also* Supreme
  Court
COWPS. *See* Council on Wages and Price
  Stability
Cox, James, 71
CPI. *See* Consumer Price Index
Crisis of Confidence speech (Carter), 62–63
Culver, John C., 128, 130, 131, 191
Cummings, Homer, 215, 269, 276–277
Cuomo, Mario, 319
Currie, Lauchlin, 124
CWA. *See* Civil Works Administration
CWRA. *See* California Welfare Reform Act

D'Amato, Alfonse, 227
Daniels, Josephus, 70, 71
Darman, Richard
  background, 161
  on Baker, 158
  as Baker's assistant, 157, 159, 242
  responses to Democratic attacks, 316
  role as Reagan adviser, 161–162, 241
  on social security, 231
  tax cut compromises, 234
  at Treasury department, 242
Darrow, Clarence, 202
Davis, Chester, 131, 190, 191
Davis, John W., 73, 324, 330
Davis, Kenneth S., 74, 75, 137, 146, 183
Dawes, Charles, 20
Dawson, Molly, 250
Deaver, Michael
  conflicts with other advisers, 154, 162–163

Darman and, 161
  as deputy chief of staff, 154, 158, 225
  Legislative Strategy Group and, 158
  media relations, 160, 164, 318, 360
  Nancy Reagan and, 163, 164–165
  public relations expertise, 163, 164–166
  relations with Reagan, 91
  responses to Democratic attacks, 316
Defense spending, 224, 227, 232, 295, 313
Deficit Reduction Act (DEFRA) of
  1984, 239
Deflation, 29
DEFRA. *See* Deficit Reduction Act
Degler, Carl, 322, 323
Deindustrialization, 309–310
Delano, Frederic A., 194
Democratic Leadership Council, 309
Democratic National Committee, 333, 342
Democratic Party
  African American voters, 329–330,
    345–346
  Boll Weevils, 234, 235, 236
  Carter's leadership, 57–58
  civil rights issues, 314
  conservatives, 331, 332–334, 335
  decentralized organization, 326, 327,
    332, 334
  divisions, 48, 57–58, 265, 305–310, 331,
    332–334
  identification with welfare state, 313–315
  immigrant services, 323
  labor and, 58
  in 1920s, 324
  opposition to Reagan's policies, 233–235,
    305–319, 365–366
  presidential leadership, 326–327, 332
  presidential nomination process, 330
  in Southern states, 324, 330–331,
    333–334, 336, 342
  special interest domination, 49, 307–309,
    343–344, 345, 366
  urban machines, 323, 324, 325
  urban voters, 323–324, 329, 336
  See also Liberal regime (1932-80);
    New Deal electoral coalition; Party
    leadership, of Roosevelt
Depression
  bank failures, 29, 179, 180, 185
  economic impact, 28–29
  effects on agriculture, 28
  end, 118
  global impact, 31

Hoover's responses, 10, 35–42
pessimism, 29, 30, 31
significance, 30
stock market crash, 23–28, 35, 40
unemployment, 28–29, 249
victims, 29–30
Depression, causes of
agricultural problems, 185
Berle on, 115
FDR on, 79
Federal Reserve policies, 21
Hoover on, 39
Moley on, 104
Morgenthau on, 120
overproduction, 206
Tugwell on, 110–111
underconsumption, 124, 206
DePriest, Oscar, 330
Deregulation, 10, 302. *See also* Regulation
Dewey, John, 328, 337
Dickinson, John, 195, 196
Dictator bill, 258, 333
Dionne, E. J., 49–50, 61
Disjunction, politics of. *See* Politics of
disjunction
Dole, Robert J., 231, 233, 234, 235, 239, 240
Domenici, Pete, 233
Donovan, Raymond, 165
Douglas, Lewis, 101, 120–122, 125, 187,
196, 359
Douglas, Paul, 328
D'Souza, Dinesh, 97, 157, 343
Duberstein, Kenneth, 156, 158
Dubofsky, Melvyn, 211
Due process clause
Fifth Amendment, 271, 275, 281, 284
Fourteenth Amendment, 270, 272,
281, 284
Dunn, Susan, 147, 192–193

Eccles, Marriner, 124, 145, 205
Economic conditions
consumption, 21–22, 23, 47, 297
deindustrialization, 309–310
in 1920s, 19–23, 24–25
in 1970s, 45–47, 52, 152, 224, 342
in 1980s, 310–313
service orientation of U.S. economy, 293,
295–296, 312
See also Depression; Inflation; Recession
Economic growth
consumption-driven, 21–22, 297

in 1920s, 20, 21–22, 24, 25
in 1960s, 47
in 1980s, 291, 292–294, 297, 298,
317–318, 319, 354, 355
results of Reagan policies, 287, 291, 298,
317–318, 354, 364
Economic policies
Carter administration, 50, 52, 59–61, 152
Coolidge administration, 20, 33
Hoover administration, 33–42
New Deal, 124–125, 126, 145, 147, 359
Republican regime (1860–1932), 19–21,
28, 35
Roosevelt administrations, 78, 285
See also Federal budgets; Fiscal policies;
Keynesian economics; Monetary
policy; Reaganomics; Supply-side
economics
Economic Recovery Tax Act (ERTA),
233–238, 244, 245, 288
Economy Act of 1933, 186, 255
Eisenach, Eldon J., 8
Eisenhower, Dwight D., 151, 256, 344
Eizenstat, Stuart, 54, 58, 60, 61, 62
Electoral coalition, New Deal. *See* New
Deal electoral coalition
Electoral coalition, of Reagan, 349–353
Democrats, 61, 344, 349, 351, 352
groups included, 11, 241, 343, 344,
349–350, 354, 366
independent voters, 352
labor voters, 61, 344, 349–350
Southern whites, 344, 345, 347, 349
Electoral coalitions
divergent views within, 16
loose, 11
of Nixon, 344
realignments, 350, 351
of reconstructive presidents, 13–14,
321, 365
for regime change, 13
Republican regime (1860–1932), 322–324
See also Party leadership
Electric power companies, 21
Eliot, Martha, 250
Emergency Banking Act of 1933,
181–183, 186
Emergency Committee for Employment,
36
Emergency Farm Mortgage Act, 187
Emergency Relief and Construction Act,
36–37

Employment
  affirmative action, 314, 315, 342
  created by Reagan policies, 287, 294
  federal government, 247, 249–253
  manufacturing, 293, 295, 309–310, 312
  New Deal policies, 194
  service sector, 295–296, 312
  See also Labor
Energy crisis, 58, 59, 62–63, 293
Entitlements, 221
ERTA. *See* Economic Recovery Tax Act
Europe, unemployment, 294–295
Executive branch
  FDR's management, 255
  New Deal agencies, 248, 254, 255
  patronage, 248–249, 250
  power, 256–261, 326–327, 363
  reorganization bill, 257–261, 333
  See also Administrative state; Regulatory
    agencies
Executive Council, 255
Executive Office of the President, 150, 260,
  261. *See also* White House staff

Fairness issue
  criticism of Reagan, 162, 310, 316, 352
  as Democratic issue, 242, 310, 316, 346,
    352
  tax reform, 242
  See also Income inequality
Farley, James, 104, 107, 113, 248–249,
  250, 333
Farm Bureau Federation, 187, 193
Farm Credit Administration, 119, 189, 249
Farmers
  credit, 189–190
  criticism of NRA, 205
  incomes, 28, 80, 192
  mortgage foreclosures, 189
  numbers of, 22
  political views, 22
  Republican voters, 193, 329
  security for, 129
  views of New Deal, 329
  See also Agriculture
Farm Mortgage Foreclosure Act, 272
Fascism, 31, 194
FDIC. *See* Federal Deposit Insurance
  Corporation
Federal budgets
  Carter's cuts, 61
  defense spending, 224, 227, 232, 295, 313

deficits, 37, 47, 60, 226, 238, 361
  effects of Depression, 37
  emergency, 121, 122
  expenditures, 37, 39, 365
  FDR's policies, 113, 120–121
  of Hoover, 37–38
  pork barrel spending, 227–228
  Reagan's cuts, 224, 225, 226–228,
    232–233, 238
  revenues, 365
  social programs, 227, 232
  Stockman's balancing efforts, 224, 225, 226
Federal courts. *See* Courts, federal;
  Supreme Court
Federal Deposit Insurance Corporation
  (FDIC), 184, 185
Federal Emergency Relief Act, 254
Federal Emergency Relief Administration
  (FERA), 133, 137
Federal Farm Board, 34–35, 119
Federal government, economic role
  development promotion, 135
  expansion in New Deal, 248, 269,
    362–363
  expansion with social security, 221
  FDR's view, 78, 79–82, 116–117, 179,
    358, 362, 366–367
  Hoover's view, 33–34, 36, 134
  Hopkins on, 135, 265
  liberal view, 269, 308, 310
  national planning, 110–111, 194, 204
  in 1920s, 39
  public views, 352–353, 354–355
  Reagan's view, 93, 94–95, 96, 98, 289,
    358, 367
  relationship with business, 205
  relief programs, 41, 134–136
  Stockman's view, 224
  Supreme Court decisions, 270, 271, 275,
    276, 281, 284
  union views, 207–208
  See also Laissez-faire doctrine; Regulation
Federal government employees
  civil service coverage, 249, 256
  during New Deal, 247, 249–253
  numbers, 247
  political activities, 334–335
  See also Executive branch; Regulatory
    agencies
Federal land banks, 189
Federal Open Markets Committee
  (FOMC), 299–300, 301

Federal Reserve Act of 1913, 179, 184
Federal Reserve Bank of New York, 26, 180, 300
Federal Reserve Board
  banking crisis and, 180, 182
  bank regulation, 179
  Depression blamed on, 21
  discount rates, 21, 25, 301
  Eccles as chairman, 145
  establishment, 247
  Greenspan as chairman, 304
  policies in 1920s, 20, 26, 35
  powers expanded, 254
  recession of 1937 and, 124
  See also Monetary policy; Volcker, Paul
Federal Trade Commission (FTC), 247, 252, 273
Feldstein, Martin, 290
FERA. *See* Federal Emergency Relief Administration
Ferraro, Geraldine, 348
Fifth Amendment
  due process clause, 271, 275, 281, 284
  interpretations, 272
  liberty of contract, 276
Fiscal policy
  anti-inflation policies, 124
  Keynesian, 291
  link to monetary policy, 291, 303
  New Deal, 124
  See also Federal budgets; Taxes
Flynn, Ed, 104
Foley, Michael, 44, 63–64
FOMC. *See* Federal Open Markets Committee
Food processors, 187, 190, 274
Ford, Gerald, 51, 89, 158, 341, 345, 346
Forest Service, 259–260
"Forgotten Man" speech (FDR), 79–80, 103
Fortas, Abe, 190, 251
Four Horsemen of the Apocalypse, 270, 276
Fourteenth Amendment
  due process clause, 270, 272, 281, 284
  interpretations, 275–276
Frank, Jerome N., 131, 188, 190, 191, 195, 251–252
Frankfurter, Felix
  Adkins v. Children's Hospital, 271
  antitrust policies, 104, 106
  New Deal lawyers recruited, 251, 252
  New York state minimum wage law, 275
  as Roosevelt adviser, 274

Supreme Court reforms, 277
  on White House staff organization, 147
Freidel, Frank, 143, 210
Friedersdorf, Max, 231
Friedman, Benjamin, 301
Friedman, Milton, 291, 298–299, 301, 315
Friedman, Rose, 315
FTC. *See* Federal Trade Commission
Fuller, Craig, 158
Fuller, Melville, 271

Galbraith, John Kenneth, 310
Galombe, Carter, 185
Garner, John Nance, 38, 184, 337
General Electric (GE), 86–87, 194, 340
General Motors, 22, 211–212
George, Walter, 333–334
Gerard, James W., 71
Gergen, David, 158, 163, 164, 316
Germany, social insurance, 213
Gillon, Steven M., 48, 49, 51–52, 62
Gingrich, Newt, 350, 367
Glass, Carter, 145, 183, 279
Glass-Steagall Act (Banking Act of 1933), 183–185
Goldwater, Barry, 87–88, 97, 108, 341, 342, 344
Gompers, Samuel, 208
Gorbachev, Mikhail, 170
Gordon, John Steele, 184
Gould, Lewis, 169–170
Graham, Otis, Jr., 259
Great Depression. *See* Depression
Great Society programs, 58, 94, 367
Great War. *See* World War I
Green, William, 208, 209, 210
Greenspan, Alan, 224, 238, 239–240, 304
Gulick, Luther, 255, 257

Hamby, Alonzo, 49, 203, 204, 205, 258, 290
Hamilton, David, 22, 56
Hamilton, David E., 193
Hamner v. Dagenhart, 271
Hance, Kent, 234, 235
Harding, Warren, 19, 32, 71, 126, 127
Hargrove, Erwin C., 52, 53, 54–55, 56, 59, 60
Harper, Edwin, 152
Harriman, Harry, 194
Harris, Joseph P., 255
Harrison, George, 180
Hart, Gary, 308, 345

Hatch, Orrin, 228
Hatch Act, 334–335
Haugen, Gilbert, 23
Havenmeyer Sugar Trust, 270–271
Hawley, Ellis W., 197, 248, 253–255, 261
Hayek, Friedrich A., 263, 315
Health and Human Services, Department
    of, 230, 231
Heclo, Hugh, 96
Helms, Jesse, 228
Helvering et al. v. Davis, 282
Henderson, Leon, 124
Herk, I. 'Izzy', 201
Hertsgaard, Mark, 164
Hess, Stephen, 55
High, Stanley, 129
Hirschman, Albert O., 314, 315
Hiss, Alger, 190, 191, 251
Hofstadter, Richard, 204
Holmes, Oliver Wendell, 74, 271
Home Owners Loan Corporation, 249
Hoover, Herbert
    administrative skills, 31, 40, 357
    advisers, 33
    agricultural policies, 34–35
    background, 31–32
    banking crisis response, 180–181, 183
    as commerce secretary, 32, 127
    comparison to Carter, 54, 63
    economic policies, 33–42
    election campaign (1928), 19, 31, 32–33,
        74, 323–324
    election campaign (1932), 41, 79–80,
        325–326, 335
    expansion of federal government role,
        245, 248
    failures, 38, 41–42
    on FDR, 77
    humanitarian missions, 32
    investments, 27
    judicial nominations, 270
    labor legislation, 207
    moral code, 34, 38, 39–40, 43
    on New Deal, 262, 263–264
    political career, 32–33
    political philosophy, 33–34, 37, 39–40
    political skills, 40–41
    politics of disjunction and, 357
    responses to Depression, 10, 35–42
    ties to declining regime, 31
    trade association movement, 194

view of federal government role, 33–34,
    36, 134
Hopkins, Harry, 132–139, 265
    advocacy of federal spending, 124–125
    background, 132–133, 250
    as commerce secretary, 133, 136
    death, 133
    on government role, 135, 265
    personality, 133–134, 136, 149
    political activities, 332, 333
    political philosophy, 134–137
    presidential ambitions, 133
    relationship with FDR, 133, 137–139,
        149
    religious beliefs, 133
    social security program, 215, 216–217
Hopkins, June, 133, 134, 135
House of Representatives
    Budget Committee, 228
    Ways and Means Committee, 218–219,
        233, 235, 241–242, 244
    See also Congress
Howe, Louis
    background, 69
    death, 138
    as FDR's assistant, 71, 72, 74, 76, 104,
        105, 107, 113, 324
    Moley and, 103, 108, 148
    political advice, 325
    relationship with FDR, 69–70
Hughes, Charles Evans, 269, 270, 271, 273,
    274, 275, 280–282, 286
Hughes, Emmet John, 54
Hull, Cordell, 101, 105, 130, 148
Humphrey, Hubert, 341
Humphrey's Executor v. the United States, 273
Hunt, Albert, 244
Huntington, Samuel P., 247
Hutcheson, "Big Bill," 211
Hyde, John, 128, 130, 131, 191

Ickes, Harold, 138, 198–199, 259–260, 332
Immigrants, 208, 322, 323
Income inequality
    growth, 310–312, 318–319, 320
    income mobility and, 316–317
    in 1920s, 23
Income taxes
    corporate, 227, 237, 241, 243, 244
    loopholes, 235, 237, 239, 241, 242
    reforms (1986), 241–244, 245

Income tax rates
  bracket creep, 46
  cuts in 1920s, 20, 95
  cuts in 1930s, 37
  cuts in 1960s, 95
  increases in 1930s, 38
  increases in 1980s, 238–239, 320
  in 1970s, 46
  progressive, 38, 95, 245, 361
  See also Tax cuts, Reagan administration
Individualism, 247, 263–264
Industrial Emergency Committee, 255
Industrial policy, 309–310
Inflation
  Carter's anti-inflation policies, 60–61
  decline in 1980s, 288, 303
  in 1970s, 46, 48, 59–61, 299, 342
  in 1980s, 298
  political effects, 342
  Reagan's anti-inflation policies, 47, 152,
    290, 298–299, 317, 364
  Social Security cost-of-living
    adjustments, 228, 240
  stagflation, 47, 90, 152, 223
Interest-group liberalism, 307–309. *See also*
  Special interests, in Democratic Party
Interest rates
  in 1920s, 20–21, 26
  in 1980s, 47, 61, 224, 288, 298, 300, 301,
    302, 303–304
Interior, Department of, 259–260
Interstate commerce, congressional
  regulation, 193, 269, 270–271, 273,
    281, 284
Investment
  foreign capital, 297–298, 365
  rates, 296–297
  See also Capital markets
Iran-Contra scandal, 156–157, 163,
  170, 174
Iranian hostage crisis, 59, 63, 64, 90,
  342, 344
Isaacson, Walter, 159

Jackson, Andrew, 177, 330
Jackson, Gardiner, 131
Jackson, Jesse, 319, 345, 346
Jackson, Robert, 251, 279
Jacobson, Gary, 353
Jefferson, Thomas, 6, 177, 324, 326
Jobs. *See* Employment; Labor

Johnson, Hugh
  campaign speeches written by, 113
  industrial regulation proposals, 195,
    196, 204
  as NRA director, 198–200, 201, 202,
    203, 206
  parity concept, 22–23
Johnson, Lyndon B.
  Great Society programs, 58, 94, 367
  presidential campaign (1964), 87–88,
    97, 341
  support of FDR's court reform bill, 283
Jones, Charles O., 56
Jones, Jesse, 138, 184
Jordan, Hamilton, 53, 57, 63
Judges, federal, 268–269
Judicial Procedures Reform Act, 278–280,
  282–284
Judiciary branch. *See* Courts, federal;
  Supreme Court

Karaagic, John, 11
Karl, Barry, 40, 213, 261
Katz, Michael B., 36, 221
Kellerman, Barbara, 305–307
Kemp, Jack, 300
Kennedy, David M., 39, 79, 80–81, 128, 133,
  191, 192, 193, 198, 206, 212, 213, 214, 221
Kennedy, Edward, 56, 58–59, 300, 309
Kennedy, John F., 95
Kennedy, Joseph P., 27, 71, 106, 109, 252
Kennedy, Robert, 87
Kettl, Donald, 26, 301, 302
Keynes, John Maynard, 170
Keynesian economics
  fairness issue, 310
  fiscal policy, 291
  in 1930s, 124, 145, 147
  in 1960s, 47
  seen as failure, 46
Keyserling, Leon, 209
Kingdon, John W., 12–13
Kiplinger Washington Letter, 180
Kirkendall, Richard S., 262–263
Kirkland, Lane, 313
Kirkpatrick, Jeane, 152, 163
Kirschten, Dick, 154
Klein, Maury, 25, 27, 39
Knox, Frank, 266, 267
Krock, Arthur, 105, 136, 334
Krugman, Paul, 294

Kurtzman, Joel, 293
Kuttner, Robert, 308
Kuznets, Simon, 310

Labor
    child, 199, 206, 271
    collective bargaining and organizing
        rights, 196, 197, 202–203
    electoral power, 58
    electoral support for FDR, 211, 212
    FDR's alliance with, 207, 210–211,
        222, 336
    government protections, 199, 214, 271
    incomes, 80, 312
    minimum wages, 199, 264, 271, 275,
        280–281, 315
    New Deal policies, 69, 195, 197, 199,
        202–203, 206, 207–213
    problems in 1920s, 23
    productivity, 23, 45–46, 47, 292
    Republican voters, 48, 61, 322, 344,
        349–350
    strikes, 202, 211–212
    Supreme Court decisions, 211, 281
    ties to Democratic Party, 58
    wages, 23
    working conditions, 69, 214
    working hours restrictions, 195, 199,
        264, 271
    yellow dog contracts, 196, 197, 207
    See also Unions
Labor, Department of, 214, 215
Labor force, women in, 293, 294, 295
Labor's Nonpartisan League, 211
Ladd, Everett Carl, 341–342, 349
LaFollette, Phillip, 109, 328
LaFollette, Robert M., 109, 323, 328
LaGuardia, Fiorello, 118
Laissez-faire doctrine
    American belief in, 247
    criticisms, 110
    FDR's view of, 80
    Hoover's opposition, 33, 34, 38
    judicial support, 268–269, 271
    supporters, 121–122, 135
    See also Liberty of contract
Lance, Bert, 53
Landis, James, 251, 252–253
Landon, Alfred, 31, 265–268
Langston, Thomas, 101–102
Lash, Joseph P., 191
Lawyers, 190, 191, 251–253, 269

Leadership. *See* Party leadership;
        Presidential leadership model
League for Independent Action, 328
Legislative Strategy Group (LSG),
        158–159, 162, 231, 234
LeHand, Marguerite "Missy," 71, 76
Lemann, Nicholas, 347
Lenroot, Katharine, 250
Leuchtenburg, William E., 24, 30, 67, 77,
        180, 185, 186–187, 201, 207, 208, 214,
        250, 273, 274, 324
Lewis, Drew, 227
Lewis, John L., 209, 210–211, 212
Liberalism
    activist government, 269, 308
    criticism of Reagan, 169–170
    criticism of social security, 220–221
    equality goals, 341
    of FDR, 78, 141, 361
    interest-group, 307–309
    liberty and, 247
    neo-, 308–309
    in 1970s, 341–342
    in 1980s, 169–170, 307–309, 352–353
    popular policies, 355, 366
    public disaffection, 49
    Reagan's criticisms, 95, 99, 100
    "tax and spend" caricature, 95,
        136–137, 345
    See also Democratic Party; Fairness issue;
        Income inequality; New Deal electoral
        coalition
Liberal regime (1932–80)
    achievements, 47
    activist government, 269, 308, 352–353
    Carter's attempts to save, 50, 64
    decline, 47–50, 55, 308, 341–342
    foreign policy, 47
    Great Society programs, 58, 94, 367
    institutionalization, 338, 361, 365
    legitimization, 362–364
    persistence, 228, 240, 352–353, 355, 360,
        364–365
    political philosophy, 47
    See also New Deal electoral coalition
Liberty League, 264
Liberty of contract, 271, 275, 276, 281, 284
Lincoln, Abraham, 4, 5, 14, 177, 322
Lippmann, Walter, 31, 40, 75, 102,
        147–148, 278, 358
Lipset, Seymour Martin, 247
Lochner v. New York, 271

London Economic Conference, 108
Long, Huey, 140, 328
Long, Russell, 57
Lowi, Theodore, 51, 307
LSG. *See* Legislative Strategy Group

Magaziner, Ira, 309
Manufacturing jobs, 293, 295, 309–310, 312
Martin, George, 218
Marx, Karl, 95
Mason, Alphonse T., 280
Mayer, Jeremy, 345, 346, 347
MCA, 86, 87
McAdoo, William, 73, 330
McElvaine, Robert S., 23, 25
McFarlane, Robert, 163, 174
McGovern, George, 48, 341
McIntyre, James, 53, 54, 60
McJimsey, George, 30, 81, 140, 145, 181
McKenna, Marian C., 281, 282–283
McKinley, William, 265, 322
McNary, Charles, 23
McNary-Haugen bill, 23, 127, 186
McReynolds, James, 270, 271, 275, 277, 282
Means, Gardner, 114
Media advisers. *See* Public relations
    practitioners
Medicare, 227, 228, 313, 367
Meese, Edwin, 154–156
    as attorney general, 156
    conflicts with other advisers, 154,
        162–163, 165
    conservatism, 152, 315
    on economic policies, 223, 225
    lack of organizational skills, 155, 225
    Legislative Strategy Group and, 158
    on Reagan, 168
    relationship with Reagan, 155–156
    White House staff organization, 151
Mellon, Andrew, 19–20, 35, 37, 38, 95
Meltzer, Allan, 29
Mencken, H. L., 19, 77
Merriam, Charles, 255
Meyer, Eugene, 37
Military. *See* Defense spending
Milkis, Sidney M., 53, 82, 117, 324, 326,
    327, 331, 334, 348
Miller, Nathan, 189
Miller, Warren, 352
Mills, Ogden, 180, 183, 263
Minimum wages, 199, 264, 271, 275,
    280–281, 315

Mitchell, Arthur W., 330
Mitchell, Charles, 40
Moley, Raymond, 103–108, 249
    banking crisis and, 180, 181
    Berle and, 114
    campaign participation, 327
    on causes of Depression, 104
    character, 103
    criticism of FDR, 107–108, 339
    on Hopkins, 137
    policy recommendations, 104–105, 195,
        196, 204
    political views, 103, 104, 112
    positions in FDR's administration,
        105–108, 148
    relationship with FDR, 105, 107–108, 250
    resignation, 108
    role, 104, 105–106
    speeches written by, 91, 103, 106, 108
    on Tugwell, 109
Mondale, Walter
    presidential campaign (1984), 241, 307,
        308–309, 317, 345–346, 348, 352
    as vice president, 53, 54, 60, 62
Monetarism, 298–299, 301
Monetarists, 291
Monetary policy
    gold standard, 37, 121
    interest-rate targeting, 303–304
    link to fiscal policy, 291, 303
    in 1920s, 20, 26
    in 1930s, 124, 142, 144
    in 1970s, 60
    in 1980s, 320
    Reagan's anti-inflation policies, 47, 152,
        290, 317
    recession of 1937 and, 124
    Volcker's anti-inflation policies, 61, 289,
        298, 299–301, 302–305, 364
    See also Federal Reserve Board
Money, velocity of, 302
Money supply
    controlling growth, 291, 298
    decline during Depression, 29
    effects of tax cuts and budget deficits, 291
    Federal Reserve targets, 299, 301, 302
    in 1980s, 291, 301–302
    relationship to inflation, 298–299
Montgomery, Robert, 85
Moore, Frank, 53, 57
Morehead v. New York ex rel. Tipaldo,
    275–276, 280, 281

Morgan, Edward, 247
Morgan, Ted, 114
Morgenthau, Henry, Jr., 118–126
  background, 118
  budget policies, 120, 145
  on causes of Depression, 120
  conflicts with other advisers, 109
  at Farm Credit Administration, 119, 189
  fiscal conservatism, 120–121, 122,
    125–126, 148
  Moley and, 108
  personality, 119
  positions in FDR's administration, 119
  relationship with FDR, 118–119, 123,
    125–126
  social security program, 215, 218, 219
  as treasury secretary, 119, 120–121,
    122–126, 145, 148
  view of federal government role, 120
  Wallace and, 127
Morris, Edmund, 91–92, 170
Mortgages
  foreclosures, 29, 189
  interest rates, 288
Morton, Rogers, 158
Moynihan, Daniel Patrick, 231, 239,
  308, 316
Muir, William, 100
Murphy, Charles, 69, 71
Murphy, Frank, 211–212
Murray, Charles, 315
Myers, William, 189

Namorato, Michael V., 110, 111
Nasar, Sylvia, 296, 312
National Association of Manufacturers,
  204, 209
National City Bank, 40
National Commission on Social Security
  Reform, 238, 239–240
National Credit Corporation (NCC), 37
National Emergency Council, 203, 255
National Industrial Recovery Act (NIRA)
  of 1933
  administration, 254
  employment codes, 85
  failure, 106, 194
  fair practice codes, 197, 204
  labor standards, 196, 197, 202–203, 206
  passage, 196
  problems, 204
  provisions, 196–197

  roots, 194–196
  Supreme Court decision on, 192, 206,
    207, 210, 222, 254, 272, 273–274
  See also National Recovery
    Administration
National Labor Board, 202
National Labor Relations Act (Wagner
  Act), 207, 209–210, 211, 254, 281–282
National Labor Relations Board, 85, 209,
  210
*National Labor Relations Board v. Jones and
  Laughlin Steel Company*, 211, 281–282
National planning, 110–111, 194, 204
National Recovery Administration (NRA)
  as bargaining forum, 199, 200, 203
  constitutionality, 199
  contradictions, 203, 204
  criticism of, 204–205
  directors, 198–200
  failure, 200–202, 203–204, 206–207
  goals, 197–198
  labor issues, 202–203
  production codes, 194, 200, 201, 204,
    206, 273
  public relations, 199–200
  relations with business, 201, 203, 204–205
National Security Council (NSC), 154, 155,
  162–163
Nativism, 323
NCC. *See* National Credit Corporation
Nebbia v. New York, 271–272, 276
Neibuhr, Reinhold, 51
Nelson, Michael, 53
Neoliberalism, 308–309
Neustadt, Richard, 61, 169
New Deal
  administrative state, 248–250, 253–261,
    262, 285, 362–363
  agricultural policies, 185–193, 329
  banking policies, 179–185
  business opposition, 146, 204–205, 206,
    212–213, 264
  Commonwealth Club speech, 81–82,
    116–118, 222, 359
  communicating to public, 327–328
  comparison to Reagan Revolution, 3
  constitutional issues, 268–270, 271–
    276, 284
  core policies, 179, 194, 222
  economic policies, 124–125, 126, 145,
    147, 359
  economic social contract, 81–82, 117

experimentation, 112, 131, 141, 142–143, 144, 179
failures, 285, 359
federal budgets, 120–122, 145
first, 104, 222, 254
labor policies, 69, 195, 197, 199, 202–203, 206, 207–213
Landon's view, 265–267, 268
legitimation by Supreme Court, 280–282, 286, 364
new federal employees, 249–253
progressive influences, 78, 81
Reagan's view, 94
relief programs, 84, 133, 137, 138
Republican opposition, 136–137, 261–268, 285–286, 331, 363
second, 104, 254–255
security as goal, 80–81, 115–116, 215, 222, 338, 360–361
social justice goals, 147
in Southern states, 330–331
third, 255
unconstitutional laws, 192, 206, 207, 210, 254, 272, 273–275, 276, 363
See also Liberal regime (1932–80); National Industrial Recovery Act; Social security
New Deal electoral coalition
African American voters, 329–330, 345–346
building, 328, 329, 336–337, 338, 363
election campaign (1932), 335–336
erosion, 342, 349, 364
groups included, 47, 325, 329–330, 336
labor, 207, 210–211, 212, 222, 336
opposing groups in, 11, 325
rural voters, 325
urban voters, 325, 329, 336
New Freedom, 11, 78, 116, 205
New Nationalism, 11, 78, 194
New Right, 343, 354, 364
New York City
Tammany Hall, 69, 71, 75, 208, 264–265
Triangle Shirtwaist Company fire, 69, 214
New York Factory Commission, 69
New York state
minimum wage law, 275
relief programs, 133, 137
Roosevelt as governor, 73–74, 79, 118–119, 133, 215, 325
New York Stock Exchange (NYSE), 24, 25, 27, 180. *See also* Stock market

Nicaragua, 174. *See also* Iran-Contra scandal
NIRA. *See* National Industrial Recovery Act
Niskanen, William, 159–160, 302, 304
Nixon, Richard M., 48, 49, 53, 89, 341, 344
Nofziger, Lynn, 86
Noonan, Peggy, 44, 152, 171, 174–175
Norris, George, 41
Norris–La Guardia Act, 207
North, Oliver, 156, 174
NRA. *See* National Recovery Administration
Nye, Gerald, 202, 204
NYSE. *See* New York Stock Exchange

Obey, David, 306
O'Connor, Basil "Doc," 113
O'Connor, John H., 333
Office of Management and Budget (OMB), 224–226. *See also* Stockman, David
Office of the Comptroller, 179, 181, 182
Oil prices, 45, 62, 293
Old age benefits, 213, 217–218, 220, 228, 282. *See also* Social security
Olsen, Floyd, 328
OMB. *See* Office of Management and Budget
Omnibus Budget Reconciliation Act of 1981, 232–233
O'Neill, Thomas "Tip," 57, 231, 236, 239, 306, 313, 355
OPEC (Organization of Petroleum Exporting Countries), 45, 62
Orren, Karren, 10, 11

Paine, Thomas, 96, 175
Panama Refining Co. et al. v. Ryan, 272
Parity, 22–23, 186, 187, 193, 205
Parrish, Michael, 20, 37
Partisan regimes. *See* Regimes
Party leadership
by Carter, 57–58
of reconstructive presidents, 13–14, 321–322
by Wilson, 332
Party leadership, of Reagan, 343–349, 353–355, 365–366
coattails, 348, 350, 352
conservatism, 13
public perception of party changed, 348–349, 352–353, 354
skills, 340
unification of party, 340, 348
See also Electoral coalition, of Reagan; Republican Party

Party leadership, of Roosevelt
  coattails, 327, 350
  criticism of, 338–339
  dominance, 337
  liberalism, 13
  purge of anti-New Dealers, 146, 331,
    332–334
  transformation of party, 322, 325–327,
    330, 333, 337–338, 365
  See also Democratic Party; New Deal
    electoral coalition
Patman, Wright, 123
Patronage, 248–249, 250
Patterson, James T., 92, 329
Payroll taxes, 217, 219, 220, 221, 229,
  240
Peabody, Endicott, 67–68
Peek, George, 22–23, 131, 188, 189, 190,
  198, 251
Pensions, 213, 214, 227, 272. *See also* Social
  security
Pepper, Claude, 332
Perkins, Frances
  background, 214, 250
  on FDR, 144
  on Hopkins, 138
  on Hugh Johnson, 203
  industrial recovery proposals, 195, 196
  as labor secretary, 214, 215
  New York Factory Commission, 69
  social security program, 215, 216–217,
    220–221
Phillips, Kevin, 305
Pioneer Hi-Bred Company, 127
Poindexter, John, 156, 174
Polenberg, Richard, 256, 259, 260
Political cycles, 2, 3, 12. *See also* Presidential
  leadership model
Political parties
  identification with, 351, 354
  ideological polarization, 13, 354, 366
  See also Democratic Party; Electoral
    coalitions; Party leadership; Regimes;
    Republican Party
Political time, waning of, 6, 10, 12, 16, 177,
  356, 360
Politics of articulation, 4
Politics of disjunction, 4, 18, 19, 42–43,
  357. *See also* Carter, Jimmy; Hoover,
  Herbert
Politics of preemption, 4

Politics of reconstruction
  conditions prepared by disjunctive
    presidents, 18
  presidential leadership, 2
  variations, 2, 5–6
  waning of political time and, 6
  See also Reconstructive presidents
The Politics Presidents Make (Skowronek), 1–2
Ponzi, Charles, 23–24
Populism, 22, 49, 162, 236, 243, 247
Populist commonwealth, 253
Post Office, 248, 249
Poverty
  of elderly, 213
  in 1920s, 23
  in 1970s, 45
  in 1980s, 310, 312, 317, 319
  permanence, 136
  war on, 48
Powell, Jody, 53
Power
  executive branch, 256–261, 326–327, 363
  presidential, 3–4, 258
PRA, 199
Pragmatism
  of FDR, 141–142
  of Reagan, 175, 176
Pragmatists (Reagan advisers), 156–163, 360
  conflicts with other advisers, 152, 153,
    157, 166
  influence, 154–155, 165, 171, 173, 234, 241
  roles, 152
  See also Baker, James; Darman, Richard
Preemption, politics of, 4
Presidential leadership model, 1–6
  agenda setting, 12–13
  categories, 3, 4
  contexts, 1–2, 4, 66
  cycles, 2, 3, 7–11, 12
  personification of regimes, 17, 55, 64
  political role of presidency, 3–4, 11–16
  See also Politics; Reconstructive
    presidents; Regimes
President's Committee on Unemployment, 36
President's Reemployment Agreement
  (PRA), 199
Pressman, Lee, 131, 190, 191
Progressive party, 127
Progressives
  FDR's support of policies, 77–78, 359
  influence on New Deal, 78, 81

isolationists, 130
labor reforms, 207, 214
Republicans, 323, 328, 363
third parties, 323, 328
view of bureaucracy, 34
western, 265–266
Wilson and, 70
See also Moley, Raymond
Prohibition, 323
Property taxes, 46
Protectionism, 35–36, 39–40
Public administration scholars, 255–258
Public policy, presidential role, 11–16
Public relations practitioners (Reagan
advisers), 163–166, 360
Baker and, 160, 161
conflicts with other advisers, 152, 153,
154, 165–166
defenses against Democratic criticisms,
315–316
influence, 163, 169, 171
media relations, 160
public image management, 156, 245, 318
See also Deaver, Michael
Public Works Administration (PWA),
198–199
Public works programs, 36–37, 135, 197, 259

Race
affirmative action, 314, 315, 342
Reagan's attitudes, 346–347
school integration, 48
segregation, 219, 331, 346
white voters, 48–49, 349
See also African Americans
Railway Workers' Pension Act, 272
Raskob, John J., 25, 74, 324
Reagan, Nancy Davis
influence on Reagan, 160, 171
marriage, 85–86, 91
relations with presidential advisers, 86,
154, 160–161, 163, 164–165, 382n14
Reagan, Ronald
acting career, 84–85, 87, 340
on American exceptionalism, 96–97
anecdotes told, 92–93, 98, 168, 170
assassination attempt, 153, 164–165
background, 82–87, 99, 100, 357–358
as California governor, 88–89, 154, 164, 173
communication skills, 87, 97, 100, 163,
164, 168, 169, 340

core policies, 224
decision-making style, 166–175, 176,
177, 244
as Democrat, 84, 85, 100
election campaign (1976), 89, 158,
346–347
election campaign (1980), 56, 63–64,
89–90, 158, 344–345, 347, 352
election campaign (1984), 163, 241, 307,
313–314, 317, 345–346, 347–348, 352
goals as president, 166–167, 225, 233, 358
on government role, 93, 94–95, 96, 98,
289, 358, 367
intellectual passivity, 168, 177, 225
intelligence questioned, 170, 358
legislative agenda, 158–159, 225, 307
management style, 88, 171–173
optimism, 83, 166–167, 174
personality, 83, 90–93, 166–167, 174,
175, 358
policy reversals, 173
political career, 87–90
political philosophy, 93–99, 100, 167,
243, 245
political skills, 307, 340
pragmatism, 175, 176
public approval ratings, 163, 165, 238,
290, 292, 353
public image, 156, 173, 245, 318
racial attitudes, 346–347
as reconstructive president, 2, 174–175,
177
religious beliefs, 96–97, 167, 175, 358
Republican Party membership, 87–88
self-confidence, 167, 175, 358
skepticism toward experts, 171, 175
social security reform, 228–232
speeches, 86–88, 92, 97–99, 169, 241, 243
weaknesses, 173–174
See also Advisers, Reagan; Electoral
coalition, of Reagan; Party leadership,
of Reagan
Reagan, Ronald, comparisons to FDR, 2–3
advisers, 2, 358–360
backgrounds, 357–358
decision-making styles, 175–177
goals, 166–167, 358
party leadership, 350
personal characteristics, 166–167, 358
policies, 3
as reconstructive presidents, 100

Reaganomics
  anti-inflation policies, 47, 152, 290,
    298–299, 317, 364
  budget cuts, 224, 225, 226–228,
    232–233, 238
  Bush's criticism in primary campaign,
    226
  campaign promises, 344
  consequences, 238, 287, 291, 317–318,
    319, 361–362, 364, 365
  contradiction between tax-cutting and
    budget-balancing goals, 233, 320,
    361–362
  as core policy, 223
  defense spending, 224, 227, 232, 295, 313
  Democratic criticism, 305–319
  economic policies, 289–292
  failures, 296
  growing income inequality, 310–312,
    316–317, 318–319, 320
  inconsistencies, 226, 245
  legacy, 318–319
  political aspects, 227–228, 241
  priorities, 224, 361
  supply-side economics and, 95–96,
    224, 344
  tax cuts, 47
  tax increases, 238–239, 245
  tax reform, 241–244, 245
  See also Tax cuts
Reagan Revolution, 166
  comparison to New Deal, 3
  Democratic criticism, 305–319, 365–366
  legacy, 367
  legitimization, 287, 364–365
  obstacles, 364–365
  supporters, 11
Recession of 1937, 124, 146
Recession of 1981–1982, 61, 238, 288–291,
    300
  Carter's role, 292
  Reagan's approval ratings, 163, 290
  Reagan's reaction, 289–290
  recovery, 292–294, 301
  unemployment, 238, 288, 294
Recession of 1990–1991, 296
Reconstruction Finance Corporation (RFC)
  agricultural loans, 189
  bank investments, 181–182
  establishment, 10, 37, 247
  Hoover's policies, 36–37, 41
  proposed revival, 309

Reconstructive presidents
  authority warrants, 2
  blame avoided for policy failures, 206
  changes made by, 12
  constraints, 6
  electoral coalitions, 13–14, 321, 365
  failures, 6
  in future, 12, 16, 356–357
  influence on subsequent presidents, 367
  legitimacy, 5
  party leadership, 13–14, 321–322
  personification of regimes, 17
  as politicians, 14, 365
  replacement of old regime, 4
  waning of political time and, 6, 12, 16,
    177, 356
  See also Politics of reconstruction; Reagan,
    Ronald; Roosevelt, Franklin D.
Reed, Stanley, 277–278
Reedy, George, 107
Rees, Albert, 300
Reeves, Richard, 93, 170
Regan, Donald
  as chief of staff, 153, 154, 156, 170, 242
  firing of, 165
  Legislative Strategy Group and, 158
  pragmatism, 382n14
  relations with Reagan, 91, 172
  as treasury secretary, 158, 172, 233, 234,
    241, 289, 300
Regimes, 7
  affiliated presidents, 4, 18, 357
  constitutional procedures, 7, 9, 12
  core policies, 178
  decline, 4–5, 8, 9–10, 357
  hybrid, 11, 177, 353, 355
  institutionalization, 7–8, 10
  opposition to, 4
  persistence, 10–11
  political philosophies, 8, 9
  pressures for change, 9
  represented by presidents, 17, 55, 64
  resilient, 2, 4
  supporters of existing, 6, 9
  transitions, 9–10
  vulnerable, 2, 4
  waning of political time and, 10, 177, 360
  See also Electoral coalitions; Liberal
    regime; Reconstructive presidents;
    Republican regime
Regulation
  banking, 116, 179, 183–185

business, 104, 105, 110–111
child labor, 199, 206, 271
congressional powers, 193, 269, 270–271, 273, 281, 284
criticism of, 46
expansion of federal power, 252–253, 281
FDR's policies, 82
labor protections, 195, 199, 214, 264, 271
NRA production codes, 194, 200, 201, 204, 206, 273
securities markets, 40, 116, 252
Regulatory agencies
constitutional issues, 252–253
history, 247
New Deal, 248, 254, 262
See also Administrative state; Executive branch
Reich, Robert, 309
Relief programs
Civil Works Administration, 84, 133, 138
distinction from social security, 221
Federal Emergency Relief Administration, 133, 137
federal role, 41, 134–136
Hoover's policies, 36–37, 134
New Deal, 84, 133, 137, 138
New York state, 133, 137
private charities, 36, 41
Works Progress Administration, 84, 133, 254, 333
See also Public works programs
Religious right, 343, 348
Republican National Committee (RNC), 342–343
Republican Party
business support, 264, 268
Contract with America, 367
control of Senate, 345, 348
Democratic voters attracted to, 48–49, 61, 344
farmers' support, 193, 329
New Right and, 343, 354, 364
in 1930s, 261–262, 337
in 1970s, 48–49, 342–343
in 1980s, 344
opposition to New Deal, 136–137, 261–268, 285–286, 331, 363
opposition to social security, 219
probusiness policies, 323, 324
progressive reformers, 323, 328, 363
supply-side economics, 348–349
tax policies, 235

See also Electoral coalition, of Reagan; Party leadership, of Reagan
Republican regime (1860–1932)
control of presidency and Congress, 322
economic conditions in 1920s, 19–23
economic policies, 19–21, 28, 35
electoral coalition, 322–324
factors in declining support, 323–324, 325
FDR's criticism, 366–367
Hoover's efforts to save, 38, 41–42
legitimacy questioned, 41–42
Resettlement Administration, 191
Reuss, Henry, 306
Revenue Act of 1932, 38
Revue Productions, 86
RFC. *See* Reconstruction Finance Corporation
Richberg, Donald
court-packing plan and, 277–278
on FDR's political skills, 146
New Deal policies, 196
at NRA, 197–198, 200, 202, 203, 206
Rickover, Hyman, 50, 52
RNC. *See* Republican National Committee
Roberts, Owen, 270, 272, 274, 275, 276, 280, 286, 364
Roberts, Paul Craig, 316–317
Robinson, Frances, 203
Robinson, Joseph, 283–284
Rockman, Bert, 169
Rohatyn, Felix, 309
Rohr, John, 246–247, 270
Roosevelt, Eleanor, 68, 72, 74, 109, 329
Roosevelt, Franklin D.
background, 66–68, 99, 357–358
blame avoided for policy failures, 206
communication skills, 146, 327–328
decision-making style, 123, 131, 139–148, 175–177
economic policies, 78, 285
election campaign (1932), 41, 79–82, 102, 103, 113, 116–118, 222, 325–326, 335–336
election campaign (1936), 113, 211, 222, 265–268, 336
election campaign (1940), 133, 212, 337
fireside chats, 182, 197, 279, 327, 332–333
on government role, 78, 79–82, 116–117, 179, 358, 362, 366–367
on Hoover, 32

Roosevelt, Franklin D. (*continued*)
  inaugural addresses, 141, 268–269,
    361, 362
  information sources, 143
  intelligence questioned, 74, 75, 91–92,
    102, 358
  judicial nominations, 269, 284
  leadership style, 78, 147, 338
  as New York governor, 73–74, 79,
    118–119, 133, 215, 325
  optimism, 139–140, 146
  partnership of business and government,
    106
  party leadership, 13, 146, 322, 324–
    335, 365
  personality, 73, 74–76, 139–140, 146,
    166–167, 176, 326, 358
  polio, 72–73
  political career, 68–71, 72–74
  political philosophy, 72, 77–82, 99–100,
    116–117, 141, 326
  political skills, 146, 147, 176, 187,
    337–338, 359, 365
  pragmatism, 176
  presidential ambitions, 76, 99
  public approval ratings, 260, 337
  as reconstructive president, 2, 140–141,
    177, 326
  regulatory policies, 40
  relations with Congress, 278
  religious beliefs, 75, 140–141, 175, 358
  self-confidence, 67, 78, 175, 358
  skepticism toward experts, 142–143, 175
  vindictiveness, 282–283, 284
  weaknesses, 147–148
  See also Advisers, Roosevelt; New Deal;
    Party leadership, of Roosevelt; Reagan,
    Ronald, comparisons to FDR
Roosevelt, James, 73, 125, 332
Roosevelt, Theodore
  comparison to FDR, 66, 68
  leadership style, 72
  New Nationalism, 11, 78, 194
  political career, 68, 70
  progressive views, 323
  view of business/government
    relationship, 205
  World War I and, 71
Rosen, Elliot, 104, 113
Rosenman, Samuel, 113, 147, 251, 277–278
Rosenof, Theodore, 205

Rossiter, Clinton L., 81
Rostenkowski, Dan, 233–235, 244, 306

SAG. *See* Screen Actors Guild
Saloutos, Theodore, 193
Samuelson, Paul, 309
Savings rates, 47, 290, 296–297
*Schecter Poultry Corporation v. The United
    States*, 206, 210, 273–274
Schlesinger, Arthur M., Jr., 20, 37, 70,
    75, 78, 101, 106, 119, 128, 130–131,
    133–134, 136, 138, 140, 145, 183, 186,
    193, 196, 199, 201, 262, 263
Schmitt, Jack, 228
Schrieber, Sylvester I., 214, 216
Schroeder, Patricia, 308
Schulman, Bruce, 174
Schultze, Charles, 60, 292, 309–310
Schweiker, Richard, 230, 231
Screen Actors Guild (SAG), 85, 86, 87
Sears, John, 159
SEC. *See* Securities and Exchange
    Commission
Securities and Exchange Commission
    (SEC), 40, 106, 252, 254
Securities markets. *See* Stock market
Security
  compatibility with liberty, 286
  for farmers, 129
  as New Deal goal, 80–81, 115–116, 215,
    222, 338, 360–361
  See also Social security
Sell, Bertrand, 181
Senate
  Finance Committee, 219, 235, 239
  Judiciary Committee, 283–284
  Labor Committee, 209
  See also Congress
Shaw, Arch W., 33
Sherman Antitrust Act, 87, 270
Sherwood, Robert, 76, 138–139
Shoven, John B., 214, 216
Shultz, George, 153, 163, 170, 174
Silk, Leonard, 235
Sinclair, Barbara, 336
Skowronek, Stephen
  on Carter, 50, 51
  on Democratic regime, 49
  on FDR's administrative reform, 261
  importance of context for presidential
    leadership, 66

on political role of presidency, 11–12
on politics of disjunction, 18, 19, 357
presidential leadership model, 1–6
on regimes, 7, 10, 11
on Roosevelt's religious rhetoric, 141
on waning of political time, 6, 12, 16, 177, 356, 360
Smith, Alfred
New York Factory Commission, 69
as New York governor, 71
presidential candidacy, 33, 73–74, 127, 323–324, 325, 330
Smith, 'Cotton Ed', 191, 333–334
Smith, Hedrick, 159
Smoot-Hawley tariff, 35–36, 39–40
Social insurance, 213, 221
Socialism, 263, 328–329
Social justice, 147, 318–319, 320. *See also* Income inequality
Social programs
entitlements, 221
Great Society, 58, 94, 367
Reagan's cuts, 227, 232, 238
See also Welfare programs
Social security
congressional hearings, 218–219
constitutionality, 282
cost-of-living adjustments, 228, 240
Democratic defense against Reagan, 307
development of program, 141, 215–218
distinction from relief, 221
expenditures, 228
funding, 217–218, 220, 229
implementation, 220
liberal criticism, 220–221
need for, 213
obstacles, 213, 217, 219
passage, 219–220
payroll taxes, 217, 219, 220, 221, 229, 240
political sensitivity, 221, 229, 231
programs, 220, 221, 228
projected deficits, 229
public support, 366
racial issues, 219
Reagan's inability to cut, 227, 240, 307
Reagan's reform proposals, 228–232
reform commission, 238, 239–240
successes, 222
Social Security Act, 218–220, 254
Social Security Administration, 249

Social workers, 134, 250–251. *See also* Hopkins, Harry; Perkins, Frances
Soil Conservation and Domestic Allotment Act, 192
Southerners
African American tenant farmers and sharecroppers, 131, 190–191
Democrats, 324, 330–331, 333–334, 336, 342
farm landlords, 190–191
FDR as, 73, 325
Reagan voters, 344, 345, 347
support of FDR, 325, 330
See also Carter, Jimmy
Southern states
New Deal in, 330–331
race relations, 190–191, 219, 331, 342, 346
states' rights issue, 347
union membership, 212
Soviet Union, Afghanistan war, 59, 90
Speakes, Larry, 163, 172
Special interests, in Democratic Party, 49, 307–309, 343–344, 345, 366
Specter, Arlen, 227
Spencer, Stuart, 88, 154, 229
Spoils system, 249. *See also* Patronage
Sprinkel, Beryl, 291, 298, 300
Stagflation, 47, 90, 152, 223. *See also* Inflation
State Department, 105, 148
Steagall, Henry B., 183, 184
Steel industry, 211, 212
Stein, Herbert, 33
Stern, Robert, 273, 284
Steuerle, C. Eugene, 237–238, 239, 244
Stevenson, Adlai, 190, 251
Steward Machine Company v. Davis, 282
Stewart, Joseph, Jr., 335, 336
Stockman, David
economic program, 224–226
on equality principle, 316
on government role, 224
Legislative Strategy Group and, 158
relations with Reagan, 91, 168, 172, 173, 225
on social security reform, 229, 230–232
on tax reform, 233, 234, 235, 236, 361–362
Stock market
bull market of 1980s, 291, 292, 301

Stock market (*continued*)
  crash, 23–28, 35, 40
  effects of Reagan tax cuts, 288
  lack of regulation, 24
  number of investors, 25
  regulation, 40, 116, 252
  risks, 24, 25
  speculative booms, 23–26, 179
Stone, Harlan Fiske, 270, 273, 274,
  275–276, 282
Strauss, Jesse Isador, 133
Strong, Benjamin, 26
Sumners, Hatton, 278
Sundquist, James L., 313–314, 328, 338,
  348–349, 351, 352–353
Supply-side economics
  adoption by Republican Party, 348–349
  defense of income inequality, 316–317
  Reagan's view, 95–96, 224, 344
  savings and investment rates, 296–297
  tax cuts, 95, 224, 225, 237, 288, 310
Supreme Court
  conflict with FDR, 271–276, 279–280,
    282–284, 286, 363–364
  justices, 270
  legitimation of New Deal, 280–282,
    286, 364
  New Deal laws found unconstitutional,
    192, 206, 207, 210, 254, 272, 273–275,
    276, 363
  probusiness perspective, 270–271
Supreme Court, FDR's court-packing plan,
  276–280, 282–284, 363–364
  label, 258, 333
  motives, 146
  opposition, 278–280, 332
  public opinion, 279
Supreme Court cases
  Adkins v. Children's Hospital, 271, 272,
    275, 280, 281
  Ashwander v. TVA, 275
  Carmichael v. Smith Coal and Coke Co., 282
  Carter v. Carter Coal Co., 275, 276, 281, 282
  Hamner v. Dagenhart, 271
  Helvering et al. v. Davis, 282
  Humphrey's Executor v. the United States,
    273
  Lochner v. New York, 271
  Morehead v. New York ex rel. Tipaldo,
    275–276, 280, 281
  *National Labor Relations Board v. Jones and
    Laughlin Steel Company,* 211, 281–282

Nebbia v. New York, 271–272, 276
Panama Refining Co. et al. v. Ryan, 272
*Schecter Poultry Corporation v. The United
  States,* 206, 210, 273–274
Steward Machine Company v. Davis, 282
United States v. Butler, 193, 274, 282
United States v. E. C. Knight, 270–271
West Coast Hotel v. Parrish, 280–281
Wickard v. Filburn, 193
Sutherland, George, 270, 271, 273, 275, 281
Swope, Gerard, 194, 204

Taber, John, 219, 264
Taft, William Howard, 270, 323, 332
Tammany Hall, 69, 71, 75, 208, 264–265
Tax cuts, Reagan administration
  Economic Recovery Tax Act, 233–238,
    244, 245, 288
  effects, 291, 365
  fairness, 316
  as priority, 152, 224, 225, 245, 288, 361
  rate reductions, 227, 242
  rationale, 95–96, 288, 310
Tax Equity and Fiscal Responsibility Act
  (TEFRA) of 1982, 171, 239, 291
Taxes
  Hoover's policies, 37–38
  payroll, 217, 219, 220, 221, 229, 240
  property, 46
  Reagan's reforms, 171, 291
  reform efforts, 46–47
  See also Income taxes
Tax Reform Act (TRA) of 1986, 242–244, 245
Taylor, Telford, 190
Teamsters Union, 208
Teapot Dome scandal, 19
TEFRA. *See* Tax Equity and Fiscal
  Responsibility Act
Temporary Emergency Relief Agency
  (TERA), 133, 137
Tennessee Valley Authority (TVA), 41, 87,
  141, 249, 275
Tenth Amendment, 274, 282
TERA. *See* Temporary Emergency Relief
  Agency
Thomas, Elmer, 186–187
Thomas, Norman, 328–329
Thurow, Lester, 312
"A Time for Choosing" (Reagan), 87–88,
  97–99
Time magazine, 132
Tindall, George B., 330–331

Tipaldo. See Morehead v. New York ex rel. Tipaldo
Tobin, Dan, 208
Tobin, James, 291, 309
Townsend, Francis, 214
Townsend Plan, 214
Toynbee, Arnold, 31
TRA. *See* Tax Reform Act
Trade association movement, 194, 200
Trade policies
  differences among FDR advisers, 105
  reciprocal agreements, 130
  Smoot-Hawley tariff, 35–36, 39–40
Trading with the Enemy Act, 180–181
Transformational leadership, 13–14, 62, 147
Trattner, Walter I., 220, 221, 250–251
Treasury, Department of
  Baker as secretary, 242
  banking crisis and, 180–181, 182, 183
  bonds, 120, 297–298
  Morgenthau as secretary, 119, 120–121, 122–126, 145, 148
  New Deal financing, 120–121
  Office of the Comptroller, 179, 181, 182
  Regan as secretary, 158, 172, 233, 234, 241, 289, 300
  tax reform plans, 242, 244
  war bonds, 24
Triangle Shirtwaist Company fire, 69, 214
Truman, Harry, 85, 127
Tsongas, Paul, 308, 309
Tugwell, Rexford, 108–114
  at AAA, 190, 191, 195
  agricultural policies, 186, 190
  background, 108–109
  on causes of Depression, 110–111
  conflicts with other advisers, 109
  economic policies, 110–111, 113, 148, 194, 204
  on FDR, 166–167
  on Hugh Johnson, 203
  Moley and, 107, 109
  personality, 109
  political views, 109–110
  relationship with FDR, 111–113
  resignation, 113–114
  social security program, 217
Tully, Grace, 119
TVA. *See* Tennessee Valley Authority
Tydings, Millard, 331, 334
Tygiel, Jules, 83–84, 87
Tyrell, R. Emmett, 96

Uchitelle, Louis, 319
UMW. *See* United Mine Workers
Unemployment
  in Depression, 28–29, 249
  in Europe, 294–295
  in 1970s, 59, 60
  in 1980s, 61, 238, 288, 294
  relief programs, 36–37, 41, 134–136
  social insurance programs, 213
  stagflation, 47, 90, 152, 223
  urban, 194
  See also Employment
Unemployment insurance, 216, 220, 232, 282
Unions
  accomplishments, 211
  company, 202, 203
  craft, 208
  FDR's relationship with, 207, 210–211
  industrial, 208, 210–211
  leaders, 207–208, 210–211, 212, 313
  majority votes, 202–203, 207, 210
  membership, 207, 211, 212, 295, 312
  in 1920s, 23
  Screen Actors Guild, 85, 86, 87
  view of government intervention, 207–208
  See also Labor
United Auto Workers, 211–212, 295
United Mine Workers (UMW), 209
United States, founding, 6–7, 96–97, 247
United States Chamber of Commerce, 194, 204, 206, 209
United States Steel, 211
United States v. Butler, 193, 274, 282
United States v. E. C. Knight, 270–271

Vance, Cyrus, 54
Vandenberg, Arthur, 184, 185, 265, 331
Van Devanter, Willis, 270, 271, 279, 280, 283
Van Hise, Charles, 104
Van Riper, Paul, 249, 250, 334–335
Velocity of money, 302
Vietnam War, 47–48, 342
Volcker, Paul
  anti-inflation policies, 61, 289, 298, 299–301, 302–305, 364
  appointment by Carter, 61, 299, 304
  criticism of, 300
  money supply expansion, 291, 320
  reappointment by Reagan, 302, 304, 320
  recession blamed on, 289
Von Damm, Helene, 165, 171–172

Wagner, Robert, 36, 69, 195, 196, 202, 208–209

Wagner Act (National Labor Relations Act), 207, 209–210, 211, 254, 281–282

Waligorski, Conrad, 315

Walker, Charles, 237

Walker, Jimmy, 75

Wallace, George, 48, 344, 346

Wallace, Henry A., 126–132
  as agriculture secretary, 127, 128–132, 148, 186, 188, 189, 191, 193, 247, 260
  background, 126–127
  beliefs, 128
  as commerce secretary, 127
  contributions to New Deal, 131
  reform policies, 130
  relationship with FDR, 127, 130–131
  social security program, 215
  as vice president, 127

Wallace, Henry C., 126, 127

Waning of political time, 6, 10, 12, 16, 177, 356, 360

Warburg, James, 142

Warburg, Paul, 27

Ward, Geoffrey, 69, 70, 72–73

War Industries Board, 194, 195, 198

Warm Springs, Georgia, 73, 74

Warm Springs Foundation, 99

War Trade Board, 195

Washington state minimum wage law, 280–281

Wasserman, Lew, 85, 86

Watt, James, 153, 173

Wayne, John, 169

Weed, Clyde, 28, 263, 265

Weidenbaum, Murray, 289

Weinberger, Caspar, 163, 173, 174

Weisman, Steven R., 169, 171

Welfare programs
  distinction from social insurance, 221
  Reagan's budget cuts, 232
  reforms, 89, 367

Welfare queen anecdote, 96, 170, 346–347

Welfare state
  conservative criticisms, 314–316
  construction, 251, 285, 362
  FDR's support, 327
  identification with Democrats, 313–315
  problems in 1970s, 48, 308
  public ambivalence, 353, 355, 362
  Reagan's criticisms, 224, 353

West Coast Hotel v. Parrish, 280–281

Wheeler, Burton, 196, 278, 280

White, William Allen, 278

White House staff
  Carter administration, 53–54, 56, 63, 151
  chiefs of staff, 56, 63, 150, 151, 256
  growth, 150
  Roosevelt administrations, 147
  See also Advisers; Executive office of the president

Whitney, Richard, 27, 180

Wickard v. Filburn, 193

Will, George, 312, 364

Williams, Aubrey, 124, 137, 250

Williams, Walter, 169

Willkie, Wendell, 138–139, 212

Wills, Garry, 92–93, 97, 348

Wilson, H. L., 127

Wilson, James Q., 305, 344

Wilson, M. L., 186, 191

Wilson, Woodrow
  antitrust policies, 106
  election, 323
  FDR as assistant secretary of navy, 70–71
  Hoover and, 32
  judicial nominations, 270
  New Freedom, 11, 78, 116, 205
  party leadership, 332
  political skills, 70
  reform policies, 324, 328
  supporters, 103

Wirthlin, Richard, 163, 165, 317

Witt, Nathan, 190

Witte, Edwin, 215, 216, 217, 218, 219

Witte, John, 234, 236, 242, 243, 244

Women, in labor force, 293, 294, 295

Woodin, William H., 119, 121, 180, 181, 183

Woods, Arthur, 36

Woodward, Ellen, 250

Workers. *See* Employment; Labor; Unions

Work relief, 135. *See also* Public works programs; Relief programs

Works Progress Administration (WPA), 84, 133, 254, 333

World War I
  agricultural exports, 22
  FDR's view, 71
  German war reparations, 20
  relief efforts led by Hoover, 32
  Treaty of Versailles, 20
  U.S. national debt incurred, 20

veterans' bonus payments, 123
war bonds, 24
War Industries Board, 194, 195, 198
World War II
economic growth, 118
Reagan's activities, 84–85
WPA. *See* Works Progress Administration
Wright, Jim, 300, 307
Wyman, Jane, 84, 85

Yellow dog contracts, 196, 197, 207
Young, James Sterling, 52
Young, Owen, 20, 27

Zelizer, Julien E., 120–121, 122, 124, 126